D0938941

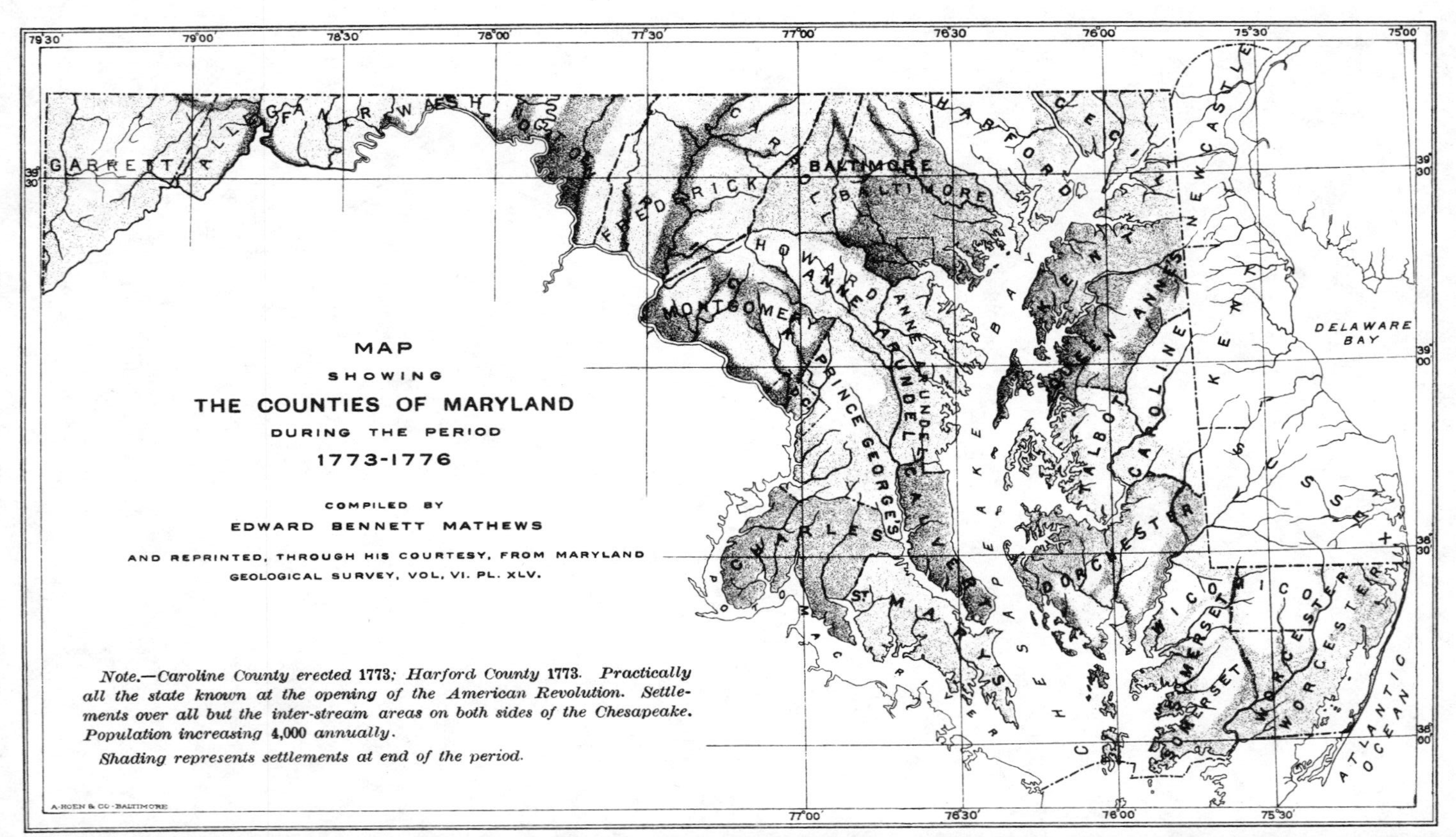
MAP
SHOWING
THE COUNTIES OF MARYLAND
DURING THE PERIOD
1773-1776
COMPILED BY
EDWARD BENNETT MATHEWS
AND REPRINTED, THROUGH HIS COURTESY, FROM MARYLAND
GEOLOGICAL SURVEY, VOL. VI. PL. XLV.
Note.—*Caroline County erected* 1773; *Harford County* 1773. *Practically all the state known at the opening of the American Revolution. Settlements over all but the inter-stream areas on both sides of the Chesapeake. Population increasing* 4,000 *annually.*
Shading represents settlements at end of the period.
GARRETT
ALLEGANY
WASHINGTON
FREDERICK
CARROLL
BALTIMORE
HARFORD
CECIL
NEWCASTLE
KENT
QUEEN ANNES
CAROLINE
TALBOT
DORCHESTER
SUSSEX
WICOMICO
WORCESTER
SOMERSET
HOWARD
ANNE ARUNDEL
MONTGOMERY
PRINCE GEORGES
CALVERT
CHARLES
ST. MARYS
DELAWARE BAY
ATLANTIC OCEAN
CHESAPEAKE BAY
POTOMAC RIVER
79°30′
79°00′
78°30′
78°00′
77°30′
77°00′
76°30′
76°00′
75°30′
75°00′
39°30′
39°00′
38°30′
38°00′
A. HOEN & CO. BALTIMORE

MARYLAND RECORDS

COLONIAL, REVOLUTIONARY, COUNTY AND CHURCH

FROM

ORIGINAL SOURCES

BY

GAIUS MARCUS BRUMBAUGH, M.S., M.D.

Member Maryland Historical Society, Pennsylvania, German Society, American Association for Advancement of Science, National Genealogical Society, American Medical Association, Medical Society of the District of Columbia, Etc.

VOLUME I

Baltimore

GENEALOGICAL PUBLISHING CO., INC.

1985

Originally Published: Baltimore, 1915
Reprinted, Genealogical Publishing Co., Inc.
Baltimore, 1967, 1975, 1985
Library of Congress Catalogue Card Number 67-24374
International Standard Book Number, Volume I: 0-8063-1131-2
Set Number: 0-8063-0059-0
Made in the United States of America

PREFACE

Some year ago the compiler was searching for certain early marriage records, and was directed by the Right Reverend Alfred Harding, D.D., Bishop of Washington, to the Broad Creek or Piscataway Parish Records. These are the oldest records for Washington, and are amongst the oldest for the Province and State of Maryland. They begin in 1693, and have been prepared in manuscript to appear in the subsequent volume, with other valuable and hitherto unpublished records.

The early Parish Records contain the compulsory recording of marriages, births, deaths, trials, etc., *irrespective of religious affiliations*, and were the public records kept before the formation of the counties. These records are not complete, but every entry has a bearing historically and genealogically upon localities and families throughout the United States and England.

COLONIAL CENSUS OF 1776

The deficiencies in the preserved Church Records, inscriptions, etc., led the compiler to search for other collateral data. A valued friend suggested the Archives of Maryland as containing valuable material, and they were drawn upon through the active coöperation of the Maryland Historical Society.

A Century of Population Growth in the United States, 1790–1900, Washington, 1909, pp. 3–4, says:

> The necessity for a national census, comprehending all the states, became apparent early in the Continental period (1774–1789). During the War of the Revolution, the Continental Congress had authorized and directed the issue of $3,000,000.00 in bills of credit. It had also resolved that the credit of the Thirteen United Colonies should be pledged for the redemption of these bills; that each colony should provide ways and means to redeem its proportion in such manner as it should see fit; that the proportion of each colony should be determined by the number of its inhabitants of all ages, including negroes and mulattoes; and that it should be recommended to the colonial authorities to ascertain in the most confidential manner their respective populations, and to send the returns, properly authenticated, to Congress. Massachusetts and Rhode Island took a census upon this recommendation in 1776, but most of the colonies failed to comply.

Page 185 of the same publication gives "An Account of the Number of Souls in the Province of Maryland, in the Year 1755" from the *Gentle-*

man's Magazine, Vol. xxxiv, page 261. Nowhere do we find any reference to the Maryland Census of 1776.

Through the active interest and assistance of Hon. Edwin Warfield, President of the Maryland Historical Society, and of its Council and Library Committee, permission was granted to photograph and reproduce important documents in connection with the related Parish and other records. A portion of the Census of 1776 is therefore herein reproduced as an important historical contribution to the early history of Maryland.

Heads of Families, First Census of the United States, 1790, enumerates the *male head* of the family, and gives the number of children, including the mother, etc. The *Colonial Census of 1776, Maryland*, part of which is herein reproduced in facsimile, enumerates "*all souls*," largely by names, even of babies, giving all ages at the time of enumeration. Peculiar value attaches to such information from whatever angle the data may be considered. One subscriber summarizes by saying "There is nothing to be found like this publication."

The expense involved in reproducing pages in facsimile, upon permanent uncoated paper, is deemed to be justified by reason of the resulting accuracy and permanency. To avoid all possibility of error through cleaning the plates, artistic appearance has been sacrificed, and the perpetuated blemishes occurring in the old and yellow documents bear mute testimony to the accuracy of the facsimiles. The remainder of the valuable Census of 1776 will probably be later published, if the support for the project justifies the expenditure. Those who desire such additional publication of the record will confer a favor upon all concerned if they will soon communicate with the compiler of this volume.

Especial attention is directed to the fact that this Census of 1776 (Frederick County in this volume, and certain unpublished parts of the census) is a census not only of Maryland, but also of the twenty-mile strip of former Pennsylvania soil and inhabitants brought into Maryland by the location of the Mason and Dixon Line (1763–1767). This should broaden the support accorded the publication, as the title might be made to read "Maryland and Pennsylvania Records, etc."

In using the Census of 1776 deduct from 1776 the figure following the individual enumerated, and you have the year in which the said individual was born. In the Census for Prince George's County, pp. 18–88 the ages of all male members of the family follow the name of the male head, and the ages of the female members follow the name of the female head, without giving the separate names of the children and servants. It gives the dates of birth of all living members of the family and is a valuable check list on the membership of the special families in 1776. It enables the reader to see what probable omissions occur in the enumerated births, etc., of the same families as given in the later volume of Parish records.

Cordial thanks for active coöperation are hereby extended to Hon. Edwin Warfield, President of the Maryland Historical Society, Mr. Richard H. Spencer, Corresponding Secretary, Mr. Robert F. Hayes, Jr., Acting Librarian, Mr. Charles Fickus, and others connected with the said Society; to Mr. Chas. W. Stewart, Superintendent Library and Naval War Records, Washington, D. C., for important suggestions, etc.; to Mrs. Margaret Roberts Hodges and her husband, Mr. George W. Hodges, Annapolis, Md., for important assistance in research and in furnishing valuable manuscript; to Mrs. Bell Merrill Draper (Mrs. Amos G.), Washington, D. C., for research and manuscript; to Mr. Leroy Stafford Boyd, Washington, D. C., for manuscript; to Hon. Hammond Urner, Chief Judge Circuit Court for Frederick County, Frederick, Md., for his interest and consent to publish records, and to Miss Nellie Carter Garrott, Frederick, Md., for copying the said records; to Mr. Ernest Helfenstein, Frederick, Md., for research and for manuscript. The accomplishment of the latter gentleman in perpetuating old tombstone records about to be forever lost is especially commended to numerous others who are in position to copy valuable records in the older portions of the United States. Dr. Edward B. Mathews, Baltimore, Md., very kindly granted the use of the Map of Maryland, etc., from his admirable *The Counties of Maryland*, etc., elsewhere acknowledged.

Cordial thanks are also extended to Mr. Ernest Lindsley Crandall for his skillful photographs of the original records; to the Joyce Engraving Company for skillfully making most of the illustrations, and to the Waverly Press, Messrs. Williams and Wilkins, Baltimore, Md. (especially Mr. John K. Mount who has shown continuous interest in the solution of the problems encountered in the work). Further mention will be made of the Right Reverend Alfred Harding, Bishop of Washington, and to other friends who have materially assisted in furthering the success of this undertaking, in connection with the subsequent volume to be issued next year. Further assistance by directing attention to unknown and newly discovered Maryland records, and by stimulating increased subscriptions for the several volumes will be greatly appreciated. To all the numerous active co-workers warmest thanks are hereby extended, and the hope is expressed that this volume may prove to be one of much interest and permanent value.

Gaius Marcus Brumbaugh (M.D.)

July 1, 1915, Washington, D. C.

Contents of Volume I

PRINCE GEORGE'S COUNTY

LIST OF INHABITANTS IN ST. JOHN'S AND PRINCE GEORGE'S PARISHES

Prince George's County

["List of Inhabitants in St. John's and Prince George's Parishes contained in Prince George's County, Maryland", August 31, 1776.]

[Page 1]

	Years of age	Free Negroes under the age of 16	Free Negroes above the age of 16	Males whites between 16 & 50 y. old	Males white under the age of 16	Do. white males above 16	Females whites	Slaves above 16	Slaves under 16
Thomas Clagett	35								
Horatio Clagett	19			3					
David Boswell	25								
Mary Clagett	30						2		
Mary Clagett	5								
Judson M. Clagett	7								
Thomas Clagett	3								
Hector Clagett	3 Mo.				3				
Negroes James Graham	22		1						
Nancy	30								
Charles	35								
Dick	50								
Frank	32								
Ninian	55								
Sarah	25								
Jenny	18								
Nanny	56								
Jane	35								
Hagar	30								
Hannah	17								
Isaiah	16							12	
Andrew	6								
Jesse	5								
Frederick	3								3
John					3		2	12	

2		Free Negroes under the age of 16	Free Negroes above the age of 16	Male Whites between 16 & 50	Male Whites under 16	Defective Male Whites above 16	Female Whites	Slaves above	Slaves
Thomas Dent	41.		1	3	3		2	12	3
John Clark	40.			2.					
George Fairfax Dent	2.								
George Washington Dent	2 Mo								
George Hardey	14 yr				3				
Elizabeth Dent	28.								
Judah Murrey	35.						2		
Negroes Thomas free	23		1						
Fendah	30								
Henney	21								
Judah	18								
Paisley	25								
Poll	25								
Babb	28								
Jack	19.							7	
Luke	10								
Pompey	13								
Sall	14								
Henney	10								
Minta	6								
Hannah	2								
Jack	3								
Glasgow	3								
Vinah	6								
Susan	3								
Anne	4.								11
John Adams	36.								
Mary Adams	43						1		
			2	6	6		5	19	

3

Name	Age	Free Negroes under 16	Free Negroes above 16	Male whites between 16 & 50	Male whites under 16	[illegible] male Whites above 16	Female whites	Negroes above 16	[illegible]
			2	6	6		5.	19.	16
Abraham Cox	25.			1					
Mary Cox	24.						1		
Jesse Cox	5								
Zachariah Cox	2.				2				
John Chapman	50.					1			
Sarah Chapman	42								
Elizabeth Lattimore	13.						2		
James Vermillion	34.			1					
Rachell Vermillion	34.								
Elizabeth Vermillion	15								
Elianor Vermillion	7.						3.		
Abraham Vermillion	5.				1				
Thomas Martin	40.			1					
Rozia Martin	37								
Smith Martin	12.				1				
Amelia Martin	10								
Susanna Martin	1.						3.		
Negroes. Jack	27								
Charity	17							2.	
James Adams	35			2					
George Dement	26.								
Walter Adams	1.				1				
Elizabeth Adams	5								
Susanna Adams	28.						2.		
John Vincent	25								
Joseph Vincent	3 Mo								
Prudence Vincent	30 yrs			1.			5.		
Mary Vincent	3								
Frances Vincent	27								
	13								
Negro Paul			2	12	11	1	21	21	16

		Free negroes under 16	Free negroes above 16	Male whites between 16 & 50	Male whites under 16	Decrepit male whites above 16	Female whites	Slaves	[illegible]
Richard Dent	28		2	12	11	1	21	21	14
Mary Dent	67								
Elizabeth Dent	49								
Elizabeth Hardey	12								
Elizabeth Welch	16						4		
Negroes . . Harry	56								
Jenny	60								
Daphne	30								
Harry	27								
Nanny	50								
George	21								
Charles	19								
Cloe	18							8	
Phill	12								
Tomm	11								
Jemm	9								
Jenny	7								
Bazell	5								
Will	3								
Billey	6								7
Walter Dent	32			1					
Elizabeth Dent	35								
Margarett Mongomery	29								
Cloe Dent	9								
Jane Dent	5								
Walter C. Dent	4				1		5		
Ann Dent	2								
Negroes . Margarett	25								
Timothy	20							2	
			2	14	12	1	30	31	21

5

Name	Age	Free negroes under 16	Free negroes above 16	Male whites between 16 & 50	Male whites under 16	Defective male whites above 16	Female whites	Slaves above 16	Slaves under 16
			2	14	12	1	30	31	21
Salome Edelen	50								
Catherine S. Edelen	22								
Margarett Edelen	20								
Sarah Edelen	16								
Betty Gill	44								
Catherine Curtain	60						6		
Edward Edelen	29								
Joseph Edelen	19			2					
Saml. Edelen	14								
James Edelen	12				2				
Negroes Nancy	40								
George	20								
Dick	55								
Tomm	27								
Dinah	50								
Patt	20								
Bess	44								
Cecelia	20								
Jack	40								
Ruth	30								
Stephen	60								
Peter	60								
Nann	65								
Charity	22								
Dobb	19							15	
Children Will	15								
Watt	12								
Henney	12								
Tom	11								
Bazell	12								
Nany	8								
Judah	3								
Alice & Jennet	1								
Billy	2								10
			2	[illegible]	[illegible]	1	36	46	31

6		Free negroes under 16	Free negroes above 16	Male whites between 16 & 50	Male whites under 16	[illegible] male whites above 16	Female whites	Slaves above 16	Slaves under 16
			2	16	14	1	36	46.	31
John Turton	32			1					
Harrison Turton	2								
Fielder Turton	6 mo.				2				
Acquilla Turton	28 yrs.						1		
Henry Hines	25		1						
Negroes Bobb	15								
Jessee	15								
Sarah	4								
Jesse	6								
Hariot	2								
Charles	3								
Betty	1								7
Thomas Dent Hardey	21			1					
Ann Hardey	22								
Mary Hardey	17								
Letty Hardey	6						3		
Negroes Frank	17		1						
~~Charles~~	~~[illegible]~~								
Linda	33								
Roger	36							2	1
Anna	3								
James Smith	43								
John Shine	33			2					
Ann Leach	37								
Ann Beneham	27								
Sarah Smith	15								
Elianor Smith	14								
Rebecca Smith	10						5		
Joseph Holmes	55					1			
Negroes Jack Wood	30		1					1	
Pegg	28				1				
Walter Smith	11								
			5	20	17	2	45	49	39

7		Free negroes under 16	Free negroes above 16	Male whites between 16 & 50	Male whites under 16	Defective male whites above 16	Female whites	Slaves above 16	Sla[illegible]
			5.	20	17	2	45	49.	39
James Holliday	35.			1					
William Holliday	1.				1				
Elizabeth Holliday	25								
Elizabeth Holliday	8						3		
Mary Holliday	7.								
William Fuller	40.			1					
James Fuller	7				2				
William Fuller	5.						1		
Elizabeth Fuller	35.								
Joseph Simpson	35								
Solomon Lanham	21.			2					
Charity Simpson	30								
Salome Simpson	6						3		
Amelia Simpson	2.								
Tennally Simpson	14								
Levey Simpson	12								
Thomas Simpson	10								
George Simpson	8.				4				
Negroes. Rose	16							2	
Sam	24								
John Casey	35								
John Gill	30								
John Lillis	19								
William Jones	15								
Patrick Fren[illegible]	25.			4	1				
Negroe Dick	30							2	
Betty	18								
Elias Lanham	25.			1	1				
John Lanham	4								
Ann Lanham	30						2		
Betty Lanham	1								
			5	[illegible]	26	2	54	51	39

8

Name	Age	Free negroes under 16	Free negroes above 16	Male whites [illegible]	Male whites between 16 [illegible]	Male whites under 16	Females [illegible] above 16	Slaves above	Slaves [illegible]
Enoch Magruder	53		5	29	26	2/1	54	53	39
Dennis Magruder	18			1					
Thomas Noble	14				1	–			
Meek Magruder	54								
Elizabeth Magruder	24								
Elianor Magruder	22						3		
Negroes Lander	54								
Will	24								
Walter	25								
Peter	25								
Naran	36								
Lucy	38								
Phillis	28								
Dinah	24								
Henney	24							9	
Nace	15								
Tom	15								
Dick	14								
Josias	13								
Phill	14								
Tom	13								
Ben	12								
Charles	2								
Jack	1								
Jessee	1								
Dore	6 mo.								
Henney	15 y.rs								
Milley	14								
Beck	10								
Peg	10								
Lydia	5								17
Bett	5								
			5	30	37	3	57	62	56

9		Free negroes under 16	Free negroes above 16	Male whites between 16 & 50	Male whites under 16	defective male whites above 16	Females whites	Slaves above 16	Slaves under 16
			5	30	27	3	57	62	56
Benjamin Duvall	59								
Moreen Duvall	12				1				
Ann Duvall	45								
Mary Bonifant	12								
Nancy Duvall	70								
Rosey Galiham	17						4		
Saml. Hawkins Bayne	28			2					
Thomas Bayne	48								
Elizabeth Bayne	50								
Ann Bayne	24								
Henrietta Bayne	1						3		
Negroe Bess	30								
Sambo	48							3	
Combo	53								1
Ann	12								
Thomas Welling	25			1					
Saml. Parkim	13				2				
William Welling	6								
Ann Welling	30								
Raihell Parkim	10						3		
Ann Parkins	8								1
Negroe George	15								
Thomas Jones	32	1744		1					
William Jones	7				2				
Thomas Jones	5								
Susanna Jones	30	b 1746							
Elianor Jones	2								
Ann Brooks	19						3		
Thomas Neydin	39								
Hector Neydin	31			2					
Mary Neydin	1						1		
			5	36	32	4	71	65	58

10		Free negroes under 16	Free negroes above 16	Male whites between 16 & 60	Male whites under 16	defective whites	Female Whites	Slaves above 16	Slaves under 16
			5	36	32	4	71	65	58
William Swink	34			1					
George Swink	5								
John Swink	3				2				
Mary Swink	27								
Elizabeth	10								
Susanna Swink	8								
Catherine Swink	7						5		
Mary Swink	5 Mo.								
Peter Hoggin	50								
John Hoggin	20								
Richard Hoggin	16			3					
Peter Hoggin	12								
William Hoggin	10								
Soloman Hoggin	8				3				
Catherine Hoggin	46								
Elizabeth Hoggin	84								
Elizabeth Hoggin	15								
Rebecca Hoggin	6								
Catherine Hoggin	3						5		
Negroes Tom	12								
David	3								
Phillis	11								
Rose	3								
Charity	1								5
Elisha Lankam	52					2			
John Rollins	13				1				
Jeminah Lankam	36								
Charity Bayne	17								
Meriah	7						3		
Negroes Frank	40							1	1
Cloe	10								
			5	40	38	5	84	66	64

11

Name	Age	Foreigners under 16	Foreigners Above 16	Male whites between 16 & 50	Whites under 16	[illegible]	Whites Females	Slaves Above 16	Slaves under 16
			5	40	38	5	84	66	64
John Worland	56				1	1			
William Worland	15								
James Worland	13								
Thomas Worland	2								
Walter Worland	1				4				
Rebecca Brady	65								
Mary Worland	39								
Stacy Worland	27								
Elianor Worland	24								
Mary Worland	20								
Elianor Murtle	17								
Ann Murtle	11						7		
Negroes Fortune	41								
Tom	21							2	
Phillip Locker	57					1			
Phillip Locker	23								
James Locker	22								
David Locker	20								
Thomas Locker	16			4					
Isaac Locker	8				1				
Elizabeth Locker	50								
Elizabeth Locker	17								
Amelia Locker	13						3		
Joseph Willson	56					1			
Nathaniel Willson	23			1					
Jane Willson	53								
Martha Willson	18								
Elizabeth Willson	14						3		
Negroes Nan	27							2	2
Harry	17								
Watt	8								
Dick	3								
			5	45	43	8	97	70	66

12

Name	Age	Free negroes under 16	Free negroes above 16	Male whites between 16 & 50	Male whites under 16	Captive whites above 16	Female whites	Slaves above 16	Slaves under 16
			5.	45	43	8.	97	70	66
John Nevel Jun.r	29								
Thomas Nevel	1			1	1				
Mary Nevel	23								
Ann Gates	14						2.		
Negroes Jenny	33								
Joe	8								
Bazell	6								
Harry	4								
Mill	2								
Edmond	1							1	5
Charles Landale	34								
Richard Littlemore	44								
John Scarfe	36			3	1		5.		
Harry Landale	5								
Elizabeth Wheeler	68 — b 1708								
Catherine Landale	40								
Elizabeth A Landale	7								
Susanna Landale	1 Mo.								
Elizabeth Scarfe	40 yrs								
Negroes Ben	55								
Cesar	40								
Lucy	18							3	2
Sam	12								
George	2								
Edward Simms	38 — 1738								
Charles Braddicum	10			1	1		1		
Ann Simms	32								
Negroes Susan	32								
Stephen	19							2	5
Moses	11								
Bob	9								
Toma	6								
Hannah	5								
Judah	2								
			5	50	46	8	105	76	78

.13		Free negroes under 16	Free negroes above 16	Male whites between 16 & 50	Males whites under 16	[illegible]	Females whites above 16	Females under 16	Slaves [illegible]
			5	50	46	8	105	76.	78
John Clarvoe Junr.	27								
William Clarvoe	2								
Henry Clarvoe	2			1.	2		1		
Mary Clarvoe	25								
Negroes Beck	15								
Lucy	15								2
John Tennally	27								
Joanna Tennally	52								
Elizabeth Tennally	30			1			3		
Sarah Tennally	20								
William Tennally	29								
Thomas Tennally	5:4								
Lydia Tennally	27:21			1	2		3		
Tracy Tennally	2								
John Keech	40								
Edward Keech	8								
William Keech	4								
Thomas Thompson	14								
Clotilda Keith	41								
Eleanor Stuart	17			1.	3		2		1
Negroe Francis	13								
John Nevet	53								
James Nevet	23								
Richard Nevet	13								
Joseph Nevet	11								
Ann Nevet	47								
Ann Nevet	16								
Ann M. Nevet	1								
Negroes Susan	25			1	2	1	3.	1	1
Clem	1								
			5	55	55	9	117	77	82

14

Name	Age	Free negroes under 16	Free negroes Above 16	Male Whites between 16	Male Whites Under 16	Defective Whites Ab. 16	Female whites	Slaves Above 16	Slaves
			5	55	55	9	117	77	82
William Norton Junior	36								
Walter Mudd	12								
John Mudd	8								
Mary Norton	33								
Amelia Norton	3			1	2		2	1	2
Negroes. Cate	45								
Tadge	14								
Nedd	12								
Zachariah Wade	56								
George Wade	34								
Zachariah Wade Jr.	28								
Ann Wade	50								
Hester Saxton	36								
Lionora Saxton	2								
Negroes Harry 14. Phill. 8.				2		1	3		2
Edward Clarkson	54								
Harry Clarkson	19								
Edward Clarkson Jr.	15								
Martha Clarkson	53								
Sarah Clarkson	23								
Martha Clarkson	21								
Negroes. Sam 51, Robin 45.									
Nan	20								
Rachell 8. Michael 7.									
Milla	5			1	1	1	3	3	3
James Harvey	30								
Thomas Harvey Jr.	6								
George Harvey	3								
Mary Harvey	30								
Elizabeth Harvey	2			1	2		2		
			5	60	60	11	127	81	89

15

Name	Age	Free negroes under 16	Free negroes Above 16	Male whites between 16 & 50	Male whites under 16	Capitation Males / Whites above 50	Female Whites	Slaves above 16	Slaves under 16
			5	60	60	11	127	81	89
Henry Aiton	44								
Henry Aiton Jr.	21								
Smallwood Aiton	17								
Ignatius Farrell	36								
Richard Smallwood	9								
Hester Aiton	45								
Ann Aiton	9								
Elizabeth Aiton	7								
Mary Aiton	4								
Negroes Sarah	35								
Area 2. George 14: Watt	6.								
Will	4			4	1		4	1	4
George Summers	54								
George Summers Jr.	17								
Paul Summers	10								
Thos. Bean Glasgow	6								
Elizabeth Summers	54								
Ann Summers	22								
Virlinda Summers	15								
Negroes Cate	28								
Jack	4 Mo.			1	2	1	3	1	1
Thomas Harvey	55								
Henry Harvey	21								
Osborn Mears	9								
Elianor Harvey	59								
Virlinda Harvey	17								
Negroes Peter	80								
Tamar	10			1	1	1	2	1	1
John Hilleary	35								
Thomas Hilleary	2 Mo.			1	1		2		
Mary Hilleary	24 4th		5	67	65	13	138	84	95
Elianor Hilleary	3								

16		Free negroes Under 16	Free negroes Above 16	Male Whites between 16 & [illegible]	Male whites Under 16	Decrepit Males Ab. 16	Female Whites	Slaves Above 16	Slaves under 16
			5	67	65	13	138	84	95
John Harris Jur.	50								
Phillip Smallwood	32								
Francis Smallwood	23								
Benjamin Smallwood	17								
Precilla Smallwood	30								
Martha Smallwood	20								
Negroes Bowles 34. Daniel	32								
Apollo 28. Jenny	57								
Sylvia	30								
Cloe 18. Nell	15								
Will 18. Ophia	8								
Cate 8 Mo. George	6 Mo.								
Charity	11 yrs			4			2	~~5~~	6
George Boswell	27								
Peter Boswell	22								
Elizabeth Boswell	65								
Mary Redman	20								
Rebecca Redman	6			2			3		
James Beall	47								
Samuel Beall	6								
Elizabeth Beall	42								
Mary A. Beall	18								
Elizabeth Beall	16								
Rebecca Beall	14								
Elianor Beall	12			1	1		7		
Casandra Beall	9								
Sarah Beall	3								
			5	74	65	13	150	90	101

17		Free negroes Under 16	Taxables	Male whites	[illegible]	Males under 16	Female whites	Slaves above 16	Slaves under 16
Michael Lowe	35		5	74	66	13	150	90	101
John Long	45								
Lloyd M. Lowe	9								
Henry Lowe	7								
John Long	6 Mo.								
Ann Lowe	30								
Elizabeth Lowe	6								
Barbary Lowe	10								
Ann Tomlin	15								
Venia Long	23								
Negroes Benjamin (free at 31)	18		1	2	3		5	2	2
Jack 35 . . Sarah	34								
Daniel 11 . . Amey	5								
Richard Bryan	46								
Rachel Bryan	33								
Elisabeth Cox	16								
Edward Lanham	14								
Robert Poor Lanham	10								
Ann Gilder	6								
Negroes Darkus	16			1	2		3	1	3
Pricilla	9								
Jeames	14								
Anthony	12								
Henry Evans. 44: 30: 9:									
Elizabeth Evans 36: 17: 14: 12: 7: 5: 1				2	1		7	1	2
Male Slaves 25: 12:									
female do. 15.									
			6	79	72	13	165	94	108

18

	Free negroes Under 16	Free negroes above 16	Male Whites above 16 & below 50	Male Whites Under 16	Defective Male Whites abv. 16	Female Whites	Slaves above 16	Slaves Under 16
		6	79	72	13.	165	94	108
Richard Carns 39: 30: 24: 23: 17: 13: 3: Mary Carns. 38: 15: ~~13~~: 11: 9: 7: 1. free Negroe 30: 28: Male Slaves 54: female do. .26.		2	4	2		6	2	
William Sutton 27: 1: Mary Sutton 67: 23: 3: Male Slaves. 31: 29: – 11: 4: 3. female do. 50: 28: 17: .. 2: 1.			1	1		3	5	5
Benedict Hardey. 26. Male Slaves. 49: 30: 25: 19: ... 8. female do. 35. ... 2.			1				5	2
Christopher Lowndes 61: 26: 27: 24: 20: 23: 26: 13: 11. Elizabeth Lowndes 48: 27: 18: 35: 26: 50 Male Slaves 35: 33: 30: 32: 36: 27: 24: 35: 21: 46: 17: 50: 46: 53: 45: 50: 40: 37: 23: 47: 52 = 15: 14: 14: 13: 1: 13: 5: 1: 1. Female Slaves 56: 50: 32: 30: 10: 8: 6: 39: 7: 3.			6	2	1	7	25	16
[illegible] 26: 30: 3: [illegible] 20: 2			2	1		2		
James Hunt. 41. 20: 18: 16.. 13: 9 Ruth Hunt. 47. Male Slave 50. female do. 22: 16 = 5: 4: 1: 1			4	2		1	3	4
		8	97	80	14	184	134	135

19

	Free negroes Under 16	Free negroes Above 16	Male Whites between 16 & 50	Male Whites Under 16	defective m Whites Ab 16	Female Whites	Slaves Above 16	Slaves under 16
	8	97	80	74	184	132	135	

Edward Gale 26
Margaret Barnes. 50
Male Slaves. 30: 30: 20: 17. . 6.
female do 26: 16: 16: 27: . 8: 3: 1. . . . 1. . . . 1. 8 4

William Foard Jur 47: 19: . 8: 6: 4: 2. .
Susanna Foard 43: 18: 16: 13: 12. . .
Male Slave 16. female do 50. . . . 2 . . 4 . . . 5 . 2.

David Ross 60: 22: 20: Servant 35.
12.
Annanias Ross. 44: 14: 10: 8: 4: Serv. 17. 4
Male Slaves 44: 40: 50: 45: 80: 35: 30: 25 . . . 3 . . 1 . . 1 . 6 . 14 19 . .
12: 10: 8: 6: 4: 1: 11: 7: 5: 1: 10: 4: 5: 4 mo
female do 40: 30: 28: 24: 22: 25: . .
10: 3: 9: 3: 7 mo 8 mo

William Deakins 56: 25: 20:
Elizabeth Deakins. 64: 64: 18.
Free black Males. 7: . . .
female do 30: 11: 9: 4: . . . . 4 . 1 . 2 . . . 1 . 3 . 4 4 . .
Male Slave 52 = 15: 11: 4: 2
female do 70: 31: 45

James Miller 33: 33: 28: . .
Jean McDonald. 28: 2.
Male Slaves. 40: 16: . . 12: 5. . . . 3 . . . . 2 . . 5. 4 .
female do. 35. 28: 16: . . 9: 7. . .

Francis Hatfield 52: 70: 29
Margaret Adams 43. . . . 1. . . . 2 . 1. 5. 6 . .
Male Slaves 25: 20: 16 = 10: 6: 6 mo
female do 55: 25: = 14: 10: 4

9 109 85 18 202 172 172

20	Free negroes Under 16	Free negroes Above 16	Male Whites between 16 & 50	Male Whites Under 16	Decrepit male Whites Above 50	Female Whites	Slaves Above 16	Slaves under 16
Robert Buchan 59: 19: 16: 24: 23: 12: 5: 1		9	109	85	18	202	172	172
Mary Buchan 46: 14: 9: Male Slaves 12: 7 female d°. 29: ~~13~~: 10: 4: 1 M°.			4	3	1	3	1	5
George Bence. 21: 23: . . 15: 13: 11: Barbara Bence 37: 8: 6: Male Slave 7: female d°. 27: 13:			2	3		3	1	2
Joshua Beall. 57: Amelia Beall. 28: 24: Male Slaves. 39: 33: 29: 25: 24: 16. 5: 4: 4 M°. 4 M°. Female d°. 50. 42: 28: 20: 18: 20: 6. 4: 11: 2.					1	2	12	8
George Beall 30 Ann Beall . . 26: 3: 3 M°. Male Slaves 18: 8: 6: 1: 1 female d°. 24: 17: . 3.			1			3	3	5
Thomas Thorn. 46: 16. 13: 10: 5: 3. Cassandra Thorn ~~18~~: 11: 8: 7: 4: 6 M°.			2	4		6		
William Lowe 55. 19 10 Eleanor Lowe 53: 20: 16: 50: 14: 6			1	1	1	6		
Robert Dick 40: 19: 15: 3: 2 M°. Mason Dick. 36: 55: . . 8: 7: 4: 2 Male Slaves 35. 13: 10: 6: 5: 4: 3: 2. Female d°. 50: 36: 20: 19. 3: 3: 9.			2	3		6	5	10
		9	121	99	21	231	194	202

21	Free negroes Under 16	Free negroes Above 16	Male whites between 16 & 50	Male Whites Under 16	[illegible] Whites Ab. 16	Female Whites	Slaves Above 16	Slaves under 16
		9	121	99	21	231	194	202
Andrew Beall. 55: 21: 25: 19: 2 Margaret Beall. 54. 25: 16. Male Slaves 60: 50: 47: 45: 20: 50: 15. female do. 40: 35: 34: 23: 19: 51. 11: 8: 5: 5: 2: 2:			3	1	1	3	12	7
George Conn 44: 14: 13. Sarah Conn. 32: 12: 8: 6: 3. Male Slaves 70: female do. 20: 16: 15. 4: 2.			1	2		5	3	3
Richard Isaac. 55. Sarah Isaac. 57: 25: 22: 16: 8: Male Slaves 25: 17: female do. 30: 17: 6.					1	5	4	1
Christian Hilragle 25: 23: Polsin Hilragle 23:			2			1		
Sam.l Shackells. 26. Ann Shackells 23: 4: 1. Male Slaves 47. 14 female do. 14.			1			3	1	2
Jonathan Slater 45: 30: Serv.t 24. 11: 9. Ann Slater. 35: 50: 7. Male Slaves 50: 35: 35: 20: 16: 19: 16: 14: 12: 7. 5 Mo. female do. 45: 44: 27: 24: 15: 8: 8: 5: 5: 3: 5. 2: 1			3	2		3	11	13
Francis Jenkins 29: 20.			2					
William Nevet. 27: Margaret 15 Male Slave. 1. female do. 29: 3.			1			1	1	2
		9	134	104	23	252	226	230

22	Free negroes Under 16	Free negroes Above 16	Male Whites between [illegible]	Male Whites Under 16	Reputed M[illegible] Whites Ab[ove] 16	Female Whites	Slaves Above 16	Slaves Under 1[6]
		9	134	104	23	252	226	200
Mary Carroll 32: 30: Patrick Law Overseer 45: 12:10:8 Male Slaves 45:45: 25: 14:4:2 female ditto 35: 26: 12:8:6			1	3		2	5	6
Elisha Crown 33. 2 Mo. Elizabeth Crown 21:			1	1		1		
Benjamin Berry Jur. 35: 26: Senr. 40 1 Mo. Deborah Berry 28: 35: 35: 8: 7: 5: 4: 2: 8: Male Slaves 26: 25: 25: 21: 50: 18: 18 7:1 female do. 50: 40: 28: 18: 17: 15: 4 15: 14: 7: 2: 1			3	1		10	12	7
John Ryan 63: 20: Sarah Ryan 70: 50 Male Slaves 60: 21			1		1	2	2	
Andrew Rantzell 32: 23: 7:5:1: Catherine Rantzell 30: 8: 4: 3:			2	3		4		
Richard Henderson 40. Senr. 30. 7: Sarah Henderson 41: 12: 10: 9: 3: 19 Male Slaves 35: 40: 35: 30: 8:6:3 female do. 30: 40: 26: 10: 5: 1: 6 Mo.			2	1		6	7	7
James Willson 66 8 Mary Willson 65 Male Slaves 69: 67: 47: 20: 19: 17: 15: 10: 7: 7: 3: 3: 1 Mo. female do. 72: 66: 32: 30: 23: 9: 4: 3:				1	1	4	11	14
		9	144	114	25	277	263	260

23	Free negroes Under 16	Free negroes Above 16	Male Whites Between 16 & 50	Male Whites Under 16	Defective Male Whites All Ages	Female Whites	Slaves Above 16	Slaves Under 16
		9	144	114	25	277	263	260
Jonathon Wyght 27: 7: 4: Sarah Wyght 28: 18: 16: Male Slave 13: female Slave 13			1	2		3		2
John Halsall 61: 17: 15: 13: 11: 9: Mrs Halsall 38: 6: 3: 3:			1	4	1	4		
Elizabeth Gordon 46: 18: 15: Charles Gordon 13				1		3		
Jane Clagett 51: 20: 16:						3		
Charles Faldo 52					1			
Nathaniel Parr 22 Hannah Maudate 50: 15 Male Slaves 70: 45: 16: 12: 2 Mo. female do 32: 21: 21: 2			1			2	6	3
John Ray Senr. 69: 27: 18: 40: 30: Sarah Ray 62: 20			4		1	2		
Abraham Boyd 40: 16: 9: 1: Barbara Boyd 36: 12: 11: 6: 3: Male Slaves 28: 26: 12: 6 female do 35 3: 1			2	2		5	3	4
James White 62: 18: Elianor White 62: Male Slaves 70: 45: 24: 27: 15: 2 femal do 26: 7: 7:			1		1	1	5	4
		9	154	123	29	300	277	273

24	Freenegroes Under 16	Freenegroes Above 16	Male Whites between 16 & 50	Male Whites Under 16	Defective Whites Ab. 16	Female Whites	Slaves Above 16	Slaves Under 16
		9	154	123	29	300	277	273
Edmond Turner 52. Catherine Turner 57: 37: 18: 9. Male Slaves 50: 30: 50: 30: 10: femal d° 50					1	4	5	1
Benjamin Tucker Junr. 3 Martha Bonithan 57: 27: 21: 5				1		4		
William Ferguson 31. 15: 2 Elizabeth Ferguson 25: 7: 5: 2 femal Slave 13			1	2		4		1
Enoch Jenkins 45: 16: Mary Jenkins 47: 15 Male Slave 24: female Slave 15.			2			2	1	1
John Thomas Boucher 30: 26: 25 Mary Boucher 30 Male Slaves 45: 20: 19: 9 female d° 50 12			3			1	4	2
Ephraim Thorn 43: 23: 6: 2: Elianor Thorn 46: 34: Male Slaves 50: 29: 17: 14: 12			2	2		2	3	2
John Willson 30			1					
William Stephens 24			1					
John Parker Junr. 23: 22 Mary Parker 24: 26: 2: 1 Male Slave 3 female d° 24 1			2			4	1	2
Oliver Burch 28: 7: 5: 2: Virlinda 29 Male Slave 42: female d° 30			1	3		1	2	
		9	167	131	30	322	293	282

25

	Free negroes Under 16 / Free negroes Above 16	Male Whites between 16 & 50	Male Whites Under 16	Collective Whites ab. 16	Female Whites	Slaves above 16	Slaves under 16
	9	167	131	90	322	293	282
John Parker 48. 15:13:11:5. Drusilla Parker 29:10:4:2:6 Mo. Male Slaves 14:13 female do. . . 16.		1	4		5	2	2
William Lucas 51. 14:10 Ann Lucas 63:27: 1 Mo.			2	1	3		
George Boulton 35: 23: Catherine Boulton 23		2			1		
Notley Jones . . . 50 14:12:7:5. Eleanor Jones 45:17:2. Male Slaves. 48: 7. female do. 20: 3: 4 Mo.		1	4		3	2	3
Richard Jameston 45: 20: 4:7 Mo. Ann S. Jameston 25:15:10:2:		2	2		4		
John Davies 30: Jane Davies 23		1			1		
Edward Hardin 53. Margaret Hardin 61: 38.				1	2		
William Duley 21. 1 Mo. Ann Duley. 19		1	1		1		
John Ford . . . 22.		1					
John Robinson: . . 30 5 Elizabeth Robinson 33:3:1.		1	1		3		
Nathan Lanham 52: 23: 20: 18: 12:2. Sarah Lanham 41: 18.		3	2	1	2		
James Campbell 22. Male Slaves 22:17 female do. 20:14		1				3	1
	9	181	147	33	247	299	288

26

	Free negroes Under 16	Free negroes Abt 16	Male Whites between 16 & 50	Male Whites Under 16	Decrepit Men Whites Abv 50	Female Whites	Slaves Abv 16	Slaves Under 16
		9	181	147	38	247	299	288
Elianor Free 49:17:10:7 Charles Free 14:12 female Slave 13				2		2	0	1
Bazell Stonestreet 21: 13 Elizabeth Stonestreet 19: 9 Mo Male Slave 1: female do 28: 3			1	1		2	1	2
Joseph Downing 28: 4:2: Jemimah Downing 21:3			1	2		2		
William Annear 57: Ann Annear 55					1	1		
William Harper 32. 7:4:9 Mo Stella Harper 27:8. Male Slaves 40 female do 48. 3.			1	3		2	2	1
Jeremiah Moore 27:40:30 Enesent Moore 28:57			3			2		
Nicholas Whealand 52 12:8:4: Sarah Whealand 42:14.				3	1	2		
Jane Coun 40:17:9 William Coun 5:11.				2		3		
Ann Hall. 20:2						2		
John Barren 53:16. 9 Jane Barren 38:19:13:9:7:5:3:2			1	1	1	8		
James McBew 22 Susanna McBew 21: 4 Mo Male Slaves 23: female do 25:23: 15 12:2			1			2	3	3
		9	189	161	36	277	305	295

27

Name	Free negroes Under 16	Free negroes Abv. 16	Male whites between 16 & 50	Male Whites Under 16	Defective Male Whites Abv. 16	Female Whites	Slaves Abv. 16	Slaves Under 16
		9	189	161	36	277	305	295
William Brown Senr. 88:28:21:18:25: 11:9:4: Ruth Brown 49:29:23:15:13:4 Mo.			4	3	1	6		
Edward Janes 65:22:16: 9 Ann Janes 50:17:13:12. Male Slave 58.			2	1	1	4	1	
William Janes, 34: 8:6:3 Jane Janes 40 Male Slave 13 female do. 15:13			1	3		1		3
Thomas Tucker 41. 18 13:6: Deanna Tucker 43:16:15:1			2	2		4		
John Wyght Senr. 63:23: 14 Ann Wyght 57:21:18: Male Slave 22. female do. 48:45:33:17: 11:1 Mo.			1	1	1	3	5	3
Henry Duly 45: 15:12:9:2. Mary Duly 39:20:17:5:9 Mo. female Slave 12.			1	4		5		1
Thomas Wise 50 13:11:7:3:1. Sarah Wise 46:9:6.			1	5		3		
Shadrick Lanham 47:17 15:13:10 Sarah Lanham 35:19:16:12:7:4:2			2	3		7		
Thomas Eales 53. 10:7:5:1 Elizabeth Eales 35:16:14:12				4	1	4		
Christopher Beanes Sr. 70:49:21: 15:12:6 Jane Beanes 37:19:14:10:4:2			2	3	1	6	0	0
		9	205	190	41	326	311	302

28	Free negroes Under 16	Free negroes Above 16	Male Whites between 16 & 50	Male Whites Under 16	Collectivum Whites Ab. 50	Female Whites	Slaves Ab. 16	Slaves under 16
		9	205	190	41	320	311	302
Thomas Gentle 35: Dianna Gentle 25: 7: 4: 2			1	1		3		
John Hill 58: 31: 17: Mary Hill 56: 21 Male Slaves 42: 18: 38: 22: 50: 37: 21 10: 6: 1: 1: 6: 13: 15: 7: 5: 11: 4: 4 Female do. 40: 22: 20. 16: 52: 38: 37: 35 12: 8: 4: 8: 12: 3: 15: 8: 6: 4: 4: 9			2		1	2	15	24
Ninian Beall 25: 20: Ann Beall 21: 3: 1			2	1		2		
John Brown Planter 56: 14: 9 Elizabeth Brown 52: 17: 12: Female Slave 20				2	1	3	1	
John Brown of Jno. 31: Elizabeth Brown 24: 2 Female Slave 40			1			2	1	
John Brown Shoemaker 52: 30: Elianor Brown 50: 16. 18: 2 Male Slaves 18: 16:			1	1	1	3	2	
Thomas Beall 34: 7: 5: 1. Female Whites 6: 2 Male Slaves 3: 1 Female do. 20.			1	3		2	1	2
John Beale 27: Elianor Beall 20.			1			1		
Neamiah Norton 41. Ann Norton 15: 6: Male Slaves 60: 40: 10: 7: 3 20: Female do. 9: 2: 1: 6 26 3			1	2		5	2	5
		9	215	200	44	343	333	333

29	Free negroes Under 16	Free negroes Above 16	Male Whites above 16	Male Whites under 16	Defective Males	Whites all female	Slaves above 16	Slaves under 16
		9	215	200	44	343	333	333
James Crafford 80 Mary Crafford 70 Male slaves 32:30:25:17 female do 60:60:21: 15:13:12:10:7:4					1	1	7	6
Niman Beall Senr 53:22:19: 15:13:10 Cathirine Beall 52:11:7:4: Male Slaves 60:40.			2	3	1	4	2	
Jonathan Simmons 30:40. 4:3. Elizabeth Simmons 26:1. Male Slaves 20:16 4. female do 26 15.			2	2		2	3	2
Thomas Sparks 65:18: 14: Elizabeth Sparks 58:16:14.			1	1	1	3		
Richard Beall 40:50:30. 12:9:7:5. Rebecca Beall 41:17:15:13:2:1. Male Slaves 25:24:30: 12:2. femae do 25: 12:8.			3	4		6	4	4
Edward Cook 28. 2 Precilla Cook 30:4:1 Mo.			1	1		3		
Joseph Hinton 32: 6:5:3 Mary Hinton 37:17:15:12:8.			1	3		5.		
John Norton Senr 36:30: 3:7 Elizabeth Norton 28:5:4:2			2	2		4		
Edmond Willson 55 4 Lucy Willson 40:16:12:7				1	1	4		
		9	227	217	48	375	349	345

30

Names	Ages	Free negroes Under 16	Free negroes Above 16	Male Whites between 16 & 50	Male Whites Under 16	Defective Male Whites Above 16	Female Whites	Slaves Above 16	Slaves Under 16
			9	227	217	48	375	349	345
Orlando Smith Martha Smith	52:16 10:8 35:17:14:12:6:4:2			1	2	1	7		
Bazell Willson Lucy Willson Male Slave Female do.	38 25 35 50			1			3		
John Harvey Elizabeth Harvey	24 12 35:14:4:2			1	1		4		
Anthoney Page Winifred Page Male Slave Female do.	32 10:3 31:8:5 20 21:16			1	2		3	3	1
Hezekiah Chaney Elianor Chaney Female Slaves	34 27:2 35 [illegible]			1			2	1	1
Mary Able	50:20:12						3		
Thomas Tucker Elizabeth Tucker	64:22 1 62:20			1	1	1	2		
Denoney Price Mary Price Female Slave	50:16: 15:13:12:8 40:18:16:7:5 2[illegible]			2	4		5	1	
Ignatius Price Ann Price Male Slaves Female do.	22 40 14:9 50 12:6			1			1	1	4
			9	236	227	50	405	355	350

31

	Freenegroes Under 16	Freenegroes Above 16	Male Whites between 16 &	Male Whites Under 18	Defective Males Whites Above	Female Whites	Slaves Above	Slaves Under
		9	206	227	50	405	355	350
Timothy Ragan . . 26. . Elizabeth Ragan . 16			1			1		
Thomas Norton . . . . 30 Catherine Norton 29:10:8:6:4:2			1			6		
~~Jacob Martin~~ Rachell Willson 40:10:6:1 Norindo Willson 14:12:7:2. Male Slave . . . 45 female do . . . 30			1	4		4	2	
Richard Chew . . . 55. Ann Chew . 70:44					1	2		
Jane Taylor . . . 50:20:18:13.						4		
Sarah Grant . . 40:12:11:7:4. Richard Grant . 14:8:1.			1	3		5		
Alice Trigg . . . 45:17:7:3. Samuel Trigg 16: 13:9:4			1	3		4		
Daniel Broga . . . . 26. Mary Broga . . 35.			1			1		
Mathew Sparks . . . 61:27:17 15:11:7 Elianor Sparks . . 45:23:3.			2	3	1	3		
Jane Beans . . . . 40 Samuel Beans . 14				1		1		
John Merick . . . . 40: 15:14:12 Elianor Merick . 55:20:18:16:12:8.			1	3		6		
		9	243	244	52	442	357	350

32

	Free negroes Under 16	Free negroes Above 16	Male Whites between 16 & 60	Male Whites under 16	Decrepit Male Whites Ab. 16	Female Whites	Slaves [above] 16	Slaves under 16
		9	243	244	52	442	357	350
James Robinson . . . 30: 5.			1	1		2		
Ann Robinson . . . 27: 2								
John Hamilton . . . 31: 40: 39. 6.			3	1		3		
Sarah Hamilton . . 37: 4: 2.								
John Jenkins . . . 53: 21: 17: 13: 9.								
Frances Jenkins . . 42: 19: 3.			2	2	1	3	5	2
Male Slaves . . . 30: 23: 54.								
Female do. . . . 30: 22: 9: 8.								
Adam Crafford . . . 54: 17. 9: 7.								
Elizabeth Crafford . 47: 19: 13: 11: 5: 70.			1	2	1	6	5	
Male Slave . . . 40.								
Female do. . . 54: 30: 55: 22.								
Mary Suit . . . 40: 18: 14: 10: 6.								
Nathanl. Suit . . 19. 15: 13: 4.			1	3		5	2	
Male Slave . . 30.								
Female do. . . 50.								
Gilbert Gray . . . 39: 16: 2.			2	1		2		
Elizabeth Gray . . . 32: 7:								
Josiah Gordon . . . 30: 4: 2: 2.			1	3		3		
Lucy Gordon . . . 26: 20: 6.								
Abednigoe White . . . 42: [illegible]			1			3		
Mary White . . 24: 4: 3								
Robert Ridgeway . . . 35. 4: 1								
Martha Ridgeway . 35: 8: 6: 5: 2			1	2		5		1
Male Slave . . 14								
		9	256	259	54	474	369	353

33

	Free negroes Under 16	Free negroes Above 16	Male Whites	between 16 & ... Male Whites	Under 16 Rejective M...	Whites Abt 16 Female Whites	Slaves Above	Slaves Under
		9	256	259	54	474	369	353
Joseph Cook .... 27 11:4:2: Martha Cook ... 30:10:9			1	3		3		
John Mullican Jun . 40:20:17 14:13:11:9:1 Sarah Mullican .. 40			3	5		1		
John Mullican ... 70: Catherine Mullican 50:26 Male Slave .. 42 female do. ... 5					1	2	1	1
Thomas Mullican ... 38 14 Elizabeth Mullican .. 50: female Slave .. 16			1	1		1	1	
Elizabeth Warring . 55:26:24:22:18 James Warring 21: 15 Male Slaves .. 55:19:21 14:9:2 female do. 50:24: 15:7			1	1		5	5	5
Hazwell Magruder ... 40: 10:9:6 Charity Magruder 36:13:7 Male Slave 10			1	3		3		1
Joseph Conn ... 35 2 Elizabeth Conn . 32:4:1:3 female Slaves .. 30 13			1	1		4	1	1
Josiah Willson .... 35 5 Mary Willson .... 28:4:3 Male Slave 30: female do. 22			1	1		3	2	
		9	265	274	55	496	379	361

34

Name	Ages	Free negroes Under 16	Free negroes Above 16	Male Whites between 16 & 50	Male Whites Under 16	Defective Males Ab. 16	Female Whites	Slaves Above 16	Slaves Under 16
			9	265	274	55	496	379	362
William Ross	36:22								
Susanna Ross	3 / 29:4			2	1		2		
Thomas Salter	25								
Margaret Salter	1 / 20			1	1		1		
Sarah Beall	45:16:10:6: ~~[struck out]~~								
Jeremiah Beall	17:21:70:22:								
	14:9:7			3	3	1	4	2	5
Female Slaves	39:19								
	13:12:9:5:1								
Isaac Sansbury	44:								
	15:14:11:7:2			1	5		3	3	1
Mary Sansbury	32:13:8								
Male Slave	30								
Female Do.	25:24 / 6								
John Cissell	55					1	3	1	
Susanna Cissell	20:17:14								
Female Slave	32								
Thomas Gordon	57					1	5	2	1
Drucilla Gordon	17:7:54:20:53;								
Male Slaves	53:52: / 7								
Bazill Crafford	30								
Margaret Crafford	35			1			1		1
Female Slave	13								
John Thompson	60								
Elianor Thompson	23					1	1		
William Willson	30:28			2	1		3		
Elizabeth Willson	1 / 22:16:3								
			9	275	285	59	519	387	369

35		Free negroes Under 16	Free negroes Above 16	Male Whites between 16 & 50	Male Whites Under 16	Defective m Whites All ages	Female Whites	Slaves Above 16	Slaves Under 16
			9	275	285	59	519	387	369
Philip Cissell	40 / 14:3:1			1	3		5	1	1
Elizabeth Cissell	35.12:10:7:5								
Female Slaves	40 / 13								
Mary Cissell	33:12:2				1		3		
William Cissell	4								
William Brooke Junr.	45:40 / 7			2	1		6		
Mary Brooke	38:10:9:8:6:5								
George Fraser	70 / 15				1	1	1		
Hannah Fraser	60								
David Willson	33			1			3		
Rebecca Willson	30:20:7								
Elizabeth Willson	45:20:18			3	1		3	1	3
James Willson	31:30:42								
Male Slave	6 / 3:2								
female do.	40 / 1								
Mary Heron	40:16:20:9:7			1			5		
John Heron	16								
John Willson	32 / 2			1	1		2		
Barbary Willson	29:4								
Joseph Cole	56:22 / 13:11			1	2	1	5		
Rachell Cole	46:20:18:16:6								
John Crecraft	48 / 14:13			1	2		5		1
Mary Crecraft	40:20:17:7:5								
female Slave	8								
			9	286	297	61	557	389	374

36		Freenegroes Under 16 / Freenegroes Above 16	Male Whites Above 16	Male Whites between 16 & 50 / Male Whites Under 16	Decrepit m	Whites All 16 / Female Whites	Slaves Above 16	Slaves Under 16
		9	286	297	61	557	389	374
Ignatius Willson	40:28 / 1		2	1		1		1
Elianor Willson	30:							
Male Slave	7							
Josiah Shaw	32:40 / 9:7		2	2		5	3	1
Mary Shaw	28:23:30:16:4							
Male Slaves	35:16							
Female do	32:5							
Nathaniel Hall	48 / 3		1	1		1		1
Ann Hues	20							
Female Slave	12							
Ninian Beall Sen.	80:27 / 2		1	1	1	3	1	
Catherine Beall	30:36:4							
Female Slave	76							
Clement Trigg	40 / 14:7:1		1	3		5		
Mary Trigg	41:17:15:14:1							
John Gover	45 / 6:2		1	2		4		
Elizabeth Gover	40:16:13:8							
Edward Legg	28 / 2:1		1	2		1		
Mary Legg	20							
John Robinson	28 / 4:2		1	2		2		
Keziah Robinson	28:20							
Anthoney Beek	38 / 7:4:1		1	3		2	1	
Elizabeth Beek	26:17							
Male Slave	27							
		9	297	314	61	581	394	377

37

Names	Ages	Free negroes Under 16 / Free negroes Above 16	Male Whites between 16 & 50	Male Whites Under 16	[illegible] Whites Ab. 16	Femaly Whites	Slaves Above 16	Slaves Under 16
		9	297	314	61	581	394	377
Isaac Robinson	49:17: 4							
Elizabeth Robinson	51:23							
Male Slaves	65:23:21		2	1		2	4	4
Femal Do	45 7 14:12:3							
Thomas Hamilton	62:21:25							
Ann Hamilton	45:20:19:16:14		2		1	5		
Thomas Webb Senr	70:23							
Elizabeth Webb	65:20:17:3 7		1	1	1	4		
John Hopper	45: 4:2		1	2		3		
Sarah Hopper	40:13:3							
John Riddell	72							
Elizabeth Riddell	70:17							
Male Slaves	10:4:1				1	2	2	5
Femal Do	28:20 6:2							
Shadrick Turner	48:25:22: 15:8							
Sarah Turner	38:14:10:20:6:1		3	2		6		4
Male Slaves	11:9:6:4							
Solomon Graves	38:24:23: 14:10:7:1							
Elizabeth Graves	30:65:20:13:6:2		3	4		6		
James Baldin	55:31: 11:8		1	2	1	3		
Elizabeth Baldin	49:17:13							
Thomas Hinton	46: 15:6:1							
Ann Hinton	30:12:9:4		1	3		4		
		9	311	329	65	616	400	390

38

	Free blacks under 16	free blacks above 16	Male whites between 16&50	Male whites under 16	Ditto above Male Whites	Female whites	Slaves above 16	Slaves under 16
		9	311	329	65	616	400	390
John Baynes 50: Mary 49 Male Slaves 52:51:40:40:28:23:20 5: 3: 2:1:1 female d°. 50:40:34:30:22:38:40: 15:17:6:6:5:3:1:3:17:					1	1	14	15
Joseph Noble Baynes. 25. Male Slaves 31:20:12:17:9:5:2:1. female d° 60:30:15:12:12:10:7:3			1				4	11
John Baynes Jun.r 24: Mary 22:20:1 Male Slaves 50:26:15:13:12:15:7:7:2:1 female d° 70:33:24:17:6:5:3:6:4:2:10:3:1			1			3	5	17
Catherine Noble . . 50 Male Slaves 43:18:2:1 female d° 33:19:9:4:1						1	4	4
Francis Jenkins 57:14:14:12: Ann 46:25:10 Male Slaves 6:4: female d° 34:30:11:7:1:1.				3	1	3	2	7
Charles Walker 23:1: Jane 20: Male Slave 9:			1	1		1		1
William Jenkins 33:			1					
James Short. 54:16: Jane 60:14:				1	1	2		
William Tiston 26:38: Catherine 69:30			2			2		
Mathew Clubb 60: 24: Mary 52:36.			1		1	2		
William Hutchison 54:18: Ann 60: 21:3			1		1	3		
Robert Ogdon 26:7: Dorothy Marrow 28. Male Slaves 43:27:18: female d° 50:9			1	1		1	4	1
Ann Smallwood 41 17:7						3		
Stephen Gerenan 23:16:2: Sarah 53:76:66:28:26:22:12:17:13:10.			2	1		10		
Joseph Mitchell 52:26:16:12 Elizabeth 48:60:18:8 Male Slave 7: female d° 40:18:16:14			2	1	1	4	3	2
		9	324	337	71	652	436	448

39

	Free Blacks under 16	Free blacks above 16	Male whites above 16	Do. under 16	Defective Male whites	Female whites	Slaves above 16	Do. under 16
		9	324	337	71	652	436	448
Henry Cassell 44:4:2:9 Mary Ann 32:16 Male black 9			1	3	2			1
Thomas Blacklock 60:20:18 Charity 58: Male Slaves 40:21:15:12:6:1 Female do. 40:33:30:21:15:12:10:8:4:2			2		1	1	6	10
William Hugar 33:18:7:4 Ann Ogdon 58:38:25			2	2		3		-
William Eats 35:23:12:9:2 Christian 30:14:7:15:4			2	3		5		
John Frammile 30:12:9:7:3 Ann 30:11			1	4		2		
Elisha Turner 26: Ann 17 Male slaves 40:32:30:7:5:4:1 Female do. 36:12:7:5			1			1	4	7
Samuel Townshend 61:20:16:9:8 Ann 47:22:16:11:7:4 Female Slaves 100:60:21:16:2:2 Male Slaves 26:16			2	2	1	6	6	2
John Webster 40:10:5: Joanna 25:12:2 1 Male Slave 18: female do. 12			1	2		3	1	1
Josias Beall 51:15:13:11:9:5:1: female 25 Male Slaves 43:27:22:21:20:7:12:10:7: 4:1:1:1 Female do. 65:35:30:23:22:18:8:7:4:2:			1	6	1	1	11	8
William Beanes Jr. 27: Sarah 26 Male Slaves 23:21:20:14:10:5:3:1 Female do. 20:16:10:5			2			1	4	7
Thomas Clarkson 61:28:19:8 Sarah 59: 30. Female Slaves 31:7:1 Male Slaves 70:40:25:14:10:7:5			2	1	1	2	4	6
William Lyles Jr. 26:21:27 Sarah 21 Male Slaves 55:50:35:24:19:18:20:15:14:13: 11:9:7:5:3:1 Female do. 60:50:35:24:22:18:6:10:4			3			1	14	11
		9	344	360	77	678	486	501

40	Free blacks under 16	Do. above 16	Male whites between 16 & 50	Do. under 16	Do. defective	Female whites	Slaves above 16	Do. under 16
		9.	344	360.	77.	678:	486	501
William Digges 63:30 Female whites 20:21:22:23 Male Slaves 58:28:39:25:22:40:70 20:25 = 14:13:12 Female do 48:39:50:39:30:50:23:22: 19:16:16:10:9:4:6:4:2:11:9:5:2:1 11:7:4:14:2:12:3			1		1	4	20	21
at Bladensburgh Male Slaves 30:28:31 25:50:48:26:39:40:21:18:35:30:45 50:53:27:31:25:22=15:14:13:14:15 13:9:1:9:5:3:1:3:1:4:1:10:3:6:7:5 2:1:3 Female do 70:65:55:60:50:70:73:30 28:24:20:50:30:28:23:24:30:25 31:20:25:50:45=15:13:12:14:13:5:7 2:5:3:1:3:4:6:7:5:6:3:12:10:							73	44
Henry Riddell 30:23: Male Slaves 45:25:21:15:4 female do 24:14:2			2				5	4
John Evans 23:14:12:10:7 Mary 43:20:16:5 = Male Slaves 36:8 Female Slaves 38:17:15:12:10:2			1	4		4	3	4
Mary Talbot 34:16:11:9:1 her sons 13:6				2		5		
Adam Lucas 33:26:8:1 Sarah 27:6:3:25			2	2		4		
John Manning 40:10:8:6:5:3 Mary Ann 35:75 Male Slaves 30:29:28:26:24:17:14:8:2 Female do 27:16:15:11:9:6			1	5		2	8	7
Thomas Young 43:16:14:12:2 Eleanor 36:10:8:6:1:1 Male Slaves 30:14:12:7:5:2 Female do 36:9:			2	3		6	2	6
		9	353	376	78	703	567	587

41

	Free blacks under 16	Do above 16	Total Males between 16 & 50	Do under 16	Do defective	Females Whites	Negroes above 16	Do under 16
		9	353	376	78	705	567	587
Samuel Bond 29: Clarissa 20 Male Slaves 33:32:38:22:15:11:11:9:8: 7:6:4:4:4:2:1:1: Female do 40:32:29:15:14:13:9:8:			1			1	7	18
James Gantt 22 Ann 16:32 Male Slaves 42:15:11:9 female do 23:21:39:29:14:5			1			1	5	5
William Turner 27: Mary 18. Male Slave 28: female do 5:2			1			1	1	2
Robey Worland 48:16:6:1 Edey 48:23:21:10: Male Slaves 14:7:5:2: female do 36:11:9:4			2	2		3	1	7
Thomas Howell 22: Maryann 25:40 Male Slaves 25:21:			1			2	2	
John Davidson 43:10:8:7:5: Elizabeth 31 Male Slave 2: female do 20:16:16			1	4		1	3	1
Thomas Morris 56:12:11 Elizabeth 50:23:20: Male Slave 30			1	2		3	1	
Richard Jenkins 35:10:2 Henrietta 30:12:8:6			1	2		4		
Joseph Shaw 40: Ann 48								
Thomas Mudd 36:4:2 Ann 28:1:1 Male Slave 12: female do 35:16:12:9:5			1	2		3	2	4
John Edelen Senr 62: Jane Edelen 32: 24:18 Male Slaves 21:18:10:1 female do 40:38:15:12:4:7					1	3	2	6
		9	363	388	79	725	593	630

42

	Free Blacks under 16	D° above 16	Male whites between 16 & 50	D° under 16	D° Defective	Female whites	Slaves above 16	D° under
		9	363	388	79	725	593	630
William Harris 30:5:3 Susanna 23			1	2		1		
William Toard 70:18:16:13. Elizabeth .. 66: 40: Male Slaves 50:20:17:7:5 Female d°... 50:45			2	1	1	2	5	2
William Jones 60:28:20:16:13 Mary 48:26:18:11:9 Male Slaves 28: female d° 50:10			3	1	1	5	2	1
Philip Lewin Jones 27:17:12:10:6 Charity 31:7:1			2	3		3		
Charles Jones 25:13 Mary 27:23 Male Slaves 25:9 female d° 67:14			1	1		2	2	2
Benjamin Turner 47: Patience 38:8 Male Slave 22: female d° 4	1	2					1	1
Henry Herns 55:15:12:9:8:3 Elizabeth 49:21:16:7: Male Slaves 9:8:6 female d° 20				5	1	4	1	3
Edward Longly 44:13: his Wife 32:11:9:4:2			1	1		5		
Luke Marbury 31:5 Elizabeth 39:3:2 Male Slaves 50:50:31:24:15. Female d° 50:28:36:13:13:13			1	1		3	7	4
James Lowry 30:30			2					
Bazell Green 22: Elianor 23:60 Male Slaves 40:16:4 female d° 30:12:10:3:1			1			2	3	5
	1	11	377	403	82	752	614	648

43

	Free blacks under 16	D° above 16	White males above 16	D° under 16	D° defective	Female Whites	Slave above 16	D° under 16
	1	11	377	403	82	752	614	648
Henry Downing 40: Sarah 32:1 Male Slave 40.			1			2	1	-
Robert Davies & Mary 60:55.					1	1		
Thomas Edelen 55:16:18:14:10:8:5 Precilla 51:20:18: Male Slaves 16:14 Female d° 40:2			2	4	1	3	2	2
Josias Harris 20:15:14:13:6 Edith 51:17: Male Slave 25			1	4		2	2	1
George Lee 40:20: Cloe 33:12:10: Male Slaves 50:35:25:25:18:50:16 15 40:35:35:30:30: 14:10:8:5:1:2:4 9:5:1:1:10: Females 45:40:25:20:30:50:25:25:30 12:10:8:6:4:10:5:6:2:2:4:2:8:6:4:2:4			2			3	21	29
John Addison 34:24: Elizabeth 27:10:6 Male Slaves 70:65:43:40:26:22 38:25:18: 12:10:9:6:8. 34 Female d° 80:50:40:28:23:17:14: 10:7:4:17:2:1:5			2			3	15	14
Rebecca Addison 26:15:5:9:8 Daniel Moris 33:11:6:7:1 Male Slaves 56:43:28:19:32:38:36 46:40:36:64:52:23:26:30:19:16 77 17:76:72:67:[illegible]7:27:23:17: 13:5:15:9:4:1:7:2:4:1:12:8: Female d° 60:26:25:54:40:27:13:60 18:23:24:16:16: 15:14:12:11:8:5:2:4 3:1:1:1:7:7:10:5:2			1	4		5	38	29
Zachariah Jenkins 50:18:[illegible]:14:9:6:4:2 Martha 28:14:11:22:1 Male Slaves [illegible]:8:4:1 Female d° 30:29:15			2	5	1	5	2	4
	1	11	388	420	85	776	695	727

44

	Free blacks under 16	Do. above 16	Male whites above 16	Do. under 16	Do. defective	Female whites	Slaves above 16	Do. under 16
Overton Carr 25:30:[30]22:25:19:15:7:4:4:1	1	11	388	420	85	776	695	727
Ann 30:34:24:30:2 Male Slaves 22:33:24:24:31:16:23:35:19 20:=14:10:8:5:3:1:9:8:1:1:6:4:13:14:5:2: 3:2:14: Female do 28:27:21:38:30:36:36: 77 38:20:16:35:16:18:7:5:3:3:4:13 10:2:15:9:10:7:7:4:10:7:12:1:2			6	5		5	23	38
William Bayne 47:12:8:3 Mary 43 17:14:1 Male Slaves 25:35:25:8:6 Female do 31:22:14:15:11:2:1			1	3		4	5	7
James Smith 52:20:15:10:5. Mary 40:18:13:26:12:3:2			1	3	1	7	-	-
John Marlow 52:22:19:17 Elianor 53:15				2	1	2		
Sarah Lantham 41:17:6. Son 6				1		3		
Patrick Beall 41:12:10:5:2 Elianor 41:19:15:8 Male Slaves 60:33:20:13:10:9:8:5:2:1 Female do 41:25:25:14:10:7:7:1			1	4		4	6	12
John McDowell 52:8:6:2:1 Elianor 37:3 Male Slave 25:				3	1	2	1	
Alexander Lovejoy 45:15:13:12:10:9:6: Mary 39:14:8:4:			1	6		4	-	
Benjamin Musgrave 84: Jemimah 27 Ann Brown 60:10. Sons 21:16 Male Slave 12: female do 80:12	1	3			1	1	1	2
Benjamin Brown 35:33		2						
	2	16	398	447	89	808	731	785

45

	Free blacks under 16	Do. above 16	Male whites above 16	Do. under 16	Do. defective	Female whites	Slaves above 16	Do. under 16
	2	16	398	447	89	808	731	785
John Thompson I.S. 40:7: Mary 38:13:11:4:1 Male slave 40:			1	1		5	1	
Francis Wheat 38:12:12:12:6: Female, white 70:4: Female Slaves 30:14: Male do. 3:			1	4		2	1	2
Elizabeth Alder 43:18:13:1. George 20:15:7. Male Slave 15: female do. 18:5			1	2		4	1	2
Notley Rozer. Male Slaves 45:22:17:34:20: 14:10:9:2:6:2:3 Female do. 78:40:24:54:24:=13:5:2.							10	10
Samuel Snowden 48:50:40:25:25:13:11:2. Elizabeth 43:40:18:17:15:6:4: Male Slaves 70:65:60:55:40:40:38:35:35: 33:30:28:27:26:25:20:20:19 18:17:16:16:16 13:13:10:10:8:8:4:3:3:1:1:1:1: Female Slaves 50:50:40:25:22:20:17:16:15:15 12:11:8:6:3:3:3:1:1			4	3	1	7	31	24
Thomas Snowden 27:40:30:30:27:24:22:2 Mary 48:21:6. Male Slaves 50:60:45:45:25:25:22:22:45:30: 30:22:40:25:40:20:20:35:=14:12:12:7:6:5:12:4 3:3:3:2:1:12:7:4:2:2:2 Female Slaves 50:40:30:25:22:40:20:17:35: 25:22:_ 14:12:12:5:5:3:3:1:2:6:4:3:4:8:6 3:6:2:2:1:1.			7	1		3	29	40
Nathan Prather 34:4: Ann 33:8:6:1 Male Slave 14: female do. 18:14:11			1	1		4	1	3
Elisha Hoskins 28			1					
John Gordon 27: Ann 24:3:1.			1			3		
	2	16	415	458	90	836	805	866

46	Free blacks under 16	D° above 16	Male whites above 16	D° under 16	D° defective	Female whites	Slaves above 16	D° under 16
	2	16	415	458	90	836	805	866
Joseph Prather 46:16: Ruth 46. Male Slave 40:13 female d° 15			2			1	1	2
Joseph Hughs 50:10: Phebe 43				1	1	1		
James Laughlin 33:2: Mary 30:4 Female Slave 15			1	1		2		1
William Hall 61: Margery 44 Male Slaves 35:17: female d° 4					1	1	2	1
Isaac Fowler 33:12:6. Elizabeth 28:7:1			1	2		3		
Jeremiah Fowler 65:27:21:17:13:10 Drucilla 53:38:16:7: female Slave 53			3	2	1	4	1	
William Willet 33:15:13:4:1 Mary 32:12:8: Female Slaves 22:11:4			1	4		3	1	2
Samuel Jones 48:24:11:5: Catherine 36:17:13:9:7:3 Male Slaves 25:24:8:6:4:4 Female d° 30:29:2:2:1			2	2		6	4	7
Bazell Maunew 28:5:1: Frances 26 Female Slave .34			1	2		1	1	
James Selby 29:25: Ruth 23:1			2			2		
Nathan Selbey 41:8:5: Agnes 28:2			1	2		2		
Lingan 23:1: Drucilla 20			1	1		1		
William W. Selbey 47:31:14:12:4:2 Elizabeth 30:17:9:6			2	4		4		
William & Elizabeth Tracy 26:20			1			1		
	2	16	433	479	93	868	815	879

47

	Free blacks under 16	D° above 16	Male whites above 16	D° under 16	D° Defective	Female Whites	Slaves above 16	D° under do 16
	2	16	433	479	93	868	815	879
Thomas Richardson 33:5:3:1 Anne 30:24:9:7 Male slaves 25:15:8:6:5:3:3:1:1 Female d° 34:32:9:7			1	3		4	2	2
Thomas Thompson 27: Rachel 21			1			1		
William Thomas 31:3:1 Amelia 27:15:2 Female Slave 10			1	2		3		1
Richard Lonsdale 53:28:10:6: his Wife 47:25:13 Male Slaves 34:26:23:10:8:4:1 Female d° 48:34:23:18:12:3			1	2	1	3	7	6
John Turner 38:36:34:26:20:13:14:14:13: Jane 73:40:36:21: Male Slave 12 Female d° 5			5	4		4		2
Richard Wheeler 29:15:5:2: Lydia 23:3:1. Male Slaves 31:8:4:2 Female d° 29:15			1	3		3	2	4
Robert Hardesty 49:19:12:9:7:2 Elizabeth 48:75:16:14			2	4		4		
Joshua Selby 35: Sarah 35:11			1			2		
Thomas Fowler 30:21: Females 3:3:1			2			3		
James Crow 28:23:25:17: Mary 58:32 Male Slaves 60:27:19:18:15:10:4 Female d° 62:52:40:1			4			2	7	4
Lewis Duvall 55:16:14: Alice 53:28:26:23:20 Male Slaves 60:55:32:25: Female d° 60:23:9:6:1			1	1	1	5	6	3
William Hyat 57:19:17:14:12:6 Elizabeth 48:13:9			2	3	1	3		
Christopher Hyat 25: Male Slave 75			1				1	
	2	16	456	501	96	905	840	901

48	Free black under 16	D° above 16	Male whites above 16	D° under 16	D° defective	Female whites	Slaves above 16	D° under 16
	2	16	456	501	96	905	840	901
William Kyal 28:3: Martha 28:6:4:1.			1	1		4		
John McDougle 44:17:16:13:1: Charity 42:15:12:7:5			3	2		5		
Richard King 85:30:16:15:13:4:1. Jane 68:43:22:8:6			2	4	1	5	-	
Richard Simmons 28:15:9:1: Tabitha 24:12:5:4:1. Male Slave 1 Female Slaves 33:30:7:2.			1	3		5	2	3
William M Selbey 67: Martha 63:16 Male Slaves 30:17: female d° 46:20:12:2.					1	2	4	2
Bazell Shaw 20:2:1: Susanna 20:30:1.			1	2		3	-	-
William Savil 42: Ann 46:			1			1	-	
William Willson 28: Margaret 26:6:3. Male Slaves 33:20:9:8:6:4 Female d° 29:11:7:6:5:2:			1			3	3	9
Zephaniah Prather 35:14:8:6 Rachell 34:17:11:4:1: Male Slave 18			1	3		5	3	3
William Prather 76:15: Martha 69 Male Slaves 26:8:5:5:5: Female d° 52:32:22:15:2				1	1	1	4	6
Josias Hoskins 20.			1					
Benjamin Owen 60:27:16:11 Anne 51: Male Slaves 32:26:20:11:10:7 female d° 47:29:17:16:9:8:1			2	1	1	1	7	6
Robert Adams 30:5: Jane 23:7:2	3	2						
Margaret Turner 45:16.						2		
William Higgins 29: Precilla 27:5:3:1 Female Slaves 30:14			1			4	1	1
	5	18	471	518	100	946	864	931

49	Free blacks under 16	D° above 16	Male whites above 16	D° under 16	D° defective	Female whites	Slaves above 16	D° under 16
	5	18	471	518	100	946	864	931
Jacob Aldridge 35:7:5:3: Elizabeth 27:4 Male Slaves 28:26:1. female D° 18:15:11:1.			1	3		2	3	4
Thomas Watkins 20:15: Jane 42:8:6 Male Slaves 34:35: female D° 50:25:7:2:1.			1	1		3	4	3
Van Simmons 24:19:1 Mary 21 Female Slaves 50:7			1	2		1	1	1
James Greenwell 54:15:9: Elizabeth 18:12				2	1	2		
Shadrick Beall 31:5:2: Agnes 26:7:1. Female Slave 15			1	2		3		1
Ninian Edmonston 41:13:11:9:4:1: Dorety 35:6 Male Slave 35			1	5		2	1	
George Willson 73:17:15: Mary 59:33:27:23:14:5 Male Slave 12: female D° 15			1	1	1	6		2
Isaac Short 36:24:13:6:4: Mary 34:12:8:4			2	3		4		
Thomas Gales 37:8: Sarah 47:15			1	1		2		
Edmond Hardesty 55:1 Elizabeth 28				3		1		
Robert Owens 34:16:5:2:1. Precilla 37:6:3			2	3		3		
Daniel Gloyd 40:15:13:4:1. Joanna 37:8:5			1	4		3		
Sarah Shaw 70:40:2 Male Slave 60						3	1	
Archibald Lanham 25:1. Jane 27:1			1	1		2		
Richard Bulger 48:7: Margaret 38:13:13			1	1		3		
James Calling 30:23:1. Sarah 65:20			2	1		2		
	5	18	487	551	102	988	874	942

50	Free blacks under 16	D° above 16	Male whites above 16	D° under 16	D° defective	Female whites	Slaves above 16	D° under 16
	5	18	487	551	102	988	874	942
William Sainsberry 40:15:12:9:7:5:1 Sarah 40:2			1	6		2		
William Thomas of Thos 20:17:1 Eleanor 63:18: Male Slaves 15: female d° 50:7:1			2	1		2	1	3
Ignatius Calicoe 35:6:2:1 Elizabeth 35:7:4 Female Slaves 19:3			1	3		3	1	1
James Cecil 42:12:8:3:1 Elizabeth 15:10:10: female Slave 5			1	4		3		1
George Hoskins 43:6:4:1 Mary 42:9 Male Slave 13: female d° 26			1	3		2	1	1
Middleton Belt 20: Ruth 64:23:23: Male Slaves 43:6:2 female d° 25:8:5			1	3		3	2	4
Benjamin Belt, Quarter Male Slaves 43:33:25:22:5 female d° 50							5	1
Joseph Jones 45:26:24:19:17:15 Margaret 53:23:13:6 Male Slaves 3:3:1:1 female d° 27:25:18:13:6:5			5	1		4	3	7
Anthoney Smith 48:5 Male Slave 9			1	1		1		
Archibald Elson 36:2. Mary 30:5. female Slaves 22:12:2			1	1		2	1	2
	5	18	501	571	102	1010	888	962

51

	Free blacks under 16	D° above 16	Male whites above 16	D° under 16	D° Defective	Female whites	Slaves above 16	D° under 16
	5	18	501	571	102	1010	888	962
Josiah Jones 22:1 Anna 27: Male Slaves. 24:14:13:9:7:5:2:1. Female D° 36:28:17:1:1.			1	1		1	4	9
Thomas Welch 54:24:15:5:5 Darcas 53:28:20:13:11:4 Male Slaves 55:37:25 female D° 36:13:10			1	3	1	6	4	2
Henry Norton 40			1					
Samuel Cheney 46:15:13:11:1 Martha 34:16:12			1	4		3		
John Duvall 32:6:5:3. Sarah 24:2:1			1	3		3		
Benjamin Duvall 63:24:21 Mary 60:4: Male Slave 25			1	1	1	2	1	
Thomas Duvall 37:14:12:6:4: Sarah 40:16:11:8:6:2:1 Male Slave 19			1	4		7	1	
William Hancock 75:14:1 Melkiah 46:15:10:				2	1	3		
Isaac Taylor 24:14:4 Mary 22:2:1 Male Slaves 23:22: free black 9	1		1	2		3	2	
Robert Langwell 25: Elizabeth 18			1			1		
Charles Shaw 27:2:1. Keziah 20			1	2		1		
William Mullican 42:10:8:6:1: Mary 40:12:2			1	4		3		
	6	18	512	597	105	1063	900	973

52

	Free blacks under 16	Do. above 16	Male whites above 16	Do. under 16	Do. Defective	Females Whites	Slaves above 16	Do. under 16
	6	18	512	597	105	1043	900	973
Joseph Walker 54:23:20:14 Elizabeth 52:18:16:13:9:2 Male Slaves 30:27:23:15:3 Female do. 27:14:1			2	1	1	5	4	4
James Comm 50:16:3 Ruth 32:24:15:11:5 Male Slaves 5:2:9 Female do. 34:14:13			1	1	1	5	1	5
Nathan Orme 42:5 Ann 29:14:7:2 Male Slaves 50:7 Female do. 32:2			1	1		4		
John Pitman 27 Jane 46:17:15			1			3		
Jeremiah Breashears 25:2 Jemima 22			1	1		1		
Charles Case 41 Martha 36:6:1			1			3		
Thomas Finch 62					1			
John Mackintosh 50:9:7:5 Priscilla 34:14:12				3	1	3		
John Beall of Jno. 42:7:5:1 Tabitha 32: Female Slave 8			1	3		1		1
James Ferguson 56:5 Catherine 57:28:17:9				1	1	4		
Marsham Beall 38:8:5 Frances 32:3:1			1	2		3		
James Beall of Jno. 40:14:12:4 Ann 40:14:2			1	3		3		
	6	18	522	61[illegible]	110	1078	905	983

53

	Free blacks under 16	D° above 16	Male whites above 16	D° under 16	D° defective	Female whites	Slaves above 16	D° under 16
Asa Nickols 20 14 4 2 Jemima 16	6 3	18	522	613	160	1078	905	983
Jacob Isaac 30: 3 2 Jane 22			1	2		1		
Jonathan Church [illegible] Joseph Carrol 20: 15: 13: 12 Keziah 41			1	3		1		
Thomas Beall Jun.r 76 11: 7: 4: Priscilla 33: 12			1	3		2		
William Waters 43 21 female slave 41			1	1		.	1	
Philip Hall 41 21: 15 11: 9. 5. 3: 1. Anna 41: 14: 12: 7.			2	6		4		
Ignatius Lucas 45 16: 14 6: 1: 1 Catherine 42 20: 18 13: 11: 7: 4			2	4		7		
Benjamin May 48 37: 21: 7: Elizabeth 37 22: 1			3	1		3		
John Harris 97 Female 30					1	1		
James Downing 50 9: 7 Sarah 54 35: 22 Male Slave 47. female d° 60 18				2	1	3	3	
John Redman 60 18 14 Sarah 50: 12			1	1	1	2		
Elizabeth Green 65. 15 12 Robert Wade 40. Male Slaves 35 10 9 female d° 40. 35			1			3	3	2
Samuel Tilles 50. female 3	1	1						
Joseph Hyton 45. 9. 7 Ann 40 11			1	2		2		
John Manates 32 Charity 25. 6. 5. female slave 14			1			3		1
William Stephens 62 18 11 Rebecca 58 18. 15			1	1	1	3		
James Green 37: 4: Elizabeth 30 17 6 1 Male Slaves 37 14: female d° 22 12 13. 11. 1			1	1		4	2	5
Benjamin Higdon 52: 5. 1 Ann 49: 25: 17: 7				2	1	4		
	10	21	539	642	115	1121	914	991

54

Name	Ages	Free negroes Under 16	Free negroes Above 16	Male Whites between 16 & 60	Male Whites Under 16	Capable of bearing arms [illegible]	Female Whites	Slaves Above 16	Slaves under 16
		10	21	539	642	115	1121	914	991
James Beck	40. 12:11:9:7:5:1								
Rebecca Beck	33:16:10:4:1			1	6		5	2	6
Male Slaves	30 12:4:1								
female do.	30: 10:7:5								
Samuel Bonifield	32: 15:7:3:4:13:11:1			1	7		2	2	7
Sarah Bonifield	36:5								
Male Slaves	10:2:6								
female do.	28:25: 7:2:1:1								
Susanna Pierce	38:17:10				2		3		
John Pierce	15:8:								
Simon Scott	45:20: 15:10:8:1			2	4		5		
Mary Scott	38:22:17:10:5								
Thomas Webb	43:25:19 14:9:7:4:2			3	5		2		
Rebecca Webb	38:15:								
John Sheriff	30: 1			1	1		2		
Ruth Sheriff	20:2								
Ezekiel Burque	30:75			1		1	4		
Elizabeth Burque	25:60:3:1								
John Beggerly	39. 4.			1	1		5		
Abigail Beggerly	30.60:11:8:5								
Isaac Walker	55:18:15:18 15			2	1	2	1	1	3
Elizabeth Walker	42:								
Male Slave	1.								
female do.	25: 4:3.								
		10	21	551	669	118	1150	919	1007

55

Name	Ages	Freemen Upwds 45	Freemen Above 16	Male whites between 16 & 50	Male Whites Under 16	Defective	White Females	White Slaves Above 16	Slaves under 16
		10	21	551	669	118	1150	919	1007
Thomas Shrife	40:								
Catherine Shrife	20:4:2			1			3		
James Edmonstone	31:30								
Ruth Edmonstone	32			2			1	1	4
Male Slaves	12:9:6								
Female do	23: 11								
Ignatius Breashears	43: 11:8:6:3:1			1	5		4	3	7
Frances Breashears	41:16:14:13:								
Male Slave	32: 12:6:5:3								
Female do	29:30: 15:8:1								
Job Jenkins. R. Peters	28:20:40								
Male Slaves	30:30:21:22:25:20 8:6:4								
Female do	25: 2			3				7	4
William Digges Junr	50								
Catherine Digges	40:21								
Male Slaves	40:30. 15:14:14:11:8:12:6:4					1	2	5	8
Female do	40:30:30:								
William Webster	83					1	1	2	1
Elizabeth Webster	50								
Male Slave	25								
Female do	20 3								
William Webster Junr	45:16 12:5:3:1								
Ann Webster	40:19:14:10			2	4		4		
James Webster	39:1 12:10:8:[illegible]:1			1	4		6		
Mary Ann Webster	35:20:17:6:4:2								
		10	21	561	682	120	1171	937	1031

56

Name	Ages	[illegible]	[illegible]	[illegible]	[illegible]	[illegible]	[illegible]	[illegible]	[illegible]
		10	21	561	682	120	1171	937	1031
Thomas Webster	50:19: 14								
Mary Webster	48:21:17:9:11:6			2	1	1	6		
James Campbell	42 12								
Elizabeth Campbell	48:23			1	1		2		
John Emerson	70:34: 13								
Lucy Emerson	20:18			1	1	1	2	1	
Male Slave	45								
James King Taylor	28								
Elianor King	18 6Mo			1			2		
Benjamin Athey	41:20 15:7:1			2	3		5		
Edea Athey	40:21:18:13:10								
Margaret Edwards	70:35:8						3		
John B. Boswell	45: 7:6:4								
Rebecca Boswell	40:3:1			1	3		3	2	1
Male Slaves	35 1								
Female do	30								
Joseph Willson Junr	30 6:3:1			1	3		1	2	3
Cloe Willson	27:								
Male Slave	13								
Female do	30: 13:3								
Ann Downes	58:34:30:13:4				2		6		
White Males	14:9								
Lewis Graves	58:25								
Elianor Graves	18			1	1	1	1	1	3
Male Slaves	50								
Female do	7:4:1 35								
		10	21	570	6971	123	1202	962	1038

57

Name	Ages	Free negroes Under 16	Free negroes Above 16	Male whites between 16 & 50	Male whites Under 16	Ditto upwards of 50	Female whites	Slaves Above 16	Slaves Under 16
		10	21	570	697	783	1202	942	1038
James Wood	45: 12:9			1	2		1		
Catherine Wood	40								
John Shaw	65:25:20: 1			2	1	1	5		1
Sarah Shaw	60:40:20:4:1								
Male Slave	7								
Neamiah Traherne	49: 7:5:1			1	3		2	4	1
Amelia Traherne	30:9								
Male Slaves	27:30:50								
female do	50: 12								
Edward Delozier	53:90:19 14:5:9			1	3	2	3		
Ann Delozier	50:20:11								
Richard Stonestreet	22 14			1	1		2	7	4
Ann Stonestreet	18:15								
Male Slaves	55:20:22:20 14								
female do	50:30:20 10:8:1								
Jonathan Turner	36 7:5:4			1	3		3	1	2
Mary Turner	25:9:1								
Male Slaves	6:3								
female do	26								
Josias Lanham	47:21 11			2	1		4	2	1
Elizabeth Lanham	30:15:5:3								
Male Slaves	30:22								
female do	15								
John Poor	47 6:1			1	2		4		1
Elizabeth Poor	30:24:6:4								
Male Slave	7								
		10	21	580	713	126	1226	956	1048

58

		Free negroes Under 16	Free negroes above 16	Male Whites between 16 & 50	Male whites Under 16 & above 50	Deserters & Orphans	Whites all Females	Slaves Above 16	Slaves Under 16
		10	21	580	713	126	1226	956	1045
Joseph Boarman	44:21:18. 15:10.								
Mary Boarman	40.								
Male Slaves	20:22:20 15:4:5:2:1			3	2		1	6	8
female do.	25:20:20: 9:6:1.								
John Halley	37. 10:8:4:1								
Elizabeth Halley	40:14:12:7:2			1	4		5		
John Dunn	70: 14								
Mary Dunn	52:18								
Male Slaves	58:40 8:6				1	1	2	2	5
female do.	9:4:2								
Hezekiah Athey	38. 15:9:4								
Rebecca Athey	40:10:2			1	3		3		
Robert Vermilion	51:19:16 13:10								
Elizabeth Vermilion	47:27:24			2	2	1	3		1
female Slave	7								
Mary Lanham	47:18:16:13:				1		4	2	8
Male White	11.								
Male Slaves	5:4								
female do.	40:27 13:9:7:7:6:2								
Charles Marr	26								
Hester Marr	26:20:3			1			3		
Joseph Carlton	22:17:35								
White females	58:32:5:1			3			4		
Jacob Funk	51:..9				1	1	2		
Ann Funk	49:12.								
		10	21	591	727	129	1253	966	1070

59

		Free negroes Under 16	Free negroes Above 16	Male Whites Above 16	Male Whites Under 16	[illegible]	Females Whites	Slaves Above 16	Slaves Under 16
		.0	21	591	727	129	1253	966	1070
Nichola Boswell	30								
Rachell Boswell	18.			1			1		1
Female Slave	15								
Samuel Nalley	33. 3								
Sarah Nalley	24:2			1	1		2		1
Female Slave	15								
Robert Lashley	60:28:								
Lucy Lashley	55:19								
Male Slave	40			1		1	2	1	
Richard Edelen Sen.r	60:22:17 14:12:4 M.o								
Sarah Edelen	45:21:18:10:7:4			2	3	1	6	1	1
Female Slaves	30 14								
Robey Tucker. 23: Hester Tucker 23.				1			1		
George M.cClane	27 5								
Mary M.cClane	37.			1	1		1		
John M.cClane 64: Precilla M.cClane 60.						1	1		
Joseph Sparrow	43. 12:10:8								
Ann Sparrow	32:6:5			1	3		3		
Thomas Dougal	56. 10								
Ann Dougall	51.				1	1	1		
Robert Hadrick	61 11:4:1								
Margaret Hadrick	40:14				3	1	2		
Peter Miller	43 5								
Elizabeth Miller	30:10			1	1		2	1	1
free female Blacks	20: 2								
		10	21	600	740	134	1275	969	1074

60

Name	Ages	Free negroes Under 16	Free negroes Abt 16	Male Whites between 16 & 60	Male Whites Under 16	[illegible]	White females	Slaves Abt 16	Slaves Under 16
		10	21	600	740	134	1275	969	1074
Anthony Gabriel	30:25:26:25:22 20:18: . . 1	1	10						
females	30:22:23:								
Abell Longdon	38:7:4			1	2		4		
Margaret	38:14.9:1								
William Collins	30: 2:1			1	2		2		
Ann Collins	28: 4								
Robert Bigner	30:40								
Margaret Bigner	[illegible]			2			1		
Richard Queen	51:22:20:28:9			3	1	1	3	7	3
Mary Queen	24:18:15								
Male Slaves	47:45: . . 2								
Female do.	52:23. 21:16:19 13:10								
John Tucker	74 . . 14								
Drucilla Tucker	64:14:12				1	1	3		
John Robey	62:23:17: . . 10:8								
Mary Robey	55:20:18:13:10			2	2	1	5		
Benjamin Tucker	31: 23: . . 5								
White females	55:18:25:17			2	1		4		
Joseph Williams	55: 7:5:4								
Sarah Williams	33:9:7:1				3	1	4		
Jasper Wirt	45:25:15:10								
Catherine Wirt	47:20:18:6			2	2		4		
Walter Queen	21:20:								
Elizabeth Queen	18:6:21:								
Male Slaves	40:30: 11:13:10:8:6:			2			3	7	7
Female do.	16:50:22:21:30:12:9:								
		11	31	615	754	138	1308	983	1084

61

Name	Ages	Free negroes Under 16	Free negroes Above 16	Male Whites between 16 & 50	Male Whites Under 16	Male Whites Above 50	Female Whites	Slaves Above 16	Slaves Under 16
		11	31	615	754	138	1308	983	1084
John Reagar	53								
Sophia	60					1	1		
Moses Graham	35: 13			1	1		2		
" Elizabeth	47:7								
George Beggarly	40:6:2:1			1	3		4	2	
Margaret	35:12:9:7								
Male Slaves	30:20								
William Bowen	21: 13:1								
Jemimah	52:17:15			1	2		3	3	1
Male Slaves	38:								
Female do.	60:34: 10								
Alexander White	28: 2			1	1		1		
Hannah	27								
Thomas Pearce	50:21:17: 14:7:3:1								
Martha	43:16:12:9			2	4	1	4	2	
Female Slaves	25:23								
David Bowen	30: 4								
Ann	30:23			1	1		2	2	2
Male Slaves	20:16:14								
Female do.	12								
William Pearce	52:25:14:9								
Rachell	52:21:11			1	2	1	3	6	
Male Slaves	24:20:16								
Female do.	46:50:30								
William Mahew	43:70:27::15			2	1	1	4		
Charity	23:65:11:1								
Robert Hissick	28:								
Jane	44:10:9			1			3	1	5
Male Slaves	30:8:7:3:1:10								
Clement Woodward	45:18:13:11:1			2	3		5		
Frances	40:15:9:7:5								
		11	31	628	772	142	1340	999	1092

62

Name	Ages	Free negroes Under 16	Free negroes Above 16	Male Whites Above 16	Male Whites between	Male Whites Under 16	Defective Whites Ab 16	Female Whites	Slaves Abe 16	Slaves Under
		11	31	628	772	142	1340	999	1092
William Trimbles	26: 1								
Elizabeth	18: 1			1	1		2	—	—
Timothy Canady	37:								
Ann	30:8:4			1			3		
William Cofsey	26								
Margaret	26: 14			1			2		
Walter Evans	55: . 5								
Elizabeth	36: . 1				1	1	2	6	3
Male Slaves	50:55: 30								
female do	60:32:16:13:11:9								
Jeremiah Reyley	46:18:20: 14:12:8:1:1			3	5		5	1	5
Elianor	23:40:22:20:1								
Male Slaves	8:5								
femal do	37:15:13:2								
John Halley	37:19:17:13:5:3								
~~Winifred~~ Mary	36:36:16:7:5:1			3	3		6	1	
female Slave	21								
Benjamin Downs	62:30:								
Mary	59: 24:20:17:2:1			1	0	1	6	4	5
Male Slaves	25:13:4								
female do	60:30:26:10:5:2								
Henry Downs	26: . 3								
Winefred	24:1			1	1		2	2	—
Male Slave	26								
female do	16								
William Tuels	69:								
Elianor	60:24:20:17					1	4		
Edward O. Herbin	45:21:18:17:10:4			4	2		7	3	—
Lydia	50:21:14:12:21:3:1								
Male Slaves	50:25:17								
		11	31	643	785	145	1374	1016	1105

63.

	[illegible] Under 16	[illegible] Above 16	Male [illegible]	Male [illegible]	[illegible]	[illegible]	Slaves	[illegible]
	11	31	643	765	145	1379	1016	1105
Joseph Coomes . . . 36: 5: 1 Sarah . . . . 30: 10: 8: 6: 3 Male Slave . . . . 1 Female do 17			1	2		5	1	
William Young . . . 70: 30: 22 Elianor . . . 68: 35 Male Slaves 40: 35: 24: 10: 9: 6: 6: 12 Female do . . 60: 50: 40: 35: 21: 40: 17: 16: 12: 4			2		1	2	11	7
Stephen Field . . 21 Precilla Lucus . . 38: 13: 7 Male Slaves . . 36: 18: 14 Female do . . . 60: 33: 11			1			3	4	2
Joseph Shirtcliff . . 26: 16 Dorithey . . . 35: 14: 11: 9: 7: 3: 2			2			7		
Mrs Scott Eastern branch 50: 26: 22: 22: 20 Male Slaves 45: 17: 4: 10: 3 Female do, 56 50: 37: 15: 12: 13: 5 3: 6						5	5	9
Henry Berkley . . 49: 9: 7: 5: 32: 32: 1 Elizabeth . . . 34: 11. 18:			2	6		3		
John Mahew . . 50: 12: 10: 9: 7: 5 Mary Ann 45: 35: 13: 4: 2: 1			0	5	1	6		
Elizabeth Willcoxen . 51: 13: 10: 5: Thomas Willcoxen . 29: 25: 7 Male Slaves . 38: 19: 9: 7: 3 Female do . 45: 35: 14			2	1		4	4	4
Robert Soper . . . 66: 1 Sarah 40 10 Male Slaves 30: 10: 8: 5: 4: 2: 2 Female do 25: 23: 22: 21: 17: 15: 14: 12: 4: 1				1	1	2	6	11
Rebecca Hardey . . 62: 33: 21 George Hardey 16.			1			3		
	11	31	[illegible]	[illegible]	[illegible]	1419	1047	[illegible]

4.

Name	Ages	Freenegroes Under 16	Freenegroes Older 16	Male Whites Above 16	Male Whites Under 16	Upwards of 60 [illegible]	Females Whites	Slaves Above 16	Slaves Under 16
		11	31	654	805	148	1419	1047	1138
Leonard Soper	39: 12: 10								
Mary	39: 18: 17 16: 7 3								
1 Male slave	28			1	2		5	1	
Thomas Upton	22			1			2		
Keziah	20: 5								
John Hardey	41: 3: 6: 2			1	3		4		
Mary	31 12: 4. 1								
Baptist Hardey	23: 2			1	1		2		
Rachel	25 1								
Joseph Dorsey	39: 23: 14: 12: 2			2	3		3	1	1
Elizabeth	23: 7: 4								
Male slave	50 14								
John Soper	52: 16: 14: 8: 6								
Martha	50: 20: 18: 12: 4			1	3	1	5	1	4
Male slave	4								
Female do	28: 8: 6: 1								
Thomas Ray	32: 5. 1								
Mary	31: 6: 2			1	2		3		
Leonard Gray	52: 18: 16: 14			2	1	1	3		
Elizabeth	56: 21: 10								
Isaac Darnal	44: 19: 14: 12: 10								
Susanna	45: 18: 13: 8: 5: 3			2	3		6		
Robert Fish	48: 11: 8: 6: 4: 3			1	5		3		
Rebecca	32: 10: 1								
John Nedden	34: 7								
Ruth	32: 13: 3: 2			1	1		4		
Jacob Weaver	32: 10: 2: 7								
Ann	32: 60: 6			1	3		3		
Charles Piles	28								
Mary	20: 2			1			3		1
Female slave	7								
John Warringford	56: 20: 10				3		3		
Joseph	15: 15: 7								
		11	31	670	835	150	1467	1050	1144

65

Name	Ages	Foreigners Under 16	Foreigners Above 16	Male Whites betw. 16 & 50	Male Whites Under 16	Defective Mle Whites Ab. 16	Female Whites	Slaves Under 16	Slaves Abv. 16
		11	31	670	835	150	1467	1050	1144
George Warringford	23:1								
Amminta	21:								
Males slaves	55								
female do	10:7			1	1		1	1	2
Richard Ridgeway	36:5								
Mary	40:16:14:11			1	1		4		
Giles Vermillion	23:5:3			1	2		2		
Mary	27:14								
John Upton	24:3			1	1		1		
Keziah	24								
Elizabeth Morgan	67:26						2		
Silvester Jones	35:13:5:								
Sarah	29:3:2			1	2		3		
James Mahew	52:22:20:12:9:7:5:2			2	5	1	3		
Elizabeth	45:17:4:								
Thomas Vermillion	57:22:16:15:15:10:5			2	4	1	2		
Sarah	51:13:								
Nathaniel Pope	40:17:15:8:5								
Elizabeth	38:13:11:3:1			2	3		5		2
Male Slaves	12:9								
Monica Johnson	60:24						2		
Ann Russell	38:10:1								
White Males	7				1		3		
Elizabeth Carrol	49:20:								
White Males	18:12:3			1	2		2		
Joseph Pope	51:15:13:9:6								
Elizabeth	45:24:23:20:3								
Males Slaves	40:25:21:12:10:7:4:6:1				4	1	5	6	8
female do	40:23:16:3:1								
Daniel Ferrol	57:60:28:13			1	1	2	4		
Ruth	52:28:23:16:								
		11	31	683	862	155	1506	1057	1156

Name	Ages	Free negroes Under 16	Free negroes above 16	Male whites above 16 [illegible]	Male whites Under 16	Decrepit white [illegible]	female whites	Slaves above 16	Slaves Under 16
		11	31	683	862	155	1506	1057	1156
[illegible] Hamilton	42:15:7:3								
Ruth	36:16:[illegible]:6:1			1	3		5		
[illegible] Beall	42:15:3:2								
Ruth	34:11:6:5			1	3		4	1	
Male Slave	32								
Joseph Willson	38:11								
Agnes	86:12			1	1		2	1	4
Males Slaves	7:6								
female do	25:3:1								
John Lowe	52:11:1								
Mary	52:17:15				2	1	3		
Clement Chamberlain	30:								
Mary	60:24			1			2		
Mary Marshall	53:15								
White Males	21:20:17:13			3	1		2	4	2
Male Slaves	24:22:14:								
female do	52:20:2								
James Tawnihill	71:32:41:18:7			3	1	1	2		
White females	48:15								
Babtist Riston	20								
Mary	30:5			1			2		
Luke Jefferson	44:8								
Elizabeth	43			1	1		1		
Andrew Hamilton	60:14:9:7								
Mary	40:10:								
Male Slaves	40:18:5:3			1	3	1	2	3	3
female do	22:1								
Mathew Wigfield	41:27:5:3:1			2	3		4	[illegible]	[illegible]
Elizabeth	36:12:10:7:								
Male Slave	15								
female do	14:7:5								
Robert Thompson	85:19								
Agnes	54:33:14:12:3			1		1	5	3	7
Male Slaves	60:40:20:14:12:7:3								
female do	14:7:5								
		11	31	698	880	159	1540	1069	1176

67	Ferreigners Under 16	Ferreigners Above 16	Male Whites between 16 & 50	Male Whites Under 16	Decrepit M. Whites above 50	Female Whites	Slaves Above 16	Slaves Under 16
	11	31	698	880	179	1540	1069	1176
Notley Gatton . . . 37:5 Mary . . . 32:7:4:1 . . .			1	1		4		
Richard Kirbey . . . 50:22:14:12:1 Mary . . . 55:18: Male Slaves . . 35:22:10 . . . female do . . 40:15			2	3	1	2	3	2
Thomas Willmot . . . 39:6:3:1 Mary . . . . . . 26:8 . . . female Slave . . . 14			1	3		2		1
Robert St Clair . . . . 53:13:7 Rebeccah 34				2	1	1		
James Reddin . . . 46:16:3:1 Rebecca . . . . 40:12:10:7 . . .			2	2		4		
George Bean . . . . 53:18:7:4 White females . . 16:15:13 Male Slaves . . . 25:12:6 female do . . . 40:7			1	2	1	3	2	3
Obeddo Philips . . . 36:11 . . . Jane 22:20			1	1		2		
Ann McDonald . 50: White Males . . 20:17 Male Slaves . . 30 female do . . . 50:29			2			1	3	
Richard & Martha Jones . 40: & 35 .			1			1		
William Masters Jr. . 22: Mary . . . . 29:6:1 . . female Slave . . 22			1			3	1	
William Masters Senr. 53:12:10:8:6: Tryphenia . . . 43:20:15:4:3 Male Slaves . . . 4:2 female do . . . 35:7:5				4	1	5	1	4
John & Mary Brown 28:30 . . .			1			1		
	11	31	710	898	163	1569	1079	1186

68

Name	Ages	Free negroes Under 16	Free negroes Above 16	Male whites between 16 & 50	Male whites Under 16	Overseers Mulattoes ab. 16	Female whites	Slaves Ab. 16	Slaves Under 16
Thomas Standage	63:27	11	31	710	893	163	1569	1079	1186
Margaret	55:25:22:19:16			1		1	5	1	3
Male Slave	8								
Female Do.	40:13:3								
Notley Claxon	45:15:10:5:2:1			1	5		3	1	3
Violetta	38:8:3								
Male Slaves	6:4:1								
Female Do.	23								
Azariah Gatton	26:								
Elizabeth	24:31:5:1:3			1			5	5	4
Male Slaves	50:5:								
Female Do.	50:37:30:20:9:3:2								
Ann Norton	55:19								
Male Slaves	4:2			1		1	2	2	3
Female Do.	60:40:4								
Robert Naxton	29:7:1								
Chloe	27:5:4:3			1	2		4		
William Tuell Jr.	38:13:7:2			1	3		2		
Rachelle	33:10								
Tobias Talbot	29:								
Sarah	26:8:6			1			3		
John Allen Hoskins	36:6								
Susanna	36:13:8:1			1	1		4		
Elsworth Bean	57:15:7								
Susanna	47:23:20:13:11:9								
Male Slaves	45:17:15:7:3:5				2	1	6	4	6
Female Do.	35:23:9:3								
John Bean	33:								
Male Slaves	36:27:22:22:7			1			5	2	2
Female Do.	76:28:15:1								
John Weldon Jr.	40:12:6			1	2		3		1
Ann	50:13:10								
Male Slave	14:								
Josias Bean	33:10:8			1	2		4		
Ann	32:6:4:1								
		11	31	720	915	165	1615	1094	1208

69

Name	Ages	Free negroes under 16	Free negroes above 16	Male whites above 16 & under 50	Male whites under 16	Male whites above 50	Female whites	Slaves above 16	Slaves under 16
Henry Biggs	51:21:19:14:17:11	11	31	720	915	165	1615	1096	1208
Sarah	40			2	3	1	1		
John Allen	54:15:12:9 (0722)								
Dorithy	40:7:2				3	1	3		
Henry Jones	39:6								
Ann	28:30:8:4:10:1								
Female Slaves	28:11:8:5:4:1			1	1		6	1	5
William Talbott	66:20:21:18:16:12:10:8:6			4	4	1	5		
Sarah	41:20:14:2:2								
Edward Boswell	52:38:6:6:1			1	3	1	4		
Elizabeth	40:24:8:3								
Rachell Neagle	27:25:10				1		3		
Male White	5								
John Martin	43:30:16:12:8:1								
Mary	40:30:14:11			3	3		4		
James Ewart	59:1								
Catherine	36:9				1	1	2		
Adam Craig	36:21:6:12			2	2		3	1	4
Ann	35:10:5								
Male Slave	3:2								
Female do.	20:5:1								
Prudence Coonel	20:26						2		
Alexander Crawford	36:8:6:3								
Elizabeth	40:7:5			1	3		3	1	1
Male Slave	11								
Female do.	17								
Thomas Crawford	39:12:10:5			1	3		3		1
Elizabeth	39:14:7								
Female Slave	15								
Bazell Crawford & Mary	33:&36			1			1		1
Female Slave	10								
Thomas Brown	35								
Grace	35:19			1			2		
		11	31	737	942	170	1656	1097	1220

70

		Foreigners Under 16	Foreigners Above 16	Male whites betw. 16 & 50	Male whites Under 16	Males above 50	Female whites	Slaves Above 16	Slaves under 16
John G. Hamilton	28:6:	11	31	737	942	170	1656	1097	1220
Susanna	28:57:23:1			1	1		4		
Nicholas Free	41:25:13:7:6:2								
Catherine	40:12:7:4:1			2	4	1	5		
John Frances	57:50:25			1		2	1		—
White female	25								
Philip Miller	35:								
Elizabeth	21:17:2			1			3		
Henry Bradford	48:20:27:15								
Elianor	31:19:8:6:								
Male Slaves	40:25:14:13			4	1		4	3	5
Female do.	23:8:6:2								
Christian B. Reyly	40:9:4:1			1	3		2		
Margaret	33:12								
Felty Waghler	22:22:			2					
Richard Stone	62:36:19:16:13:12			3	2	1	2	2	
Susanna	36:4								
Male Slave	18: female do. 65.								
John Fergusson	51:8.								
Bershiba	37:20:16:14:11				1	1	5	2	
Male Slaves	37:24								
Samuel Collard	50:66:7:4								
Agnes	43:12:								
Male Slaves	35:30:6				2	2	2	4	2
Female do.	35:30:16								
David Scarce	30:10:8:6			1	3		3		—
Cascendra	27:4:2								
William Santam	26								
Catherine	21:18			1			2		
William Tawnihill	28:1								
Elizabeth	25:34			1	1		2		
Thomas Adams	49:17:11:8								
Elizabeth	46:22:15:13:6:			2	2		5	4	1
Male Slaves	19:16: female do. 20:16:1	11	31	758	901	177	1696	1112	1228

71

Names and ages	Foreigners Under 16	Foreigners above 16	Male Whites between 16 & 50	Male Whites under 16	Male Whites above 50	Female Whites	Slaves above 16	Slaves under 16
Thomas & Lucy Adams. 24:20	11	31	758 / 1	961	179	1696 / 1	1112	1228
Samuel Santham 30:13:9:1; Charity ... 31:14			1	3		2		
Thomas Worrell ..58:40:11; Elizabeth Champlin 37:50:16:44:16:6:1:3; female Slave 7			1	1	1	8		1
Nicholas Fair .. 55:19:15:12:3.; Alice 46:17:13:9:5			1	3	1	5		
Jeremiah Tawnihill .. 41:6; Lettice 33			1	1		1		
Jonathan Church ... 31:35:35:3:1; Sarah ..... 45:29:18:7:10:1.; female Slave ...... 15.			3	2		6		1
William Sydebotham .38:25:25:22:22:; female white ... 22:; Male Slave ..... 25; female do. 50			5			1	2	
John Stuart .... 25:19:1; Sarah ..... 23:4:3.			2	1		3		
Benjamin Stoddert .. 24:21.			2					
Francis Wheeler ... 85:28.; Elizabeth ... 55; Male Slaves . 50:13			1		1	1	1	1
Richard Walace .. 36:2; Ann .... 25:60:8:6:4:20.			1	1		6		
Henry Scott ..... 49:14:10:7:4:1; Mary .... 42:38:17; Male Slaves .. 38:13		1	1	5		3	1	1
William Corn ... 26:; Rachell ... 20:40:3:2; Male Slave 9			1			4		1
	11	31	579	978	180	1737	1116	1233

72

	Free negroes under 16	Free negroes above 16	Male whites between 16 & 50	Male whites under 16	Whites above 50	Female whites	Slaves above 16	Slaves under 16
	11	31	579	978	180	1737	1116	1233
Thomas McGill . . 30:3 Rachell . . 30:22			1	1		2		
Peter Carnes . . 27:27:40:15:6:3 Henrietta . . 37:11:8:6 Male Slaves . . 6:2:1. female do: 27:27:4:3:2:1			3	3		4	2	7
William Datford . . 40:24 Sarah . . 25:6:4:2			2			4		
Richard Beall . . 41:11:8:6:4 . . 70:27 Rebecca . . 40:17:15:13:2:1 Male Slaves . . 30:25:20:7:2: female do . . 23:11:7			2	4	1	6	4	4
John Perry . . 41:3: Penelope . 32:77:20:15:5:1 Male Slaves . 41:36:5:3: female do . . 70:35:8:6:7:1			1	1		6	4	6
James Perry . . 49:25:14:11:7 Marcia Perry: 42:20:16:6:3 Male Slaves . 18:6:1: female do . . 38:14:9:8:3			2	3		5	2	6
John Boswell . . . 36:11:4 Elizabeth . . . 29:7:2			1	2		3		
Thomas Henry . 23 . Ann . . 22:1			1			2		
Robert Vinn . . 25:1: Elizabeth . . 21			1	1		1		
William Dickerson . . 23: Male Slaves . . 13:11:9:3 female do . 30:20:7:1:1			1				2	7
Thomas Shanks . . . 29:1 Susanna . . 20. Male Slaves . . 22:13:9:3:1:1: female do . . 38:27:16:35:15:14:12:8:6:3			1	1		1	5	11
Thomas Henry . 73:7: Mary . 31:70:21:8				1	1	4		
John Henry . . . 30:6:4:1: Martha . 33:25:3			1	3		3		
Thomas Wright . 34:2: Ruth . . . 21			1	1		1		
	11	31	597	999	182	1779	1135	1274

73

	Free negroes Under 16	Free negroes Above 16	Male Whites Above 16	Male Whites Under 16	Do.	White Females	Slaves	Slaves Above 16
	11	31	597	999	182	1779	1135	1274
Thomas Crampton . . 61:34 Pricilla . . 29 Male Slaves . . 56:46:42:33:24:20: female do. . . 56:48:35:34:26:19:52:16 Male do. 14:8:6:4:3:2:1: female do. 6:6:5:6			1		1	6	14	11
Catherine Hallum . 30:25:3 White Males . . 7:1				2		3		
Thomas Cissell . . . 50:15:5. Mary 50:15: Male Slaves . . . 28: female do. 40:25:8. free Black . . . . . . 15.	1			2	1	2	3	1
James Page . . 48:8: Frances 50:25:81.			1	1		4		
Henry Purdie . . . 30:17:14:12:10:1 White females 26:8			2	4		2		
Robert Tilley . . 19: Mary . . 41 Male Slaves . 50: 8:5:3:2 female do. . . 53:30:26:13:1:1:			1	1		1	4	7
Jonathan Roberts . 73: Jane . 63:19:17					1	3		
John Turnbull . 29:26:25:22:19:3. Sarah . . . 20:23:2:1 female Slave . . . 8.			5	1		4		1
John T. Bobey . . . 48:16:13:9:6:2 Margaret . . 36:11			2	4		2		
John Beall Junr. . . . 48:25:19:11:6:3 Mary . . . . 45:22:14:8:22 . . Male Slaves . 60:48 [illegible] 14:13:4:6 female do. 38 [illegible] 2:9			3	3		5	4	6
Martha McNew . 44:12: James . 6				1		2		
Alexander Jackson . 54:12:14 Deborah . . . . . 47:19:16:7 Male Slaves . . . 60:24:10:6:3:4:1 female do. . . . 40:30:12:2:				2	1	4	4	7
Thomas Tilley . . . 48:27:19:7 Mary . . . . . 47:17:14:12:10 Male Slave . . . 24			3	1		5	1	
	12	31	615	1020	186	1817	1165	1307

74

	Freemen Under 16	Freemen Above 16	Male whites below 16 & 59	Male whites Under 16	Confessive or Whole All 16	female Whites	Slaves Above 16	Slaves Under 16
Samuel Lindsey . . 48:15:13. Sarah: 44:12:10	12	31	615	1020	126	1817	1165	1307
			1	2		3		
Thomas Tilley Jun. 25:1. Elizabeth . . 25. female Slaves . . 23:20: 4			1	1		1	2	1
William Jackson . 26:25: Elizabeth . . 22 Males Slaves . 17:12: female d°. 30:16:4:2:1			2			1	3	4
Michael Martin 42:9:7 Mary 50:15:6:4 Male Slaves . . 23: 13:6:1. female d°. 30			1	2		4	2	3
Bennett Taylor . 35:10:1. Sarah 28:14:11:4 Male Slaves . . 38:65:40:26:21:22:13 female d°. . . 70:24:26:22:11:1:1			1	2		4	10	4
John Peirce . 30:8:5:1: Mary . . 30:36			1	3		2		
William Clagett. 27:1: Harriet . . 17 Male Slaves . 55:50:27:27:22:16:15:14:14:12:2:1 female d°. 36:36:36:17:14:14:12:8:6:4:2			1	1		1	10	13
William Duvall. 29:23:19: Eleanor. 30:34			3			2		
Clem. Dyar . 30:1. Anna . . 24 Male Slaves . . . . 25 female d°. 13:7			1	1		1	1	2
William Hazwell 46:18:16:13. Anna 40:20			3	1		2		
Benjamin Caywood Jun. 64:24:18:13:15:13 Eleanor 41:12			2	3	1	2		
Philip Edelen . 45:13:11:5: Mary 33:9:7:3:1. Male Slaves . . . 40:25			1	3		5	2	
Richard Clagett. 40:13:11 Mary . . 26:2 Male Slaves . . 36:21:2 female d°. 45:21:13:6:2			1	2		2	4	4
Ignatius Fenwick Male Slaves 55:35:30: 23:12:4. female d°. 50:50:35.							7	2
John Lowe. 60:28: Ann . 65 Male Slaves . 58:40:25:14:15:9 female d°. 22:18:3 15:6:1			1		1	1	5	7
Peter Boswell . . 21: Mary . . 30:5			1		1	2		
Jonathan Burch 68:33:15:6. Elizabeth 58:20:18:3 Male Slaves 50:35:18: female d°. 30:24:24 13:1 14:5:3			1	2	1	4	6	5
Jonathan Burch Jun. 36:9. Anna. 42:12 Male Slaves 22:[illegible]:15:13:3 female d°. 30:21:18:8:6:1			1	1		2	4	6
	12	31	638	1044	189	1856	1221	1358

75

	Foreigners Under 16	Foreigners above 16	Male White between 16 & 50	Male White Under 16	Decrepit m[ales] White above 16	Female White	Slaves above 16	Slaves Under 16
Smith Middleton. 56: Mary. 45:15	12	31	638	1044	189	1856	1221	1358
Male Slaves 62:60:54:26:21:15:14					1	2	8	5
female do 60:26:16:12:10:1								
Edward Lanham. 45:16:11:2								
Susanna. 45:14:7:4:								
Male Slaves. 45:44:19:5:4:3:2:1:1			2	2		4	7	9
female do 40:36:24:20:14:6:2								
Notley Mitchell. 56: Elizabeth 54								
Male Slaves 43:21: female do 70:37:37:37 15:14:9:5:3:1					1	1	6	6
Francis Mudd 30:15:3. Sarah 28:5:1								
Male Slaves. 17:16: female do 12:11:1			1	2		3	2	3
Samuel Clubb. 28:2: Mary. 26			1	1		1		
George F Hawkins. 35:7: Susanna. 26:3								
Male Slaves 56:52:50:45:40:29:21:26:15:8			1	1		2	12	9
female do 28:32:16:14:7:4:3:2:2:5:3:19								
Thomas Shearwood. 71:24:18: Ann. 50:17:12			2		1	3		
John Price. 33:8: Mary. 35			1	1		1		
Joseph Simpson. 71:26:13: Sarah 71:38:24			1	1	1	3		
Jeremiah Shrieves 33:6: Ann. 25:20:6:8			1	1		4		
Joseph Stonestreet 36: Alice 28:1			1			2		
Samuel Mahew 26:14:2:1: Lydia 20			1	3		1		
Humphry Whitmore 60:27:18:9 Elianor 50:22:14			2	1	1	3		
John Calchorn 63:28:11:7:5 Elianor 38:25:23:19:10			1	3	1	5		
Thomas Howe. 46:12: Elizabeth 45:8:6			1	1		3		
Solomon Lanham 21: Lucy 40:11:8			1			3		
Henry Nichols 51:7: Mary. 41				1	1	1		
Thomas Lanham 75:7: Margaret 55				1	1	1		
James Jarboe 40:1= Martha 29:1			1	1		2		
Leonard Fry 26:13:10= Christian 46:15:12			1	2		3		
William Palmer 24			1					
	12	31	658	1366	197	1904	1256	1390

76

	Free negroes under 16	Free negroes above 16	Male whites between 16 & 50	Male whites under 16	Superannuated whites above 50	Female whites	Slaves above 16	Slaves under 16
	12	31	658	1066	197	1904	1256	1390
William Lewis. 26: Sarah 19.			1			1		
Keizer Nighton 33:5= Mary 28:3.			1	1		2		
John James. 38:7= females 13:5.			1	1		2		
John Stonestreet 25: Ann 19: 28:26:8:4:4. Male Slaves 60:50:35:21:35:7:2. Female do. 23:5.			1			6	6	3
Ann Gibbs. 52:14= John Harris Gibbs 23:100. Male Slaves 60:17: female do. 70:12.			1		1	2	3	1
Benjamin Thorn. 43:6:2= Amelia 24:9:4:1. Female Slave 15			1	2		4		1
Ann Athers. 70.						1		
Thomas Dawson 41:13:10:6= Mary 38:12:3:1.			1	3		4		
Ann Dawson 59: 27:13:8:3 Male Slave 4: female do. 27:11.						5	1	2
Daniel Fraser. 59:16: Elizabeth 48:18:13:7			1		1	4		
Thomas Wright. 43:10:3:1: Elizabeth 38:9:1			1	3		3		
John Scott. 42:14:9:3 Mary 42:14:12:11:10:3.			1	3		6		
Nathell Weathers 52: free black. 64 Male.		2						
John Cassell. 51:15:11: Rebecca 40:1. Female black free 2. Do. Slave 40.	1		1	1	1	2	1	
Benjamin Jones. 40:13:10:7= Elizabeth 39:12:1			1	3		3		
Mary Paice. 25. her son 1.				1		1		
John Paine. 30:8: Mary: 36:6:4:2 Female Slave 14.			1	1		4		1
Jesse Lanham. 42:14:10:9: Elizabeth 37:17:14: 8:4:2.			1	3		6		
James Robinson 54: Mary 53:16:14.					1	3		
Thomas P. Edelen. 37: Susanna. 35:11. Male Slaves 20:15:14: female do. 17.			1			2	2	2
George Rowe. 25: Sarah 19:1			1			2		
	13	33	674	1088	101	1969	1264	1400

77

	Free negroes under 16	Free negroes above 16	Male whites between 16 & 50	Male whites under 16	Males above 50	Female whites	Slaves above 16	Slaves under 16
	13	33	674	1088	101	1967	1269	1400
Henry Fraser 22:1: Virlinda . . 22			1	1		1		
Edward Jones Jun.r 28:3: Elizabeth 30: Male Slave 10			1	1		1		
William Norton Jun. 60: 20:16:10:8:6:1. Elianor . . . . . 38:18:14:12:4. Male Slave . . 19: female d.o 17			1	1	1	5	2	
John Jones. 45.13: Elianor. 29:11:1 Male Slaves. 21:11; female d.o 27:14:2:12:1			1	1		3	2	5
Thomas Clarkson Jun. 28:2:1 Elizabeth 37:3 Male Slave 9: female d.o 40:7			1	2		2	1	2
Benjamin Gilpin 39:13: Ann:16:28:10:8:4.			1	1		5		
John Goldrope 52:25: Mary 52:22:12:			1		1	3		
Mary Jones 60: her son . . 14 female Slave . . . 14				1	1			1
Notley Jones 27:1. Ann 23:4.			1	1		2		
John Wheal 43:12:9:7:1. Mary 11:5. female Slave 19			1	4		2	1	
John Breashears 53:22:14. Mary 57:19			1	1	1	2		
John P: Breashears 24:4: Ann 24:1			1	1		2		
Samuel Mullican 27:5:2:1: Ruth 27:2			1	3		2		
Nathaniel Talbot & Ann . 56 & 58 Male Slaves 36:20					1	1	2	
Ignatius N. Dennis 31:1: Lucrecia 33:8:4.			1	1		3		
Susanna Kinsberry 20			0			1		
Thomas Kindrick 51:23:18:12:6 Sarah 45:28:16:6			2	2	1	4		
Richard Ridgeway 24:4:1 = Charity 28:8:6			1	2		3		
Jonathan Ridgeway 57:21:16: Elizabeth 57:			2		1	1		
Henry Humphry. 29:6:4:2: Elizabeth 24 Male Slaves. 26:10: female d.o 24:14:14:3			1	3		1	2	4
Susanna Jones 26						1		
	13	33	693	1114	108	2012	1279	1412

78

	Free negroes under 16	Free negroes above 16	Male whites between 16 & 50	Male whites under 16	Upwards of 50 whites	Female whites	Slaves above 16	Slaves under 16
	13	33	693	1114	103	2012	1279	1412
John Galworth. 29: Sarah 23: 2			1			2		
Sarah Humphray. 58: 26: 24: 20: her son 15: Male Slaves 26: 11. female do 36: 26: 10: 4				1		4	3	3
James Simpson. 39: 12: 10: 8 Precilla 38: 5: 3: 1			1	3		4		
Henry Hardey. 56: Mary. 60: 23: 1 Male Slave. 8					1	3		1
Richard Adams 20: 2: 1 Elizabeth 20: Male Slave. 20: female do 6.			1	2		1	1	1
William Walker. 25: 2: Elizabeth 24: 1			1	1		2		
Samuel Dorr. 35: Martha 26: 6: 3			1			3	1	
John Thompson Sen. 67: 16: 15: 10: 3 Sarah 45: 18: 13			1	3	1	3		
Mathew Day Jr. 30: 9: 4: 2 Ann. 25: 11: 6			1	3		3		
William Thompson 38: 17: 23: 15: 10: 8: 6: 5: 3 Mary 29: 16			3	6		2		
Henry Walker. 45: 16: 3: Elianor 29: 60: 22: 8: 6			2	1		5		
Robert Barrot. 53: 16: 14: 1. Sarah 40: 80: 31			1	2	1	3		
George Keath 51: 20: 12: 6: 4. Monica 49: 17: 15: 12: 9: 2. Male Slaves 4: 2: 1: female do 48: 25			1	3	1	6	2	3
John King 38: 7: Elianor 39: 12: 13: 11: 9: 5: 1. Male Slave 14			1	1		7		1
Thomas Lewis. 34: 9: 6: 12. Elizabeth 35: 16: 11: 1			1	3		4		
Joseph Stone 37: 16: 10: 7: 6: 4: 1. Elianor 35: 12: 11: 3			2	5		4		
Barton Morris 20: 1: Mary. 18: 2 free female black 12			1	1		2		1
Mary Davies 40: 19: 16: 15						4		
William Bryan 63: 23: 19: Diana 45: 33: 15: 12: 6: 4: 11. Male Slave 19: female do 30: 40			2		1	7	3	
George Bryan 34: 4: 3: 1. Anna 24			1	3		1		
Sarah Ball 60						1		
	13	33	715	1152	113	2083	1288	1422

79

	Foreigners under 16	Foreigners above 16	Male whites betw. 16 & 50	Male whites under 16	[illegible] whites ab. 50	Female whites	Slaves above 16	Slaves under 16
	13	33	715	1152	113	2083	1288	1622
Martha Walker 30:2 her sons 4:1				2		2		
Richard Grigory 32:5:1: Violetta 31:11:8:3			1	2		4		
Richard Barrel 51:24:19:16:15:9: Ann 53:21:12: Female Slaves 33:1			3	2	1	3	1	1
Martha Burgess 50:18:17:9:5. sons 21:1			1	1		5		
Elizabeth Rollins & Robert Ellis 57 & 47						1		
Reubin McDaniel 29:5:1: Catherine 25:7			1	2		2		
Nathaniel Willson 60:19:17:14: Elizabeth 53:27:24:22:11 Male Slaves 17:7: female do 54:40:14:13:11			2	1	1	5	3	4
Sarah Mason 45:57:13:6: Sons 19:4			1	1		4		
Samuel Lusby 50:23:22:6:4:1 Susanna 41:18:12:9 Male Slaves 38:14:12 female do 50:35:5			2	3	1	4	3	3
Christopher Edelen 28:21: Mary 28:3:1 Male Slave 7. female do 12			2			3		2
Henry Dyar 26: Ann 21 Male Slave 7. female do 12			1			1		2
Richard Edelen 53:14:7: Mary 52:17:12:10:5:4 Male Slaves 35:14: female do 35:33:34:17:8:1				2	1	6	5	3
Mathew Day 66:14:13:11 Ann 55:30:28:26:20:9				3	1	6		
Clement Mattinly 28:11: Frances 44:20:18:15:9:2:9			1	1		7		
Benjamin Gilpin 60:14: Sarah 60:18:16:10				1	1	4		
Charles Worland 29:23:4 Winefred 20:4 Male Slaves 13:9:7			2	1		2		3
John Walker 25:6: Elizabeth 29:64:5:2 Male Slave 12			1	1		5		1
Richard Ball 40:9:7:1 Sarah 28:12:8:6 Male Slaves 60:26: female do 40:2			1	3		4	3	1
	13	33	734	1178	120	2151	1302	1642

80

	13	33	734	1178	120	2151	1302	1442
John Reeves. 51: 11: Sarah 61				1	1	1		
Elizabeth Wheeler 67: 43: 32: 27: 24: 12: 8. Male Slaves 20: 22: 25: female do 25: 13: 11: 4: 1						7	5	3
James Reed 27: Male Slave 30			1				1	
Eleanor Stonestreet 25: 8: 4: 2: her son 1 Female Slaves 20: 3: Male do 1				1		4	1	2
Henrietta Dyar 55: 20: 20: 16: 13: 4. her sons 23: 25: 1 Male Slaves 100: 60: 50: 30: 9: 7 female do 35: 27			2	1		6	6	2
Charles Edelen 49: 16: 13: 7: 5: Catherine 47: 12: 9. Male Slaves 39: 17: 13: 10: 1 female do 28: 19: 8: 7: 5			2	3		3	4	6
Darius Simms 52: 13: 10: Mary 30: 25: 17				2	1	3		
Hannah Smith [illegible] 40: 22: 13: 7: 5: 1 free black her sons 12: 9	6	2						
Zadok Jenkins 34: 10: 7: Precilla 34: 21: 12: 5: 1 female Slave 12			1	2		5		1
Zachariah Scott 39: 13: 9: 8: 4: 1 Elizabeth 40: 11: 6: 2			1	5		4		
Samuel Club 37: 12: 7: 5. Keziah 36: 3: 1			1	3		3		
George Grymes 50: 19: 13: 11: 7: 1 Catherine 42: 16: 7: 3: 3			1	4	1	5		
Paul Talbot 51: 13: 11: 6: 1 Martha 38: 15: 12: 8: 4				4	1	5		
Robert Grymes 34: 4: Hester 31: 12: 10: 1			1	1		4		
John Talbot 51. Ann 76: 30. Male Slaves 22: 21: 16: 9: 7: 4: 10: female do 48: 18: 15: 4: 4					1	2	5	7
Abraham Fisher 55: Elizabeth 50 Male Slaves 30: 12: 1 female do 30: 30: 10: 8: 6: 4: 2					1	1	3	7
John Stone 55: 8: 6: 2: Margaret 60: 13: 4				3	1	3		
	19	35	744	1208	127	2207	1327	1470

81

	Free negroes Under 16	Free negroes above 16	Male whites between 16 & 50	Male whites Under 16	Upwards of 50	Whites abo. 16 female	Whites Slaves above 16	Slaves under 16
	19	35	744	1208	127	2207	1327	1470
Cheyney Joyce 53: Sarah 37:6					1	2		
Azariah Lanham 45. Femal Slaves 27:17:9:6:1			1				2	3
Hillary Bell 49:16:13:14:3:2 Elizabeth . . . 39:17:10:9:7			3	3		5		
Joseph Clarkson 27. Male Slaves - 27:10: female do. 24:5:1			1				2	3
Thomas Bryan 25:1 Anna: 21			1	1		1		
Winefred Bayne 54: 20:18:15: Sons 22:12			1	1		4		
Sarah Smallwood 38:13						2		
Joseph Adams 55: Winefred 66: 14:40: Male Slaves 30:24:24:5:2 female do. 49:49:22:7:1					1	3	6	4
Stephen Robinson 51:14:10:1 Jane 37:19:12:6:3				3	1	5		
Benjamin N. Vermilion 28:5: Hester 22:3:1			1	1		3		
James Havis 39:6:3: Catherine 23:4			1	2		2		
John Simpson 51:22:12: Sarah 48:19:17:14:11:4			1	1	1	6		
James Brown 26:26			2					
Elias Harvin 23:23:2:1 Mary 24:25			2	2		4		
Sarah Jones 31:12:11. her Son 1				1		3		
Lydia Summers 65:25:12: her son 17			1			3		
Joseph Waters 40: Margaret 9			1			1		
Thomas Williams 82:35:29: Ruth 73:36:17:14 Male Slaves 70:69:25:23:15:12:10:9:6:4:2:2: 15:1:2 Femal do. 69:26:26:18:20:9:8:5:2:11			2	1	1	4	9	16
~~Mary Talbot 34:43:5: [illegible]~~								
Dominicar Haviner 46:11:11:10:4 Mary 38			1	4		1		
Ignatius Hardey 39:17:10: Elizabeth 38:15:14:9:8:6:2 Male Slav . . . 1. female do. 21			2	1		7	1	1
Nathan Scarce 35:10: Sarah 33:8:6:3 Male Slave 12			1	1		4		1
	19	35	766	1230	132	2265	1347	1498

82

	Free negroes Under 16	Free negroes Above 16	Male whites between 16&50	Male whites Under 16	Defective m	Whites W. F. female	Slaves	Slaves above 16
	19	35	766	1230	122	2265	1347	1498
William Cary .50.					1			
John King 74: Mary 29:18:16					1	3		
Simon Dimmilion .24.			1					
James Moore 40:16:21 female 12: Male Slaves 31:4: female do 16			3	0		1	2	1
Benjamin Moore 64:21: female 16			1		1	1		
Thomas Parkins 20: Casandria 18:69:11			1			3		
Ignatius Wheeler 45:12:8: Elizabeth 38:19:16:2 Male Slaves 50:38:16:12:9:3. female do 58:38:14:9			1	2		4	5	5
Stephen Coton 30:5:3:1. Eleanor 27:14 Male Slave 14			1	3		2		1
Bartholomew Jenkins 49:14:12:10 Mary 44:6:4:2 Male Slaves 44:15:12:5:3: female do 15:30:11			1	3		4	2	6
Francis Warner 30:6:4:2: Catherine 24: Male Slaves 7:4:1: female do 32:13			1	3		1	1	4
Ann Lowe 60: Male Slaves 50:36:27:20:7:4 female do 36:1						1	5	3
Joseph Hurley 50:78: Ann 48:			1		1	1		
Owen Athey 40:13:11:5:5:1:2: Lucy 43:22:12:7:1			1	6		5		
Thomas Hurley 41:13:11:6:3:1 Jane 36:15:9			1	5		3		
Daniel Hurley 75: female White 35:2					1	2		
Josias Saunders 25:5:4: Jemima 32:2			1	2		2		
John Minnis 36:4:1 Dorithy 37:11:7:5			1	2		4		
Joseph Wigfield 40:4 Elizabeth 28:6:3:1			1	1		4		
Thomas Magruder 38: Mary 39:4 Male Slaves 8:1: female do 30:4:3			1			2	1	4
Demillion Kingsberry 50:16:10: Elizabeth 51:14:13:1			1	1	1	4		
Edward Brown 35:4:2 Hannah 20: Male Slave 22:14			1	2		1	1	1
Leonard Soper 34:6:5:3: Elizabeth 26:9:7:2 Male Slaves 22:1 female do 25:4			1	3		4	2	2
	19	35	786	1263	138	2319	1366	1528

83

	Free negroes Under 16	Free negroes above 16	Male white between 16 & 50	Male whites Under 16	[illegible] Whites ab. 50	Female White	Slaves ab. 16	Slaves under 16
	19	35	786	1263	138	2317	1366	1525
Thomas Wigfield 33:20:13:2 Radie 34:7:3:			2	2		2		
Richard Lowe 30:1: Sarah 20:2: Male Slave 2:			1	1		2		1
Raichell Wheeler 40: Son 15				1		1		
Christopher Arnold 50:10:6:3:1: Mary 30:13: Male Slave 1: female do 18				4	1	2	1	1
Mrs Allen 56: Male Slaves 26:7:5: female do 26						1	2	2
Francis Spinkes 39:8:6:2: Sarah 34:14:11:4. Male Slave 43			1	3		4	1	
Cornelius Hurley 46:19:11:3 Mary 46:16:14:8 Male Slave 30. female do 15			2	2		4	1	1
Edward Magruder 28: Male Slave 11			1					1
Thomas Grymes 52:14:10:2 Margaret 4:5				3	1	2		
Joseph Clarkson 26:1 Male Slaves 12: female do 26:1			1	1			1	2
John Smith 53:8: Sarah 55 Male Slaves 10:6:4:2. female do 40:36:6:4:4:3:1				1	1	1	2	9
John Nowland 31: Elianor 23:2			1			2		
James Robinson 33: Mary Knight 33			1			1		
Thomas Lanham 70:8: Margaret 60				1	1	1		
Thomas Masey 50:19:6: Lucy 46:17:15:12			1	1	1	4		
Edward King 48:5:1. Ann 30:13:10:6:3			1	2		5		
John Hall 35:7: Elizabeth 30			1	1		1		
Anthoney Hardey 31: Lydia 19:1 Male Slave 1: female do 17:1			1			2	1	2
Nicholas Nicklson 40: Mary 47:13:9:5			1			4		
Dorithy Piles 45: 28:21:19:17:9:5:2 Male 15				1		8		
Nicholas Lowe 28:10: Sarah 23:8:6:4 Male Slaves 48:45:15:14, female do 48:34:16:4			1	1		4	5	3
Josiah Bayne 31:9:7: Ann 30:5:3:1			1	2		4		
	19	35	803	1290	143	2072	1380	1547

84

	Free negroes under 16	Free negroes above 16	Male whites between 16 & 50	Male whites under 16	Ditto above 50	Females whites	Slaves above 16	Slaves under 16
	19	35	803	1290	143	2372	1380	1547
Harry Soor 27: Elizabeth 21: 50 Male Slaves 35:22:8 female do. 32:16:11:6:13:1			1			2	4	5
James Waugh 39:28:9:1 Mary 40:13:11:7			2	2		4		
Mary Minnis 45						1		
Thomas Fry 29:6:4:1 Sarah 28:3			1	3		2		
John Strong 38:5: Ann 25:3:1			1	1		3		
Richard Knell 51:18:12:10:8:6:2 Sarah 42:15:4:1 Male Slaves 18: female do. 30:15			1	6	1	4	2	1
John Walker 31:6:4:2: Rachell 25			1	3		1		
Francis Jones 51:18:17:15:12:3: Ann 38:8:6			2	3	1	3		
Mary McDaniel 46:19						2		
Robert Wade Junr. 50:21:15:13:7:4: Mary 45:15:11:9 Male Slaves 34:31:19:15:12: female do. 40:37:16:8:4:1			1	4	1	4	6	5
Ann Wade 38:13:10:3: Males 8:6. Male Slave 35				2		4	1	
Elizabeth Lanham 26:16: Sons 6:4:2				3		2		
John Clifford 43:22:15:12. Monica 39:14:8:2 Male Slave 12: female do. 15			2	2		4		2
Charles Robinson 57: Elizabeth 49					1	1		
Henry Lowe 43:18:10:8:6:3:10:1 Ann 40:19:16:14:12:4			2	6		6		
Margaret Herbert 53:15: Sons 26:18:8			2	1		2		
Andrew All 65: Margaret 56					1	1		
John B. Hardey 67: Mary 63:26:17:15:12					1	5		
Peter Robinson 60:8:4: Wife 30:1				2	1	2		
William Pumphrey 49:15:14:11:7:6 Elizabeth 38:20:17:5:2			1	5		5		
Ralph Pickerson 57:31:22:16:14:5 Elizabeth 53:28:26:24:20:18:12:10			3	2	1	8		
James Jarbo 45:1: Elizabeth 43:1			1	1		2		
	19	35	824	1336	151	2440	1393	1560

85

	Free negroes under 16	Free negroes above 16	Male whites between 16 & 50	Male whites under 16	[illegible] above 16	females White	Slaves above 16	Slaves under 16
	19	35	824	1336	151	2440	1393	1560
Henry Hardey J. S. 45:11:4. Mary 32:30:15:13:6:6 Male Slaves 30:25:22:20:16:9:8:5:3:1:8:3 female do 30:25:20:16:16:13:10:6:6:3:1:1:1			1	2		6	10	15
William Hurley 37:14:12:11:8:3: Male Slave 20:9 Rachell 32:7:5:1. . female do. 10:			1	5		4	1	2
~~[illegible]~~ ~~[illegible]~~						~~[illegible]~~	~~[illegible]~~	~~[illegible]~~
Giles Vermilion 68:36:25:20: Sarah 21:66:			3		1	2		
George Hall & Mary 45:50			1			1		
Thomas Johnson 30: Margery 27:7:4:1			1			4		
Ann Tolon 43:10: her son 14				1		2		
Henry Stonestreet 24: Mary. 23. Male Slaves 27:21:9:7:7:1 female do 24:24:26: 4:6:3:6:2:			1			1	5	9
Thomas Stephens 30:9 Mary 26:50:4:1 female Slave . . . 6			1	1		4		1
William Stephens Jr 26:4:3:1 Elizabeth 24: Male Slave . . — — 40			1	3		1	1	
John McDaniel 39:7: Mary 30:5:1: Male Slaves 30:20. female do 9			1	1		3	2	1
John Redman J. S. 30:4:2: Cloe 25:6			1	2		2		
Walter McDaniel 21: Jane 20:15:1.			1			3		
Joseph Hatton 55:32:27:21:19:15: Mary. 53:26:24:22:10 Male Slaves 60:40:18:14:14:12:8:6:4 Female do 54:37:35:22:19:14:13:7:15:22:			4	5	1	6	9	10
Henry Rozer 51:19:19:17:26:30:6 Elianor . 48:26:12:8:3 Male Slaves 50:22:35:26:33:18:27:40:30:28:22: 53:24:40:18:13:11:12:10:10:8:6:12:2:2:9:1:2:2: 5:9:1:7:2 Female do 52:18:20:16:20:18:46:30:20:16:40:40:46 34:37:24:48:19:17:11:19:4:10:9:1:8:4:6:3:6:4:2:2:1			5	5	1	5	34	34
	4 & 19	35	846	1353	154	2485	1456	1632

86

	Foreigners under 16	Foreigners above 16	Male white between 16 & 50	Male white under 16	Other free Whites ab° 16	Female Whites	Slaves above 16	Slaves under 16
Nolley Young white Males above 16	19	35	846	1353	154	2483	1456	1632
White Females			6	3				
Male Slaves above 16 . . . 25						6		
Female d° . . . 23							48	
Male d° under 16 . . . 21								
Femal d° . . . 21								42
Thomas Moore 31: Hester 26: 3 Male Slaves 55:27:20:12:10:3:1. female d° 31:17:8:			1			2	5	5
Hezekiah Wheeler 37 Male Slaves 50:30:13:11:6:5:3:2 female d° 60:38:34:13:5:1			1				5	9
Thomas Dyar 32:7:2:1. Ann 28:10:4 Male Slave 27: female d° 22			1	3		3	2	
Nathaniel Newton 39:30: females 50:43:33:30:22 Male Slaves 36:29:29:27:26:22:17:16:12:9:6:6:5:5:4:4:1:1:1 Female d° 47:45:42:39:35:33:22:20:19:18:16:12:12:11:10:8:5:4:3:1:1			2			5	19	21
James Hawkins 42 Elizabeth 44 Male Slaves 70:48:40:35:25:15:11:10:9:9:7:3:3:1. female d° 40:35:34:15:13:11:7:5:4:2:1			1			1	8	47
Elizabeth Beall 70:38:27: Male 10 Male Slaves 50:28:26:23:11:3: female d° 41:25:21:39:13:8:5:11:				1		3	8	6
Susanna Dyar 75:29: her Sons 28:27: female Slaves 60:36:36			2			2	3	
John Dowling 43:13:6:1. Mary 38:15:11:8:4:25: Male Slaves 48:30:22:16:15:13:12:10:3:1 female d° 36:20:7:5:5:2			1	3		6	6	10
William L: Dowling 28:24: Mary 74:26:22 Male Slaves 51:H. female d° 51:18;			2			3	3	1
Samuel Coe 32:18:9:1. Phebe 33			2	2		1		
Mary Coe 50:23:18:16: Sons 26:21:6			2	1		4		
Elizabeth Simpson 70:14:10: Green 27 Male Slaves 60:48			1			3	2	
	19	35	868	1366	154	2522	1565	1748

87

	Foreigners under 16	Foreigners above 16	Male whites above 16	Male whites below 16	Male whites above 50	Females whites	Slaves	Slaves under 16
	19	35	868	1366	154	2522	1565	1743
Althea S. Parker 45: John Simpson 34: Male Slaves 30:12:7:6:4:1. female do. 30:30:29:20:14:15:14:12:10:7:4			1			1	5	11
Thomas L. Green 29:2: Cathirine 28:5:3. Male Slaves 26:13:7: female do. 35			1	1		3		
Christopher Edelen 53:18:2 Elizabeth 42:16:14:12:9:6. Male Slave 9			1	1	1	6		1
William Winn 24: Ann 21			1			7		
Henry Spalding 27:1. Ann 24:4 Male Slaves 11:1. female do. 21			1	1		2	2	1
John Spalding 24:20: Male Slaves 30:18: female do. 45:46			2				4	
John King 25:16:11: Kersey 20:14:9:7			2	1		4		
Nathaniel Hatton 55:56 Mary 63 Male Slaves 60:44:25:20=14:13:10:8:3:1. Female do. 60:28:20:21:35:23:16:14:13:10:6:11:5:9:4				2	2	1	11	14
Nicholas Miles 35:10: Ann 28:3. Male Slave 23:22:			1	1		2	2	
Anthoney Addisons List cannot be got								
Wm. Addisons Quarter Male Slaves 70:50:40:31:21:=13:14:11:10:8. 7:5:5:3:4:1. Female do. 67:60:35:30:23 8:7:6:4:4:4:9:1							10	19
John Winn 56:17: Sarah 54:15:14:12:9 Male Slaves 35:34:10: female do. 100:16:1			1		1	5	4	2
John Winn Jr. 37:9:7:4:1: Mary 30:10:5			1	4		3		
William Smallwood 54:19: Mary 56:20:14			1		1	3		
John Berry 24: Male Slave 30 female Slaves 36:16:4:2			1				2	3
	19	35	882	1375	159	[illegible]	1605	[illegible]

88

	Free Negroes Under 16	Free Negroes above 16	Male whites above 16	Male whites Under 16	Aged Males above 50	Females Whites	Slaves above 16	Slaves under 16
Bazil Russell ... 32	19	35	282	1375	159	2553	1605	1794
Robert Phelps 45:12:10:8:6:4: Sarah 40:60: Female Slave 14:		1	1	5		2		1
Gilbert Simpson 26: 16: Mary 40:18:14:12:10:8:7			2			7		
	19	36	285	1380	159	2562	1605	1795

89

The Number of Inhabitants contain'd in the parts of St Johns & Wm Williamson's Parish lying in Prince Georges County

Free blacks under 16	Free blacks above 16	White Males between the age of 16 & 50	White Males under the age of 16	White Males above the age of 50	Female Whites	Slaves above the age of 16	Slaves under the age of 16
19	36	885	1380	159	2562	1605	1795

The foregoing is the list of Inhabitants the parts of St John Parish & Prince Georges Parish contained in Prince Georges County taken by Order of the Committe of this County by

Thoms Dent

N.B. Richard Thrawls & James Prather refuse to give in a list of their families and Anthoney Addison neglects to do it after several applications by Tho Dent

Prince Georges County ss Augt 31st 1776
I hereby Certify that this day Capt Thomas Dent returned His list of Inhabitants in ~~Prince~~ Prince Georges & Saint Johns Parishes being in the County aforesaid to the Committee of Observation Agreable to resolve of Convention

Micah Lyon Clk

Accounts upon the Covers (inside) of "Census of 1776,"* Prince George's County

36 MARYLAND JUNE Y^{e} 2^{d} 1736
Mr. Robt Carrol Dr.
To 10 y^{ds} fine Drugget @ 2/4^{d} p.£ 1-3-4
To 4 Doz Coat Buttons @ 0-2-0
To 3 Doz breass Do 0-1-0
To 5 Sticks mohair @ 0-1-3
To 7 y^{d} Shalloon @ 15^{d} p. 0-8-9
To 1/2 y^{d} Irish Linen 0-1-0
To 2 hanks Silk 0-0-10
To ¼ (?) Coll^{d} thread 0-0-9
To 1 Romale handkf 0-3-6
To 1 p mens Cotton hose 0-4-6 S45-£2-s6
Mrs Catherine Plassey Dr.
To 2 Casks Rum No. q^{t} 224½ Gal @ 41 p £44-18
To 2 Casks Ale Bottled q^{t} 20 Doz £12-0
To 6 Doz bottles Do @ 12/p £ 3-12
S9-£60-10
Mr Henry Brooke Dr.
To 7½ (?) D D Sugar @ 1/p £2-6
To 1 Single Do 6 (?) @ 9 4-6
To 1 p^{r} mens thread hose 3-6
S44-£0-16
Supra Cr.
By J^{no} Cresswell S44-£0-16.
51 MARYLAND JUNE Y^{e} 7th 1736.
Mr Robt Wade Junr. Dr.
10 1 q^{t} Rum S10-£0-s0-d9½.
Mr. Thos. Middleton Senr. Dr.
To Cash £2 Cu (?) S21-£2
To 2 felt hatts 3-6
To 1M pinns 1-2
To 2 Combs & cases 1-2
To 2 Ivory Combs 1-4
To 1 Gall Rum 2-6—S21-£0-s9-d8
Mr. Thos. Owen Dr.
To Rum and other items (indistinct) amounting to S45-£0-s16-d17.
Mr. Jno Winn Dr.
To 5 Clasp knives s2-d6
To 2 coco knives & forks s1-d5
To other items (indistinct)

* Apparently pages 36 and 51 of an old account book pasted on the inside of cover.

Prince George's County

"At the time Prince George's County was erected [1695] there were settlements along the Patuxent nearly up to Laurel, but there were few if any settlements on the Potomac side in the vicinity of Piscataway Creek on account of the presence of the friendly Indians, who had reserved to themselves this territory for a permanent abode. There were, however, settlements or small outposts at the mouth of Rock Creek within the present limits of Georgetown and along the Anacostia River in the vicinity of Hyattsville and Bladensburg, and as far up the Northwest Branch as the present Montgomery line."

"Within the next two decades these settlements had extended beyond the present limits of Prince George's County although they were at that time within its limits. During these same years the whites began to settle on the territory formerly claimed by the Indians, who ultimately left the Europeans in undisputed possession."

"The first curtailment of territory assigned Prince George's County occurred in 1748 when the county was reduced to its present limits, including the District of Columbia, by Chapters 14 and 15 of the Laws of Md. for 1748. According to the first act which was stimulated by a petition by some of the freeholders in Prince George's County who found it inconvenient to attend the County Court at Upper Marlboro, it was enacted:

" 'That from and after the Tenth Day of December, in the year One thousand seven hundred and forty eight the Land lying at present in Prince George's County, and contained within the bounds following, viz., by a Line drawn from *Mattawoman* run, in the Road commonly called the *Rolling Road*, that leads from the late dwelling Plantation of Mr. *Edward Neale,* through the lower Part of Mr. *Peter Dent's* Dwelling Plantation, until it strikes Patowmack River, at or near the bounded Tree of a Tract of Land whereon *John Beall, junior* now lives (standing on the Bank of the aforesaid River, at the lower end of the aforesaid *Beall's* Plantation) then with the River to the Mouth of *Mattawoman* Creek, shall be and for ever hereafter deemed as a Part of *Charles* County . . . .' "

"The second act passed in 1748 related to the erection of Frederick County from all the less settled portions of Prince George's County. According to this law it was enacted:

" 'that all the land lying to the westward of a line beginning at the lower side of the mouth of Rock Creek and thence by a straight line joining to the east side of *Seth*

Hyatts plantation, to the Patuxent River shall be taken from Prince George's County and made into a new jurisdiction to be called Frederick County.' "

"A portion of this line still forms the boundary between Montgomery and Prince George's counties."

"The final change in the boundaries of Prince George's County was made in 1791 when the District of Columbia was ceded to the National Government from portions of Montgomery [erected 1776] and Prince George's counties."*

HUNDREDS OF PRINCE GEORGE'S COUNTY

Prince George's County was established in 1695; and is divided into nineteen hundreds, viz., Prince Frederick, Washington, Mattawoman, Mount Calvert, Patuxent, Upper Marlborough, Charlotte, Horsepan, King George, Piscataway, Hanson, Oxen, Bladensburg, Eastern Branch, Rock Creek, Western Branch, Collington, Grubb, and New Scotland.†

The Census of 1776 was taken by *parishes* in Prince George's County (see pp. 1–89), and in Anne Arundel County (see pp. 407–431). The admirable returns for the said counties herein reproduced in facsimile, and the returns for the several hundreds of Frederick County (see pp. 177–257), and of Charles County (see pp. 297–312) are unfortunately all of this census which have been preserved for the said localities.

Note: In pages 93–172 a few names are out of alphabetical order, due to errors in name being corrected in the page proof and therefore the position was not changed. Not all the licensees are repeated in the alphabetical positions, therefore see the general index for all names.

G. M. B.

* *The Counties of Maryland*, Mathews, pp. 526–527, 1907.

† *A Geographical Description of the States of Maryland and Delaware*, Joseph Scott, Philadelphia, 1807, p. 122.

Marriage Licenses Issued at Upper Marlborough, Prince George's County, Maryland—1777 to 1801.*

Abbigell, Thomas	Hughes, Sarah	Feb. 4, 1788
Adams, Anny	Contee, Zachariah	Dec. 12, 1797
Adams, Elizabeth	Grimes, Isaac	Mch. 23, 1799
Adams, George	Wright, Mary	Jan, 21, 1783
Adams, Joseph	Nevitt, Ann	Nov. 5, 1791
Adams, Josephus	Watson, Eliza	Oct. 24, 1777
Adams, Judy	Barten, John	June 1, 1792
Adams, Levisa	Smute, Thomas Barton	Jan. 16, 1788
Adams, Luke	Thorn, Susanna	June 2, 1781
Adams, William	Howard, Rebecca	July 12, 1796
Addeton, Richard	Clarke, Elizabeth	Apr. 25, 1787
Addison, Anthony	Murdock, Rebecca	June 26, 1794
Addison, Eleanor	Corliss, Garland	Dec. 22, 1779
Addison, Henry	Clagett, Eliza	Feb. 22, 1794
Addison, Mary	Ridout, Samuel	Dec. 21, 1790
Addison, Rebecca	Hanson, Thomas H	Mch. 21, 1778
Adkins, Thomas	Berry, Lucy	Mch. 11, 1780
Albey, Alminta	Riston, Elisha	Jan. 11, 1779
Albey, Ann	Higdon, Thomas	June 10, 1797
Albey, Walter	Smith, Elizabeth	Feb. 26, 1783
Albey, William	Riston, Keziah	Jan. 21, 1778
Alder, Elizabeth	Fry, Robert	Dec. 13, 1792
Alder, George	Wynn, Lucy Ann	Oct. 31, 1778
Alder, James	Atchison, Rebecca	Jan. 6, 1790
Alder, Joanna	Ryon, Philip	Mch. 23, 1778
Alder, Ruth Hawkins	Haye, William	Jan. 6, 1798
Alexander, Eliza	Thompson, Electius	Aug. 14, 1780
Alexander, Rachel	Hayes, William	Sept. 5, 1795
Allein, Sarah	Wood, James G.	Dec. 4, 1798
Allen, Elizabeth	Arnold, William	Aug. 30, 1786
Allen, George	Lowe, Sarah	Jan. 5, 1782
Allen, John	Lanham, Verlinda	Oct. 29, 1781
Allen, Thomas	Piles, Jemima	Oct. 11, 1786

* Carefully transcribed and compared with the original records by Mrs. Amos G. Draper, Washington, D. C. Alphabetically arranged by the compiler of this volume.

Allingham, Stephen.......Richards, Jemima............Mch. 30, 1781
Amberson, William........Simpson, Mary Ann...........Dec. 21, 1789
Ambler, Elizabeth........Pearce, Thomas.............Jan. 21, 1783
Ambler, Mary............Lee, Richard.................Nov. 9, 1779
Anderson, Comfort........Peters, John Saml............Feb. 27, 1779
Anderson, Absalom.......Burrell, Ann.................June 6, 1794
Anderson, Benjamin.......Davis, Beno..................Feb. 12, 1800
Anderson, George.........Sutherland, Barbara...........Apr. 18, 1788
Anderson, Jesse...........Riley, Mary...................July 19, 1800
Anderson, Samuel.........Taylor, Martha................Feb. 19, 1787
Anderwig, Lancelot.......Turner, Sarah.................Dec. 19, 1797
Armistead, Mary.........Carter, Landon.................Jan. 1, 1800
Arnold, Richard..........Talbert, Susannah............Dec. 16, 1800
Arnold, William..........Allen, Elizabeth..............Aug. 30, 1786
Askey, Mary.............Wells, Nathan..................Jan. 14, 1785
Askey, Priscilla...........Hinton, Gideon...............Dec. 24, 1798
Atcheson, Chloe..........Vernem, Caleb................Nov. 30, 1790
Atchison, Henry..........Hilton, Susannah.............Feb. 17, 1800
Atchison, James..........Darien, Ann...................Feb. 8, 1783
Atchison, Rebecca.........Alder, James...................Jan. 6, 1790
Atcherson, Mildred.......Jenkins, Thomas.............Nov. 10, 1787
Athey, Elizabeth..........Robey, George Dement........Dec. 16, 1791
Athey, Hezekiah..........Tilley, Rebecca...............Dec. 10, 1799
Athey, Rhodoe...........Thompson, James.............Nov. 25, 1788
Athey, Zephaniah.........Duckett, Lucy................Nov. 11, 1790
Atwell, James............Owens, Elizabeth............Sept. 16, 1799
Austin, Eleanor...........Naylor, Baston................Nov. 6, 1778
Austin, Elizabeth.........Robinson, Benjamin............Feb. 7, 1793
Austin, Samuel...........Davis, Ann....................Jan. 18, 1793
Austin, Sarah............Wheeler, Jacob................Feb. 10, 1786
Avans, Sarah.............Barnes, John..................Feb. 19, 1785
Awl, Martha.............Daugherty, James..............June 9, 1795
Ayres, Robert............Hardey, Ann.................Sept. 10, 1784

Bacon, Benjamin.........Downes, Elizabeth............Dec. 23, 1797
Baden, Alexander.........Steel, Mary...................June 3, 1797
Baden, Elizabeth.........Marlow, John.................Oct. 29, 1791
Baden, Elizabeth.........Emberson, Henry.............Dec. 31, 1800
Baden, James............Gibbons, Susannah.............Dec. 4, 1799
Baden, Martha...........Naylor, Joshua.................Dec. 2, 1799
Badon, Rebecca..........Noble, Richard..............Sept. 26, 1796
Baden, Robert, Jr.........Gover, Frances...............Nov. 10, 1779

Badon, Robert...........Gover, Elizabeth.............May 12, 1796
Baden, Sarah.............Cater, Thomas...............Aug. 31, 1791
Baden, Thomas...........Dorrett, Sarah.................Feb. 6, 1797
Baine, Quintin............Brewer, Mary...............Sept. 13, 1792
Baker, Philip Thomas.....Bayly, Maria A...............Dec. 19, 1799
Baker, Samuel H..........Paca, Elizabeth.............June 30, 1797
Baker, William...........Greenfield, Susanna............May 2, 1789
Baldwin, Amelia..........Bright, Stephen..............Sept. 21, 1796
Baldwin, Catherine.......Simmons, Robert..............May 9, 1781
Baldwin, Susannah........Riddle, Samuel................Dec. 2, 1791
Baldwin, Thomas.........Webster, Christian............July 23, 1790
Baldwin, William.........Sheriff, Elizabeth............. Dec. 7, 1799
Baldwin, Zachariah.......Beckett, Margaret............Feb. 21, 1783
Ball, Ann Busey..........Bryan, Richard..............Jan. 27, 1786
Ball, Bennett.............Morris, Ann ....Jan. 6, 1789
Ball, Druscilla............Jones, Moses.................Nov. 30, 1790
Ball, Isaac................Leach, Mary.................Apr. 20, 1799
Ball, John................Fowler, Ann...................Apr. 4, 1795
Ball, Priscilla.............Crow, John....................Oct. 25, 1780
Ball, Stephen.............Jones, Monica...............July 16, 1781
Ball, Susanna.............Lawson, William...............Oct. 5, 1782
Ball, Thomas.............Beane, Eleanor..............June 15, 1799
Ballett, John.............Gloyd, Joanna................Nov. 29, 1782
Barclay, William..........Evans, Mary.................Dec. 17, 1794
Barnes, Basil.............Lanham, Mary...............Jan. 22, 1791
Barnes, Bridget..........Cofield, Owen...............June 15, 1782
Barnes, Daniel...........Wilson, Ann..................Feb. 21, 1783
Barnes, Henry...........Lanham, Ann.................Feb. 3, 1790
Barnes, John.............Avans, Sarah.................Feb. 19, 1785
Barnes, Margaret.........Lane, John....................Feb. 21, 1781
Barnes, Mary A..........Wilson, James C...............Feb. 1, 1782
Barnes, Milicent ....Berry, Hezekiah..............Dec. 19, 1797
Barnes, Oliver...........Wilson, Sarah..................Feb. 8, 1785
Barrett, Ann.............Milliken, William............Mch. 25, 1780
Barrett, John............Price, Mary...................Dec. 11, 1781
Barrott, John............Newman, Catherine............Jan. 8, 1799
Barrett, Jonathan........Gilpin, Margaret.............Mch. 20, 1779
Barrett, Richard..........Brown, Lucy..................Dec. 18, 1784
Barrett, Sarah............Roberts, John................Aug. 10, 1781
Barrett, Sarah............Loveless, Isaac................Jan. 7, 1794
Barron, Oliver...........Beall, Elizabeth.............May 28, 1800
Barron, Rebecca.........Burch, Benjamin..............Sept. 6, 1784

Barry, William............Smith, Mary Ann.............June 19, 1778
Barten, John.............Adams, Judy..................June 1, 1792
Bartley, George...........Cross, Mary...................Jan. 26, 1798
Bartley, Sarah............Cross, Thomas................Nov. 1, 1798
Bartly, Elizabeth.........Riston, Zadock.................Jan. 7, 1786
Bassford, Chrissy.........Ferrall, Thomas...............Dec. 4, 1794
Bassford, Thomas.........Waters, Casandra..............Apr. 2, 1784
Batt, Dorcas.............Turner, William...............Feb. 21, 1784
Batt, Elizabeth...........Quinn, Thomas................May 26, 1792
Bayly, Maria A...........Baker, Philip Thomas.........Dec. 19, 1799
Bayne, Amelia............Hurley, Daniel................Dec. 21, 1784
Bayne, Daniel............Pope, Ann......................Feb. 4, 1795
Bayne, Elizabeth.........Crow, Lancelot...............Nov. 26, 1794
Bayne, George............Jones, Ann.....................Apr. 24, 1779
Bayne, Martha...........Howsley, Henry...............Apr. 14, 1783
Bayne, Mary.............Noland, Thomas...............June 13, 1796
Bayne, Milly.............Talburt, Josias.................June 4, 1796
Bayne, Prescilla..........Masters, John..................June 3, 1778
Bayne, Sarah.............Moore, George D..............Dec. 16, 1795
Baynes, Chloe ....Finley, Thomas................Jan. 29, 1791
Baynes, John.............Beall, Catherine...............Nov. 3, 1784
Baynes, Mary Fell........Stewart, Philip................Dec. 15, 1792
Beach, William...........Medley, Mary..................May 9, 1797
Beale, Alethea............Dorsey, Jesse...................Jan. 7, 1797
Beall, Alethea Elizabeth...Vanhorn, Archibald...........July 26, 1797
Beall, Andrew............Beall, Mary.....................Nov. 9, 1782
Beall, Ann...............Wilson, Thomas...............Sept. 7, 1783
Beall, Aquilla............Duvall, Sophia.................Dec. 21, 1798
Beall, Catherine..........Baynes, John....................Nov. 3, 1784
Beall, Catherine..........Beanes, William...............Dec. 20, 1788
Beall, Christopher........Brooke, Ann....................Jan. 11, 1780
Beall, David F...........McDaniel, Elizabeth..........June 28, 1800
Beall, Eleanor...........Macgill, Robert...............Apr. 28, 1789
Beall, Elizabeth..........Brown, Peter...................May 11, 1781
Beall, Elizabeth..........Duvall, Zachariah..............Apr. 1, 1791
Beall, Elizabeth..........Barron, Oliver..................May 28, 1800
Beall, Elizabeth..........Crawford, James..............June 11, 1799
Beall, George............Beall, Elizabeth..............Sept. 13, 1800
Beall, James.............Mitchell, Ann...................May 9, 1787
Beall, John F.............Hanson, Margaret B............Apr. 4, 1787
Beall, Jonathan...........Williams, Elizabeth............May 6, 1794
Beall, Joshua.............Waring, Elizabeth.............Feb. 3, 1787

Beall, Lethea............White, Samuel B..............Feb. 21, 1781
Beall, Mary..............White, James.................Oct. 31, 1781
Beall, Mary..............Beall, Andrew................Nov. 9, 1782
Beall, Mary..............Duvall, John................Mch. 29, 1793
Beall, Mary..............Belt, Hiram..................Oct. 6, 1796
Beall, Nancy.............Mullikin, Richard.............Dec. 14, 1785
Beall, Nancy Dent........Hewitt, Thomas..............Dec. 15, 1789
Beall, Rachel............Walker, Richard..............Dec. 13, 1785
Beall, Rebecca...........Belt, Tobias..................Jan. 31, 1789
Beall, Richard, Jr.........Hilleary, Cassandra...........Dec. 16, 1794
Beall, Robert B...........Berry, Elizabeth E.............Jan. 5, 1791
Beall, Sarah.............Hanson, Samuel...............Jan. 9, 1795
Beall, Sarah.............Harrison, Elisha.............Mch. 25, 1796
Beall, Sarah.............Williams, Humphrey..........Jan. 21, 1794
Beall, Taris.............Brashears, John Ducker........Nov. 5, 1788
Beall, Thomas............Brown, Catherine.............Jan. 13, 1779
Beall, Upton.............Clagett, Sarah M..............Nov. 5, 1800
Beall, Walter Brooke......Waring, Jane.................May 1, 1794
Beall, William D..........Brookes, Sarah A.............Aug. 30, 1786
Beall, Zephaniah..........Ferguson, Verlinda.............Jan. 5, 1783
Bean, Benjamin...........Evans, Rebecca...............Dec. 8, 1779
Beane, Ebbsworth........McDaniel, Mary.............Dec. 12, 1798
Beane, Eleanor...........Ball, Thomas................June 15, 1799
Beane, Elizabeth..........Webster, Philip Lewin.........May 20, 1793
Beane, John.............Brightwell, Rebecca..........Mch. 10, 1784
Beane, Milicent..........Magruder, James A...........June 10, 1794
Beane, Rebecca..........Lucker, Thomas...............Feb. 7, 1785
Beane, Thomas...........Brown, Sarah.................Jan. 13, 1794
Beane, Walter............Wade, Meakey.................Oct. 22, 1785
Beanes, Colmow..........Tyler, Milicent..............Apr. 10, 1778
Beanes, Eleanor..........Milliken, James.............Mch. 30, 1781
Beanes, Esther...........Pennefield, Thomas...........July 20, 1790
Beanes, Henrietta.........Tyler, Robert Bradley..........Dec. 1, 1779
Beanes, John H...........Dyar, Henrietta..............Dec. 23, 1785
Beanes, Mary............Cooke, Jeremiah.............Dec. 14, 1785
Beanes, Mary B...........Duckett, Baruch..............Jan. 11, 1783
Beanes William...........Beall, Catherine..............Dec. 20, 1788
Beavin, Ann.............Trueman, Henry...............Apr. 3, 1790
Beaven, Charles..........Sasser, Sarah.................Jan. 13, 1778
Beavin, Charles..........Sasser, Mary.................Dec. 13, 1791
Beavin, Charles..........Lang, Catherine.............Mch. 28, 1792
Beaven, Eliza............Sasser, William...............Dec. 5, 1781

Beven, Elizabeth	Magruder, Nathan	Aug. 12, 1790
Beaven, Henrietta	Cooke, William	Aug. 28, 1777
Beaven, Jane	Sasser, William	Apr. 3, 1779
Beavin, John	Gibbons, Verlinda	Dec. 6, 1796
Beaven, Martha	Naylor, Benjamin	Dec. 23, 1793
Beavin, Mary	Watson, James	Dec. 25, 1799
Beavin, William	Ellixon, Ann	Feb. 2, 1787
Beck, John	Hamilton, Sarah	Nov. 18, 1778
Beck, Ruth	Williams, William	Dec. 11, 1792
Beck, Samuel D.	Webb, Martha	Aug. 19, 1793
Beck, Sarah	Turner, John	Feb. 5, 1799
Beckett, Ann	Moons, Francis	Sept. 25, 1779
Beckett, Easter	Clarke, Henry	Dec. 20, 1777
Beckett, Humphrey	Shreves, Mary	Feb. 22, 1786
Beckett, John	Walker, Mary	Sept. 29, 1778
Beckett, Margt.	Baldwin, Zachr.	Feb. 2, 1783
Beckett, Sarah	Newcome, William	Dec. 19, 1780
Beckwith, Rezin	Hopkins, Mary.	Mch. 31, 1798
Beckwith, William	Jenkins, Prescilla	Sept. 23, 1778
Bedden, Catherine	McClish, Robert	Dec. 14, 1785
Bedder, Elizabeth	Hooper, Thomas	Aug. 18, 1784
Bedder, Jonathan	Hooper, Martha	May 25, 1778
Bedder, Thomas	Sullavan, Sarah	Jan. 8, 1785
Belt, Ann	Belt, Middleton	Aug. 26, 1782
Belt, Benjamin	Wells, Mary	Feb. 6, 1782
Belt, Dreyden G.	Tyler, Robert B.	Mch. 17, 1783
Belt, Elizabeth	Magill, John	Nov. 13, 1786
Belt, Elizabeth Bowie	Smith, Samuel Lane	Nov. 26, 1799
Belt, Esther	Soper, Alexander	Nov. 9, 1796
Belt, Hiram	Beall, Mary	Oct. 6, 1796
Belt, Humphrey, Jr.	Tyler, Elizabeth	Feb. 4, 1792
Belt, James	Lansdale, Elizabeth	Dec. 2, 1794
Belt, Jeremiah, Jr.	Gantt, Priscilla	Mch. 4, 1778
Belt, Joseph	Brashears, Rachel	Jan. 12, 1791
Belt, Joseph Sprigg	Burgess, Sarah	Apr. 28, 1790
Belt, Lucy	Watkins, Thomas	Dec. 6, 1779
Belt, Margaret	Bowie, Thomas	Jan. 23, 1794
Belt, Margery	Duvall, Beale.	Apr. 28, 1800
Belt, Mary	Jackson, William John	Apr. 29, 1788
Belt, Middleton	Belt, Ann	Aug. 26, 1782
Belt, Rachel	Duvall, Elisha	June 17, 1785
Belt, Stephen	Hilleary, Rebecca	Jan. 18, 1786

Belt, Tobias..............Beall, Rebecca................Jan. 31, 1798
Bennett, Mary...........Rhodes, John.................Jan. 30, 1782
Benson, Sarah............Danielson, Zochariah..........Dec. 29, 1777
Benson, Thomas..........Tate, Margaret...............Feb. 11, 1790
Bentenning, Benjamin Smith Willet, Susana..............May 15, 1783
Berckley, Henry............Nicholson, Frances..........Nov. 22, 1788
Berry, Ann..................Walker, Mareen D...........Jan. 15, 1787
Berry, Deborah.............Hodges, Thomas Ramsey....Dec. 30, 1797
Berry, Eleanor.............Naylor, George..............June 2, 1785
Berry, Eleanor.............Beall, Samuel Brooke........Nov. 3, 1785
Berry, Eleanor.............Jeffries, Benjamin Berry.....Oct. 18, 1791
Berry, Elizabeth...........Swain, Gardiner.............Jan. 3, 1798
Berry, Elizabeth E..........Beall, Robert B..............Jan. 5, 1791
Berry, Hezekiah............Barnes, Millicent...........Dec. 19, 1797
Berry, Lucy................Adkins, Thomas...........Mch. 11, 1780
Berry, Margaret............Waring, Thomas...........Mch. 21, 1795
Berry, Nicholas.............Eversfield, Eleanor.........June 16, 1784
Berry, Rebecca.............Hodges, John of Thomas....Jan. 12, 1799
Berry, Thomas.............Smallwood, Susanna........Aug. 25, 1781
Berry, William.............Wells, Martha..............Apr. 7, 1792
Berry, William E...........Harwood, Elizabeth........Mch. 23, 1799
Biggs, John................King, Susanna..............Dec. 11, 1779
Biggs, Priscilla.............Boteler, Henry..............Feb. 9, 1789
Bignell, John...............Weiders, Catherine.........Aug. 21, 1786
Billings, Daniel.............Thompson, Jane...........Sept. 26, 1791
Brown, George.............McDowell, Ann.............May 27, 1799
Bird, Francis...............Ryon, Elizabeth............Oct. 14, 1785
Bird, John.................Swain, Elizabeth............Sept. 5, 1788
Bird, Thomas..............Wheeler, Jemima...........Dec. 14, 1780
Blackburn, John...........Magruder, Elizabeth.........Feb. 4, 1787
Blacklock, Nicholas........Cawood, Elizabeth.........Nov. 24, 1786
Blacklock, Thomas..........Sansbury, Sarah............Jan. 30, 1783
Blacklock, Thomas..........Wynn, Ann.................Nov. 22, 1783
Blanford, Henrietta.........Miles, Harry................June 9, 1783
Blanford, Rebecca..........White, William.............Oct. 11, 1783
Blanford, Susan............Hamilton, Francis...........Jan. 27, 1785
Boarman, Juliet............Spalding, Edward............Oct. 8, 1789
Boarman, Rebecca..........Edelen, George.............Dec. 31, 1790
Bonafin, Sarah.............Havener, Adam............Dec. 12, 1792
Bonnafill, Ann.............Riston, Basil................Dec. 4, 1787
Bonifant, Elizabeth.........Davis, Joshua..............Dec. 24, 1793
Bonefant, Keziah...........Townshend, William........Oct. 12, 1795

Bonifant, Mary	Gray, Thomas	June 2, 1781
Boone, Eleanor	Spalding, James	Dec. 16, 1797
Boone, Electius	Smith, Mary	Jan. 8, 1779
Boone, Francis	Sansbury, Mary	Oct. 16, 1785
Boone, Francis	Neale, Henrietta	Aug. 13, 1795
Boone, Ignatius	Boone, Martha	Apr. 21, 1790
Boone, Ignatius	Sansbury, Eleanor	Jan. 14, 1796
Boone, John	Hardey, Ann	Jan. 12, 1782
Boone, Joseph	Boone, Priscilla	Jan. 3, 1795
Boone, Margaret	Jameson, Benedict	Mch. 12, 1796
Boone, Martha	Boone, Ignatius	Apr. 21, 1790
Boone, Priscilla	Boone, Joseph	Jan. 3, 1795
Boone, Oswald	Jenkins, Ann	Apr. 14, 1800
Boone, Stanislaus	Gardiner, Eleanor	Jan. 2, 1796
Boone, Susannah	Mitchell, Samuel	Jan. 2, 1794
Boone, Walter	Edelen, Mildred	Oct. 9, 1783
Boswell, Clement	Collard, Eleaner	May 18, 1796
Boswell, Hendley	Johnson, Henrietta	Dec. 15, 1792
Boswell, Peter	Findlay, Ann	May 4, 1783
Boteler, Ann	Cox, Thomas Smith	Feb. 2, 1785
Boteler, Catherine	Selby, Philip	Aug. 24, 1778
Boteler, Charles	Robinson, Sarah	Jan. 22, 1785
Boteler, Charles	Brashears, Harriet	Jan. 25, 1799
Boteler, Edward	Sanders, Elizabeth	Jan. 31, 1781
Boteler, Elizabeth	Price, James	Jan. 28, 1779
Boteler, Henderson S.	Hawkins, Susannah G.	Nov. 7, 1799
Boteler, Henry	Biggs, Priscilla	Feb. 9, 1789
Boteler, Joseph	Reynolds, Sarah	Dec. 22, 1783
Boteler, Margaret	Brooke, Leonard John	Oct. 29, 1793
Boteler, Mary	Naylor, James	Dec. 31, 1800
Boteler, Milly	Lovejoy, Alexander	Sept. 6, 1794
Boteler, Sophia	Hodgkin, Philip	Dec. 26, 1789
Boteler, Thomas	Clarke, Ann	May 24, 1784
Bowie, Ann	Brookes, John Smith	Oct. 31, 1780
Bowie, Ann	Chew, Philemon Lloyd	Oct. 27, 1790
Bowie, Elizabeth Margaret	Waring, John, Jr.	Dec. 30, 1800
Bowie, John F.	Hawkins, Susanna A.	Apr. 23, 1784
Bowie, Margaret	Duckett, Isaac	Jan. 24, 1792
Bowie, Margaret S.	Brookes, Benjamin, Jr.	Dec. 24, 1785
Bowie, Mary M.	Wootton, Turnor	Mch. 27, 1794
Bowie, Thomas	Belt, Margaret	Jan. 23, 1794
Bowie, William S.	Sprigg, Elizabeth	Dec. 18, 1781

Bowling, Basil..............Hardey, Mary..............Dec. 31, 1799
Bowling, Levinah...........Nevitt, Charles.............Jan. 18, 1780
Bowling, Thomas...........Nevill, Ann.................Aug. 4, 1783
Boyd, Abraham............Iglehart, Elizabeth..........Jan. 23, 1800
Boyd, Archibald............Scott, Ann...................Nov. 9, 1777
Boyd, Eleanor.............Shekells, Cephas...........Sept. 27, 1796
Boyd, Joseph..............Tait, Elizabeth..............Jan. 14, 1800
Boyd, Thomas, Jr..........Magruder, Mary............Oct. 13, 1788
Bradford, Eleanor..........Walker, Isaac...............July 27, 1790
Bradley, Catherine.........Williams, Abraham.........Dec. 13, 1794
Bradley, Susanna...........Jones, David................Nov. 16, 1779
Brandtt, Richard...........Mitchell, Lucy Ann.........Dec. 15, 1792
Brant, Margaret............Tarman, Richard............Feb. 12, 1795
Braner, John H.............Clagett, Harriett...........May 20, 1795
Branham, Mary............White, Richard.............Nov. 14, 1798
Brashears, Cassia...........Duvall, Charles.............Mch. 27, 1778
Brashears, Eliza............Ridgway, Basil.............Jan. 18, 1779
Brashears, Elizabeth........Orme, Moses...............Feb. 27, 1795
Brashears, Harriot..........Boteler, Charles............Jan. 25, 1799
Brashears, Henrietta........Hoskinson, Elisha...........July 21, 1777
Brashears, Henry...........Ferguson, Aggy..............Apr. 7, 1792
Brashears, John P..........Pumphrey, Ann.............Dec. 9, 1778
Brashears, John Ducker.....Beall, Taris..................Nov. 5, 1788
Brashears, Jonathan........Brown, Mary..............June 12, 1781
Brashears, Joseph...........Cross, Mary................Dec. 10, 1780
Brashears, Lilburn..........Proctor, Eleanor............Feb. 14, 1795
Brashears, Margaret........Cross, Fielding.............Dec. 12, 1794
Brashears, Martha..........Hodge, James...............Jan. 22, 1790
Brashears, Mary............Willcoxon, Levin...........Feb. 11, 1780
Brashears, Mary............Lattin, Plummer............Jan. 25, 1798
Brashears, Mary............Thomas, Nathan............Jan. 17, 1799
Brashears, Nathaniel........Page, Mary.................Feb. 17, 1792
Brashears, Rachel...........Belt, Joseph.................Jan. 12, 1791
Brashears, Rebecca.........Ray, Walter..................Dec. 31, 1791
Brashears, Ruth............Miles, Frederick............Feb. 11, 1784
Brashears, Wilkinson.......Brown, Hannah..............Feb. 4, 1788
Brashears, Zachariah........Crutchly, Ann...............Jan. 22, 1785
Brashears, Zadock..........Drane, Elizabeth............Feb. 9, 1790
Brewer, Mary..............Baine, Quintin.............Sept. 13, 1792
Brice, Richard.............Isaac, Hannah.............Nov. 22, 1781
Brent, Ann................Roberts, Edward...........Dec. 29, 1797
Brentt, Mary..............Sewell, Robert..............Feb. 16, 1789

Brian—see Bryan.
Briges, Aquilla.............Robinson, Jane.............Apr. 4, 1795
Bright, Stephen.............Baldwin, Amelia...........Sept. 21, 1796
Brightwell, Allen...........Moran, Rebecca...........Oct. 15, 1785
Brightwell, Jno.............Swann, Eleanor............Sept. 6, 1782
Brightwell, Mary...........Cave, Thomas..............Apr. 15, 1782
Brightwell, Rebecca.........Beane, John...............Mch. 10, 1784
Brightwell, Richard.........Pierce, Mary...............May 3, 1785
Brightwell, Richard C.......Thomas, Fanoni............Dec. 26, 1794
Biscoe, Eliza...............Calvert, Edward H..........Feb. 29, 1796
Bromley, William...........Sansbury, Sarah............Jan. 29, 1794
Brooke, Ann...............Beall, Christopher..........Jan. 11, 1780
Brooke, Ann...............Wheeler, Joseph............Apr. 23, 1785
Brooke, Barbara............Eversfield, John............June 2, 1778
Brooke, Catherine..........Lansdale, Isaac............Mch. 27, 1792
Brooke, Henry.............Waring, Eleanor.............Oct. 8, 1798
Brooke, Hetta..............Hill, Henry, Jr.............Apr. 23, 1781
Brooke, Isaac..............Magruder, Sarah Ann.......Oct. 20, 1780
Brooke, Leonard John.......Boteler, Margaret...........Oct. 29, 1793
Brooke, Richard............Otway, Eleanor.............June 5, 1800
Brooke, Thomas F..........Duckett, Ann...............June 20, 1791
Brookes, Benjamin..........Johnson, Sarah.............Nov. 7, 1782
Brookes, Benjamin, Jr.......Bowie, Margaret S..........Dec. 24, 1785
Brookes, Benjamin..........Halkerstone, Elizabeth......Feb. 18, 1799
Brookes, John Smith........Bowie, Ann................Oct. 31, 1780
Brookes John Smith.........Harwood, Eleanor...........June 3, 1786
Brookes, Sarah A...........Beall, William D...........Aug. 30, 1786
Brown, Andrew.............Crawford, Margaret........Mch. 14, 1797
Brown, Ann................Hutchinson, Samuel..........June 3, 1786
Brown, Catherine...........Beall, Thomas..............Jan. 13, 1779
Brown, Edward.............Speake, Catherine...........Mch. 8, 1780
Brown, Elizabeth...........Hooper, John................July 7, 1788
Brown, Elizabeth...........King, Richard..............Feb. 11, 1795
Brown, Hannah............Brashears, Wilkinson.........Feb. 4, 1788
Brown, Harriet S...........Brooke, Henry..............Jan. 13, 1798
Brown, Jennett.............Carroll, Charles John.......May 26, 1795
Brown, Letitia.............Wheeler, John..............Dec. 11, 1792
Brown, Mary..............White, John...............Dec. 20, 1780
Brown, Mary..............Brashears, Jonathan........June 12, 1781
Brown, Milly..............Riley, Joseph..............July 23, 1794
Brown, Peter..............Beall, Elizabeth............May 11, 1781
Brown, Priscilla............Hunt, John................Jan. 10, 1789

Brown, Sarah	Manley, William	Jan. 7, 1789
Brown, Sarah	Beane, Thomas	Jan. 13, 1794
Brown, Thomas	Taylor, Sarah	June 29, 1777
Brown, Thomas	Low, Mary	Nov. 9, 1778
Brown, Walter	Sheriff, Ruth	Dec. 21, 1799
Brown, Zachariah	Ricketts, Jane	Apr. 4, 1787
Brunt, Thomas	Smith, Verlinda	Aug. 2, 1796
Brian, Rachel	Wheat, Joseph	Dec. 12, 1791
Brian, William	Padgett, Sarah	Jan. 13, 1787
Bryan, Eliza	Church, Thomas	Dec. 6, 1777
Bryan, Elizabeth	Mayhew, Henry	July 10, 1800
Bryan, Jane	Stewart, William	June 6, 1783
Bryan, Lewis	Church, Margt.	Jan. 16, 1779
Bryan, Margaret	Manning, William W	June 30, 1800
Bryan, Richard	Ball, Ann Busey	Jan. 27, 1786
Bryan, Richard	Steel, Mary	Sept. 29, 1796
Bryan, Sarah Ann	Talbutt, Paul	Mch. 4, 1791
Bryan, William Thomas	Smith, Lucy	Mch. 23, 1778
Bryant, Mary	Davis, John	Oct. 20, 1779
Bryant, Richd.	Harris, Eleanor	May 17, 1782
Buchanan, Mary	Pottinger, Robert	Feb. 15, 1785
Buckingham, Nancy	Curting, Dennis	Feb. 13, 1797
Buchanan, Sophia	Duckett, Richard Jacob	Mch. 30, 1795
Buckland, William	Lynn, Ann	Nov. 24, 1795
Budd, Allen	Rawlings, Catherine	June 27, 1787
Burch, Ann	Godfrey, Samuel	July 3, 1798
Burch, Benjamin	Townsend, Mary	Feb. 22, 1784
Burch, Benjamin	Barron, Rebecca	Sept. 6, 1784
Burch, Edward	Spink, Ann	Oct. 15, 1779
Burch, Elizabeth	Talbott, Lewin	Nov. 17, 1794
Burch, Francis	Vermilion, Penelope	Jan. 26, 1783
Burch, Jane	Hamilton, Andrew	Apr. 17, 1783
Burch, Margt.	Humphries, Thomas	Nov. 22, 1781
Burch, Thomas	Talburt, Susanna	July 26, 1780
Burch, Thomas	Harvey, Linny	Sept. 5, 1794
Burgess, Edward	Thompson, Margaret	June 25, 1781
Burgess, John M	Magruder, Eleanor	Oct. 18, 1779
Burgess, John M	Cooledge, Eliza	Feb. 26, 1794
Burgess, Joseph	Gray, Sarah	Dec. 31, 1779
Burgess, Keziah	Walker, Henry	Dec. 8, 1780
Burgess, Massey	Stewart, James	Dec. 30, 1790
Burgess, Mildred	White, Allen	July 9, 1785

Burgess, Rachel............Thompson, Richard.........Oct. 20, 1779
Burgess, Richard...........Coolidge, Mary............Sept. 17, 1782
Burgess, Sarah.............Bell, Joseph Sprigg..........Apr. 28, 1790
Burns, Elizabeth...........Wilson, Josiah...............Apr. 1, 1789
Burrell, Allen..............Wood, Susannah...........Mch. 18, 1789
Burrell, Ann...............Anderson, Absalom..........June 6, 1794
Burrell, Mary..............Wells, James.................Feb. 6, 1795
Burrell, Sarah..............Denoon, John..............Jan. 17, 1798
Burroughs, George..........Wailes, Rebeccah............July 6, 1792
Bury, William..............Cole, Mary.................Dec. 18, 1797
Busey, Ann.................Walker, Benjamin..........June 13, 1798
Busey, Eleanor.............Littleford, Thomas.........Feb. 11, 1797
Busey, Elizabeth...........Howse, Zacha...............Nov. 3, 1779
Busey, Mary...............Vermilion, Caleb...........Dec. 20, 1794
Busey, Samuel.............Roberts, Sarah.............July 13, 1777
Butler, Ann................Garner, William............Dec. 30, 1799
Butt, Eleanor..............Philips, Samuel.............Jan. 12, 1790
Buttelor, Walter............Davis, Jemima.............Dec. 15, 1785
Butterworth, William.......Darbyshire, Eliza...........Jan. 31, 1779

Cage, Mary................Mayhew, William............Apr. 7, 1794
Cage, Peter B..............Parker, Mary...............Jan. 20, 1783
Cage, William..............Mayhew, Mary.............Dec. 18, 1777
Cain, Michael..............Craver, Elizabeth...........Jan. 27, 1800
Calahan, Catharine.........O'Mara, Philip.............Sept. 8, 1798
Callahan, Eleanor...........Newton, John.............May 27, 1781
Callahan, John.............Sherwood, Susanna.........Feb. 21, 1778
Callahan, Rosamond........Prather, Zacha.............Mch. 2, 1778
Callicoe, Joseph............Demar, Amelia..............Dec. 5, 1781
Calvert, Ann...............Lovelis, Ignatius...........Dec. 23, 1799
Calvert, Edward H..........Biscoe, Eliza..............Feb. 29, 1796
Calvert, Elizabeth..........Stewart, Charles...........June 14, 1780
Campbell, Ann.............McKay, Alexander..........Dec. 16, 1778
Campbell, Arthur..........Lovejoy, Ann.............Dec. 29, 1788
Campbell, Sarah............Lovejoy, Josias.............Feb. 19, 1789
Carr, Eleanor B............Carr, Samuel..............Apr. 28, 1795
Carr, John.................Purnell, Rachel..............Feb. 8, 1779
Carr, Samuel...............Carr, Eleanor B............Apr. 28, 1795
Carren, John...............Page Ann...................Jan. 4, 1790
Carrick, Ann...............Warfield, John.............Dec. 19, 1784
Carrick, Mareen............Jones, Eliza..............Sept. 30, 1782
Carrick, Mareen............Duvall, Mary.............Feb. 23, 1791

Carrick, Mareen............Webb, Margaret............Jan. 7, 1795
Carrick, Sarah............Carroll, Thomas............Mch. 8, 1788
Carrick, William............Shreeves, Eliza............Feb. 13, 1795
Carrington, Alexander.......Magruder, Harriet..........Dec. 16, 1797
Carrington, Leonard........Summerville, Susannah......Oct. 22, 1789
Carrington, Levin...........Mackall, Rebecca..........Mch. 25, 1796
Carroll, Charles John.......Brown, Jennett............May 26, 1795
Carroll, Ignatius............Lynch, Jane..............Dec. 15, 1800
Carroll, James.............Galwith, Susannah..........Apr. 6, 1792
Carroll, John..............Duvall, Mary..............Nov. 8, 1800
Carroll, Mary..............Sim, Patrick..............July 11, 1777
Carroll, Mary..............Fenwick, Ignatius..........June 10, 1780
Carroll, Patrick............Hayes, Mina..............Dec. 31, 1794
Carroll, Thomas............Carrick, Sarah.............Mch. 8, 1788
Carson, Elizabeth...........Johnson, James............Sept. 12, 1800
Carter, Elizabeth...........Hilton, George............Sept. 23, 1796
Carter, Landon.............Armistead, Mary............Jan. 1, 1800
Casey, John...............Edgeworth, Philorlea........Aug. 12, 1778
Cassell, Mary..............Swain, Isaac..............Dec. 24, 1787
Cassell, William............Cole, Margery..............Dec. 2, 1793
Cassell, Amine.............Ridgway, Basil............Dec. 18, 1798
Cater, Elizabeth............Swan, Thomas............Feb. 11, 1793
Cater, Mary...............Weedon, Nathaniel.........Dec. 15, 1794
Cater, Sarah..............Thompson, Thomas..........Feb. 7, 1785
Cater, Thomas.............Baden, Sarah..............Aug. 31, 1791
Cater, William.............Clubb, Elizabeth............Feb. 1, 1792
Cave, Elizabeth............Lee, Henry...............Dec. 15, 1781
Cave, Mary...............Thomas, Caleb.............Dec. 29, 1784
Cave, Sarah...............Eddis, Leonard............Aug. 24, 1780
Cave, Sary................Rollings, John Adam........Apr. 10, 1787
Cave, Thos................Brightwell, Mary...........Apr. 15, 1782
Cave, Thomas..............Pierce, Elizabeth..........Nov. 18, 1786
Cawood, Benjamin..........Shield, Martha.............May 8, 1798
Cawood, Elizabeth.........Blacklock, Nicholas.........Nov. 24, 1786
Cawood, Stephen...........Fendall, Elizabeth Ann.......June 1, 1792
Champline, Alice...........Francis, John..............Nov. 5, 1781
Chaney, Abraham..........Woodfield, Diana..........Sept. 22, 1797
Cheney, Ann..............Shekells, John.............Aug. 14, 1799
Chaney, Deborah...........Russell, Joseph............May 16, 1797
Cheney, Eleanor............Wells, William.............Mch. 30, 1793
Cheney, Henrietta..........Hardesty, John............July 23, 1788
Cheney, Henry.............Duvall, Susannah..........Nov. 28, 1785

Chaney, John	Ferrall, Elizabeth	Dec. 12, 1780
Cheney, Rebecca	Watson, William	Dec. 19, 1793
Chaney, Rebecca	Sheppard, John	Feb. 27, 1797
Chatham, Ann	Parsons, Joseph	July 22, 1798
Chesley, Joseph	Thompson, Rachel	Sept. 19, 1789
Chew, Ann	Perry, Levi	Feb. 20, 1797
Chew, Philemon Lloyd	Bowie, Ann	Oct. 27, 1790
Childs, Joseph	Soper, Eleanor	June 20, 1793
Childs, William	Willett, Mary	Dec. 13, 1781
Church, Elizabeth	Smith, Richard	Jan. 12, 1785
Church, Joseph	Fassett, Ann	Dec. 23, 1800
Church, Margt.	Bryan, Lewis	Jan. 16, 1779
Church, Susanna	Mobley, Jonathan	Feb. 5, 1793
Church, Thomas	Bryan, Eliza	Dec. 6, 1777
Clagett, Eleanor	Scott, Judson	Dec. 3, 1785
Clagett, Eliza	Addison, Henry	Feb. 22, 1794
Clagett, Harriett	Braner, John H.	May 20, 1795
Clagett, James W.	Diggs, Eleanor	May 21, 1782
Clagett, Margaret	Marlow, Thomas D.	Mch. 10, 1787
Clagett, Mary	McElderry, Patrick	June 5, 1789
Clagett, Mary	Scott, Edward	Jan. 9, 1790
Clagett, Mary	Duckett, Thomas	Jan. 5, 1796
Clagett, Mary Ann	Eversfield, John	Feb. 22, 1800
Clagett, Priscilla	Wood, Thomas	Mch. 10, 1787
Clagett, Sarah M.	Beall, Upton	Nov. 5, 1800
Clagett, Wiseman	Lyles, Priscilla	Jan. 16, 1779
Clare, Melicent S.	Tarman, William	Mch. 12, 1781
Clarke, Abraham	Willett, Priscilla	Dec. 14, 1786
Clarke, Ann	Mockbee, William	Feb. 29, 1780
Clarke, Ann	Boteler, Thomas	May 24, 1784
Clark, David	Hall, Eleanor	Mch. 25, 1788
Clarke, Elizabeth	Addeton, Richard	Apr. 25, 1787
Clarke, Henry	Beckett, Easter	Dec. 20, 1777
Clarke, James	Hogan, Rachel	Feb. 9, 1781
Clark, John	Willett, Ann	Dec. 18, 1788
Clarke, Levin	Gibbons, Elizabeth	Dec. 13, 1796
Clarke, Lurana	Perry, Edward	July 12, 1777
Clark, Margaret	Duvall, Calmore	Jan. 3, 1789
Clarke, Martha	Parrott, Chrisr.	Jan. 20, 1781
Clarke, Mary	Green, Elisha	May 1, 1783
Clarke, Mary	Magruder, Thomas	Jan. 4, 1800
Clarke, Sarah	Hyatt, Christopher	Sept. 3, 1793

Clarke, Susanna............Perkins, William...........June 17, 1777
Clark, Thomas.............Hall, Ann..................Dec. 21, 1781
Clark, Thomas.............Wailes, Ann................Oct. 29, 1791
Clark, Thomas.............Mitchell, Eleanor............Dec. 9, 1797
Clark, Thomas.............Jones, Elizabeth..........Sept. 20, 1799
Clarke, Willicy.............Riley, John.............Aug. 9(2?), 1790
Clarkson, Edward..........Edelen, Lucy...............July 19, 1782
Clarkson, Elizabeth.........Spink, Ignatius.............Dec. 15, 1794
Clarkson, Joseph...........Eaglin, Jane................Apr. 11, 1788
Clarkson, Sarah............Dyer, George...............May 27, 1784
Clarkson, Thomas..........Edelen, Tracy..............Nov. 18, 1797
Claud, Ephana.............Grant, John.................Oct. 21, 1777
Clements, Edward H........Sansberry, Minty...........Jan. 15, 1796
Clements, Martha..........Grimes, John...............Jan. 11, 1785
Clemmens, Catherine.......Wright, Samuel..............Jan. 9, 1786
Clifford, Wilder (Milder?)...McEver, Charles............Oct. 17, 1778
Clubb, Elizabeth...........Cater, William...............Feb. 1, 1792
Club, John.................Taylor, Sarah..............Dec. 23, 1799
Club, Levin................Short, Rhoda..............Aug. 25, 1786
Clubb, Rebecca............Mitchell, John..............Jan. 29, 1791
Clubb, William.............Nothey, Ann.................Jan. 2, 1797
Cockler, John..............Shoemaker, Ann............May 13, 1799
Coe, Elijah................Smallwood, Ann............Oct. 23, 1779
Coe, Marsilva..............Smallwood, Bayne..........Dec. 19, 1780
Coe, Milburn..............Tongue, Mary................Jan. 8, 1783
Coe, Richard...............Wood, Margaret.............May 8, 1784
Cofield, Owen..............Barnes, Bridget.............June 15, 1782
Coghlan, Dennis............Smith, Rebecca.............July 18, 1777
Coicel, Susannah...........Wilson, Clement............Sept. 5, 1778
Cole, George..............Hooker, Priscilla............May 6, 1778
Cole, Margery.............Cassell, William.............Dec. 2, 1793
Cole, Mary................Jacob, Mordecai.............June 6, 1789
Cole, Mary................Bury, William..............Dec. 18, 1797
Collard, Eleaner............Boswell, Clement...........May 18, 1796
Collard, Elizabeth..........Kirby, Francis..............Jan. 11, 1783
Collea, William.............Trass, Ann.................Nov. 7, 1786
Collins, Elizabeth...........Right, James...............July 27, 1796
Collins, Sarah..............Davis, Thomas..............Mch. 8, 1791
Collings, Elizabeth..........Silk, Samuel...............July 26, 1779
Collings, Rose.............Jones, Henry...............Aug. 29, 1781
Collings, Sarah.............Hoye, Cephas..............Dec. 27, 1784
Compton, Henry T..........Swann, Ann................Nov. 17, 1797

Conley, Adera..............Newhouse, William..........Jan. 10, 1786
Conley, Ann...............Mayhew, Brian...........June 19, 1779
Conley, Mary..............Magruder, Alexander Wilson Nov. 16, 1785
Conn, Ruth................Nevitt, James.............May 31, 1777
Conner, John..............Tracy, Eleanor W...........Dec. 1, 1778
Connor, Solomon...........Griffin, Susannah..........July 16, 1789
Conner, Thomas............Hutchinson, Elizabeth........Feb. 3, 1781
Connock, William..........Ryon, Elizabeth............Jan. 31, 1798
Constable, John...........Fuller, Ann.................Dec. 4, 1780
Contee, Ann...............Magruder, Dennis..........Sept. 23, 1779
Contee, Eleanor...........Wallace, Michael...........Aug. 18, 1780
Contee, Jane..............Worthington, William.......Feb. 28, 1782
Contee, Richard A..........Craufurd, Mary............June 16, 1785
Contee, Sarah.............Slater, David..............May 29, 1790
Contee, Zachariah..........Adams, Anny...............Dec. 12, 1797
Cooke, Elizabeth..........Hinton, Joseph.............Dec. 22, 1796
Cooke, Jeremiah...........Beanes, Mary..............Dec. 14, 1785
Cooke, Joseph, Jr..........Russell, Elizabeth..........Dec. 11, 1792
Cooke, Rebecca............Deakin, Michael.............Oct. 7, 1779
Cooke, Robert.............Hagan, Henrietta...........July 27, 1790
Cooke, William............Beaven, Henrietta..........Aug. 28, 1777
Cooke, William............Mudd, Elizabeth...........May 28, 1796
Cooke, Zadokiah...........King, Hetty................Dec. 26, 1794
Cooksey, Andrew...........Perrie, Sarah..............Feb. 18, 1800
Cooksey, Sarah............Watson, Leonard.............Jan. 7, 1792
Cooledge, Eliza............Burgess, John M............Feb. 26, 1794
Coolidge, Mary............Burgess, Richard..........Sept. 17, 1782
Coolidge, Samuel Judson....Hepburn, Mary.............Feb. 20, 1798
Cooley, Jane..............Earley, Benjamin...........Jan. 27, 1789
Coombes, Joseph...........Sherkliff, Dorothy...........May 4, 1783
Coombes, Joseph...........Lyles, Mary................Oct. 23, 1797
Coombes, Terissa..........Hardey, Nathan.............May 16, 1783
Corliss, Garland ....Addison, Eleanor...........Dec. 22, 1779
Coughland, Richard Johnson Mitchell, Eliza.............Feb. 28, 1785
Cowles, William...........Earlie, Ann.................July 29, 1777
Cox, Sarah Ann............Harwood, Richard..........Oct. 28, 1799
Cox, Thomas Smith.........Boteler, Ann.................Feb. 2, 1785
Cox, Walter B.............Hollyday, Ann.............Nov. 19, 1778
Cox, William..............Taylor, Charlotte...........May 25, 1796
Crabb, Charles............Smith, Susanna.............Feb. 13, 1792
Crabb, Priscilla...........Drane, Stephen.............Dec. 24, 1793
Craycroft, Elizabeth........Duvall, Jesse..............Sept. 23, 1789

Crandell, Elizabeth.........Fry, Thomas...............June 29, 1795
Crandall, Sarah............Dorsett, Thomas M..........Sept. 3, 1799
Craver, Elizabeth...........Cain, Michael..............Jan. 27, 1800
Craver, Jacob..............Evans, Ann................Apr. 13, 1800
Crawford, Hugh............Jeans, Mary...............Nov. 28, 1780
Craufurd, James............Beall, Elizabeth............June 11, 1799
Crawford, Margaret.........Brown, Andrew.............Mch. 14, 1797
Craufurd, Martha..........Walker, George............Dec. 16, 1794
Craufurd, Mary............Contee, Richard A..........June 16, 1785
Craufurd, Sarah............Forrest, Richard...........Sept. 15, 1789
Creaton, John.............Lanham, Massey Ann.......Feb. 21, 1783
Crimpton, Thomas..........Waring, Margery...........Jan. 28, 1779
Croner, Margaret G.........Edmonston, Edward........June 27, 1800
Crooke, John..............Gray, Cassandra............Dec. 23, 1797
Crook, Mary...............Taylor, John...............Feb. 16, 1798
Crosby, Walter.............Ryon, Ann................Nov. 16, 1799
Cross, Edward.............Scott, Elizabeth............June 19, 1780
Cross, Eleanor.............Simmons, Jacob............Apr. 19, 1780
Cross, Fielding............Brashears, Margaret........Dec. 12, 1794
Cross, Joseph.............Brashears, Lucy............May 20, 1783
Cross, Mary...............Brashears, Joseph..........Dec. 10, 1780
Cross, Mary...............Bartley, George............Jan. 26, 1798
Cross, Thomas............Vermilion, Eliza...........Oct. 14, 1780
Cross, Thomas............Bartley, Sarah..............Nov. 1, 1798
Crouse, George............Sparrow, Ann..............Sept. 24, 1796
Crow, John...............Ball, Priscilla...............Oct. 25, 1780
Crow, Lancelot............Bayne, Elizabeth...........Nov. 26, 1794
Crown, Elizabeth...........Wood, Leonard.............Sept. 9, 1781
Crown, Joseph............Guy, Anne................May 12, 1795
Crown, William...........Ferguson, Janet............Oct. 19, 1799
Crutchly, Ann.............Brashears, Zachariah.......Jan. 22, 1785
Crutchly, Delia............Popham, Samuel...........Dec. 25, 1783
Cunningham, John.........Simms, Margaret............Aug. 4, 1792
Curcaurd, Mary J..........Hodgkin, Theodore..........Apr. 9, 1787
Curting, Dennis...........Buckingham, Nancy........Feb. 13, 1797

Dabney, Mary.............Young, Charles, Jr..........Aug. 17, 1796
Dailey, Moses.............Wiley, Ann.................Oct. 7, 1797
Danforth, Nancy (Mrs.).....White, John M..............Oct. 30, 1797
Danielson, Benjamin........Pearce, Drusilla............Oct. 26, 1779
Darbyshire, Eliza..........Butterworth, William.......Jan. 31, 1779
Darcey, John..............Hardey, Rebecca...........Nov. 21, 1786

Darcey, Mary	Wellen, William	Jan. 30, 1793
Darien, Ann	Atchison, James	Feb. 8, 1783
Darnall, Gerrard	Hurley, Sarah	Jan. 31, 1781
Darnall, Gerrard	Summers, Henrietta	Nov. 7, 1785
Darnall, John	Hurley, Barsheba	Dec. 11, 1782
Darnall, Sarah	Lowe, John	June 24, 1782
Darnall, Susanna	Owen, George	Jan. 25, 1783
Davidson, Ann	Hatton, Henry	July 19, 1781
Davidson, Plinny	Harrison, Mary Henry	Aug. 31, 1793
Davis, Ann	Talbott, John	Oct. 1, 1777
Davis, Ann	Austin, Samuel	Jan. 18, 1793
Davis, Beno	Anderson, Benjamin	Feb. 12, 1800
Davis, Eleanor	Thompson, Zacha	Dec. 9, 1783
Davis, Eleanor	Wailes, Levin	Oct. 28, 1796
Davis, Elizabeth	Orme, Moses	Oct. 22, 1781
Davis, Henry	Morris, Mary Norman	Oct. 23, 1790
Davis, Jemima	Buttelor, Walter	Dec. 15, 1785
Davis, John	Bryant, Mary	Oct. 20, 1779
Davis, Jonathan	Watson, Sarah	Dec. 26, 1787
Davis, Joshua	Bonifant, Elizabeth	Dec. 24, 1793
Davis, Minty	Swann, Henery	Jan. 8, 1789
Davis, Sarah	White, Walter	Jan. 14, 1789
Davis, Sophia	Green, William	Feb. 26, 1778
Davis, Thomas	Collins, Sarah	Mch. 8, 1791
Day, Martha	Jenkins, Thomas	Oct. 28, 1780
Dayley, Thomas	Jones, Bini	Aug. 23, 1793
Deakin, Michael	Cooke, Rebecca	Oct. 7, 1779
Delehaye, Joseph	Miles, Mary	June 22, 1788
Demar, Amelia	Callicoe, Joseph	Dec. 5, 1781
Demely, John	Frowmay, Margaret	Nov. 7, 1784
Danielson, Zachariah	Benson, Sarah	Dec. 29, 1777
Denoon, John	Burrell, Sarah	Jan. 17, 1798
Dent, Cloe Hanson	Stoddert, Thomas James John	Sept. 21, 1790
Dent, Eleanor	Hattin, George	June 27, 1786
Devaughn, Susannah	Johnson, John	Feb. 2, 1788
Dick, Mary	Laird, John	Jan. 28, 1797
Digges, Ann	Plummer, John	Nov. 28, 1780
Diggs, Eleanor	Clagett, James W.	May 21, 1782
Digges, Jane	Fitzgerald, John	Jan. 2, 1779
Diggs, Terissa	Forster, Ralph	May 27, 1783
Dijean, Peter	Stoddert, Letitia Dent	Jan. 18, 1785
Donlevy, Charles	Newton, Eleanor	Aug. 12, 1799

Dority, William............Hurdle, Mary..............Jan. 13, 1798
Dorrett, Sarah.............Baden, Thomas.............Feb. 6, 1797
Dorsett, Fielder............Young, Jane Joan G.........Apr. 19, 1794
Dorsett, Samuel............Skinner, Mary...............Jan. 4, 1794
Dorsett, Thomas...........Selby, Ann...............Dec. 16, 1784
Dorsett, Thomas M.........Crandall, Sarah.............Sept. 3, 1799
Dorcey, Ann...............Soper, Nathan.............Nov. 21, 1791
Dorsey, Edward............Peach, Hannah.............Dec. 28, 1799
Dorsey, George.............Scarce, Milly..............Dec. 27, 1798
Dorsey, Henrietta..........Nevitt, Thomas..............Jan. 3, 1798
Dorsey, Jesse..............Beale, Alethia...............Jan. 7, 1797
Dorsey, Joshua.............Hall, Martha...............Dec. 17, 1798
Dougherty, James..........Awl, Martha................June 9, 1795
Douglass, Elizabeth.........Hamilton, Gavin............July 26, 1800
Dove, Deborah.............Pearce, Joshua.............Apr. 16, 1785
Dove, Eliza...............Russell, Philip.............Feb. 17, 1781
Dove, Elizabeth............Hooper, John...............June 5, 1779
Dove, Elizabeth............Fendley, Charles............Dec. 5, 1797
Dove, Mary...............Stuart, John...............Feb. 3, 1790
Dove, Mary Ann...........Hooper, John.............Feb. 20, 1784
Dove, Thomas.............Hopkins, Elizabeth.........Dec. 18, 1797
Dowell, Richard............Journey, Margaret...........Apr. 4, 1795
Downes, Amy..............Holly, Thomas ....Jan. 29, 1800
Downes, Elizabeth..........Bacon, Benjamin...........Dec. 23, 1797
Downs, John..............Underwood, Sarah..........Dec. 11, 1789
Downes, Lucy.............Halsal, John..............Feb. 15, 1779
Doxy, Susannah............Plum, Lewis W.............Nov. 6, 1799
Drane, Ann...............Lamar, Richard.............Nov. 9, 1790
Drane, Anthony............Smith, Ann...............Dec. 23, 1778
Drane, Anthony............Scott, Catherine...........Mch. 29, 1792
Drane, Eleanor............Moore, George............Nov. 19, 1792
Drane, Eliza Piles..........Woodward, John............Nov. 9, 1796
Drane, Elizabeth...........Brashears, Zadock...........Feb. 9, 1790
Drane, James.............Lamar, Priscilla............Feb. 18, 1789
Drane, Stephen............Crabb, Priscilla............Dec. 24, 1793
Drane, Thomas.............Wells, Martha...............Feb. 4, 1786
Duckett, Ann.............Brooke, Thomas F..........June 20, 1791
Duckett, Baruch...........Beanes, Mary B.............Jan. 11, 1783
Duckett, Charity...........Moore, Josiah.............Apr. 21, 1778
Duckett, Isaac............Bowie, Margaret............Jan. 24, 1792
Duckett, Jacob............McElderry, Mary...........May 4, 1799
Duckett, Jane.............Waters, Stephen...........Mch. 25, 1794

Duckett, Lucy.............Athey, Zephaniah..........Nov. 11, 1790
Duckett, Richard Jacob.....Buchanan, Sophia..........Mch. 30, 1795
Duckett, Thomas...........Clagett, Mary...............Jan. 5, 1796
Duckrell, Eleanor...........Lyles, Thomas.............Apr. 10, 1779
Duke, Mary...............Morse, William.............Mch. 6, 1780
Dulaney, Benjamin Tasker. . Rozer, Eliza................Feb. 13, 1796
Duley, John...............Wilson, Mary..............June 14, 1800
Duley, Sophia..............Wells, Nathan.............Nov. 12, 1798
Dunkin, Grace.............Shaw, William.............Dec. 13, 1797
Dunn, Elizabeth...........Moore, Joseph.............July 11, 1798
Durity, Sarah..............Joy, Joseph.................July 4, 1795
Duvall, Beale..............Belt, Margery..............Apr. 28, 1800
Duvall, Benjamin...........Higgins, Eleanor.............July 4, 1787
Duvall, Calmore............Clark, Margaret.............Jan. 3, 1789
Duvall, Charles............Brashears, Cassia..........Mch. 27, 1778
Duvall, Elisha.............Belt, Rachel...............June 17, 1785
Duvall, Jesse..............Craycroft, Elizabeth........Sept. 23, 1789
Duvall, John..............Beall, Mary...............Mch. 29, 1793
Duvall, Joseph, Jr..........Redden, Mary.............Aug. 26, 1800
Duvall, Mareen............Duvall, Mary..............Oct. 26, 1780
Duvall, Mark Brown........Duvall, Sarah..............June 14, 1793
Duvall, Marsh M...........Ijams, Susanna.............June 4, 1785
Duvall, Mary..............Duvall, Mareen.............Oct. 26, 1780
Duvall, Mary..............Carrick, Mareen............Feb. 23, 1791
Duvall, Mary..............Carroll, John...............Nov. 8, 1800
Duvall, Rachel.............Lucas, John..............Sept. 12, 1787
Duvall, Ruth..............Morica, William............Oct. 29, 1778
Duvall, Sarah..............Duvall, Mark Brown.......June 14, 1793
Duvall, Sophia.............Beall, Aquilla.............Dec. 21, 1798
Duvall, Susannah...........Cheney, Henry.............Nov. 28, 1785
Duvall, Tobias.............Willett, Sarah...............Feb. 5, 1795
Duvall, Zadock (Zachariah?). Beall, Elizabeth.............Apr. 1, 1791
Dyer, George..............Clarkson, Sarah............May 27, 1784
Dyar, Henrietta............Beanes, John H.............Dec. 23, 1785
Dyer, Henny...............Finley, James...............Feb. 7, 1800
Dyer, Martha Ann..........Smith, Nicholas............Oct. 23, 1790
Dyer, Mary Henrietta.......Gibbs, John H..............July 20, 1778
Dyer, Milley..............Johnson, Alexander.........Dec. 24, 1798
Dyer, Robert..............Speake, Lucy..............Jan. 21, 1800

Eaglin, Jane...............Clarkson, Joseph...........Apr. 11, 1788
Eaglin, Thomas............Hinton, Sarah..............July 25, 1795

Eales, Susannah	Stallons, Thomas Harvey	Dec. 21, 1798
Earlie, Ann	Cowles, William	July 29, 1777
Earley, Benjamin	Cooley, Jane	Jan. 27, 1789
Earle, John	Hodgkins, Barbara	June 9, 1798
Earley, Martha	Piles, Francis	Apr. 6, 1795
Earley, Thomas	Slye, Willimina	Jan. 1, 1784
Eastep, Benjamin	Tayler, Sarah	Sept. 27, 1793
Easton, Eliza	Riston, Allen	Apr. 5, 1779
Eastwood, Eliza	Waljon, Alexander	Jan. 9, 1796
Eastwood, Sarah	Rawlings, William	Oct. 9, 1799
Eddis, Leonard	Cave, Sarah	Aug. 24, 1780
Edelen, Catherine	Edelen, Joseph	Feb. 26, 1788
Edelen, Clary	Edelen, Jesse	Feb. 7, 1800
Edelen, Clement	Simpson, Ann	Nov. 6, 1780
Edelen, Edward	Hatton, Mary	Feb. 7, 1800
Edelen, Eleanor	Mitchell, Thomas	Nov. 9, 1778
Edelen, Elizabeth	Mudd, Hezekiah	May 12, 1779
Edelen, Elizabeth	Hogan, Ignatius	Jan. 28, 1792
Edelen, George	Boarman, Rebecca	Dec. 31, 1790
Edelen, Jeremiah	Jenkins, Sally	Feb. 11, 1792
Edelen, Jesse	Edelen, Clary	Feb. 7, 1800
Edelen, Joseph	Watkin, Catherine	Apr. 3, 1786
Edelen, Joseph	Edelin, Catherine	Feb. 26, 1788
Edelen, Lucy	Clarkson, Edward	July 19, 1782
Edelen, Martha	Jenkins, Leonard	Feb. 10, 1798
Edelen, Mary	Jenkins, Jachin	Feb. 18, 1784
Edelen, Mildred	Boone, Walter	Oct. 9, 1783
Edelen, Samuel	Suit, Mary	Dec. 14, 1787
Edelen, Sarah	Rozer, Henry J	Sept. 13, 1779
Edelen, Tracy	Clarkson, Thomas	Nov. 18, 1797
Edgeworth, Philorlea	Casey, John	Aug. 12, 1778
Edmonston, Edward	Croner, Margaret G.	June 27, 1800
Edmonston, Nathan	Welsh, Deborah	Dec. 19, 1788
Eigleheart, Martha	Farall, Benjamin	Feb. 16, 1787
Elery, Charity	Trigg, David	Jan. 11, 1796
Ellecon, Hannah	Swain, Benjamin	Feb. 1, 1794
Elliott, Anne	Smith, John	Feb. 5, 1796
Ellis, Elijah	Watson, Susannah	Dec. 27, 1779
Ellis, Leonard	Pierce, Jane	Nov. 15, 1780
Ellixon, Ann	Beavin, William	Feb. 2, 1787
Ellixson, Mary	Thomas, Samuel	Apr. 18, 1797
Ellon, Anne	Magruder, Edward	Oct. 23, 1800

Elson, Joseph P.	Isaac, Carolina M.	Jan. 30, 1795
Elson, Rachel	Moore, Zadock	Nov. 22, 1782
Elson, Richard	Roberts, Hannah	Nov. 3, 1782
Elson, Sarah	Kirby, John Baptist	Sept. 23, 1779
Emberson, Henry	Baden, Elizabeth	Dec. 31, 1800
Emberson, John	Simpson, Rebecca	Oct. 25, 1790
Emerson, Aquila	Simpson, Susannah	Nov. 13, 1792
Essex, Francis	Shekell, Deborah	Aug. 21, 1792
Estep, Henry	Garner, Sarah	Dec. 4, 1798
Estep, John	Wailes, Kitty B.	May 30, 1795
Estep, Sarah	Oden, Michael	Mch. 12, 1796
Estep, Susannah	Pierce, Richard A.	Jan. 24, 1787
Estep, Thomas	Letchwalt, Mary	Mch. 4, 1797
Evans, Ann	Craver, Jacob	Apr. 13, 1800
Evans, Casandra	Fraser, John T.	Aug. 30, 1777
Evans, Guy	Twain, Christian	Sept. 16, 1779
Evans, John	Wilcoxon, Verlinda	Dec. 19, 1786
Evans, John	Wright, Elizabeth	Aug. 25, 1798
Evans, Mary	Hurley, William	Aug. 12, 1778
Evans, Mary	Barclay, William	Dec. 17, 1794
Evans, Philip	Hurley, Mary	Jan. 9, 1786
Evans, Rebecca	Bean, Benjamin	Dec. 8, 1779
Evans, Ruth	Smith, Thomas	Aug. 18, 1777
Evans, Sarah	Hurley, John	Dec. 19, 1787
Everheart, Caspar	Keadle, Mary	Dec. 11, 1792
Eversfield, Charles	Gantt, Elizabeth	Feb. 13, 1786
Eversfield, Eleanor	Berry, Nicholas	June 16, 1784
Eversfield, John	Brooke, Barbara	June 2, 1778
Eversfield, John	Clagett, Mary Ann	Feb. 22, 1800
Eversfield, Mary	Readmond, Matthias	Oct. 27, 1785
Eversfield, Verlinda	Mundell, Thomas	Feb. 28, 1794
Fair, Ann	Gray, Hezekiah	Jan. 2, 1782
Farr, Bennett	Hall, Elizabeth	Nov. 28, 1795
Farr, Elizabeth	Warner, Henry	Nov. 29, 1794
Farr, George	Maddox, Frances	Feb. 12, 1798
Farr, Joshua	Hull, Margaret	Nov. 8, 1800
Farr, John Baptist	Vermillion, Mary	Nov. 23, 1780
Far, Mary	Gray, Elias	Apr. 11, 1785
Farr, Priscilla	Vermillion, Benjamin	Jan. 8, 1788
Farr, Samuel	Isaac, Rachel	Oct. 17, 1795
Farall, Benjamin	Eigleheart, Martha	Feb. 16, 1787

Farrall, John	Wheeler, Susanna	Jan. 13, 1786
Fassett, Ann	Church, Joseph	Dec. 23, 1800
Fendall, Elizabeth Ann	Cawood, Stephen	June 1, 1792
Fendley, Charles	Dove, Elizabeth	Dec. 5, 1797
Fenley, Mary	Gill, Joseph	Dec. 16, 1794
Fenley, Martha Hawkins	Wade, Lancelot	Nov. 1, 1785
Fenton, Sarah	Morris, Andrew	Oct. 16, 1800
Fenwick, Ignatius	Carroll, Mary	June 10, 1780
Ferguson, Aggy	Brashears, Henry	Apr. 7, 1792
Ferguson, Ann S.	Wilson, Joseph	Aug. 29, 1777
Ferguson, James	Halsall, Ruth	Aug. 23, 1780
Ferguson, Janet	Crown, William	Oct. 19, 1799
Ferguson, Jennett	West, Henry	Jan. 15, 1795
Ferguson, Rebecca	Wilson, William	Oct. 1, 1777
Ferguson, Ruth	Wilson, Joseph	Oct. 5, 1793
Ferguson, Ruth	Young, Samuel	Dec. 8, 1798
Ferguson, Susan	McCray, Farquire	Apr. 21, 1781
Ferguson, Verlinda	Beall, Zephaniah	Jan. 5, 1783
Ferrall, Elizabeth	Chaney, John	Dec. 12, 1780
Ferrall, Jason	Johnson, Mary Ann	Feb. 4, 1800
Ferrall, Rebecca	Upton, Archibald	Dec. 30, 1795
Ferrall, Thomas	Bassford, Crissy	Dec. 4, 1794
Ferrall, William	Hyatt, Elizabeth	Feb. 26, 1783
Fields, Elisha	Naylor, Margaret	Feb. 12, 1780
Fields, Lettie	Jarman, Benjamin	Mch. 7, 1791
Fields, Margaret	Wills, John	Dec. 24, 1788
Findlay, Ann	Boswell, Peter	May 4, 1783
Finly, Elizabeth	Sutton, John	Dec. 21, 1797
Finley, James	Dyer, Henny	Feb. 7, 1800
Finley, Thomas	Baynes, Chloe	Jan. 29, 1791
Fitzgerald, John	Digges, Jane	Jan. 2, 1779
Fitzgerald, Rachel	Russell, William	Jan. 6, 1795
Flemmin, Frederick	Hogan, Ann	Dec. 18, 1798
Fling, James	Frazer, Rebecca	Apr. 20, 1783
Foard, Charlotte	Marlow, Buttler	Dec. 21, 1782
Foard, Mary	Ward, Benjamin	July 17, 1784
Forguson, Sarah	Habiner, Dominick	Nov. 13, 1790
Forrest, Richard	Craufurd, Sarah	Sept. 15, 1789
Forster, John	Smith, Linny	Feb. 11, 1792
Forster, Ralph	Diggs, Terissa	May 27, 1783
Forster, Richard	Tyler, Priscilla	Apr. 5, 1784
Forster, Thomas	Watson, Catherine	Aug. 29, 1781

Forster, Thomas	Magruder, Mary	June 2, 1794
Foster, Mary	Kidwell, Leonard	Aug. 1, 1798
Fowler, Abraham	Stamp, Willey	Dec. 23, 1790
Fowler, Abraham	Mills, Hester	Nov. 28, 1794
Fowler, Ann	Ball, John	Apr. 4, 1795
Fowler, Elizabeth	Price, Frederick	Oct. 27, 1798
Fowler, Jemima	Sappington, John	Jan. 29, 1781
Fowler, Margaret	Hopkins, Philip	June 6, 1794
Fowler, Mary	Wells, Martin	Jan. 5, 1799
Fowler, Richard	Summers, Ann	Jan. 14, 1779
Fowler, Samuel	Selby, Margaret	Feb. 2, 1798
Fowler, William	Lovejoy, Eleanor	Feb. 24, 1786
Fowler, William	Sanders, Lydia	Nov. 25, 1788
Fowler, William	Simpson, Priscilla	Jan. 29, 1799
Fox, William	Wade, Letty	Nov. 18, 1794
Framnay, James	Love, Margaret	Mch. 8, 1782
Francis, Alexander	Lovelace, Mellesent Ann	Dec. 22, 1783
Francis, John	Champline, Alice	Nov. 5, 1781
Frank, Catherine	Green, James	Nov. 9, 1796
Fraser, Andrew	Lanham, Catherine	Dec. 31, 1791
Frazier, Archibald	Taylor, Sarah	Apr. 15, 1800
Fraser, John	Lanham, Mary	Oct. 24, 1789
Frazer, John T.	Evans, Casandra	Aug. 30, 1777
Fraser, Nellie	Southerland, John	Nov. 20, 1777
Frazer, Rebecca	Fling, James	Apr. 20, 1783
Fraser, Rebecca	Linsey, Thomas	June 20, 1789
Frazier, Sarah	Lindsay, George	Dec. 6, 1798
Free, Elizabeth	Scott, Samuel	Apr. 19, 1796
Free, John	Wallace, Sarah	Jan. 25, 1796
Frowmay, Margaret	Demely, John	Nov. 7, 1784
Fry, Robert	Alder, Elizabeth	Dec. 13, 1792
Fry, Thomas	Crandell, Elizabeth	June 29, 1795
Fuller, Ann	Constable, John	Dec. 4, 1780
Galwith, Mary	Jenkins, Isaac	June 5, 1787
Galwith, Rachel	Simpson, Joseph	Jan. 31, 1788
Galwith, Rebecca	Morris, Benjamin	Feb. 4, 1783
Galwith, Susannah	Carroll, James	Apr. 6, 1792
Gantt, Ann	Wood, Peter	Apr. 3, 1793
Gantt, Elizabeth	Eversfield, Charles	Feb. 13, 1786
Gantt, Henry	Weems, Wilhelmina	Mch. 3, 1798
Gantt, John Mackall	Heermance, Mary Sprigg	Dec. 18, 1798

Gantt, Mary...............Mewburn, James............May 7, 1791
Gantt, Priscilla.............Belt, Jeremiah, Jr...........Mch. 4, 1778
Gantt, Robert..............Maynard, Elizabeth........Aug. 21, 1790
Gantt, Sarah...............Sprigg, Osborn.............Apr. 3, 1779
Gardiner, Eleanor..........Boone, Stanislaus............Jan. 2, 1796
Gardiner, Elizabeth.........Poston, William............Dec. 25, 1797
Gardiner, Henry............Queen, Mary..............June 30, 1798
Gardiner, Joseph James.....Hamilton, Winefred.........Jan. 16, 1795
Gardiner, Mary............Smith, Benedict.............Feb. 7, 1795
Gardiner, Abraham.........Webb, Sarah................Apr. 5, 1783
Gardiner, Benjamin.........Hardey, Sarah..............May 4, 1783
Garner, Benjamin..........Hyde, Ann.................Feb. 8, 1793
Garner, Joseph............Newell, Sarah.............Feb. 25, 1794
Garner, Michael...........Poston, Sarah..............Dec. 19, 1798
Garner, Patsy.............Wooton, William............June 4, 1799
Garner, Sarah..............Estep, Henry...............Dec. 4, 1798
Garner, Thomas............Naylor, Mary..............Jan. 27, 1798
Garner, William............Butler, Ann...............Dec. 30, 1799
Garrett, Elizabeth..........Husten, William...........Nov. 18, 1797
Gates, Eleanor............Ryon, John................Mch. 7, 1786
Gatton, Ann...............Jones, Samuel.............Oct. 11, 1800
Gebby, Elizabeth...........Osbon, Alvin...............May 3, 1794
Gentle, Linney............Jones, Perry...............Feb. 6, 1793
Gibbons, Alexander........Leith, Rebecca.............Oct. 2, 1792
Gibbons, Ann..............Turner, George............Sept. 5, 1797
Gibbons, Elizabeth.........Clarke, Levin..............Dec. 13, 1796
Gibbons, Elizabeth.........Wilson, James............Mch. 16, 1798
Gibbons, Frances...........Howse, Charles..............Dec. 7, 1779
Gibbons, George...........Grear, Mary...............Dec. 31, 1778
Gibbons, George Wailes.....Naylor, Susannah..........Jan. 26, 1793
Gibbons, Jane.............Richards, James............Jan. 27, 1795
Gibbons, John.............Wright, Rebecca............Jan. 15, 1799
Gibbons, Susannah.........Baden, James...............Dec. 4, 1799
Gibbons, Susannah.........Wilson, William.............May 5, 1800
Gibbons, Verlinda..........Beavin, John...............Dec. 6, 1796
Gibbs, John H.............Dyer, Mary Henrietta.......July 20, 1778
Gibling, William............Hygdon, Lydia............Sept. 21, 1793
Gill, Joseph...............Fenley, Mary..............Dec. 16, 1794
Gill, Thomas..............Jones, Sarah..............Aug. 30, 1777
Gilpin, Margaret...........Barrett, Jonathan..........Mch. 20, 1779
Gilpin, Mary..............Walker, Richard...........Aug. 23, 1778
Givens, Arter.............Givens, Elizabeth..........Dec. 11, 1800

Glasgow, Theodore........Irvington, Ann..............Dec. 1, 1800
Gloyd, Joanna.............Ballett, John..............Nov. 29, 1782
Glover, Mary..............Mahew, Thomas............Apr. 14, 1781
Goddard, John.............Knott, Elizabeth...........July 14, 1795
Godfrey, Samuel...........Burch, Ann..................July 3, 1798
Goodman, Peter............Turner, Rebecca...........May 15, 1793
Gordon, Elizabeth..........Wilson, John...............Feb. 11, 1795
Gordon, George............Kelly, Jane..................June 9, 1796
Gordon, John..............Wilson, Ann.................June 5, 1797
Gordon, Mary.............Sollars, Sabret.............May 10, 1787
Gordon, Rebecca...........Marshman, James..........Oct. 22, 1779
Gordon, Thomas...........Hardy, Ann................June 11, 1777
Gotherd, Stephen...........Osburn, Anna...............Apr. 9, 1798
Gott, Ezekiel..............Soper, Susanna Jackson.....Apr. 23, 1792
Gover, Elizabeth...........Badon, Robert.............May 12, 1796
Gover, Frances............Baden, Robert, Jr..........Nov. 10, 1779
Grant, Catherine...........Mackay, Hugh.............Feb. 11, 1790
Grant, John...............Claud, Ephana.............Oct. 21, 1777
Grant, Mary..............Riley, John................Dec. 10, 1788
Gray, Ann................:Walker, George.............Dec. 7, 1779
Gray, Cassandra...........Crooke, John..............Dec. 23, 1797
Gray, Catherine............Padgett, Benedict...........Apr. 13, 1789
Gray, Charles.............Ware, Sarah................Dec. 3, 1778
Gray, Elias...............Far, Mary...................Apr. 11, 1785
Gray, Eleanor.............Kidwell, William............Jan. 14, 1783
Gray, Elizabeth...........Wood, William..............Dec. 7, 1780
Gray, Elizabeth...........McDaniel, Cephas..........Feb. 20, 1797
Gray, Hezekiah...........Fair, Ann...................Jan. 2, 1782
Gray, Hugh...............Stevens, Elizabeth...........Aug. 8, 1795
Gray, James..............Osborn, Linny...............Feb. 7, 1785
Gray, Mary...............Rastridge, James.............Apr. 7, 1798
Gray, Rebecca.............King, Thomas M............Jan. 18, 1790
Gray, Richard.............Wilson, Rebecca............Aug. 30, 1778
Gray, Sarah...............Burgess, Joseph............Dec. 31, 1779
Gray, Thomas.............Bonifant, Mary.............June 2, 1781
Grear, Ananias............Lang, Ann...................Feb. 6, 1781
Grear, Mary..............Gibbons, George............Dec. 31, 1778
Green, Basil..............Lanham, Sarah Ann.........Jan. 18, 1780
Green, Charles............Mackay, Barbara............Dec. 1, 1785
Green, Elisha.............Clarke, Mary...............May 1, 1783
Green, James.............Frank, Catherine............Nov. 9, 1796
Green, Sarah..............Powell, William............Mch. 17, 1785

Green, William.............Davis, Sophia.............Feb. 26, 1778
Greenfield, Ann.............Wood, John Thomas........June 22, 1799
Greenfield, Susanna.........Baker, William..............May 2, 1789
Greentree, Benjamin........Roberts, Sarah.............May 16, 1782
Greenwell, Jesse............Moore, Ann...............Jan. 21, 1795
Greenwell, Jesse............Low, Leithy................Jan. 6, 1790
Greenwell, Joseph..........Lowe, Winefred.............Jan. 7, 1793
Gregory, James.............Jones, Ann................Dec. 13, 1792
Gregory, Susannah.........Lewis, Hugh...............Jan. 12, 1790
Griffin, Deborah............Jones, James..............Oct. 29, 1785
Griffin, Edward............Shekalls, Agnes............May 24, 1781
Griffen, Edward............Harvey, Tomsey............Dec. 22, 1785
Griffin, Margaret...........Shekell, Richard...........July 29, 1789
Griffin, Susannah...........Connor, Solomon...........July 16, 1789
Griffin, Thomas............Notley, Ann..............Aug. 30, 1790
Griffith, Ann...............Reynolds, William...........Dec. 5, 1777
Griffith, Ann...............Walker, Benjamin N........Apr. 18, 1794
Griffith, Howard...........Jacob, Jemima..............Feb. 4, 1782
Grimes, Benjamin..........Grimes, Mary..............Jan. 17, 1789
Grimes, Charles............Stone, Ann...............Feb. 17, 1787
Grimes, George............Parrett, Elizabeth..........Jan. 11, 1786
Grimes, Isaac..............Adams, Elizabeth.........Mch. 23, 1799
Grimes, Jeremiah...........Talbott, Susannah..........Jan. 8, 1793
Grimes, John..............Clements, Martha..........Jan. 11, 1785
Grimes, John..............King, Sarah................Jan. 3, 1789
Grimes, Mary..............Short, James...............Feb. 9, 1779
Grimes, Mary..............Taylor, Thomas............Dec. 21, 1785
Grimes, Mary..............Grimes, Benjamin..........Jan. 17, 1789
Gunn, Rebecca.............Molleson, William...........May 5, 1781
Guy, Anne.................Crown, Joseph.............May 12, 1795
Gwinn, Ann...............Summers, Jonathan.........Dec. 23, 1782
Gwinn, Bennett............Hilleary, Susannah.........Feb. 21, 1797

Haas, Rachel..............Vermilion, Osborn...........May 5, 1798
Habiner, Dominick.........Forguson, Sarah...........Nov. 13, 1790
Hagan, Henrietta..........Cooke, Robert.............July 27, 1790
Halkerstone, Elizabeth......Brookes, Benjamin.........Feb. 18, 1799
Hall, Amelia...............Magruder, John...........Sept. 13, 1794
Hall, Ann.................Clarke, Thomas.......Dec. 21, 1781 (82?)
Hall, Ann.................Wood, Thomas............May 25, 1782
Hall, Eleanor..............Clark, David.............Mch. 25, 1788
Hall, Eleanor..............Hall, Francis, Jr...........June 25, 1791

Hall, Elizabeth............Farr, Bennett............Nov. 28, 1795
Hall, Francis, Jr............Hall, Eleanor............June 25, 1791
Hall, Francis Magruder.....Hill, Mary............Oct. 20, 1795
Hall, John Henry............Straw, Terrissa............Feb. 22, 1791
Hall, Martha............Hall, William............Jan. 13, 1779
Hall, Martha............Dorsey, Joshua............Dec. 17, 1798
Hall, Mary............Weems, James William Loch..May 6, 1786
Hall, Nathaniel............Hughes, Mary............Dec. 23, 1777
Hall, Richard D............Perkins, Elizabeth............Jan. 8, 1799
Hall, Samuel............Mayhew, Frances............July 5, 1779
Hall, William............Hall, Martha............Jan. 13, 1779
Halsal, John............Downes, Lucy............Feb. 15, 1779
Halsall, Ruth............Ferguson, James............Aug. 23, 1780
Hamilton, Andrew............Burch, Jane............Apr. 17, 1783
Hamilton, Eliza............Sansbury, Alexius............Feb. 16, 1789
Hamilton, Francis............Blanford, Susan............Jan. 27, 1785
Hamilton, Gavin............Douglass, Elizabeth............July 26, 1800
Hamilton, Hezekiah............Higgins, Ann............Nov. 1, 1794
Hamilton, Martha............Morgan, Robert............May 30, 1780
Hamilton, Sarah............Beck, John............Nov. 18, 1778
Hamilton, Thomas............Hodgkin, Ann............Apr. 17, 1781
Hamilton, Wilemina............Nicholls, Edward............Aug. 15, 1780
Hamilton, Winefred............Gardiner, Joseph James......Jan. 16, 1795
Hammerstone, Richard......Wouster, Mary............Dec. 17, 1777
Handling, James............Magruder, Priscilla............May 22, 1787
Handling, Joseph............Harden, Bridgett............May 15, 1782
Hanes, Elizabeth............Reed, Isaac............Oct. 11, 1800
Hanson, Bryan............Hatton, Lucy............Feb. 9, 1793
Hanson, Cloe............Vermilion, Jacob............Jan. 29, 1781
Hanson, Margaret B............Beall, John F............Apr. 4, 1787
Hanson, Martha............Wilson, Nathaniel............June 15, 1779
Hanson, Rachel............Sebbald, George............Jan. 5, 1786
Hanson, Samuel............Marshall, Elizabeth Fendall..July 29, 1788
Hanson, Samuel............Beall, Sarah............June 9, 1795
Hanson, Thomas H............Addison, Rebecca............Mch. 21, 1778
Harbin, Rezin............Macnea, Mary............Nov. 14, 1778
Harden, Bridgett............Handling, Joseph............May 15, 1782
Hardesty, Elisha............Wells, Sarah............Aug. 24, 1780
Hardesty, John............Cheney, Henrietta............July 23, 1788
Hardesty, Richard G............Hodges, Mary............June 1, 1799
Hardey, Anastasia............Reynolds, Patrick............Dec. 29, 1792
Hardey, Anthony............Hatton, Mary Green......Sept. 29, 1796

Hardy, Ann................Gordon, Thomas...........June 11, 1777
Hardey, Ann...............Ayres, Robert............Sept. 10, 1784
Hardey, Ann...............Boone, John...............Jan. 12, 1782
Hardey, Baptist............Osborn, Ester...............Apr. 3, 1786
Hardey, Benedict...........Jones, Charity.............Nov. 21, 1785
Hardey, Eleanor...........Hughes, George............Oct. 24, 1797
Hardey, Elizabeth..........Soper, Robert.............Nov. 19, 1784
Hardy, Elizabeth...........Mullican, Henry............Jan. 13, 1796
Hardey, George............Stone, Eleanor..............Feb. 7, 1782
Hardey, George............Jenkins, Priscilla............July 13, 1786
Hardey, Jesse..............Wheat, Sarah..............Oct. 31, 1789
Hardey, Jonathan..........Soper, Mary Ann...........Jan. 31, 1799
Hardey, Margaret..........Marshall, Richard...........Mch. 5, 1782
Hardey, Mary.............Ridgway, Benjamin.........Dec. 14, 1779
Hardey, Mary.............Wilcoxon, Thomas, Jr.......Apr. 23, 1781
Hardey, Mary.............Underwood, George.........Aug. 31, 1789
Hardey, Mary.............Bowling, Basil.............Dec. 31, 1799
Hardey, Mary D............Wade, Benoni Hamilton.....May 31, 1796
Hardey, Nathan............Coombes, Terissa...........May 16, 1783
Hardey, Noah..............Stone, Mary ....Jan. 13, 1784
Hardey, Rebecca...........Younger, Gilbert...........June 12, 1784
Hardey, Rebecca...........Darcey, John.............Nov. 21, 1786
Hardey, Rebecca...........Scott, William..............Feb. 22, 1792
Hardey, Sarah.............Gardiner, Benjamin..........May 4, 1783
Hardey, Susanna...........Harvey, Richard............Feb. 8, 1798
Hardey, Terrasa Catherine...Redmond, Matthias........May 21, 1791
Hardy, Thomas............Wilcoxen, Margaret..........Feb. 9, 1780
Harding, William..........Lamar, Rachel............Mch. 22, 1784
Harris, Eleanor...........Bryant, Richard............May 17, 1782
Harris, Josias.............Morton, Catherine.........Aug. 29, 1781
Harris, Sarah.............Marshall, Josias............Apr. 18, 1797
Harrison, Elisha...........Beall, Sarah..............Mch. 25, 1796
Harrison, Joseph...........Perry, Rachel..............Oct. 23, 1778
Harrison, Mary Henry......Davidson, Plinny...........Aug. 31, 1793
Harrison, Thomas..........White, Jane................Dec. 4, 1779
Harrison, Thomas..........Stamp, Mary.............May 30, 1783
Hart, Margaret............Hinton, Benjamin..........Feb. 17, 1798
Harvey, Alexander..........McCauley, Rebecca.........July 19, 1777
Harvey, Eleanor............Jackson, John.............Dec. 31, 1796
Harvey, Elizabeth..........Hern, James................Apr. 7, 1798
Harvey, Henry.............McDaniel, Sarah...........Apr. 20, 1791
Harvey, James.............Selby, Ann...............Mch. 25, 1796

Harvey, Linny............Burch, Thomas............Sept. 5, 1794
Harvey, Lucy............Swain, John............Apr. 11, 1797
Harvey, Moses............Macatee, Clarissa............Dec. 15, 1780
Harvey, Richard............Hardey, Susannah............Feb. 8, 1798
Harvey, Thomas............Simpson, Eliza Ann............Apr. 18, 1794
Harvey, Tomsey............Griffen, Edward............Dec. 22, 1784
Harwood, Eleanor............Brookes, John Smith............June 3, 1786
Harwood, Elizabeth............Berry, William E............Mch. 23, 1799
Harwood, Richard............Cox, Sarah Ann............Oct. 28, 1799
Harwood, Thomas............Mayhew, Ann............Apr. 16, 1794
Harwood, Thomas, 3rd............Whyte, Ann............Oct. 29, 1778
Hattin, George............Dent, Eleanor............June 27, 1786
Hatton, Henry............Davidson, Ann............July 19, 1781
Hatton, Joseph............Jones, Martha............Oct. 14, 1777
Hatton, Josias............Mitchell, Mary............Feb. 22, 1793
Hatton, Lucy............Hanson, Bryan............Feb. 9, 1793
Hatton, Mary............Edelin, Edward............Feb. 7, 1800
Hatton, Mary Green............Hardey, Anthony............Sept. 29, 1796
Havener, Adam............Bonafin, Sarah............Dec. 12, 1792
Havener, Domineek............Upton, Eleanor............Jan. 31, 1789
Havener, John............Wheat, Linny............Jan. 19, 1788
Havener, Michael............Soper, Elizabeth............Feb. 5, 1793
Hawkins, Henry............Swan, Jennett............Dec. 26, 1790
Hawkins, Margaret............Washington, Nathaniel............Nov. 24, 1790
Hawkins, Susanna............Bowie, John F............Apr. 23, 1784
Hawkins, Susannah G............Boteler, Henderson S............Nov. 7, 1799
Hay, Robert............Magruder, Ann............Mch. 9, 1791
Haye, William............Alder, Ruth Hawkins............Jan. 6, 1798
Hayse, Catherine............James, Daniel............Nov. 7, 1777
Hays, Eleanor............Kidwell, John............Jan. 5, 1785
Hayes, Mina............Carroll, Patrick............Dec. 31, 1794
Hayes, Verllinda............Lowe, Nathaniel............Sept. 9, 1797
Hayes, Thomas............Padget, Rebecca............Sept. 9, 1784
Hayes, William............Alexander, Rachel............Sept. 5, 1795
Heermance, Mary Sprigg............Gantt, John Mackall............Dec. 18, 1798
Hellen, Jane............Muran, James............May 6, 1780
Hellen, Susannah............Wall, Thomas............Dec. 5, 1791
Helsell, Catherine............Husther, Jacob............Mch. 2, 1793
Henderson, Ariana............Sim, Patrick............Aug. 28, 1787
Hennis, Ann............Olbee, John............Oct. 21, 1786
Henness, Margaret............Mockbee, William, Jr............Dec. 24, 1780
Hennis, Rebecca............Wight, John............Apr. 15, 1786

Henry, John	Taylor, Linny	Apr. 18, 1797
Henry, Mary	Lowe, William	Apr. 19, 1783
Henry, Sarah	Lowe, Elias	Aug. 9, 1785
Hepburn, Henrietta Maria	Walker, Joseph, Jr.	Dec. 7, 1779
Hepburn, Mary	Coolidge, Samuel Judson	Feb. 20, 1798
Hern, James	Harvey, Elizabeth	Apr. 7, 1798
Hewitt, Thomas	Beall, Nancy Dent	Dec. 15, 1789
Hickman, John	Boston, Viasia	Nov. 3, 1798
Hickman, Joseph	Jinkins, Margaret	Aug. 18, 1780
Hide, George	Webster, Sarah	Dec. 16, 1783
Higdon, James	Rawlings, Ann	Aug. 18, 1779
Higdon, James	Linton, Ann	Jan. 28, 1797
Higdon, Joshua	Roberts, Mary	Oct. 11, 1783
Higdon, Mary	Mahew, Timothy	Mch. 17, 1787
Higdon, Mary Ann	Long, John	Apr. 27, 1798
Higdon, Phebe Eleanora	Lambert, John B.	Dec. 17, 1793
Higdon, Thomas	Albey, Ann	June 10, 1797
Higgins, Eleanor	Duvall, Benjamin	July 4, 1787
Higgins, Richard	Macgill, Eleanor	Mch. 21, 1783
Higgins, Samuel	Willett, Tabitha	Dec. 13, 1799
Hill, Elizabeth	Mudd, Joseph	June 2, 1787
Hill, Henry, Jr.	Brooke, Hetta	Apr. 23, 1781
Hill, Mary	Hall, Francis Magruder	Oct. 20, 1795
Hill, Mary	Kidwell, Theodore	Jan. 12, 1799
Hilleary, Ann	Wheeler, Samuel	Dec. 4, 1782
Hilleary, Cassandra	Beall, Richard, Jr.	Dec. 16, 1794
Hilleary, Eleanor	Woodward, Thomas	Apr. 18, 1788
Hilleary, Eliza	Magruder, William	Feb. 5, 1796
Hilleary, Elizabeth	Waring, James	Jan. 4, 1787
Hilleary, George	Smith, Sarah	Nov. 29, 1781
Hilleary, John	Williams, Verlinda	Feb. 22, 1791
Hilleary, Mary	Magruder, Samuel	June 11, 1792
Hilleary, Rebecca	Belt, Stephen	Jan. 18, 1786
Hilleary, Sarah	Wheeler, Edward	Dec. 21, 1785
Hilleary, Susannah	Gwinn, Bennett	Feb. 21, 1797
Hilleary, Tilghman	Wheeler, Ann	Jan. 9, 1782
Hilseagle, Barbara	Veitch, Alexander	July 11, 1798
Hilton, Susannah	Atchison, Henry	Feb. 17, 1800
Hines, Elizabeth	Pierce, John	Feb. 3, 1786
Hinton, Ann	Miller, John	Dec. 26, 1800
Hinton, Benjamin	Hart, Margaret	Feb. 17, 1798
Hinton, Gideon	Askey, Priscilla	Dec. 24, 1798

Hinton, John	Ray, Mary	Jan. 1, 1795
Hinton, Joseph	Cooke, Elizabeth	Dec. 22, 1796
Hinton, Sarah	Taylor, John	Feb. 16, 1784
Hinton, Sarah	Eaglin, Thomas	July 25, 1795
Hodge, James	Brashears, Martha	Jan. 22, 1790
Hodge, Lucy	Osborn, Dennis	Dec. 14, 1784
Hodge, Sarah	Plummer, John	Aug. 1, 1782
Hodges, Benjamin	Oden, Susan	Feb. 6, 1787
Hodges, Benjamin M.	Tyler, Susannah	Apr. 18, 1797
Hodges, Charles Drury	Watkins, Elizabeth	Feb. 3, 1798
Hodges, Elizabeth	Hodges, Walter	Dec. 22, 1794
Hodges, John of Thomas	Berry, Rebecca	Jan. 12, 1799
Hodges, Mary	Hardesty, Mary G.	June 1, 1799
Hodges, Thomas	White, Elizabeth	Oct. 26, 1797
Hodges, Thomas Ramsey	Berry, Deborah	Dec. 30, 1797
Hodges, Walter	Hodges, Elizabeth	Dec. 22, 1794
Hodgkin, Ann	Hamilton, Thomas	Apr. 17, 1781
Hodgkin, Mary	Townsend, Samuel	Aug. 27, 1781
Hodgkin, Mary	Skinner, Walter	June 10, 1791
Hodgkin, Philip	Boteler, Sophia	Dec. 26, 1789
Hodgkin, Theodore	Curcaurd, Mary J.	Apr. 9, 1787
Hodgkins, Barbara	Earle, John	June 9, 1798
Hodgkinson, Agnes	Selby, Magruder	Feb. 11, 1788
Hogan, Ann	Flemmin, Frederick	Dec. 18, 1798
Hogan, Ignatius	Edelen, Elizabeth	Jan. 28, 1792
Hogan, Rachel	Clarke, James	Feb. 9, 1781
Holland, Susannah	King, William	Oct. 22, 1796
Hollingsford, Susanna	Lowe, Barton	Feb. 10, 1782
Holly, Penelope	Peacock, William	June 28, 1792
Holly, Thomas	Downes, Amey	Jan. 29, 1800
Hollyday, Ann	Cox, Walter B.	Nov. 19, 1778
Hollyday, Clement	Priggs, Hedwick	Jan. 18, 1784
Holliday, Mary	Waring, Marcus S.	Jan. 9, 1794
Hoofman, John	Scott, Mary	Apr. 24, 1781
Hooker, Priscilla	Cole, George	May 6, 1778
Hooper, Anne	Lang, John	Dec. 17, 1779
Hooper, John	Dove, Elizabeth	June 5, 1779
Hooper, John	Dove, Mary Ann	Feb. 20, 1784
Hooper, John	Brown, Elizabeth	July 7, 1788
Hooper, Martha	Bedder, Jonathan	May 25, 1778
Hooper, Samuel	Ryon, Ann	Dec. 31, 1785
Hooper, Thomas	Bedder, Elizabeth	Aug. 18, 1784

Hopkins, Ann..............Tarman, Richard...........May 30, 1785
Hopkins, Elizabeth.........Dove, Thomas.............Dec. 18, 1797
Hopkins, Francis...........Sansbury, Mary............Jan. 29, 1786
Hopkins, Mary.............Beckwith, Rezin...........Mch. 31, 1798
Hopkins, Mary.............Steel, Alexander............Mch. 6, 1800
Hopkins, Philip............Fowler, Margaret............June 6, 1794
Hopkins, Philip............Ryon, Susanna.............Aug. 22, 1798
Hoskinson, Elisha..........Brashears, Henrietta........July 21, 1777
Howard, John..............Linton, Martha............Sept. 16, 1791
Howard, Rebecca...........Adams, William............July 12, 1796
Howe, Ignatius.............Willett, Rachel.............Nov. 27, 1798
Howe, Stanislaus...........Willett, Elizabeth..........Dec. 6, 1797
Howerton, Sarah...........Owens, John...............Mch. 8, 1780
Howse, Charles............Gibbons, Frances............Dec. 7, 1779
Howse, Zachariah..........Busey, Elizabeth...........Nov. 3, 1779
Howsley, Henry............Bayne, Martha.............Apr. 14, 1783
Hoxton, Julia..............Middleton, Theodore.......Nov. 20, 1789
Hoxton, Stanislaus..........Semmes, Mary.............Jan. 17, 1799
Hoye, Cephas.............Collings, Sarah............Dec. 27, 1784
Hoye, Cephas.............Ryon, Elizabeth............Sept. 9, 1786
Hoye, Thomas.............Scott, Agnes..............Apr. 22, 1786
Hughes, George...........Hardy, Eleanor.............Oct. 24, 1797
Hughes, Jane.............Simms, William............Nov. 24, 1787
Hughes, Mary.............Hall, Nathaniel............Dec. 23, 1777
Hughes, Sarah............Abbigell, Thomas...........Feb. 4, 1788
Hull, Margaret............Farr, Joshua...............Nov. 8, 1800
Humphreys, Ann..........Taylor, Allen..............June 10, 1799
Humphreys, Mary.........Scott, James...............Feb. 4, 1797
Humphrey, Sarah Ann......Ranter, John...............Dec. 9, 1778
Humphries, Thomas........Burch, Margaret...........Nov. 22, 1781
Hunt, James..............Loveless, Unice............Jan. 12, 1793
Hunt, John...............Brown, Priscilla............Jan. 10, 1789
Hunter, Richard...........Whiten, Rachel............Jan. 19, 1782
Hurdle, Lucretia...........Parsons, Barnaba...........June 8, 1799
Hurdle, Mary.............Dority, William...........Jan. 13, 1798
Hurdle, Rebecca...........Ridgway, James...........Feb. 23, 1797
Hurley, Barsheba..........Darnall, John.............Dec. 11, 1782
Hurley, Basil.............Soper, Mary...............Feb. 3, 1789
Hurley, Cornelius..........Wade, Linny...............Apr. 4, 1795
Hurley, Daniel............Bayne, Amelia............Dec. 21, 1784
Hurley, Daniel............Jones, Mary..............Sept. 8, 1797
Hurley, John..............Evans, Sarah.............Dec. 19, 1787

Hurley, Mary..............Evans, Philip................Jan. 9, 1786
Hurley, Rhoda.............Taylor, Samuel.............Apr. 10, 1793
Hurley, Salem..............Summers, Anna.............Dec. 8, 1784
Hurley, Sarah..............Darnall, Gerrard............Jan. 31, 1781
Hurley, William............Evans, Mary..............Aug. 12, 1778
Hurley, William............Taylor, Sarah................Jan. 4, 1790
Hurley, William............Soaper, Rebecca............Dec. 21, 1790
Hurley, William............Soper, Sarah...............Aug. 12, 1795
Husther, Jacob.............Helsell, Catherine...........Mch. 2, 1793
Husten, William............Garrett, Elizabeth..........Nov. 18, 1797
Huston, William............Randall, Elizabeth..........Dec. 22, 1798
Hutchinson, Elizabeth.......Conner, Thomas.............Feb. 3, 1781
Hutchenson, George........Lowe, Rachel..............Nov. 13, 1781
Hutchinson, Nathan........Tredwell, Tracy.............June 2, 1777
Hutchinson, Samuel.........Brown, Ann.................June 3, 1786
Hutchinson, William........Willett, Christian...........Apr. 18, 1780
Hyatt, Cris................Peach, Lucy...............Sept. 10, 1777
Hyatt, Christopher.........Clarke, Sarah..............Sept. 3, 1793
Hyatt, Elizabeth...........Ferrall, William............Feb. 26, 1783
Hyde, Ann.................Garner, Benjamin...........Feb. 8, 1793
Hyde, Priscilla.............Lawson, Thomas...........Feb. 26, 1791
Hyde, Sarah...............Mason, Thomas............July 21, 1787
Hygdon, Lydia.............Gibling, William...........Sept. 21, 1793

Iglehart, Elizabeth..........Boyd, Abraham............Jan. 23, 1800
Iglehart, Susannah..........Wheeler, Jacob.............June 2, 1787
Iglehart, William...........Soper, Susanna...........Mch. 17, 1781
Ijams, Isaac...............Williams, Elizabeth..........Aug. 4, 1795
Ijams, Susanna.............Duvall, Marsh M............June 4, 1785
Irwin, John................Stonestreet, Eleanor.........June 2, 1784
Irvington, Ann.............Glasgow, Theodore..........Dec. 1, 1800
Isaac, Carolina M..........Elson, Joseph P.............Jan. 30, 1795
Isaac, Hannah.............Brice, Richard.............Nov. 22, 1781
Isaac, Rachel..............Farr, Samuel...............Oct. 17, 1795
Isaac, Sarah...............Ray, John................Mch. 24, 1787

Jackson, Alexander.........McLish, Margaret..........Apr. 30, 1784
Jackson, John.............Williams, Cave.............Feb. 1, 1788
Jackson, John.............Harvey, Eleanor............Dec. 31, 1796
Jackson, William..........Virmeer, Jane..............Jan. 31, 1789
Jackson, William John......Belt, Mary................Apr. 29, 1788
Jacob, Allice..............Waters, Thomas Jones......July 14, 1787

Jacob, Jemima............Griffith, Howard............Feb. 4, 1782
Jacob, Mordecai............Cole, Mary................June 6, 1789
Jacob, Richard ....Wells, Susanna.............Apr. 8, 1778
James, Ann................Sparrow, Henry............Jan. 21, 1791
James, Daniel..............Hayse, Catherine............Nov. 7, 1777
Jameson, Benedict..........Boone, Margaret...........Mch. 12, 1796
Jarmain, Ann..............Lanham, George............Feb. 23, 1781
Jorman, Benjamin..........Fields, Lettie..............Mch. 7, 1791
Jarman, Elizabeth..........Robey, Michael............Dec. 21, 1790
Jarvis, Jonathan............Mahorney, Edelburgodis....May 23, 1787
Jeans, Mary...............Crawford, Hugh............Nov. 28, 1780
Jeffries, Benjamin Berry.....Berry, Eleanor............Oct. 18, 1791
Jeffreys, William...........Robinson, Priscilla..........Dec. 14, 1799
Jenkins, Ann..............Turton, Josey Harrison.....Nov. 19, 1794
Jenkins, Ann..............Boone, Oswald.............Apr. 14, 1800
Jenkins, Francis............Day, Martha...............Oct. 28, 1780
Jenkins, Isaac..............Galwith, Mary..............June 5, 1787
Jenkins, Jachin.............Edelen, Mary..............Feb. 18, 1784
Jenkins, Joseph............Wilson, Margery...........June 25, 1780
Jenkins, Leonard...........Edelin, Martha.............Feb. 10, 1798
Jenkins, Mary.............Summers, Zadock..........Nov. 13, 1794
Jenkins, Massy M..........Scott, Thomas.............Nov. 23, 1795
Jenkins, Prescilla...........Beckwith, William.........Sept. 23, 1778
Jenkins, Priscilla...........Hardey, George............July 13, 1786
Jenkins, Sally..............Edelen, Jeremiah...........Feb. 11, 1792
Jenkins, Thomas...........Atcherson, Mildred........Nov. 10, 1787
Jenkins, Winifred...........Masters, Nathan.............Jan. 8, 1794
Jenkins, Zadock............Summers, Ann.............Jan. 12, 1798
Jenners, Abriel.............Young, Deborah...........May 17, 1796
Jenings, Peter.............Waters, Jemima............Jan. 15, 1794
Jerman, Sarah.............Robinson, Benjamin........May 13, 1794
Jinkins, Margaret..........Hickman, Joseph...........Aug. 18, 1780
Jinkins, William............Masters, Dorcas............Dec. 31, 1778
Jockherer, Alexander Lewy..Sandford, Nancy...........June 13, 1796
Johnson, Alexander.........Dyer, Milly................Dec. 24, 1798
Johnson, Benjamin.........Sansbury, Anne............Feb. 11, 1792
Johnson, Eliza.............Tucker, Richard............Jan. 21, 1794
Johnson, Elizabeth.........Lynn, Colerrton............Sept. 21, 1795
Johnson, Henrietta.........Boswell, Hendley...........Dec. 15, 1792
Johnson, James............Weil, Catherine.............Dec. 5, 1782
Johnson, James............Carson, Elizabeth..........Sept. 12, 1800
Johnson, John.............Devaughn, Susannah.........Feb. 2, 1788

Johnson, Joseph	Winsett, Mary	Feb. 2, 1799
Johnson, Mary	Yates, Joseph	Oct. 12, 1781
Johnson, Mary Ann	Ferrall, Jason	Feb. 4, 1800
Johnson, Rinaldo	Trueman, Rebecca	Feb. 1, 1779
Johnson, Sarah	Brookes, Benjamin	Nov. 7, 1782
Johnson, Verlinda	Robertson, George	Sept. 29, 1781
Joiner, Joseph	Merritt, Elizabeth	Aug. 19, 1800
Jones, Ann	Bayne, George	Apr. 24, 1779
Jones, Ann	Reynolds, Thomas	Feb. 24, 1784
Jones, Ann	Gregory, James	Dec. 13, 1792
Jones, Ann	Talbott, Levin	Feb. 11, 1797
Jones, Anne	Lovelace, Elisha	Jan. 6, 1789
Jones, Arey	Jones, Josias	Mch. 23, 1785
Jones, Benjamin	Young, Ruth	Oct. 11, 1786
Jones, Bini	Dayley, Thomas	Aug. 23, 1793
Jones, Butler	Lindsey, Elizabeth	Feb. 8, 1790
Jones, Charity	Hardey, Benedict	Nov. 21, 1785
Jones, David	Bradley, Susanna	Nov. 16, 1779
Jones, David	Wells, Margaret	Nov. 4, 1797
Jones, Edward	Jones, Susannah	May 8, 1799
Jones, Elijah	Manley, Elizabeth	May 15, 1784
Jones, Eliza	Carrick, Mareen	Sept. 30, 1782
Jones, Elizabeth	Clark, Thomas	Sept. 20, 1799
Jones, Elizabeth	Waters, Richard	Oct. 5, 1782
Jones, Elizabeth	Wedderal, John	Apr. 14, 1786
Jones, George	Roberts, Ann	Jan. 4, 1785
Jones, George	Sinclair, Elizabeth	Aug. 25, 1787
Jones, George	Wilson, Elizabeth	Jan. 29, 1788
Jones, George	Tarman, Ann	June 25, 1799
Jones, Henry	Collings, Rose	Aug. 29, 1781
Jones, James	Griffin, Deborah	Oct. 29, 1785
Jones, James	Smith, Rosanah	Mch. 19, 1785
Jones, Josias	Jones, Arey	Mch. 23, 1785
Jones, Leithy	Robinson, Charles	Jan. 21, 1790
Jones, Margaret	Wilson, William	Nov. 7, 1781
Jones, Martha	Hatton, Joseph	Oct. 14, 1777
Jones, Mary	Patterson, William	Nov. 23, 1779
Jones, Mary	Tilley, John	Mch. 29, 1780
Jones, Mary	Lyles, Thomas	Oct. 23, 1790
Jones, Mary	Hurley, Daniel	Sept. 8, 1797
Jones, Mary	Rawlings, John	May 25, 1798
Jones, Monica	Ball, Stephen	July 16, 1781

Jones, Moses..............Ball, Druscilla.............Nov. 30, 1790
Jones, Perry..............Gentle, Linney.............Feb. 6, 1793
Jones, Rebecca............Taylor, John..............Aug. 23, 1780
Jones, Richard............Ladyman, Priscilla...........Jan. 4, 1783
Jones, Richard............Wilson, Ann..............Dec. 10, 1796
Jones, Samuel............Welch, Dorcus.............Nov. 4, 1788
Jones, Samuel............Gatton, Ann..............Oct. 11, 1800
Jones, Sarah..............Gill, Thomas..............Aug. 30, 1777
Jones, Sarah..............Magruder, John Bowie.......Feb. 3, 1791
Jones, Susanna............Jones, Edward.............May 8, 1799
Jones, Thomas............Thorn, Winny.............Dec. 26, 1789
Jones, William............Mockbee, Darkey..........June 25, 1791
Jones, William............King, Sabret..............Feb. 11, 1793
Journey, Margaret..........Dowell, Richard.............Apr. 4, 1795
Joy, Joseph..............Durity, Sarah..............July 4, 1795

Kayhawley, David..........Kerrick, Elizabeth.........Mch. 28, 1780
Keadl, Elizabeth...........Moore, John...............May 3, 1783
Keadle, Mary.............Everheart, Caspar..........Dec. 11, 1792
Keadle, Wiseman..........Wightt, Ann..............Aug. 25, 1787
Keech, William............Williams, Jane.............Sept. 6, 1780
Keith, Edward............Lisby, Ann................Feb. 9, 1793
Keith, Gerard.............Lusby, Eleanor.............Dec. 27, 1782
Keith, Rebecca............Gibbons, Alexander..........Oct. 2, 1792
Kelly, Jane...............Gordon, George.............June 9, 1796
Kelly, Mary..............Roberts, Henry............Aug. 10, 1778
Kelton, George............Carter, Elizabeth..........Sept. 23, 1796
Kennedy, James...........Wailks, Susanna..........Dec. 16, 1799
Kerrick, Elizabeth..........Kayhawley, David.........Mch. 28, 1780
Key, Ignatius.............Queen, Henrietta...........July 14, 1785
Key, Richard.............Mason, Sarah.............Feb. 16, 1784
Kiddle, Thomas...........Perry, Mary..............June 15, 1784
Kidwell, Eliza.............Mobberly, Hezekiah.........Dec. 5, 1796
Kidwell, George...........Smith, Ann................Dec. 6, 1800
Kidwell, James............Mudd, Mary.............Dec. 18, 1790
Kidwell, John.............Lawson, Mary.............Feb. 22, 1784
Kidwell, John.............Hays, Eleanor..............Jan. 5, 1785
Kidwell, Josias............Ladymer, Elizabeth.........Dec. 17, 1799
Kidwell, Leonard..........Foster, Mary..............Aug. 1, 1798
Kidwell, Margaret.........Webster, John............Dec. 26, 1784
Kidwell, Mathew..........Moore, Priscilla...........Dec. 20, 1781
Kidwell, Sarah............Strickland, William.........Dec. 20, 1784

Kidwell, Sophia Mary	Simpson, Thomas	May 21, 1782
Kidwell, Theodore	Hill, Mary	Jan. 12, 1799
Kidwell, Thomas	Wentfield, Mary Ann	Mch. 23, 1781
Kidwell, William	Gray, Eleanor	Jan. 14, 1783
King, Ann	Moore, Zadock	Mch. 6, 1779
King, Eleanor	Wilson, Joseph H.	Aug. 24, 1782
King, Elisha	Spalding, Elizabeth	Feb. 18, 1800
King, Elizabeth	Simm, Robert	Jan. 5, 1786
King, Elizabeth	Pumphrey, Richard	Feb. 21, 1786
King, Hetty	Cooke, Zadokiah	Dec. 26, 1794
King, Isaac	Weaver, Sarah	Mch. 16, 1799
King, James Swan	Lanham, Sarah Lee	Dec. 22, 1800
King, Jane	Wise, George	Mch. 7, 1799
King, John	Leach, Susannah	Nov. 25, 1777
King, John	Upton, Keziah	June 5, 1779
King, John of Richard	McDowell, Elizabeth	July 30, 1791
King, John	Lewis, Ann	Jan. 10, 1794
King, Leonard	Watson, Susanna	Nov. 15, 1780
King, Mary	Hulliken, Thomas	Jan. 5, 1799
King, Richard	Brown, Elizabeth	Feb. 11, 1795
King, Richard	Weaver, Anamina	Feb. 27, 1795
King, Ruth	Simpson, Thomas	Apr. 7, 1787
King, Sabret	Jones, William	Feb. 11, 1793
King, Sarah	Grimes, John	Jan. 3, 1789
King, Susanna	Biggs, John	Dec. 11, 1779
King, Susannah	Watson, John	Feb. 28, 1789
King, Susannah	Thomas, Caleb	Apr. 14, 1798
King, Thomas	Mitchell, Mary	Oct. 16, 1787
King, Thomas M.	Gray, Rebecca	Jan. 18, 1790
King, William	Holland, Susannah	Oct. 22, 1796
Kingsbury, Elizabeth	Rawlings, Luke	Jan. 30, 1786
Kirby, Francis	Collard, Elizabeth	Jan. 11,'1783
Kirby, John Baptist	Elson, Sarah	Sept. 23, 1779
Kirby, Richard	Talburt, Susanna	Sept. 9, 1783
Kirby, Sarah	Neal, Theodore	Apr. 25, 1778
Knighton, Samuel	Ryon, Susannah	Feb. 11, 1791
Knighton, Thompsey	Nicholls, John	Jan. 29, 1791
Knott, Elizabeth	Goddard, John	July 14, 1795
Ladyman, Priscilla	Jones, Richard	Jan. 4, 1783
Ladymer, Elizabeth	Kidwell, Josias	Dec. 17, 1799
Laird, John	Dick, Mary	Jan. 28, 1797

Lamar, Priscilla	Drane, James	Feb. 18, 1789
Lamar, Rachel	Harding, William	Mch. 22, 1784
Lamar, Richard	Drane, Ann	Nov. 9, 1790
Lamar, Susannah	Watson, Cornelius	Dec. 28, 1791
Lambert, John B.	Higdon, Phebe Eleanor	Dec. 17, 1793
Lane, John	Barnes, Margaret	Feb. 21, 1781
Lang, Ann	Grear, Ananias	Feb. 6, 1781
Lang, Catherine	Beavin, Charles	Mch. 28, 1793
Lang, John	Hooper, Anne	Dec. 17, 1779
Lanham, Acquilla	Thompson, Ann	Jan. 28, 1788
Lanham, Ann	Barnes, Henry	Feb. 3, 1790
Lanham, Catherine	Fraser, Andrew	Dec. 31, 1791
Lanham, Charity	Lanham, Solomon	Jan. 14, 1778
Lanham, Elizabeth	Smith, Robert	Sept. 5, 1785
Lanham, George	Jarmain, Ann	Feb. 23, 1781
Lanham, Hilleary	Upton, Eliza	Apr. 5, 1783
Lanham, John	Mockbee, Linna	Mch. 6, 1800
Lanham, Josias	Mason, Chloe	Feb. 14, 1790
Lanham, Layor	Selby, Charles	Dec. 18, 1787
Lanham, Mary	Fraser, John	Oct. 24, 1789
Lanham, Mary	Barnes, Basil	Jan. 22, 1791
Lanham, Massey Ann	Creaton, John	Feb. 21, 1783
Lanham, Mildred	Talbott, Jesse	Nov. 12, 1794
Lanham, Sarah Ann	Green, Basil	Jan. 18, 1780
Lanham, Sarah Lee	King, James Swan	Dec. 22, 1800
Lanham, Solomon	Lanham, Charity	Jan. 14, 1778
Lanham, Stephen	Selby, Eleanor	Oct. 4, 1779
Lanham, Susannah	McSherry, Hugh	Apr. 13, 1790
Lanham, Verlinda	Allen, John	Oct. 29, 1781
Lansdale, Ann	Robb, Adam	Sept. 8, 1789
Lansdale, Elizabeth	Belt, James	Dec. 2, 1794
Lansdale, Isaac	Brooke, Catherine	Mch. 27, 1792
Lansdale, Isaac	Whitaker, Elizabeth	June 19, 1794
Lattin, Plummer	Brashears, Mary	Jan. 25, 1798
Lattin, Rebecca	Owen, Joseph	June 12, 1781
Lawry, Elizabeth	Sandfield, George	Dec. 9, 1800
Laws, William	Walker, Martha	May 26, 1784
Lawson, Mary	Kidwell, John	Feb. 22, 1784
Lawson, Thomas	Hyde, Priscilla	Feb. 26, 1791
Lawson, William	Simpson, Eleanor	Nov. 16, 1778
Lawson, William	Ball, Susanna	Oct. 5, 1782
Leach, James	Watson, Jane	Jan. 13, 1790

Leach, Mary............... Ball, Isaac................. Apr. 20, 1799
Leach, Susanna............ King, John................ Nov. 25, 1777
Leach, Thomas............. Wells, Bridgett............ July 11, 1789
Leach, Verlinda........... Smith, Thomas............ Mch. 19, 1789
Leach, Tabitha............ Tippett, John.............. July 30, 1796
Lecompt, Rezin............ Piper, Margaret........... Sept. 10, 1800
Lee, Henry............... Cave, Elizabeth........... Dec. 15, 1781
Lee, Richard.............. Ambler, Mary.............. Nov. 9, 1779
Lee, Thomas.............. Wilson, Elizabeth.......... Sept. 29, 1792
Leitch, Benjamin.......... Wells, Mary................ Oct. 1, 1781
Leitch, Margaret.......... Sydebotham, William....... Sept. 23, 1778
Letchwalt, Mary........... Estep, Thomas............. Mch. 4, 1797
Letchworth, John.......... Sothoron, Deborah......... Dec. 10, 1798
Lewis, Ann............... King, John................ Jan. 10, 1794
Lewis, Daniel............. Martin, Mildred............ Jan. 2, 1792
Lewis, Hugh.............. Gregory, Susanna........... Jan. 12, 1790
Lewis, Mary.............. Thompson, Clark........... May 20, 1783
Linch, John S............. Watson, Rebecca............ Jan. 5, 1782
Lind, Amelia.............. Simpson, Thomas.......... Sept. 17, 1787
Lindsay, George........... Frazier, Sarah.............. Dec. 6, 1798
Lindsey, Elizabeth......... Jones, Butler................ Feb. 8, 1790
Linsey, Thomas............ Fraser, Rebecca........... June 20, 1789
Linton, Ann............... Higdon, James............. Jan. 28, 1797
Linton, Martha............ Howard, John............. Sept. 16, 1791
Linton, Mary.............. Warne, John.............. Dec. 24, 1783
Lisby, Ann............... Keith, Edward.............. Feb. 9, 1793
Littlefield, Mary........... Walker, Benjamin Neill..... Mch. 25, 1788
Littleford, John........... Piles, Ann.................. Jan. 2, 1799
Littleford, Mary........... Walker, Thomas............ Dec. 24, 1780
Littleford, Thomas......... Busey, Eleanor............ Feb. 11, 1797
Livingston, John........... Lyle, Martha.............. Dec. 19, 1793
Locker, David............. Page, Sarah............... July 30, 1794
Locker, Isaac............. Miles, Sarah............... Jan. 14, 1795
Locker, Philip............. Tongue, Margaret.......... Feb. 25, 1785
Loflin, Mary.............. Watkins, Gassoway......... Apr. 17, 1784
Long, John............... Higdon, Mary Ann......... Apr. 27, 1798
Long, Samuel............. Ransom, Martha........... Feb. 13, 1784
Long, William............. Pickrell, Rebecca.......... Feb. 11, 1781
Love, Margaret............ Framnay, James............ Mch. 8, 1782
Lovejoy, Alexander........ Sullivan, Mary............ May 10, 1779
Lovejoy, Alexander........ Boteler, Milly............. Sept. 6, 1794
Lovejoy, Ann.............. Campbell, Arthur.......... Dec. 29, 1788

Lovejoy, Eleanor	Fowler, William	Feb. 24, 1786
Lovejoy, George N.	Smallwood, Rebecca	June 10, 1794
Lovejoy, Josias	Campbell, Sarah	Feb. 19, 1789
Lovejoy, Lettice	Mitchell, Alexius.	Oct. 7, 1794
Lovejoy, Michael	Poston, Christian	Oct. 1, 1788
Lovejoy, Samuel	Mockbee, Verlinda	Dec. 13, 1793
Lovelace, Johannah	Padgett, Josias	Dec. 31, 1796
Lovelace, Mellesent Ann	Francis, Alexander	Dec. 22, 1783
Loveless, Isaac	Barrett, Sarah	Jan. 7, 1794
Loveless, Unice	Hunt, James	Jan. 12, 1793
Lovelis, Ignatius	Calvert, Ann	Dec. 23, 1799
Lovelis, Luke	Ridgway, Mary	Dec. 18, 1800
Lowden, Rachel	Thompson, Moses	Dec. 22, 1783
Lowe, Ann	Urquhart, John	Feb. 22, 1793
Lowe, Ann	Moore, James	Feb. 3, 1796
Lowe, Barton	Hollingsford, Susanna	Feb. 10, 1782
Lowe, Barsheba	Luxon, Anthony	Nov. 6, 1786
Lowe, Basil	Wood, Tracy	Aug. 15, 1785
Lowe, Charles F.	Sutton, Mary B.	Oct. 26, 1795
Lowe, Dennis	Wood, Ann	Dec. 3, 1785
Lowe, Elias	Henry, Sarah	Aug. 9, 1785
Lowe, Elizabeth	Rugless, William	Oct. 31, 1789
Lowe, Esther	Wallingsford, Joseph	Feb. 25, 1782
Lowe, George	Moore, Mary	Dec. 12, 1794
Low, James	Wig, Elizabeth	July 26, 1790
Low, Mary	Brown, Thomas	Nov. 9, 1778
Lowe, John	Wilcoxon, Ann	June 29, 1781
Lowe, John	Darnall, Sarah	June 24, 1782
Lowe, John	Riddle, Susanna	July 10, 1784
Lowe, John H.	Magruder, Barbara	Jan. 2, 1788
Lowe, Keziah	Talbott, Basil	June 17, 1788
Low, Leithy	Greenwell, Jesse	Jan. 6, 1790
Lowe, Nathaniel	Hayes, Verllinda	Sept. 9, 1797
Lowe, Priscilla	Milburn, Robert	Dec. 29, 1798
Lowe, Rachel	Hutchenson, George	Nov. 13, 1781
Lowe, Rachel	Smith, John Willing	Feb. 27, 1788
Lowe, Rebecca	Pickrell, Henry	Apr. 6, 1779
Lowe, Sarah	Allen, George	Jan. 5, 1782
Lowe, William	Henry, Mary	Apr. 19, 1783
Lowe, Winifred	Greenwell, Joseph	Jan. 7, 1793
Lowndes, Rebecca	Stoddert, Benjamin C.	June 7, 1781
Lucas, John	Simmons, Mary	Dec. 14, 1780

Lucas, John	Duvall, Rachel	Sept. 12, 1787
Lucker, Thomas	Beane, Rebecca	Feb. 7, 1785
Lusby, Eleanor	Keith, Gerard	Dec. 27, 1782
Lusby, John	Wilson, Martha	Feb. 24, 1778
Luxon, Anthony	Lowe, Barsheba	Nov. 6, 1786
Lyle, Martha	Livingston, John	Dec. 19, 1793
Lyles, Elizabeth	Simmons, Thomas	May 26, 1795
Lyles, Mary	Coombes, Joseph	Oct. 23, 1797
Lyles, Priscilla	Clagett, Wiseman	Jan. 16, 1779
Lyles, Richard	Magruder, Harriet	Jan. 11, 1786
Lyles, Thomas	Duckrell, Eleanor	Apr. 10, 1779
Lyles, Thomas	Jones, Mary	Oct. 23, 1790
Lynch, Jane	Carroll, Ignatius	Dec. 15, 1800
Lynn, Ann	Buckland, William	Nov. 24, 1795
Lynn, Colerrton	Johnson, Elizabeth	Sept. 21, 1795
McAtee, Ann	Owens, Thomas	Apr. 27, 1793
McCartey, Sarah M.	Warrensford, Joseph	Dec. 20, 1800
McCarthy, Daniel, Jr.	Magruder, Matilda Margaret Snowden	Oct. 4, 1800
McCarthy, Dennis	Mudd, Mary Tabatha	Sept. 16, 1791
McCartney, Fanny	Mead, William	Aug. 7, 1796
McCauley, Rebecca	Harvey, Alexander	July 19, 1777
McClerren, John	Macgill, Ann	Dec. 18, 1788
McClish, Robert	Bedden, Catherine	Dec. 14, 1785
McCormick, Andrew T.	Ponsonby, Sarah	Aug. 27, 1796
McCoy, Priscilla	Rawlings, Isaac	Feb. 11, 1782
McCray, Farquire	Ferguson, Susan	Apr. 21, 1781
McDaniel, Elizabeth	Beall, David F.	June 28, 1800
McDaniel, Archibald	Tull, Eleanor	June 25, 1798
McDaniel, Cephas	Gray, Elizabeth	Feb. 20, 1797
McDaniel, Janephene	Vermilion, John	July 15, 1780
McDaniel, Mary	Beane, Ebbsworth	Dec. 12, 1798
McDaniel, Sarah	Harvey, Henry	Apr. 20, 1791
McDaniel, William	Wynn, Priscilla Ann	Nov. 29, 1779
McDonogh, Morris James	Wheeler, Elizabeth	Nov. 4, 1789
McDougall, Alexander	Nawood, Margaret	Feb. 25, 1783
McDowell, Ann	Brown, George	May 27, 1799
McDowell, Elizabeth	King, John (of Richard)	July 30, 1791
McDowell, William	Mitchell, Mary	Oct. 24, 1788
McElderry, Mary	Duckett, Jacob	May 4, 1799
McElderry, Patrick	Clagett, Mary	June 5, 1789

McEver, Charles..........Clifford, Wilder............Oct. 17, 1778
McKay, Alexander.........Campbell, Ann.............Dec. 16, 1778
McKenzie, James..........Magruder, Casandra........Mch. 9, 1781
McKenzy, John............Talbott, Salomy...........Mch. 19, 1794
McKnight, John...........Piercy, Catherine...........Oct. 29, 1799
McLish, Margaret..........Jackson, Alexander.........Apr. 30, 1784
McNauty, Cephas..........Wilson, Ann..............Aug. 19, 1800
McSeney, Deborah.........Pearce, Edward.............June 3, 1784
McSherry, Hugh...........Lanham, Susannah.........Apr. 13, 1790
Macatee, Clarissa..........Harvey, Moses.............Dec. 15, 1780
Maccastle, Mary..........Short, James..............Dec. 12, 1791
Macgill, Ann..............McClerren, John...........Dec. 18, 1788
Macgill, Eleanor...........Higgins, Richard...........Mch. 21, 1783
Macgill, Elizabeth..........Rawlings, Elijah............Aug. 6, 1778
Macgill, Robert...........Beall, Eleanor..............Apr. 28, 1789
Mackall, John.............Magruder, Jane.............Jan. 11, 1788
Mackall, Mary.............Magruder, Alexander........Feb. 27, 1790
Mackall, Rebecca..........Carrington, Levin..........Mch. 25, 1796
Mackay, Barbara..........Green, Charles..............Dec. 1, 1785
Mackay, Hugh.............Grant, Catherine...........Feb. 11, 1790
Mackeney, Zachariah......Simmons, Martha...........Feb. 23, 1789
Mackness, Samuel.........War, Ann..................Sept. 2, 1779
Macnea, Mary.............Harbin, Rezin.............Nov. 14, 1778
Maddocks, Nathan.........Robey, Meshal........Dec. 18 (11?), 1781
Maddox, Frances..........Farr, George..............Feb. 12, 1798
Magill, John..............Belt, Elizabeth.............Nov. 13, 1786
Maginnes, Elizabeth........Wilson, Barnaba............Jan. 11, 1786
Magruder, Alexander.......Mackall, Mary.............Feb. 27, 1790
Magruder, Alexander Wilson Conley, Mary.............Nov. 16, 1785
Magruder, Ann.............Hay, Robert................Mch. 9, 1791
Magruder, Barbara.........Lowe, John H...............Jan. 2, 1788
Magruder, Casandra........McKenzie, James...........Mch. 9, 1781
Magruder, Dennis..........Contee, Ann..............Sept. 23, 1779
Magruder, Edward.........Wade, Elizabeth...........May 22, 1782
Magruder, Edward.........Ellon, Anne...............Oct. 23, 1800
Magruder, Eleanor.........Burgess, John M...........Oct. 18, 1779
Magruder, Elizabeth........Blackburn, John.............Feb. 4, 1787
Magruder, Elizabeth........Williams, Osborn...........Oct. 15, 1787
Magruder, Elizabeth
Hawkins..............Somerville, James...........Nov. 7, 1792
Magruder, Enoch...........Sprigg, Elizabeth...........Feb. 27, 1781
Magruder, Francis..........Williams, Barbara..........Dec. 23, 1786

Magruder, Harriet..........Lyles, Richard..............Jan. 11, 1786
Magruder, Harriet..........Carrington, Alexander.......Dec. 16, 1797
Magruder, James A..........Beane, Milicent ....June 10, 1794
Magruder, Jane.............Mackall, John...............Jan. 11, 1788
Magruder, John Bowie.......Jones, Sarah.................Feb. 3, 1791
Magruder, John Read, Jr....Hall, Amelia...............Sept. 13, 1794
Magruder, Kitty............Skinner, Adderton...........Aug. 29, 1798
Magruder, Mary.............Boyd, Thomas, Jr............Oct. 13, 1788
Magruder, Mary.............Forster, Thomas..............June 2, 1794
Magruder, Matilda Margaret
Snowden..............McCarthy, Daniel, Jr.........Oct. 4, 1800
Magruder, Nathan...........Beven, Elizabeth............Aug. 12, 1790
Magruder, Priscilla........Handling, James.............May 22, 1787
Magruder, Rebecca..........Turnbull, John.............Sept. 24, 1789
Magruder, Samuel...........Hilleary, Mary..............June 11, 1792
Magruder, Sarah............Stanley (Shaney?), Bernard...Feb. 3, 1785
Magruder, Sarah............Osborn, John................Jan. 12, 1788
Magruder, Sarah Ann........Brooke, Isaac...............Oct. 20, 1780
Magruder, Thomas...........Clarke, Mary.................Jan. 4, 1800
Magruder, William..........Hilleary, Eliza..............Feb. 5, 1796
Mahew, Alice...............Wallace, William............Apr. 23, 1778
Mahew, Eleanor.............Mahew, Jonathan.............Feb. 11, 1784
Mahew, Mary................Cage, William...............Dec. 18, 1777
Mahew, Thomas..............Glover, Mary................Apr. 14, 1781
Mahew, Timothy.............Higdon, Mary................Mch. 17, 1787
Mahoney, Edward............Taylor, Alis................Dec. 18, 1786
Mahoney, John..............Moore, Elizabeth............May 14, 1785
Mahorney, Edelburgodis.....Jarvis, Jonathan............May 23, 1787
Maitland, James............Taylor, Mary................June 17, 1800
Malone, Catherine..........Teasdale, John...............May 5, 1778
Maloney, Ann...............Whiting, Gilbert............Nov. 21, 1794
Manders, Basil.............Piles, Mary..................July 3, 1781
Mangum, Eleanor............Wilson, Norando.............Dec. 26, 1785
Mangum, Henry..............Tarman, Eleanor.............Jan. 25, 1797
Mangum, John...............Piles, Elizabeth.............Aug. 4, 1785
Manley, Elizabeth..........Jones, Elijah...............May 15, 1784
Manley, Elizabeth..........Summers, John...............Dec. 11, 1785
Manley, John...............Shagnasha, Mary.............July 22, 1786
Manley, Thomas.............Ray, Priscilla..............July 15, 1785
Manley, William............Brown, Sarah.................Jan. 7, 1789
Manning, William W.........Bryan, Margaret.............June 30, 1800
Marlow, Abraham............Marlow, Sarah...............Sept. 6, 1779

Marlow, Amelia	Pickrell, Richard	July 24, 1779*
Marlow, Buttler	Foard, Charlotte	Dec. 21, 1782
Marlow, John	Baden, Elizabeth	Oct. 29, 1791
Marlow, Sarah	Marlow, Abraham	Sept. 6, 1779
Marlow, Thomas D.	Clagett, Margaret	Mch. 10, 1787
Marlow, William	Willett, Mary	Dec. 29, 1786
Marlows, Butler D.	Webster, Elizabeth	Aug. 30, 1796
Marr, Joshua	Speak, Joanna	Jan. 2, 1779
Marshall, Benjamin	Upton, Sarah	Jan. 17, 1778
Marshall, Elizabeth Fendall	Hanson, Samuel	July 29, 1788
Marshall, Josias	Harris, Sarah	Apr. 18, 1797
Marshall, Mary	Steward, Philip	Feb. 26, 1787
Marshall, Richard	Hardey, Margaret	Mch. 5, 1782
Marshall, Thomas	Mockbee, Eleanor	Dec. 22, 1783
Marshman, James	Gordon, Rebecca	Oct. 22, 1779
Martin, Mildred	Lewis, Daniel	Jan. 2, 1792
Martin, Richard	Russell, Ann	Jan. 1, 1780
Martin, Zephaniah	Robinson, Sarah Eliza Ford	Dec. 30, 1795
Mason, Chloe	Lanham, Josias	Feb. 14, 1790
Mason, Sarah	Reeves, John	Apr. 19, 1781
Mason, Sarah	Key, Richard	Feb. 16, 1784
Mason, Thomas	Hyde, Sarah	July 21, 1787
Mason, Verlinda	Wilson, William	Jan. 10, 1780
Masters, Dorcas	Jenkins, William	Dec. 31, 1778
Masters, Ezekial	Norton, Cassandra	Apr. 11, 1789
Masters, John	Bayne, Prescilla	June 3, 1778
Masters, Mary	Waugh, John	Nov. 2, 1793
Masters, Nathan	Jenkins, Winifred	Jan. 8, 1794
Mattingly, Joseph	Scott, Margaret	Jan. 24, 1785
Mayhew, Ann	Harwood, Thomas	Apr. 16, 1794
Mayhew, Brian	Conley, Ann	June 19, 1779
Mayhew, Frances	Hull, Samuel	July 5, 1779
Mayhew, Henry	Bryan, Elizabeth	July 10, 1800
Mayhew, James	Ryon, Mary	May 14, 1788
Mayhew, John	Soper, Massy	Dec. 9, 1795
Mayhew, Mary	Watson, Isaac	Mch. 21, 1786
Mayhew, Susanna	Poston, John Stone	Dec. 24, 1797
Mayhew, William	Cage, Mary	Apr. 7, 1794
Mayhew, William	Talburt, Elizabeth	Dec. 23, 1795
Maynard, Elizabeth	Gantt, Robert	Aug. 21, 1790

*Also given as Oct. 30, 1779—same contracting parties.

Mayoh, Ann	Riston, Elisha	Feb. 6, 1790
Mead, William	McCartney, Fanny	Aug. 7, 1796
Medley, Mary	Beach, William	May 9, 1797
Meek, Western	Perkins, Susannah	Nov. 11, 1800
Merritt, Elizabeth	Joiner, Joseph	Aug. 19, 1800
Merroll, Philip	Trueman, Mocky	Feb. 10, 1798
Mewburn, James	Gantt, Mary	May 7, 1791
Middleton, Ann	Tolson, Francis	Feb. 21, 1782
Middleton, Theodore	Hoxton, Julia	Nov. 20, 1789
Mier, Elizabeth	Waters, Joseph	Aug. 25, 1779
Milburn, Robert	Lowe, Priscilla	Dec. 29, 1798
Miles, Eleanor	Rabbitt, John	May 4, 1778
Miles, Frederick	White, Eliza	Dec. 31, 1781
Miles, Frederick	Brashears, Ruth	Feb. 11, 1784
Miles, Harry	Blanford, Henrietta	June 9, 1783
Miles, James	Pearce, Jane	Nov. 30, 1780
Miles, John	Pearce, Rebecca	Jan. 21, 1783
Miles, Mary	Mitchell, Francis	Apr. 26, 1786
Miles, Mary	Mockbee, Breck	June 11, 1788
Miles, Mary	Delehaye, Joseph	June 22, 1788
Miles, Priscilla	Nevitt, Miles William	Jan. 1, 1779
Miles, Sarah	Locker, Isaac	Jan. 14, 1795
Millard, William	Webb, Elizabeth	June 22, 1780
Miller, John	Hinton, Ann	Dec. 26, 1800
Milliken, James	Beanes, Eleanor	Mch. 30, 1781
Milliken, Walter	Russell, Elizabeth	Oct. 3, 1799
Mills, Hester	Fowler, Abraham	Nov. 28, 1794
Mills, John	Waters, Eliza	Jan. 18, 1782
Mills, Zachariah	Waters, Elizabeth	Dec. 21, 1787
Mitchell, Alexius	Lovejoy, Lettice	Oct. 7, 1794
Mitchell, Amelia	Ray, Benjamin	Dec. 26, 1782
Mitchell, Ann	Beall, James	May 9, 1787
Mitchell, Eleanor	Clark, Thomas	Dec. 9, 1797
Mitchell, Eliza	Coughland, Richard Johnson	Feb. 28, 1785
Mitchell, Frances	Pool, John	Sept. 4, 1784
Mitchell, Francis	Miles, Mary	Apr. 26, 1786
Mitchell, John	Newton, Peggy	Apr. 14, 1781
Mitchell, John	Sweeny, Drury	May 10, 1788
Mitchell, John	Clubb, Rebecca	Jan. 29, 1791
Mitchell, Lucy Ann	Brandtt, Richard	Dec. 15, 1792
Mitchell, Mary	King, Thomas	Oct. 16, 1787
Mitchell, Mary	McDowell, William	Oct. 24, 1788

Mitchell, Mary............Hatton, Josias............Feb. 22, 1793
Mitchell, Middleton........Riston, Rebecca............Apr. 21, 1792
Mitchell, Mordecai Miles....Wilson, Sarah..............Nov. 26, 1779
Mitchell, Priscilla...........Upton, Thomas.............Feb. 19, 1798
Mitchell, Samuel...........Boone, Susanna..............Jan. 2, 1794
Mitchell, Sarah.............Stallings, Thomas, Jr........Nov. 25, 1791
Mitchell, Susanna..........Parsons, James.............Apr. 22, 1782
Mitchell, Theodore.........Wells, Mary...............Nov. 27, 1777
Mitchell, Thomas...........Edelen, Eleanor.............Nov. 9, 1778
Mitchell, Thomas...........Wood, Elizabeth............Aug. 20, 1781
Mitchell, William...........White, Mary...............Dec. 10, 1792
Mobberly, Elizabeth........Windsor, Luke.............Jan. 23, 1797
Mobberly, Hezekiah........Kidwell, Eliza...............Dec. 5, 1796
Mobberly, Mary...........Winser, Ignatius............Dec. 21, 1792
Mobley, Jonathan..........Church, Susanna............Feb. 5, 1793
Mockbee, Ann.............Mockbee, Basil.............Nov. 5, 1779
Mockbee, Breck............Miles, Mary...............June 11, 1788
Mockbee, Darkey..........Jones, William.............June 25, 1791
Mockbee, Eleanor..........Marshall, Thomas..........Dec. 22, 1783
Mockbee, John.............Robinson, Mary............Aug. 20, 1777
Mockbee, Linna...........Lanham, John..............Mch. 6, 1800
Mockbee, Rachel...........Ridgway, John..............Dec. 2, 1778
Mockbee, Rebecca..........Sansbury, Thomas..........Feb. 25, 1797
Mockbee, Verlinda.........Lovejoy, Samuel...........Dec. 13, 1793
Mockbee, William..........Clarke, Ann................Feb. 29, 1780
Mockbee, William, Jr.......Henness, Margaret..........Dec. 24, 1780
Molan, James.............Montgomery, Catherine......Oct. 20, 1780
Molleson, William..........Gunn, Rebecca..............May 5, 1781
Montgomery, Catherine.....Molan, James..............Oct. 20, 1780
Moons, Francis............Beckett, Ann..............Sept. 25, 1779
Moore, Ann...............Greenwell, Jesse............Jan. 21, 1795
Moore, Elizabeth...........Mahoney, John............May 14, 1785
Moore, George............Drane, Eleanor............Nov. 19, 1792
Moore, George D...........Bayne, Sarah.............Dec. 16, 1795
Moore, James..............Lowe, Ann.................Feb. 3, 1796
Moore, John..............Keadl, Elizabeth............May 3, 1783
Moore, Joseph............Dunn, Elizabeth............July 11, 1798
Moore, Josiah.............Duckett, Charity...........Apr. 21, 1778
Moore, Mary.............Lowe, George..............Dec. 12, 1794
Moore, Priscilla...........Kidwell, Mathew...........Dec. 20, 1781
Moore, Sarah.............Thompson, James Fraser.....June 5, 1778
Moore, Zadock............King, Ann.................Mch. 6, 1779

Moore, Zadock	Soper, Mary	June 5, 1779
Moore, Zadock	Elson, Rachel	Nov. 22, 1782
Moran, Rebecca	Brightwell, Allen	Oct. 15, 1785
Moreland, Elias	Tenly, Letty Ann	Feb. 6, 1798
Moreland, Philip	Southwell, Lydia	July 18, 1781
Moreland, Thomas B.	Wheat, Mary	Oct. 17, 1799
Morgan, John	Wood, Hannah	Apr. 20, 1779
Morgan, Robert	Hamilton, Martha	May 30, 1780
Morica, William	Duvall, Ruth	Oct. 29, 1778
Morris, Ann	Ball, Bennett	Jan. 6, 1789
Morris, Andrew	Fenton, Sarah	Oct. 16, 1800
Morris, Benjamin	Galwith, Rebecca	Feb. 4, 1783
Morris, John	Payne, Lucy	Dec. 17, 1799
Morris, Mary Dent	Simpson, John	Apr. 10, 1788
Morris, Mary Norman	Davis, Henry	Oct. 23, 1790
Morse, William	Duke, Mary	Mch. 6, 1780
Morton, Catherine	Harris, Josias	Aug. 29, 1781
Mosley, Stacey	Walker, John	Dec. 16, 1796
Moulton, Willimina M.	Baden, Jere	Jan. 12, 1782
Mudd, Ann	Williams, John F.	Jan. 9, 1782
Mudd, Elizabeth	Simms, Joseph Milburn	Feb. 10, 1790
Mudd, Elizabeth	Cooke, William	May 28, 1796
Mudd, Hezekiah	Edelen, Elizabeth	May 12, 1779
Mudd, Joseph	Hill, Elizabeth	June 2, 1787
Mudd, Mary	Kidwell, James	Dec. 18, 1790
Mudd, Mary Tabatha	McCarthy, Dennis	Sept. 16, 1791
Mullican, Henry	Hardy, Elizabeth	Jan. 13, 1796
Mullican, Joseph	Mitchell, Massy Ann	Oct. 10, 1797
Mulliken, Lucy	Thralls, Richard	Dec. 31, 1787
Mulliken, Richard	Beall, Nancy	Dec. 14, 1785
Mulliken, Thomas	King, Mary	Jan. 5, 1799
Mundell, Thomas	Eversfield, Verlinda	Feb. 28, 1794
Muran, James	Hellen, Jane	May 6, 1780
Murdock, Rebecca	Addison, Anthony	June 6, 1794
Murray, John	Thompson, Eleanor	Dec. 10, 1789
Murray, Margaret	Sutherland, John	Nov. 30, 1780
Nash, Christopher	Young, Mary	Sept. 4, 1782
Nawood, Margaret	McDougall, Alexander	Feb. 25, 1783
Naylor, Ann	Wailes, Samuel	Feb. 8, 1783
Naylor, Ann	Watson, Walter	Dec. 23, 1783
Naylor, Ann	Wright, Joseph	Feb. 26, 1788

Naylor, Benjamin	Selby, Deborah	Aug. 31, 1785
Naylor, Benjamin	Beaven, Martha	Dec. 23, 1793
Naylor, Benjamin	Wilson, Mary	Dec. 14, 1797
Naylor, Baston	Austin, Eleanor	Nov. 6, 1778
Nayler, George	Berry, Eleanor	June 2, 1785
Naylor, James	Wilson, Priscilla	Sept. 5, 1797
Naylor, James	Boteler, Mary	Dec. 31, 1800
Naylor, Joshua	Nutwell, Martha	Jan. 17, 1781
Naylor, Joshua	Baden, Martha	Dec. 2, 1799
Naylor, Margaret	Fields, Elisha	Feb. 12, 1780
Naylor, Martha	Walls, George	Feb. 25, 1783
Naylor, Mary	Garner, Thomas	Jan. 27, 1798
Naylor, Nicholas	Selby, Mary	Feb. 15, 1783
Naylor, Susannah	Gibbons, George Wailes	Jan. 26, 1793
Neale, Henrietta	Boone, Francis	Aug. 13, 1795
Neal, Theodore	Kirby, Sarah	Apr. 25, 1778
Neal, Thomas	Whitemore, Elizabeth	Aug. 7, 1779
Neale, William	Veitch, Rachel	Aug. 1, 1798
Nelson, Eliza H.	Wilson, Nathaniel	Mch. 30, 1782
Nesmith, Ebenezer	Trother, Jane	May 20, 1796
Nevill (Nevitt ?), Ann	Bowling, Thomas	Aug. 4, 1783
Nevitt, Ann	Adams, Joseph	Nov. 5, 1791
Nevitt, Charles	Bowling, Levinah	Jan. 18, 1780
Nevitt, James	Conn, Ruth	May 31, 1777
Neavitt, Levinia	Perry, Elisha	Sept. 30, 1799
Nevitt, Mary	Yates, Martin	Dec. 31, 1798
Nevitt, Miles William	Miles, Priscilla	Jan. 1, 1779
Nevitt, Richard	Ridgeway, Eleanor	Sept. 10, 1787
Nevitt, Thomas	Dorsey, Henrietta	Jan. 3, 1798
Newcome, William	Beckett, Sarah	Dec. 19, 1780
Newell, James	Ryon, Elizabeth	Feb. 6, 1798
Newell, Sarah	Garner, Joseph	Feb. 25, 1794
Newhouse, William	Conley, Adera	Jan. 10, 1786
Newton, Eleanor	Donlevy, Charles	Aug. 12, 1799
Newton, John	Callahan, Eleanor	May 27, 1781
Newton, Peggy	Mitchell, John	Apr. 14, 1781
Newton, Rachel	Wheeler, Ignatius	Jan. 28, 1794
Nicholls, Edward	Hamilton, Wilemina	Aug. 15, 1780
Nicholls, John	Knighton, Thompsey	Jan. 29, 1791
Nicholls, William	Smith, Martha	Jan. 20, 1778
Nicholson, Frances	Berckley, Henry	Nov. 22, 1788

Nicholson, Jeremiah........Sparrow, Isabella...........Jan. 30, 1800
Noble, Richard.............Badon, Rebecca............Sept. 26, 1796
Noland, Edward............Soper, Rachel.............Dec. 27, 1796
Noland, Thomas...........Bayne, Mary..............June 13, 1796
Norton, Cassandra..........Masters, Ezekial...........Apr. 11, 1789
Norton, Sarah..............Stonestreet, Buttler E........Jan. 6, 1778
Notley, Ann...............Slye, William..............June 19, 1783
Notley, Ann...............Griffin, Thomas............Aug. 30, 1790
Nothey, Ann...............Clubb, William..............Jan. 2, 1797
Notley, Mary..............Ryan, Clement..............Feb. 1, 1779
Nutwell, Catherine.........Watson, Thomas...........Feb. 11, 1784
Nutwell, Elias.............Shekells, Deborah..........May 11, 1781
Nutwell, Martha...........Naylor, Joshua.............Jan. 17, 1781

Oden, Benjamin............West, Rachel Sophia........Jan. 25, 1790
Oden, Eleanor..............Williams, Calvert...........Dec. 20, 1792
Oden, Michael.............Estep, Sarah...............Mch. 12, 1796
Oden, Susan...............Hodges, Benjamin...........Feb. 6, 1787
Oden, Sarah Biggs.........Wailes, Edward Lloyd......Mch. 22, 1780
Ogden, Catherine...........Wakin, Nathaniel..........Sept. 24, 1788
Ogden, John..............Willett, Salome.............Nov. 2, 1782
Ogden, Robert.............Wynn, Ann................Oct. 17, 1778
Ohio, John................Tarman, Susannah.........June 30, 1786
Olbee, John...............Hennis, Ann...............Oct. 21, 1786
Oliver, Cornelius...........Wells, Elizabeth.............Jan. 9, 1784
Oliver, Martha.............Wells, Samuel..............Aug. 10, 1778
Oliver, Rhoda.............Wells, William...............Jan. 4, 1790
O'Mara, Philip............Calahan, Catharine..........Sept. 8, 1798
ONeil, Bernard............Waring, Elizabeth............Jan. 5, 1782
O'Neal, Nathan............Taylor, Ann.................June 5, 1789
Orme, Ann................Willett, Samuel............June 27, 1784
Orme, Moses..............Davis, Elizabeth............Oct. 22, 1781
Orme, Moses..............Brashears, Elizabeth........Feb. 27, 1795
Orme, Sabinah.............Selby, John Smith..........Apr. 14, 1780
Osbon, Alvin..............Gebby, Elizabeth............May 3, 1794
Osburn, Anna..............Gotherd, Stephen............Apr. 9, 1798
Osborn, Cristey...........Pumphrey, James..........Dec. 23, 1786
Osborn, Dennis............Hodge, Lucy...............Dec. 14, 1784
Osborn, Ester.............Hardy, Baptist..............Apr. 3, 1786
Osborn, Francis...........Pope, Charity..............July 19, 1778
Osborn, John.............Magruder, Sarah...........Jan. 12, 1788
Osborn, Linny............Gray, James...............Feb. 7, 1785

Otway, Eleanor............Brooke, Richard............June 5, 1800
Owen, George..............Darnall, Susannah..........Jan. 25, 1783
Owen, Joseph..............Lattin, Rebecca............June 12, 1781
Owens, Elizabeth..........Atwell, James.............Sept. 16, 1799
Owens, John...............Howerton, Sarah............Mch. 8, 1780
Owens, Joseph.............Waters, Jane...............Feb. 19, 1787
Owens, Thomas.............McAtee, Ann.................Apr. 27, 1793

Paca, Elizabeth...........Baker, Samuel H............June 30, 1797
Padgett, Benedict.........Gray, Catherine............Apr. 13, 1789
Padgett, Joseph...........Reeves, Mary...............Oct. 11, 1785
Padgett, Josias...........Lovelace, Johannah.........Dec. 31, 1796
Padget, Rebecca...........Hayes, Thomas..............Sept. 9, 1784
Padgett, Sarah............Brian, William.............Jan. 13, 1787
Page, Ann.................Carren, John................Jan. 4, 1790
Page, Daniel..............Piles, Leanora.............Nov. 16, 1777
Page, Mary................Brashears, Nathaniel........Feb. 17, 1792
Page, Mary................Veatch, James..............Jan. 25, 1798
Page, Sarah...............Locker, David..............July 30, 1794
Page, Verlinda............Strickland, Joseph.........Jan. 19, 1789
Parker, Elizabeth.........Townshend, Leonard........Dec. 16, 1796
Parker, Mary..............Cage, Peter B..............Jan. 20, 1783
Parker, Thomas............Shekells, Mary.............Mch. 25, 1785
Parrott, Chris[r].........Clarke, Martha.............Jan. 20, 1781
Parrett, Elizabeth........Grimes, George.............Jan. 11, 1786
Parsons, Barnaba..........Hurdle, Lucretia............June 8, 1799
Parsons, James............Mitchell, Susanna..........Apr. 22, 1782
Parsons, Joseph...........Chatham, Ann...............July 22, 1798
Patterson, William........Jones, Mary................Nov. 23, 1779
Payne, Lucy...............Morris, John...............Dec. 17, 1799
Peach, Hannah.............Dorsey, Edward.............Dec. 28, 1799
Peach, Joseph.............Peach, Mary................Dec. 24, 1799
Peach, Lucy...............Hyatt, Cris...............Sept. 10, 1777
Peach, Mary...............Peach, Joseph..............Dec. 24, 1799
Peacock, William..........Holly, Penelope............June 28, 1792
Pearce, Charles...........Pearce, Ann................July 31, 1780
Pearce, Drusilla..........Danielson, Benjamin........Oct. 26, 1779
Pearce, Edward............McSeney, Deborah...........June 3, 1784
Pearce, Jane..............Miles, James...............Nov. 30, 1780
Pearce, John..............Taylor, Elizabeth...........Apr. 9, 1789
Pearce, Joshua............Dove, Deborah..............Apr. 16, 1785
Pearce, Rebecca...........Miles, John................Jan. 21, 1783

Pearce, Thomas............Ambler, Elizabeth..........Jan. 21, 1783
Pearre, Joshua.............Woodward, Margaret........Dec. 6, 1786
Peck, John................Woodward, Druscilla........Feb. 17, 1798
Pennefield, Thomas.........Beanes, Esther.............July 20, 1790
Perkins, Elizabeth..........Upton, George..............Jan. 6, 1778
Perkins, Elizabeth..........Hall, Richard..............Jan. 8, 1799
Perkins, Rachel............Smith, James..............July 13, 1781
Perkins, Samuel............Warner, Mary..............Feb. 11, 1797
Perkins, Susannah..........Meek, Western............Nov. 11, 1800
Perkins, William...........Clarke, Susanna............June 17, 1777
Perrie, Francis.............Swann, Letty..............Jan. 19, 1798
Perrie, Margaret...........Terrason, Bartholomew......May 6, 1781
Perrie, Sarah..............Wailes, Levin Carrington....Dec. 17, 1789
Perrie, Sarah..............Cooksey, Andrew...........Feb. 18, 1800
Perry, Edward.............Clarke, Lurana.............July 12, 1777
Perry, Elisha...............Neavitt, Levinia...........Sept. 30, 1799
Perry, Ester...............Warman, Benjamin.........Feb. 20, 1779
Perry, Levi................Chew, Ann................Feb. 20, 1797
Perry, Mary...............Kiddle, Thomas............June 15, 1784
Perry, Rachel..............Harrison, Joseph...........Oct. 23, 1778
Perry, William.............Soper, Rachel.............Dec. 26, 1796
Peters, John Samuel........Anderson, Comfort.........Feb. 27, 1779
Phelps, Benjamin...........Wheat, Priscilla............Dec. 10, 1795
Phelps, Jesse..............Pumphrey, Sarah...........Sept. 2, 1795
Phenix, Thomas............Symmes, Elizabeth.........Feb. 26, 1791
Philips, Mary..............Thompson, James..........Dec. 27, 1790
Philips, Samuel............Butt, Eleanor.............Jan. 12, 1790
Philips, Sarah.............Simpson, Josiah............Dec. 1, 1789
Philips, Stephen............Pumphrey, Rachel.........Nov. 11, 1795
Pickrell, Henry.............Lowe, Rebecca..............Apr. 6, 1779
Pickrell, Rebecca...........Long, William.............Feb. 11, 1781
Pickrell, Richard...........Marlow, Amelia...........July 24, 1779*
Pierce, Elizabeth...........Cave, Thomas.............Nov. 18, 1786
Pierce, Jane...............Ellis, Leonard.............Nov. 15, 1780
Pierce, John...............Hines, Elizabeth.............Feb. 3, 1786
Pierce, John...............Trueman, Rebecca.........Mch. 29, 1798
Pierce, Letetia.............Sheriden, James P..........June 11, 1793
Pierce, Mary...............Brightwell, Richard..........May 3, 1785
Pierce, Rachel.............Taylor, Gedion.............Dec. 29, 1788
Pierce, Richard A..........Estep, Susannah............Jan. 24, 1787

*Oct. 30, 1779, also given, with the same principals.

Piercy, Catherine............McKnight, John............Oct. 29, 1799
Piles, Ann.................Littleford, John..............Jan. 2, 1799
Piles, Elizabeth............Mangum, John..............Aug. 4, 1785
Piles, Elizabeth............Wall, William...............Jan. 9, 1786
Piles, Francis..............Early, Martha...............Apr. 6, 1795
Piles, Henry...............Wallingsford, Elizabeth......Aug. 6, 1779
Piles, Hilleary.............White, Ariana...............Jan. 7, 1795
Piles, Jemima..............Allen, Thomas..............Oct. 11, 1786
Piles, Leanora.............Page, Daniel...............Nov. 16, 1777
Piles, Mary................Manders, Basil..............July 3, 1781
Pindell, Philip.............Pratt, Lucy.................Oct. 5, 1787
Pindall, Philip.............Pratt, Priscilla..............Nov. 1, 1796
Piper, Margaret............Lecompt, Rezin............Sept. 10, 1800
Plum, Lewis W.............Doxy, Susannah.............Nov. 6, 1799
Plummer, Abiezer..........Wells, Susannah............Nov. 3, 1795
Plummer, John.............Digges, Ann...............Nov. 28, 1780
Plummer, John.............Hodge, Sarah...............Aug. 1, 1782
Ponsonby, Sarah...........McCormick, Andrew T......Aug. 27, 1796
Pool, John................Mitchell, Frances...........Sept. 4, 1784
Pope, Amelia..............Pope, Joseph, Jr............Dec. 11, 1787
Pope, Ann.................Bayne, Daniel...............Feb. 4, 1795
Pope, Charity..............Osborn, Francis.............July 19, 1778
Pope, Elizabeth............Soper, Philip Evans.........July 30, 1794
Pope, Humphrey...........Thompson, Eleanor........Nov. 17, 1783
Pope, Joseph, Jr............Pope, Amelia..............Dec. 11, 1787
Pope, Margaret............Soper, Mareen Duvall.......Feb. 13, 1798
Popham, Samuel...........Crutchly, Delia............Dec. 25, 1783
Poston, Christian...........Lovejoy, Michael............Oct. 1, 1788
Poston, John Stone.........Mayhew, Susannah.........Dec. 24, 1797
Poston, Sarah..............Garner, Michael............Dec. 19, 1798
Poston, William............Gardiner, Elizabeth.........Dec. 25, 1797
Pottinger, Robert...........Buchanan, Mary............Feb. 15, 1785
Powell, William............Green, Sarah..............Mch. 17, 1785
Power, Thomas............Watson, Elizabeth...........July 1, 1795
Pownall, Thomas...........Selby, Sybal...............Dec. 27, 1787
Prather, Benjamin..........Walker, Rachel.............Jan. 15, 1782
Prather, Joseph............Welsh, Elizabeth............June 1, 1781
Prather, Massey...........Welch, Richard..............Oct. 1, 1781
Prather, Zachariah..........Callahan, Rosamond........Mch. 2, 1778
Pratt, Eleanor.............Shekells, Cephas...........Sept. 14, 1780
Pratt, Lucy...............Pindell, Philip..............Oct. 5, 1787
Pratt, Priscilla............Pindall, Philip.............Nov. 1, 1796

Pratt, Thomas	Souther, Elizabeth	Dec. 30, 1796
Pratt, Thomas	Tyler, Christy	Oct. 16, 1799
Price, Frederick	Fowler, Elizabeth	Oct. 27, 1798
Price, James	Boteler, Elizabeth	Jan. 28, 1779
Price, Mary	Barrett, John	Dec. 11, 1781
Price, Richard	Willett, Rachel	Dec. 17, 1782
Priggs, Hedwick	Hollyday, Clement	Jan. 18, 1784
Proctor, Eleanor	Brashears, Lilburn	Feb. 14, 1795
Pumphrey, Ann	Brashears, John P.	Dec. 9, 1778
Pumphrey, James	Osborn, Cristey	Dec. 23, 1786
Pumphrey, Mary	Walker, Benjamin	Dec. 31, 1778
Pumphrey, Rachel	Philips, Stephen	Nov. 11, 1795
Pumphrey, Richard	King, Elizabeth	Feb. 21, 1786
Pumphrey, Sarah	Phelps, Jesse	Sept. 2, 1795
Pumphrey, William	Rollings, Mary	Feb. 4, 1792
Purnell, Rachel	Carr, John	Feb. 8, 1779
Pye, Charles	Rogers, Sarah	Dec. 4, 1784
Queen, Henrietta	Key, Ignatius	July 14, 1785
Queen, Mary	Gardiner, Henry	June 30, 1798
Quinn, Thomas	Batt, Elizabeth	May 26, 1792
Rabbitt, John	Miles, Eleanor	May 4, 1778
Ragon, Basil	Trott, Sarah	June 24, 1789
Randall, Elizabeth	Huston, William	Dec. 22, 1798
Randal, Sarah	Tarman, Quillar	Dec. 25, 1786
Ransom, Martha	Long, Samuel	Feb. 13, 1784
Ranten, Susannah	Summers, Paul	Apr. 11, 1789
Ranter, John	Humphrey, Sarah Ann	Dec. 9, 1778
Rastridge, James	Gray, Mary	Apr. 7, 1798
Rawlings, Ann	Higdon, James	Aug. 18, 1779
Rawlings, Catherine	Budd, Allen	June 27, 1787
Rawlings, Elijah	Macgill, Elizabeth	Aug. 6, 1778
Rawlings, Elizabeth	Smith, John	Aug. 20, 1777
Rawlings, Isaac	McCoy, Priscilla	Feb. 11, 1782
Rallings, Jane	Watson, Levin	Oct. 11, 1785
Rawlings, John	Watson, Verlinda	Apr. 12, 1792
Rawlings, John	Jones, Mary	May 25, 1798
Rawlings, Luke	Kingsbury, Elizabeth	Jan. 30, 1786
Rawlings, Richard Smith	Rawlings, Susannah	May 17, 1793
Rawlings, William	Eastwood, Sarah	Oct. 9, 1799
Ray, Basil	Wall, Rebecca	Jan. 19, 1782

Ray, Benjamin	Mitchell, Amelia	Dec. 26, 1782
Ray, Jesse	Wall, Mary	Jan. 24, 1782
Ray, John	Isaac, Sarah	Mch. 24, 1787
Ray, Mary	Hinton, John	Jan. 1, 1795
Ray, Priscilla	Manley, Thomas	July 15, 1785
Ray, Walter	Brashears, Rebecca	Dec. 31, 1791
Readmond, Matthias	Eversfield, Mary	Oct. 27, 1785
Redmond, Matthias	Hardy, Terrasa Catherine	May 21, 1791
Redden, Mary	Duvall, Joseph, Jr	Aug. 26, 1800
Reed, Isaac	Hanes, Elizabeth	Oct. 11, 1800
Reeves, John	Mason, Sarah	Apr. 19, 1781
Reeves, Mary	Padgett, Joseph	Oct. 11, 1785
Reiley, Margaret	Winslow, John C.	Feb. 22, 1784
Reynolds, Patrick	Hardey, Anastasa	Dec. 29, 1792
Reynolds, Priscilla	Wheat, Zachariah	Feb. 4, 1782
Reynolds, Sarah	Boteler, Joseph	Dec. 22, 1783
Reynolds, Thomas	Jones, Ann	Feb. 24, 1784
Reynolds, William	Griffith, Ann	Dec. 5, 1777
Rhodes, John	Bennett, Mary	Jan. 30, 1782
Richards, James	Gibbons, Jane	Jan. 27, 1795
Richards, Jemima	Allingham, Stephen	Mch. 30, 1781
Richardson, Elisha	Werrald, Sarah	Dec. 3, 1782
Richardson, Martha	Sasser, Jonathan Thorne	Jan. 16, 1797
Ricketts, Jane	Brown, Zachariah	Apr. 4, 1787
Riddell, Samuel	Baldwin, Susannah	Dec. 2, 1791
Riddle, James	Stuart, Ariana	May 8, 1800
Riddle, Susanna	Lowe, John	July 10, 1784
Riddle, Verlinda	Tyler, Samuel	Jan. 19, 1782
Ridgway, Basil	Brashears, Elizabeth	Jan. 18, 1779
Ridgeway, Basil	Cassell, Amine	Dec. 18, 1798
Ridgway, Benjamin	Hardey, Mary	Dec. 14, 1779
Ridgeway, Eleanor	Nevitt, Richard	Sept. 10, 1787
Ridgeway, Eleanor	Wells, Walter	Jan. 25, 1800
Ridgway, Elizabeth	Soper, Benjamin Nony	July 23, 1792
Ridgway, James	Hurdle, Rebecca	Feb. 23, 1797
Ridgway, John	Mockbee, Rachel	Dec. 2, 1778
Ridgway, Mary	Lovelis, Luke	Dec. 18, 1800
Ridgway, Mordecai	Soper, Eleanor	Nov. 24, 1794
Ridout, Samuel	Addison, Mary	Dec. 21, 1790
Right, Elizabeth	Watson, William	July 20, 1784
Right, James	Collins, Elizabeth	July 27, 1796
Riley, George	Sansbury, Alice	Dec. 25, 1797

Riley, John................Grant, Mary...............Dec. 10, 1788
Riley, John................Clarke, Willicy..........Aug. 2 (9?), 1790
Riley, Joseph..............Brown, Milly..............July 23, 1794
Riley, Margaret............Talbert, Tobias.............Aug. 9, 1800
Riley, Mary................Anderson, Jesse............July 19, 1800
Riston, Allen..............Easton, Elizabeth............Apr. 5, 1779
Riston, Basil..............Bonnafill, Ann..............Dec. 4, 1787
Riston, Elisha.............Albey, Aminta..............Jan. 11, 1779
Riston, Elisha.............Mayoh, Ann.................Feb. 6, 1790
Riston, Keziah.............Albey, William.............Jan. 21, 1778
Riston, Rebecca............Mitchell, Middleton.........Apr. 21, 1792
Riston, Zadock.............Bartly, Elizabeth............Jan. 7, 1786
Robb, Adam.................Lansdale, Ann..............Sept. 8, 1789
Roberts, Ann...............Jones, George...............Jan. 4, 1785
Roberts, Edward............Brent, Ann................Dec. 29, 1797
Roberts, Elizabeth.........Walker, Elisha.............Dec. 31, 1792
Roberts, Hannah............Elson, Richard..............Nov. 3, 1782
Roberts, Henry.............Kelly, Mary...............Aug. 10, 1778
Roberts, John..............Barrett, Sarah............Aug. 10, 1781
Roberts, Mary..............Higdon, Joshua.............Oct. 11, 1783
Roberts, Sarah.............Busey, Samuel..............July 13, 1777
Roberts, Sarah.............Greentree, Benjamin........May 16, 1782
Robertson, Elizabeth.......Smith, Thomas..............Nov. 16, 1793
Robertson, George..........Johnson, Verlinda.........Sept. 29, 1781
Robey, George Dement.....Athey, Elizabeth............Dec. 16, 1791
Robey, Meshal..............Maddocks, Nathan..........Dec. 11, 1781
Robey, Michael.............Jarman, Elizabeth..........Dec. 21, 1790
Robinson, Benjamin........Austin, Elizabeth............Feb. 7, 1793
Robinson, Benjamin........Jerman, Sarah..............May 13, 1794
Robinson, Charles..........Jones, Leithy..............Jan. 21, 1790
Robinson, Elijah...........Talburt, Ann...............Nov. 24, 1788
Robinson, Hezekiah........Robinson, Mary............Oct. 10, 1782
Robinson, Jane.............Briges, Aquilla...............Apr. 4, 1795
Robinson, Mary.............Mockbee, John.............Aug. 20, 1777
Robinson, Mary.............Robinson, Hezekiah.........Oct. 10, 1782
Robinson, Mary.............Wells, Martin..............Feb. 26, 1783
Robinson, Milly............Wise, Thomas................Dec. 1, 1787
Robinson, Priscilla..........Jeffreys, William...........Dec. 14, 1799
Robinson, Sarah............Boteler, Charles............Jan. 22, 1785
Robinson, Sarah Eliza Ford..Martin, Zephaniah..........Dec. 30, 1795
Rogers, Sarah..............Pye, Charles.................Dec. 4, 1784
Rollings, Catherine Estep....Rollings, John..............Oct. 22, 1783

Rollings, John Adam........Cave, Sary..................Apr. 10, 1787
Rollings, Mary.............Pumphrey, William..........Feb. 4, 1792
Rose, Thomas...............Smith, Mary...............Oct. 22, 1777
Ross, Ariana...............Stewart, John.............Dec. 13, 1791
Ross, Elizabeth............Smith, Jeremiah...........Mch. 8, 1797
Ross, Margaret.............Sheriff, Benedict.........Jan. 28, 1797
Rozer, Eliza...............Dulaney, Benjamin Tasker...Feb. 13, 1796
Rozer, Francis H...........Rozer, Maria..............Dec. 15, 1792
Rozer, Henry J.............Edelen, Sarah.............Sept. 13, 1779
Rozer, Maria...............Rozer, Francis H..........Dec. 15, 1792
Rugless, William...........Lowe, Elizabeth...........Oct. 31, 1789
Russell, Ann...............Martin, Richard............Jan. 1, 1780
Russell, Ann...............Sollars, Sabret............Mch. 3, 1785
Russell, Elizabeth.........Cooke, Joseph, Jr..........Dec. 11, 1792
Russell, Elizabeth.........Milliken, Walter...........Oct. 3, 1799
Russell, Joseph............Chaney, Deborah...........May 16, 1797
Russell, Philip............Dove, Elizabeth...........Feb. 17, 1781
Russell, William...........Fitzgerald, Rachel..........Jan. 6, 1795
Ryan, Clement..............Notley, Mary...............Feb. 1, 1779
Ryan, Elijah...............Wilburn, Sarah..............Jan. 2, 1798
Ryley, Margaret............Thompson, Luke............Feb. 15, 1793
Ryon, Ann..................Hooper, Samuel............Dec. 31, 1785
Ryon, Ann..................Sansbury, William Richard..Dec. 29, 1792
Ryon, Ann..................Crosby, Walter............Nov. 16, 1799
Ryon, Elisha...............Sansburry, Sarah..........Feb. 16, 1779
Ryon, Elizabeth............Bird, Francis..............Oct. 14, 1785
Ryon, Elizabeth............Hoye, Cephas..............Sept. 9, 1786
Ryon, Elizabeth............Connock, William..........Jan. 31, 1798
Ryon, Elizabeth............Newell, James..............Feb. 6, 1798
Ryon, Fielder..............Smith, Rachel..............June 3, 1797
Ryon, Jeremiah.............Smith, Fanny..............Dec. 24, 1791
Ryon, John.................Gates, Eleanor.............Mch. 7, 1786
Ryon, Mary.................Mayhew, James.............May 14, 1788
Ryon, Philip...............Alder, Joanna.............Mch. 23, 1778
Ryon, Priscilla............Tarman, Henry..............May 2, 1779
Ryon, Susannah.............Knighton, Samuel..........Feb. 11, 1791
Ryon, Susanna..............Hopkins, Philip...........Aug. 22, 1798

Sadler, Rebena.............Turner, Abraham...........Nov. 27, 1781
Safell, Lucy...............Thomas, Anthony...........Jan. 30, 1782
Sanders, Elizabeth.........Boteler, Edward...........Jan. 31, 1781
Sanders, Lydia.............Fowler, William...........Nov. 25, 1788

Sandfield, George............Lawry, Elizabeth............Dec. 9, 1800
Sandford, Nancy............Jockherer, Alexander Lewy..June 13, 1796
Sanford, Presley............Taylor, Mary.............Dec. 19, 1792
Sansberrie, Rebecca.........White, Osborn.............Dec. 24, 1792
Sansbury, Alexius..........Hamilton, Eliza............Feb. 16, 1789
Sansbury, Alice............Riley, George..............Dec. 25, 1797
Sansbury, Ann.............Johnson, Benjamin.........Feb. 11, 1792
Sansbury, Eleanor..........Boone, Ignatius.............Jan. 14, 1796
Sansbury, Joseph...........Spalding, Elizabeth.........Nov. 30, 1798
Sansbury, Mary............Boone, Francis.............Oct. 16, 1785
Sansbury, Mary............Hopkins, Francis...........Jan. 29, 1786
Sansberry, Minty...........Clements, Edward H........Jan. 15, 1796
Sansbury, Sarah............Ryan, Elisha...............Feb. 16, 1779
Sansbury, Sarah............White, Fielder..............Feb. 16, 1782
Sansbury, Sarah............Blacklock, Thomas..........Jan. 30, 1783
Sansbury, Sarah............Bromley, William...........Jan. 29, 1794
Sansbury, Thomas..........Mockbee, Rebecca..........Feb. 25, 1797
Sansbury, William Richard..Ryon, Ann................Dec. 29, 1792
Sappington, John...........Fowler, Jemima............Jan. 29, 1781
Sasser, Elizabeth...........Sasser, Jonathan T.........Sept. 29, 1783
Sasser, Jonathan Thorne....Richardson, Martha........Jan. 16, 1797
Sasser, Mary..............Beavin, Charles............Dec. 13, 1791
Sasser, Sarah..............Beaven, Charles............Jan. 13, 1778
Sasser, William............Beaven, Jane...............May 3, 1779
Sasser, William............Beaven, Eliza..............Dec. 5, 1781
Saucer, Ann...............Thursby, Edward...........Jan. 25, 1786
Savory, Peter..............Smith, Jane..............Nov. 18, 1782
Scarce, Milly..............Dorsey, George............Dec. 27, 1798
Scarce, Rebecca............Summers, John............Feb. 26, 1794
Scarce, Sarah.............Summers, Nathaniel.........June 2, 1793
Scissell, Eleanor...........Suit, John Smith...........Nov. 28, 1784
Scissell, Elizabeth.........Woodward, Benedict........Dec. 15, 1778
Scissell, Mary.............Tracy, William............Sept. 18, 1777
Scofield, Ann..............Scott, William Ashford......Dec. 13, 1796
Scott, Agnes..............Hoye, Thomas.............Apr. 22, 1786
Scott, Ann................Boyd, Archibald...........Nov. 9, 1777
Scott, Ann................Wilson, Basil..............Aug. 9, 1779
Scott, Catherine...........Drane, Anthony...........Mch. 29, 1792
Scott, Edward.............Clagett, Mary..............Jan. 9, 1790
Scott, Eliza...............Sherwood, Thomas..........Feb. 1, 1779
Scott, Elizabeth...........Cross, Edward.............June 19, 1780
Scott, James..............Humphreys, Mary..........Feb. 4, 1797

Scott, Judson.............Clagett, Eleanor............Dec. 3, 1785
Scott, Margaret............Mattingly, Joseph..........Jan. 24, 1785
Scott, Mary..............Hoofman, John............Apr. 24, 1781
Scott, Mary..............Turner, Rezin.............Dec. 12, 1799
Scott, Samuel.............Wilson, Ann Dickson.......Nov. 19, 1784
Scott, Samuel.............Free, Elizabeth............Apr. 19, 1796
Scott, Thomas.............Jenkins, Massy M..........Nov. 23, 1795
Scott, William.............Hardey, Rebecca...........Feb. 22, 1792
Scott, William Ashford......Scofield, Ann..............Dec. 13, 1796
Sebbald, George...........Hanson, Rachel.............Jan. 5, 1786
Selby, Ann...............Dorsett, Thomas..........Dec. 16, 1784
Selby, Ann...............Harvey, James............Mch. 25, 1796
Selby, Charles.............Lanham, Layor............Dec. 18, 1787
Selby, Deborah............Naylor, Benjamin..........Aug. 31, 1785
Selby, Eleanor............Lanham, Stephen............Oct. 4, 1779
Selby, John Smith.........Orme, Sabinah.............Apr. 14, 1780
Selby, Magruder..........Hodgkinson, Agness.........Feb. 11, 1788
Selby, Margaret...........Fowler, Samuel.............Feb. 2, 1798
Selby, Mary..............Naylor, Nicholas...........Feb. 15, 1783
Selby, Philip.............Boteler, Catherine.........Aug. 24, 1778
Selby, Sybal.............Pownall, Thomas...........Dec. 27, 1787
Semmes, Mary............Hoxton, Stanislaus.........Jan. 17, 1799
Sewell, Robert............Brentt, Mary..............Feb. 16, 1789
Shagnasha, Mary..........Manley, John..............July 22, 1786
Shannon, Luke............Wade, Dely...............Mch. 24, 1794
Shaw, William............Dunkin, Grace.............Dec. 13, 1797
Shekell, Deborah..........Essex, Francis.............Aug. 21, 1792
Shekell, Richard...........Griffin, Margaret...........July 29, 1789
Shekalls, Agnes...........Griffin, Edward...........May 24, 1781
Shekells, Cephas..........Pratt, Eleanor............Sept. 14, 1780
Shekells, Cephas..........Boyd, Eleanor............Sept. 27, 1796
Shekells, Deborah.........Nutwell, Elias............May 11, 1781
Shekells, John............Cheney, Ann..............Aug. 14, 1799
Shekells, Mary............Parker, Thomas...........Mch. 25, 1785
Shelton, Thomas..........Webb, Elizabeth............Aug. 6, 1777
Sheppard, John...........Chaney, Rebecca...........Feb. 27, 1797
Sheriff, Benedict..........Ross, Margaret.............Jan. 28, 1797
Sheriff, Elizabeth..........Baldwin, William............Dec. 7, 1799
Sheriff, Joshua............Sherwood, Rhoda..........June 29, 1781
Sheriff, Ruth.............Brown, Walter............Dec. 21, 1799
Sheriden, James P.........Pierce, Letatia............June 11, 1793
Sherkliff, Dorothy.........Coombes, Joseph............May 4, 1783

Sherly, Theodore	Watkins, Nancy	Mch. 28, 1797
Sherwood, Job	Shreves, Casandra	Aug. 7, 1781
Sherwood, Rhoda	Sheriff, Joshua	June 29, 1781
Sherwood, Susanna	Callahan, John	Feb. 21, 1778
Sherwood, Thomas	Scott, Eliza	Feb. 1, 1779
Shield, Martha	Cawood, Benjamin	May 8, 1798
Shoemaker, Ann	Cockler, John	May 13, 1799
Shooff, John Thomas	Sydebotham, Mary	Dec. 18, 1800
Short, James	Grimes, Mary	Feb. 9, 1779
Short, James	Maccastle, Mary	Dec. 12, 1791
Short, Rhoda	Club, Levin	Aug. 25, 1786
Shreves, Casandra	Sherwood, Job	Aug. 7, 1781
Shreeves, Eliza	Carrick, William	Feb. 13, 1795
Shreves, Mary	Beckett, Humphrey	Feb. 22, 1786
Silk, Samuel	Collings, Elizabeth	July 26, 1779
Sim, Patrick	Henderson, Ariana	Aug. 28, 1787
Sim, Patrick	Carroll, Mary	July 11, 1777
Simm, Robert	King, Elizabeth	Jan. 5, 1786
Simms, Elizabeth	Tolson, Francis	Feb. 27, 1794
Simms, Joseph Milburn	Mudd, Elizabeth	Feb. 10, 1790
Simms, Margaret	Cunningham, John	Aug. 4, 1792
Simms, Mary Anne	Vermillion, William	Apr. 19, 1778
Simms, William	Hughes, Jane	Nov. 24, 1787
Simmons, Isaac	Simmons, Susanna	Nov. 19, 1777
Simmons, Jacob	Cross, Eleanor	Apr. 19, 1780
Simmons, Jesse	Wells, Rachel	Sept. 13, 1781
Simmons, Martha	Mackeney, Zachariah	Feb. 23, 1789
Simmons, Mary	Lucas, John	Dec. 14, 1780
Simmons, Richard	Willett, Mary	Mch. 7, 1779
Simmons, Robert	Baldwin, Catherine	May 9, 1781
Simmons, Susanna	Simmons, Isaac	Nov. 19, 1777
Simmons, Susannah	Welch, Richard	June 5, 1793
Simmons, Thomas	Lyles, Elizabeth	May 26, 1795
Simpson, Ann	Wornald, Henry	Apr. 15, 1780
Simpson, Ann	Edelen, Clement	Nov. 6, 1780
Simpson, Ann	Turton, Fielder	May 4, 1799
Simpson, Eleanor	Lawson, William	Nov. 16, 1778
Simpson, Eliza Ann	Harvey, Thomas	Apr. 18, 1794
Simpson, Isabella	Weaver, William	Apr. 2, 1782
Simpson, John	Whiting, Rebecca	Sept. 9, 1784
Simpson, John	Morris, Mary Dent	Apr. 10, 1788
Simpson, Joseph	Galwith, Rachel	Jan. 31, 1788

Simpson, Josiah............Philips, Sarah...............Dec. 1, 1789
Simpson, Mary Ann........Amberson, William.........Dec. 21, 1789
Simpson, Priscilla...........Fowler, William............Jan. 29, 1799
Simpson, Rebecca..........Emberson, John............Oct. 25, 1790
Simpson, Susannah.........Emerson, Aquila...........Nov. 13, 1792
Simpson, Thomas..........Kidwell, Sophia Mary.......May 21, 1782
Simpson, Thomas...........King, Ruth.................Apr. 7, 1787
Simpson, Thomas...........Lind, Amelia.............Sept. 17, 1787
Sinclair, Elizabeth..........Jones, George..............Aug. 25, 1787
Skinner, Adderton..........Magruder, Kitty...........Aug. 29, 1798
Skinner, Mary.............Dorsett, Samuel.............Jan. 4, 1794
Skinner, Walter............Hodgkin, Mary............June 10, 1791
Slater, David..............Contee, Sarah.............May 29, 1790
Slye, William..............Notley, Ann...............June 19, 1783
Slye, Willimina ....Earley, Thomas..............Jan. 1, 1784
Smallwood, Ann............Wynn, John...............Dec. 12, 1778
Smallwood, Ann............Coe, Elijah.................Oct. 23, 1779
Smallwood, Bayne..........Coe, Marsilva..............Dec. 19, 1780
Smallwood, John...........Wilson, Clowe..............Dec. 15, 1787
Smallwood, Milicent........Wynns, William............May 20, 1778
Smallwood, Rebecca........Lovejoy, George N..........June 10, 1794
Smallwood, Rebecca M......Wynne, Hezekiah...........Jan. 12, 1779
Smallwood, Susannah.......Berry, Thomas.............Aug. 25, 1781
Smith, Ann................Sparrow, Joseph............Dec. 9, 1778
Smith, Ann................Drane, Anthony............Dec. 23, 1778
Smith, Ann................Wallace, William...........Feb. 14, 1780
Smith, Ann................Kidwell, George.............Dec. 6, 1800
Smith, Benedict............Gardiner, Mary.............Feb. 7, 1795
Smith, Elizabeth...........Swain, Thomas.............Feb. 17, 1779
Smith, Elizabeth...........Albey, Walter.............Feb. 26, 1783
Smith, Elizabeth...........Warman, Edmund.........Sept. 22, 1788
Smith, Elizabeth...........Wilson, Joseph............Mch. 17, 1795
Smith, Fanny..............Ryon, Jeremiah...........Dec. 24, 1791
Smith, Henrietta...........Young, David.............Dec. 17, 1784
Smith, James..............Perkins, Rachel............July 13, 1781
Smith, Jane...............Savory, Peter.............Nov. 18, 1782
Smith, Jane...............Summers, George...........May 19, 1787
Smith, Jeremiah...........Ross, Elizabeth.............Mch. 8, 1797
Smith, John...............Rawlings, Elizabeth........Aug. 20, 1777
Smith, John...............Elliott, Anne................Feb. 5, 1796
Smith, John Willing........Lowe, Rachel..............Feb. 27, 1788
Smith, Linny..............Forster, John..............Feb. 11, 1792

Smith, Martha............Nicholls, William...........Jan. 20, 1778
Smith, Mary..............Rose, Thomas..............Oct. 22, 1777
Smith, Lucy..............Bryan, William Thomas....Mch. 23, 1778
Smith, Mary..............Boone, Electius..............Jan. 8, 1779
Smith, Mary Ann..........Barry, William.............June 19, 1778
Smith, Nicholas..........Dyer, Martha Ann..........Oct. 23, 1790
Smith, Rachel.............Ryon, Fielder...............June 3, 1797
Smith, Richard............Church, Elizabeth...........Jan. 12, 1785
Smith, Robert.............Lanham, Elizabeth..........Sept. 5, 1785
Smith, Rosanah............Jones, James..............Mch. 19, 1785
Smith, Samuel Lane........Belt, Elizabeth Bowie......Nov. 26, 1799
Smith, Sarah..............Wear, James...............July 19, 1777
Smith, Sarah..............Hilleary, George............Nov. 29, 1781
Smith, Susanna............White, Charles.............July 30, 1777
Smith, Susanna............Crabb, Charles.............Feb. 13, 1792
Smith, Thomas.............Evans, Ruth...............Aug. 18, 1777
Smith, Thomas.............Leach, Verlinda............Mch. 19, 1789
Smith, Thomas.............Robertson, Elizabeth.......Nov. 16, 1793
Smith, Ursula..............White, John...............Sept. 20, 1780
Smith, Verlinda............Brunt, Thomas..............Aug. 2, 1796
Smute, Thomas Barton......Adams, Levisa..............Jan. 16, 1788
Snowden, Mary............Thomas, John Chew........Sept. 16, 1788
Sollars, Sabret.............Russell, Ann................Mch. 3, 1785
Sollars, Sabret.............Gordon, Mary..............May 10, 1787
Somerville, James..........Magruder, Elizabeth
Hawkins..............Nov. 7, 1792
Soper, Alexander...........Belt, Esther................Nov. 9, 1796
Soper, Benjamin Nony......Ridgway, Elizabeth.........July 23, 1792
Soper, Eleanor.............Childs, Joseph.............June 20, 1793
Soper, Eleanor.............Ridgway, Mordecai.........Nov. 24, 1794
Soper, Elizabeth...........Havener, Michael............Feb. 5, 1793
Soper, Mareen Duvall......Pope, Margaret.............Feb. 13, 1798
Soper, Mary...............Moore, Zadock..............June 5, 1779
Soper, Mary...............Hurley, Basil................Feb. 3, 1789
Soper, Mary Ann...........Hardey, Jonathan...........Jan. 31, 1799
Soper, Massy..............Mayhew, John..............Dec. 9, 1795
Soper, Nathan.............Dorcey, Ann...............Nov. 21, 1791
Soper, Philip Evans.........Pope, Elizabeth.............July 30, 1794
Soper, Rachel..............Perry, William.............Dec. 26, 1796
Soper, Rachel..............Noland, Edward............Dec. 27, 1796
Soaper, Rebecca............Hurley, William............Dec. 21, 1790
Soper, Robert..............Hardey, Elizabeth..........Nov. 19, 1784

Soper, Sarah..............Hurley, William............Aug. 12, 1795
Soper, Sarah..............Wheat, Jesse..............Dec. 2, 1795
Soper, Susannah............Iglehart, William...........Mch. 17, 1781
Soper, Susanna Jackson.....Gott, Ezekiel..............Apr. 23, 1792
Sothoron, Deborah..........Letchworth, John...........Dec. 10, 1798
Sout, Edward..............Wilson, Mary..............July 12, 1779
Souther, Benjamin..........Taylor, Mary Ann...........Dec. 2, 1778
Souther, Elizabeth..........Pratt, Thomas.............Dec. 30, 1796
Southerland, John..........Fraser, Nellie..............Nov. 20, 1777
Sotherlin, James...........Mulliken, Mary.............Aug. 8, 1799
Southwell, Lana (Pana?)....Steuart, William............Feb. 21, 1778
Southwell, Lydia...........Moreland, Philip...........July 18, 1781
Spalding, Edward...........Boarman, Juliet.............Oct. 8, 1789
Spalding, Elizabeth.........Sansbury, Joseph...........Nov. 30, 1798
Spalding, Elizabeth.........King, Elisha...............Feb. 18, 1800
Spalding, James............Boone, Eleanor.............Dec. 16, 1797
Sparrow, Ann..............Crouse, George............Sept. 24, 1796
Sparrow, Henry............James, Ann................Jan. 21, 1791
Sparrow, Isabelle...........Nicholson, Jeremiah.........Jan. 30, 1800
Sparrow, Joseph............Smith, Ann.................Dec. 9, 1778
Speake, Catherine..........Brown, Edward.............Mch. 8, 1780
Speak, Joanna.............Marr, Joshua...............Jan. 2, 1779
Speake, Lucy..............Dyer, Robert...............Jan. 21, 1800
Spiden, Robert.............Williams, Ann...............Apr. 3, 1797
Spink, Ann................Burch, Edward.............Oct. 15, 1779
Spink, Ignatius.............Clarkson, Elizabeth.........Dec. 15, 1794
Sprigg, Elizabeth...........Watkins, Thomas, Jr.........Jan. 7, 1778
Sprigg, Elizabeth...........Magruder, Enoch...........Feb. 27, 1781
Sprigg, Elizabeth...........Bowie, William S...........Dec. 18, 1781
Sprigg, Osborn.............Gantt, Sarah...............Apr. 3, 1779
Stallings, Sarah............Strickland, John.............Feb. 8, 1790
Stallings, Thomas, Jr........Mitchell, Sarah............Nov. 25, 1791
Stallons, Thomas Harvey....Eales, Susannah............Dec. 21, 1798
Stamp, Mary..............Harrison, Thomas...........May 30, 1783
Stamp, Willey.............Fowler, Abraham...........Dec. 23, 1790
Standage, Eleazer..........Wigfield, Mary.............Dec. 23, 1783
Standage, Elizabeth........Talbott, Zadock............Dec. 30, 1778
Standage, Margaret.........Talburt, Henry............Sept. 26, 1780
Stanley (Shaney?), Bernard..Magruder, Sarah............Feb. 3, 1785
Steel, Alexander...........Hopkins, Mary.............Mch. 6, 1800
Steel, Mary...............Bryan, Richard............Sept. 29, 1796
Steel, Mary...............Baden, Alexander...........June 3, 1797

Stephens, James	Steward, Winifred	Feb. 3, 1787
Stephens, John	Turner, Susannah	Feb. 28, 1798
Stephens, William	Taylor, Ann	Dec. 31, 1785
Stevens, Elizabeth	Gray, Hugh	Aug. 8, 1795
Stevens, William	Tilley, Rebecca	Jan. 15, 1785
Stewart, Ann Eustatia	Watson, Richard	Feb. 19, 1781
Stewart, Ann M.	Winfield, Jonas	Apr. 13, 1781
Stewart, Charles	Calvert, Elizabeth	June 14, 1780
Stewart, Henrietta	Townley, Thomas	Jan. 15, 1782
Stewart, James	Burgess, Massey	Dec. 30, 1790
Stewart, John	Ross, Ariana	Dec. 13, 1791
Steward, Philip	Marshall, Mary	Feb. 26, 1787
Stewart, Philip	Baynes, Mary Fell	Dec. 15, 1792
Steuart, William	Southwell, Pana	Feb. 21, 1778
Stewart, William	Bryan, Jane	June 6, 1783
Steward, Winifred	Stephens, James	Feb. 3, 1787
Stoddert, Benjamin C.	Lowndes, Rebecca	June 7, 1781
Stoddert, Letitia Dent	Dijean, Peter	Jan. 18, 1785
Stoddert, Thomas James	Dent, Cloe Hanson	Sept. 21, 1790
Stone, Ann	Grimes, Charles	Feb. 17, 1787
Stone, Eleanor	Hardey, George	Feb. 7, 1782
Stone, Leonora	Talburt, Nathan	Apr. 19, 1783
Stone, Mary	Taylor, Edward	Jan. 13, 1784
Stone, Mary	Hardey, Noah	Jan. 13, 1794
Stone, Nemiah	Wilson, Sarah	Mch. 3, 1778
Stone, Rachel	Watson, Walter	Oct. 8, 1779
Stonestreet, Buttler E.	Norton, Sarah	Jan. 6, 1778
Stonestreet, Edward	Wright, Margery	May 10, 1780
Stonestreet, Eleanor	Irwin, John	June 2, 1784
Straw, Terrissa	Hall, John Henry	Feb. 22, 1791
Strickland, John	Stallings, Sarah	Feb. 8, 1790
Strickland, Joseph	Page, Verlinda	Jan. 19, 1789
Strickland, Linny	Swain, Isaac	Dec. 28, 1795
Strickland, William	Kidwell, Sarah	Dec. 20, 1784
Stuart, Ariana	Riddle, James	May 8, 1800
Stuart, John	Dove, Mary	Feb. 3, 1790
Suit, John Smith	Scissell, Eleanor	Nov. 28, 1784
Suit, Mary	Edelen, Samuel	Dec. 14, 1787
Suit, Rebecca	Coghlan, Dennis	July 18, 1777
Sullivan, Mary	Lovejoy, Alexander	May 10, 1779
Sullavan, Sarah	Bedder, Thomas	Jan. 8, 1785
Summers, Ann	Fowler, Richard	Jan. 14, 1779

Summers, Ann	Jenkins, Zadock	Jan. 12, 1798
Summers, Anna	Hurley, Salem	Dec. 8, 1784
Summers, Eleven	Wilcoxon, Elizabeth	Dec. 30, 1786
Summers, George	Smith, Jane	May 19, 1787
Summers, Henrietta	Darnall, Gerrard	Nov. 7, 1785
Summers, John	Manley, Elizabeth	Dec. 11, 1785
Summers, John	Scarce, Rebecca	Feb. 26, 1794
Summers, Jonathan	Gwinn, Ann	Dec. 23, 1782
Summers, Nathaniel	Scarce, Sarah	June 2, 1793
Summers, Paul	Ranten, Susannah	Apr. 11, 1789
Summers, Zadock	Jenkins, Mary	Nov. 13, 1794
Summerville, Susannah	Carrington, Leonard	Oct. 22, 1789
Sutherland, Barbara	Anderson, George	Apr. 18, 1788
Sutherland, John	Murray, Margaret	Nov. 30, 1780
Sutton, John	Finly, Elizabeth	Dec. 21, 1797
Sutton, Mary B.	Lowe, Charles F.	Oct. 26, 1795
Swain, Benjamin	Ellecon, Hannah	Feb. 1, 1794
Swain, Elizabeth	Bird, John	Sept. 5, 1788
Swain, Gardiner	Berry, Elizabeth	Jan. 3, 1798
Swain, Isaac	Cassell, Mary	Dec. 24, 1787
Swain, Isaac	Strickland, Linny	Dec. 28, 1795
Swain, John	Harvey, Lucy	Apr. 11, 1797
Swain, Thomas	Smith, Elizabeth	Feb. 17, 1779
Swann, Ann	Compton, Henry T.	Nov. 17, 1797
Swann, Eleanor	Brightwell, John	Sept. 6, 1782
Swann, Henery	Davis, Minty	Jan. 8, 1789
Swan, Jennett	Hawkins, Henry	Dec. 26, 1790
Swann, Letty	Perrie, Francis	Jan. 19, 1798
Swan, Thomas	Cater, Elizabeth	Feb. 11, 1793
Sweeny, Drury	Mitchell, John	May 10, 1788
Sweeney, Lloyd	Walker, Ann	Jan. 10, 1790
Sydebotham, Mary	Shoof, John Thomas	Dec. 18, 1800
Sydebotham, William	Leitch, Margaret	Sept. 23, 1778
Symmes, Elizabeth	Phenix, Thomas	Feb. 26, 1791
Tait, Elizabeth	Boyd, Joseph	Jan. 14, 1800
Talbott, Basil	Lowe, Keziah	June 17, 1788
Talbot, Basil	Wilson, Susannah	July 5, 1800
Talbott, Jesse	Lanham, Mildred	Nov. 12, 1794
Talbott, Lewin	Burch, Elizabeth	Nov. 17, 1794
Talbott, Levin	Jones, Ann	Feb. 11, 1797
Talbott, Salomy	McKenzy, John	Mch. 19, 1794

Talbott, Susannah..........Grimes, Jeremiah............Jan. 8, 1793
Talbott, Zadock............Standage, Elizabeth........Dec. 30, 1778
Talburt, Ann..............Robinson, Elijah...........Nov. 24, 1788
Talburt, Elizabeth..........Mayhew, William..........Dec. 23, 1795
Talburt, Henry.............Standage, Margaret........Sept. 26, 1780
Talbott, John..............Davis, Ann..................Oct. 1, 1777
Talburt, Josias.............Bayne, Milly...............June 4, 1796
Talburt, Nathan...........Stone, Leonora.............Apr. 19, 1783
Talbutt, Paul..............Bryan, Sarah Ann...........Mch. 4, 1791
Talburt, Susannah..........Burch, Thomas.............July 26, 1780
Talburt, Susannah..........Kirby, Richard.............Sept. 9, 1783
Talbert, Susannah..........Arnold, Richard............Dec. 16, 1800
Talbert, Tobias............Riley, Margaret.............Aug. 9, 1800
Tarman, Ann..............Jones, George.............June 25, 1799
Tarman, Benjamin.........Fields, Lettie...............Mch. 7, 1791
Tarman, Eleanor...........Mangum, Henry............Jan. 25, 1797
Tarman, Henrietta.........Taylor, William..............Jan. 9, 1794
Tarman, Henry............Ryon, Priscilla..............May 2, 1779
Tarman, Mary............Venables, Theodore.........May 24, 1799
Tarman, Quillar............Randal, Sarah.............Dec. 25, 1786
Tarman, Richard...........Turton, Mary A............Feb. 22, 1784
Tarman, Richard...........Hopkins, Ann..............May 30, 1785
Tarman, Richard...........Brant, Margaret............Feb. 12, 1795
Tarman, Sarah.............White, Jonathan...........Mch. 27, 1785
Tarman, Susannah..........Ohio, John...............June 30, 1786
Tarman, William...........Clare, Melicent S...........Mch. 12, 1781
Tate, Margaret.............Benson, Thomas............Feb. 11, 1790
Taylor, Alis...............Mahoney, Edward..........Dec. 18, 1786
Taylor, Allen.............Humphreys, Ann...........June 10, 1799
Taylor, Ann..............Stephens, William..........Dec. 31, 1785
Taylor, Ann..............O'Neal, Nathan.............June 5, 1789
Taylor, Charlotte..........Cox, William.............May 25, 1796
Taylor, Edward...........Stone, Mary...............Jan. 13, 1784
Taylor, Elizabeth...........Pearce, John...............Apr. 9, 1789
Taylor, Gedion............Pierce, Rachel.............Dec. 29, 1788
Taylor, John..............Jones, Rebecca............Aug. 23, 1780
Taylor, John..............Hinton, Sarah.............Feb. 16, 1784
Taylor, John..............Crook, Mary..............Feb. 16, 1798
Taylor, Linny.............Henry, John..............Apr. 18, 1797
Taylor, Martha............Anderson, Samuel.........Feb. 19, 1787
Taylor, Mary.............Sanford, Presley...........Dec. 19, 1792
Taylor, Mary.............Maitland, James..........June 17, 1800

Taylor, Mary Ann..........Souther, Benjamin...........Dec. 2, 1778
Taylor, Samuel.............Hurley, Rhoda.............Apr. 10, 1793
Taylor, Sarah..............Brown, Thomas.............June 29, 1777
Taylor, Sarah..............Hurley, William..............Jan. 4, 1790
Taylor, Sarah..............Wilson, Aquila.............Nov. 21, 1791
Tayler, Sarah..............Eastep, Benjamin..........Sept. 27, 1793
Taylor, Sarah..............Club, John................Dec. 23, 1799
Taylor, Sarah..............Frazier, Archibald..........Apr. 15, 1800
Taylor, Thomas............Grimes, Mary.............Dec. 21, 1785
Taylor, William............Tarman, Henrietta...........Jan. 9, 1794
Taylor, William............Townshend, Elizabeth.......Dec. 30, 1795
Teasdale, John.............Malone, Catherine...........May 5, 1778
Tenly, Letty Ann...........Moreland, Elias.............Feb. 6, 1798
Terrason, Bartholomew.....Perrie, Margaret............May 6, 1781
Thomas, Anthony..........Safell, Lucy................Jan. 30, 1782
Thomas, Caleb.............Cave, Mary................Dec. 29, 1784
Thomas, Caleb.............King, Susannah.............Apr. 14, 1798
Thomas, Fanoni............Brightwell, Richard C.......Dec. 26, 1794
Thomas, James.............Willett, Ann...............Aug. 10, 1781
Thomas, John Chew........Snowden, Mary............Sept. 16, 1788
Thomas, Nathan...........Brashears, Mary............Jan. 17, 1799
Thomas, Samuel...........Ellixson, Mary.............Apr. 18, 1797
Thomas, William...........Taylor, Ann...............Aug. 12, 1799
Thompson, Andrew.........Tull, Elizabeth.............July 20, 1798
Thompson, Ann............Lanham, Acquilla...........Jan. 28, 1788
Thompson, Clark..........Lewis, Mary...............May 20, 1783
Thompson, Eleanor.........Pope, Humphrey...........Nov. 17, 1783
Thompson, Eleanor.........Murray, John..............Dec. 10, 1789
Thompson, Electius........Alexander, Eliza............Aug. 14, 1780
Thompson, George.........Tippett, Mary Atway........May 4, 1798
Thompson, James..........Athey, Rhodoe.............Nov. 25, 1788
Thompson, James..........Philips, Mary..............Dec. 27, 1790
Thompson, James Fraser....Moore, Sarah...............June 5, 1778
Thompson, Jane...........Billings, Daniel............Sept. 26, 1791
Thompson, Luke...........Ryley, Margaret............Feb. 15, 1793
Thompson, Margaret.......Burgess, Edward...........June 25, 1781
Thompson, Mary...........Williams, Lelburn............Oct. 8, 1782
Thompson, Minta..........Yearbey, Benjamin.........Feb. 14, 1785
Thompson, Moses..........Lowden, Rachel............Dec. 22, 1783
Thompson, Philip..........Whitney, Ann..............May 30, 1796
Thompson, Rachel.........Chesley, Joseph............Sept. 19, 1789
Thompson, Richard........Burgess, Rachel............Oct. 20, 1779

Thompson, Samuel.........Walker, Ann...............Jan. 10, 1790
Thompson, Thomas.........Cater, Sarah................Feb. 7, 1785
Thompson, Zachariah.......Davis, Eleanor..............Dec. 9, 1783
Thorn, Henry..............Wilson, Elizabeth..........May 29, 1779
Thorn, Henry Burch........Thorn, Mary...............Feb. 25, 1790
Thorn, Susannah...........Adams, Luke...............June 2, 1781
Thorn, Winny..............Jones, Thomas.............Dec. 26, 1789
Thralls, Richard...........Mulliken, Lucy............Dec. 31, 1787
Thursby, Edward..........Saucer, Ann...............Jan. 25, 1786
Tilley, John...............Jones, Mary..............Mch. 29, 1780
Tilley, John...............Wirt, Barbara...............Jan. 6, 1790
Tilley, Rebecca............Stevens, William............Jan. 15, 1785
Tilley, Rebecca............Athey, Hezekiah...........Dec. 10, 1799
Tippett, John..............Leach, Tabitha.............July 30, 1796
Tippett, Mary Atway.......Thompson, George..........May 4, 1798
Togood, Sarah.............Vellum, Henry.............June 29, 1791
Tolson, Francis............Middleton, Ann............Feb. 21, 1782
Tolson, Francis............Simms, Elizabeth...........Feb. 27, 1794
Tongue, Margaret..........Locker, Philip.............Feb. 25, 1785
Tongue, Mary.............Coe, Milburn...............Jan. 8, 1783
Townley, Thomas..........Stewart, Henrietta..........Jan. 15, 1782
Townsend, Mary...........Burch, Benjamin...........Feb. 22, 1784
Townsend, Samuel.........Hodgkin, Mary............Aug. 27, 1781
Townshend, Ann...........Wright, John Watson........Jan. 8, 1794
Townshend, Elizabeth......Taylor, William............Dec. 30, 1795
Townshend, Leonard........Young, Sarah Eleanor........Dec. 8, 1789
Townshend, Leonard.......Parker, Elizabeth...........Dec. 16, 1796
Townshend, William........Bonefant, Keziah...........Oct. 12, 1795
Tracy, Eleanor W..........Conner, John..............Dec. 1, 1778
Tracy, William.............Scissell, Mary.............Sept. 18, 1777
Trass, Ann...............Collea, William.............Nov. 7, 1786
Tredwell, Tracy...........Hutchinson, Nathan.........June 2, 1777
Trigg, David..............Elery, Charity..............Jan. 11, 1796
Trother, Jane.............Nesmith, Ebenezer.........May 20, 1796
Trott, Sarah..............Ragon, Basil...............June 24, 1789
True, John...............Waters, Mima...............Jan. 9, 1797
Trueman, Henry...........Beavin, Ann................Apr. 3, 1790
Trueman, Mocky...........Merroll, Philip............Feb. 10, 1798
Trueman, Rebecca..........Johnson, Rinaldo............Feb. 1, 1779
Trueman, Rebecca..........Pierce, John..............Mch. 29, 1798
Trunnell, Rachel...........Wilson, Lancelot...........Feb. 14, 1792

Tucker, Benjamin	Wornald, Ann	Feb. 11, 1778
Tucker, John	Weeden, Jane	Feb. 7, 1782
Tucker, Richard	Johnson, Eliza	Jan. 21, 1794
Tull, Eleanor	McDaniel, Archibald	June 25, 1798
Tull, Elizabeth	Thompson, Andrew	July 20, 1798
Turnbull, John	Magruder, Rebecca	Sept. 24, 1789
Turner, Abraham	Sadler, Rebena	Nov. 27, 1781
Turner, George	Gibbons, Ann	Sept. 5, 1797
Turner, John	Beck, Sarah	Feb. 5, 1799
Turner, Philip	Williams, Rachel	Sept. 14, 1787
Turner, Rebecca	Goodman, Peter	May 15, 1793
Turner, Rezin	Scott, Mary	Dec. 12, 1799
Turner, Richard	Williams, Eleanor	Jan. 10, 1791
Turner, Sarah	Anderwig, Lancelot	Dec. 19, 1797
Turner, Susannah	Stephens, John	Feb. 28, 1798
Turner, William	Batt, Dorcas	Feb. 21, 1784
Turton, Fielder	Simpson, Ann	May 4, 1799
Turton, Josey Harrison	Jenkins, Ann	Nov. 19, 1794
Turton, Mary A.	Tarman, Richard	Feb. 22, 1784
Twain, Christian	Evans, Guy	Sept. 16, 1779
Tyler, Christy	Pratt, Thomas	Oct. 16, 1799
Tyler, Elizabeth	Belt, Humphrey, Jr.	Feb. 4, 1792
Tyler, Milicent	Beanes, Colmow	Apr. 10, 1778
Tyler, Priscilla	Forster, Richard	Apr. 5, 1784
Tyler, Robert Bradley	Beanes, Henrietta	Dec. 1, 1779
Tyler, Robert B.	Belt, Dreyden G.	Mch. 17, 1783
Tyler, Samuel	Riddle, Verlinda	Jan. 19, 1782
Tyler, Samuel	Waters, Susanna	Dec. 25, 1783
Tyler, Susannah	Hodges, Benjamin M.	Apr. 18, 1797
Underwood, George	Hardey, Mary	Aug. 31, 1789
Underwood, Sarah	Downs, John	Dec. 11, 1789
Upton, Archibald	Ferrall, Rebecca	Dec. 30, 1795
Upton, Eleanor	Havener, Dominick	Jan. 31, 1789
Upton, Eliza	Lanham, Hilleary	Apr. 5, 1783
Upton, George	Perkins, Elizabeth	Jan. 6, 1778
Upton, Keziah	King, John	June 5, 1779
Upton, Sarah	Marshall, Benjamin	Jan. 17, 1778
Upton, Sarah	Wheat, Francis	Nov. 11 (1?), 1780
Upton, Thomas	Mitchell, Priscilla	Feb. 19, 1798
Urquhart, John	Lowe, Ann	Feb. 22, 1793

Vanhorn, Archibald.........Beall, Alethea Elizabeth.....July 26, 1797
Vaughan, Thomas..........Watson, Ann...............Nov. 6, 1794
Veitch, Alexander..........Hilseagle, Barbara..........July 11, 1798
Veatch, James.............Page, Mary................Jan. 25, 1798
Veitch, Rachel.............Neale, William..............Aug. 1, 1798
Vellum, Henry.............Togood, Sarah.............June 29, 1791
Venables, Theodore.........Tarman, Mary.............May 24, 1799
Vermillion, Benjamin.......Farr, Priscilla..............Jan. 8, 1788
Vermilion, Caleb...........Busey, Mary..............Dec. 20, 1794
Vermilion, Eliza...........Cross, Thomas.............Oct. 14, 1780
Vermilion, Francis Burch....Wood, Ann................Oct. 30, 1780
Vermilion, Jacob...........Hanson, Cloe..............Jan. 29, 1781
Vermilion, John............McDaniel, Janephene.......July 15, 1780
Vermillion, Mary...........Farr, John Baptist.........Nov. 23, 1780
Vermilion, Osborn..........Haas, Rachel..............May 5, 1798
Vermilion, Penelope.........Burch, Francis.............Jan. 26, 1783
Vermillion, William.........Simms, Mary Anne.........Apr. 19, 1778
Vernem, Caleb.............Atcheson, Chloe............Nov. 30, 1790
Virmeer, Jane.............Jackson, William...........Jan. 31, 1789

Wade, Benoni Hamilton.....Hardey, Mary D...........May 31, 1796
Wade, Dely...............Shannon, Luke............Mch. 24, 1794
Wade, Elizabeth............Magruder, Edward.........May 22, 1782
Wade, Hetta...............Webster, William..........Aug. 13, 1792
Wade, Lancelot............Fenley, Martha Hawkins.....Nov. 1, 1785
Wade, Letty...............Fox, William..............Nov. 18, 1794
Wade, Linny..............Hurley, Cornelius............Apr. 4, 1795
Wade, Meakey.............Beane, Walter..............Oct. 22, 1785
Wailes, Ann..............Clark, Thomas.............Oct. 29, 1791
Wailes, Edward Lloyd......Oden, Sarah Biggs.........Mch. 22, 1780
Wailes, Kitty B............Estep, John...............May 30, 1795
Wailes, Levin.............Davis, Eleanor.............Oct. 28, 1796
Wailes, Levin Carrington....Perrie, Sarah..............Dec. 17, 1789
Wailes, Rebeccah...........Burroughs, George..........July 6, 1792
Wailes, Samuel............Naylor, Ann................Feb. 8, 1783
Wailks, Susanna...........Kennedy, James............Dec. 16, 1799
Wakin, Nathaniel...........Ogden, Catherine..........Sept. 24, 1788
Waljon, Alexander..........Eastwood, Eliza.............Jan. 9, 1796
Walker, Ann..............Sweeney, Lloyd............Jan. 10, 1790
Walker, Ann..............Thompson, Samuel.........Jan. 10, 1790
Walker, Benjamin..........Pumphrey, Mary...........Dec. 31, 1778
Walker, Benjamin..........Busey, Ann................June 13, 1798

Walker, Benjamin N........Griffeth, Ann..............Apr. 18, 1794
Walker, Benjamin Neill.....Littleford, Mary...........Mch. 25, 1788
Walker, Catherine..........Walker, Richard............Dec. 24, 1796
Walker, Elisha.............Roberts, Elizabeth.........Dec. 31, 1792
Walker, George.............Gray, Ann..................Dec. 7, 1779
Walker, George.............Craufurd, Martha...........Dec. 16, 1794
Walker, Henry..............Burgess, Keziah............Dec. 8, 1780
Walker, Isaac..............Bradford, Eleanor..........July 27, 1790
Walker, John...............Mosley, Stacey.............Dec. 16, 1796
Walker, Joseph, Jr.........Hepburn, Henrietta Maria....Dec. 7, 1779
Walker, Martha.............Laws, William..............May 26, 1784
Walker, Mary...............Beckett, John..............Sept. 29, 1778
Walker, Mary...............Whitmore, Humphrey.........Nov. 30, 1793
Walker, Mareen D...........Berry, Ann.................Jan. 15, 1787
Walker, Rachel.............Prather, Benjamin..........Jan. 15, 1782
Walker, Richard............Gilpin, Mary...............Aug. 23, 1778
Walker, Richard............Beall, Rachel..............Dec. 13, 1785
Walker, Richard............Walker, Catherine..........Dec. 24, 1796
Walker, Thomas.............Littleford, Mary...........Dec. 24, 1780
Wall, Mary.................Ray, Jesse.................Jan. 24, 1782
Wall, Rebecca..............Ray, Basil.................Jan. 19, 1782
Wall, Sarah................Wells, Thomas..............May 26, 1787
Wall, Thomas...............Hellen, Susannah...........Dec. 5, 1791
Wall, William..............Piles, Elizabeth...........Jan. 9, 1786
Wallace, Michael...........Contee, Eleanor............Aug. 18, 1780
Wallace, Sarah.............Free, John.................Jan. 25, 1796
Walace, William............Mahew, Alice...............Apr. 23, 1778
Wallace, William...........Smith, Ann.................Feb. 14, 1780
Wallingsford, Elizabeth.....Piles, Henry...............Aug. 6, 1779
Wallingsford, Joseph........Lowe, Esther...............Feb. 25, 1782
Walls, George..............Naylor, Martha.............Feb. 25, 1783
Walls, Martha..............Berry, William.............Apr. 7, 1792
War, Ann...................Mackness, Samuel...........Sept. 2, 1779
Ward, Benjamin.............Foard, Mary................July 17, 1784
Ware, Sarah................Gray, Charles..............Dec. 3, 1778
Warfield, Elizabeth.........Wells, Joseph..............Nov. 22, 1781
Warfield, John.............Carrick, Ann...............Dec. 19, 1784
Waring, Ann................Wharton, Jesse.............Apr. 6, 1779
Waring, Eleanor............Brooke, Henry..............Oct. 8, 1798
Waring, Elizabeth..........O'Neil, Bernard............Jan. 5, 1782
Waring, Elizabeth..........Beall, Joshua..............Feb. 3, 1787
Waring, James..............Hilleary, Elizabeth.........Jan. 4, 1787

Waring, Jane..............Beall, Walter Brooke.........May 1, 1794
Waring, John, Jr............Bowie, Elizabeth Margaret...Dec. 30, 1800
Waring, Marcus S...........Holliday, Mary..............Jan. 9, 1794
Waring, Margery...........Crimpton, Thomas..........Jan. 28, 1779
Waring, Thomas...........Berry, Margaret...........Mch. 21, 1795
Warman, Benjamin.........Perry, Ester...............Feb. 20, 1779
Warman, Edmund..........Smith, Elizabeth...........Sept. 22, 1788
Warman, Frances Hanslep...Watkins, Stephen..........May 18, 1784
Warne, John..............Linton, Mary.............Dec. 24, 1783
Warner, Henry.............Farr, Elizabeth............Nov. 29, 1794
Warner, Mary.............Perkins, Samuel...........Feb. 11, 1797
Warren, Patsey............Wheeler, Leonard............Dec. 7, 1797
Warrensford, Joseph........McCartey, Sarah M.........Dec. 20, 1800
Washington, Nathaniel.....Hawkins, Margaret.........Nov. 24, 1790
Waters, Casandra..........Bassford, Thomas...........Apr. 2, 1784
Waters, Eliza..............Mills, John................Jan. 18, 1782
Waters, Elizabeth..........Mills, Zachariah............Dec. 21, 1787
Waters, Henry............Waters, Mary..............Jan. 30, 1783
Waters, Jacob Franklin.....Mullikin, Martha Hall......Feb. 12, 1798
Waters, Jane..............Owens, Joseph............Feb. 19, 1787
Waters, Jemima............Jenings, Peter.............Jan. 15, 1794
Waters, Joseph............Mier, Elizabeth...........Aug. 25, 1779
Waters, Mary.............Whitehead, Thomas.........Dec. 4, 1779
Waters, Mary.............Waters, Henry............Jan. 30, 1783
Waters, Mima.............True, John.................Jan. 9, 1797
Waters, Richard...........Jones, Elizabeth.............Oct. 5, 1782
Waters, Stephen...........Duckett, Jane............Mch. 25, 1794
Waters, Susanna...........Tyler, Samuel.............Dec. 25, 1783
Waters, Thomas Jones......Jacob, Allice..............July 14, 1787
Watkin, Catherine..........Edelen, Joseph.............Apr. 3, 1786
Watkins, Elizabeth.........Hodges, Charles Drury.......Feb. 3, 1798
Watkins, Gassoway.........Loflin, Mary..............Apr. 17, 1784
Watkins, Nancy............Sherly, Theodore..........Mch. 28, 1797
Watkins, Peggy...........Wells, Joseph..............Feb. 1, 1787
Watkins, Stephen..........Warman, Frances Hanslep...May 18, 1784
Watkins, Thomas, Jr........Sprigg, Elizabeth............Jan. 7, 1778
Watkins, Thomas..........Belt, Lucy.................Dec. 6, 1779
Watson, Ann.............Vaughan, Thomas...........Nov. 6, 1794
Watson, Ann.............Wilson, Samuel Taylor......June 20, 1795
Watson, Catherine..........Forster, Thomas...........Aug. 29, 1781
Watson, Cornelius..........Lamar, Susannah...........Dec. 28, 1791
Watson, Eliza.............Adams, Josephus...........Oct. 24, 1777

Watson, Elizabeth..........Power, Thomas..............July 1, 1795
Watson, Isaac..............Mayhew, Mary............Mch. 21, 1786
Watson, James.............Watson, Sarah..............Jan. 17, 1781
Watson, James.............Beavin, Mary..............Dec. 25, 1799
Watson, Jane...............Leach, James...............Jan. 13, 1790
Watson, John...............King, Susannah.............Feb. 28, 1789
Watson, Leonard...........Cooksey, Sarah..............Jan. 7, 1792
Watson, Levin..............Rallings, Jane..............Oct. 11, 1785
Watson, Rebecca...........Linch, John S................Jan. 5, 1782
Watson, Richard...........Stewart, Ann Eustatia.......Feb. 19, 1781
Watson, Sarah.............Watson, James.............Jan. 17, 1781
Watson, Sarah.............Davis, Jonathan............Dec. 26, 1787
Watson, Susanna...........Ellis, Elijah...............Dec. 27, 1779
Watson, Susanna...........King, Leonard.............Nov. 15, 1780
Watson, Thomas...........Nutwell, Catherine..........Feb. 11, 1784
Watson, Verlinda...........Rawlings, John.............Apr. 12, 1792
Watson, Walter............Stone, Rachel...............Oct. 8, 1779
Watson, Walter............Naylor, Ann................Dec. 23, 1783
Watson, William...........Wells, Eliza................Oct. 18, 1781
Watson, William...........Right, Elizabeth............July 20, 1784
Watson, William...........Cheney, Rebecca...........Dec. 19, 1793
Waugh, John..............Masters, Mary..............Nov. 2, 1793
Wear, James...............Smith, Sarah...............July 19, 1777
Weaver, Anamina..........King, Richard..............Feb. 27, 1795
Weaver, Mary.............Wirt, Christian.............Sept. 3, 1792
Weaver, Sarah.............King, Isaac...............Mch. 16, 1799
Weaver, William...........Simpson, Isabella............Apr. 2, 1782
Webb, Elizabeth...........Shelton, Thomas............Aug. 6, 1777
Webb, Elizabeth...........Millard, William...........June 22, 1780
Webb, Margaret............Carrick, Mareen............Jan. 17, 1795
Webb, Martha.............Beck, Samuel D...........Aug. 19, 1793
Webb, Sarah...............Gardiner, Abraham..........Apr. 5, 1783
Webster, Christian..........Baldwin, Thomas...........July 23, 1790
Webster, Elizabeth.........Marlows, Butler D..........Aug. 30, 1796
Webster, John.............Kidwell, Margaret..........Dec. 26, 1784
Webster, Mary Ann........Wright, John...............Feb. 25, 1791
Webster, Philip Lewin......Beane, Elizabeth ....May 20, 1793
Webster, Sarah............Hide, George...............Dec. 16, 1783
Webster, William...........Wade, Hetta...............Aug. 13, 1792
Webster, William...........Wright, Ann..................Feb. 1, 1793
Wedderal, John............Jones, Elizabeth............Apr. 14, 1786
Weeden Henry.............Young, Sarah.............Sept. 23, 1797

Weeden, Jane.............Tucker, John..............Feb. 7, 1782
Weedon, Nathaniel.........Cater, Mary...............Dec. 15, 1794
Weems, James William Loch Hall, Mary.................May 6, 1786
Weems, Wilhelmina.........Gantt, Henry...............Mch. 3, 1798
Weiders, Catherine.........Bignell, John..............Aug. 21, 1786
Weil, Catherine............Johnson, James..............Dec. 5, 1782
Welch, Dorcus.............Jones, Samuel..............Nov. 4, 1788
Welch, Elizabeth...........Williams, William...........Apr. 4, 1797
Welch, Richard.............Prather, Massey.............Oct. 1, 1781
Welch, Richard............Simmons, Susannah.........June 5, 1793
Wellen, William............Darcey, Mary..............Jan. 30, 1793
Wells, Bridgett.............Leach, Thomas.............July 11, 1789
Wells, Eliza................Watson, William...........Oct. 18, 1781
Wells, Elizabeth............Oliver, Cornelius............Jan. 9, 1784
Wells, James...............Burrell, Mary...............Feb. 6, 1795
Wells, Joseph..............Warfield, Elizabeth.........Nov. 22, 1781
Wells, Joseph..............Watkins, Peggy.............Feb. 1, 1787
Wells, Margaret............Jones, David...............Nov. 4, 1797
Wells, Martha.............Drane, Thomas.............Feb. 4, 1786
Wells, Martin..............Robinson, Mary............Feb. 26, 1783
Wells, Martin..............Fowler, Mary...............Jan. 5, 1799
Wells, Mary...............Mitchell, Theodore.........Nov. 27, 1777
Wells, Mary...............Leitch, Benjamin............Oct. 1, 1781
Wells, Mary...............Belt, Benjamin..............Feb. 6, 1782
Wells, Nathan.............Askey, Mary...............Jan. 14, 1785
Wells, Nathan.............Duley, Sophia.............Nov. 12, 1798
Wells, Rachel.............Simmons, Jesse...........Sept. 13, 1781
Wells, Rebecca............Wells, William............Dec. 22, 1780
Wells, Samuel.............Olliver, Martha...........Aug. 10, 1778
Wells, Sarah..............Hardesty, Elisha...........Aug. 24, 1780
Wells, Susanna............Jacob, Richard.............Apr. 8, 1778
Wells, Susannah...........Plummer, Abiezer...........Nov. 3, 1795
Wells, Thomas.............Wall, Sarah...............May 26, 1787
Wells, Walter..............Ridgway, Eleanor..........Jan. 25, 1800
Wells, William.............Wells, Rebecca............Dec. 22, 1780
Wells, William.............Oliver, Rhoda...............Jan. 4, 1790
Wells, William.............Cheney, Eleanor...........Mch. 30, 1793
Welsh, Deborah............Edmonston, Nathan........Dec. 19, 1788
Welsh, Elizabeth...........Prather, Joseph.............June 1, 1781
Wentfield, Mary Ann.......Kidwell, Thomas...........Mch. 23, 1781
Werrald, Sarah.............Richardson, Elisha...........Dec. 3, 1782
West, Rachel Sophia........Oden, Benjamin.............Jan. 25, 1790

Wharton, Jesse............Waring, Ann................Apr. 6, 1779
Wheat, Francis............Upton, Sarah..............Nov. 11, 1780
Wheat, Jesse...............Soper, Sarah................Dec. 2, 1795
Wheat, Joseph.............Brian, Rachel..............Dec. 12, 1791
Wheat, Linney.............Havener, John..............Jan. 19, 1788
Wheat, Mary...............Moreland, Thomas B........Oct. 17, 1799
Wheat, Priscilla............Phelps, Benjamin...........Dec. 10, 1795
Wheat, Sarah..............Hardey, Jesse..............Oct. 31, 1789
Wheat, Zachariah..........Reynolds, Priscilla...........Feb. 4, 1782
Wheatley, Ann.............Wheatley, George............Oct. 4, 1798
Wheeler, Ann..............Hilleary, Tilghman...........Jan. 9, 1782
Wheeler, Aquila............Young, Elizabeth...........Feb. 26, 1778
Wheeler, Edward..........Hilleary, Sarah.............Dec. 21, 1785
Wheeler, Eleanor..........Wheeler, Samuel............Oct. 27, 1780
Wheeler, Elizabeth.........McDonogh, Morris James....Nov. 4, 1789
Wheeler, Ignatius..........Newton, Rachel............Jan. 28, 1794
Wheeler, Jacob............Austin, Sarah..............Feb. 10, 1786
Wheeler, Jacob............Iglehart, Susannah..........June 2, 1787
Wheeler, Jemima..........Bird, Thomas..............Dec. 14, 1780
Wheeler, John.............Brown, Letetia.............Dec. 11, 1792
Wheeler, Joseph...........Brooke, Ann...............Apr. 23, 1785
Wheeler, Leonard.........Warren, Patsey.............Dec. 7, 1797
Wheeler, Samuel..........Wheeler, Eleanor...........Oct. 27, 1780
Wheeler, Samuel..........Hilleary, Ann...............Dec. 4, 1781
Wheeler, Susannah.........Farrall, John..............Jan. 13, 1786
Whitaker, Elizabeth.......Williams, Calvert..........May 16, 1794
Whitaker, Elizabeth.......Lansdale, Isaac............June 19, 1794
White, Allen...............Burgess, Mildred............July 9, 1785
White, Ariana..............Piles, Hilleary...............Jan. 7, 1795
White, Charles.............Smith, Susanna............July 30, 1777
White, Eliza...............Miles, Frederick............Dec. 31, 1781
White, Elizabeth...........Hodges, Thomas............Oct. 26, 1797
White, Fielder.............Sansbury, Sarah...........Feb. 16, 1782
White, James..............Beall, Mary................Oct. 31, 1781
White, Jane...............Harrison, Thomas...........Dec. 4, 1779
White, John...............Smith, Ursula.............Sept. 20, 1780
White, John...............Brown, Mary..............Dec. 20, 1780
White, John M.............Danforth, (Mrs.) Nancy.....Oct. 30, 1797
White, Jonathan...........Tarman, Sarah............Mch. 27, 1785
White, Mary..............Mitchell, William...........Dec. 10, 1792
White, Osborn............Sansberrie, Rebecca.........Dec. 24, 1792
White, Richard............Branham, Mary...........Nov. 14, 1798

White, Samuel B. . . . . Beall, Lethea . . . . Feb. 21, 1781
White, Walter . . . . Davis, Sarah . . . . Jan. 14, 1789
White, William . . . . Blanford, Rebecca . . . . Oct. 11, 1783
Whitehead, Thomas . . . . Waters, Mary . . . . Dec. 4. 1779
Whitemore, Elizabeth . . . . Neal, Thomas . . . . Aug. 7, 1779
Whitmore, Humphrey . . . . Walker, Mary . . . . Nov. 30, 1793
Whiten, Rachel . . . . Hunter, Richard . . . . Jan. 19, 1782
Whiting, Gilbert . . . . Maloney, Ann . . . . Nov. 21, 1794
Whiting, Rebecca . . . . Simpson, John . . . . Sept. 9, 1784
Whitney, Ann . . . . Thompson, Philip . . . . May 30, 1796
Wig, Elizabeth . . . . Low, James . . . . July 26, 1790
Wigfield, Mary . . . . Standage, Eleazor . . . . Dec. 23, 1783
Wightt, Ann . . . . Keadle, Wiseman . . . . Aug. 25, 1787
Wight, Isle of . . . . Wilson, Elizabeth . . . . May 29, 1783
Wight, John . . . . Hennis, Rebecca . . . . Apr. 15, 1786
Wilburn, Sarah . . . . Ryan, Elijah . . . . Jan. 2, 1798
Wilcoxon, Ann . . . . Lowe, John . . . . June 29, 1781
Wilcoxon, Elizabeth . . . . Summers, Eleven . . . . Dec. 30, 1786
Willcoxon, Levin . . . . Brashears, Mary . . . . Feb. 11, 1780
Wilcoxen, Margaret . . . . Hardy, Thomas . . . . Feb. 9, 1780
Wilcoxon, Thomas, Jr. . . . . . . Hardey, Mary . . . . Apr. 23, 1781
Wilcoxon, Verlinda . . . . Evans, John . . . . Dec. 19, 1786
Wiley, Ann . . . . Dailey, Moses . . . . Oct. 7, 1797
Willett, Ann . . . . Thomas, James . . . . Aug. 10, 1781
Willett, Ann . . . . Clark, John . . . . Dec. 18, 1788
Willett, Christian . . . . Hutchinson, William . . . . Apr. 18, 1780
Willett, Elizabeth . . . . Howe, Stanislaus . . . . Dec. 6, 1797
Willett, Mary . . . . Simmons, Richard . . . . Mch. 7, 1779
Willett, Mary . . . . Childs, William . . . . Dec. 13, 1781
Willett, Mary . . . . Marlow, William . . . . Dec. 29, 1786
Willett, Priscilla . . . . Clarke, Abraham . . . . Dec. 14, 1786
Willett, Rachel . . . . Price, Richard . . . . Dec. 17, 1782
Willett, Rachel . . . . Howe, Ignatius . . . . Nov. 27, 1798
Willett, Salome . . . . Ogden, John . . . . Nov. 2, 1782
Willett, Samuel . . . . Orme, Ann . . . . June 27, 1784
Willett, Sarah . . . . Duvall, Tobias . . . . Feb. 5, 1795
Willett, Susana . . . . Bentenning, Benjamin Smith May 15, 1783
Willett, Tabitha . . . . Higgins, Samuel . . . . Dec. 13, 1799
Williams, Abraham . . . . Bradley, Catherine . . . . Dec. 13, 1794
Williams, Ann . . . . Spiden, Robert . . . . Apr. 3, 1797
Williams, Barbara . . . . Magruder, Francis . . . . Dec. 23, 1786
Williams, Calvert . . . . Oden, Eleanor . . . . Dec. 20, 1792

Williams, Calvert...........Whitaker, Elizabeth........May 16, 1794
Williams, Cave.............Jackson, John...............Feb. 1, 1788
Williams, Eleanor..........Turner, Richard............Jan. 10, 1791
Williams, Elizabeth.........Beall, Jonathan.............May 6, 1794
Williams, Elizabeth.........Ijams, Isaac................Aug. 4, 1795
Williams, Humphrey........Beall, Sarah................Jan. 21, 1794
Williams, Jane.............Keech, William.............Sept. 6, 1780
Williams, John F...........Mudd, Ann..................Jan. 9, 1782
Williams, Lelburn..........Thompson, Mary............Oct. 8, 1782
Williams, Osborn...........Magruder, Elizabeth........Oct. 15, 1787
Williams, Rachel...........Turner, Philip.............Sept. 14, 1787
Williams, Verlinda..........Hilleary, John..............Feb. 22, 1791
Williams, William..........Beck, Ruth.................Dec. 11, 1792
Williams, William..........Welch, Elizabeth.............Apr. 4, 1797
Wills, Eleanor..............Wills, Zadock..............Nov. 13, 1794
Wills, John.................Fields, Margaret...........Dec. 24, 1788
Wills, Zadock..............Wills, Eleanor..............Nov. 13, 1794
Wilson, Ann................Barnes, Daniel.............Feb. 21, 1783
Wilson, Ann................Jones, Richard.............Dec. 10, 1796
Wilson, Ann................Gordon, John...............June 5, 1797
Wilson, Ann................McNauty, Cephas..........Aug. 19, 1800
Wilson, Ann Dickson.......Scott, Samuel..............Nov. 19, 1784
Wilson, Aquila.............Taylor, Sarah..............Nov. 21, 1791
Wilson, Barnaba............Maginnes, Elizabeth........Jan. 11, 1786
Wilson, Basil...............Scott, Ann..................Aug. 9, 1779
Wilson, Clement...........Coicel, Susannah............Sept. 5, 1778
Wilson, Clowe.............Smallwood, John...........Dec. 15, 1787
Wilson, Elizabeth..........Thorn, Henry..............May 29, 1779
Wilson, Elizabeth..........Wight, Isle of..............May 29, 1783
Wilson, Elizabeth..........Jones, George.............Jan. 29, 1788
Wilson, Elizabeth..........Lee, Thomas.............Sept. 29, 1792
Wilson, James.............Gibbons, Elizabeth.........Mch. 16, 1798
Wilson, James C...........Barnes, Mary A.............Feb. 1, 1782
Wilson, John...............Gordon, Elizabeth..........Feb. 11, 1795
Wilson, Joseph.............Ferguson, Ann S............Aug. 29, 1777
Wilson, Joseph.............Wilson, Sarah...............Jan. 8, 1787
Wilson, Joseph.............Ferguson, Ruth..............Oct. 5, 1793
Wilson, Joseph.............Smith, Elizabeth...........Mch. 17, 1795
Wilson, Joseph H..........King, Eleanor..............Aug. 24, 1782
Wilson, Josiah.............Burns, Elizabeth............Apr. 1, 1789
Wilson, Lancelot...........Trunnell, Rachel...........Feb. 14, 1792
Wilson, Margery...........Jenkins, Joseph............June 25, 1780

Wilson, Martha............Lusby, John...............Feb. 24, 1778
Wilson, Mary..............Sout, Edward..............July 12, 1779
Wilson, Mary..............Naylor, Benjamin..........Dec. 14, 1797
Wilson, Mary..............Duley, John...............June 14, 1800
Wilson, Nathaniel.........Hanson, Martha............June 15, 1779
Wilson, Nathaniel.........Nelson, Eliza H...........Mch. 30, 1782
Wilson, Norando...........Mangum, Eleanor...........Dec. 26, 1785
Wilson, Priscilla.........Naylor, James.............Sept. 5, 1797
Wilson, Rebecca...........Gray, Richard.............Aug. 30, 1778
Wilson, Samuel Taylor.....Watson, Ann...............June 20, 1795
Wilson, Sarah.............Stone, Nemiah.............Mch. 3, 1778
Wilson, Sarah.............Mitchell, Mordicai Miles....Nov. 26, 1779
Wilson, Sarah.............Barnes, Oliver.............Feb. 8, 1785
Wilson, Sarah.............Wilson, Joseph.............Jan. 8, 1787
Wilson, Susannah..........Talbot, Basil..............July 5, 1800
Wilson, Thomas............Beall, Ann.................Sept. 7, 1783
Wilson, William...........Ferguson, Rebecca..........Oct. 1, 1777
Wilson, William...........Mason, Verlinda............Jan. 10, 1780
Wilson, William...........Jones, Margaret............Nov. 7, 1781
Wilson, William...........Gibbons, Susanna...........May 5, 1800
Windsor, Luke.............Mobberly, Elizabeth........Jan. 23, 1797
Winfield, Jonas...........Stewart, Ann M.............Apr. 13, 1781
Winser, Ignatius..........Mobberly, Mary.............Dec. 21, 1792
Winsett, Mary.............Johnson, Joseph............Feb. 2, 1799
Winslow, John C...........Reiley, Margaret...........Feb. 22, 1784
Wirt, Barbara.............Tilley, John...............Jan. 6, 1790
Wirt, Christian...........Weaver, Mary...............Sept. 3, 1792
Wirt, Henry...............Ferguson, Jennett..........Jan. 15, 1795
Wise, George..............King, Jane.................Mch. 7, 1799
Wise, Thomas..............Robinson, Milly............Dec. 1, 1787
Wood, Ann.................Vermilion, Francis Burch....Oct. 30, 1780
Wood, Ann.................Lowe, Dennis...............Dec. 3, 1785
Wood, Elizabeth...........Mitchell, Thomas...........Aug. 20, 1781
Wood, Hannah..............Morgan, John...............Apr. 20, 1779
Wood, James G.............Allein, Sarah..............Dec. 4, 1798
Wood, John Thomas.........Greenfield, Ann............June 22, 1799
Wood, Leonard.............Crown, Elizabeth...........Sept. 9, 1781
Wood, Margaret............Coe, Richard...............May 8, 1784
Wood, Peter...............Gantt, Ann.................Apr. 3, 1793
Wood, Susannah............Burrell, Allen.............Mch. 18, 1789
Wood, Thomas..............Hall, Ann..................May 25, 1782

Wood, Thomas	Clagett, Priscilla	Mch. 10, 1787
Wood, Tracy	Lowe, Basil	Aug. 15, 1785
Wood, William	Gray, Elizabeth	Dec. 7, 1780
Woodfield, Diana	Chaney, Abraham	Sept. 22, 1797
Woodward, Benjamin	Scissell, Eliza	Dec. 15, 1778
Woodward, Druscilla	Peck, John	Feb. 17, 1798
Woodward, John	Drane, Eliza Piles	Nov. 9, 1796
Woodward, Margaret	Pearre, Joshua	Dec. 6, 1786
Woodward, Thomas	Hilleary, Eleanor	Apr. 18, 1788
Wootton, Turnor	Bowie, Mary M.	Mch. 27, 1794
Wootton, William	Garner, Patsy	June 4, 1799
Wornald, Ann	Tucker, Benjamin	Feb. 11, 1778
Wornald, Henry	Simpson, Ann	Apr. 15, 1780
Worthington, William	Contee, Jane	Feb. 28, 1782
Wouster, Mary	Hammerstein, Richard	Dec. 17, 1777
Wright, Ann	Webster, William	Feb. 1, 1793
Wright, Elizabeth	Evans, John	Aug. 25, 1798
Wright, John	Webster, Mary Ann	Feb. 25, 1791
Wright, John Watson	Townshend, Ann	Jan. 8, 1794
Wright, Joseph	Naylor, Ann	Feb. 26, 1788
Wright, Margery	Stonestreet, Edward	May 10, 1780
Wright, Mary	Adams, George	Jan. 21, 1783
Wright, Rebecca	Gibbons, John	Jan. 15, 1799
Wright, Samuel	Clemmens, Catherine	Jan. 9, 1786
Whyte, Ann	Harwood, Thomas, 3rd.	Oct. 29, 1778
Wynn, Ann	Ogden, Robert	Oct. 17, 1778
Wynn, Ann	Blacklock, Thomas	Nov. 22, 1783
Wynn, John	Smallwood, Ann	Dec. 12, 1778
Wynn, Lucy Ann	Alder, George	Oct. 31, 1778
Wynn, Priscilla Ann	McDaniel, William	Nov. 29, 1779
Wynne, Hezekiah	Smallwood, Rebecca M.	Jan. 12, 1779
Wynns, William	Smallwood, Milicent	May 20, 1778
Yates, Joseph	Johnson, Mary	Oct. 12, 1781
Yates, Martin	Nevitt, Mary	Dec. 31, 1798
Yearbey, Benjamin	Thompson, Minta	Feb. 14, 1785
Young, Charles, Jr.	Dabney, Mary	Aug. 17, 1796
Young, David	Smith, Henrietta	Dec. 17, 1784
Young, Deborah	Jenners, Abriel	May 17, 1796
Young, Elizabeth	Wheeler, Aquila	Feb. 26, 1778
Young, Jane Joan G.	Dorsett, Fielder	Apr. 19, 1794

Young, Mary..............Nash, Christopher..........Sept. 4, 1782
Young, Ruth..............Jones, Benjamin............Oct. 11, 1786
Young, Samuel............Ferguson, Ruth.............Dec. 8, 1798
Young, Sarah.............Weeden, Henry.............Sept. 23, 1797
Young, Sarah Eleanor.......Townshend, Leonard.........Dec. 8, 1789
Younger, Gilbert...........Hardey, Rebeca............June 12, 1784

Prince George's County Militia in the French War of 1799

"A list of men enrolled in Captain Jacob Duckett's Company in the 34th Maryland Regiment of Militia under Command of Lieutt Coll H.ll—30th March 1799"—(No. 1).

Jacob Duckett, Captain
Humphrey Williams, Lieutt
John Hilleary, Ensign

	SERGEANTS	*Born*
Gun.	Basil Duckett"	26th March 1772
	Tobias Belt	9th Sept 1776*
	Samuel Magruder	25th June 1767
	Thomas Magruder	24th Novr. 1779

	PRIVATES	
Gun.	1. Jacob Wheeler, draughted on the Western expedition, born	5th Jany 1760
	2. Richard Taylor ditto ditto	15th Decr 1768
	3 Philip Turner	8th March 1778
	5. William Denune	24th May 1764
Gun.	6. William Cross	Sept 1768
	(Caleb Taylor—name crossed out)	
Gun.	Thomas Abigale	7th Feby 1758
	Lewis Lanham	14th July 1757
Gun.	Charles Soper	1770
Gun.	Belt Brashear	8th Feby 1768
ditto	Thomas Soper	10th June 1768
	William Bowie (of Walter)	29th Jany 1776
	William R. Clarke [William Russell]	1st April 1774
Gun.	John Hinton	1770
	(Thomas Magruder born 24th Novr 1779—name crossed out)	
	Philip Hacket	17th March 1764
	Zachariah Hazel	14th April 1774
	Fielder Cross	18th Jany 1772
	Richard Duvall	22nd Decr 1779

*Tobias Belt born 9th Sept. 1766—a line is drawn through this entry—see also the 1776 in date given above.

Gun. Benja Duvall (of Ben. 3d)........................8th Feby 1774
Gun. Tilghman Brashear........................22d Feby 1778
Daniel Bowie........................2nd March 1780
Michael Maw........................2nd Jany 1767
James Newel, does not know his age but believes he is about 40 years old.
John Leach........................4th Augt 1757
Gun. Isaac Magruder........................1755
Samuel Mockbee........................2nd Augt 1771
Gun. Bartin Brashear........................16th March 1766
John Riddle........................11th Octor 1762
Samuel Riddle........................1756
Gun. John Hlll
Gun. Joseph Boyd........................5th July 1766
Hezekiah Butt........................24th March 1765
John Turner........................1st March 1778
Benjamin Boyd........................24th March 1768
Gun. William Igleheart........................15th Octor 1778
Gun. Fielding Belt........................29th March 1765
William Boyd........................10th April 1781
George Page........................27th Jany 1768
Leven Beall........................Augt 1780
Gun. Nathan Soper Junr........................16th Novr 1778
Truman Duvall........................28th Feby 1781
William Clarke........................29th Jany 1779
Gun. James Waring........................12th Octor 1755
William Orme........................23d Feby 1757
Joseph Hinton........................28th Mar 1777
William Mockbee........................19th Novr 1778
Gun. 47 John Hill........................13th Jany 1766
Jacob Dines (or Dieus?)........................13th Octor 1772"

Another Muster Roll—(No. 2), *bearing the same date*, and duplicating the names, and dates of birth, but with the heading: "A list of men Enrolled in Humphrey Williams Company in the 34th Maryland Regiment of Militia under Command of Lieutt Coll Hill—30th March 1799" is headed by Humphrey Williams, Captain; John Hilleary, Lieutt; and Basil Duckett, Ensign. The Sergeants are given as Tobias Belt (date of birth here given as 9th Sept. 1766), Samuel Magruder and Thomas Magruder. The Privates are given the same, except that: Thomas Abigale is spelled "Abigail;" William R. Clarke appears as "William Russell Clarke;" "Samuel Mockbee appears as "Mocbee;" Gun. John

Hill was born 13th Jany 1766; William Mockbee appears as "Mocbee;" and the following additional names:

"Caleb Taylor.............................born 24th April 1775
Henry Brooke.............................
Henry H. M. kearn (M'Kearn, M'Keoun, or M'Hearn?)
John Hall.......................................born—1781"

Both Muster Rolls were copied May 14, 1906 from the originals by Leroy Stafford Boyd, Librarian Interstate Commerce Commission, Washington, D. C.; said Muster Rolls are owned by Mr. Boyd.

Jacob Duckett seems to have retired for some reason, and a promotion throughout the roll occurred on the same day.

FREDERICK COUNTY

CENSUS OF 1776

Census of 1776, Frederick County, Maryland*

The first settlements in Frederick County began along the Monocacy River, probably as early as 1710. As early as 1740 Pennsylvania Germans had followed the old Monocacy trail, and settled in the vicinity of Grayson, Creagerstown and Frederick. Especial attention is directed to the Census for Elizabeth Town Hundred, herein reproduced. "The growth in population in this region was very rapid, and by 1748 it appeared wise to erect a new county for this accommodation. The Act by which this was decreed enacted that:

'Beginning at the lower side of the mouth of Rock Creek, and thence by a strait line joining to the East Side of Seth Hyatt's Plantation, to Patuxent River—then with Patuxent River to the Lines of Baltimore County, and with the said County to the Extent of the Province; and that all the Land lying to the Westward and Southward of the said Lines be included in the new County aforesaid, and that after the Commencement of this Act the said new County shall be called Frederick County—'†

The Act of 1750, Chap. 13, loosely defined the boundary between Frederick and Baltimore counties, and this line continued until Carroll County was erected (Mch. 25, 1836, confirmed Jan. 19, 1837).

"Up to the outbreak of the Revolutionary War no further change was made in the limits of Frederick County. Permanent settlements of Germans had in the meantime been made at Middletown, Taneytown, Sharpsburg, Thurmont, Union Bridge, Emmitsburg and Woodsboro as well as in the Hagerstown Valley. At the Constitutional Convention of 1776 it was decided to divide this widely extended and now more or less populous Frederick County into three counties, Washington, Montgomery and Frederick, corresponding to the Upper, Lower and Middle Districts of Frederick County. The line of separation determined by this Convention was as follows: From the mouth of the Monocacy a straight line was drawn to Parrs Spring, or the headwaters of the Patuxent, and the portion of Frederick County lying to the south and east was assigned to Montgomery County. The second line ran along the crest of the South Mountain from the temporary line to the Potomac River. All the territory lying west of this was assigned to Washington County.‡

* Complete, so far as the Hundreds are preserved in the *Archives of Maryland*—a number are unfortunately missing.

† *The Counties of Maryland*, etc., Mathews, Vol. vi, Part v, pp 490–491.

‡ *The Counties of Maryland*, Mathews, pp. 490–492. See also the Frontispiece of this volume.

THE HUNDRED IN MARYLAND

"In Maryland the people settled in plantations scattered along the banks of the streams emptying into the Chesapeake Bay. They had no towns for this reason, but they had an area of local government smaller than the county [and district] during provincial times. This division was known as the Hundred, because in old English times that division was supposed to furnish that number of warriors to the army. John Fiske in his *Civil Government in the United States* says: 'In Maryland the hundred flourished and became the political unit like the township in New England. The hundred was the militia district and the district for the assessment of taxes. . . . The officers of the Maryland hundred were the high constable, the commander of the militia, the tobacco viewers, the overseer of roads, and the assessor of taxes. The last mentioned officer was elected by the people, the others were all appointed by the Governor.' The hundred was not prized by the people of Maryland, and was abolished in 1824. It was swallowed up in the county, and no small area of government has been established in the State since that time, except the municipalities."*

"Of the courts below the provincial court there were, at one time and another, the manorial courts, the hundred court, and the court of the single justice of the peace for the recovery of small debts.

Previous to 1650 it does not appear that there was any erection of counties in an express and formal way; yet, in reality, the western shore was treated as one county, called St. Mary's and the eastern shore was treated as another called Kent. The more important settlements on the western shore were erected into hundreds as constituent parts of St. Mary's County, while those on the eastern shore were erected into hundreds as constituent parts of Kent County. Whenever a hundred was erected, its head officer was constituted a justice of the peace. Under him was a constable. He was appointed either by the justice or by the governor, and was intrusted with the duties of constable and coroner. As justice of the peace, the head officer of the hundred was given such powers as belonged to one or even to two justices of the peace in England.†

* *The Institutions and Civil Government of Maryland*, Steiner, 1899, pp. 140–141.

† *Maryland as a Proprietary Province*; Mereness, 1901, p. 230.

White Male	485	Black Male	316
White Female	427	Black Female	300
White Male in G. Town Hd.	197	Black Male in G. Town Hd.	44
White Female in Do.	154	Black Female in Do.	38
Whites	1263	Blacks	698

Frederick County Lower Potomack Hundred August the 22, 1776.

Then Came Levin Magruder and made Oath on the holy Evangelist of Almighty God that the within List Contains all the Living Souls in Lower Potomack Hundred & George Town Hundred to the Best of his Knowledge

Sworne before

Robert Peter

Recd augst 2 1776 by the Committee of the Lower District of Fredk County Simon Nicholls Clk

Lower Potomack Hundred

"A LIST OF THE NUMBER OF SOULS TAKEN & GIVEN IN TO THE COMMITTEE OF OBSERVATION. THE SEX & AGES OF WHITE & BLACK, AUG. 22, 1776."

WHITE MALE	*Years*
Anderson, Robert	65
Austin, John	37
Aubrey, William	40
Atkins, Joseph	40
Adams, Edward	33
Alexander	30
John	1
Ahare, John	13
Austin, Thomas	15
Zechariah	13
James	11
John Kindrick	6
Hezekiah	4
Amos	1
Alexander	19
Benton, Joseph	52
Benjamin	16
Mordecai	10, (11?)
Nathan	12
Erasmus	10
Hezekiah	8
Belt, Leonard	49
Blackmore, James	33
Lawrence Owen	8
Samuel	4
James	2
Barnes, Prime	18
Beall, Henry	28
Blacklock, Richard	26
Richard, Junr	3
Beasley, Moses	60
Brook, Isaac	17
Burch, Zepheniah	26

	Years
Barber, John	60
Barney	7
Beall, George, Junr	46
Alexander	8
Erasmus	14
Hezekiah	10
Thomas Brook	8
Col. George	81
Josiah	18
Thomas of Saml	36
John Brook	7
Josiah	6
Baley, Edward	23
Badfoot, Bashual	22
Brown, James	25
William	20
Bonnifield, Gregory	50
Henry	10
Arnold	8
William	6
Brodie, William	30
Bucey, Joshua	65
John	25
Samuel	20
Blockley, Thomas	50
Nehemiah	3
Baley, Monjoy	21
Bryan, Philip	23
Bloyce, David	24
William	1
Broadie, John	55
Baley, William	30
Samuel	2

	Years
Belt, William	(indistinct)
Colyar, William	44
William, Junr	17
John	11
James	6
Clagett, Thomas	63
Nathan	20
John	32
Thomas	5
Ninian	2
Carnes, Arthur	19
Clagett, Rd. Keene	30
Cocendofer, Christopher	24
Michael	25
John	3
Michael	2
Carnes, William	25
Cheshire, John	23
Clark, Harmon	47*
Leonard	21
Cowan, Thomas	24
Conwell, Arthur	25
Clark, George	21
Crown, Lancelot	26
Josiah	2
Clark, Thomas	30
Benedict	23
Collings, James	33
John	7
James, Junr	5
Nathan	22
Thomas	13
John	60
Joshua	17
Zechariah	10
Chapple, John	30
William	2
Caster, Vincent	67
William	16
Thomas	10

* Indistinct.

	Years
Clagett, John	63
John, Junr	22
Walter	12
Zadock	8
Chapple, Henry	60
Thomas	21
George	16
Duly, Thomas	36
Duley, Thomas, Junr	1
Duis, Francis	33
Downing, Michael	17
Duckett, Samuel	25
Day, John	8
Douglass, John	10
Robert	8
Earley, Benjamin	43
Ellson, William	21
Evans, Samuel	51
Zechariah	17
John	16
Evans, James	14
George	12
Samuel	9
Flint, Thomas	45
Fulton, Robert	55
James	11
Frederick, George	44
George, Junr	6
Nicholas	2
Fowler, Elisha	42
Elisha, Junr	8
Thomas	6
Glaze, Joseph	64
William	23
Gittings, Benjamin	40
Kinsey	7
Gragg, Joshua	42
Gringul, George	32
Gittings, Jeremiah	30
Colmore	14
Erasmus	1

	Years
Gill, Joseph	49
John	14
Joseph, Junr	13
William	8
Thomas	6
Samuel	1
Greenfield, Walter Smith	45
Charles	15
Thomas	13
Walter, Junr	9
Graves, Thomas	47
Peregrine	26
John	16
Humphrey	13
Joshua	12
George	9
Gilham, Thomas	42
Jacob	13
Benjamin	5
Thomas, Junr	3
John	1
Godfrey, Joseph	19
Hance, Kinsey	24
Harris, Benjamin	34
John Cramphin	3
Higdon, John	60
John, Junr	20
Joseph	17
Peter	11
Hughes, Edward	25
Henman, John	23
Hurley, William	16
Hawkins, John	38
Thomas	7
Hurley, Alexander	7
Harris, George	27
Hackett, Thomas	28
Harp, William	47
William	17
Josiah	14
Erasmus	11

	Years
Harp, Samuel	6
Philip	21
Hurdle, Richard	35
Hardy, Henry	10
Hennes, David	49
John	17
Benjamin	15
Henry	14
Hill, Giles	52
John	1
Hedley, Jacob	25
Hickey, Charles	28
Heugh, Andrew	49
John	11
Andrew, Junr	6
Hurdle, John	9
William	5
Leonard	3
Jackson, John	20
James	17
William	11
Johnston, John	35
Joseph	9
William	11
John	2
Jones, Charles, C. D	64
Henry	27
John Courts	21
Charles Courts	13
Charles, R. C.	65
Jeanes, Henry	23
Janes, Willie	1
Johns, Thomas	39
Richard	1
Karr, Stephen	22
Keizer, Stophel	30
Jacob	8
John	7
Stophel, Junr	1
Kennett, Matthew	25
Keizer, John	37

	Years
Keizer, Jacob	15
John, Junr	1
King, Samuel	23
Lewis, John	4
Lingoe, Thomas	16
John	11
Lewis, Thomas	34
Benedict Woodward	4
Thomas, Junr	2
William	20
William Fardoe	20
Long, James	45
Thomas	17
John	4
Charles	1
Langton, James	43
John	17
James, Junr	11
Thomas	9
William	4
Lanham, Aaron	45
Walter	5
Low, Charles	25
Magruder, Sam Wade	48
Levin	17
Charles	15
Brooke	12
George	10
Patrick	8
Thomas	5
Mulkehy, James	25
Magruder, Nathaniel, of Alex.	50
Walter	16
Aquila	2
McCormack, John	24
James	2
Magruder, Sam Bruce	30
James	8
Ninian	4
Samuel	2

	Years
Magruder, Zechariah	65
Wm. Beall	39
Richard	26
Josiah	24
Normond Bruce	22
Nathaniel	20
Mahall, Stephen	37
Magruder, Elias	50
Samuel 3d	69
John	67
Archibald	25
Ezekiel	19
McCrown, Thos. Hughes	20
Magruder, Edward	33
Ninian	6
John	1
Moore, Andrew	20
Maffatt, Barney	30
William	3
Maccubbin,* Zechariah	25
Thomas	28
Zechariah, Junr	7
Maccattee,* Samuel	22
Charles	16
Murdock, Col. John	42
McDonald, John	30
John	30
William	50
Thomas	3
Maddox, Matthew	26
Masters, William	25
John	1
Mockby, Zechariah	24
Zephaniah	19
John	3
Dennis	1
Mills, Jacob	25
Magruder, Hezekiah	47
Daniel	12
George	10

* These names may be Manubbin and Manattee (?)

	Years
Magruder, Ninian	25
Nathaniel, of Nin	54
Enoch	17
Nathaniel, Junr	15
Middleton, Theodore	17
Mires, Adam	19
Nicholls, James	50
Thomas	9
James, Junr	7
John	4
John	26
Thomas	23
Henry	7
John	4
Odle, Baruch	21
Pierce, Nicholas	40
Poland, William	20
Parker, William, R. C.	45
David	11
William, Junr	7
Rutherford, John	23
Ramington, John	25
James	1
Ridgway, Robert	60
Isaac	24
Jonathan	27
Joseph	22
Riggs, Thomas	9
Reed, George	23
Riley, Walter	24
Ray, James	52
Riggs, Robert	14
James	35
Basil	2
Robertson, Zechariah	11
James	13
Roberts, William	1
Riley, Hugh	50
James	13
George Campden	8
Amos	6

	Years
Riley, Isaac	2
Ray, Thomas	55
Russel, Aaron	17
Robertson, Robert	34
Zechariah	14
Daniel	8
Samuel	2
Nathan	1
Rowan, William	22
Robertson, Nathan	24
Robert	4
Middleton	2
Ross, Alexander	25
Sole, Samuel	25
Scoffield, William	40
William	1
Stephens, Patrick	25
Steel, William	33
Richard	8
William	4
John	2
Shearlock, James	31
Sanndsbery, Thomas	28
Middleton	2
Solomon	1
Sargo, John	18
Steuart, Bryan	27
Sparrow, Jonathan	30
Solomon	10
William	4
Jonathan West	2
Richd. Lewis	1
Benj. Battey	23
Smith, Stephen	43
Matthew	26
Shehone, James	55
Richard	6
Joseph	1
Slicer, Nathaniel	62
James	25
Nathaniel, Junr	2

	Years
Sutton, John	29
Robert	27
Smith, Thomas	26
Summers, William	25
Simmonds, Thomas	20
Smith, David	40
Spyvey, John	35
Jonathan	5
John	1
William	2
Soper, Zadock	25
Smith, John	50
Nicholas	1
Charles	13
Sung, James	15
Speaks, Hezekiah	19
Styles, William	41
John	13
Thomas	11
William, Junr	7
Sullivan, Thomas	23
Summers, William	25
Shoemaker, Joshua	23
Jacob	3
Thomas	1
Servant: William	40
Talbot, William	35
Edward	11
Nathaniel	10
Enock	7
Daniel	4
William, Junr	1
Taylor, William	14
Benjamin	13
Tucker, Edward	56
Alexander	21
Topping, James	62
Thomas, William	24
Tucker, Walter	34
William	10
Rezin	8

	Years
Tucker, Osborn	6
Walter	4
Nathaniel	2
Benjamin	1
Benjamin	22
Joseph	25
John	4
Thompson, David	25
Tucker, Hezekiah	25
Townsend, Joseph	24
Turner, William	22
Talbott, Richard	31
Ummett, George	30
Umphress, John	20
Wallace, Herbert	50
Zepheniah	25
James	24
Herbert Alex	20
William	19
Nathaniel	15
John	8
Wilcoxon, William	43
John	20
Josiah	18
Amos	2
Jesse	38
Thomas	3
Jesse	1
Woodward, John	68
Benedict	22
Walker	15
Benjamin	13
Jonathan	4
George	2
Woodward, Thomas	30
Wood, James	32
Wallace, Nathaniel	22
William	18
James	39
John	5
William	40

	Years
Wallace, Alexander	14
William	12
James	6
Charles	3
Robert	1
Williams, John	48
James	2
Wiser, Michael	17
Wilson, Abraham	1
Young, James	25
Peter	17
Abraham	25
Total	485

WHITE FEMALE

	Years
Adams, Elizabeth	26
Mary	2
Austin, Charity	44
Hezekiah	18
Amelia	8
Mary	80
Adkins, Elizabeth	40
Ann, Mary	12
Benton, Elizabeth	48
Elizabeth	6
Belt, Rebecca	47
Blackmore, Rachel	28
Elizabeth	6
Blacklock, Mary	20
Elizabeth	1
Beasley, Elizabeth	65
Batts, Elizabeth	75
Barber, Elizabeth	39
Mary	16
Dorothy	11
Beall, Anne	42
Elizabeth	12
Anne	5
Violinda	36
Eleanor	10
Lucy	9
Beall, Ann	5
Elizabeth	4
Bonnifield, Sarah	48
Elizabeth	20
Sarah	13
Martha	16
Dorcas	3
Bucey, Eleanor	60
Blockley, Mary	33
Elizabeth	14
Mary	6
Bloyce, Mary	20
Colyar, Sarah	43
Keziah	20
Sarah	15
Elizabeth	13
Lucy	4
Ann	2
Cramphin, Jeane	66
Clagett, Ann	63
Mary	27
Mary	8
Martha	24
Sarah	5
Elizabeth	4
Cocendofer, Hannah	23
Mary	1
Carnes, Aray	18
Canady, Judea	20
Ann	1
Cheshire, Sarah	21
Clark, Mary	38
Elizabeth	2
Elizabeth	29
Crown, Mary	20
Elizabeth	1
Clark, Hannah	32
Grace	12
Rebecca	24
Mary	2
Collings, Jemima	25

	Years
Collings, Cassandra	11
Elizabeth	4
Mary	2
Elizabeth	50
Rachel	24
Chapple, Virlinda	20
Sarah	1
Caster, Elizabeth	52
Margaret	13
Mary	8
Clagett, Sarah	52
Sarah	24
Ann	10
Chapple, Uphane	55
Rebecca	19
Duley, Margaret	20
Dunley, Mary	20
Duckett, Ann	22
Day, Katharine	71
Sarah	40
Mary	16
Douglass, Ann	29
Evans, Margaret	23
Early, Sarah	43
Earley, Rachel	15
Elizabeth	12
Elder, Johannah	57
Sarah	16
Hannah	13
Eleanor	27
Amelia	7
Tressia	5
Hadassy	3
Evans, Ann	50
Hannah	11
Ann	10
Margaret	7
Mary	6
Ruth	5
Rachel	4
Eleanor	3
Ferrol, Margaret	20
Fulton, Mary	48
Frederick, Uney	35
Elizabeth	12
Mary	8
Margaret	4
Molley	10
Fowler, Mary	42
Mary	16
Rachel	14
Rebecca	3
Glaze, Ruth	60
Dorcas	20
Gittings, Ann	36
Amelia	13
Virlinda	11
Elizabeth	5
Sarah	3
Jeane	34
Virlinda	15
Cavia	12
Liley	9
Cassandra	7
Jeane	5
Gregg, Hannah	26
Gill, Ann	49
Sarah	10
Garrott, Katharine	4
Greenfield, Keziah	24
Eleanor	19
Sarah	1
Graves, Jeane	65
Chloe	23
Elizabeth	17
Cassandria	7
Grimes, Lucy	35
Gilham, Mary	38
Elizabeth	14
Margaret	11
Mary	7
Harris, Jeane	30

	Years
Harris, Jeane	5
Rachel	7
Sarah	1
Higdon, Mary	50
Susanna	23
Mary	14
Katharine	8
Hughes, Amelia	24
Hawkins, L. Elizabeth	30
Harris, Katharine	23
Sarah	1
Harp, Priscilla	48
Esther	19
Ann	10
Sarah	1
Hardy, Eleanor	8
Hennes, Sarah	40
Sarah	12
Elizabeth	6
Katharine	2
Hill, Sophia	24
House, Ann	75
Hugh, Sarah	45
Heugh, Elizabeth	21
Sarah	19
Ann	17
Margaret	15
Jeane	12
Mary	8
Harriot	2
Hurdle, Susanna	30
Ann	7
Priscilla	2
Hedley, Ann	30
James, Henrietta	16
Jackson, Mary	45
Mary	16
Susanna	15
Ann	12
Johnston, Ann	16
Sarah	26

	Years
Johnston, Precious	7
Virlinda	2
Ann	36
Elizabeth	13
Sarah	11
Eleanor	9
Ann	1
Esther	30
Ann	13
Jones, Charity	33
Eleanor	13
Malintha	10
Elizabeth	8
Keziah	6
Elizabeth	49
Mary Ann	23
Sarah	19
Henrietta	16
Eleanor Coats	15
Susanna Courts	8
Elizabeth (Servant)	51
Mary	68
Jeanes, Mary	21
Johns, Sarah	25
Mary	3
Keizer, Margaret	30
Rebecca	33
Elizabeth	11
Susanna	8
Ann	4
King, Mary	19
Lingoe, Rachel	14
Lewis, Mary	20
Lee, Lucy	50
Ruth	17
Elizabeth	16
Lucy	12
Long, Ann	45
Mary	9
Langton, Elizabeth	44
Ann	15

	Years
Langton, Elizabeth	13
Eleanor	10
Lanham, Elizabeth	25
Eleanor	4
Elizabeth	2
Magruder, Lucy	38
Elizabeth	20
Ann	19
Sarah	13
Lucy	6
Mary	1
Elizabeth	38
Elizabeth	6
Lethe	4
McCormack, Eve	19
Magruder, Rebecca	30
Charlottee	6
Sarah	56
Elizabeth	18
Mahall, Eleanor	33
Magruder, Rebecca	40
Margaret	65
Jeane	58
Mary	28
Priscilla	4
Maffatt, Susanna	22
Rachel	1
Maccubbin, Martha	28
Mary	1
Hellen	25
Maccatee, Ann	55
Mary	22
Elizabeth	24
Lucy	18
McDonald, Ann	26
Sarah	4
Mary	1
Murphey, Katharine	29
McDonald, Elizabeth	30
Martus, Henrietta	22
Maddox, Rachel	23

	Years
Maddox, Dorcas	2
Masters, Barsheba	23
Margaret	50
Mockby, Ann	24
Joice	9
McGinnis, Alethea	26
Susanna	5
Magruder, Susanna	40
Ann	15
Mary	55
Ann	21
Mary	51
Ann	21
Amelia	12
McCoy, Katharine	13
Needham, Ann	31 (34?)
Sarah	14
Nichols, Charity	30
Susanna	1
Elizabeth	26
Mary Ann	1
Ann	48
Offutt, Ursula	16
Purliven, Elizabeth	30
Parker, Mary	42
Elizabeth	18
Ann	16
Margaret	9
Sarah	5
Amelia	3
Martha	1
Pritchett, Margaret	63
Ridgway, Sarah	50
Jemima	16
Sarah	18
Russel, Mary	26
Reed, Sarah	22
Priscilla	2
Elizabeth	1
Ray, Mary	72
Ann	18

	Years
Riggs, Mary	27
Maxemelia	7
Mary	4
Robinson, Virlinda	32
Riggs, Sarah	50
Riley, Sarah	39
Sarah	18
Eleanor	15
Esther	13
Martha	4
Ray, Jemima	22
Mary	56
Robinson, Rachel	36
Mary	12
Susanna	4
Elizabeth	23
Eleanor	1
Schoffield, Eleanor	25
Steel, Elizabeth	33
Sarah	6
Martha	1
Shearlock, Jeane	37
Sansberry, Elizabeth	35
Sparrow, Elizabeth	30
Tidings	6
Dinah	8
Elizabeth	20
Luranah	3
Mary	1
Shehone, Eleanor	16
Luranah	35
Luranah	14
Ann	12
Lucy	9
Thomason	3
Slicer, Mary	21
Sarah	1
Smith, Sarah	40
Elizabeth	11
Spyvey, Barsheba	25
Ann	4

	Years
Soaper, Ann	26
Mary	5
Rachel	2
Esther	1
Smith, Sarah	48
Ann	9
Rebecca	11
Redy	5
Sarah	20
Steel, Mary	8
Priscilla	5
Susanna	3
Speaks, Mary	18
Elizabeth	41
Styles, Virlinda	33
Sarah	2
Summers, Montha	23
Shoemaker, Mary	21
Thomas, Elizabeth	34
Tucker, Elizabeth	56
Eleanor	14
Topping, Margaret	62
Jude	24
Taylor, Susanna	69
Tucker, Susanna	26
Elizabeth	28
Susanna	2
Elizabeth	1
Elizabeth	31
Mary	35
Truman, Ann	24
Ummell, Elizabeth	25
Weston, Ann	13
Wallace, Eleanor	50
Mary	21
Elizabeth	17
Anne	12
Wilcoxon, Rebecca	44
Elizabeth	17
Rachel	14
Ann	12

	Years
Wilcoxon, Sarah	1
Elizabeth	25
Ruth	4
Woodward, Mary	66
Walker, Vineay	48
Elizabeth	11
Susanna	8
Woodward, Martha	23
Wood, Chloe	37
Sarah	9
Charlotte	5
Ann	2
Wallace, Frances	50
Martha	30
Margaret	27
Mary	25
Barbara	20
Eleanor	29
Eleanor	4
Susanna	35
Mary	16
Eleanor	10
Wallace, Ann	8
Susanna	4
Wilson, Sarah	22
Wager, Jeane	7
Wade, Jeane	23
Whittle, Elizabeth	48
Williams, Elizabeth	22
Mary	5
Weldon, Rachel	3
Young, Eleanor	40
White Female in the whole,	427

BLACK MALE

Anthony 8; Adam 11; Aaron 23; Alex 2; Aaron 4; Adam 2; Anthony 16; etc., etc.—316 given names in all.

BLACK FEMALES

Amelia 7; Alice 5; Alice 7; Alley 23; Amey 13; etc., etc.—300 given names in all.

"A List of the George Town Hundred," Frederick County, Aug. 22, 1776

WHITE MALE	Years
Asbeld, John	22
Branen, Thomas	46
George	19
Thomas	15
Jeremiah	13
John	10
Jesse	5
Samuel	2
Bisbind, James	53
Beall, John	48
S. Sebert	14
Baker, William	27
Samuel Henson	3
Phillip Thomas	1
Belt, Joseph	60
William	21
Barber, Thomas	25
Been, Thomas	18
Borough, Volendine	33
Volendine, Junr	8
Blacamore, Loyd Beall	11
Bulgar, Daniel	17
Borough, Simon	36
John	6
Simon, Junr	4
Volendine	2
Brooks, Thomas	30
Joseph	12
George	12
Thomas	2
Bonser, Joseph Tompson	13
John Tompson	12
James Tompson	7
Barrett, Thomas	33
Becraft, Benjamin, Junr	35

	Years
Cammel, John	17
Carter, William	24
Cokendofer, Federick	22
Casner, Michael	17
Cammel, Gollings	30
Clevley, Henry	40
Chue, Daniel	22
Conley, Thomas	16
Conner, Paull	43
Corner [Conner?] John	6
Collings, Hezekiah	7
Donboch, Frederick	50
Michael	13
Caltron	8
Daley, John	26
Dave, Charles	22
Dixon, William	23
Simon	1
Earp, Caleb	22
Faulks, John	45
Farbairn, Wm.	30
Gussaler, Anthony	40
John	9
George	2
Graver, Philip	27
Jacob	1
Garrin, Daniel	17
Gittings, Levy	1
Hatt, Samuel	58
Hess, Jacob	36
House, John	63
Jingrims, Thomas	23
Kiphart, John	38
John, Junr	12
Jacob	9

	Years
Kiphart, George	5
Phillip	4
Leonard	1
Kirtze, Nicholas	16
Kraus, Theodoris	39
Peter	5
John	2
Jacob	1
Kennerson, John	38
Kizer, Frederick	50
Frederick, Junr	9
John	3
Kurtze, Peter	26
Lanham, William	23
Lingan, Nicholas	17
Linenbery, Nicholas	48
Benjamin	6
John	1
Lange, Peter	22
Lingan, James	22
Joseph	1
Leech, Jeremiah	27
McKenery, Thomas	30
John	4
James	2
Manen, James	35
Moses, Robert	35
Murphey, William	27
Mounce, John	36
John, Junr	4
Jacob	2
Mungle, Michael	29
Mirey, Frederick	13
McFercen, William	10
Monger, William	22
Murphey, Antoney	28
McFadden, Alexander	25
Morry, James	27
Milley, Jacob	18
Messor, Thomas	7
Marques, Kidd	32

	Years
Marques, James	6
William	4
Paul, Nicholls	38
Petor	9
Jacob	8
Pringle, John	28
Putty, Charles	8
Purdy, Thomas	14
Pearce, Benjamin Nolley	48
Pasley (Pafley ?) John	36
Petor, John	20
Robert	50
Robert, Junr	19
Thomas	8
Alexander	7
Robert	3
Risoner, Jacob	26
Rigdon, Thomas	29
Right, Henry	21
Rigdon, John Edward	4
Ravenscroft, John	42
Rowen, Daniel	22
Roberts, Arthur	28
Roberson, Zachariah	15
Runhel, Valentine	56
Daniel	20
Valentine, Junr	15
John	9
Randle, John	39
Richardson, Thomas	35
Stewardweall, William	25
Smith, John	2
Schoolfield, Andrew	14
Joseph	15
Summers, Thomas	25
Schoolfield, Issachar	10
Maland	6
John	55
Smith, Walter	32
Walter, Junr	3
Patrick	2

	Years
Smith, Clement	18
Sloven, William	16
Sisor, Joseph	8
Stonestreet, Butlar	19
Siles, John	50
John, Junr	6
Jacob }	4
George }	4
Sweeny, Major	32
Threlkield, Henry	60
Threlkild, John	17
Tucker, Thomas	59
John	13
David	5
Trissoler, Jacob	32
George	4
John	2
Jacob, Junr	1
Tomson, Richard	38
Taylor, Richard	15
Upright, Jacob	54
Vessel, Even	25
Wise, John	36
John, Junr	6
Winard, Abraham	4
Winbargle, George	30
John	6
Jacob	4
Waggoner, John	22
Wickel, Adam	19
Wingle, John	5
Wilson, William	20
Wingal, Lazurus	27
Lazuress, Junr	7
Yates, Joseph	26
Youst, Tobias	21
Phillip	14
John	33
John, Junr	5
Young, Thomas	33
George	28
Young, Thomas, Junr	1
William	15
Youst, Casbery	64
White Male, the whole	197

WHITE FEMALE

	Years
Adley, Elizabeth	30
Anderson, Rachel	20
Mary	45
Branen, Elizabeth	39
Mary	17
Bisbend, Eles	60
Bores, Ann	13
Beall, Mary	36
Ruth	13
Mary	21
Baley, F. Susanna	25
Bayley, P. Mary	6
Brigg, Mary	50
Brotan, Elizabeth	19
Baley, Ann	20
Baker, Mildred	30
Belt, Esther	53
Ann	25
Barber, Ann	18
Borough, Margaret	26
Sarah	5
Margaret	2
Elizabeth	1
Margaret	32
Elizabeth	1
Brooks, Mary	26
Amelia	9
Bonser, Christian	44
Bramley, Elizabeth	20
Barrett, Mary	25
Ann	1
Cammel, Ann	21
Martha	14
Conner, Eleanor	25
Casner, Christian	22

	Years
Colbrock, Harriott	21
Corner, Margaret	31
Susanna	10
Margaret	7
Febe	5
Elizabeth	2
Mary	1
Cammel, Ann	19
Clarion, Mary	3
Chew, Cassandra	47
Donboch, Elizabeth	48
Elizabeth	18
Mary	6
Drusilla	2
Duncastle, Sarah	20
Daley, Elizabeth	27
Dixon, Ann	20
Ellett, Marthe	41
Gussaler, Katharine	28
Rebecca	10
Elizabeth	5
Katherine	4
Mary	1
Graver, Katherine	28
Margaret	7
Elizabeth	3
House, Margaret	50
Harmon, Margaret	66
Hatt, Susanna	50
Hess, Barbary	29
Jinnings, Lucy	19
Johnston, Mary	16
Jinkins, Elizabeth	26
Kiphart, Susanna	34
Elizabeth	13
Katherine	8
Kraus, Dorothy	30
Susanna	11
Katherene	8
Kizer, Elizabeth	40
Elizabeth	16
Kizer, Katharine	14
Susanna	12
Margaret	11
Christine	7
Kagan, Margaret	22
Linnenbery, Christene	30
Rusener	14
Elizabeth	10
Mary	4
Lewis, Martha	50
McKenery, Mary	26
Margaret	1
Moses, Margaret	25
McCloud, Sarah	8
Mounce, Elizabeth	30
Katharine	8
Elizabeth	1
Messay, Evey	8
Mungle, ———	22
Murphey, Elizabeth	26
Rebecca	1
Messor, Alse	25
Marques, Eleanor	30
Mary	2
Orme, Lucy	53
Ruth	15
Eleanor	15
Paul, Elizabeth	26
Margaret	10
Elizabeth	4
Pearce, Ann	3
Petor, Elizabeth	33
Elizabeth	6
Margaret	1
Risoner, Elizabeth	20
Mary	2
Eleanor	14
Rigdon, Mary	36
Runhel, Sarah	54
Mary	13
Katharine	11

	Years
Ready, Sophiah	11
Strannum, Mary	20
Smith, Mary	30
Scholfield, Rachel	46
Ann	18
Smith, Esther	31
Elizabeth	1
Siles, Ann	30
Susanna	1
Smith, Margaret	31
Servant—Ann	24
Threlkild, Mary	58
Tucker, Mary	52
Mary	10
Trissoler, Mary	23
Elizabeth	7
Taylor, Margaret	67
Upright, Katharine	52
Vessel, Eleanor	15
Wise, Elizabeth	30
Katharine	4
Elizabeth	1
Winard, Elizabeth	21
Elizabeth	1
Wiseam, Elizabeth	17
White, Katharine	39
Winbargle, Margaret	30
Susanna	1
Wingal, Elizabeth	28
Elizabeth	1
Youst, Eleanor	58
Susanna	17
Rebecca	27
Katharine	7
Elizabeth	2
Mary	4
Young, Sarah	19

White Female, the whole 154

BLACK MALE

Andrew 1; Adam 4; Able 2—etc., 44 single names in all.

BLACK FEMALE

Ann 33; Age 12; Bett 2; Babb 1; Cass 58; Charity 17—etc. 38 single names in all.

Number of Souls, With Names and Ages, ——— Hundred, Frederick County, Maryland, August 1776: Section now Embraced in Montgomery County*

	Age
Dowden, Thomas	31
Johnas	5
Archabald	6 mos.
John, St.	17
Sary (?)	25
Martha	7
Richd. (?)	3
Jones, Mary, St.	23
Davis, Bexly	22
Poly Carp	8
Joseph	3
Elizabeth	31
Maryan	6
Elizabeth	1
Hickman, Arthur	63
Margt.	11
(Illegible)	35
Mary	63

Peter a Negroe 56; illegible 25
Nancy 11; John 9; Samson 7;
Peter 3; Hannah 30; Ruth 7.

Meginias, Neal	30
Thomas	2 mos.
Catarin	22
Mary	5
Alleyfar	2
Brandon, Abraham St.	22
Patience, a Negroe	12

	Age
Hickman, William	30
Rossel	2
Jean	25
Bety	1
Ruth, a Negroe	30
Watson, Samuel	48
Elkanah	20
Sary G.	11
Sary	49
Lucy	15
Rebecca	8
Elizabeth	4
Dyer, Jonathan	21
Jackson, Bennett	48
Jafaras	15
John	18
Sary	54
Ellenner	16
Warker, Thomas	39
William	9
Cassandra	28
Virlinder	5
Lovlis, Benjamin	49
Eleanah	21
Barton	19
Zadock	16

* Sheets before unidentified in the *Archives of Maryland* (Md. Hist. Soc.), and evidently including part of the Montgomery County portion of Frederick County (Old). The name of the Hundred has not yet been identified. Spaces indicate family, or plantation, divisions—G. M. B.

	Age
Lovlis, Reson	12
Benjn	2
Sary	41
Sary	6
Willson, Mary	23
George	30
William	8
Michel	6
George	4
Lidia	26
Elisabeth	1
Hools, Joseph	37
Shaw, Benjamin	13
Hibbey, John	8
Robey, Elizabeth	56
Shaw, Dorraty	20
Gentle, Stephen	66
George	23
Stephen	21
John	15
William	10
Samuel	8
Sary	52
Mary	23
Ellender	17
Dianna	13
John, an infant	4 mos.
Owen, John	70
Owen, Thomas	17
Riggs, Charles	5
Owen, Elizabeth	68
Riggs, Ann	33
Colliar, Elizabeth	24
Riggs, Mary	8
Jancy a Negroe 30—Clar	2
Dowel, Phillip	24
Bachelder	4

	Age
Dowel, Prissiller	22
Elisabeth	3
Allay	1
Robinson, James	49
Charles	12
John	7
Susey	36
Ann	16
Mary	14
Elisabeth	10
Charity	4
Sary	2
Ale, Robert	14
Sinclear, Dunkin	26
Mary	18
Robinson, John	33
William	9
Carlos	7
Tolbert, George	16
Rockford, Edward	28
Robinson, Jaen	31
Tolbart, Basil	22
Mary	44
Robinson, Elisabeth	1
Briggs, William	36
Catron	6
Mary	4
Ann	1
Ashen, Ellender	39
Samuel	16
William	12
John	14
James	8
Rigney, Terance	30
Lusey	25

Name	Age
Rigney, Ann	2
Sambo a Negroe 48; Jose 16—Heney 20.	
Walter, David	35
Thomas, Notley	21
Marten, John	21
Brannen, Lawrence	21
Marten, Samuel	10
Walter, Stephen	4
Ann	26
Mearet, Margaret	18
Green, Sary	5
Walter, Sary	2
Arnold, Joseph	33
Ellenner	35
Talbert, Ellenner	14
Ann	9
Notley	19
Lewis	12
Leven	6
Reson	3
Case, Israel	27
John	4
Margaret	22
Lowrey, John	20
Dyson, Philip	30
Mash,	20
Rabaca	1
Smith, Johanah	6
Mcdaniel, William	47
William, Junr	23
Hennary	19
Daniel	6
Ann	47
Linder	16
Mary	13
Mcdaniel, Ann	3
Poplin, Elisabeth, St.	29
Hannah, a Negroe	40
Mcdanniel, Elisabeth	23
Hoskinson, Mary	16
Fyffe, James, Senr	63
James, Junr	23
Jonathan	21
John	16
Sary	56
Elisabeth	18
Abija	30
James	8
Daniel	8 mos.
Ellenner	25
Elisabeth	5
Sary	3
Will a Negroe 50; Sam 40; Little Sam 35; James 15; Will 6; Joe 5; Ned 4 mos.—Phillis 30; Hester 20; Ann 3.	
Fyffe, Joseph	25
Samuel	5
William	3
Drusiller	25
Sary	1
Burk, John	30
Jacob a Negroe 25; Joe 18; Andrew 13; Harry 1; Beck 20. Mary Brown 14—Wm. Brown 4 mos.	
Neall, Doct. Charles	71
Ralph	36
Will a Negroe 70; Humphra 55; Ned 34; Charles 35; Joe 71; Ned 5; Ralph 2—Sary 60; Sang 35; Bett 20; Nell 12; Hester 7; Mary 50.	

Name	Age
Henry, Daniel	21
Elizabeth	19
Been, 66—Terry, 50.	
Lanner, Thomas	23
Longenston, Daniel	46
Cleckett, Nin'n	26
Windham, George	16
Elizabeth	52
Robert	9
Clear, a Negro W. 12.	
Heard, Bennet	25
Swann, Zephaniah	36
Jesse	1 mo.
Mary	25
Orpha	5
Anna	2
Short, Richard	22
McCanna, Patrick, St.	18
Barker, Elisabeth	18
Smith, Nathan	41
Ali	19
Archabald	16
Leander	14
Benja	9
Nathan	4
Rebaca	44
Preshey	12
Drusiller	10
Roda	3
Sweatman, Susannah	23
Randell, Elisabeth	50
Purdom, John	37
Walter	11
Joshuah	9
Kesiah	36

Name	Age
Purdom, Kisiah	4
Henna	7
Love, Leonard	30
Thomas	27
Levy	1
Elisabeth	35
Ann	8
Sary	5
Elisabeth	3
Cole, Barnett	26
Tunons (?)	3
William	1
Susannah	19
Veares, Nehemiah	43
Daniel	20
Brice	12
Elisha	10
Basil	3
Luranar	39
Sary	17
Elisabeth	15
Ann	13
Ellender	11
Cassandra	2
Case, Jean	58
More, Mary	24
Case, Elizabeth	22
More, Martha	4 mos.
More, Nathon	27
Samuel	25
Jack a Negroe 21.	
Dyson, Matdox	32
Bennett	8
Aquely	6
John	3
Jean	40

	Age
Dyson, Mary	1
Mary	56
Swann, Thomas	15
Ann	10
Clark, Nester	38
Prilley a Negroe 56.	
Dyson, Zaphaniah	26
Thomas	18 mos.
Dorraty	19
Veares, Capt. William	41
Lien	17
William	15
John	13
Edward	12
Heszakiah	8
Solomon	6
Levy	4
Mary	36
Levy	7
A infant.	
Woodfield, Mariar	19
Rose a Negroe 38.	
Purdey, Richard	45
Catron	33
Ann	13
Richard	1
Darnold, John	40
Cornelas	14
William	12
Hennary	10
Thos.	7
Ezekil	5
Rubin	1
Marion	31
Rebeca	8
Prissillar	2
Silber a Negroe	13

	Age
Mccray, Zaphaniah	30
Allnutt, Jesse	63
William	20
John	15
Joseph	13
Talbart	7
Daniel	6 mos.
Jean	40
Mary	19
Susanna	17
Rebeca	11
Drummer a Negroe 46—Luce 30.	
Allnutt, James	25
Virlinder	20
Sary	1
Patience a Negro 12.	
Dyson, Sam	33
John	11
Lydia	31
Mary	9
Sary	5
Darkes	2
Walters, William	15
Allnutt, Lawrence	26
Ellender	25
Ellender	3
Mary	1
Nan a Negro 15.	
Allnutt, Jesse	31
Ann	25
Sary	1
Mary Ruth	19
Charles a Negroe 9.	
Jones, Thos.	25
Thos.	2

Name	Age
Jones, Mary	22
Susanna	3
Nisbet, Charles	55
Barnett	17
Ann	22
Ellenner	20
Catron	15
Mary	13
Lydea	9
Metarer, Betsey	19
Burtler, Andrew	33
Susanna	23
Ellennder	5
Elisabeth	1
Lewis, Elisabeth	61
Ellenner	15
George	23
Abraham	2
Mary	19
Denton, James	29
Messicopp, Christopher	24
George	19
John	3
Margaret	33
Mary	1
Kiltey, Frances	17
Howel, Joseph	33
Harbin, James	50
Joshuah	21
Jarratt	15
Elias	13
Ellenner	47
Mary	7
Darkes	5
Norman, Phillip	76
Larnan, Ann	18
Case, Hester	20

Name	Age
Tucker, Jonathan	38
Leonard	12
Edward	10
James	4
Mary	30
Darkis	8
Miltrue	6
Sary	1
Truman, Richard	28
Sutten, William	41
Jack a Negroe 16—Teary 12.	
Currenton, John	42
Hopkins, Ann	25
Ward, Benja	22
Pomp a Negroe 40; Neo 40; Charles 13; Hack 13; David 7.	
Lewis, Saml	35
John	3
Mary	26
Margaret	8
Ann	6
Susanna	2
Ellett, March	50
Benja	20
Joseph	18
Mark	15
Richard	6
John	4
Kissiar	39
Elisabeth	13
Ann	8
Kassa	7 mos.
Tiffendale, Mary	25
Andrew a Negro 27.	
Dennair, William	40
Mary	39

	Age
McDaniel, Elisha	21
Mary	15

Sam a Negroe 30; Sam, Junr. 4; Moses 4; Dick 2; Jacob 2 mos.; Silby 30; Patt 24; Nan 4; Kis 3.

	Age
Locker, Patrick	40
Jesse	10
John	7
Elisabeth	4
Ellenner	2
Holland, Joel	27
Lydia	26
Steall, William	67
James	26
John	21
Saml	19
Joseph	3
William	1
Elisabeth	48
Mary	28
Mary	14
Elisabeth	7
Margaret	4
Farguson, John	53
Daniel	19
Elias	16
Reson	14
Mordecai	12
Ellenner	55
John	26
Mary	24
Elisabeth	4
Ellenner	2
Whalen, Daniel	30
Rabaca	20

Will a Negroe 27; Jack 27—Priss 20; Patt 2; Priss 1.

	Age
Downden, Michel	39
Ward, Matten	17
Beard, William	7
Beall, Edward	13
William	10
Dowden, Elisabeth	40
Robinson, Mary	20

Toney a Negroe 46.

	Age
Williams, James	23
Davis, William	30
Byrn, Charles	29
Beegding, Hennary	27
Hutts, Andrew	36
Cartwright, Saml	42
Walter, Levy	27
Woodyard, Jesse	25
Taylor, John	24
Gillom, John	23
Stalons, William	19
Gentle, George	23
Hopkins, Leven	35
Stephen	4

Ruth a Negroe 9.

	Age
Hennary, John	27

Name	Age
Lucas, Chas.	29
Lindoes	18
Richard	2
Susanna	26
Nancy	4
Jamima	3
Mary	3 mos.
Orne, Michel	9

Name	Age
Young, John	33
William	7
Benjamin	3
Kessiah	29
Nancy	7 mos.

Joe a Negroe 25; Bobb 16—Dyner 19; Racel 6 mos.

Name	Age
Lucas, Thos	25
Kissiah	26
Woodyard, John	20

Bobb a Negroe 1; Feby 26; Siegn 3.

Name	Age
Hoskinson, George	25

Name	Age
Locker, Joseph	43
Shaderick	18
Joseph, Junr	14
Lusey	47
Virlinder	17
Marick, John	16
Tolbart, Ellenner	30
Rebaca	8

Feeb a Negroe 8.

Name	Age
Johnson, Batholomew	35
Joseph	6
John	4
Iisbell	35
Rebaca	9
Iisbell	2

Name	Age
Lintrage, Saml	27

Name	Age
Hyser, Martain	25

Name	Age
Hardey, Zadock	20
Mary	29

Prince a Negroe 24.

Name	Age
Miles, John	37
Nicholas	10
James	4
Mary	42
Elisabeth	6
Baker, Bartain	21

Name	Age
Lewis, Richard	27
Hyrom	3
Ann	21

Name	Age
Blackmore, Saml	40
James	12
Saml. Junr	5
William	2
Abriller	35
Ellenner	17
Mary	16
Elisabeth	14
Ann	10
Amma	8
An infant 1 month.	
Heughes, John	34
Hennabon, Patrick	19
Lockton, Michel	18

Clear a Negroe 35; Cass 11; Lidia 6; Dillila 4; Lettes 2.

Name	Age
Allison, Charles	25

Name	Age
Swearinger, Van	29
Leonard	9
Samuel	5

Name	Age
Swearinger, Clemmcy	2
Lacy	34
Mary	7
Servants	
hortley, John	29
ford, Ralph	23
Byrn, Matthias	33
Patrick	1
Martha Ann	22
Mary	50
Catharine	22
Clementena	18
Mary	15
Verlinder	13
Curtin, John	17
Margarate a Negroe 42; Lucey 43.	
Jewell, William	35
Bassel	11
William	2
Ann Tabitha	38
Rebecak	15
Amay	7
Betty	5
Rose 33.	
Hickman, William	21
Stephen	14
Richard	12
Jeane	18
Ann	16
James a Negroe 14; Jesse 4—Dark 24; Lib ?; Eave 2.	
Arnold, William	35
John	6
Ann	26
Elisabeth	11
Mary	8
Arnold, Anna	3
Infant, 2 months.	
Robertson, Andrew Green	22
Beeding, Joseph	25
Beeding, Edward	35
Jacob	8
John	5
Solomon	2
Tabitha	25
Gillum, Thomas	23
Thompson, William	37
John	15
William	8
Joseph	1
Susanah	37
Susanah	6
Nancy	3
Perryman, Richard	45
Ellgin, Mary	12
Woodgerd, William	32
John	6
Jisse	3
William	1
Dennis	21
Elisabeth	23
Jene	4
Jerry	26
Chilton, Mark	22
Draper, William	22
Thomas, Martin	25
Campbell, Eneas, Senr	46
Eneas, Junr	18
Magrate	45

	Age
Campbell, Hester	17
Lidia	15
Ann	8
Ketty White	4 mos.
Connor, Cattrine	20
Linn, Barbra	23

Sam a Negroe 35; Tom 15; Sam 16; Jack 18; Phill 17—Monica 48; Sary 65; Pegg 48; Christian 25; Mill 14; Nell 12; Eve 7; Cass 3.

Hickman, Gilbert	7
Lidia	10
Tall (Lall?), Arthur	28
Benj	4
Pentacast	3
Maryann	33
Melarve, John	25
Osben, Hannah	19
Fealds, Joseph	33
Thompson, John	13
Fowller, Ann	28
Elisabeth	10
Hennaritter	8
Fealds, Mathew	41
Fealds, James	35
William	5
Joseph	3 mos.
Martha	23
Sary	3
Landard, Johnana	27
Flether, Abraham	51
George	29
John	13
Elias	3

	Age
Flether, Prisilla	47
Hannah	34
Sary	24
Betty	20
Pressella	16
Rachel	6 mos.
Carsey, Daniel	24
Ann	23
Elisabeth	14
Ealce	8
Sary	5
An infant, a week.	
Eales	49
Ferguson, Basil	21
Beckwith, Mary	1
Ann	29
William	6
Jones, Joseph	40
Osborn, Ann	42
Mary	12
David	14
Benja	21
Wallace, Mathew	45
Fedrick, Grace	30
Milkey	10
Walter, Clement	32
Rebaca	32
Sary	2
Elisabeth	6 mos.
Hardesty, Hennary	10
Miller, Thomas	15
Stallons, Margaret	13
Green, Mary	10
Mcintoush, Alexander	47
Alexsander	11

	Age
Mcintoush, William	9
Lowre	7
Macke	5
Benja	3
Ann	40
Ellender	12

Culley a Negroe 36; Boson 33; George 30; Peter 22—Febey 30; Rachel 16.

Johnjones, John	20

Poldore a Negroe 28; Charles 18; Tom 16; Frank 7—Betty 60; Mill 20; Sall 18.

Evens, William	52
Mary	41
Essex, Elisabeth	13
Davis, Joseph	25
Farguson, Nathaniel	22
Peggey	21
Prissilla	1
Barlow, John	31
Zachariah	3
Ann	21
Zachariah	66
Mary	78
Susanna	29
Elisabeth	21
Martain, Virlinder	7
Davis, Efrom	41
Jaramiah	4
Darkis	35
Anna	8
Mary	6
Nansey	3

	Age
Dickson, John	52
William	19
John	17
Zachariah	3
Hannah	44
Mary	14
Ruth	8
Ellenner	6
Susanna	1
Elgin, Christopher	63
Jesse	8
John	6
William	1
Mary	34
Ann	14
Mary	13
Anabella	10
Cloe	3
Duglace, William	37
Saml	13
George	8
William	6
Sue	10
Haris, John	23
Robert	2
Vinaford	32

Ben a Negroe 13—Sal 9; Rachel 4.

Walter, George	88
Thomas	5
Mary	37
Elisabeth	15
Sary	13
Rebaca	11
Mary	8
Osborn, Thomas	13

Nan a Negroe 24; Pris 24; Lid 6; Diner 4; Nell 1.

	Age
Crips, Edward	25
Jones, Lewis	37
James	10
Jeane	28
Elisabeth	7
Backster, Gabriel	30

Old Dick a Negroe 90; Vinser 60; James 5—Hannah 70; Bett 33; Jean 30; Sall 21; Lib 14; Nan 7; Bett 5; Charity 5; Nell 1; Mime 6 months; Phill 14.

	Age
Jewel, Arnay, (Amay?)	64
John	3
Elisabeth	6
Sary	1
Backster, Betty	27

Sam a Negroe 25—Peg 24; Peg 1.

	Age
Hickman, Prisilla	48
Chilton, Mary	37
Jewell, Jonathan	14
Elisha	12
George	10
David	5
Smallwood	1
Mary	3

Nan a Negroe 26; Sary 7; Jean 3; Phillis 2; Samson 5—Sam 2 mos.

	Age
Hall, Sillar	30
Margaret	12
Ann	10
Mary	5
Susan	4
Elisabeth	2 mos.
Basil	7

	Age
Howman, Benja	36
Isaac	10
Benja	8
Stayson	6
Jesse	5
Martha	21
Elisabeth	3
Maxley, John	31
John	1
ann	25
Susanna	8
Elisabeth	4
Ann	48
Daniel	17
Sillavin, Philip	30

Jude a Negroe 32—George 14; Jack 9; Cate 7; Patt 4—Spence 2.

	Age
Fagin, John	25
Howley, William	22
Walter, John	43
John	11
Daniel	5
Sary	39
Crips, Mary	21

George a Negroe 20; Tom 6; James 4 mos.—Meriar 30.

	Age
Rigeaway, William	30
John	1
Sary	31
Elisabeth	5
Hathaliah	3

Kitt a Negroe 15.

	Age
Gatten, James	38
Azariah	14

Age

Gatten, Elisha.................. 7
Mary.................. 35
Rebaca.................. 10
Elisabeth.................. 3
Will a Negroe 16.

Botts, Aron.................. 68
Margaret.................. 58
Susannah.................. 23
Francis.................. 18

Hunter, Joshua.................. 26
Sary.................. 28
Martha.................. 3
Mary.................. 1
Otten, John.................. 28
James a Negroe 27; Absolon 18; George Beall 20—Feeb a Negroe 42; Sue 31; Bett 13; Vine 7; Dafna 3; Lusey 10 months—Charles 20; Jack 7; Sam 6 mos.

Bright, Fannah.................. 22
Margaret.................. 3

Allison, John.................. 36
John.................. 2
Hennary, an infant.
Mathew.................. 30
Osiller.................. 8
Rachel.................. 5

Henwood, Ann.................. 26
Azariah.................. 2

Chilton, James.................. 36
John.................. 7
Jesse.................. 4
James.................. 1
Ann.................. 28
Sary.................. 8
Hall, Richard.................. 18

Age

Collop, George.................. 20
George a Negroe 27; Flower 25; Will 2—Lusey Barlay 4 —Jack, 1 month.

Jones, Daniel.................. 45

Green, John.................. 50
Thomas.................. 23
Isaac.................. 21
William.................. 10
Jamima.................. 45
Dianna.................. 19
Martha.................. 13

Franklin, Joseph.................. 46
William.................. 19
Barker.................. 15
Zaphaniah.................. 9
Maryan.................. 46
Ann.................. 12
Benedicter.................. 5
Driver, Edward.................. 20

Hurnman, Jacob.................. 30
Thomas.................. 4
William.................. 12
Saml.................. 10
John.................. 3
Allexeander.................. 1
Ann.................. 30

Taylor, John.................. 28
Delitha.................. 20
Ann.................. 1
Hickman, Elihu.................. 15
Mary.................. 14
Joshuah.................. 12
Samn a Negroe 37; Samson 33; George 22—Merear 50; Vin 14; Rett 12; Nell 8; Jean 18; Beck 4; Bett 13.

	Age
Wilkerson, William	27
Chitton, Thomas	24
Suffiah	20
Barlow, Bettey	5
Cartwright, Thomas	50
John	7
Barbary	30
Beard, Jean	18
Richards, John	23
Lawder, Mary	17

Joe a Negroe 23; Jacob 6 mos. —Jean 20; Nell 3; Cloe 18.

Rigg, Benja	45
Charles	11
Benja	4
Rebaca	13
Ann	8
Hennaritta	2
Davis, William	22
Cassadra	16
Saml	24
Hennary	3
Levisa	35
Ann	1

Samson a Negroe 70—Sary 40; Moll 12; North, James, Servant 36.

Williams, Andrew	36
William	6
Allen, Archabald	35
Elisabeth	34
Elisabeth	5
Woodgard, Ann	22

Seser a Negroe 30; Sie 21; Jack 12; Primas 7—Vilett 20; Beck 8.

	Age
Sible, James	25
Harwood, John	32
Gasaway W	3
John H., infant.	
Mary	23

Jacob a Negroe 28; Benn 18; Tom 8; Peter 2–Moll 30; Poll 22; Viller 16; Nan 12; Lusey 7; Pegg 5; Jean 2; Hester an infant.

Green, Phillip	22
Ann	26
Mary	1
Yates, Mary	66
Newton, Mary	38
James	7

Suck a Negroe 15.

Lazenby, Robert	26
Thomas	21
Joshua	1
Margery	25
McCarty, Flurrance	21
Elles, John	24
John, Junr	3
Mary	21
Prisila	52
Zachariah	43
Shadrack	21
Christopher	12
Zacha., Junr	1
Ann	43
Elisabeth	17
William	17
Rule	15
Ann	8
Charity	6

Negro Moll 49; Led 14—George 10.

	Age
Luckett, John	25
Phillip H.	10 mos.
Moley Ann	21
Mcdaniel, John	24
Wats, James	14
Fitchgarrel, Margaret	25
Barbary, Ann	15

Frank a Negroe 25; Peter 17; Joe 14; Butler 2—Florer 24.

Burn, Adom	40
William	14
Sary	12

Bob a Negroe 26; Add 17; Will 13; Fender 75–Grace 45; Bess 27; Fann 11.

McCullugh, James	26

Mires, Conrod	38
John	11
Margaret	45
Mary	10
Lestenbarro, Hennary	16
Solomon, John	30

Harding, Walter	22
Elias	4 mos.
Mary	26
Anna	1

Frank a Negroe 30; Joseph 5; Ben 3; Nace 2—Nan 30; Nell 8.

Green, Benedict	34
Francis	4
Margaret	35
Cloe	7
Jean	6 mos.
David	20

	Age
Davis, Ann	62
Susanna	40
Ann	36
Cresey	29
Aza	38
Moses	8
Azariah	2
Rohdom	2 mos.

Nobbs, John	64
Hennary	26
Elisabeth	58
Nansey	17

Hardey, Fielder	40
Sary	17
Rebaca	12
Fealder	10
Mary	9
Elisabeth	7
Barbary	3
Elias	15
Kenzey	14
Saml	5
Self, John	16

Williams, John	48
John J	17
Rezen	11
Thomas	9
Jesse	6
Daniel	4
Sary	44
Ellenner	15
Prissilla	12
Cassander	6
Sary	2
Lalar, Hennary	24
Mccomb, John	21

Jones, Phillip	24
Elisabeth	24

	Age
Jones, Susanna	1
Joseph	23
Elisabeth	22
Sary	2
Margaret, 18 months.	

Dick a Negroe 44; Jack 33—Backeas 21; Peter 1—Charity 31; Hester 30; Rose 18; Clea 16; jone 13; pol 4.

Wallase, William	52
Susanna	57
Rilay, Danais	10
Fanning, Thomas	37
Bowan, John	29

Draper, John	62
Ellener	40
Elisabeth	14
Ann	4

Fennamoe, William	65

Henson, Patrick	30

Edelin, Thos	26
Bartholomew	28
Monica	24
Ann	1

Phillis 18; Nell 10; Jeane 1.

Luckett, Capt. William	65
Charity	59
Virlider	29
Susanna	18
Leven	13
Walch, Mary, servant	34

Harrey a Negroe 35; Dick 29; Sago 24; Teary 24; Joe 21; Charles 20; Phill 24; Benn 16; Natt 13; Nace 12; Benn 9; Dick 6; Jim 4; Nace 2; Solomon 1—Nell 32; Nann 30; Hannah 25; Floer 25; Clear 25; Dill 10; Nell 2.

	Age
Beggerly, Charles	25
Isaac	5
Saml	3
Ann	22

Warker, James	39
William	5
Archa'd	1
Elisabeth	8

Hocker, William, Senr	55
William	24
Susanna	60
Margaret	21
Dianner	19
Elisabeth	15
Swann, Heza	7

Charles a Negroe 45.

Duglace, Saml	33
Heza	11
John	8
Charles	4
Rebaca	27
Elisabeth	6
Mary	2
Ann	9 mos.
Hoskison, Ruth	16

Beeding, Thomas	37
William	9
James	7
Thomas, Junr	5
Mary	34
Susanna	3
Elisabeth	3

	Age
Biggs, Saml.	46
Hannrator	47
McGlocklanen, Mary	30

Mollow a Negroe 35; Bob 11; Jack 2; Dick 4 mos.—Jude 24; Nan 9; Stace 7; Moll 3.

	Age
Dyson, Basil	27
George	3
Jamima	27
Margaret	1
Taylor, Griffin, servant	28
Belt, Carlton	32
Watson	7
Carlton	2 mos.
Mary	32
Molley	2
Neall, Thomas	34
Baker, John	31
Adams, Thomas	33
Head, William	26
Chiliten, William	24
Riley, Patrick	24
Evens, Sary, Sarvents	26

Dafuy a Negroe 45—Poll 15; Jean 9; Charity 4—Jim 14; Bill 2.

	Age
Tully, James	33
John	3
Ann	33
Ellenner	8
Mary	5
Elisabeth	1
Peddicoat, Nicholas	26
Morrow, John	24
Roach, Richard	22
Kirck, William	13
Willson, Josiah	45
Absolon	14
Thomas	7
James	1
Jamima	35
Nansey	13
Rebacah	4
Willson, William	43
Heza	12
Elisabeth	33
Sary	10
Elisabeth	8
Mary	6
Margaret	4
Priscilla	2

Ned a Negroe 12—Nell a Negroe 17—Bob 16—Dyner 3.

	Age
Warner, Saml.	57
Hennary	3
Druslla	16
Mary	10
Haes, William	25

Ned a Negroe 27—Alexander 6.

	Age
Shabord, Saml.	31
Saml., Junr	8
Benony	5
Middleton	3
Sary	25
Rachel	7
Sary	1 mo.
Fealds, George, St.	32
Veatch, Ninian, Junr	51
Nin	21
John	19
James	18
Solomon	15
Elisabeth	46
Jamima	13

	Age
Tobey a Negroe 15.	
Seares, James	78
Elisabeth	70
Hickman, Sary	13
Bec a Negroe 32—Adom 15; Tobe 9.	
Seares, William, Junr	48
James	16
William	14
Israel	12
John	10
Elias	7
Joshua	6
Elisabeth	36
Prissilla	13
Anna	1
Mary, an infant.	
Power, Nicholas	32
Veatch, Richard	34
Sary	37
Rebaca	11
Matha	2
Russell, Thomas	18
Andrew a Negroe 5.	
Willson, Wodsworth	51
James	16
Leven	3
Ellenner	49
Francis	24
Mary	14
Ellenner	9
Peter a Negroe 50; Pomp 12; Beckwith 11; George 6—Bess 35; Teny 8; Bett 1.	
Veatch, Thomas	40
Elijah	14

	Age
Veatch, Hensenk	12
John T	10
Thomas	4
Lurana	31
Barshaba	8
Mary	1 mo.
Phillips, Jesse	12
Amos	7
Howard, Thomas	3
Sary	2
Conner, Mary, St	22
Mahannah, Ellenner, St	20
Margaret	1
Conner, Richard	3
Frances	4 mos.
Eve a Negroe 34; Rose 17; Suck 12; Ruth 7; pasience 4—Ned 2.	
Veatch, Grase	60
Silas	45
William	20
Silas	9
Lander	7
Jean	45
Kissiah	16
Susanna	14
Cate a Negroe 40—Bess 12; Sall 8; Amay 6.	
Gatten, James	38
John	15
Richard	14
Thomas	12
James	5
Zachariah	2
Elisabeth	41
Susanna	16
Elisabeth	10
Anna	8
Virlinder	6

	Age
Hannah a Negroe 35; Moll 20; Cate 12—Swan 21; Michael 1.	
Shekelworth, Phillip	28
Luranah	24
Leatch, Catron	34
Mary	11
John	12
James	3

	Age
Ragen, Andrew	8
Ogden, Heugh	54
David	14
Heugh	12
Charles	8
Mary	48
Dorraty	17
Ann	11
Ruth	9

"Number of Souls in Sugar Land Hundred. By Samuel Blackmore; Sept. 2, 1776*"

	Age
Speight, Robert	37
William	12
"——son"	8
Robert	6
Elisabeth	38
Ann	4
Mary	2
Hickman, Solomon	40
Joshua	14
Jesse	9
Geats, James	34
Taylor, Ruth	23
an infant.	
Carter, Pegey	21
George a Negroe	35
Nan	56
Hickman, Ellenor	32
Nansey	11
Sarey	3
Henry	12
Elisha	5
Barlow, Zachariah	26
Collings, John	24
Thompson, Mary	17
Charles a Negroe	28
Mackall, Benja	41
John	1
Mary	31

	Age
Mackall, Elizabeth	11
Mary	8
Darke	6
Rebaca	4
Kelley, Mary	29
Davis, John	8
Major, a Negroe	40
Luce, 38; Moll 21.	
Dyson, Barton	25
William	5 mos.
Anna	25
Martha	2
Dignum, Lusey	18
Williams, Elisha	41
Hazel	18
John	14
Thomas	12
Jarred	10
Elisha	6
Ann	40
Mary	16
Martha	3
Ford, Jean	28
Sebon, John	26
Dowden, John	35
John B.	5
Thomas P.	3

*The 12 sheets included in this part of the Census of 1776 are 12¼ in. x 4 in., and are loose, hence the order of enumeration, and of plantations cannot be known. Small lines in the original sheets separate the males, females, and slaves.

	Age
Dowden, Michael A.	1
Jean	25
Beck, Negroe	37
Dowden, Mary	70
Warde, Elizabeth	19
Phil, a Negroe	30
Charles 14; Hen 35.	
Ellis, Solomon	32
Charles	4
Solomon	2
James	12
Margaret	32
Verlinder	12
Martha	10
Ann	8
Gibson, John	18
Nan a Negroe	27
Tomlinson, Heugh	24
John	2
Mary	20
Kelley, Frederick	19
Jacobs, Jaramiah	58
Zachariah	23
Edward	16
John	12
Rachel	56
Rebaca	20
Ruth	13
Ben a Negroe	56
Will 57; Jean 50; Hager 49.	
Willson, Hannah	22
John	1
Clearwaters, Silvester	64
Lettes	62
Elisabeth	25

	Age
Hoskinson, Heugh	21
Charles	18
Josiah	12
Charles	7 mos.
Margaret	19
Stimpson, Capt. Solomon	40
Dorkus	35
Sango a Negroe	23
Charles 15; Ned 7; Hary 9 mos.; Sary 20; Lid 7.	
Rian, William	25
Joshua	1
Jamima	18
Worker, William	21
John	12
Agnes	85
Margaret	38
Ellis, Samuel	55
Samuel, Jr.	10
Mary	52
Cassandra	17
Anna	14
Suger, William	18
Ellis, Zaphaniah	21
Thomas	2
Hannah	20
Colliar, William	31
James	6
William	4
John	1
Jean	25
Rachel	58
Wood, John	47
James	19

	Age
Wood, John, Junr.	5
Walter	3
Thomas	9 mos.
Anna	43
Mary	13
Charity	10
Elizabeth	8
Ginkinks, Edward	20
Warren, George	54
Johan	24
George	21
Mary	35
Alley	16
Mary	8
Mary	64
Warren, Thomas	26
Charles	3
Elisabeth	25
Mary	5
Sary	2
Henley, James	40
Johnson, Isaac	24
Horasha	2
Elisabeth	20
Mary	6 mos.
Yeates, John, Sr.	25
Whitaker, Alexander	30
Hester	25
Elisabeth Magruder	2
Price, Thomas	23
Gilks, Mary	21

Tom a Negroe 40; Clem 20; Ned 1—Sall 17; Nan 11; Semos 5.

	Age
Soper, James	44
Thomas	7
Soper, Alvan	5
John	3
Mcreen	1
James	7
Ann	26

Sam a Negroe 12; Tobe 11; Dave 3—Gin 32; Fillis 25; Feby 15; Dyner 13; Hannah 7; Merear 6.

	Age
O'Neal, John	57
Peter	22
Barton	16
Joseph	10
Margaret	49
Margaret	18
Phebe	16
Janet	14
Mary	10
Willson, Mathew	35
Henry	7
Benja	5
Rachel	26
Rachel	3
Wood, Zophonioh	32
Eli	4
Lucas, Mary	43
Nansy	10
Charles	23
William	19

Dyner a Negroe 46; Hannah 31; Dill 4; George 13; Sam 12.

	Age
Gatten, Benjamin	42
Benjamin	1 mo.
John	10
Elisabeth	33
Phillinder	15

	Age
Medly, George	13
Prusten, Edward	40
Niles, George	30

Hester a Negroe 28; Moll 28; Nan 3; Jean 2—Jose 13; Harry 8; George 7; Bob 1 month.

Else & Blackburns quorter: Harry a Negroe 50; Kippen 37; Charles 25 Jean 40; Bab 20; Cris 14; Bet 6; Rach 1.

	Age
Smallwood, Derecter	24
Palmer, Tobitha	40
Jariat	3
Hopkins, Ann	28
Lear	4
Allison, Hendery	56
Silvester	22
Hendery	18
Ellenner	91
Elisabeth	48
Ellenner	24
Maryan	14

Hester a Negroe 38; Luce 17; Feby 14; Rachel 11; Nell 8; —Sezer 7; Jaramiah 4; Phill 2 months.

	Age
Sanders, Charles	45
Edward	3
John	1
Hennaratter	23

Agnes a Negroe 55; Charity 33; Rachel 11; Nan 8; Monoca 4—Charles 44; Charles 1.

	Age
Adams, Ann	56
Maryan	16
Cassandra	12
Jesse	18
Rullan, Rachel	10
Riggs, Thos	31
Azariah	22
John	7
Ophea	6
Rachel	25
Nansey	4
Ruth	1
Tomlinson, William	26
Hester	18
Martha	1
Casey, James	22
Riggs, Elisabeth	14
phelps, Margaret	9
Hardy John	46
George	15
Ashford	9
Hennary	4
Anna	43
Mary	18
Anna	13
Darcus	6
Martha	2

Nan a Negroe 15.

	Age
Dowell, Peter	57
Peter	27
John	25
William	15
John, son of John	1
Elisabeth	59
Mary	27
Mary	1

	Age
Doll a Negroe 22; Lusey 15; Rachel 8; Clea, 7—Batchelder 5; Daniel 1.	
Belt, Higinson	31
Alley	20
Elisabeth	1
Harris, James	18
Cato a Negroe 21; Efrom 31; Nase 3—Hannah 24; Sue 30.	
Atchinson John	26
Efrom	2
Lody	19
Ruth	18
Wood, Stephen	25
Bennet	1
Preasha	23
Amma	3
Elisabeth	12
Fletchall, John	49
Thomas	16
John	6
Elisabeth	45.
Ann	19
Elisabeth	14
Cintha	12
Warters, James	30
Grimes, Ann	28
Fox, Ann	25
(Sarvts 3)	
Samson a Negroe 25; Frank 31; Charles 20; Jack 17; Joseph 5; Jacob 3; Samson 30—Phillis 38; Cato 13; Alley 4; Rachel 3 months; Frank 1.	
Coarts, Charles	62
James	23

	Age
Coarts, Notley	21
Jean a Negro 55; Clea 7; Harry 3.	
Pool, Joseph	38
Joseph	10
Benja	4
Mary	28
Mary	6
Rachel	2
Mccolley, Sary	14
Felphs, Sary	11
Pool, John	43
John	7
Sary	28
Elisabeth	6
Ann	4
Tary	1
Riggs, John	12
Crellin, James	15
Blackmore, William	31
Dawson	4
Sary	28
Sary	4 mos.
Savents:	
Burch, Holford	48
Dixon, James	30
Brubly, Joseph	26
Frahser, Andrew	23
Bowers, Jeae	9
Jean a Negroe 27; Siss 10; Ned 6 mos.	
Mackall, Mary	65
Darbay, Asa	2
Moll a Negroe 29; Sall 12; Rachel 6—Harry 15; Ned 13.	

	Age
Perry, Charles at his quarter:	
William a Savent	42
Sam a Negroe	20
Perry, James at his quarter:	
James a Negroe	54
Patrick	25
Cass	20
Brown, James	52
Pollixfin, John Willis	36
John W.	9
James W.	2
Matthew W.	5 mos.
Mary W.	31
Ellennas W.	14
Elisabeth W.	13
Victory W.	11
Tomeny (Jemeny ?) W.	7
Ann W.	4
Willett Griffeth	26
Henson, Saml.	12

Number of Souls in Sugar Land Hundred. By Saml. Blackmore

White Males	744
White Females	630
Black Males	206
Black Females	241
Total	1821

Frederick City Sept. 2d 1776. then Came Samuel Blackmore before the SubScriber and made oath on the holy vanjels that to the best of his knowledge the foregoing is a true list of all the souls and their ages in Sugerland Hundred. Sworn before
David Lynn.

Dr. 1776 the Committee of the Lower District of Frederick County in actt with Samuel Blackmore to 12 Days Riding to take the number of Souls in the Sugerland Hundred at 7/6 p Day £ 4–10–0

Frederick City Septr. 2, 1776 Came Samuel Blackmore before the subscriber and made oath on the holy vanjils that the above acctt is just and true as it Stands Stated. Sworn before David Lynn.

Received Sept. 2d 1776 By the Committee of the Said district Fredk. County.
Simon Nicholls Clk.

North West Hundred. Number Taking By Robt. Beall of Ja[s.]*

	Age
Trundle, Thomas	65
Johanah	43
Johannah J	5
Rachol	3
Mila	1
Darkus Kor	14
Negor Dottor	50

Janney 30; Lib 22—Jacob 19; florah 14; Tom 13; Dottor 14; Jenney 11; Will 9; Peg 5; Ester 6; nan 4; Ann 2.

	Age
Housle, Robert	56
Sarah	43
Elizabeth	23
Mary	17
Robert, Junr	15
Johnathan	11
Sarah	9
Proscolah	7
Lucy	5
Saml	3
Malmaduke	6 mos.
Leviah	4 mos.
Wood, Thoma	58
Rache	19
Tracy, William	53
Elenorr	53
Philip	19
Elnor	17
James	10

	Age
Marchlo, James	50
Mary	34
Grootroo, Benjm	14
Williams, John	35
Mary	32
Nancy	12
Elizabeth	10
Charles	8
Basol	3
William	1
Lashloo, William	30
Margry	25
Robert	6
Rebackah	5
Aaron	3
Moses	5 mos.
Lashloo, John	40
Rachel Lee	46
Mary	9
Arnold	6
John, Junr	3

Negro Toney 30; Alse 1.

	Age
Kusol (?), Mary free Malatoe	78
forrel, Ann free Malatoe	52
Lee, John	45
Elizabeth	52
Daniel	18
James	15

* The pages of this record are 6½ in. x 15¼ in. 16 in number. The letters "o" and "e" are often made alike in the record.

	Age
Lee, Elizabeth	13
Dan (?)	11
Emelia	9
Ferrel, Joseph	60
Tharasher, William	45
Margrett	39
Mary	17
Elizabeth	13
John, Junior	11
Sarah	8
Thomas	5 weeks
William	3
Goodrick, Benjman	30
Rachel	25
Elender	8
Elizabeth	6
Benjman Jonson	4
John	2
Negro Osburn	11
Jennens, John	56
"Jennins," Sarah	35
Elizabeth	14
Ann	11
Sarah	9
John, Juner	7
Mary	5
Rachel	2
Margaret	2 weeks
Higdon, Thomas	25
Rachel	30
John	3
Margaret	1
Negro Bassel	11
King, Edward	36
Rebackah	34

	Age
King, Elizabath	13
Sarah	12
Mary	9
Charrity	7
Benjaman	4
Edward, Junor	2
Rebackah	5 mos.
Madding, Joseph	48
Mary	43
Ann	21
James	20
Joseph	17
Benjaman	15
Thomas	14
Sarah	11
Elizabath	9
Margra	8
Rebackah	6
Hezekiah	4
Catharine	2
John	24
Margratt	21
Collens, John	34
Sarah	30
Mary	9
John, Junor	6
Elizabath	2
Maddox, Thomas	38
Jannet	28
Elizabath	4
John Mad	2
Jacob wood	4 mos.
Wilson, Sarah	9

Neger Mol 29—Bil 10; Hirro 7; Sall 7; Emalia 5; Jaratt 3.

Gentle (written "Gontlo"), Elizabeth	23

Darkey 2 months.

	Age
Holmod, Antony	52
Susanah	42
Jane	16
John	14
Sarah	12
Antony, Juner	10
Goorge	8
Loveday	2

Negroe Peg; Sue 50; Bet 38; Sharper 11; Dinnar 8—Sam 4; Mingo 5 months.

	Age
Taylor, William	52
Elizabeth	49
Gentle, Rebecker	4
Gimlish, Frances	42
Mary	39
Charlot	12
Mary	9
Ariat	7
Michel	5
Macket	2 mos.
Ozburn, William	53
Mary	37
Elander	18
Archabald	15
Charlot	14
Ann	12
Isac	9
Lenerd	7
Potter	4
Toppon William	15
Evens Joh	19
Hill, John	36
Kesiah	34
Sarah	13
Joseph	11
Jonathan	9

	Age
White, Mary	45
James	16
Saml	14
Jach	12
Elsie (Elmer ?)	10
Mary	8
Robert Beall	6
Negro Dinah	21
Peirce, Margratt	55
Catharin	26
John Baptis	22

Negros Charles 23; Sam 24; Tobe 20; Dave 15—Charlot 12; Nace 6; Arch 4; Margary 1.

	Age
Harroson, Priscilla	23
Crown, Joseph	66
Elizabeth	50
Catharin	17
Sarah	15
Arter	12
Thomas	7
Whitnoll, Solaman	50
Evens, Mary	18
Young (written "Toung"), John	54
Jane	35
Mary	14
Jane	11
Elenor	5
John, Juner	1
Goodman, Humphry	40
Kesiah	32
Ann	15
Jeramiah	13
Patsey	11
Betsy	9

	Age
Goodman, Tomma	7
Kesiah	6
Saml	4
Rebeckah	2
Charlot	8 mos.
Srt Carthew, Edmond	20
Conn, Mary	21
Wilson, Henry	51
folander	47
Zadock	19
Lucy	16
Thomas	13
Mary	11
Elender	7
Lanclot	9
Henry	5
folandor	3
Negro Sall	17
Trundle, John	27
Ruth	22
David	3
John Lowos	8 mos.
Negro Toney 24; Tom 3.	
Madding, John	84
Sarah	68
Negro Robben (?)	60
Gittings, Henry	46
Elizabeth	14
William	10
fletcher, Sarah	43
Gordon, Joseph	23
Lowe, William	30
Sarah	18
Speaks, William	60
Mary	55

	Age
Hufman, Martain	41
Barbro	35
John	14
Elizabath	12
Joseph	10
Hannah	8
Mary	4
Day, Lenerd	40
Tobitha	36
Saml	14
Susanah	11
Ezekel	9
Sarah	7
Bazel	5
Tobitha	2
Lambeth, Saml	33
Mary	35
Ann	3
John	2
Lucy	2 mos.
Higgens, Joseph	30
Martha	26
Ann	6
Elizabeth	4
Elender	4 mos.
Hennes, Mary	18
Stallons, Griffon	27
Elizabeth	17
Susanah	2 mos.
Stallons, Jacob	25
Margratt	20
Susanah	1
Cash, Calan (?)	15
Wilson, James	13
Cumphen, James	70
Bearlander	22
William	4

	Age
Harres, Ezekel	36
Maggon, Philip	26
William, Ann	60
Daniel	20
Elizabeth	21
Cooke, William	45
Sharrad, John	8
Beall, Richard	54
Elener	47
Priscilla	22
Margaret	19
Elizabeth	13
Wiloba	11
Beall, Saml, Sr	70
Jane	61
Jemima	32
Margre	22
Joseph Belt	22
Alexander Robt	19
Dickson, Susanah	16

Negro Mingo 18; feebe 58; fillis 32; Somus 11; Vino 3.

Beall, Richd. of Saml	38
Sarah	38
Saml. Brook	14
Thos. Brook	13
Mary	11
Robt. Brook	7
Walter Brook	5
Asa Brook	2

Negro Jane 36; Juno 9; Isaac 7; John 4—Mary 1; Isabel 21—Harculs 6 months; Charles 6 Do.; Jack 38; John 24; Cato 14; Suba 14; Humphry 27—Bess 13; Sarah 11; Conbr 13; Antejey 30; 8 males—9 females.

	Age
Beall, Clemt	42
Priscilla	35
Perry	9
Elizabeth	3
Normand	1
Cassandra	7

Negro Diner 90; James 38; Charles 21; Cloar 20; Philis 12; Bed 11; Will 2.

Ward, Andrew	48
Rachel	32
Ann	7
Mary	4
Tracy	1
Alby, Joseph	30
Cassandra	24
Joseph, Junor	4
Ann	2
Barratt, Ninian	25
Mary	24
Isac	1
Richd	12
Moore, Benjamin	23
Sarah	21
Elizabeth	1
Lee, John	21
Dickson, Sarah	11
Bocraft, Petter	35
Mary	25
Jonathan Nixon	6 mos.
Day, Elizabeth	11

Negro Charles 36; Estorr 26; Affor 20; Tom 20; Job 14; Camby 3; Sam 2; Jack 1.

Bocraft, Benjaman	67
Deborah	57

	Age
Whitehead, Timothy	67
New, Mary	40
Jones, Abraham	22
Negro Toby 50; Bet 52; Richd 30; Dol 28; Boson 20; Joney 22; Easter 12; Toney 10; Alse 8; Rachel 6; Sarah 4; Aaron 3.	
Abington, John	40
Lucy	18
Bob (Bole?)	15
Elizabeth	13
John, Juner	11
Henry	9
Sert. Mackeay, William	30
Agga	6
Negros Sal 27; Dinar 52; hannah 17; Dick 5; Dafna 3.	
Mackette, James	43
Mary	39
Mary	16
Joseph	14
Elisha	12
Agness	10
Ignashus	8
Cloa	4
Loweser	2
Tyson, Ann	60
Mary	29
Beall, Mary	9
Alarina	6
Negro Bob	50
Begarly, Henry	30
Elizabeth	26
Hezekiah	3
Ann	1
Sert. Wood, John	17

	Age
Whallen, Michel	60
Bridgett	50
Mathew	20
Margratt	18
Mark	15
Thomas	9
Martin	6
Mary	2
Dulany, Bridgett	21
Roe, Robert	21
Wood, Robert	35
Elizabeth	34
Ama	5
Zadock	3
Mary	67
jay, Sarah	22
Servant Grindle, Elizabeth	33
Negro Sal 40; Nan 26; Jac 26; Toys 3; Abagil 4 months; Tom 3 months.	
Cash, Calab	41
Elennor	48
Ruth	19
Mary	14
Dawson	11
Rachel	6
Plommer, Sarah	18
Wilson, Verlander	80
Zachariah	45
Plommer, Jane	50
Mary	20
Rebackah	16
Kesiah	15
Elizabeth	12
Robeson, Elizabeth	13
Mitchel, Mordeca	50
Sarah	51

	Age
Mitchel, Lucy	18
Bathsheba	15
Notly	13
Barbara	12
Lankford, frosman James	40
Mackdonald, Olson Edward	4
Tucker, William	63
Elizabeth	49
Henry	17
Sarah	15
Jemima	14
Sebina	12
Alen	7
Tucker, William, Juner	29
Margary	25
Levi	2
A Son 1 Month old.	
Stallons, Joseph	60
Elezebeth	53
Thomas	19
Negros Hanner 40; Rose 22—Charles 10; Nell 8; Tobe 6; Sal 4.	
Tannehill, William	55
Sarah	59
Rebeckah	25
Anne	18
Wm. Harres	16
Negros Dinah 36; Leartos 33; Lidde 14; Magor 11.	
Nixson, Jonathan	19
Servunt Boy herod	18
Bloys, David	26
Mary	25
William, Juner	2

	Age
Bloys, William, Senr	63
Sarah	50
Elizabeth	24
Mary	22
Rebeckah	17
Charls	15
Ann	14
Sarah	13
Mordeca	12
Zachah	10
Jonathan	8
Zadock	5
Robeson, Jams ("male")	1
Cicil, Sabrot	53
Mary	46
Saml	23
Elinor	20
John	18
James	15
William	13
Mary	11
Jemima	9
Thomas	4
Anne	1
Hall, Rebeckah	6
Negro Hanner	70
Lashlee, Thomas	23
Elizabeth	27
Harris, Zadock	26
Sarah	27
Ann	2
Elizabeth 7 months old.	
Negros Dick 31; Harry 7.	
Larrow, Michel	23
Jane	23
Clark, Henry	42
Nancy	42

	Age
Clark, Seven	14
Walter	12
Hennerietta	11
Henry, Juner	9
Baless	8
Nancy	7
Lesson	5
Thomson	5
Justson	3
Johnson	1

Negros Joney 50; Maloy 35; Cato 30; Margery 25; Peg 18; Dick 17; Will 15; Anica 15; Mingo 9; Priss 6; Jene 3; Lott 2; Bett 20.

Larrow, Frances	23
Martha	31
Abraham	10
Elizabeth	8
James	6
George	3
John 6 months old.	
Sarvant Colbo, John	21

Harris, Aaron	30
Mary	26
Sarah	9
Elizabeth	6
Walter	3
Thomas 3 months old.	
Sarvants Camblo, Daniel	20
Knight, John	30

Negros frank 28; Easter 40; Charles 15; Isaac 2.

Frances, Joseph	34
Elizabeth	28
Lucy	7
Elizabeth	6
Jacob	4

	Age
Frances, Hessa (?)	2
and a Son 4 months old.	
Elemont, Elizabeth	32

Clark, William	26

Honnos (Hennes ?), Cavea	24

Beall, Robert of James	54
Servants Brigges, Richd	22
Mackgyer, Andrew	18
Negro Henne ("female")	27

Summers, Hezekiah	26
Rebacker	32
William Dent	3
Benjamin (?)	1
Glaz, Charaty	53
Elennor	23

Harwood, Saml	29
Mary Elizth	24
Elizabeth Ann	3
Thomas Noble	2
Mary Ann 2 months old.	

Negros George 60; Lucy 50; Garey 40; Charles 28; Tuba 29; Sarey 21; Janey 19; Bacon 16; Hagea 14; Will 14; Charaty 15; Priss 14; Jack 13; George 8; Nan 8; Jack 5; Lucy 3; Milly 1; John 8 months old, Pag 2 months old—8 black males, 12 black females.

Beall, Zachariah	33
Rebackah	23
Orasha	2
A Gairl 2 months old.	
Negro Candos	80

	Age
Doxse Elennor	20
Martha	2
Woodard, Frances	63
Weneford	55
Frances	19
Hezekiah	16
Zachariah	13
Sarah	11
Weneford	6
Stallons, Elizabeth	27
Patsa	4
William	1
Stallons, Isaac	66
Ezable	53
Sarah	17

Negros philos 80; Sarah 67; Rachel 30; Ned 15; Jane 12; Sam 10; frank 8; Dick 6.

Tucker, Martha	32
Catharine	11
Susanna	10
Negro Tamar	3
*Watson, John	42
Sarah	38
John Wright	5½
Sally	2½
Abington, Elizth	13
Murdock, Martha	25

Servants:

Dixon, Richard	45
McCoy, Janet	17

Hired for Year:

McGirtt, James	45
Bannerman, Betsey	54

Negroes, Jack 32; Will 40; Brumley 54; Charles 11; Negroes, Isaac 9—Lucy 29; Sophia 15; Ursula 6.

	Age
Carroll, Daniel	46

Servants:

Condon, John	25
John	45
Kelly, Tom	16
Kenney	24
Bush	23

Negroes—Joe 28; Deb 28; Tom 10; Kate 8; Bill 4; Babb 3; Henny 1; Rachell 23; Diana 3; Flora 1; Will 18, Roe, Robert, Overseer.—

Dixon, James	6
Sarah	40
Carroll, Mrs. Ellr	67
Mary	34
Elizth	31
John	40

Negroes—Frank 68; Johnny 28; Tom 36; Johnny 25; Ned 25; Zanga 45; Archy 21; Will 21; Tom 16; Dick 13; Tom 11; Nelly 60; Hanna 20; Pig 45; Nanny 35; Ciss 18; Judith 50; Nanny 18; Nanny 20; Mary 35; Kitt 23; Jett 21; Sue 20; Magg 14; Sall 16; Bett 12; Poll 14; Bett 12; Rose 5; Mary 10; Rachell 7; Nell 1; George 2; Nan 1; Kate 7; Tom 1; Henny 4; Sandy 9; Isaack 25; Isaack 22; Jack 12; Betty 60; Nell 55; Nell 17; Dick 70; Nanny 68—17 black males, 29 black females.

* At this point a bold, experienced penmanship appears in the original record.

	Age
Nickolls, Thos	47
Casandra	39
Ann	75
William	17
Daniel	13
Thos., Junr	11
Saml	6
Isaiah	4
Benjn	2
Rebekah	15
Elizabeth	9

Negroes—Tom 55; Daniel 28; Sam 19; Richard 17; Davy 15; Neasey 15; Sam 13; James 13; Joseph 9; Leonard 8; Abraham 6; Hardus 5; Jacob 2; Stephen 1; George 1; Nelly 37; Sarah 24; Sal 20; Bithy 12; Nanny 3; Ally 3; Cate 1—15 black males, 7 black females, 1 female servant.

Carroll, Daniel, Junr	23
Elizth	23

Servants:

Vaun, Betty	45
Buckley, John	40
Gilligan, John	30
Purley, Ned	10

Negroes—Michael 40; Rose 20; Pall 10, Sall 4; Joe 12.

*Barrett, Elizabeth	53
Ann	20
John	19
Isaac	11

	Age
Mackmaness, Thomas	30
Ann	22
Mackmaness, Thomas	3
May, Ann	21

The Number of Dent Sumers family is 9 But he wont make a Return of Names no ages

Bazil white wont make a return of nether Number Names. nor ages But I think 8 in his family.

The Number of White males is	272
and the Number of females	283
	555
the Number of Black males	112
and of females	138
Totle 805	250

Fredk City Sept[t] ye[e] 2[d] 1776 then Came Robert Beall of Ja[s]. and Made oath on the holy Evengelist of Almighty God that he has to the Best of his knowledge taken the Number and ages of persons White and black male and female in the Northwest Hundred as they was given to him. Sworn before

David Lynn.

Recd Sept 2[d] 1776 by the Committee of the Lower district of Frederick County Simon Nickolls Clk.

* Here the handwriting of Robt. Beall reappears.

Aug[t] 10, 1776 the Committee of the Lower District of Frederick County Dr.

To Six days Numbering the Souls in the Northwest Hundred at Seven Shillings and Six pence p day £2–5–0.

Fredk City Sep[t] 2[d], 1776 then Came Rob[t] Beall of Ja[s]. before me one of his Lordships Justes of the peace and Made oath on the holy Evengalist of Almighty God that the above Account is Just and true and that he has not Rec[d] any part or parcel or Sattesfaction for the Same Sworn before

David Lynn

HUNDREDS OF FREDERICK AND MONTGOMERY COUNTIES

Volume 1, *Scharf's History of Western Maryland*, p. 419, enumerates the original hundreds of Frederick County, as established in 1749 (county erected in 1748), together with the constables for the hundreds. In 1759 Piney Creek, Burnt House Woods, Fredericktown, and Old Town hundreds first appear in the records.

The records of the Maryland Historical Society give the following hundreds, alphabetically arranged, for Frederick (Old) County before 1776:

Upper Antietam, Lower Antietam, Burnt Woods, Conococheague, Cumberland, Elizabeth, Fort Frederick, Fredericktown, Georgetown, Kitocton, Upper Kitocton, Linganore, Linton, Manor, Marsh, Upper Part Monocacy, Middle Monocacy, Lower Monocacy, Upper Part Newfoundland, Lower Part Newfoundland, North West, Old Town, Piney Creek, Pipe Creek, Upper Part Potomack, Lower Part Potomack, Rock Creek, Salisbury, Seneca, Sharpsburgh, Shipton, Sugar Land, Sugar Loaf, Tom's Creek.

Montgomery and Washington counties were carved out of Frederick County by "resolve of the Convention on 6th September, 1776," but were not organized until 1777, at which time (Scharf, Vol. 1, p. 658) the Montgomery County Hundreds were:

(1) Upper Part Newfoundland, (2) Lower Part Newfoundland, (3) Upper Part Potomack, (4) Lower Part Potomack, (5) Seneca, (6) North West, (7) Georgetown, (8) Rock Creek, (9) Sugar Land, (10) Sugar Loaf, (11) Linganore.

"Of these (1) to (4), and (8) to (11), inclusive, are the old Frederick County names, while the others are new names, but the new hundreds must have been carved out of the originals as they came from Frederick."*

* Wm. H. Talbott, Esq., Rockville, Md., who also assisted in identifying the —— Hundred of Frederick County (198–216) as being a Montgomery County Census.

ELIZABETH HUNDRED

"TRUE LIST OF ALL THE SOULS BOTH WHITE AND BLACK, AND THEIR AGES LIVING IN ELIZABETH HUNDRED IN THE COUNTY OF FREDERICK" AS TAKEN BY JOHN MILLER, AUGUST, 1776

An Act of Legislature of January 26, 1814, read "to alter and change the name of Elizabeth Town, Washington County, to Hager's Town, and to incorporate the same."

Elizabeth Hundred

Negroes Aged 16 Years and upwards	
Daniel Aged	30 Years
Toby	25
Cufe	27
Peter	55
Sam	20
Bose	26
Born	56
James	21
Bob	23
Peter	19
Chiff	95
Ned	25
Will	25
Bose	22
Charls	21
George	35

Males Aged 16 Year and upwards

Males 16 } 38
Females 22
More Females then Males 6

unter 16 Years old
Males 19 } 41
Females 22
More Females then Males 3

Total 79

Ditto Females Aged 16 and upwards	
Filis Aged	18 Years
Nany Mulatre	23
Peap	26
Heger	43
Sure	22
Eastes	30
Mary	50
Beky	24
Elizabeth	17
Luly	30
Sill	40
Mekin	60
Buye	20
Rachel	30
Sary	20
Hanah	45
Nell	21
Sall	19
Fider	40
Bett	40
Rachel	25
Abigal	23

Ditto Males Aged 16 y[ears and under]	
Edward Aged	9 Years
Tom	10
Manmouth	1
Tomra	7
Ritchard	10
Charls	8 months
Richard	3
Jacob	1
Martin	15
Ginn	2
James	1
Tom	14
Henry	13
Will	5
Zoney	1
Herculous	13
Daniel	15
Sandy	10
Nacy	7
	19

Neg. Females Aged 16 years and under	
Susy Aged	4 Years
Dine	7
Jane	5
Susy	4
Mary	6
Pegg	5
Dyan	16
Rose	6
Pol	3
Gate	15
Filis	5
Dyan	9 months
Milly	8
Sarey	4
Beck	2
Jonney	3
Suck	7
Dynah	13
Isabell	15
Rose	3
Margret	8
Susy	12
	22

(2) Males from the Age of 16 to 50 in Elisabeth Hundred

Name	Age
Rudolph Bley aged	30
Martin Steck	28
Ernst Dietz	28
Francis Wagoner	25
Michael Fessler	35
Jacob Whymer	49
Jacob Wolfleger	27
Frederick Rohrer	34
John Krumbach	40
David Hellen	40
Michael Kline	50
Jacob Hoober	50
William Kiefer	44
John Stinesifer	33
Andrew Filler	27
John Unfill	32
George Zinn	27
Jacob Bardon	37
Jacob Fisher	46
Nicolaus Hagan	23
John Ofter	26
Edward Br[illegible]	39
Melker [illegible]	37
Henry Duer[illegible]	38
Joseph George	50
Henry Dud[illegible]	30
Jonathan [illegible]	31
William [illegible]	33
John [illegible]	35
Bal[illegible] Goll	50
Michael Ott	28
William Mofoy	17
Daniel McCardon	24
Nathaniel Morgan	28
Philip Badolph	18
Joseph Gelfin	20
David Morgin	23
Thomas Foot	22
John Reab	29

Name	Age
George Booke Aged Years	19
David Herry	25
Martin Herry	20
Jacob Herry	19
Mathias Ned	50
Benjamin Campbell	27
Jacob Ott	27
Peter Bell	40
Adam Dile	37
John Backes	39
George Woltz	33
John Ronin	25
Adam Smith	25
Peter Woltz	30
Herman Crealy	28
Francis Crealy	24
Andrew Backes	26
William Co[illegible]	27
Eustatious Young	50
John Robinson	27
Isaac Yourdy	36
Simon Hauschelder	31
Jost Wayand	27
John Fackler	47
Henry Wilde	27
Philip Ofter	32
George Arnold	31
Andrew Miller	45
Peter Wagoner	39
Peter Hauf	48
[illegible]	
Daniel Callaghan	24
George Sheaner	25
George Squiers	21
Leonhard Dave[illegible]	19
George Bayerly	20
Martin [illegible] Peyfer	24
William [illegible] Coker	29
James Farney	18
Thomas Loyfine	20
John [illegible] Lee	20
Jacob Shryock	30
Jacob Hoogel	27
John Michael	20

(5) Males from the Age of 16 Years to 50 in Elizabeth 100

Name	Aged
Jacob Hoober	20
James Dunken	18
William Welsh	19
John Maguain	29
Gotlieb Willerd	33
Peter Deved	20
Samuel Young	28
Phily Greegbaum	17
William Brown	17
James Fegor	20
Jones Emry	34
Jacob Rolf	43
Jacob Belshoober	27
George Rinehart	31
John Sneyder	44
Jacob Nicolous	24
John Feisy	28
Stephan McCafby	37
William Muffet	44
John Adear	50
Thomas Simmons	29
Henry Shryock	39
Michael Fackler	36
Frederick Heidinger	50
Noah Hart	30
Frederick Highshill	24
Peter Hoefligh	34
Michael Domer	30
John Shryock	28
Moses Chaplin	22
William Pullin	29
Christopher Alder	29
Peter Hoze	28
Jacob Hoze	34
Charles Heterick	26
Adam Wise	24
Christopher Trapp	40
John Wraken	24
Samuel Paten	20
John Hoefligh	25
John Wolecock	36
Philip Riefinagh	25
Mathew Horne	25
Alexander Megare	20

Name	Aged Years
Frederick Alder	35
Michael Walter	26
John Rosepening	26
Michael Yegley	36
Conrad Stitz	26
Joseph Hanfman	25
James Clark	35
Leonhard Shryock	37
Christian Mantle	49
Matheus Fleeger	36
Michael Hohelltier	28
Dewalt Gellhoober	30
George Young	35
Frances Bruges	35
Moritz Bruer	49
William Bishop	23
George Ablater	50
Abraham Bouer	33
Barney Reily	22
George Lile	27
Martin Shese	39
Thomas Rinehart	33
Thomas George	31
Felix Meyer	30
John Klabe	38
Daniel Ward	23
Philip Harnish	21
Henry Baumward	22
George Gray	30
William Lewis	20
John Swan	29
Horn	18
Peter Grofe	29
Benjamin Moll	25
Joseph Dawney	21
William Dawney	22
Michael Bear	22
Peter Stuky	42
James Watson	21
Francis Meyer	21
Jacob Rohrer	32
Herman Klaber	42
Christian Rohrer	49
John Braun	33
Jost Kline	49
John Stull	49
Daniel Stull	43 21
Feodorus Folmet	20

(4) Males from the Age of 16 Years to 50 Years in Elisabeth 100

Name	Age	Name	Age
William Porksey Aged Years	22	[illegible] Rufe Aged Years	34
Frederick Craft	35	Stephen Brown	25
Peter Giden	50	Andrew Rench	48
James Nox	40	George Boughmen	22
John Seiman	37	Isaac Rewsinger	24
Paul Christman	38	George Green	32
Matthias Reitenauer	20	Ludwig Young	47
Philip Renner	28	Samuel Baghtel	45
Imanuel Smith	21	Samuel Baeghtle	22
George Smith	38	Isaac Baghtle	22
Henry Manigher	27	Martin Funk	22
Henry Miller	33	Conrad Brendlinger	48
Peter Prakunier	49	Baltzer Shirracker	40
George Draxel	41	Henry Funk	24
Michael Haushalter	20	John Funck	26
Jacob Reitenauer	37	Peter Sailor	23
Thomas Clasby	30	John Sailor	21
Rasper	18	George Nave	21
Joseph Peifer	24	Philip Dusner	30
Michael E[illegible]	40	John Henry Snyder	47
Robart G[illegible]	49	Michael Whare	26
John [illegible]	20	George Suan	31
John Seiler	35	William Garmont	31
George Frien[illegible]	24	Henry Hinkle	23
David Frien[illegible]	22	Thomas Gross	32
Philip Friend	21	William Beard	17
Ludwig [illegible]nauer	26	Samuel Dawney	23
Joseph [illegible]	30	John Dilles	44
Henry Stoneman	28	William Dilles	17
John [illegible]	20	Simon Foghler	44
Henry Blume	39	Christian Foghler	[illegible]
John Meyer	20	Augustin Liphard	42
Jacob Meyer	18	George Hutson	30
Martin Snyder	49	William Shenafield	40
Nicolaus Ellis	19	John Thomsan	28
John Bunes	26	Samuel Finley	47
Peter Rench	20	Jacob Deibley	42
John Rench	19	Joseph Sprigg	40
John Mowen	24	Thomas Belt	34
George ~~Holl~~ Charles	24	John Lincoler	23
Lawrence Breyner	18		
George Dunn	23		
Henry Moll	34		

(5) Males from the Age of 16 to 50 Years in Elizabeth 100.

Name	Aged Years
Thomas Sprigg Aged Years	[illegible]
Brian M'Connal	30
Martin Robinson	28
Michael Cary	29
James Cullin	30
James M'kay	30
Timothy	40
Martin Bauman	32
Samuel Dugles	23
John Dugles	18
Robert Dugles	26
Christian [illegible]	46
William Martin	40
Daniel Gleabfuller	42
John Lebis	31
Henry Smith	23
Joseph Biddle	17
John Scot	50
David Scot	17
Peter Simon	50
Peter Beaker	38
Frederick Egle	23
Andrew Maggey	28
Andrew [illegible]man	26
Frederick Hau	24
Albertous Hiffner	49
John Hiffner	21
[illegible] Hiffner	19
[illegible] Sneyder	30
[illegible] Heller	49
Martin Jacob	46
James Dawney	22
Jacob Smith	29
Michael Boyer	29
Henry Klaber	26
Peter Shees	21
Christian Grove	28
Abraham Daruse	35
Henry Fore Aged Years	50
Michael Fore	18
Christian Leyder	40
Christian Metz	24
Christian Bentz	36
Leonhard Sheafer	25
Christian [illegible]	21
John Sitze	29
Adam Leeser	17
Henry Rowe	27
Dewalt Rowe	22
Henry Brete	33
Baltzer Lanabach	49
Frederick Nicodemus	44
Conrad Nicodemus	20
Henry Sneyder	44
Philip Reimal	50
George Reimal	17
Jacob [illegible]	50
Elias [illegible]	20
Abraham Leyder	35
Jacob Leyder	27
Andrew Fuller	28
Ludwig M[illegible]	20
Ludwig [illegible]	30
Robard Gray	26

Total 321

(6) Females Aged from 16 years To 50 years in Elisabeth 100

Name	Aged
Barbara Bley	22
~~Mary Winkel~~	~~65~~
Catharina Steck	23
Catharina Dietz	24
Sharlote Wagner	21
Catharina Fessler	28
Mary Salome	46
Susanna Sander	50
Catharina Wolfleger	26
Catharina Rohrer	30
July Crumbach	47
Susanna Hellin	36
Christiena Stober	46
Ann Heiser	32
Margaretha Stinesaiver	31
Magdalane Filler	19
Magdalen Unsel	27
Mary Zinn	26
Margaretha B[illegible]	30
Elisabeth [illegible]	47
Elisabeth [illegible]	19
Elisabeth [illegible]	25
Elisabeth Hellybauer	34
Catharina [illegible]	36
Mary [illegible]	24
Mary [illegible]	46
Dorathea [illegible]rry	27
Ann [illegible]	28
Francia Miller	30
Elisabeth Goll	46
Margaretha Ott	23
Mary Monger	27
Christiena Sneyder	35
Catharina Hellybauer	46
Margaretha Weiser	46
Catharina Burger	18
Mary Kropfin	17
Susanna Fisher	20
Ann Magin	20
Magdalena Gies	20
Christiana Sauders	22

Name	Aged Years
Barbara Reed	17
Mary Ebey	40
Margaretha Meglin	19
Lidia Shockan	18
Margaretha Gollin	20
Catharina Soin	19
Christiana Miller	21
Catharina Fackler	19
Catharina Reed	44
Mary Link	25
Mary Campbell	18
Catharina Ott	20
Catharina Hogh	28
Elisabeth [illegible]ell	35
Mary [illegible]	35
Margaretha Barker	32
Jane Long	31
Charlote Wolf	25
~~[illegible]~~	~~[illegible]~~
Susanna Frantz	27
Mary Smith	21
Mary Wolf	22
Catharina Creily	27
Elisabeth Blakb[illegible]	33
Charlote Bakes	27
Catharina Conrad	20
Margaretha Young	42
Elisabeth Robinson	20
Elisabeth Gneadig	29
Elisabeth Householder	24
Margaretha Weyand	26
Mary Miller	44
Eve Fackler	39
Susana Weikle	20
Magdalina Bowman	30
Catharina Ofler	34
Catharina Arnold	26
Mary Miller	26
Margaretha Wagoner	35
Elisabeth Herman	24
Catharine Creily	24
Elisabeth Wagner	22
Catharina Grime	18
Mary Young	2[illegible]

Females Aged from 16 Years to 50 in Elisabeth 100

Name	Age	Name	Age
Elisabeth Moll Aged Years	28	Eve Wise Aged Years	42
Elisabeth Riche	19	Barbara Traff	36
Ann Chaplin	23	Margret Alter	29
[illegible] Caldwell	17	Mary Silhard	46
Elisabeth Mantle	18	Catharina Walter	23
Margaret Mowen	18	Mary Horspening	19
Ann Haefley	25	Catharina Yegly	34
Martha Sneyder	20	Margret Shit	22
Catharina ~~[illegible]~~ Davis	30	Margaretha Hinsman	33
~~[illegible]~~	~~[illegible]~~	Jane Clark	35
Elisabeth ~~[illegible]~~ Silhard	22	Margaretha Shryock	29
Magdalane ~~[illegible]~~ Metter	48	Ann Doose	43
~~[illegible]~~	~~[illegible]~~	Barbara Mantle	28
Susanna [illegible]	28	Catharina Heeger	23
Mary [illegible]	31	Margaretha Dahlber	26
Catharina [illegible]	23	Mary Gillheober	29
Mary Hall	31	Mary Beward	46
Julianna Hooser	18	Margret Young	22
Eve Reigel	48	Elisabeth Burgess	30
[illegible]	22	Ann Bauer	17
Catharina Hak	27	Margret Bishop	47
Mary Belsheober	26	Margret Bishop	17
Barbara Rinehard	36	Catharina Bough	50
Mary Sneyder	43	Eve Bauer	31
Eve Nicolous	20	Fronica [illegible]	25
Ann Muffet	24	Elisabeth [illegible]	27
Sarah Veat	26	Eve Rinehart	28
Ann Kinmns	20	Christianna Rohrer	28
Cathrin Shryock	29	Cathrin [illegible]	28
Sarah ~~[illegible]~~ Johnson	43	Fronica Rohrer	35
Helfena Hackler	32	Catharina Brown	28
Rachel Hart	27	Mary Kling	48
Catharine Highskil	19	Marey Stull	30
Ann Hoeflich	37	Martha Stull	19
Ann Dower	21	Susanna Stull	17
Ann Shryock	28	Elisabeth Craft	25
Mary Chaplin	20	Jane Nox	38
Mary Pullin	31	Ann Seiman	27
Susanna Alter	25	Catharina Hart	19
Salmey Hose	23	Ann Bowman	39
Elisabeth Donelley	38	Magdalena Christman	32
Magdalena Hoge	31	Magdalena Ritenour	17
Elisabeth Setzler	43	Magdelena Smith	36
Susanna Helbrick	22	Elisabeth Maninger	26
Elisabeth Wise	26	Catharina Miller	20
		Margret Drakune	42

Females Aged from 16 Years to 50 in Elisabeth 100.

Margretha Prakunier aged years 17
Elisabeth Dragel — 26
Margret Houshelder — 19
Barbara H Reitenauer — 22
Hannah Gare — 18
Dorathea Hoffman — 30
Elisabeth Loafer — 20
Cathrin Ekenbergh — 34
Ester Gutry — 46
Ann Gutry — 21
Pheeb Gutry — 18
Elisabeth Steiles — 35
Elisabeth Friend — 50
Dorethe Friend — 18
Rosina Reitenauer — 24
Susanna Hix — 30
Eve Stertzman — 33
Cathrin Blume — 34
Elisabeth Mayer — 49
Margret Mayer — 21
Mary Sneyder — 34
Margret Rench — 43
Ann White — 19
Margret Rench — 43
Rosina Smith — 28
July Boyer — 20
Susanna Dunn — 17
Ester [illegible] — 40
Ann Evely — 30
Elisabeth Mull — 24
Margret Roofe — 20
Mary Mowen — 20
Elisabeth Rench — 38
Margret Darton — 22
Mary Green — 21
Magdalena Young — 38
Magdalena Young — 20
Margret Young — 19
Ann Beaghtle — 41
Magdalena Beaghtle — 18
Mary Brendlinger — 42
Rosina Brendlinger — 18

Christianna Shoomaker aged 40
Ann Funck — 23
Barbara Funck — 23
Elisabeth Messer — 19
Barbara Sailor — 21
Magdalena Sailor — 47
Magdalena Nave — 24
Ann Dusinger — 23
Susanna Sneyder — 33
Ann Where — 28
Eve Smith — 18
Ann Stuard — 34
Rebecca [illegible]ment — 37
Ann Hinkle — 19
Sharlote Gross — 36
Ester Beard — 18
Elisabeth Dawney — 22
Margret Dilles — 43
Catharine Dilles — 19
Elisabeth Foghler — 46
Dorethea Lekron — 42
Elisabeth Roush — 40
Elisabeth Roush — 17
Catharina Lipshard — 46
Jane Hutsen — 24
Ann Shenafeeld — [illegible]
Susanna Thampson — 28
Ann Deibely — 40
Hanna Sprigg — 40
Elisabeth Lawson Belt — 22
Amilia Sprigg — 22
Elisabeth Lauman — 26
Rachel Dugles — 47
Elisabeth Koenig — 46
Rosina Martin — 40
Catharina Kletsadler — 36
Elisabeth Smith — 26
Mary Scot — 47
Mery Joss — 21
Catharina Simon — 26
Christiana Beaker — 32

9) Females Aged from 16 Years to 50 in Elisabeth 100

Elisabeth Hittler Aged Years — 22
Jane Maggal — 27
Barbara Hittler — 19
Elisabeth Reab — 22
Cathrin Hiffner — 43
Cathrin Hitter — 45
Babara Jacob — 48
Mary Jacob — 18
Rosina Dawney — 18
Ann Smith — 23
Margret Bower — 27
Christiana Klaber — 50
Cathrin Klaber — 20
Elisabeth Klaber — 17
Fronica Klaber — 17
Margret Reab — 42
Elisabeth Shees — 43
Susanna Shees — 19
Cathrin Grove — 25
Elisabeth Darise — 26
Cathrin Fore — 42
Elisabeth Leyder — 34
Cathrin Metz — 19
Magdalena Bentz — 30
Margret Sheafer — 24
Hannah Sitze — 48
Barbara Sitze — 23
Cathrin Leisor — 38
Mary Rowe — 23
Elisabeth Rowe — 17
Elisabeth Brate — 25
Elisabeth Rowe — 30
Elisabeth Lanebach — 34
Christianna Sneyder — 32
Cathrin Reimal — 44
Mary Reimal — 23
Elisabeth Reimal Aged — 20
Judith Ritter — 44
Ann Ritter — 22
Cathrin Ritter — 17
Cathrin Leyder — 35
July Leyder — 24
Ester Fuller — 19
Cathrin Mowen — 18
Margret Heard — 18

Total 300

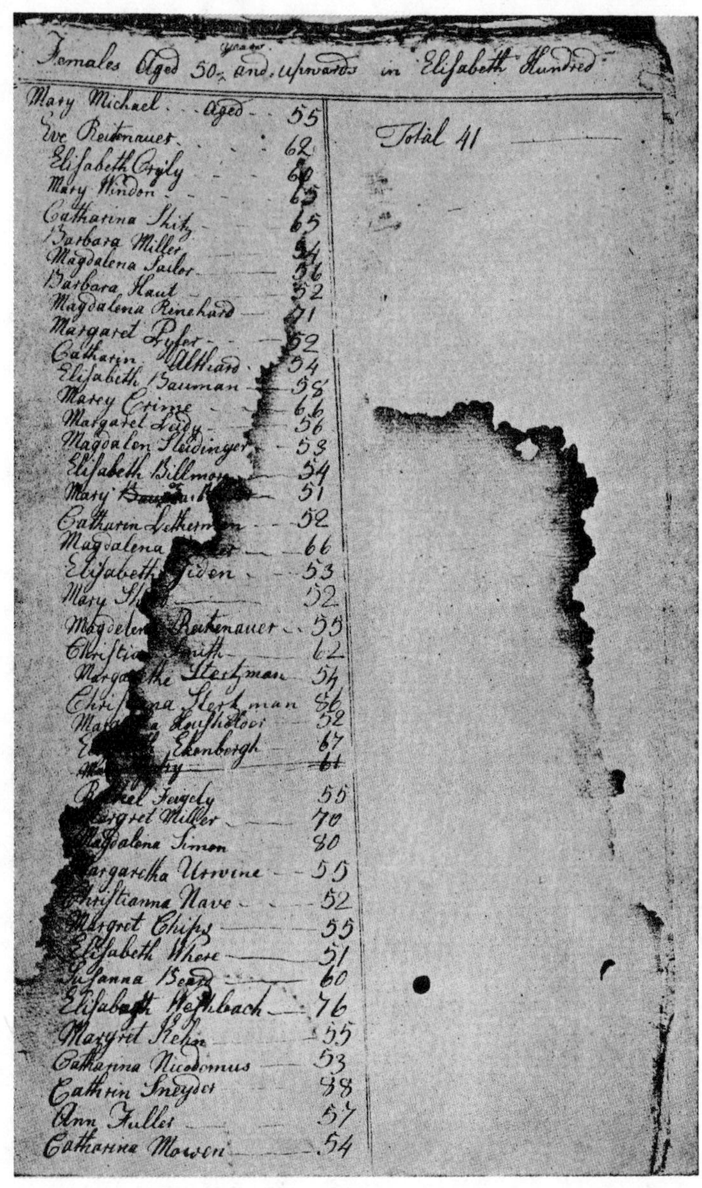

Females Aged 50 years and upwards in Elisabeth Hundred

Name	Age
Mary Michael Aged	55
Eve Reitenauer	62
Elisabeth Crily	60
Mary Windon	65
Catharina Shitz	65
Barbara Miller	54
Magdalena Sailor	56
Barbara Haut	52
Magdalena Rinehard	71
Margaret Pyfer	52
Catharin Altheard	54
Elisabeth Bauman	58
Marey Crime	66
Margaret Lady	56
Magdalen Steidinger	53
Elisabeth Billmore	54
Mary [illegible]	51
Catharin Letherman	52
Magdalena [illegible]	66
Elisabeth [illegible]iden	53
Mary Sh[illegible]	52
Magdalena Reitenauer	55
Christian Smith	62
Margarethe Steitzman	54
Christiana Steitzman	86
Ma[illegible] Houshelooi	52
E[illegible] Ekenbergh	67
~~[illegible]~~	~~61~~
Rachel Feigely	55
Margret Miller	70
Magdalena Simon	80
Margaretha Urvine	55
Christianna Nave	52
Margret Chips	55
Elisabeth Where	51
Susanna Beard	60
Elisabeth Weshbach	76
Margret Kehn	55
Catharina Nicodemus	53
Cathrin Sneyder	88
Ann Fuller	57
Catharina Mowen	54

Total 41

12 Females Aged 16 Years and under in Elisabeth Hd

Name	Age	Name	Age
Mary Stall Aged	2	July Stetzman Aged Years	2
Madilta Stull	4 months	Barbara Myer	15
Sarah Seiman	4	Christianna Sneyder	7
Elisabeth Braghin	15	Elisabeth Sneyder	4
Elisabeth Beker	4	Mary Sneyder	1
Margaretha Mequine	6	Cathrin Rench	16
Elisabeth Christman	1	Ester Rench	10
Cathrin Reitenauer	15	Catharin Rench	12
Rosina Reitenauer	11	Elisabeth Rench	10
Elisabeth Smith	2	Mary Wise	10
Salome Smith	1	Elisabeth Wise	8
Magdalena Smith	3 months	Catharin Wise	6
Susanna Berry	4	Margret [illegible]	2
Susanna Brakeneer	15	Elisabeth Mull	4
Elisabeth Brakeneer	13	Cathrin Mull	3
Barbara Brakeneer	6	Susanna Rench	10
Magdalena Draxel	14	Elisabeth Rench	8
Catharina Draxel	2	Ann Green	2
Elisabeth Kaufholder	15	Margret Young	8
Cathrin Kaufholder	11	Ester Beaghtle	16
Barbara Kaufholder	9	Susanna Beaghtle	14
Susanna Reitenauer	10	Ann Beaghtle	[illegible]
Dorothy Reitenauer	8	Elisabeth Beaghtle	[illegible]
Mary Reitenauer	4 months	Barbara Beaghtle	[illegible]
Christianna Hoffman	15	Sarah Brendlinger	[illegible]
Margret Ekenbergh	5	Christianna Brendlinger	13
Mary Guiry	16	Elisabeth Brendlinger	8
Sarah Guiry	11	Catharin Shoomaker	[illegible]
Sarah Jane	1	Susanna Shoomaker	3
Rachel Sciles	10	Elisabeth Wise	12
Cathrin Sciles	1	Elisabeth Funck	3 months
Chathanna Friend	16	Elisabeth Sneyder	13
Elisabeth Friend	10	Susanna Tallor	15
Dorothy Feigely	9	Catharina Urwine	9
Christiana Feigely	7	Margret Nave	15
Eave Reitenauer	3	Sophia Nave	8
Elisabeth Reitenauer	2	Cathrin Trisinger	6 months
Elisabeth Magdalena Reitenauer	2	Barbara Sneyder	6
Rosina Reitenauer	2 months	Susanna Sneyder	2
Mary Hix	2	Susanna White	11
Susanna Hix	4 months	Christiana White	8
Margret Stetzman	3	Elisabeth White	2
		Mary Garment	6

Females Aged 16 Years And Under in Elisabeth 100

Name	Age	Name	Age
Rebecca Garment Aged years	1	Elisabeth Koenig Aged years	4
Ester Gross	14	Magdalena Koenig	2
Elisabeth Gross	[illegible]	Catharina Smith	8
Elsy Gross	8	Mary Scot	12
Susanna Gross	[illegible]	Martha Scot	8
Ruth Beard	[illegible]	Susanna Beaker	7
Mary Dilles	[illegible]	Elisabeth Beaker	3
Elisabeth Dilles	11	Margret Hiffner	13
Magdalena Dilles	2	Elisabeth Hiffner	10
Sophia Dilles	7	Mary Hiffner	6
Dorethea Dilles	5	Cathrin Hiffner	4 months
Margret [illegible]	[illegible]	Mary Snyder	16
Dorethea [illegible]	2	Margret Hitler	17
Catharina Roush	15	Eve Hitler	3
Susanna Roush	14	Catharina Jacob	9
Magdalena Roush	7	Mary [illegible]	13
Margret Roush	8	Mary Rease	14
Elisabeth Lisshard	13	Eve Rease	3
Sarah Hutton	[illegible]	Catharin Shees	14
Eve Dimbelton	16	Elisabeth Shees	12
Margret Shenafield	7	Magdalena Shees	2
Susanna Shenafeeld	5	Elisabeth Grove	2
Catharina Shenafield	2	Cathrin Danish	3
Hanna Thamson	3	Elisabeth Fore	11
Margret Deibly	12	Susanna Fore	9
Catharina Deibley	9	Cathrin Fore	3
Littica Sprigg	14	Susanna Leyder	[illegible]
Corbin Sprigg	9	Elisabeth Leyder	[illegible]
Ann Sprigg	10	Magdalena Leyder	[illegible]
Hannah Sprigg	6	Mary Leyder	[illegible]
Isabella Frasier	3	Cathrin Bentz	[illegible]
Elisabeth Frasier	7	Margret Sheaffer	6 months
Catharina Lauman	4	Cathrin Feitz	14
Elisabeth Lauman	1 month	Hannah Feitz	10
Martha Dugles	16	Margret Leiser	9
Rachel Dugles	10	Cathrin Leiser	7
Mary Dugles	5	Christianna Leiser	4
Catharin Koenig	15	Susanna Leiser	3
Mary Koenig	[illegible]	Elisabeth Bread	1

Females Aged 16 Years and under in Elisabeth 100

Name	Aged Years
Christiana Bley	1
Mary Steck	2
Sofhia Fesler	8
Mary Fesler	4
Sofphia Sauder	14
Elisabeth Sauder	12
Barbara Rohrer	8
Eve Sneyder	12
Ann Hellin	13
Jane Hellin	12
Susanna Hellin	8
Dorathea Hoober	15
Christiana Hoober	13
Catharina Heiser	11
Elisabeth Heiser	[illegible] Months
Elisabeth Stinefeiver	3
Catharina Stinefeiver	2
Mary Stinefeiver	10 Weeks
Margaretha Kulin	15
Elisabeth Ansel	3
Elisabeth Lean	1
Catharina Barron	4
Barbara Fisher	15
Magdalena Fisher	8
Elisabeth Oster	7
Catharina Oster	5
Mary Oster	1
Catharina Belshoober	4
Mary Henry	3
Sarah Scot	6
Ann Scot	4
Catharina Miller	9
Elisabith Goll	1
Sophia Gilhard	12
Sutey Bell	9
Elisabeth Bell	5
Margaretha Bell	3
Margaretha Dile	6
Elisabeth Robinson	10 Months

Name	Aged Years
Mary Gneadig	5
Susana Gneadig	1
Margaretha Sneyder	13
Elisabeth Sneyder	9
Mary Sneyder	5
Elisabeth Heusholder	2
Elisabeth Weyand	1
Margaretha Miller	15
Mary Miller	12
Elisabeth Seller	11
Magdalena Fackler	14
Margaretha Fackler	11
Barbara Fackler	8
Hellina Fackler	[illegible] months
Susanna Bouman	11
Catharina Gessiner	7
Elisabeth Miller	7
Eve Miller	6
Elisabeth Wagoner	10
Suley Reed	10
Sharlote Reed	3
Elisabeth Link	1
Margarethe Campbell	8 months
Elisabeth Kogh	1
Elisabeth Barker	5
Jane Barker	4
Margaretha Kogh	4
Elisabeth Long	10
Margarett Long	[illegible]
Margaretha Long	3
Elisabeth Wolt	6
Mary Wolt	2
Dorathea Shooman	10
Magdalane Shooman	7
Magdalane Smith	8 Months
Susanna Blackburn	12
Mary Becks	1
Catharina Henman	3
Mary Herman	1
Margaretha Haul	14
Magdalena Cirily	1
Margaretha Reight	1
Magdalena Emry	2
Elisabeth Emry	3 Months
Elisabeth Katz	2
Catharina Katz	6 months

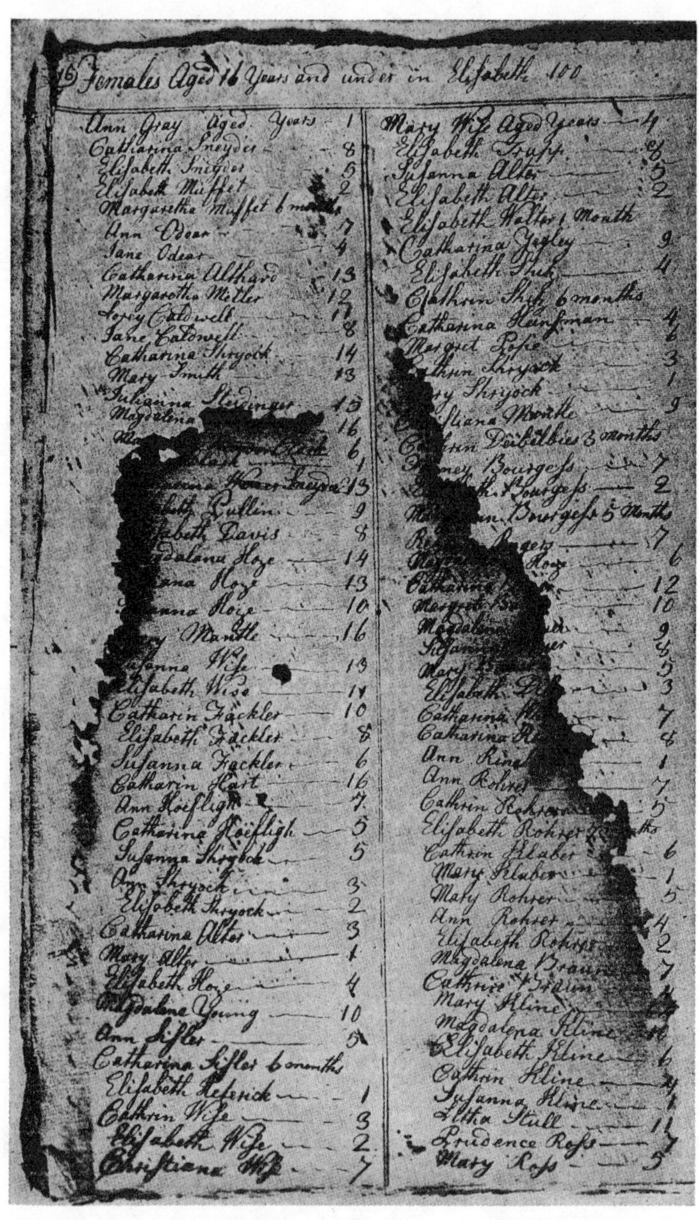

16 Females Aged 16 Years and under in Elisabeth 100

Name	Age	Name	Age
Ann Gray aged Years	1	Mary Wise Aged Years	4
Catharina Sneyder	8	Elisabeth Trapp	8
Elisabeth Sneyder	5	Susanna Alter	5
Elisabeth Muffet	2	Elisabeth Alter	2
Margaretha Muffet 6 months		Elisabeth Walter 1 Month	
Ann Odear	7	Catharina Yegley	9
Jane Odear	4	Elisabeth Shuk	4
Catharina Althard	13	Cathrin Shuk 6 months	
Margaretha Mettler	12	Catharina Heinsman	4
Sorry Caldwell	11	Margret Rose	6
Jane Caldwell	8	[illegible]athrin Shryock	3
Catharina Shryock	14	[illegible]y Shryock	1
Mary Smith	13	[illegible]stiana Mantle	9
Julianna Steidinger	15	Ca[illegible]n Daubelbies 3 months	
Magdalena [illegible]	16	[illegible]ney Bourgess	7
[illegible]	6	[illegible]abeth Bourgess	2
[illegible] Black	1	Ma[illegible] Bourgess 5 Months	
[illegible] Sneyder	13	Re[illegible]	7
[illegible] Pullin	9	[illegible] Hoze	6
[illegible]abeth Davis	8	Catharina [illegible]	12
[illegible]dalena Hoze	14	Margret [illegible]	10
[illegible]na Hoz	13	Magdalena [illegible]	9
[illegible]nna Hoze	10	Susanna [illegible]	8
[illegible] Mantle	16	Mary [illegible]	5
[illegible]sanna Wise	13	Elisabeth [illegible]	3
Elisabeth Wise	11	Catharina [illegible]	7
Catharin Fackler	10	Catharina R[illegible]	8
Elisabeth Fackler	8	Ann Rinal[illegible]	1
Susanna Fackler	6	Ann Rohrer	7
Catharin Hart	16	Cathrin Rohrer	5
Ann Hoeflich	7	Elisabeth Rohrer [illegible] months	
Catharina Hoeflich	5	Cathrin Klaber	6
Susanna Shryock	5	Mary Klaber	1
Ann Shryock	3	Mary Rohrer	5
Elisabeth Shryock	2	Ann Rohrer	4
Catharina Alter	3	Elisabeth Rohrer	2
Mary Alter	1	Magdalena Braun	7
Elisabeth Hoze	4	Cathrine [illegible]	4
Magdalena Young	10	Mary Kline	[illegible]
Ann Sifler	5	Magdalena Kline	[illegible]
Catharina Sifler 6 months		Elisabeth Kline	6
Elisabeth Hefenck	1	Cathrin Kline	4
Cathrin Wise	3	Susanna Kline	1
Elisabeth Wise	2	Letha Stull	11
Christiana Wise	7	Prudence Ross	7
		Mary Ross	5

47 Females Aged 16 Years And under in Elisabeth 100 —

Mary Lannabach Aged — 13
Catharina Lannabach — 9
Susanna Lannabach — 7
Elisabeth Lannabach — 4
Cathrin Sneider — 11
Christianna Sneyder — 7
Mary Sneyder — 4
Elisabeth Sneyder — 3
Margret Ritter — 14
Elisabeth Ritter — 8
Berbara Ritter — 4 months
Susanna Leyder — 12
Judith Leyder — 10
Cathrin Leyder — 8
Elisabeth Leyder — 7
Julyanna Leyder — 6
Eve Leyder — 4
Elisabeth Leyder — 1
Mary Mowen — 1
Magdalena Mowen — 4

Total 359

Males Aged 16 Years and under in Elisabeth 100

Name	Aged Years	Name	Aged Years
John Rohrer — Aged Years	9	Jacob Sciles Aged Years	12
Jacob Rohrer	3	John Sciles	6
Henry Klaber	12	William Sciles	3
John Klaber	3	Christopher Friend	12
Christian Rohrer	11	Peter Feigely	15
John Rohrer	9	Andrew Hix	10
Samuel Rohrer	7	William Hix	8
George Braun	1	Joseph Hix	6
Jacob Gidigh	12	Timothy Hix	4
John Kline	11	Martin Sterkman	7
William Kline	8	Henry Sterkman	5
Henry Furnear	11	Christian Meyer	14
Frederick Craft	7	Abraham Meyer	11
Henry Giden	5	Henry Meyer	6
James Nox	3	Jacob Sneyder	6
John Seiman	6	Henry Sneyder	5
Valentine Seiman	1	Peter Sneyder	4
Jonathan Heked	15	Levy Sneyder	2
William Chessman	6	John Rench	15
Philip Ch[illegible]	3	Peter Rench	12
Jacob Sm[illegible]	7	Joseph Rench	8
John Sm[illegible]	5	David Rench	5
George S[illegible]	3	Jacob Rench	14
Adam Sterkman	14	John Duarn	1
Peter Sterkman	11	Jacob Wise	13
David Sterkman	8	Adam Wise	4
Peter Prakunier	11	Samuel Wise	2
David Prakunier	9	Christian Wise	1 month
Henry Prakunier	4	Henry Moll	1
Jacob Prakunier	4	John Roof	2 months
Peter Draxel	11	Leonhard Moiven	1
Abraham Draxel	7	Michael Rench	13
Daniel Draxel	6 months	Daniel Rench	7
George Housholder	9	Jacob Young	15
John Housholder	6	Isaac Young	13
George Miller	9 months	Ludwig Young	11
Peter Reitenauer	7	Martin Baeghtle	8
Joseph Reitenauer	2	Jacob Baeghtle	6
George Peifer	5 months	George Brendlinger	
John Ekenbergh	3	Andrew Brendlinger	8
Jacob Ekenbergh	2	Michael Shoomaker	
James Guthry	14	Jacob Shoo[illegible]	13
Richard Guthry	9	John Shoomaker	10
Robert Guthry	6	Martin Funk 6 months	7
		Henry Funk	3
		John Funk	2

29 Males Aged 16 Years and under in Elizabeth 100

Name	Age	Name	Age
Michael Nave Aged Years	14	Robert Digles Aged Years	3
Henry Nave	12	Jost Koenig	12
Henry Sneyder	10	Mathias Koenig	10
John Sneyder	9	Peter Konig	6
Arnold Sneyder	4	James Martin	10
Valintine Sneyder	3	Samuel Martin	6
Christian Whore	2 months	John Wine	14
Abeija Garment	3	Robert Macal	3
Feremia Gross	11	Eckard Smith	16
Humfry Gross	9	James Scot	15
Wiliam Gross	7	John Scot	7
Wiliam Bears	14	Melker Scot	3
John Dilles	1	John Simon	3
Henry Fo[illegible]	13	Peter Simon	1
Sabastian Rau[illegible]	14	John Beaker	5
George Rau[illegible]	7	Wiliam Welsh	12
John Rau[illegible]	4	Valentin Kiffner	15
Henry L[illegible]	15	Frederick Kiffner	8
Isa[illegible] Hutson	8	Peter Kiffner	4
Charles Hutson	6	Conrad Kiffner	2
Jacob Shenafield	12	George [illegible]	11
John Shenafield	10	George [illegible]	14
Henry Shenafield	8	Henry Jacob	12
Wi[illegible]am Shenafield	4	Michael Jacob	7
[illegible] Thomson	5	John Smith	[illegible] months
John Thomson	1	Henry Boyer	3
George Debley	7	John Boyer	2
Frederick Dabley	2	Herman Klaber	[illegible]
Philip Sprigg	15	Ludwig Klaber	7
Casper Sprigg	13	Peter Real	13
Joseph Sprigg	11	John Real	6
Thomas Sprigg	7	John Grove	4
Wiliam Sprigg	6	Abraham Grove	4 months
[illegible]		Abraham Darise	13
[illegible]		John Darise	1
John Bauman	2	Jacob Fore	15
Samuel Digles	8	Henry Fore	10
Joseph Digles	12	Felix Fore	7
		Abraham Leyder	15
		John Leyder	10

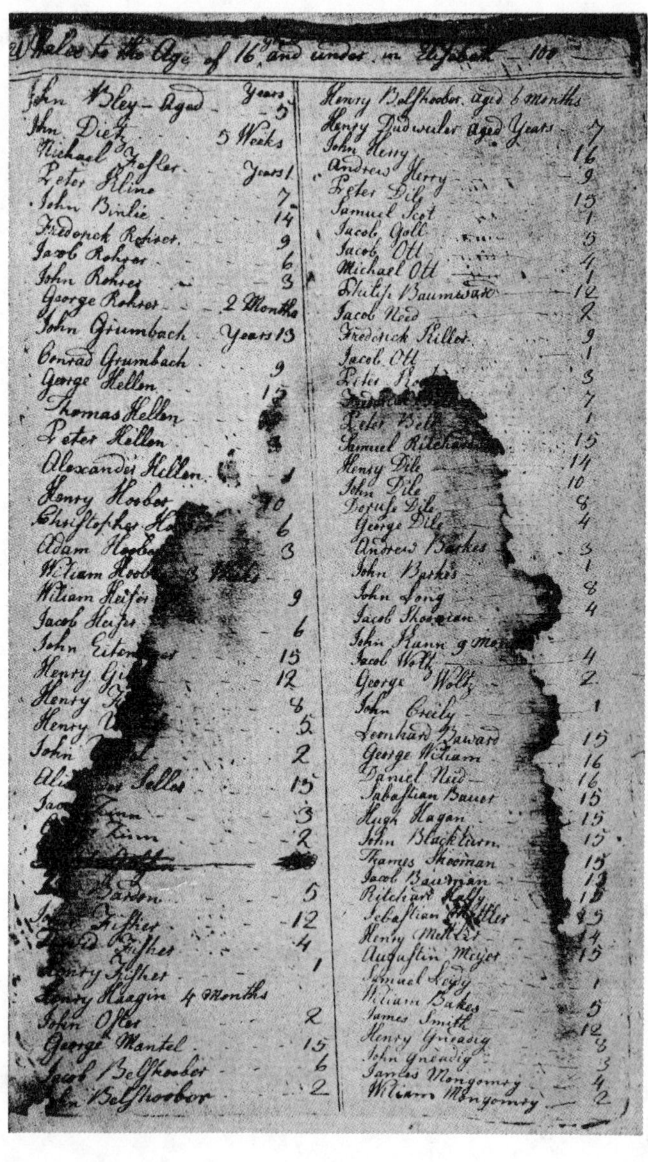

Males to the Age of 16 and under in Elizabeth — 100

John Bley — Aged Years 5
John Dietz 5 Weeks
Michael Fesler Years 1
Peter Kline 7
John Binlie 14
Frederick Rohrer 9
Jacob Rohrer 6
John Rohrer 3
George Rohrer 2 Months
John Grumbach Years 13
Conrad Grumbach 9
George Hellen 12
Thomas Hellen
Peter Hellen
Alexander Hellen 1
Henry Horber 10
Christopher H… 6
Adam Hoob… 3
William Hoob… 3 Weeks
William Heiser 9
Jacob Heiser 6
John Eitem… 15
Henry Gi… 12
Henry … 8
Henry … 5
John … 2
Ali… Sellers 15
Jac… Kinn 3
… Kinn 2
~~Thomas …~~
… Bardon 5
… Fisher 12
David Fisher 4
Henry Fisher 1
Henry Haagin 4 Months
John Ofter 2
George Mantel 15
Jacob Belshoober 6
…n Belshoober 2

Henry Belshoober, aged 6 months
Henry Dudweiler Aged Years 7
John Henry 16
Andrew Henry 9
Peter Dile 15
Samuel Scot 1
Jacob Goll 5
Jacob Ott 4
Michael Ott 1
Philip Baumwart 12
Jacob Need 2
Frederick Killer 9
Jacob Ott 1
Peter Ro… 3
… 7
Peter Belt 1
Samuel Ritchar… 15
Henry Dile 14
John Dile 10
Joseph Dile 8
George Dile 4
Andrew Barkes 3
John Barkes 1
John Long 8
Jacob Shooman 4
John Kann 9 mon
Jacob Woltz 4
George Woltz 2
John Creily 1
Leonhard Baward 15
George William 16
Daniel Need 16
Sabastian Bauer 15
Hugh Hagan 15
John Blackburn 15
Thomas Shooman 15
Jacob Bauman 13
Ritchard Kelly 1…
Sebastian Shiller 15
Henry Miller 14
Augustin Meyer 15
Samuel Leedy 1
William Bakes 5
James Smith 12
Henry Greadig 8
John Greadig 3
James Mongomery 4
William Mongomery 2

22 Males Aged 16 Years and under in Elisabeth Hundred

Name	Age
Jacob Weyand Aged - Years	3
Daniel Sneyder	1
Henry Miller	10
George Fackler	15
Peter Fackler	5
Jacob Weickle	1
John Bauman	9
Frederick Arnold	5
John Arnold	4
Daniel Arnold	2
George Miller	3
Valintine Wagoner	7
Conrad Wagoner 8 months	
Jacob Heafl[illegible]	12
George He[illegible]	11
Michael [illegible]ine	14
Jacob S[illegible]	9
John Sn[illegible]	9
Henry Sneyder	3
Jacob Sneyder 3 months	
Jacob Nicolaus 5 months	
Jacob Hoze	12
Is[illegible] Mcardell	10
[illegible]iliam Mcardell	8
[illegible]jamin Obeare	9
Jam[illegible] Rerrone	6
Jacob Shryock	10
Henry Shryock	7
George Shryock	1[illegible]
David Furney	16
Samuel Sprigg	16
John Fackler	4
Jacob Fackler	2
Thomas Barry	15
Daniel Bitlier	15
George Wentel	15
[illegible]rance Wistler	12
[illegible]lke Sywire	15
George Wise	16
George Gerdig	14
John Wise	15
Henry Sauder	12
Frederick Sweier	16
Charles White	1
John Highskill	1
Peter Hoeflighe	11
John Hoefligh 3 months	
Michael Domer Aged Years	4
Frederick Domer 3 months	
John Shryock 3 months	
Adam Beck	8
Peter Hoze	1
Frederick Hoze	9
Henry Hoze	5
Peter Hoze	2
Henry Siffler	3
Charles Hederick 1 month	
Ludwig Wise	9
Jacob Trapp	6
Henry Trapp	4
Philip Sillhard	9
Frederick Sillhard	4
Christian Yegley	6
John Yegley	3
Christopher Yegly 7 months	
Henry St[illegible]	2
John He[illegible]man	2
Samuel Clark	8
John Clark	4
Henry Shryock	10
John Shry[illegible]	5
Nicolaus [illegible]tel	7
Christian [illegible] 1 Month	
Michael Deibel[illegible]	5
John Deibelbies	3
Christopher Gellhover	5
Henry Gellhover [illegible] months	
Peter Baward	7
John Young	1
Jacob Bishop	15
George Bishop	13
Jacob Ile 8 months	
Peter Where	5
Henry Where	2
George Rinehard	6
Benjamin Elke	9
Jacob Lekron	13
Simon Lekron	10

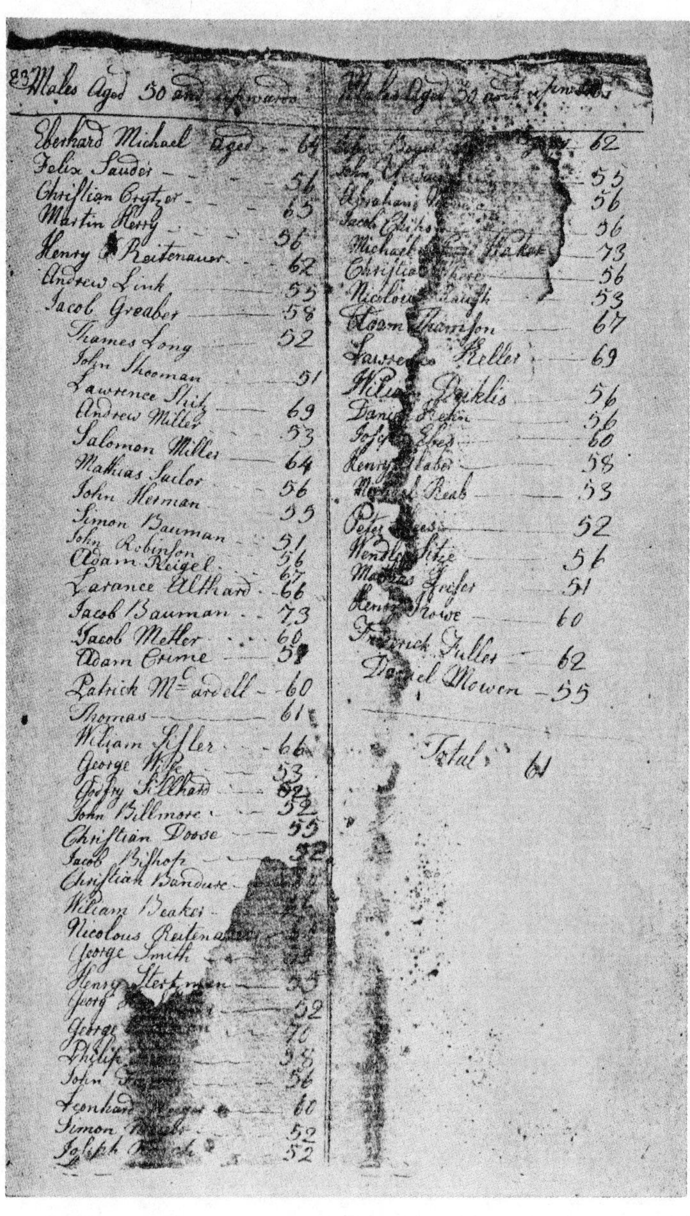

23 Males Aged 50 and upwards		Males Aged 50 and upwards	
Eberhard Michael Aged	64	[illegible] Boyer	62
Felix Sauder		John [illegible]	55
Christian Crytzer	56	Abraham [illegible]	56
Martin Herry	65	Jacob Chips	56
Henry Reitenauer	56	Michael [illegible] Waker	73
Andrew Link	62	Christian [illegible]	56
Jacob Greaber	55	Nicolous [illegible]	53
Thames Long	58	Adam Thompson	67
John Shooman	52	Lawrence Keller	69
Lawrence Shitz	51	William [illegible]kles	56
Andrew Miller	69	Daniel [illegible]	56
Salomon Miller	53	Joseph [illegible]	60
Mathias Sailor	64	Henry [illegible]	58
John Herman	56	Michael Reab	53
Simon Bauman	55	Peter [illegible]	52
John Robinson	51	Wendle Stice	56
Adam Reigel	56	Mathias [illegible]	51
Larance Althard	67	Henry Rowe	60
Jacob Bauman	66	Frederick Fuller	62
Jacob Metter	73	Daniel Mowen	55
Adam Crime	60		
Patrick McCardell	58		
Thomas	60	Total	61
William Sifler	61		
George Wi[illegible]	66		
Godfry Stillhard	53		
John Billmore	62		
Christian Doose	52		
Jacob Bishop	55		
Christian Banduse	52		
William Beaker	[illegible]		
Nicolous Reitena[illegible]	[illegible]		
George Smith	[illegible]		
Henry Steckman	53		
Georg [illegible]	52		
George [illegible]	70		
Philip [illegible]	55		
John [illegible]	56		
Leonhard [illegible]	60		
Simon [illegible]	52		
Joseph [illegible]	52		

25 Males Aged 16 Years And Under — in Elisabeth 100

Christian Motz Aged 3 months
Christopher Bentz Aged Years — 7
George Bentz — 4
John Bentz 7 months
John Sheafer — 5
Andrew Sheafer — 3
Henry Sitze — 16
Peter Sitze — 12
George Sitze — 5
William Leiser — 14
George Leiser — 12
Peter Leiser — 6
Henry Leiser 3 months
Henry Rowe 5 Months
Henry Breat — 3
Jacob Lanebach — 2
Andrew Nicodemus — 16
John Sneyder — 5
Frederick Sneyder — 2
Christian Sneyder 3 months
Elias Reimel — 15
John Reimel — 13
Philip Reimel — 7
Jacob Reimel 3 months
Andrew Maggry — 3
Tobias Ritter — 11
Jacob Ritter — 5
Andrew Sneyder — 6
Jacob Sneyder — 4
John Sneyder — 2 months
Baltzer Mowen — 15
George Mowen — 13
Daniel Mowen — 11
Peter Mowen — 8
Jacob Hart — 6 months

Total 375

(24) July the 22d - - 1776

An Abstract of the Return made by John Miller Constable of Elisabeth Hundred in the County of Frederick

White Persons

Of all Ages Males 757: Females 700:— 1457

More Males than Females 57

16 Years old and under Males 375: Females 359

More Males than Females 16: [734

from 16 to 50: Males 321: Females 300 - - 621 1457

More Males than Females 21:—

from 50: to 80: Males 61: Females 38 - - 99

More Males than Famales 23.

Eighty and upwards Males 0: Famales 3 . . 3 1457

More Females than Males 3:

Negroes

Sixteen Years old and under Males 19: Females 22: 41

Sixteen Years and upwards Males 16: Females 22 38

Total 79

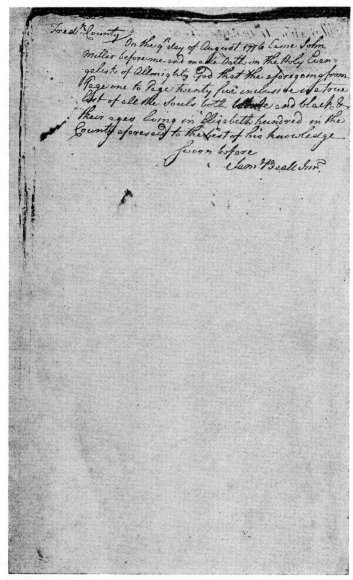

Fredk County

On the 9th day of August 1776 Came John Miller before me and made Oath on the Holy Evangelist of Allmighty God that the aforegoing from Page one to Page twenty five inclusive is a true List of all the Souls both white and black & their ages living in Elizabeth hundred in the County aforesaid to the best of his knowledge

Sworn before

Saml Beall Junr

Note: Pages 11, 13 and 18 are blank in the original Elizabeth Hundred Census. Pages 24 and 25 of the original are here transposed, to bring the summary last.

Earliest Records of All Saints' Parish, Frederick, Maryland, 1727-1781*

Barnhart, Benjamin *m* Rachael Wood, daughter of Joseph and Catharine Wood, April 3, 1773.

Biggs, Benjamin *m* Hennaratta Prudence Deborah Margaretta Munday, daughter of Henry Munday, Sept. 26, 1745.

Burroughs, John *m* Priscilla Rue, Mch. 17, 1760.

Bushelle, Elizabeth daughter of Samuel Bushelle and Allatha his wife, Buried April 6, 1743.

Byer, John *m* Ann Arnold April 3, 1743.

Carmack, William and Jane. Children:

Cornelius, *b* June 18, 1736.
William, *b* Nov. 10, 1738.
Evin, *b* Feb. 25, 1740.
John, *b* May 12, 1742.
Nathan, *b* Nov. 17, 1748.
Levi, *b* Nov. 3, 1750.
Quilah, *b* Jan. 13, 1754.

Chapline, Joseph *m* Ruhamah daughter of Rev. William Williams, October 22, 1741. Children:

William Williams, *b* Aug 20, 1742.
Ruhamah, *b* Jan. 7, 1743-4.
Joseph and Deborah, *b* Sept. 9, 1746.
Jane, *b* Sept. 18, 1748. "Jane daughter of Joseph Chapline and Ruhamah his wife Buried July 19, 1754."
James, *b* Sept. 28, 1750.
Ruhamah, *b* July 12, 1752. "Ruhamah, Daughter of Joseph Chapline and Ruhamah his wife Buried Sept. 6, 1748.
Sarah, *b* July 10, 1754.
Jeremiah, *b* June 24, 1756.
Jane, *b* Mar. 23, 1758.
Theodoras, *b* Mar. 14, 1760.

* "These will probably seem meagre and incomplete, but they are an exact and complete copy of the only records All Saints' has for the period covered"—Ernest Helfenstein.

The fragmentary records have been carefully transcribed, and grouped into the alphabetical form in which published, by the compiler of this volume—the general style adopted for the Church Records of births, &c.

Charlton, Arthur *m* Eleanor Harrison July 14, 1742. Children:
Alice, *b*. Aug. 11, 1743.
Thomas, *b*. Nov. 21, 1745.
Elenor, *b*. June 25, 1748.
Mary, *b* Jan. 31, 1750.
John Usher, *b* June 21, 1753.
Ann Phebe Penn, *b*. Feb. 6, 1756.
Jane, *b* Dec. 23, 1757.
Elizabeth Lettice, *b* Jan. 1, 1763.

Crisap, Thomas and Hannah. Children:
Daniel, *b* Feb. 29, 1727/8.
Thomas, *b* Feb. 28, 1732/3.
Elizabeth, *b* Jan. 19, 1736/7.
Sarah, *b* Apr. 21, 1740.
Michael, *b* June 29, 1742.

Edelin (also spelled "Edelen"), Christopher *m* Rebecca Johnson, daughter of George Johnson, July 24, 1757. Children:
Elizabeth, *b* June 19, 1760.
Eleanor, *b* Oct. 19, 1762.
Rebecca, *b* Oct. 10, 1765.

Elrood, "Sarah, wife of Jeremiah Elrood Buried Mar. 27, 1743."

Fryer, George *m* Mary Merrill May 22, 1743.

Harlan, Jacob and Deborah. Daughter:
Phebe, *b* Oct. 10, 1752.

Harlan, Jacob *m* Deborah Barton July 27, 1751.

Hedges, John and Mary—see Wilson, John.

Hedges, Joseph and Mary. Daughter:
Rebecca, *b* April 6, 1751.

Huffman, Jacob and Catharine. Children:
Jacob, *b* Nov. 2, 1753.
Mary, *b* Jan. 30, 1755.
Estor, *b* Jan. 6, 1757.
John, *b* Mar. 3, 1759.
Catharine, *b* Aug. 9, 1761.
Elizabeth, *b* May 9, 1764.

Humphrey, Owen and Mary. Children:
Owen, *b* Aug. 7, 1748.
John, *b* Sept. 29, 1750.

Hunter, Samuel "Clerk," *m* Mary Ann Carter, daughter of Richard Carter of Queen Anne Co. Feb. 16, 1749/50.

"Henry, son of Rev. Samuel Hunter and Mary Anne his wife born Dec. 3, 1750."

"Sarah, daughter of Rev. Samuel Hunter and Mary Anne his wife born April 7, 1752."

"Mary, daughter of Rev. Samuel Hunter and Mary Anna his wife born Oct. 1, 1753."

Johnston, Israel *m* Jean Dorsey April 7, 1743.

"Parmanes, son of Israel Johnston and Jane his wife born Jany. 12, 1743/4."

Julien, Allatha wife of Stephen Julien Buried Apr. 6, 1743.

Isaac, son of Stephen Julien *m* Susannah Hedges, daughter of Charles Hedges June 3, 1770.

Julien (Julion), Jacob *m* Catharine Hedges Feb. 2, 1743/4. "Jacob Julion Buried Mar. 26, 1747." Daughter:

"Rachel Julion *b* June 26, 1746." "Rachel Julion Daughter of Jacob Julien and Catharine his wife Buried Apr. 25, 1751."

Julien, Stephen. "Allatha, Wife of Stephen Julien Buried Apr. 6, 1743." "Stephen Julien *m* Ann Hedges July 14, 1743."

"Julien, Isaac son of Stephen, *m* Susannah Hedges, daughter of Charles Hedges June 3, 1770."

"Julien, John son of Stephen Julien, *m* Elizabeth Butler, dau of Peter Butler June 14, 1770."

Kimble, John *m* Agnes Beatty May 19, 1743.

Lane, Tydings *m* Hester Bobby May 9, 1743.

Mark, Robert *m* Catharine Scharlott, daughter of Thos. Scharlott, Nov. 7, 1743. Children:

Margaret, *b* Oct. 23, 1744.
Thomas, *b* Oct. 1, 1747.
Robert, *b* Jan. 2, 1750/1.

Martin, John and Ann ("Anne"). Children:

Demarius, *b* Apr. 10, 1740.
Zadock, *b*. Nov. 18, 1742.
Aquiah, *b* Feb. 6, 1745/6.
Ava (son), *b* Sept. 20, 1749.
Asenath, *b* Sept. 13, 1751.

Ogle, Joseph and Sarah. Children:

John, *b* Aug. 5, 1731.
Mary, *b* Apr. 15, 1735.
Sarah, *b* Apr. 22, 1739.
Eleanor, *b* Mch. 2, 1741.
Joseph, *b* Oct. 10, 1743.
Benjamin, *b* Jan. 13, 1747.
Thomas, *b* Jan. 23, 1749.
William, *b* Apr. 18, 1751.
James, *b* June 1, 1753.

Ogle, Joseph Buried Apr. 29, 1756.
Prather, Thomas and Elizabeth. Daughter:
Elizabeth, *b* Jan. 10, 1742/3.
Reed, James and Mary. Daughter:
Ann, *b* Mar. 26, 1740.
Reynolds, Thomas son of Thomas, *m* Catharine Wood, daughter of Joseph and Catharine Wood, June 26, 1766.
"Elizabeth, daughter of Thomas Reynolds and Catharine his wife born Nov. 26, 1767."
"William Reynolds," *b* Mar. 26, 1770.
Ridole, Benjamin *m* Jane McMurrey Apr. 7, 1742.
Rue, Isaac and Elizabeth. Daughter:
Presilia, *b* Aug. 11, 1742.
Shaaf, Casper *m* Allice Charlton daughter of Arthur and Elenor Charlton Nov. 12, 1759. Children:
"Mary daughter of Casper Shaff and Allice his Wife born Aug. 30, 1761."
John Thomas ("Shaff"), *b* Dec. 1, 1763.
Arthur ("Shaff"), *b* Oct. 7, 1765.
Casper ("Shaff"), *b* Jan. 24, 1775.
Smith, Peter and "Eave." Son:
John, *b* June 24, 1748.
Stephenson, Richard and Jane. Children:
Anne, *b* Feb. 11, 1736/7.
Mary, *b* Sept. 4, 1740.
Richard, *b* Aug. 9, 1742.
Elizabeth, *b* Mar. 17, 1744/5.
Jane, *b* Feb. 18, 1746/7.
Rosanah, *b* Sept. 15, 1749.
Story, Thomas *m* Patience Richards Jan. 13, 1743/4.
Swearingen, Samuel *m* Anne Wickham May 28, 1752.
Whitecar, Mark *m* Abigal Johnston Feb. 6, 1743/4.
Wickham, Nathaniel, the 3d, *m* Sarah Wood daughter of Joseph and Sarah Wood, Sept. 1, 1755."
Wilson, John *m* Mary Hedges widow of Joseph Hedges Sept. 17, 1753. Children:
Mary, *b* Aug. 14, 1754.
Sarah, *b* Mar. 19, 1756.
Wilson, Thomas son of Wm. Wilson, *m* Elisabeth Wood daughter of Joseph and Catharine Wood Aug. 6, 1769.
Winders, James *m* Elizabeth Sherwood May 9, 1743.

Wood, Joseph and Sarah. "Wood, Sarah Wife of Joseph Wood Buried July 11, 1747." Children:

Robert, *b*. Aug. 12, 1736.
Sarah, *b*. Jan. 10, 1738/9—see Wickham.
Joseph, *b*. Sept. 17, 1743.
Mary, *b*. Aug. 7, 1746.
Joseph Wood *m* Catherine Julion Sept. 11, 1747.
Catharine, *b*. Apr. 9, 1749—see Reynolds.
Elizabeth, *b*. Feb. 5, 1750/1.
Abraham, *b*. Feb. 7, 1753.
John, *b*. Nov. 29, 1754.
Rachel, *b* Feb. 5, 1757—see Barnhart.
Rebecca, *b* Sept. 12, 1759.
Ruth, *b*. Nov. 24, 1761.

Wood, Joseph son of Joseph and Sarah Wood *m* Anne Reed, daughter of James and Mary Reed Apr. 9, 1869.

Children of "Joseph Jr. and Ann his wife:"
Mary, *b* June 25, 1772.
Sarah, *b* June 21, 1774.
Elizabeth, *b* Feb. 10, 1777. "Elizabeth Wood daughter of Joseph Wood Jr. and Ann his Wife Buried March 31, 1777."
Catharine, *b* Mar. 22, 1778.
Joseph Wood 3d, *b* Jan. 9, 1781.

Wood, Robert *m* Catharine Dorsey daughter of Nicholas Dorsey Oct. 13, 1763. Children:

"Sarah daughter of Robert Wood and Katharine his Wife *b* June 1, 1764." "Wood, Sarah Daughter of Robert Wood and Katharine his Wife Buried Aug. 21, 1767."

Joseph, *b* May 19, 1765. "Wood, Joseph son of Robert Wood and Katharine his Wife Buried Nov. 5, 1768."

Nicholas, *b* May 13, 1766.
Martha *b* Jan 19th, 1768.

"Wood, Martha Daughter of Robert Wood and Katharine his Wife Buried Oct. 31, 1768."

Charles Dorsey, *b* Sept 29, 1769.
Amelia, *b* July 26, 1772.
Jesse, *b* Sept. 27, 1775. "Wood, Jesse son of Robert Wood and Katharine his Wife Buried Oct. 31, 1775."
Dennis, *b* Dec. 12, 1776.
Katherine, *b* Dec. 11, 1778.
Robert, *b* Dec. 18, 1781.

Tombstone Inscriptions from the Original Church Yard of All Saints' Parish, Frederick, Maryland (Complete)*

All Saints', the mother parish of Western Maryland, was created by Act of Assembly October 29, 1742: An "Act for dividing Prince George's Parish, in Prince George's County, and for erecting a parish out of the same, called by the name of 'All Saints' Parish.'" About three years later, when the town of Frederick was laid out by Dulaney, three lots on All Saints' Street were obtained, on a portion of which the parish church was built, and the surrounding church yard became the parish burying ground. Its use as such continued until 1852, and during this period it became the place of interment of many of the most prominent and influential citizens of Frederick County. Revolutionary heroes and men prominent in church and state were buried there, amongst the vaults erected being those of Thomas Johnson, Maryland's first governor; Worthington Johnson, John Grahame, Col. John McPherson and A. B. Hanson. In the early days of its history a definite portion of the lot was reserved for burial of bodies of slaves; but, as the demand for space increased with time and use, restrictions became necessary and a graveyard for colored members and slaves of church families was provided on an adjoining lot, outside of the church yard proper. The removal of the church building in 1814 provided additional space for burying purposes, but this relief was merely temporary and soon again all available space was in use. Efforts to purchase adjoining land came to naught, so that the church authorities were forced to again use the land that already contained graves. It was largely as a result of this condition, and through the efforts of men identified with All Saints' congregation, that the present Mt. Olivet Cemetery, of Frederick, was organized in 1852. After this date interments in the old church yard virtually ceased. The removal of the remains of some of the most prominent members began soon after this date, resulting in a lack of interest in the old yard, with consequent neglect. There still remained however a feeling of sentiment which prevented action on the part of the vestry until in 1914 it was able to reverently and carefully remove to a well selected and amply large section of Mt. Olivet all that could be found of those formerly

* By Mr. Ernest Helfenstein, Frederick, Md., who carefully matched fragments of stones, superintended the raising of stones buried under accumulated soil, etc., and has thus perpetuated this record which otherwise would have been destroyed.

buried in All Saints' Grave Yard. Of the total of three hundred and twenty-four bodies thus removed to Mt. Olivet, only seventy could be identified; while of the three hundred and eighty removed to the colored cemetery, virtually all were of unknown persons and from unmarked graves. The old yard is a vacant lot and for sale. Only about ten of the old tombstones were re-erected in Mt. Olivet, the remaining ones were placed under ground with the remains. These inscriptions are therefore especially important.

ALCOCK: "To the memory of | George Alcock | of the —— | Nottinghamshire | England | Died Dec 30 1852 | In the 76th year of | his age | After a residence of about | twenty years in this country | A christian communicant | of the P. E. Church |"

BAER: "In memory of | Charles D. Baer | son of Jacob and | Elizabeth Baer | died Sept. 5 1822"

BAKER (?) : (Stone broken) "Baker | . . . . Born–9th 1789 | and departed this | life May 5th 1798 |"

BARTHOLOW: "In memory of | Prudence Isabella | Daughter of | E. M. & M. J. Bartholow | born April 8th 1811 | died July 21 1811 | Aged 3 months | and 13 days |"

BEALL: "In memory of | William Murdock Beall | who died on the 5th of | November 1823 | in the 82nd year of | his age |"

"In memory of | Mary Ann Beall | Daughter of W M Beall | and Mary his wife | who died on the 29th | November 1817 | in the 46th year of | her age |"

"In memory of | Mary Beall | wife of William M Beall | who died on the 26th | of April 1810 | in the 68th year of | her Age |"

Rebecca (Beall) Willson—see Willson, Thomas P.

Upton, Rev. and L.—see Ogle, Louisa.

BISHOP: In memory of | Mark Bishop | who was born Sept 30 | 1786 | and died Oct 16, 1836 | Aged 50 years, 16 days."

BLAIR: Mary True, daughter of Marbow Blair, Esq., of Charles Co.—(see True).

BOTELER: "Sacred | to the memory of Elias | Boteler who was born | the 15th of September | 1767 and departed this | life the 14th of October | Anno Domini 1807 | Aged 39 years 10 months | and 29 days | Ann Maria Boteler | was born on the 5th of July 1806 and died | 15th of October 1807 | In the midst of life | we are in Death."

BOYD: "In memoriam | Margaret Boyd que | obyt quinto die | Januarii 1774 | Aetatis que ano | 25 Corpus cujus in | spem resurrectionis | benedicto his post- | tumest Archibaldus | Boyd Conjux ejus | dolore affectus hoc | monumentum confectavit."

BRADFORD: "In memory of | William Ringgold Bradford | the son of | William & Jane Bradford | who died July 20th 1824 | aged 15 months | And of | Alexander Ringgold Bradford | the son of | William & Jane Bradford | who departed this life | July 4 1825 | Aged 10 months | Sleep soft sweet babes. no | dreams disturb your rest | Your spirits flew from pure | spotless breasts | Sleep then sweet innocents | nor do you dread | The surging storm that | threatened o'er your head |"

BUTLER: "Here | Lyeth the body | of | Elizabeth Butler | who departed | this life October | Anno Domini 1753 | Aged 48 years |"

"In | Memory of | Tobias Butler | Died 15th April 1815 | AE 68 | his granddaughter | Elizabeth Houston | daughter of | ——s F & Agnes Houston | died 18 Nov 1816 |"

CAMPBELL: "Sacred | to the memory of | William Campbell | who was born August | 8th 1756 | & died Sept 11, 1821 | His character | Is drawn in the xxlx | chapter of Job | And | His name | It is humbly hoped | and believed will | appear at the last | day recorded in some | page of the book of Life | Blessed are the | dead who die in | the Lord |"

DORSEY: "In memory of | Joshua Dorsey | who | departed this life | November 15, 1848 | Aged 57 years The noblest work of God | An honest man |"

"In memory of | Alexander Fridge | son of | Ely and Sarah Dorsey | who departed this life | Jany 24 1827 | Aged 2 years 11 months | & 3 days |"

EASTBURN: "Sacred | to the memory of | Dr. Edward R. Eastburn | who departed this life | October 22nd, 1821 | Aged 19 years, 10 months | and 7 days | It is finished said his | dying breath | Again he said I fear not death | Oh let me mount and | soar away | To the bright world of | endless day."

GOLDSBOROUGH: "Sacred | To the Memory of Eliza Margaret | daughter of | Edward & Margaret Goldsborough | who departed this life | July 25th 1834 | Aged 18 months."

HANSON: See Wilson, Alexander B. & Susan W. Hanson.

HARDESTY: "In memory of | Richard Hardesty | son of | John S & Eleanor D | Hardesty | of Charles County, Md | who was born Nov | 30th 1809 | and departed this life | Jan 25th 1830 | Aged 20 years."

HARPER: "Mariah Harper | Born Dec 23, 1806 | Died Oct 1st, 1884 | Aged 77 years 9 months | and 8 days |"

HARRISON: "October 1841 | H. F. Harrison | Lieut in the Navy of the U. S. | Feb 16 1806 | Aged 36 years |"

HENDERSON: "In Memory of Lucy | Henderson Consort | of | Robert Henderson | who departed this | transitory life on the | 29th of June in the year | of our Lord 1814 | Aged 35 years |"

HOUSTON: See Butler,Tobias.

HOWARD: "Departed | this life March 7 | 1844 | Margaret Howard| in the 65th year | of her age |"

JOHNS: "In memory of | Mary Lavinia | daughter of | Revd. Henry V.D.& | Lavinia Johns | Born 20th of Feby 1831 | Died Decr 16th 1832."

"In memory of | John Henry | son of the | Revd John & Juliana Johns | Born 29th of April 1827 | Died July 6th 1829."

JOHNSON: "In memory of | Col James Johnson | of Springfield | who died on the 3d | day of December | 1809 in the 74th | year of his age |"

"In memory of | Mrs Margaret Johnson | Consort of Col. James | Johnson who departed | this life on the 3d | day of September 1813 | Aged 64 years | "

"Here lies | Miss Rebecca Johnson | the dear beloved and only | Daughter of | Col James Johnson | who died in the | nineteenth year of her age | A D 1797 |"

"Thomas Johnson | Nov 4, 1732 Oct 26, 1819 | The first Governor of | the State of Maryland | 1777 to 1779 |"

"Thos W. Johnson M.D. | died April 30th 1847 | In the 54th year of | his Age | "Blessed are the dead which | die in the Lord" |"

"On this spot affection | drops a tear | to | the memory of | Mrs Elizabeth Johnson | only daughter of Joshua and | Jane Dorsey, | and wife of Doct. Thomas W. Johnson who on | the 20th day of March 1829 | fell a-sleep in the arms of | Jesus, | in the 52nd year of her age | And also | in memory of her infant | Son Thomas A. Johnson | who departed this life Febr | 11th 1825 aged 19 months |"

"Sacred | To the memory of | William H. Johnson | Second Son of | D. T. W. & Elizabeth | Johnson | who departed this life | Jany 5th 1846 | in the 25th year of his age | How short the race our | son has run | Cut down in all his | bloom | The course but yesterday | begun | Now finished in the | Tomb |"

"Sacred | To the memory of | Jane Catharine | oldest daughter of | Thos W & Elizabeth Johnson | who departed this life | on the 19th day of Septr 1852 | in the 17th year of her age | Hear what the voice from | Heaven declares | To those in Christ who die | Relieved from all their | Earthly cares | They'll reign with him on high |"

JONES: "In memory of | William, son of | Thomas W. & Virginia J. | Jones | Born Sept 10, 1847 | Died Jany 23, 1848 | Aged 4 months & 13 days | also | Henry Clay son of | Thomas W. & Virginia J. | Jones | Born Aug 13, 1844 | Died May 18, 1850 | Aged 5 years 9 months | & 5 days | Suffer little children | to come unto me and | forbid them not for of | such is the Kingdom | of God |"

MCPIKE: "Here lyeth the | Body of Sarah McPike | 6th Regt | who

Departed This Life | the 28 Jany 1781 aged 38 yrs | A wife most kind, Gentle, | Deer, A faithful friend | that Lyeth Here | (Compass and square) | My days was spent my | glass was run | O Children deer |, prepare to come |"*

MALAMBRE: "Sacred | To the memory of | George Malambre | Born July 5, 1804 | departed this life | March 11, 1845 | Aged 40 years, 8 mo | and 6 days |"

"Sacred | to the memory of | Rachel Malambre | consort of | George Malambre | who departed this life | Feb 17, 1843 | Aged 34 yrs 11 months | and 17 days | Lord I commit my soul to thee | Accept the sacred trust | Receive this nobler part alone | And watch my sleeping dust |"

MARSHALL: "In Memory of | Miss Chloe Marshall | who departed this life | The 1st of May 1807 | Aged 39 years 4 months | & 23 days | Thus when the night | of death did come | My flesh shall rest | beneath the ground | And wait thy voice to | rouse my tomb | With sweet salvation | in the sound |"

MAULSBY: "Mrs Sarah Maulsby | wife of | Dr. David I. Maulsby | Born Feby 24 1807 | Died Jany 2 1880 | in the 73rd year of her age | Requiescat in pace |"

"Israel Davidson | first son of | Wm. P. & Emily C. T. Maulsby | who died Feb 14th 1837 | Aged 4 months & 11 days | And of | Elizabeth Harrison | daughter of | Wm. P. & Emily C. T. Maulsby | who died July 12th 1838 | Aged 4 months & 11 days | All thats sweet was made | But to be lost when sweetest |"

MAYHEW: "Here | Lieth the Body | of | Joseph Mayhew | who was born at | Hartwell | in | North Hamptonshire | in the kingdom of | Great Britain | and who departed this life | ———1763 |"

NEILL: "In memory of | Elizabeth Neill | Wife of | John Neill | Merchant | Daughter of Thomas and | Jane Lang | who departed this life | April 3d 1786 | Aged 20 years | also James Neill | who departed this life | January 28th | 1787 | Aged 10 months | and also | James Neill | who departed this life | March 1788 | Aged 5 months."

"Sarah | the late consort of | Thomas Neill, Merchant | and Daughter of | The Revd Hugh Neill | Aug 4, 1775 Aged 18 yrs | Since beauty, and useful | acquirements | Could not ward off the | early stroke | Well we may conclude | That Heaven intends | the virtuous soul | For nobler purposes | Than to be for years | distinguished on this | fluctuating stage."

*"The copy appears exactly as the stone is inscribed. What her connection with the '6th Regt' was I do not know, nor why the Masonic emblems were used on her stone"—E. H.

NELSON: "In memory of | Gen Roger Nelson | who died on the 7th June 1815 | Aged 56 years | He lived more for his country | than for himself. He was | engaged amongst others in | the battles of Eutaw, Guilford, | Camden and was present at | the surrender of Cornwallis | at YorkTown: He bore upon | his body the scars of sixteen wounds | received during the Revolutionary | War. Many years of the afterpart | of his life were spent in | both branches of the Legislature | of Maryland and in the | Congress of the U. S. and in his | declining years he served | as one of the Judges of the | 6th Judicial district of M. D. | As a husband and Father is held in most affectionate | remembrance |"

"To the Memory of | Mrs Eliza Nelson | widow of General | Roger Nelson | who departed this life | on the 23d day of | March 1855 | Aged 81 years |"

"Sacred | To the memory of | Harriott Love Nelson | who died Aug. 15th 1823 | Aged 8 months & 7 days | and her sister | Frances Columbia Nelson | who died March 22nd 1832 | Aged 23 months & 6 days | daughters of | John & Frances Harriott Nelson | The Lord gave and the Lord | hath taken away | Blessed be the name of the Lord"

"In memory of | Frederick | youngest son of | Roger & Eliza Nelson | who died Jan 27th 1823 | Aged 19 years & 3 months | He was distinguished | alike for nobleness of | heart and for superiority | mind and even in the | buoyancy and carelessness | of youth gave flattering | promises of a manhood | full of glory, of honour | and of worth. He was a dutiful son and | affectionate brother |"

OGLE: "Louisa Ogle | daughter of | Rev Upton & | L. Beall | born Dec 6 | 1838 | died July 2 | 1839 |"

PARROT: "In | Memory of | Mary Parrot | who was born in | England & died at Mr. | Ross's in this Town | on the 26th of Jany | A. D. 1818 Aged 74 | yrs |"

PIGMAN: "In memory of | W. P. Pigman | who died 23d August | 1815 Aged Nineteen | months | In the morn of life | God was pleased to | take him from the | evil to come |"

"In memory of | Ann Pig M——— | who Died in December | In the 75th years of | Her Age Her | Evening closed | in Peace |"

PRICE: "James G. Price | died Aug 14, 1834 | In the 27th year of his Age | A native of Cathel | County of Tipperary | Ireland | Erected by his brother | Wm. G. Price

SAUNDERS:

SHERWOOD: "Cemented by Love | (Compass and square) | Wm. Saunders | died Octr 18th 1827 | Aged 41 years | also | Abm Sherwood | died April 5th 1829 | Aged 42 years | Natives of England |"

SHANKS: "In memory of | Mrs Elizabeth Shanks | who departed this life | February the 15th 1825 | this stone was erected | by her friend |"

SNYDER: "In memory of | Alexander Snyder | Son of Doctr & | Rachel Snyder | born Augst 29th A D | 1797 | Departed this life | Decr 19th Aged 3 mo | & 21 Days |"

SPRINGER: "In the memory of | William Springer | , who died Nov 22 1804 | Aged 6 months 2 weeks | Fond affections nere | could save | A beautiful infant | from the grave."

STAYMAN: "Laura V | Daughter of | G F & R A | Stayman | died 19th March 1841 | in the 6th year of | her Age | "

TANNEHILL: "In Memory of | Verlenda Tannehill | who died on the 15th March | 1818 | in the 77th year of her | age daughter of | William & Mary Tannehill | "

THOMSON: "In | Memory of | Peter U. Thomson | of | St Marys County | Died Augt 29th 1825 | Aged 38 years."

TRUE: "In memory of | Mary True | Daughter of | Marbow Blair Esq of | Charles County, Md. formerly | of Glasgow, Scotland | She died as she had | always lived in the | confidence of a certain | faith, in the comfort of | a reasonable and holy | hope, in favor with God | and in perfect charity with the world | Feb 4, 1818."

TRUSCOTT: "In memory of | Alexr Truscott | who died April 10, 1840 | Ages 53 years 4 mo | and of his wife | Cate Truscott | who died April 15th 1840 | Aged 55 years 5 mo | Natives of England | Honora Patrem et matrem tuum | "

TYLER: "To the memory of | John Tyler | a distinguished | Physician & Surgeon | who was born on the 29th | of June 1763 | and died Oct 15, 1841 | "

"Catharine Contee | wife of | Dr. John Tyler | died September 17, 1831 | Aged 61 years | This tribute to worth and virtue is erected | by her affectionate and | afflicted husband."

VERNON: "Emma H. Vernon | Daughter of | Nathaniel and Charlotte | Aug 19, 1829 | Aged 15 months | "

WILSON: "In memory of | Margaret Wilson | daughter of | Alexander B & | Susan W. Hanson | who died Augt. 22nd 1833 | Aged 15 months | 22 days"

WILLSON: "Thomas P. Willson | was born April 6th | 1768 | and died Decr 26th | 1832 | Aged 64 years 8 | months & 20 days | "

"In memory of | Rebecca Willson | Wife of Thomas Willson | & Daughter of | William M & Mary Beall | who died on the 1st of | October 1807 | in the 32d year of her | age | "

WOLFENDEN: "Sacred to the | memory of | John Wolfenden | A native of the County Down | Ireland | who departed this life | on the 16th of May 1807 | Aged 41 years | As a husband, Father and Friend | He was equalled by few | Goodness, Mildness and | Christian Patience he | eminently possessed | His short and blameless | life was an uniform | preparation for a | Better World."

(?) "Frederick Elsw-orth | ——re | ——the 7th June | 1827——the 29th year of | His Age."

Official Poll of Presidential Election in Frederick County, Md., November 9 to 12, 1796; 1917 Voters*

"Poll taken at the Court House in Frederick Town in and for Frederick County. Begun on the Second Wednesday of November 1796, being the Ninth day of the same Month and continued by Adjournment from day to Day untill the Twelfth day of the same Month inclusive for Electing an Elector of the President and Vice-President of the United States of America to wit:"

[Candidates: John Tyler (Federalist voters marked F), and Geo. Murdock (Democrat-Republican voters marked D-R).]

Voters' Names:		*Voters' Names:*	
Tobias Butler	(F)	Jacob Meddert	(F)
Adam Fischer	(D-R)	John Baltzer	(F)
William Duvall	(F)	Francis Mantz	(D-R)
Henry Kuhn	(F)	Adam Cramer	(D-R)
Henry Bear	(D-R)	Daniel Jacobs	(D-R)
Woodward Evitt	(F)	Montjoy Bailey	(D-R)
Adam Frushour	(F)	John Neill	(D-R)
Samuel Templing	(F)	William M. Beall	(D-R)
Lloyd Ward	(F)	Roger Nelson	(F)
John Winemiller	(F)	Joseph Ogle	(F)
Samuel Duvall	(F)	Jacob Steiner, Jr.	(D-R)
William Brandenburgh	(F)	Henry Myers	(F)
Boltzer Koonz	(F)	Andrew Low	(F)
Walter Funderbergh	(F)	George Cook	(D-R)
George Creager	(F)	Philip Jacobs	(D-R)
George Zealer	(F)	Peter Brown	(D-R)
Gotlep Miller	(F)	Henry Brown	(D-R)
Samuel Miller	(F)	John Smay	(D-R)
Henry Zealer	(F)	Thomas Johnson	(D-R)
Jacob Wisie	(F)	Christian Smay	(D-R)
Henry Bontz	(F)	Henry Brother	(D-R)
Richard Harding	(F)	David Mantz	(D-R)

* Published under consent of Hon. Hammond Urner, Chief Judge, Circuit Court for Frederick County, Md., copied from the original at Frederick, Md., by Miss Nellie Carter Garrott, Frederick, Md.

Voters' Names:		*Voters' Names:*	
Peter Coblentz	(F)	Michael Creahbaum	(F)
Elijah Beatty	(F)	John Gantt	(F)
John Shriner	(F)	Jacob Levy	(F)
Jestian Maberry	(F)	Benjamin Ogle	(D-R)
Joseph Walling	(F)	Samuel Lilly, Jr.	(D-R)
John Schley	(D-R)	Isaac Fry, Jr.	(F)
John Getzandanner	(D-R)	Peter Crise	(F)
Peter Howman	(F)	Ralph Cato	(F)
John Lingenzelter	(F)	John Turner	(F)
Michael Weever	(F)	William Crossman	(F)
John Wigle	(F)	Frederick Kinkloy	(F)
John Weaver	(F)	James Whaling	(F)
Christian Getzandanner	(F)	Charles Sefton	(F)
Peter Walter	(F)	Christian Road	(F)
Jacob Klind	(F)	Phillip Keller	(F)
Francis Gisinger	(F)	Phillip Thomas	(D-R)
Henry Gorden	(F)	Adam Goyer	(F)
John Burkett	(F)	Adam Shisler	(F)
Christopher Hochwarter	(F)	Daniel Cost	(F)
Stephen Kline	(F)	Casper Mantz	(D-R)
George Tiyer	(F)	Jacob Hilderbrand	(F)
John Stonebraker	(F)	Henry Cose	(F)
John Hall	(F)	Samuel Levy	(F)
Stopherl Bomhisee	(F)	Tobias Butler, Jr.	(F)
Jacob Zermeman	(F)	John Morgan	(F)
Thomas Kirk, Jr.	(D-R)	Daniel Cossell	(F)
David Levy, Jr.	(F)	John Lutes	(F)
Thomas Taylor	(D-R)	Basil Williamson	(F)
Casper Shaaff	(D-R)	John Walling	(F)
Isrell Tayler	(F)	Lewis Gardner	(F)
Edward Boteler	(F)	John Deall	(F)
John Hedge	(F)	John Keller	(F)
John Wayne	(F)	William Markell	(F)
Michael Hainer	(F)	Benjamin Johnson	(D-R)
Mathias Shrub	(F)	Adolf Everhart	(D-R)
Jacob Lott	(F)	John Stinger	(D-R)
Thomas House	(F)	Casper Hane	(D-R)
Jacob Boyer, Jr.	(F)	John Custoler	(D-R)
Leonard Storm	(F)	George Craumer	(D-R)
George Trisler	(F)	Philip Eppert	(D-R)
Jacob Brengle	(D-R)	Henry Kulp	(D-R)

Voters' Names:		*Voters' Names:*	
George Burkett	(F)	Adam Creager	(D-R)
Elisha Whiting	(F)	Peter Cramer	(D-R)
Isaac Hedges	(F)	John Barrick, Sen.	(D-R)
Henry Sivers	(F)	John Ringer	(D-R)
James Tidy	(F)	Simon Waltz	(D-R)
Alexander Rait	(F)	John Crum	(D-R)
Conrad Whiltisis	(D-R)	Wm Barrick	(D-R)
John Frank	(D-R)	Christopher Binjer	(D-R)
Michael Houck	(F)	William Rice	(D-R)
Baker Johnson	(D-R)	Peter Barrick	(D-R)
Benjamin Duvall	(F)	Jacob Cramer	(D-R)
Abraham Titlow	(F)	Jacob Weaver	(D-R)
Abraham Deaver	(D-R)	John Hoffman	(D-R)
George Stockman	(F)	John Barrick Jr.	(D-R)
Richard Potts	(D-R)	Jacob Thomas	(D-R)
Benj. West	(D-R)	Daniel Buzzard, Jr.	(D-R)
Adam Shindler	(F)	Jacob Hoffman	(D-R)
Henry Stophell	(F)	Christian Creager	(D-R)
John Gittinger	(F)	Christian Champer	(D-R)
Enoch Fry	(F)	John Buzzard	(D-R)
Philip Fegie	(F)	David Barrick	(D-R)
William Everan	(D-R)	Peter Fout	(F)
Jeramiah Belt	(D-R)	Edward Bannister	(D-R)
William Potts	(D-R)	Wm Jas Turner	(D-R)
John Clink	(F)	Jacob Creager	(D-R)
Abraham Stofell	(F)	David Arnold	(D-R)
Joshua Dorsey	(D-R)	Samuel Arnold	(F)
Nicholas Rittenhouse	(D-R)	John Cramer	(D-R)
Michael Casner	(F)	William Cramer	(D-R)
Upton Sheridine	(D-R)	John Hoover	(D-R)
John Rogers	(D-R)	George Morgan	(D-R)
Valentine Black	(D-R)	George Keller	(D-R)
Henry Maynard	(D-R)	John Fleming	(D-R)
Ephriem Howard	(D-R)	William Murphey	(D-R)
John Hammond of John	(D-R)	John Hartsock	(D-R)
Joseph Arnold	(D-R)	Jefes Bennet	(D-R)
John Bryan	(D-R)	Melchor Tabler	(D-R)
David Bryan	(D-R)	Christian Roop	(D-R)
John Staley	(F)	Nicholas Shiffers	(D-R)
Henry Barrick	(D-R)	Jacob Missell	(F)
Daniel Buzzard	(D-R)	John Martin	(F)

Voters' Names:	
Jacob Lowman	(F)
Samuel Ureley	(F)
Philip Lambright	(F)
Michael Metz	(F)
Levy Thompson	(F)
Joshua Dorsey, Jr.	(D-R)
Christian Weaver	(F)
Stephen Hedges	(F)
Benj. Stallings	(F)
William Hedges	(F)
Valentine Weaver	(F)
John S. Hall	(D-R)
William Beall	(F)
Jacob Fister	(F)
William Cockran	(F)
Christian Coogle	(F)
Michael Culler	(F)
Lewis Mahoney	(F)
Peter Smith	(F)
Henry Scifer	(F)
Cornelius Stigers (or Meyers)	(F)
Samuel Bugdon	(F)
Henry Lambright	(F)
Henry Crise	(F)
Jesse Bennett	(D-R)
Elec Breshares	(D-R)
Andrew Michael	(F)
Jacob Adams	(D-R)
John Sifers	(F)
Richard Ijams	(D-R)
Abraham Crabster	(D-R)
Henry Wimemuler	(F)
Balser Cramer	(D-R)
William Breshares	(D-R)
John Albaugh	(D-R)
Daniel Albaugh	(D-R)
Nathaniel Marshall	(D-R)
Jacob Stofell	(F)
Geo. Ramsbergh	(F)
Richard Gaff	(D-R)
Henry Kitterllech	(F)

Voters' Names:	
Martin Englebright	(F)
John Lucorst	(F)
Jacob Shingle	(F)
Michael Strafer	(F)
William Waugh	(F)
Peter Kemp	(D-R)
John Boyer	(F)
Solomon Kemp	(D-R)
Richard Colgate	(F)
Thos. Lucorst	(F)
Dennis Hensey	(D-R)
Roger Edmonston	(D-R)
Thos. Busey	(D-R)
John Ensey	(D-R)
Solomon Creager	(D-R)
George Carr	(D-R)
George Buchey	(D-R)
Francis Sappington	(D-R)
John Hilleary	(D-R)
Joseph Gwenn	(D-R)
George Reppert	(D-R)
Henry Romsower	(D-R)
Thomas Walter	(D-R)
Elec Hyat	(D-R)
Lewis Mobberley	(D-R)
Christian Cramer	(D-R)
Hugh Coblence	(F)
Geo. Hoffman	(D-R)
Francis Hoffman	(D-R)
Jacob Champer	(F)
Jonathan Gisberd	(D-R)
Jacob Ennglebe rd	(F)
Peter Crist	(F)
Moses Spoon	(F)
Henry Crist	(F)
Michael Englebright	(F)
Michael Tabler	(F)
Peter Shaffer	(F)
Joseph Hilderbrand	(F)
Davalt Viel	(F)
Charles Catrow	(F)

Voters' Names:		*Voters' Names:*	
Ephriel Maynard	(D-R)	Echart Kels	(F)
Jacob Stone	(F)	Lawrence Brengle, Sr.	(D-R)
Thomas Williamson	(F)	John McPherson	(D-R)
Samuel Mumma	(F)	Conrad Dutrow	(D-R)
Geo. Bear, Senr	(D-R)	Joseph Wood	(D-R)
Peter Shriner	(D-R)	Michael Spansetler	(D-R)
Jacob Harmon	(F)	John Brafield	(D-R)
John Shechells	(D-R)	John Wise	(D-R)
Geo. Dutrow	(D-R)	John Fry	(F)
William Albaugh	(D-R)	Jonathan Fry	(F)
Frederick Reel	(F)	Elijah Wise	(D-R)
Stephen Ramsberght	(F)	Samuel Coats	(D-R)
Alexander Warfield	(D-R)	Jo. Swearinger	(F)
Henry Shell	(F)	Henry Stemple	(F)
John Carney	(F)	Daniel Fisler	(F)
Peter Garver	(D-R)	Leonard Yeast	(F)
Frederick Barrick	(D-R)	James Philips	(F)
Geo. Catrow	(F)	Philip Goodman	(F)
Joseph Browning	(F)	Richd Templing	(F)
Joshua Boran	(F)	Chrisn Long	(F)
Michael Dutrow	(F)	John Flide	(F)
Valentime Woolf	(D-R)	Barnard Beard	(F)
James Murphey	(D-R)	Andw Long	(F)
Jeramiah Browning	(F)	Arther Boteler	(F)
Joseph Beall	(D-R)	Peter Kile	(F)
John Peter	(D-R)	Henry Martin	(F)
Bett Breshares	(D-R)	Michael Rummer	(F)
Jonathan Rose	(D-R)	John Lambert	(F)
Charles Baltzell	(F)	Peter Keal	(F)
Henry Straleman	(F)	Nicholas Powlos	(F)
Daniel Baltzel	(F)	Andrew Smith	(F)
Joseph Richard	(D-R)	Philip Wise	(F)
John Thomas	(D-R)	John Shaffer	(F)
John Darnall, Junr	(D-R)	Westel Ridgley	(F)
George Shaff	(D-R)	Jacob Dippis	(F)
Jacob Trout	(D-R)	Jacob Powlas	(F)
Michael Reed	(D-R)	Isaac Runner	(F)
William Wennell	(F)	John Stone	(F)
Thomas Darnell	(D-R)	Conrad Baker	(F)
Jacob Getzandanner	(F)	George Dutrow	(F)
Michael Myers	(F)	Isaac Ren	(F)

Voters' Names:	
Jacob Carne	(F)
Godfrey Brier	(F)
John Ren	(F)
Henry Otto	(F)
George Martz	(F)
Henry Koontz	(F)
John Heson	(F)
John Cane	(F)
William Crum	(D-R)
Jacob Nicewanger	(F)
Fredk Biser	(F)
Jacob Smith	(F)
George Kolp	(F)
Jacob Staley	(F)
Francis Bean	(F)
Nicholas Hoy	(D-R)
Phillip Matton	(F)
Jacob Dutrow	(F)
Silas Baley	(D-R)
Jacob Snuke	(F)
Rezin Simpson	(D-R)
Benjn. Uncle	(F)
John Springer	(D-R)
John Grahame	(D-R)
John Dagon	(D-R)
Mathias Bemer	(D-R)
George Cramer	(D-R)
David Shryer	(F)
Richard Shechells	(D-R)
Richard Jones	(D-R)
Daniel Young	(D-R)
Wm. McPherson	(D-R)
Nathan Sheridine	(D-R)
Thomas Hammond	(D-R)
Sabrett Sollers	(D-R)
Samuel Rister	(D-R)
Nathan Vickrey	(F)
Michael Bost	(F)
Charles Armstrong	(F)
Hugh Reed	(D-R)
John Adlum, Senr	(D-R)

Voters' Names:	
Samuel Curry	(D-R)
Abraham Eater	(D-R)
Adam Jacobs	(D-R)
David Eater	(D-R)
Joshua Heard	(D-R)
John Morrison	(D-R)
James Newport	(D-R)
Alexander Nailer	(D-R)
Soloman Shue	(F)
Lawrence Everhart	(F)
Samuel Cock	(D-R)
William Cock	(D-R)
John Prichard	(D-R)
John Nelson	(D-R)
Michl Bartholo	(D-R)
Daniel Doney	(D-R)
John Landis	(D-R)
Henry Mackleferh	(D-R)
Dennis O. Trean	(D-R)
Jeramiah Tarlton	(D-R)
Wm Ahearn	(D-R)
David Nesbaugh	(D-R)
John Mick	(D-R)
Henry Wood	(D-R)
Bmn Hopkins	(F)
John Thomas	(D-R)
Geo. Leese	(D-R)
James Pool	(D-R)
James Brian	(D-R)
John Green	(D-R)
Barns Stallings	(D-R)
John Noff	(D-R)
Joseph Athen	(F)
Abraham Nesbaugh	(D-R)
John Burkett	(D-R)
Edw Dossey	(D-R)
Henry Pool	(D-R)
Samuel Nickey	(D-R)
Philip Stuver	(F)
William Shreves	(D-R)
John Smith	(D-R)

Voters' Names:		*Voters' Names:*	
Usher Charlon	(D-R)	Cornad Seltner	(D-R)
James Neill	(D-R)	John Whiteneck	(D-R)
Bennett Greenwell	(D-R)	Benjn Maherill	(D-R)
Thos. Fowler	(D-R)	Elias Harding	(D-R)
Robert Cumming	(D-R)	George Pall	(D-R)
Jacob Heard	(D-R)	Francis Smith	(D-R)
Jacob Pool	(D-R)	Wm Carbell	(D-R)
William Meyers	(D-R)	John Moran	(F)
Jacob Cramer	(D-R)	James Plummer	(D-R)
Patrick Mc lamorrow	(D-R)	Robert Pickens	(D-R)
Francis Hagon	(D-R)	Saml Stevens	(D-R)
March Moreen Duvall	(D-R)	John Stoner	(F)
Zachariah Sinton	(D-R)	Jacob Frushour	(F)
Daniel Baley	(D-R)	Roger Edmonson	(F)
Gilbert Rulluf	(D-R)	Michl Reed	(F)
Fredk Peneberger	(D-R)	Geo. Young	(F)
Rubin Crum	(D-R)	Abraham Smith	(F)
John Stucker	(D-R)	Conrad Dutrow	(F)
Fredk Amelung	(D-R)	John Stulz	(D-R)
Benjn Smith	(D-R)	Jacob Hefner	(F)
Thomas Mitchell	(D-R)	Danl Lafaver	(F)
Robert Padget	(D-R)	Abraham Simmons	(D-R)
Jacob Raymer	(D-R)	Adam Stull	(F)
Richd Lawrence	(D-R)	John Culler	(F)
John James	(D-R)	George Young	(F)
Henry Allesson	(D-R)	Jacob Cost	(D-R)
John Stutler	(D-R)	Jacob Weddrech	(F)
Christian Butts	(D-R)	Fredk Hefner	(F)
Baales Coomes	(D-R)	John Stull	(F)
Adam Showalker	(F)	Andw Tanner	(F)
Henry Struble	(D-R)	John Carty	(F)
Henry Horrell	(D-R)	Geo. Engles	(F)
John Moloy	(D-R)	John Lorntz	(F)
Wm Hurley	(D-R)	Adam Woolf	(F)
Wm Griffith	(D-R)	Michal Waugter	(F)
John Leather	(D-R)	Richard Ridgley	(F)
John Clancy	(D-R)	Solomon Shaffer	(F)
Charles Six	(D-R)	Christian Crise	(F)
Richard Clark	(D-R)	Valentine Ebert	(F)
Henry Gosling	(D-R)	Perigrine Rice	(F)
Adam Markell	(D-R)	Jno Philips	(F)

Voters' Names:	
Jesse Mathews	(D-R)
Wm Tucker	(F)
Jno Frazier	(D-R)
John Smith	(F)
John Myers	(D-R)
John Cramer	(F)
Barton Philpot	(D-R)
Bnjn Linton	(D-R)
Daniel Stauf	(F)
Roger Johnson	(D-R)
Daniel James	(D-R)
Yost Saddler	(D-R)
John Welfresh	(D-R)
Wm Markes	(D-R)
Benjn Carmel	(D-R)
Barton Garrot	(D-R)
Isaac Linton	(D-R)
Solomon Davis	(D-R)
John Brul	(F)
Adam Neff	(D-R)
John Jacobs	(D-R)
Henry Darnell	(D-R)
Richard Norwood	(D-R)
Peter France	(D-R)
Leonard Jemeson	(D-R)
Geo. Burer	(D-R)
Joseph Howard	(D-R)
Robert Adderson	(D-R)
John Brisco	(D-R)
Abid Plummer	(D-R)
John Pepper	(D-R)
Edmond Helleway	(D-R)
James Goldberry	(D-R)
Bnjn Thomas	(D-R)
Elias Thomas	(D-R)
Henry Lease	(D-R)
Daniel Gisbergh	(D-R)
Mashach Plummer	(D-R)
James Night	(D-R)
Elic Beatty	(D-R)
Joseph McElfresh	(D-R)

Voters' Names:	
John Locke	(D-R)
James Simmons	(D-R)
Phillip Sizsell	(D-R)
John Leepley	(D-R)
Abraham Albaugh	(D-R)
Jacob Whip	(D-R)
Tobias Moore	(D-R)
Daniel Gilbert	(F)
Jacob Smith	(F)
Ludwich Runner	(F)
John Snyder	(F)
Wm House	(F)
Jacob Bergesser	(D-R)
Wm Hall	(F)
Lewis Duvall	(F)
Elisha Forquare	(F)
John Williams	(F)
Chrisn Mussettle	(F)
Adam Reece	(F)
Bnjn Duvall, Jr.	(F)
Charles Turner	(F)
Geo. Abrake	(F)
Wm Anderson	(F)
Samuel Durff	(F)
Benjn Simpson	(F)
Thos. Turner	(F)
Peter Reece	(F)
Nathen Barnes	(F)
John Waggemer	(F)
Robt Anderson	(F)
James Scott	(F)
Joshua Inman	(F)
Henry Johns	(F)
Andrew Keddick	(F)
John Mussetter	(F)
Josen Frizzell	(F)
Wm Achorson	(F)
Samuel Steffer	(D-R)
Ralph Briscoe	(D-R)
Morris Albaugh	(D-R)
Geo Nichols	(D-R)

Voters' Names:		Voters' Names:	
Saml Howard	(D-R)	John Patterson	(F)
John Thomas	(D-R)	Peter Houcks	(F)
John Macy	(D-R)	Phillip Price	(F)
Edward Pope	(D-R)	Benjn. Hall	(F)
John Wayman	(D-R)	Henry Crull	(F)
John Crompton	(D-R)	Jacob Burton	(F)
Zephaniah Watson	(D-R)	Michl Lutsgesell	(F)
Nicholas Dawson	(D-R)	Jacob Wilson	(F)
Andw Michael	(D-R)	Charles Howard	(F)
John Hughs	(D-R)	Michl Mussetter	(F)
Thomas Ijams	(D-R)	Casper Ryan	(F)
Samuel Thomas	(D-R)	John Beall	(F)
Levy Phillips	(D-R)	Henry Fisher	(F)
Joshua Night	(D-R)	Michl Mussetter	(F)
Thomas Knight	(D-R)	Alexander Mussetter	(F)
Vachel Hall	(D-R)	Joseph Smith	(D-R)
Daniel Biser	(D-R)	Rezin Harris	(F)
John Phillips	(D-R)	Fredk Fogle	(F)
Joseph Howard	(D-R)	Geo. Winpigler	(F)
Lewis Browning	(D-R)	Geo. Albaugh	(D-R)
Jacob Woolf	(D-R)	Jacob Beard	(D-R)
John H. Smith	(D-R)	Wm Johnsaon	(D-R)
Garard Ricketts	(D-R)	James Eorb	(D-R)
Edward Tillard	(F)	John Julian	(F)
Christn Barrick	(D-R)	Wm Michael	(F)
Tobias Whip	(D-R)	Andrew Kesler	(F)
Phillip Grace	(D-R)	Jacob Culler	(F)
Nathaniel Hynes	(F)	Townley Rigbey	(F)
Wm Fisher	(F)	Henry Isnagle	(F)
Henry Howard	(F)	Newman Stallings	(F)
Wm Goodman	(F)	Basil Nelson	(F)
John Rian	(F)	Shaderich Hedges	(F)
Absolum Bainbridge	(F)	Moreen Duvall	(F)
Wm Cox	(F)	John Blackburn	(F)
Gelbert Wheeler	(F)	Francis Winpigler	(F)
John Mohoney	(F)	Jarom Plummer	(F)
John Beggs	(F)	Posey Stewart	(D-R)
Nathuniel Welson	(F)	George Hoffman	(F)
Jacob Layman	(F)		

Adjourned for half an our—met according to adjournment.

Voters' Names:	
Phillimon Griffith	(D-R)
Daniel Gant	(F)
Henry Carberry	(D-R)
Jonas Pusley	(D-R)
John Darnell	(D-R)
Amos Smith	(D-R)
Jacob Hohl	(F)
Abraham Adams	(F)
William Dern	(D-R)
John Boyl	(D-R)
Guy Elder	(D-R)
James McGlacklin	(D-R)
John Roberson	(D-R)
James Hawkins	(D-R)
William Dunkin	(D-R)
Jacob Ridgley	(D-R)
George Frank	(D-R)
Henry Keptart	(D-R)
Henry Swope	(D-R)
Nicholas Metsler	(D-R)
Wm McGlacklin	(D-R)
Francis Green	(D-R)
Michael Umberger	(D-R)
Peter Shawn	(F)
Michael Neill	(D-R)
George Link	(D-R)
Adam Markell	(D-R)
Hezekiah Jones	(F)
George Whitmore	(D-R)
Philip Smith	(F)
Thomas Price	(D-R)
Joseph Wayne	(F)
Peter Lamon	(F)
John Karr	(D-R)
John Ball	(D-R)
John Ball, Jnr.	(D-R)
Elisha White	(F)
William Arbaugh	(D-R)
John Ross Key	(D-R)
Thomas McGee	(D-R)
Lewis Jones	(F)

Voters' Names:	
Daniel Dorsey	(D-R)
John Larkey	(F)
John Fesler	(D-R)
Aaron Kendall	(D-R)
James McConnell	(D-R)
Charles Clabaugh	(D-R)
John Coskerry	(D-R)
Lewis Cross	(F)
Charles Clanie	(D-R)
Isaac Cood	(D-R)
John Thompson	(D-R)
Samuel Philips	(D-R)
Elie Bentley	(D-R)
Samuel Harris	(D-R)
Daniel Harrisson	(F)
Joseph McCaleb	(D-R)
Michael Flin	(D-R)
Peter Grosh	(D-R)
William Hall	(F)
Jesse Hammett	(F)
Jacob Masabaugh	(D-R)
David Laugh	(D-R)
Jacob Cover	(D-R)
Nicholas Fringer	(D-R)
Simon Grossman	(F)
John Folkner	(F)
John Mesler	(D-R)
Henry Smith	(F)
Richard Ridgley, Jr.	(F)
Joab Waters	(D-R)
Roger Brooke	(D-R)
James Adams	(D-R)
Jacob Stealy of Mel.	(F)
Mathias Fickell	(D-R)
Daniel Holler	(F)
Joseph Taney	(D-R)
Vactor Shaw	(D-R)
Joshua Grimes	(D-R)
Michael Baltzell	(F)
Thomas Bennett	(D-R)
Leonard Lantz	(D-R)

Voters' Names:		*Voters' Names:*	
Isaac Mantz	(F)	Gabriel Thomas	(D-R)
William Wood	(D-R)	Barnaby Mahoney	(D-R)
Jacob Road	(F)	John Darr	(F)
Wm. W. Cray	(D-R)	Adam Knouff	(F)
Abraham Harget	(F)	Jacob Keller	(D-R)
Michael Hefner	(F)	Jacob Anderson	(F)
Philip Hines	(F)	David Troxell	(D-R)
John Felius	(D-R)	Ezra Vanferson	(F)
John Mcleroy	(D-R)	Michael Holler, Jr.	(F)
Valentine Shriner	(F)	Adam Shivell	(F)
James Hughs	(D-R)	George Baltzell	(F)
Arthur Fleming	(D-R)	Hugh Daughlass	(F)
John Linton	(D-R)	Jacob Shaffer	(D-R)
Phillip Hardman	(D-R)	Conrad Beeker	(D-R)
John Philips, Jr.	(D-R)	Abraham Crum	(D-R)
Jacob Springer	(F)	Abraham Haff, Jr.	(D-R)
Jacob Seace	(F)	Peter Woolf	(D-R)
Fredk. Shameholtz	(F)	Jacob Barrick	(D-R)
Andrew Boyd	(F)	Francis Thomas	(D-R)
Adam Carman	(F)	Godfrey Sechrist	(D-R)
Daniel Link	(D-R)	Ephriem Crum	(D-R)
Anthony Woodward	(F)	Lloyd Belt	(D-R)
Peter Shover	(D-R)	Henry Staller	(D-R)
Michael Youtsay	(F)	Phillip Glauser	(D-R)
John Weller	(D-R)	George Dickson	(D-R)
Anthony Miller	(D-R)	Jonathan Forrist	(D-R)
Philip McElfresh	(D-R)	Daniel Curffman	(F)
Christian Ilkner	(F)	David Boyer	(D-R)
John Johnson	(D-R)	Levy Davis	(F)
John Whitmore	(D-R)	Robert McKey	(F)
Gollip Risener	(F)	George Leather	(D-R)
John Baltzell	(F)	Charles Long	(F)
Ollever Dunham	(D-R)	Phillip Senstach	(D-R)
Joseph Smith	(D-R)	Robert Conn	(F)
John Ijams	(D-R)	George Hinkell	(F)
William Emmitt	(D-R)	Phillip Keever	(F)
Phillip Winebrunner	(D-R)	John Darr	(F)
Charles Busey	(D-R)	Adam Kerkman	(F)
Benjn. Williams	(D-R)	William McCleary	(F)
Thomas Hill	(D-R)	Daniel Hook	(D-R)
Peter Hargate	(F)	Levy Hughs	(D-R)

Voters' Names:		*Voters' Names:*	
Henry Sellers	(F)	Frederick Middach	(D-R)
John Hefner	(F)	John Baer	(D-R)
Jacob Fout	(D-R)	Peter Shaffer	(F)
Christian Sheley	(F)	Aaron Ralling	(D-R)
Eli Doney	(D-R)	James Smith	(D-R)
Henry Jefferson	(D-R)	John Johnson	(D-R)
John Keller	(F)	Conrad Shaffer	(D-R)
David Martin	(D-R)	Samuel Keefer	(F)
John Brunner, Jr.	(F)	Phillip Smith	(F)
William Harding	(D-R)		

Adjourned untill Tomorrow morning 9 o'clock. Met according to adjournment.

Voters' Names:		*Voters' Names:*	
Joshua Howard	(D-R)	Henry Devilbiss	(F)
Francis Grove	(D-R)	John Bantz	(F)
Peter Decross	(F)	Geo. Newman	(F)
William Miller	(F)	Peter Brunner	(F)
Rubin Davis	(F)	George Rice	(F)
Jacob Steiner, Sr.	(D-R)	Robert Turson	(F)
Phillip Barger	(D-R)	Henry Getzandanner	(F)
Ulirich Stuller	(F)	Michl. Ott	(F)
Michael Riddlemoser	(F)	John Saddler	(F)
Adam Good	(D-R)	John Buckies	(F)
Christian Devilbiss	(F)	Henry Kallen	(F)
Johnsey Daughaday	(F)	Andrew Deall	(F)
George Kurtz	(F)	Abraham Sise	(F)
Edward Whitcraft	(F)	Michael Row	(F)
Jacob Daddisman	(F)	Geo. Ebert	(F)
Fredk. Dern	(F)	Michael Everhart	(F)
David Markell	(F)	Jacob Conrad	(F)
Henry Fogler	(F)	Joseph Staley	(F)
David Shullz	(F)	Geo. Nelson	(F)
Christopher Heckman	(F)	Henry Richter	(F)
Henry Lambright	(F)	Leonard Gavere	(F)
John Zemerman	(F)	Christn. Destenhouse	(F)
Geo. Dadisman	(F)	Fredk. Richart	(F)
Michl. Whitmore	(F)	Semon Fry	(F)
Jacob Knouff	(F)	Jacob Staley of Jas.	(F)
Jacob Bartle	(F)	Jacob Snouticle	(F)
John Rice	(F)	Jacob Snoutnocle, Jr.	(F)

Voters' Names:		Voters' Names:	
Jacob Wartentaker	(F)	George Rinehart	(F)
Martin Stuler	(F)	Adam Toms	(D-R)
Adam Keller	(F)	William Davis	(F)
John Fauble	(F)	Jacob Miller, Sen.	(D-R)
Henry Hofstatler	(F)	George Clam	(D-R)
Jacob Miller	(F)	George Kennedy	(D-R)
Geo. Getzandanner	(F)	Isaac Wayne	(D-R)
Jacob Houcks	(F)	Peter Sulser	(F)
Michl. Nuss	(F)	Peter Grunt	(F)
Charles Beutip	(F)	Jacob Young	(D-R)
Peter Beall	(F)	William Garnhart	(D-R)
Geo. Gonshawh	(F)	Joseph Norris	(D-R)
Henry Conrad	(F)	Robert McCully	(F)
Adam Hoover	(F)	Edmond Boyd	(F)
William Crum, Jr.	(F)	Michael Holler, Sen.	(D-R)
Peter Staley	(F)	Peter Storms	(D-R)
Andw. Young	(F)	Richd. Mills	(D-R)
Elisha Beall	(D-R)	George Cose	(F)
Henry Nuss	(F)	Henry Barrick	(D-R)
Jacob Boly	(F)	William Dodson	(D-R)
William Wicks	(F)	James Rice	(F)
Henry Cronise	(F)	John Adlum, Junr.	(D-R)
John Lare	(F)	Frederick Sholl	(D-R)
Martin Tigle	(F)	Henry Koontz, Junr.	(D-R)
Fredk. Nuss	(F)	Jacob Kendall	(D-R)
George House	(F)	Justice Garrick	(D-R)
Thomas Wilson	(F)	John Walker	(F)
Charles King	(F)	John Ferrill	(D-R)
John House	(F)	Henry Smith	(D-R)
Henry Garnhart	(F)	Philip Hammond	(D-R)
George Brengle	(F)	Thomas Crabb	(D-R)
Jacob Kellar	(F)	Andrew Hymes	(D-R)
George Baltzell	(F)	Geo. Jacob Schley	(D-R)
Joseph McCully	(F)	Jacob Miller Town	(D-R)
Jacob Holler	(F)	Jacob Ringer	(D-R)
Henry McCleary	(D-R)	Peter Barrick	(D-R)
Peter Raymer	(F)	Daniel Lakins (Sakins?)	(D-R)
Conrad Henry	(F)	Joseph Hardman	(F)
Jacob Weast	(F)	Michael Baugh	(D-R)
Geo. Adam Ebert	(F)	Henry Hilderbrand	(D-R)
Jacob Lusher (Susher?)	(F)	Valentine Black, Jr.	(D-R)

Voters' Names:		*Voters' Names:*	
Thomas Brawner	(F)	Samuel Brafield	(D-R)
Henry Darcas	(F)	Valentine Buchey	(D-R)
James Johnson	(D-R)	Adam Baker	(D-R)
Conrad Iler	(F)	George Miller	(D-R)
Jacob Cris	(F)	Daniel Fortney	(F)
Patrick McGill	(F)		

Adjourned untill one o'clock. Met according to adjournment.

Voters' Names:		*Voters' Names:*	
Elias Thrasher	(F)	Henry Warfield	(D-R)
John S. Lawrence	(D-R)	John Nichols	(D-R)
Barton Philpot	(D-R)	Adam Clay	(D-R)
John Campbell	(D-R)	Joel Jacobs	(D-R)
Caleb Richards	(D-R)	William Cash	(D-R)
Evin Dorsey	(D-R)	Isaac Wilson	(F)
James Campbell	(D-R)	William Gatman	(F)
Vachel Pumphrey	(D-R)	Joseph Plummer	(D-R)
Joseph Richards	(D-R)	Barnet Deall	(D-R)
John McDonald	(F)	Hezikiah Deall	(D-R)
Geo. Lafaver	(F)	Adam Hershaberger	(F)
Richard Buelay	(D-R)	John Grosman	(F)
John Long	(D-R)	George Dagon	(D-R)
Richard Taylor	(F)	John Hinkell	(F)
John Richards	(D-R)	John Gerhard	(D-R)
Fredk. Colaberger	(D-R)	Thomas Warfield	(D-R)
Daniel Galahawk	(D-R)	Stephen Musgrove	(D-R)
Jesse Wright	(D-R)	Joseph Staley	(D-R)
Frederick Young	(D-R)	Peter Stilly	(D-R)
Thomas Milton	(D-R)	Phillip Ropp	(D-R)
Thomas Sims	(F)	Conrad Coffman	(F)
John Carnes	(F)	Elias Staufer	(D-R)
Charles Busey	(D-R)	Ninian Beall	(F)
John Row	(F)	Elias Faver	(F)
Simon Kephart	(D-R)	Jacob Bower	(D-R)
George Witrick	(F)	Christian Hershman	(D-R)
Jacob Ramsberg, Sen.	(F)	John Campbell	(F)
Harry Busey	(D-R)	John Hershman	(D-R)
Nathen Hammond	(D-R)	Nicholas Ludy	(D-R)
George Hoffman	(F)	Daniel Kemp	(F)
George Slatseser	(F)	John Bergesser	(F)
Levy Thomas	(D-R)	Daniel Bergesser	(F)

Voters' Names:		Voters' Names:	
John Buyer	(F)	Boltzer Martz	(F)
Nicholas Fridenger	(F)	Lewis Kemp	(F)
John Shotz	(F)	Henry Brishe	(F)
John Hootsell	(F)	Georg W. Snyder	(D-R)
Wm. Leakens	(D-R)	Peter Flanagan	(D-R)
Christopher Bond	(D-R)	John Waskey	(D-R)
Nicholas Brengle	(D-R)	John Steiner	(D-R)
Archabold McFarling	(F)	Wm. Crum, Junr.	(D-R)
Henry Stimer	(D-R)	John Highfield	(D-R)
Frederick Siver	(D-R)	John Gittinger	(F)
Jacob Suter	(D-R)	John Ramsbergh, Jr.	(D-R)
John Allison	(D-R)	George Jacobs	(D-R)
Jacob Piman	(D-R)	Jacob Goldie	(D-R)
George Seissell	(D-R)	Conrad Ridemyer	(D-R)
Jacob Hain	(D-R)	Jacob Walter	(D-R)
Christopher Holler	(F)	Michael Bair	(D-R)
Henry Clements	(D-R)	Joseph Hughs	(D-R)
Christian Sholl	(D-R)	John Candle	(D-R)
John Stockman	(D-R)	Daniel Hughs	(D-R)
John Winter	(D-R)	Valentine Levy	(D-R)
George Snyder	(F)	Daniel Hauer, Jr.	(D-R)
Jacob Shaffer	(F)	John Smith	(F)
George Bentz	(D-R)	Mathias Smith	(F)

Adjourned untill Tomorrow morning 9 o'ck. Met according to adjournment.

Voters' Names:		Voters' Names:	
Godfrey Holler	(F)	Michl. Marquett	(F)
Samuel Lilly	(D-R)	Samuel Nixdorff	(F)
Richard Elder	(D-R)	Gadlip Basner	(F)
William Collier	(F)	Nehemiah Taylor	(D-R)
Richard Simpson	(D-R)	Phillip Keefer	(F)
Edward Salmon	(D-R)	Balser Niehooff	(D-R)
James Ogle	(F)	John Ramsbergh, Sr.	(D-R)
Wm. McCinstrey	(F)	Christian Baer	(F)
William Lamkey	(F)	Thomas Fleming	(F)
George Little John	(D-R)	Henry Staley	(F)
Jacob Ramsbergh	(D-R)	Peter Thomas	(D-R)
Godfrey Brown	(D-R)	Edmon Waymon	(D-R)
Phillip Gillion	(F)	Joshua Simpson	(D-R)
Peter Wesinger	(F)	Henry Thomas	(D-R)

Voters' Names:		*Voters' Names:*	
Solomon Pagett	(D-R)	Henry Gather	(D-R)
Thomas Brookover	(D-R)	Charles Simpson	(D-R)
Jacob Carney	(F)	Geo. Zernerman, Junr.	(D-R)
William Burgess	(D-R)	Christopher Wedagin	(D-R)
Luke Davis	(D-R)	George Scott, Junr.	(D-R)
Henry Hempy	(D-R)	Ignatius Lilly	(D-R)
Andrew Richt	(D-R)	Ignatius Davis	(D-R)
Henry Beamer	(D-R)	Jonathan Frazier	(D-R)
Christian Smith	(D-R)	Peter Smith	(D-R)
Conrad Crombaugh	(D-R)	Henry Creager	(F)
Rinehart Waltz	(D-R)	John Hilton	(D-R)
Peter Crombaugh	(D-R)	Richard Griffith	(F)
Phillip Dots	(D-R)	George Risinger	(F)
Frederick Myers	(D-R)	Valentine Brenmer	(F)
Henry Dursk	(F)	Joseph Penn	(D-R)
Jacob Shook	(D-R)	Benj. Penn	(D-R)
James Perry	(D-R)	Alexander Stewart	(D-R)
John Bagent	(D-R)	Adam Clay, Junr.	(D-R)
Absolom Warfield	(D-R)	George Holler	(D-R)

Adjourned untill one o'clock. Met according to adjnt.

Voters' Names:		*Voters' Names:*	
Lucost Fleck	(D-R)	John Marks	(D-R)
John Darcas	(D-R)	Valentine Thomas	(D-R)
John Stewart	(D-R)	George Yost	(D-R)
John Wanegardner	(D-R)	Henry Ranabarger	(D-R)
Patrick McFerrin	(D-R)	Owen Lamb	(D-R)
Henry Redburn	(D-R)	George Karse	(D-R)
Alexander Fulton	(D-R)	Benjn. Paget	(D-R)
Wm. Umbaugh	(D-R)	Samuel Hot	(D-R)
John Ott	(D-R)	Lawrence Powhorn	(D-R)
Richard Thomas	(D-R)	Hezekiah Madcolf	(D-R)
John Sowers	(D-R)	Harmon Hersh	(D-R)
James Sagafoos	(D-R)	George Yost	(D-R)
Jacob Sowers	(D-R)	Martin Whip	(D-R)
Mathias Otto	(D-R)	John Shaffer	(D-R)
John I. Coblentz	(D-R)	George Frize	(D-R)
Adam Snuke	(D-R)	John Albaugh	(D-R)
James Farthing	(D-R)	Wm. Hawk	(D-R)
Peter Albaugh	(D-R)	Paul Hoy	(D-R)
Wm. Wilson	(D-R)	John Nichols	(D-R)

Voters' Names:		*Voters' Names:*	
John Jenkins	(D-R)	John Dutrow	(D-R)
Christopher Sanher	(D-R)	Joseph Curbbey	(D-R)
William Otto	(D-R)	James Wood	(D-R)
Nicholas Baugher	(D-R)	George Koontz	(D-R)
Adam Hofman	(D-R)	Ralph Thompson	(D-R)
John Claubaugh	(D-R)	John Brunner	(D-R)
Wm. Kelley	(D-R)	Joseph Lilly	(D-R)
John Hersh	(D-R)	John Coats	(D-R)
Robert C. McGennis	(D-R)	John Stringer	(D-R)
Owen Rogers	(D-R)	Geo. Hains	(D-R)
Richard Parish	(D-R)	Joseph Piler	(D-R)
Wm. Scissell	(D-R)	Richard Stringer	(D-R)
Evin Carmick	(D-R)	Peter Otto	(D-R)
Chas. Jones	(D-R)	Peter Mort	(D-R)
Joseph Hill	(D-R)	James Stevens	(D-R)
Gisberd Gisbery	(D-R)	Geo. Charley	(D-R)
Thos. Ijams	(D-R)	Wm. Grimes	(D-R)
John Rogers	(D-R)	Jacob Shomaker	(D-R)
Mathias Mort	(D-R)	Michael Shriner	(D-R)
Henry Koontz	(D-R)	Abraham Winegardner	(D-R)
Michl. Barnhart	(D-R)	Joshua Dillaplain	(D-R)
Phillip Boyer	(D-R)	Nicholas Sythes	(D-R)
Harbard Otto	(D-R)	Wm. Hill	(D-R)
Andrew Smith	(D-R)	Wm. Busey	(D-R)
Henry Henes	(D-R)	Conrad Dutrow, Jr.	(D-R)
Joshua Clain	(D-R)	Sabastian Nagle	(D-R)
Jonathan Starren	(D-R)	Christian Zansell	(D-R)
Georg Smith	(D-R)	Wm. Gather	(D-R)
Philip Empswiler	(D-R)	Peter Beam	(D-R)
Wm. Anders	(D-R)	Lawrence Bunker	(D-R)
William Hile	(D-R)	Andrew Ebert	(D-R)
Daniel Yandis	(F)	Wm. Davis	(D-R)
George Roads	(D-R)	Henry Moore	(D-R)
Abraham Koontz	(D-R)	John Moore	(D-R)
John Yandis	(D-R)	Adam Baker	(D-R)
Geo. Overman	(D-R)	David Cromberger	(D-R)
Christian Hiner	(D-R)	Fredk. Marks	(D-R)
Amos Green	(D-R)	Jacob Wampler	(D-R)
George Toup	(D-R)	Jacob Hoof	(D-R)
George Koontz	(D-R)	John Giger	(D-R)
John Diffendall	(D-R)	Aquilla Parish	(D-R)

Voters' Names:		*Voters' Names:*	
John Gilbert	(D-R)	Wm. Walker	(D-R)
Robert Parish	(D-R)	Littleton Tucker	(D-R)
Christian Oraey	(D-R)	Abraham Steel	(D-R)
John Dellaplain, Jr.	(D-R)	Olliver Lindsey	(D-R)
John Dellaplain	(D-R)	John Boyer	(D-R)
Wm. Smith	(D-R)	Isreal Plummer	(D-R)
David Rinehart	(D-R)	Philip Cramer	(D-R)
Mathias Smith	(D-R)	Gabriel Boyer	(D-R)
Michael Olverstot	(D-R)	Samuel Linton	(D-R)
Solomon Parish	(D-R)	Thos. Ware	(D-R)
Fielder Richardson	(D-R)	Stephen Tucker	(D-R)
Jacob Holverstot	(D-R)	Elias Chrutchley	(D-R)
Michael Squire	(D-R)	Peter Orrendorff	(D-R)
Benjn. Leach	(D-R)	Geo. Ren	(F)
James Leach	(D-R)	Jacob Culler	(F)
John Hoy	(D-R)	Barnard Ren	(F)
Jacob Stripe	(D-R)	David Brishe	(F)
Aquila Taylor	(D-R)	Jesse Kilpatrick	(D-R)
Abraham Maddart	(D-R)	Edward Stewart	(D-R)
Hugh Ferrin	(F)	Geo. Yandis	(D-R)
Anthoney Boston	(F)	Aloysius Elder	(D-R)
Adam Yandis	(F)	Charles Franklin	(D-R)
Henry Freshour	(F)	John Tucker	(D-R)
Bnjn. Buson	(F)	Job. Jenkins	(D-R)
Abraham Margan	(F)	Henry Thomas	(D-R)
Wm. Smith	(F)	John Lookenpell	(D-R)
Peter Smith	(F)	Fredk. Deggensheet	(D-R)
Horatio Morlow	(F)	Elisha Griffith	(D-R)
John Copenhaver	(F)	Thos. Spurer	(D-R)
Daniel Runner	(D-R)	Theodore Breshares	(D-R)
Daniel Dellaplain	(D-R)	John Butler	(D-R)
Nicholas Kirtz	(F)	C. Joshua Grimes	(D-R)
Wm. Brackenridge	(D-R)	Jacob Smith	(D-R)
Thos. Gibson	(D-R)	Nathen Harris	(D-R)
Jacob Clabaugh	(D-R)	Jeramiah Gittings	(D-R)
Henry Smith	(D-R)	Fredk. Messell	(D-R)
John Dickenshaat	(D-R)	John Grabell	(D-R)
John Nagle	(D-R)	Jeramiah Stewart	(D-R)
Robert Brakenbridge	(D-R)	Jacob Sowers	(D-R)
Robert Lipe	(D-R)	Basil Dorsey	(D-R)
John Richards	(D-R)	Peter Sane	(D-R)

Voters' Names:		*Voters' Names:*	
Richard Roberts	(D-R)	Wm. Merryman	(D-R)
Peter Frazier	(D-R)	Jacob Keller	(D-R)
James Barnes	(D-R)	John Brunner	(D-R)
Jacob Spanseller	(F)	Elisha Barnes	(D-R)
David Barnes	(D-R)	Christopher Myer	(D-R)
Jno. Smith	(D-R)	John Speelman	(D-R)
Richd. Richardson	(D-R)	James Turner	(D-R)
Moses Given	(D-R)	Conrad Kemp	(D-R)
Thos. Russell	(D-R)	Christian Brengle, Jr.	(D-R)
Wm. Paget	(D-R)	Mathew Hilton	(F)
Zachariah Roberts	(D-R)	Thomas Wheeler	(F)
Geo. Gice	(D-R)	Michael Shaffer	(D-R)
Geo. Smith	(D-R)	Wm. Brady	(D-R)
John Renner	(D-R)	Zachariah Condon	(D-R)
Wm. Paget, Jnr.	(D-R)	Peter Kemp	(D-R)
James Jones	(F)	Jacob Lease	(F)
Jacob Gitzandanner	(D-R)	Valentine Motter	(F)
Casper Cook	(D-R)	William C. Hobbs	(D-R)
John Lashorn	(D-R)	John Welher	(F)
Baker Johnson, Junr.	(D-R)	John Stoner	(D-R)
Frederick Dellaplain	(D-R)	Aquilla Lucorst	(F)
John Henton	(D-R)	Phillip Crist	(D-R)
Jacob Smith	(F)	Peter Buckey	(D-R)
Wm. Mumphard	(D-R)	Marten Waltz	(D-R)
Elias Lafaver	(F)	David Bryan	(D-R)
John Shellman	(D-R)	Geo. Barrick	(D-R)
Joseph Stior	(D-R)	Benjn. Riddle	(D-R)
John Miller	(F)	Arasmus Gittings	(D-R)
Joseph James	(D-R)	Geo. Minnick	(D-R)
Joseph Wright	(D-R)		

Adjournment untill Tomorrow morning 9 o'clock, Met according to adjournment.

Voters' Names:		*Voters' Names:*	
Henry Hemp	(F)	Michael Allex, Sen.	(D-R)
Mathias Siner	(D-R)	Jacob Meddert, Jr.	(D-R)
Thomas Crawford	(F)	Conrad Englebright	(F)
John Campbell	(F)	Henry Koontz, Senr.	(D-R)
Geo. Castle	(F)	Daniel Hauer, Senr.	(D-R)
Anthoney Sivers, Jr.	(F)	Henry Staley	(F)
Wm. Evun	(D-R)	Rogers Landers	(D-R)

Voters' Names:		*Voters' Names:*	
Michael Trisler	(D-R)	Henry Gross	(D-R)
Wm. McClain	(D-R)	Phillip Judd	(D-R)
Jacob Sinn	(D-R)	George Zermarman	(D-R)
Jacob Routsawn	(D-R)	Jacob Segler	(D-R)
Andrew Helving	(D-R)	Jacob Mathews	(D-R)
Jacob Rohr	(D-R)	Jacob Weller	(D-R)
George Frazier	(D-R)	Joseph Brunner	(F)
Jacob Doup, Junr.	(D-R)	Vachel Hammond	(D-R)
Henry Gay	(F)	Joseph Higgins	(D-R)
Daniel Curfman	(F)	John Maynard	(D-R)
Jacob Powlas	(F)	Robert Alcook	(D-R)
James Watson	(D-R)	Henry Neat	(F)
Geo. Carnan	(F)	Henry Coleman	(D-R)
Michael Ryan	(D-R)	John Shank	(D-R)
John Harvey	(D-R)	John C. Snyder	(D-R)
John Linton	(D-R)	Valentime Steckell	(F)
John Gumber, Jr.	(D-R)	George Fulton	(F)
Thomas Neill	(D-R)	Thomas Plummer	(D-R)
Henry Ferrow	(D-R)	Joshua Plummer	(D-R)
Leonard Ferrow	(D-R)	Thomas Kirk	(D-R)
Elias Delashmutt	(F)	Hugh Jones	(D-R)
Phillip Bishop	(D-R)	John B. Busey	(D-R)
Joshua Cumston	(D-R)	Nicholas Tice	(D-R)
John Crumrine	(D-R)	Peter Sueman	(F)
Moses Grabell	(D-R)	Lewis Sigbiter	(F)
John Grove	(D-R)	John Sueman	(F)
Charles Angel	(D-R)	John Pinkley	(F)
Henry Hickley	(F)	John Wade	(D-R)
John Colglasher	(D-R)	Gazaway Selmon	(D-R)
John Cookerley	(D-R)	Jacob Shroyer	(F)
Jacob Stoner	(D-R)	Adam Reace, Jr.	(F)
Jacob Cost	(D-R)	John Lynch	(D-R)
John Baker	(D-R)	Wm. Turner	(D-R)
Philip Shade	(F)	Benjn. Turner	(F)
Robert Wickham	(F)	Barnard Otto	(D-R)
Charles Thompson	(F)	Franes Jemison	(D-R)
William Morsell	(D-R)	Seth Clark	(F)
John Roberts	(D-R)	James Smith, Jr.	(D-R)
Isreal Franks	(D-R)	John Cookerley, Sr.	(D-R)
John M. Darr	(D-R)	John Ringland	(D-R)
Phillip Mathews	(D-R)	Peter Cookerley	(D-R)

Voters' Names:	
John Strong	(D-R)
Thomas Elder	(D-R)
George Craps	(D-R)
Samuel Myers	(D-R)
James McForrin	(D-R)
Elijah Boldwin	(D-R)
Martin Ikilberger	(D-R)
Ulrick Rever	(D-R)
John Crabb	(D-R)
Frederick Black	(D-R)
Joseph Hays	(D-R)
Phillip Swartzour	(D-R)
Henry Struble	(D-R)
Jacob Stimmell	(D-R)
Wm. Currence	(D-R)
Peter Haugh	(D-R)
Nicholas Lynn	(D-R)
John Stone [or Flore]	(D-R)
Geo. Shover	(D-R)
Peter Young	(D-R)
Michael Holtz	(F)
Edmond Purdy	(D-R)
John Cramer	(D-R)
Seth Harvey	(D-R)
Elic Thrasher	(F)
John McMullen	(D-R)
Wm. Purdy	(D-R)
John Reed	(F)
Hubartus Boyer	(F)
Phillip Rohr	(D-R)
Jacob Alexander	(F)
Richd. Lemaster	(F)
John Somsell	(F)
Fredk. Miller	(F)
Adam Coblentz	(F)
Jacob Jonas	(F)
Chrisn. Routsawn	(F)
Henry Show	(F)
Davault Somsell	(F)
Jacob Smith	(F)
Peter Delashett	(F)

Voters' Names:	
Jacob Koontz	(F)
Davalt Stotlemyer	(F)
Adam Routsawn	(F)
Peter Grove	(F)
Aron Sueman	(F)
Higes Hiner	(F)
Geo. Stotlemyer	(F)
John Slanagan	(F)
Solomon Veekerey	(F)
Adam Baker	(F)
Christopher Long	(F)
John Stotlemyer	(F)
Peter Young	(F)
Jacob Markell	(F)
Jacob Stotlemyer	(F)
Henry Boteler	(F)
Saml. Brandenburg	(F)
Stofel Michael	(F)
Elias Boteler	(F)
Adam Herring	(F)
Jacob Michael	(F)
Daniel House	(F)
Jacob Coleman	(F)
Saml. McMullon	(F)
Davault Stotlemyer	(F)
Geo. Morkell	(F)
Samuel Shoup	(F)
Jacob Martin	(F)
David Shawhan	(F)
John Keller	(F)
Fredk. Miller	(F)
Martin Grove	(F)
Nathaniel Trail	(F)
Geo. Friberry	(F)
Geo. Meddert	(F)
Henry Ikelberger	(F)
Jacob Eller	(F)
Charles Balsell, Jr.	(F)
Geo. Markell	(F)
Henry Hughs	(D-R)
Casper Herring	(F)

Voters' Names:		*Voters' Names:*	
Geo. Kerrick	(F)	Jacob Maly	(F)
Michl. Miller	(F)	Henry Prutzman	(F)
Andw. Tanner	(F)	Peter Johnson	(F)
Jacob Grove	(F)	Wm. Brown	(F)
Roberson Eastburn	(F)	Geo. Madderly	(F)
Conrad Miller	(F)	Ignatius Brawner	(D-R)
Benjn. Marsell	(F)	Henry Brawner	(D-R)
Adrew Wat	(F)	Bennet Elder	(D-R)
John Swearingen	(F)	John Conn	(D-R)
Adam Booker	(F)	Thomas Cain	(D-R)
Michl. Ritter	(F)	Henry Wheeler	(D-R)
Casper Young	(F)	Wm. Shields	(D-R)
James Weakley	(D-R)	John Cain	(D-R)
Jacob Drill	(D-R)	David Martin	(D-R)
Robert Evins	(D-R)	John Woolf	(D-R)
Thomas Baker	(D-R)	John Sheppard	(D-R)
David Way	(D-R)	Thos. Fleming	(D-R)
Joseph Bartley	(D-R)	John Biard	(D-R)
Joseph Elder	(D-R)	John Lowman	(D-R)
Joseph West	(D-R)	Daniel Ballinger	(D-R)
Richd. Elder	(D-R)	John Miller	(F)
Benn. Elder	(D-R)	Wm. Butler	(F)
Christopher Meak	(D-R)	Arthur McFarling	(F)
Solomon Steel	(D-R)	Wm. Johnson	(F)
John Woolfkill	(D-R)	Jacob Eller	(F)
Benjn. Hartsock	(D-R)	John Miner	(F)
Joseph West, Jr.	(D-R)	Thos. Brawner, Jr.	(F)
Wm. Hornblower	(D-R)	Joseph Black	(F)
Charles Low	(F)	John Oharrow	(F)
Robert Plummer	(D-R)	Michl. Morningstar	(F)
Henry Poorman	(F)	Geo. Cain	(F)
John Knouff	(F)	Tobias Hammer	(F)
Charles Elder	(D-R)	Jacob Mathews	(F)
Thos. Anderson	(D-R)	Henry Graft	(F)
Wm. Kilty	(F)	Thos. Brown	(F)
Guy Elder, Junr.	(D-R)	Michl. Myers	(F)
Arnold Elder	(D-R)	Jacob Trone	(F)
Phillip Morningstar	(F)	Simon Snuke	(F)
Peter Dick	(F)	Samuel Singer	(F)
Adam Snuke	(F)	Richd. Wood	(F)
Fredk. Kimmerlin	(F)	Nathan Beall	(F)

Voters' Names:	
Stephen Handley	(F)
Daniel Burket	(F)
Robert Parsons	(F)
Henry Mane	(F)
Jacob Inch	(F)
Jacob Snider	(F)
Cornelius Redge	(F)
Christian Coon	(F)
Fredk. Ikelberger	(F)
Michl. Hefner of I.	(F)
Micheal Alle, Jr.	(F)
Ludwick Michael	(F)
Benjn. Talbert	(D-R)
Jesse Russell	(D-R)
Wm. Perkenson	(D-R)
Joseph Ramsey	(D-R)
John Pankis	(D-R)
Wm. Plummer	(D-R)
Michael Zermerman	(D-R)
Wm. Beall	(D-R)
Joseph Levers	(D-R)
John Ramsey, Jr.	(D-R)
James McCarty	(D-R)
James Atkins	(D-R)
Andw. Zermerman	(D-R)
Daniel Hand	(F)
Christopher Michael	(F)
Alexander Rankins	(D-R)
Jacob Mathews	(D-R)
George Close	(D-R)
Wm. Ragan	(D-R)

Voters' Names:	
Aaron Stevens	(D-R)
John Salkell	(D-R)
Phillip Fine	(D-R)
John Masacop	(D-R)
Michael Hagerty	(D-R)
Jacob Grabell	(D-R)
Andw. Noland	(D-R)
John F. Hopkey	(D-R)
Andrw. Carder	(D-R)
Michael Mulvy	(D-R)
Law. Powrise	(D-R)
John Evins	(D-R)
Phillip Foust	(D-R)
John Jacobs	(D-R)
George Silver	(D-R)
Balser Dutrow	(F)
Michl. Smith	(F)
Christian Miller	(F)
Jacob Bost	(F)
John Wertenbaker	(F)
Charles Harvey	(D-R)
John Glover	(D-R)
John Griffen	(D-R)
Wm. Sivers	(D-R)
Wm. Griffen	(D-R)
Chas. Stevens	(D-R)
John Caulflesh	(D-R)
John Miller	(D-R)
Lewis Harding	(D-R)
Lewis Fout	(D-R)
Jacob Stoner	(D-R)

Adjourned untill 2 o'clock. Met according to adjournment.

Voters' Names:	
Henry Thompson	(D-R)
John Evy	(D-R)
Wm. Renner	(D-R)
Samuel Stallings	(D-R)
Wm. Redburn	(D-R)
Jacob Waggerner	(F)
Michael Ressler	(D-R)

Voters' Names:	
Samuel Linton	(D-R)
John D. Mower	(D-R)
Francis McDonold	(D-R)
Wm. Cain	(D-R)
Harvy Stallings	(D-R)
John Zemerman	(D-R)
Conrad Dutrow, M.	(F)

Voters' Names:		*Voters' Names:*	
Isaac Keefers	(D-R)	John Dutrow	(F)
Daniel Niehoof	(F)	Peter Isenbergh	(D-R)
Peter Cavaridge	(F)	Wm. Stallengs	(D-R)
Michl. Keefers	(D-R)	Phillip Pipher	(D-R)
Joseph Cain	(D-R)	Charles Kelly	(F)
Jacob Ridgley, Jr.	(D-R)	Daniel Smith	(F)
Soloman Glessin	(D-R)	Peter Cramer	(F)
John Giffin	(D-R)	James Mcbride	(F)
William Wilson	(F)	Joshua Burnside	(D-R)
Daniel Ludy	(F)	Henry Pool, Jr.	(D-R)
Jacob Keller	(F)	John Montgomery	(D-R)
Peter Barnhart	(D-R)	Henry Pool, Sr.	(D-R)
John Cronise	(D-R)	Francis Kirshaw	(D-R)
Zedock Fowler	(F)	Wm. Cramer	(F)
Wm. Lease	(D-R)	James Tool	(D-R)
James Colier	(F)	James Bowdon	(D-R)
Richd. Johnson	(D-R)	Joseph Wilson	(D-R)
George Holter	(D-R)	John Fulton	(D-R)
Saml. Ford	(D-R)	Phillip Six	(D-R)
Fielder Burgee	(F)	Henry Taylor	(F)
Henry Sitsler	(D-R)	John Myer	(D-R)
Michl. Keller	(F)	John Crabbs	(D-R)
Thomas Beatty	(D-R)	John Culler	(F)
Jacob Miller	(F)	Jacob Shriner	(D-R)
Philip Fink	(D-R)	Alexander McDugel	(F)
Wm. Biggs	(F)	Nicholas Holtz	(F)
John Campbell Town	(D-R)	David McCaleb	(D-R)
Thomas Burgee	(F)	John Riley	(D-R)
Wm. Furgerson	(D-R)	Elias Harding	(D-R)
Henry Ramsbergh	(D-R)	Geo. Fox	(F)
John Redburn	(D-R)	Leonard Thomas	(D-R)
Thomas Redburn	(D-R)	Daniel Ragen	(D-R)
Fredk. Shaaff	(F)	Daniel Ragen, Jr.	(D-R)
Jacob Shellman	(D-R)	Wm. Kindley	(F)
John Woodrow	(D-R)	Edmond Byrne	(D-R)
Phillip Chepper	(F)	John Crabster	(D-R)
Wm. Frymower	(F)	Stephen Brunner	(D-R)
Adam Strickstroke	(F)	Christian Waggenner	(D-R)
John Cronise, Jr.	(D-R)	David Friddle	(F)
Conrad Iler	(F)	Jacob Brandenbergh	(F)
John Smith	(F)	Samuel Dickson	(F)

Voters' Names:		*Voters' Names:*	
John Smith	(F)	John Clay	(D-R)
Isaac Plummer	(D-R)	John Frize	(F)
Basil Richards	(D-R)	Philip Gauff	(F)
Francis McConnell	(D-R)	Thomas Spriggs	(F)
Arthur McConnell	(D-R)	Cary Thompson	(D-R)
John McConnell	(D-R)	Hugh Reynolds	(D-R)
Christian Hart	(F)	Joseph Flemming	(D-R)
Joseph Miller	(D-R)	Christian Righ	(D-R)
Michael Boyer	(D-R)	John White	(D-R)
Thomas Jones	(D-R)	James Reynolds	(D-R)
John Devilbiss of Pd. (?)	(D-R)	Benj. Stoner	(D-R)
Geo. Caufman	(F)	Garrott Haff	(F)
Amos Vanferson	(D-R)	Charles Glisson	(F)
Jacob Slicker	(F)	Charles Shell	(D-R)
Samuel Holler	(D-R)	Mathias Buckey	(D-R)
Jacob Ikelberger	(D-R)	Phillip Richt	(D-R)
Jacob McDonald	(F)	William Clements	(F)
Charles Hobbs	(F)	George Baer	(D-R)

Polls Closed Saturday Evening between 3 and 4 Clock.

1 Days Voting,	Tyler (F),	412;	Murdock (D-R),	466
2 Days Ditto,	Tyler (F),	141;	Murdock (D-R),	117
3rd Days Ditto,	Tyler (F),	47;	Murdock (D-R),	280
4th Days Ditto,	Tyler (F),	196;	Murdock (D-R),	258
		796;		1121

CHARLES COUNTY

MALE PERSONS EIGHTEEN YEARS OLD AND UPWARD IN THE LOWER HUNDRED, DURHAM PARISH

Charles County Census, 1775-1778 (1800 persons)*

MALE PERSONS EIGHTEEN YEARS OLD AND UPWARD IN THE LOWER HUNDRED, DURHAM PARISH—Uzziah Posey, Constable

Allen, Thomas
Adams, Jerimiah
Ashton, John
Ashton, Butler
Adams, Samuel
Adams, Francis
Brawner, William
Burchill, Charles
Boston, William
Bailey, Andrew
Bryan, William
Brandshaw, Uriah
Bradshaw, Joseph
Carpenter, John
Carpenter, William
Cooper, Joseph
Clane, McWilliam
Carroll, William
Carroll, Christopher
Corts, Benjamin
Collins, William
Chilton, John
Cole, Rhody
Clark, William
Cooper, John
Colly, James
Dunnington, Elijah
Dye, Reubin
Dunnington, Hezekiah
Dalrimple, George
Davis, Henry
Dunnington, Wm. Sone
Dunnington, William J.
Dunnington, Francis
Davis, Zachariah
Davis, William
Dunnington, John
Deakins, Ambrous
Elgin, Richard
Elgin, George
English, Joseph
Flanningin, Barton
Frawner, Matthew
Frawner, Joshua
Fairfax Jonathan
Ferrill, James
Fowke, Roger
Fagg, John
Fagg, William
Fagg, Joel
Griffis, Rorser
Garner, James
Gerskons, William
Gorden, William
Groves, John
Groves, William
Gray, Andrew
Greenleaves, Simon
Griffis, John
Green, Samuel, Sr.
Green, Samuel, Jr.
Harrison, Richard, Col.
Harrison, William, Col.
Hamilton, Burdit
Harrison, Hanson Josh.
Hudson, Richard
Hattur, William
Hammous, John
Howard, John
Hudson, Caleb
Howard, John, Jr.
Jenkins, Edward
Johnson, Daniel
Jones, William
Jones, Benjamin
Kennedy, Clement
Kitchen, William
Kerbert, Thomas
Kerbert, John
Knox, Robert (Capt.)
Lomax, Siffiniah
Luckett, Ignatius
Luckett, Samuel
Mordock, Godfree
Mastin, Francis (Capt.)
Morrow, Daniel
Mastin, Robert
Mastin, Alexander
Maddox, Edward
McAttee, Edmund
McPherson, Joseph
McPherson, Daniel
Maddox, Rhody
Milstead, John
Moredock, Samuel
Mondock, William

* Lib. x. fol. 630-640. State Land Office—Annapolis, Maryland. Removed to Charles Co. by Act of Legislature 1914.

Copied, verified and published through the courtesy of Mrs. Margaret Roberts Hodges (Mrs. George W.), Annapolis, Md., compiler and publisher of *Unpublished Revolutionary Records of Maryland*.

Maddox, William
Meeks, John B.
McDaniel, Patrick
Nelson, Oliver
Pritchett, Benjamin
Posey, Richard
Pattison, Perry
Posey, Richard, Jr.
Perry, John
Perry, Thomas, Sr.
Perry, Thomas, Jr.
Perkin, John
Posey, Rhody
Rye, William
Rawlings, Thomas
Resin, Peter
Resin, Chandlee
Resin, Philip
Ryon, Ignatius
Ratcliff, Joshua
Rye, John
Rye, Warren
Rye, Royle
Reede, Thomas
Reen, John
Resin, Jarot
Redman, Thomas
Ratcliff, Burdit
Ranes, Francis
Robert, Richard
Ratcliff, Rhody
Ratcliff, Joseph
Rye, Samuel
Sclothen, Walter
Simmon, Joseph
Sontoney, Lazerus
Shomat, Babtist
Stewart, William
Smith, Simon
Skinner, Jeremiah
Skinner, William, Sr.
Skinner, William
Skinner, Thomas
Skinner, James
Skinner, John, of Thos.
Skinner, Thom., of Thos.
Skinner, Ezekiah
Skinner, John of Thos.
Skinner, Emanuel
Scepon, Reubin
Simms, Thomas
Stromat, John
Simms, Joseph
Sims, James
Sheppard, John
Smith, William
Smith, John
Thompson, John
Thompson, William
Thompson, Joseph
Thompson, Richard
Thompson, Samuel
Thompson, Elijah
Talmash, James
Taylor, James
Taylor, Benjamin
Thomas, Salsbury
Thomas, Clement
Taylor, Samuel
Taylor, Francis
Wright, John
Wright, Lugar
Wright, Bucker
Waple, James
Waple, John
Waple, William
Whalen, Jeriah
Woodward, Richard
Wright, Samuel
Wright, Robert

BENEDICT HUNDRED, TAKEN BY HENRY LYON, JNR., CONSTABLE

Anderson, Joseph, Sr.
Anderson, Benjamin
Anderson, Joseph, Jr.
Anderson, William
Anderson, Edward
Adams, John B.
Adams, Samuel
Adams, John
Adams, Ignatius
Branson, Leonard
Bivings, John
Billingsly, Hezs.
Bate, James
Burch, Jesse
Burch, Edward
Bryan, Basil
Bramhall, James
Bramhall, Zachariah
Bramhall, Jonathan
Bramhall, William
Burch, Walter
Burrough, Zephaniah
Burrough, Richard
Canter, William, Jr.
Canter, William, Sr.
Canter, Isaac
Canter, James
Canell, James
Cooksey, Philip, Sr.
Cooksey, Jonathan
Cooksey, Philip, Jr.
Carter, Henry
Carter, Freeman
Carricae, Peter
Cusick, Ignatius
Davis, Luke
Davis, Thomas
Dawson, Robert
Estep, John

tep, Richard
rlter, Charles
ll, Robert, Jr.
ll, Robert, Sr.
ll, Charles
aden, Robert
rner, Richard
rner, Henry
rner, William
rner, Francis
rner, Joseph
een, James
azard, Michael
ckey, Basil
unt, Gladen
ernt, Thomas
ernt, Benjamin
hnson, Huet
hnson, Zachariah
hnson, Joseph
nes, Thomas
hnson, Nelson
each, John
adyman, William
yon, Henry
emar, Francis
yon, Joseph
yon, John
yon, Zachariah
Litchworth, Leonard
McLean, John
Moran, Andrew, Sr.
Moran, Andrew, Jr.
Moran, Gabriel
Moran, James
Moran, Jonathan
Moran, John, Jr.
Morton, John
Moran, William
Moran, John, Sr.
Ogdon, Benjamin
Ogdon, Joseph
Oden, Vincent
Oden, Thomas
Perry, Hugh
Parker, Abraham, Sr.
Parker, Abraham, Jr.
Parker, Jonathan
Rogers, William
Sorat, Alphonias
Smoot, Thomas
Smith, Charles S.
Smith, James
Taylor, John, Son of Igns.
Taylor, Stafford,
Taylor, James
Taylor, John, son of Staf'd.
Taylor, Ignatius
Taylor, Edward
Thomas, Allen
Thomas, Isaac
Thomas, John
Thomas, Calib
Thomas, Philip
Thomas, William
Venables, Theodorus, Sr.
Venables, Samuel
Venables, Theodorus, Jr.
Venable, Larance
Wales, Loyd
White, Jonathan
White, William
Wood, James G.
Wood, Peter
Wilkerston, William
Wood, Benjamin
Wallace, Basell
Wallace, Richard
Wallace, James
Wallace, William
Wonson, William
Wheatly, William
Wilson, Abraham

Port Tobacco West Hundred, taken by P. Farnandis, Constable

dams, Ignatius, Sr.
dams, Richard
dams, Ignatius
allon, John
rawiner, John
rawner, Benjamin
rawner, Henry
rawner, William
arnes, William
arnes, Matthew
utler, John (mulatto)
oswell, William
Barker, John, Sr.
Barker, John
Brogard, John (weaver)
Butts, Clement
Brown, G. Richard
Barker, Shadrick
Boswell, Jesse
Bibbins, Walter
Coley, James
Clements, Francis (of Jacob)
Clements, Leonard
Clements, Joseph
Clements, John
Clements, A. John
Clements, Walter
Clements, Walter (of Jacob)
Clements, Charles
Clements, Francis
Clements, Clement
Cheverlin, Thomas
Chatam, John
Crancroft, Nicholas

Clements, H. Bennett
Clements, Basil
Davis, William
Davis, Charles
Deen, George
Day, Benjamin
Eden, Thomas
Frazier, John
Fernandis, Peter
Farmer, Robert
Farmer, William
Flint, David
Gilpin, Leonard
Goley, Thomas
Green, Giles, Senr.
Gambro, Richard
Garner, William
Garner, Charles
Garner, John
Godfrey, George
Godfrey Landsdale
Green, Robert
Hanson, Walter, Sr.
Hanson, Walter
Hanson, Samuel
Haislip, Robert
Haislip, Henry
Haislip, John (of Robert)
Haislip, William
Haislip, John
Haislip, Samuel
Haislip, Labin
Hyfield, Thomas
Howard, Gadshall
Howard, William
Hanson, Theophilus
Hurley, Harrison
Higdon, Ignatius
Hutchison, George
Hill, William
Hill, Humphry
Hamilton, Luke
Hall, John
Hart, Michael
Herrick, James
Johnson, Archebald
John, Walter
Linkins, James
Linkins, Townly
Linkins, Hindley
Lomax, Stephen
Lomax, Luke
Luckett, Ignatius
Mushett, John
Mushett, Mungo
Mushett, William
Mud, James, Sr.
Mud, Jeremiah
Mud, John
Mud, James
Mud, Smith
Mud, William
McPherson, Thomas
McPherson, Daniel
McPherson, William
McPherson, John
McPherson, William, Jr.
McPherson, Basil
McPherson, John, Sr.
Manning, John
Manning, Joseph
Manning, Walter
Maury (Manry?), John
McCay, John
McCay, Hugh
McDonald, Zachariah
McDono, M. James
Mitchell, R. Bennett
Mitchell, Samuel
Mitchell, Richard
McBayne, William
Mankins, Joseph
Mankins, T. Richard
Mayhan, Robert
Norris, Daniel
Norris, Mark
Nelson, William
Nelson, John, Sr.
Nelson, John
Neal, Benjamin
Nelson, Joseph
Owen, Richard
Owen, Thomas, Sr.
Owen, Thomas
Ostro, Thomas
Posey, William
Peak, John
Quade, John
Quade, Ignatius
Rigg, Matthew
Roberson, John
Roberson, G. William
Ray, Charles
Ray, James
Reeder, R. Richard
Reeder, John
Simms, Roger
Sinnett, Robert
Sanders, John
Sanders, J. Foregius
Sanders, Edward
Sanders, Joseph
Sanders, Thomas
Smith, Clement
Smith, Joseph
Simpson, Ignatius
Simpson, Henry
Smallwood, John
Stone, Thomas, Esq.
Stone, J. Michael
Smoot, Thomas
Thompson, James
Tyre, Charles
Turnbull, John
Tinnus, Charles
Tinnus, John

nus, William
llace, John
eeler, William
eeler, Clement
eeler, Joshua
Wheeler, Ignatius
Wheeler, Leonard
Wheeler, Benjamin
Wheeler, Thomas
Wheeler, Benedict
Ward, John
Ward, Archilus
Ward, George
Welch, William
Welch, Edward

Upper Hundred, William and Mary Parish, taken by Wm. Roberson, Constable

teman, Benja., Sr.
teman, Benja., Jr.
uce, John
uce, Walter
uce, James
teman, George
rage, Ninion
teman, Charles
ttrell, James
ttrell, Benjamin
ggett, Hezt.
ttrell, Thomas
mpbell, James
llens, Samuel
x, John, Jr.
tton, Thomas
uglas, Joseph
uglas, John
tton, Notley
tton, Gerrard
rkin, James
ly, John
ven, James
nt, Henry
vis, Abraham
nt, George
gin, John
gin, George
nis, David
rr, William
rr, John
ndall, Benjamin
Fowler, Henry
Guy, Joseph
Glover, Philip
Green, Hugh
Gwinn, Joseph
Higgs, Jonathan
Hobart, Moses
Hobart, Edward
Hancock, Josias
Hall, Stephen
Hungerford, Thomas
Jones, Samuel
Jenkins, Abednigo
Jenkins, John
Jenkins, Thomas
Jay, Joseph
Kerton, Anthony
Kerpatrick, William
Latimer, Marcus
Lovelin, George
Lovelin, William
Lewis, Benjamin
Lee, Richard
Lee, Philip
Marshall, Philip
Marshall, H. John
Martin, Francis
Martin, Huse
Marshall, William
Marshall, John
Marshall, Robert
Marshall, Thomas
Murphey, James
Mackey, John
Money, Isaac
McWilliam, William
Marshall, Richard
Norwood, Garner
Philpot, Benjamin
Philpot, David
Posey, Blain
Procter, Basil
Pompy, Luke
Rock, William
Reeves, Upgate
Ratcliff, Richard
Ratcliff, John
Rock, James
Roberson, William
Scrogin, Barton
Smoot, Clark George
Scott, John
Smith, Peter
Swann, James
Smith, James
Shaw, John
Smith, Richard
Scott, John, Jr.
Thompson, B. John
Thomas, James
Thompson, Richard
Wakefield, Able
Winsett, Henry
Yates, Theophilus

East Hundred, Newport, taken by Zach. Churm, Constable

Amery, Samuel
Allen, Davis Joseph
Albrittian, William
Albrittian, Charles
Allen, Bartholamu
Anderson, William
Barron, Abraham
Barron, Thomas
Bond, Thomas
Brent, Robert, Sr.
Briscoe, Samuel
Brady, John
Burch, Benjamin
Burch, Walter
Burch, William
Berry, John
Brent, Robert, Jr.
Brady, Gerrard
Burch, Thos. Justinian
Burk, John
Chunn, Eleazer
Chunn, Lancelot
Campton, William
Cartwright, Gustavius
Chunn, Henry
Chunn, Zach.
Ching, Thomas
Ching, Samuel
Clarkson, Henry
Compton, W. John
Courts, R. Hendley
Dutton, Zachariah
Davis, David
Davis, Elezar
Dement, Edward
Davis, William, Jr.
Davis, William, Sr.
Davis, Edward
Davis, Benjamin
Davis, Philip
Davis, Richard
Davis, Charles
Davis, Randolph
Dent, Zachariah
Dyson, Gerard
Dyson, George
Dement, John
Davis, Gustavus
Dement, Edward, Jr.
Davis, Benjamin, Sr.
Davis, Eanus
Davis, Burnett
Dyson, A. Thomas
Dyson, George, Jr.
Dyson, Aquilla
Davis, Waters Joseph
Davis, Zephaniah
Foster, William
Ferguson, Jonathan
Gray, William
Gray, James
Gill, John
Gray, George
Gill, Adam
Gray, Joseph
Gray, William, Jr.
Huntington, Luke
Howard, Henry
Hamilton, Francis
Higdon, Baptist John
Higdon, Francis
Highfield, Jeremiah
Harrison, William
Hudson, Thomas
Higgs, George
Huntington, Luke, Jr.
Huntington, John
Hunt, Shadrick
Hardman, Ignatius
Johnson, James
Johnson, John
King, Robert
King, Williamson
Kerrick, Walter
King, Townley
Malt, Joseph
Mattingley, Zacharia
McGlue, Patrick
Murphey, Abraham
Morton, William
Matthews, Hugh
Morris, Hugh
Morris, James
Murphey, Zepheniah
Murphey, Samuel
Matthews, James
McDonald, John
Reeder, Thomas
Reeves, Samuel
Swann, Edward
Simpson, Andrew
Slye, Robert
Scallion, John
Scrogin, Walter
Stonestreet, Edward
Stonestreet, Butler
Scott, William
Swann, Thomas
Swann, Jonathan
Swann, James
Swann, Thomas, Jr.
Swann, Zachariah
Scattian, Peter
Scott, James
Swann, James, Jr.
Thom, Peregrine
Thom, Barton
Thom, Absolum
Wilder, Edward
Wood, Philip
Wood, Leonard
Wiseman, James
Wood, Gerard

PORT TOBACCO, UPPER HUNDRED, SAM'L SMALLWOOD, CONSTABLE

Athey, Hezekiah
Acton, Francis
Acton, Henry, Jr.
Acton, Henry, Sr.
Acton, John, Jr.
Acton, John, Sr.
Acton, John, of John
Atchison, James
Adams, Leonard
Athey, Elsworth
Atchison, Joshua
Ash, Charles
Bruce, James
Bell, Basil
Berry, Thomas, Sr.
Berry, John
Burch, John, Sr.
Burch, John, Jr.
Burch, Leonard
Berry, Joseph
Berry, Benjamin
Berry, Hezekiah
Berry, Humphrey
Berry, Samuel
Berry, Pryor
Berry, Thomas, Jr.
Boone, Nicholas
Blanford, James
Baden, William
Bramhall, Ignatius
Beall, Thomas
Barker, Samuel
Beale, William
Beale, Charles
Cawood, Benjamin, Jr.
Cawood, Stephen
Clements, John, of John
Clements, John, Sr.
Clements, B. Natley
Coomes, Joseph
Coomes, William, of Jas.
Coomes, Wharton, of Thos.
Cox, John
Clements, Thomas
Clements, John, of Fran.
Cawood, William
Dyar, William
Dixon, George, Sr.
Dixon, George, Jr.
Downs, William
Dyar, Annactitus.
Edelin, Francis
Ford, John
Ford, Notley
Frazier, James
Ferrall, Charles
Ferrall, Ignatius
Guy, William, Jr.
Gates, James, of James
Griffitt, John
Gwinn, John
Green, Thomas, Jr.
Green, Edward, Sr.
Green, Edward, Jr.
Green, Nicholas
Green, Peter
Green, Thomas, Sr.
Gwinn, Edward
Guy, John
Griffus, Thomas
Gates, Leonard
Gates, James, Sr.
Green, Charles
Green, Giles, Jr.
Green, Joseph
Guy, William, Sr.
Hicks, Robert
Harris, Benjamin
Hunt, Jonathan
Hill, Leonard
Hill, Clement
Hyton, Joseph
Hicks, Thomas, Sr.
Hicks, Thomas, Jr.
Harvin, Moses
Hamilton, Burnett
Hanson, Saml., Sr.
Hanson, Saml., of Saml.
Hanson, Thomas
Hagan, Henry
Hatcher, John
Hanson, Saml., Jr.
Hamilton, Patrick
Hamilton, Leonard
Hutchon, William
Haw, Thomas
Innis, Charles
Innis, James
Johnson, Hezekiah
Johnson, Benjamin
Jones, William
Key, James
Kedwell, Matthew
Lewis, Thos.
Latimer, Samuel
Luckett, Rhody Wm.
Lewis, James
Maddon, Charles
McAtee, James, of Patr.
Marlow, Richard
Marlow, William
Marlow, Butler
Marlow, James, Sr.
Marlow, Acton
Moreland, Patrick
Moreland, Isaac
Middleton, S. Isaac
Moore, Matthew, Jr.
Moreland, Richard
McLemar, Dennis
McAtee, George
Mason, Philip

McAtee, James
McCay, John
McAtee, John, Jr.
McAtee, Walter
McAtee, Henry, Jr.
Nally, Shadrick
Nott, Fillbut John
Oard, Peter
Oneal, Anthony
Paine, Ignatius
Paine, Francis, Sr.
Paine, Francis, Jr.
Paggett, Benja., Sr.
Paggett, Benja., of Wm.
Paggett, Benja., of Ben.
Paggett, Aaron
Paggett, James
Paine, Ebysworth
Permillian, Benja.
Robey, H. John
Roberson, William
Robinson, Elijah
Richardson, William
Rowland, Thomas
Smallwood, Saml.
Smallwood, Luke
Smallwood, M. Wm.
Smallwood, B. Jas.
Stewart, Walter
Stonestreet, Basil
Smallwood, Henry
Smallwood, James, of Jno.
Simpson, Thos.
Southwoll, John
Sanders, Burnett
Stewart, William
Slayter, James
Slayter, Nehemiah
Slater, Richard, Sr.
Slater, Richard, Jr.
Slater, John
Spalding, Basil
Spalding, William
Stewart, Isaac
Stone, William
Smallwood, Philip
Stewart, Henry
Smallwood, Thos., J
Simms, Edward, Jr.
Simms, Ignatius
Smallwood, Ledstone
Thomas, Thomas
Thomas, Henry
Tubman, Richard
Thompson, Smallwo
Thompson, Joseph
Wilson, Alex. Willia
Willett, Richard
Walker, Peter
Winson, Joseph, Sr.
Wilkenston, Alex.
Wilkenson, Walter
Willett, George
Winson, Joseph, Jr.

Port Tobacco Town Hundred, taken by Chas. Dodson, Constabl

Carnes, John
Cary, Francis
Cox, Benjamin
Cox, William
Crackles, Thomas
Dodson, Charles
Grey, George
Gwinn, John
Halkinton, John
Harrison, Jos. W.
Hay, David
Jenifer, Daniel
Jenifer, Walter H.
Kidgate, Thomas H.
Larmon, John C.
Luckett, George
Luckett, Ignatius
Luckett, John
Mundell, Robert
Parcells, Edward
Ridewell, Thomas
Stains, Thomas

Port Tobacco, East Hundred, taken by Peter Griffith, Constabl

Acton, Osborn
Acton, James
Acton, Henry
Adams, George
Arvin, Thomas, Jr.
Arvin, Thomas, Sr.
Arvin, Joseph
Arvin, Edward
Boswell, Edward
Boswell, Gustavis
Boswell, Matthew
Boswell, Joseph
Boswell, Josias
Boswell, Elijah
Boswell, George
Boswell, Walter
Brooke, Walter
Brooke, William
Brooke, Baker
Brooke, Walter
Baggot, John, Sr.
Baggot, Ignatius
Blanford, Charles, S
Burriss, John

Boarman, John
Beven, Saveron
Blanford, William
Boarman, Thomas
Boswell, Richard
Boswell, John
Brook, John
Burgess, Thomas
Bolton, John
Brown, Richard
Brown, John
Bean, John
Bean, Henry
Bean, Thomas
Blanford, Thomas
Blanford, Charles
Bevin, Richard
Crismond, Aaron
Chrismond, Joseph
Crismond, Mason
Cookoe, James
Comes, William, Sr.
Comes, William, Jr.
Carney, Daniel
Corbut, John
Clements, William
Cox, Thomas
Clements, Edward
Clements, William, Sr.
Clements, Edward, Son of Wm.
Chattam, John
Causeen, John
Cox, Hugh
Cox, Richard
Chandler, Stephen
Chandler, Samuel
Chandler, John
Clarke, Elias
Cox, William
Clements, George
Carrick, Edward
Chattam, James
Carrington, John
Carrington, Timothy
Curtain, Dennis
Cross, John
Clements, John
Causeen, B. Gerard
Deakins, Edward
Diggs, Henry
Dyar, Jeremiah
Davis, George
Darnal, Samuel
Darnal, Thomas, Sr.
Darnal, Thomas, Jr.
Dodson, John
Dixon, Joseph
Douglas, Thomas
Dodson, William
Dodson, Barton
Dodson, Jacob
Douglas, Richard
Douglas, Charles
Douglas, John
Dixon, Jacob
Dixon, Francis
Dixon, Samuel
Daily, John
Dodson, Charles
Douglas, Benjamin
Dunning, John
Egerton, Peter
Echison, Joseph
Freeman, Nathaniel
Freeman, Moab
Franklin, John
Griffin, John
Griffin, James
Griffin, Peter
Goodrich, Richard
Goodrich, Charles
Green, Henry
Green, T. Melchizedeck
Gilpin, Notley
Gilpin, Thomas
Garner, Benjamin
Garner, Thomas
Garner, Benja., Sr.
Green, John
Glasgow, John
Glasgow, Thomas
Godfrey, Landsdale
Hicks, Thomas
Hamilton, Ignatius
Howell, Samuel
Hugho, William
Hagan, Nathaniel
Howell, Paul
Hays, William, Sr.
Hays, Thomas
Hamilton, Baptist
Hanson, Haskins
Hanson, William, Sr.
Hanson, William
Hunter, George
Howard, Michel
Hanson, John (Capt.)
Hunt, Joseph
Hardgraves, George
Holding, James
Hanson, John
Hanson, Walter (Capt.)
Hawkins, Josias (Col.)
Hopewell, Thomas
Hanson, H. Massey
Hill, Francis
Hawkins, S. H. Alexr.
Hawkins, Henry Smith
John, James
Jenkins, Edward
Jackson, John
Jameson, John
Knott, Jesse
Kellow, William
Keech, George

Kellow, Thomas, Sr.
Kellow, Thomas, Jr.
Lamaster, Richard
Latimer, Thomas
Latimer, Jacob
Leigh, William
Luckett, Thomas
Luckett, Benjamin
Luckett, Notley
Lancaster, Joseph
Luckett, H. Thomas
Lomax, Benjamin
Latimer, Mark
Lovelace, Samuel
Lovelace, William
Lemon, John
Logins, Vincent, Jr.
Lamaster, William
Moreland, Jacob
Moreland, Zepahaniah
Moreland, Zachr.
Miles, Joseph
Miles, William
Middleton, James
Moreland, John
Montgomery, Joshua
McDonald, Jonathan
Miles, Joseph, Sr.
Miles, Henry
Moone, George
Moone, Matthew, Sr.
Montgomery, Rd.
Montgomery, Peter
Moreland, Philip
More, Hezekiah
Moreland, Stephen
Maddox, Cornelius
Morriss, Walter
Moreland, Walter
Moreland, William
Mobley, William
Murray, P. Andrew
Matthews, Joseph
Mankin, Charles
Maddox, Henry
Millar, John
Marriss, William
Martin, Michael
Martin, Leonard
McCray, Philip
McAtee, William
Maddocke, Notley, Sr.
Maddocke, Notley, Jr.
Morriss, Jacob
Moore, James
Miles, Edward
Mankin, Stephen
Manhall, Samuel
Maurey (Manrey?), Ignatius
Mead, William
Millar, Christopher
Marshall, William
McDonold, Daniel
McDonold, Olen
McDonold Isaac
Montgomery, James, Sr.
Montgomery, James
Maddocke, William
Madkin, John
Nally, Dennis
Nelson, Richard
Newman, Edward
Neale, Raphael
Newton, George
Nally, Leonard
Owen, Richard
Osbin, David
Osborn, Henry
Osborn, Thomas
Ogdon, Jonathan
Ogdon, Thomas
Osbin, Joseph
Pickell, John
Pickell, Joseph
Pickell, Thomas
Posey, Benjamin
Posey, Thomas
Paggett, Henry
Procter, Charles
Power, Walter
Pagget, Thomas
Paggett, Jonathan
Procter, Thomas
Power, Joseph
Paget, Joseph
Philips, James
Philbert, Joseph
Richards, Ceasar
Rogers, Robert
Reeves, Hezekiah
Reeves, C. Thomas
Robey, John, of Rd.
Robey, Richard
Robey, Basil
Robey, H. Peter
Robey, Thomas, Sr.
Robey, Thomas
Robey, Samuel, Sr.
Robey, Benjamin, o Rd.
Robey, Samuel, of Jo
Robey, N. John
Robey, Allexander
Robey, Leonard
Robey, Zachariah
Robey, Wm., of Wm.
Robey, Samuel, of Rd
Robey, William, of Be
Robey, Joseph
Right, Samuel
Ratcliff, Joseph
Right, John
Right, Samuel
Rupell, James
Reeves, James

les, Lewis, Benja.
aw, Benjamin
ndyford, Thomas
mms, William
nith, Walter
nallwood, Prior
eward, James
nallwood, Ledstone
nallwood, Jas., of Jas.
mms, Marmaduke
nith, Basil
nith, Basil
nith, John
nith, Matthew
nith, Thomas (Blk. Smith)
well, Charles
well, Henry
well, Francis
rogin, Obediah
ercliff, Thomas
nithton, E. Wm.
Smoot, Wm. Barton
Tubman, Samuel
Tyer, William, Sr.
Tyer, William, Jr.
Tyer, Joseph
Tyer, John
Turner, Joseph
Turner, Zephaniah
Thompson, George
Thompson, Thomas
Thompson, Joseph
Thornton, Thomas, Rev.
Taylor, James
Thomas, John (Capt.)
Thornton, George
Vincent, Philip
Vincent, Darnall Henry
Varden, John
Widding, Philip
Wathen, Jno. Baptist
Wathen, Nicholas
Williams, John
Widding, John
Wain, John
Wain, William
White, Isle, Sr.
White, William
White, of Isle
Wages, Thomas
Whitter, William
Warren, William
Widding, Thos., Sr.
Widding, John, Sr.
Widding, Thomas, Jr.
Wathen, Ignatius
Warder, William
Ware, Scott Edward
Wills, Baptist John
Ware, Francis (Col.)
Ware, Jacob
Ware, Francis, Jr.
Warren, John
Yates, Francis
Young, Robert

POMONKEY HUNDRED, TAKEN BY W. MCPHERSON, CONSTABLE

dams, James
dams, John
they, Benjamin
rawner, Basil
oarman, Bolph
riscoe, James
ennett, John
urton, James
randt, Richard
oly, Robert
oner, Owing
rown, Samuel
onoway, John
lements, Samuel
ox, Richard
lements, Walter
lements, Leonard
hapman, Pearson
Craycroft, Thomas
Dent, John
Dent, George, of John
Douglass, Jeremiah
Dent, Peter
Dent, George, of Peter
Davis, Peter
Douglass, Benjamin
Delozer, John
Dement, Charles
Downs, William
Dawson, George
Dawson, Benjamin
Fendall, Benjamin
Grant, John
Gidings, Thomas
Gray, Richard
Gray, Benjamin
Gray, William
Gorden, Robert
Hall, C. Robert
Hall, William
Hooper, Thomas
Hamilton, William
Husk, Edward, Sr.
Husk, Edward, Jr.
Haly, Nathaniel
Jenkins, William
King, John
King, Elisha
King, James
Lambeth, B. John
Lang, Thomas
Lee, William
McHoney, Ignatius
Marbury, Henry

Marbury, William
Marshall, John
Marshall, Thomas
McPherson, Walter
Monroe, John
Monroe, Thomas
Marshall, T. Hanson
Middleton, Horatio
Murphey, Zachariah
McAtee, Henry
McAtee, Thomas
McAtee, John
McDonald, Alexander
Nottingham, Stephen
Perry, John
Parmer, James
Power, John
Permillian, Edward
Permillian, James
Pye, Walter
Paggett, William
Queen, Henry
Rowe, John, Sr.
Rowe, John, Jr.
Rowe, William
Rowe, Anthony
Stewart, George
Smallwood, John
Smallwood, Thos., Sr.
Smallwood, Thos., Jr.
Smoot, Josias
Smallwood, Pryor
Smallwood, Bayne
Stoddart, K. Truma
Stone, John
Speake, Henry
Smallwood, Hezekia
Tyler, William
Tubman, George
Wheeler, Luke
Wheeler, Joseph
Wheeler, Joshua
Wade, Richard
Wade, Zachariah
Williams, John
Ward, John
Ward, William
Ward, Henry

Newport West Hundred, taken by Jas. M. Dent, Constable

Boarman, John
Boarman, Bennett
Burkett, Thomas
Boarman, Leonard
Boarman, Walter
Bradley, Charles
Banon, S. Cooksey
Banon, Daniel
Boarman, Gerrard
Boarman, Henry
Boarman, Clement
Boarman, Charles
Briscoe, Philip
Black, James
Burttes, Benjamin
Burttes, William, Sr.
Burtes, William, Jr.
Boarman, Raphael
Brooke, John
Blair, Matthew
Cooksey, R. Thomas
Cooksey, Justinian
Cooksey, Ledstone
Cooksey, Henry
Cooksey, William
Clerk, Moses
Clerk, George
Cooksey, Thomas, Sr.
Cooksey, Hezekiah
Cooksey, John
Campbell, Isaac
Dent, Hatch, Sr.
Dent, John, Sr.
Dent, Benjamin, Sr.
Dent, Michael
Dent, Thomas, Sr.
Dent, William
Dent, Walter
Dent, Thomas, Jr.
Dent, Peter
Dent, Henry
Dent, Gidian
Dent, Benjamin, Jr.
Dent, Titus
Dora, Thomas
Duggons, Robert
Duggons, Henry
Dent, Hezekiah
Edelin, John
Edelin, Edward, Sr.
Edelin, Francis
Edelin, Edward, Jr.
Ferrill, James, Sr.
Ferrill, John
Ferrill, Elisha
Ferrill, James, Jr.
Ferrill, Patrick
Garick, Francis
Hancock, John
Hancock, William
Hennican, John
Hardman, Ignatius
Higdon, Benjamin,
Hudson, Jacob
Higdon, William, Jr
Hardman, Thomas,
Hancock, Thomas
Hancock, Abram
Higdon, Leonard
Herd, John
Jamison, Thomas
Jeamson, I. Henry

ɔnes, William
IcPherson, William, Sr.
Iathews, Thomas
Iiles, James
Iugg, Peter
Iurphey, Daniel, Jr.
Iorriss, Richard
Iason, John
Iarshall, Benjamin
Iason, Richard
Iecan, Thomas
Iontgomery, Francis
Ially, Harnard
Ially, Ignatius
Ially, William
liver, William
osey, Francis

Parnham, John
Smoot, N. John
Smoot, Hendly
Smoot, B. William
Sanders, James
Smoot, Isaac
Savoy, Arthur
Savoy, William
Simms, Mark
Simms, John
Simpson, Charles
Simpson, Henry
Simpson, Ignatius
Simpson, James
Simpson, William
Simpson, William, Jr.

Simpson, L. John
Simms, James
Simms, Francis
Thompson, Thomas, Sr.
Thompson, Thomas, Jr.
Wathen, Barton
Wathen, Bennett, Sr.
Williams, Jesse
Williams, John, Jr.
Williams, John, Sr.
Winter, John
Winter, Walter
Wathen, Clements
Wathen, B. John
Wathen, Bennett, Jr.
Wathen, Basil
Wathen, B. John

William and Mary Lower Hundred, taken by Jno. Vincent, Constable

.dams, Adam
Bateman, John
Bateman, Izreel
Brandt, Randolph
Bateman, John, Jr.
Bradley, Charles
Bradley, John
Boarman, William
Boarman, William, Jr.
Boarman, Ignatius
Boarman, Richard
Brandt, Charles
Bateman, Thomas
Bateman, Benjamin
Biggs, John Benjamin
Buckman, Ignatius
Chandler, Henry
Coustes, Charles
Chunn, Levi
Cattrell, Burford
Compton, Stephen
Compton, S. William

Craycroft, Clement
Doley, Thomas
Dorrete, William
Drury, Joseph
Diggs, John
Dennis, Ezekiel
Evans, Thomas
Ford, A. Charles
Ford, Chandler
Fearson, Attevix
Fearson, Walter
French, James
Gody, Henry
Gody, Matthew
Goodrich, Walter
Goodrich, Joseph
Gwinn, John
Goodrich, Aaron
Gardiner, Philip
Goodrich, George
Harris, Thomas
Howard, Baker

Hamsley, Henry
Holmes, John
Hudson, George
Inkins, William
James, Thomas
James, George
King, Benjamin
King, Asa
Lancaster, John
Lancaster, John, Jr.
Lancaster, Thomas
McPherson, John
Minetree, Andrew
Maddox, Townley
Maddox, William
Minetree, Paul
Martingdale, John
Maddocke, James, of N.
Maddocke, George
Neale, Bennett
Neale, John
Neale, James

Neale, F. William
Neale, Joseph
Oakley, Robert
Oakley, John
Penn, Zezreel
Reeves, Thomas
Rigg, Thomas
Scrogin, John
Shaw, Joseph
Shaw, William
Smoot, Edward
Smoot, Henry
Smoot, John
Smith, James
Smoot, Edward, Jr.
Simpson, William
Steel, George
Thomas, Philip
Thomas, John
Vincent, John
Vincent, William
Vincent, William, Jr
Vincent, John, Jr.
Wilder, John
Wilder, B. John
Wilder, Benjamin
Wilder, James
Warren, Edward
Warren, John
Wheatley, Silvester
Yates, Jonathan

BRYAN TOWN HUNDRED, TAKEN BY JNO. HARBIN, CONSTABLE

Alley, Thomas
Alley, Gustavus
Anderson, James
Burrell, Allen
Bowers, Jeremiah
Bryan, James
Bryan, Cornelius
Bryan, Josias
Barker, Joseph
Barker, William
Boon, James
Billingsly, John, Sr.
Boarman, T. James, Sr.
Boarman, Ralph
Boarman, T. James, Jr.
Boarman, Ed., Jr.
Boarman, Joseph
Boarman, Edward, Esq.
Boarman, Henry
Burch, Oliver
Burch, Jesse
Basil, Edward
Bramhall, Philip
Browdy, John
Browdy, Thomas
Boarman, William
Baget, Samuel
Bevin, Charles
Bevin, Benjamin
Bevin, Richard
Bevin, Paul
Bevin, Basil, Sr.
Bevin, Wheeler
Butler, Matthias
Bolling, William
Bowling, Thomas
Bowling, Francis
Billingsly, John, Jr.
Burnes, Jonathan
Bath, William
Bryan, John
Bryan, Ignatius
Bryan, Basil
Bowling, Joseph
Bowling, John
Burch, Richard
Chahill, Roger
Carricoe, Barton
Carricoe, James, of Peter
Carricoe, James, Sr.
Carricoe, William
Carricoe, Joseph
Cambron, James
Cambron, Thomas
Clements, Charles
Clements, B. Rd.
Carricoe, James, of Jno.
Cambron, Baptist
Cambron, Henry
Cambron, Milbron
Caho, Ignatius
Cooksey, Andrew
Caho, Thomas
Davis, Zachaes
Dent, John, of John
Dent, John, of Hatch
Dement, William
Delaney, Anthony
Dowing, Abednego
Dowing, James
Davis, Jesse
Darnall, Benjamin
Edelen, James
Edelen, Richard
Edwards, John
Fowler, Jonathan
Farran, Timothy
Farran, John
Farran, Hezekiah
Gates, James
Gates, John
Gates, William
Gates, Joseph
Gardiner, Igns.
Graham, William
Gibson, John, Sr.

ibson, John, Jr.
arner, John
arner, Clement
ibbons, Thomas
ibbons, Nehemiah
ibbons, William
ibbons, Jeremiah
ibbons, George
ardiner, Richard, Jr.
ood, William
Good ros Alley"
ates, Robert
larbin, John
lagan, Jas, of Igns.
larbin, Allen
larbin, William
larbin, Elisha
lagan, John
lagan, Jas., of Wm.
lammon, Nicholas
lagan, Ralph
lagan, James
lagan, Joseph, of Thos.
laskins, Bennett
lagan, Benjamin
larbin, W. Zephaniah
lunt, Basil
ackson, William
ackson, Thomas
ohnson, John
ameson, Benjamin, Sr.
amson, Joseph
amson, James
ohnson, Matthew
ohnson, Jonias
ohnson, Huet, son of Jas.
King, Richard
Kutch, Ignatius
Kennich, William
Kennich, John
King, O. Leonard
King, Henry
King, Zephaniah
Langley, William
Littner, I. John
Lyon, Michael
Lyon, Walter
Lyon, James
Lewis, Joseph
Maddox, James, Sr.
Maddox, Ignatius
Maddox, "Jrathan" (Jonothan?)
Maddox, James, Jr.
Montgomery, Joseph
Malone, William
Montgomery, Basil
Montgomery, William
Montgomery, Charles
Malone, James
McPherson, Alexander
Mudd, Henry
Mudd, Thos. Henry
Mudd, Joshua
Mudd, Burnett
Mudd, Ignatius
Mudd, John
Mudd, Richard
Mudd, Henry
Moran, Meveral
Morris, Joshua
Murphey, Daniel
Morton, Joseph
Morton, George
Montgomery, Igns.
Ogdon, Henry
Ogdon, William
Oden, Elias
Osborn, Thomas
Perry, Edward, Sr.
Perry, Edward, Jr.
Perry, Samuel
Perry, Nathan
Procter, Francis
Procter, Charles
Procter, Henry
Procter, Benjamin
Procter, Charles, son of Wm.
Paston, Edward
Paston, Solomon
Paston, Benjamin
Paston, Botholomew
Paston, Richard
Pattison, John
Queen, William
Queen, Francis
Redman, Henry
Robey, William
Robey, Stephen
Robey, Joseph
Rawlings, David
Richards, William
Richards, Thomas
Rutter, Joseph
Rutter, Hezekiah
Rawlings, Elisha
Sanders, Joshua
Savoy, Thomas
Smoot, Arther
Smoot, Thomas, of Sam.
Sute, John
Spaulding, Igns.
Spaulding, Thos.
Spaulding, Richard
Simmons, Samuel
Smith, John, Sr.
Smith, John, Jr.
Stallions, Samuel
Steel, William
Simms, Edward, Dr.
Sothoron, John
Shude, John
Sute, Walter
Shettleworth, John

Shettleworth, Joseph
Smoot, Samuel
Stone, Matthew
Thomas, Jonathan
Townley, Thomas
Townley, Joseph
Tinch, William, Sr.
Tinch, Leonard
Tinch, Joshua
Tinch, William, Jr.
Timson, Benjamin, Sr.
Timson, Benjamin
Turner, William
Turner, Randolph
Thompson, John
Thomas, James, Sr.
Thomas, James, Jr.
Tayler, James
Thomas, Thomas
Whitherington, Thos.
Whitherington, Rd.
Whitherington, Benja.
Waters, C. John
Wheatly, Burnett
Wheatly, Francis
Wheatly, John
Waters, Joseph
Waters, William
Waters, Zephaniah
Waters, James, Sr.
Waters, Thomas
Warden, Richard
Winnett, Mark
Wood, Benjamin
Wathen, Boston
Water, James, of Jas

ST. MARY'S COUNTY

MARRIAGE LICENSES FROM A.D. 1794 to 1864

St. Mary's County Marriage Licenses (7533 Persons)

Copy of Marriage Licenses from A. D. 1794 to 1864; made by Joseph F. Neal, Deputy Clerk, under and by virtue of the Acts of the General Assembly of Maryland, Chapter 375, of the session of 1900.

ST. MARY'S CLERK'S OFFICE.*

1796	Mch. 6	Ashie, William and Eliz. Latin.
	Aug. 8	Allston, Thomas and Mary Jordan.
	Dec. 24	Abell, Philip and Eleanor Drury.
1797	Jan. 9	Anthony, Thomas and Eliz. Massey.
	Mch. 8	Aderton, Jeremiah and Mary Wise.
	Oct. 25	Abell, Ig. of Aaron and Nancy Joy.
	Sept. 10	Aderton, Jeremiah and Judith A. Biscoe.
1799	Sept. 9	Aites, Jos. and Jean Fenwick.
	Oct. 22	Abell, John and Sarah Forrost.
	Feb. 10	Armsworthy, Bennet and Susanna Scissell.
	Nov. 15	Adams, James and Eliz. Peake.
	Dec. 9	Armsworthy, Daniel and Elizabeth Newton.
	27	Atwood, John L. and Teresa Combs.
1801	June 13	Alvey, Anthony and Dorothy Walters.
	Dec. 20	Arnold, Edmund and Eleanor Ellis.
1802	Jan. 17	Allston, Jeremiah and Phillipe Chiseldine.
1803	Apr. 19	Abell, Cha. and Susa. Clarke.
1804	May 12	Ashton, Henry and Cecelia B. Key.
	June 2	Alvey, Basil and Dorothy Suttle.
	Dec. 13	Allston, Henry and Ann W. Jordan.
1805	— 19	Aud, Ignatius and Mary Sherley.
1806	Feb. 10	Abell, Philip and Helenda Peake.
	Apr. 8	Artis, Jeremiah and Eliza. Biscoe.
	Dec. 29	Abell, Jonathan and Harriet Crown.
1807	Nov. 23	Anderson, Joseph and Jane Crook.
1808	Dec. 26	Abell, Jno. of Thos. and Ann Cole.
	26	Adams, George and Sarah Lurty.
1809	Feb. 5	Aprice, Edward and Mary Locke.
1810	May 1	Abell, Philip and Julia Greenwell.
	Aug. 22	Adams, Stephen and Hannah Greenwell.
	June 2	Aderton, James and Eleanor Thomas.

*Copied, verified and published through the coöperation of Mrs. Margaret Roberts Hodges (Mrs. George W.), Annapolis, Md.

1813	Jan.	14	Abell, Matthew and Elizabeth Crane.
	Nov.	22	Armstrong, George and Rebecca Jarboe.
1814	Jan.	10	Abell, Elias and Teresia Heard.
	June	21	Armsworthy, Tho. and Elizabeth Hopewell.
1815	Jan.	16	Abell, Francis and Nancy Hebb.
	Aug.	21	Abell, Bennet and Eliza. A. Greenwell.
1816	Jan.	8	Adams, Cornelius and Maria Norriss.
	Feb.	24	Anderson, Henry and Susanna Bothwick.
	Aug.	6	Alvey, John and Mary Weatherton.
1817	Jan.	28	Abell, Matthew and Harriot Thompson.
	Feb.	9	Armstrong, Jas. and Eliza. Cole.
	July	6	Abell, Enock and Ann Norriss.
	Oct.	13	Armsworthy, Jas. and Eliza. Spicer.
1819	Jan.	18	Abell, Eliel and Susanna Clarke.
	June	12	Anderson, Jas. and Mary Jett.
1820	June	23	Abell, George and Eliza. Brewer.
1821	May	1	Aug, Ignatius and Ann Watts
	Dec.	31	Alvey, Cornelius and Susanna Cahill.
1822	Feb.	8	Alvey, James and Ann Cook.
1823	Jan.	7	Alvey, Joshua and Susanna Mattingly.
	July	26	Artis, Joseph and Mary Bennett.
1824	Jan.	13	Alvey, Aloysius and Catherine Drury.
	Feb.	9	Anderson, Thos. and Eliza. Heard.
	May	22	Alvey, Geo. N. and Elizabeth Weaklin.
	Dec.	23	Ashcom, Jno. C. and Ann Broome.
1825	Feb.	8	Alvey, Henry and Eliza. Bradburn.
	Apr.	14	Artis, Jeremiah and Susan Smith.
1826	Feb.	22	Armstrong, Henry and Christian Sothoron.
	Sept.	12	Alexander, W. P. and Julia Ann Blackiston.
	Dec.	29	Alvey, Philip and Drucilla Sothoron.
1827	May	29	Abell, Henry and Mary Yates.
1828	Feb.	18	Abell, James and Ann Gatton.
1829	Feb.	24	Abell, Henry and Mary Ann Melton.
1830	Sept.	28	Armstrong, Daniel and Maria Martin.
	Dec.	18	Ashton, Jno. N. and Ann Branagin.
1831	Feb.	7	Armsworthy, Geo. and Ann Evans.
	Feb.	8	Abell, William and Eliza. Drury.
	June	11	Anderson, Alexa. and Rose Anna Wilkinson.
	June	13	Abell, Henry and Ann Greenwell.
	Dec.	11	Anderson, Theodore and Margaret A. Knott.
		26	Anderson, Henry and Sally Davis.
1832	Mch.	5	Allbritten, Chas. and Eleanor Williams.

1833	May	8	Adams, Biscoe and Helen Redman.
		21	Armstrong, Henry and Mary E. Ford.
1834	July	8	Alvey, William and Ann Gooding.
		14	Adams, John and Dolly Owings.
1836	Apr.	5	Abell, Geo. W. and Ann J. Stone.
	June	28	Abell, James and Clara Bowes.
	Aug.	9	Allstan, James H. and Jane M. Greenwell.
1838	Jan.	5	Alvey, Joel and Elizabeth Thompson.
		15	Arnold, Edward and Julih Brown.
		17	Abell, Joseph and Hannah H. Clarke.
	Feb.	5	Aud, Ignatius and Susan Downs.
	Dec.	18	Allstan, Llewellen J. and Martha M. Dunbar.
		21	Anderson, Henry and Elizabeth Biven.
	June	6	Anderson, Charles and Margaret Owens.
	Nov.	26	Adams, John and Susan Hewett.
	Dec.	18	Aneldale, Wm. and Ann C. Tarlton.
		31	Adams, Alexa. and Mary E. Norriss.
1841	Jan.	5	Allston, William and Sophia D. Cheseldine.
		5	Alvey, James H. and Eliza Lyon.
	Dec.	6	Armsworthy, Thos. B. and Martha E. Cissell.
1842	Dec.	27	Abell, John Lewis and Susan Maria Dukes.
	May	9	Armsworthy, McKelva and Mary Eliza. Hewett.
	Dec.	20	Abercrombie, James and Attaway Garner.
1844	Jan.	2	Abell, Bend. J. and Jane A. E. Clarke.
	Feb.	13	Abell, Marcellus D. and Amanda E. Norriss.
	Nov.	16	Adams, John and Mary E. Ridgell.
1845	Jan.	23	Adams, Anselum V. and Eliza. Beckwith.
	Feb.	2	Armsworthy. George and Catherine Cole.
1846	Feb.	11	Armsworthy, Chas. W. and Eliza A. Barnes.
	Dec.	22	Alvey, W. H. and Mary E. Morriss.
1847	July	6	Adams, William and Rebecca Winters.
	Oct.	12	Armstrong, Josiah N. and Mary J. Millard.
	Dec.	28	Armstrong, Albert and Eliza McCoy.
1848	Jan.	25	Adams, Stephen W. and Anna C. Paul.
	Mch.	6	Aud, Wm. J. and Mary A. Bell.
	June	19	Abell, Jno. B. and Susan R. Clarke.
1850	Feb.	4	Armsworthy, McKelva and Clarissa P. Bennett.
	July	16	Abell, James, F. and Maria J. Nuthall.
1852	May	24	Abell, William C. and Martha H. Sutton.
		27	Alvey, William H. and Ann P. Carberry
1853	Feb.	7	Abell, Wm. T. X. and Martha Norris.
	June	14	Abell, Robert and Jane Paul.

1853	July	4	Abell, Wm. E. and Margaret A. Hayden.
1854	Jan.	31	Alvey, Ignatius B. and Priscilla Goodrick.
	Apr.	18	Abell, Enock B. and Levonia Stone.
	June	22	Abell, E. Thompson and Catherine A. H. Abell.
	Oct.	7	Alvey, Joel and Elizabeth Hazell.
1855	Jan.	17	Armstrong, Benja. and Rebecca Kirby.
	Apr.	30	Ashcom, Geo. H. and Mary E. Sollars.
	Jan.	26	Alvey, James J. and Ann R. Graves.
	June	10	Abell, Edward S. and Ann M. Smith.
1857	Jan.	7	Abell, Joseph F. and Ann M. Brown.
	June	16	Abell, B. R. and Philomina A. Roach.
	Aug.	4	Abell, Wm. E. and Jane S. H. Russell.
1859	Feb.	7	Alvey, Thos. Hilery and Jane Cornelia Hardesty.
	June	22	Adams, Biscoe and Sarah E. Parmer.
1860	Jan.	3	Abell, James T. and Susan P. Perry.
	Feb.	13	Alvey, Ignatius B. and Pheboe C. Higgs.
	Nov.	12	Abell, Dr. Wm. M. and Jennie A. Thompson.
1861	Jan.	22	Abell, J. Edwin and Susan R. Mattingly.
	July	31	Adams, Biscoe and Sallie Adams.
1862	Jan.	9	Abell, Geo. W. and Mary V. Benson.
	Feb.	7	Arnold, Richard H. and Mary C. Cheseldine.
1795	Jan.	3	Bohanan, Geo. Jr. and Catherine Sherry.
	Feb.	11	Bullock, Richard, and Rebecca Goldsmith.
1796	Jan.	13	Briscoe, William and Drayden Graves.
		17	Bean, Thomas and Nancy Hebb.
	Apr.	8	Beale, William and Susanna Heard.
	Dec.	27	Bohanan, Jonathan and Mary Richardson.
	Aug.	1	Brown, Ignatius and Elizabeth Newton.
		25	Billingsley, Thomas and Mary Barber.
	Sept.	25	Burroughs, Hezekiah and Mary Watson.
	Oct.	5	Billingsley, Allen and Sarah G. Latimer.
	Nov.	12	Burroughs, James and Elizabeth Davis.
		17	Bradburn, Charles and Frances Hayden.
	Dec.	22	Bean, William and Dicandia Martin.
		22	Burroughs, Henry and Nancy Burroughs.
		28	Baxter, John and Elizabeth Medley.
		29	Bradman, Francis and Eleanor Melton.
1797	Jan.	31	Bright, John and Eliz. Burroughs.
	Feb.	21	Bennett, Hanson and Eliza. Davis.
	Mch.	24	Bannor, Benja. and Ann Davis.
	June	3	Brookbank, John and Eliza. Brookbank.

1797	July	5	Boso, Christopher and Eliza. Howard.
	Aug.	5	Bradburn, Wm. and Jane Reeves.
	Sept.	10	Brunt, Hugh and Elizabeth Palmer.
	Nov.	1	Bryon, Francis and Mary Ann Dellaha.
	Dec.	22	Bean, Robert and Sarah Lowe.
1798	June	23	Betts, John and Monica Thompson.
	Aug.	27	Bowling, Charles and Eliza. Maryman.
	Sept.	22	Biscoe, William and Henrietta Dunbar.
	Nov.	16	Beachum, Thomas and Mary Clayton.
	Dec.	15	Burrows, William and Lydia Davis.
		27	Backster, Edward and Ann Tarlton.
		31	Brewer, Thomas and Catherine Joy.
1799	May	23	Burt, Andrew and Isabella Armston.
	Aug.	27	Bullock, James and Elizabeth French.
1800	Jan.	1	Bryan, Enock and Dorothy Leach.
		14	Bruce, John and Mary Cullison.
		21	Bunnum, Aaron, and Eleanor Peake.
	Feb.	6	Blakiston, Kenelm and Chloe Tarlton.
	Apr.	16	Bond, James and Henny Sword.
	May	3	Butler, Clement and Mary Ann Mason.
	Sept.	27	Brady, Henry and Sarah Hazel.
	Oct.	27	Bowles, John and Bibianna Spalding.
	Dec.	31	Belwood, Edward and Susanna Arles.
1801	Jan.	17	Booth, Rodolph and Monica Price.
	Feb.	9	Batinell, William and Judy Baker.
		16	Bullock, George and Ann Norris.
	Mch.	27	Barnes, Alex. and Jane Stott.
	Aug.	22	Blakistone, Nehemiah H. and Eleanor G. Hebb.
	Oct.	5	Boykin, Stephen H. and Rebecca Adderton.
		13	Bowling, William and Eleanor Heard.
		28	Booth, Mathias and Eleanor Watts.
	Nov.	28	Booth, Joseph and Mary Stephen
	Dec.	22	Biscoe, Richard and Eleanor Clarke.
1802	May	2	Barnes, John Esq. and Mary Key.
		16	Barnes, Daniel F. and Eliza Humphreys.
	Dec.	13	Boult, William and Elizabeth Hammett.
1803	Jan.	7	Brown, Martin and Eleanor Graves.
	Mch.	5	Bohanan, William and Eliza Fenwick.
	July	9	Broome, John and Ann Clarke.
	Aug.	5	Brady, John and Mary Haskins.
	Dec.	3	Brown, William H. and Mary Ann Booth.
1804	Feb.	8	Booker, James and Mary Williams.

1804	Feb.	9	Brome, Henry and Rebecca Martin.
	May	8	Bean, John and Sarah McKay.
	July	25	Booth, Charles and Henrietta Booth.
	Oct.	8	Brent, Wm. C. and Dorothy Diggs.
	Nov.	13	Biscoe, Bennet and Eliza Locke.
1805	Jan.	24	Brewer, Geo. and Sarah Berne.
	June	8	Bohanan, Moses and Darbey Rhodes.
	Oct.	8	Beck, Samuel G. and Susanna Keech.
		20	Bond, Richard and Rebecca W. Barber.
	Dec.	27	Bright, James and Mary Burroughs.
		29	Bennett, William and Mary Greenwell.
		31	Bean, John and Nancy Lynch.
1806	Jan.	6	Bean, George and Mary Wherrett.
		10	Boyd, John and Dorothy Henry.
	Feb.	11	Briscoe, James and Lettina Chesley.
	Dec.	13	Burroughs, William and Eleanor Cawood.
1807	Apr.	11	Bryan, Enoch and Elizabeth Morgan.
	July	24	Blaxsett, Joseph and Teresa Ford.
	Aug.	10	Bridget, William and Catherine Thompson.
	Nov.	14	Boothe, Jeremiah and Ann Walker.
	Dec.	24	Brewer, Richard and Eleanor Tippett.
1808	Feb.	6	Bond, Charles M. and Jane Howard.
		6	Bennett, William and Phebe Clayton.
	Apr.	23	Butler, Thomas and Milly Mason.
	July	15	Barber, Thomas and Susa. Latimore.
	Aug.	29	Burroughs, Barnet and Eliza. Burroughs.
1809	July	19	Brent, George and Matilda E. Thomas.
	Dec.	18	Bayne, John E. and Susanna Clocker.
1811	Mch.	5	Bean, Jeremiah and Eliza. Crowly.
	July	24	Bond, Richard G. B. and Sarah Parsons.
	Sept.	7	Bennett, William and Minta Hilton.
	Dec.	28	Berry, John G. and Ann Bailey.
1812	Jan.	4	Barnes, John M. and Susanna Harding.
		20	Bourgain, Nicholas and Sarah Thompson.
	Apr.	4	Butler, Lewis and Margaret Barnes.
		6	Branzel, John and Sarah Branson.
	June	10	Billingsley, Thomas and Catherine Barber.
	July	2	Burroughs, Jesse C. and Ann C. Morgan.
		18	Bryan, William and Eliza. Mason.
	Oct.	13	Bond, Samuel and Eliza Kitchen.
		31	Bryan, Enoch and Helen Alvey
	Dec.	14	Brome, James M. and Margaret Mackall.

1813 Jan. 18 Blakistone, Geo. and Rebecca Goldsmith.
May 18 Bean, Samuel and Mary Greenwell.
Dec. 31 Beverly, George and Ann Hath.
1814 Feb. 5 Branson, James and Catherine Graves.
14 Burroughs, George and Harriet Dent.
14 Barber, Walter and Mary Wainright.
Oct. 12 Brown, Leonard and Eliza. Stone.
Nov. 8 Branson, John B. and Lenna Gatton.
24 Briscoe, William H. and Rebecca W. Bond.
28 Briscoe, Thomas B. and Eleanor B. Briscoe.
1815 Sept. 7 Barber, Robert and Eliza. W. Barber.
19 Biscoe, Geo. W. and Ann Maria Hopewell.
Oct. 12 Bennett, Gerard and Lydia Jones.
1816 Jan. 4 Burroughs, Philip and Suckey Woodburn.
11 Brewer, John and Eliza. Evans.
27 Bateman, Townly and Teresa Norriss.
31 Barker, Leonard and Eliza Rogers.
Feb. 3 Burroughs, Joseph and Eliza. Dent.
6 Bean, William and Mary Combs.
26 Brown, Joseph and Susan Stone.
Apr. 13 Blake, William H. and Attaway Tippett.
22 Blakistone, Kenelm and Juliet Locke.
1817 Jan. 15 Biscoe, Samuel and Matilda Bennett.
Feb. 4 Bills, Enoch and Mary Henry.
Apr. 26 Brome, James M. and Ann Martin.
June 23 Briscoe, Saml. John and Ann Clements.
July 22 Briscoe, Philip and Maria Thompson.
Sept. 4 Burroughs, John and Ruth Ann Mills.
Nov. 4 Burroughs, James and Rebecca Davis.
Dec. 10 Beale, Zadock and Susan R. G. Morton.
1818 Jan. 20 Bufford, Robert and Eliza. Lynch.
22 Bennett, Thomas and Ann Biscoe.
26 Booth, Lewis and Ann Howard.
Mch. 7 Bowling, James and Ann Drury.
July 22 Beattey, John and Ann Drury.
Nov. 3 Bond, Th. A. and Mary Hambleton.
13 Brome, Benja. and Mary Martin.
Dec. 26 Brown, Richard and Nancy Stone.
28 Bond, James and Jamima Lynch.
1819 Jan. 26 Barnes, George and Susanna Harding.
Feb. 8 Biscoe, William and Sarah Biscoe.
July 15 Bryon, John and Cath. Lawrence.

1819	Dec.	23	Bishop, John and Darky Davis.
1820	Jan.	10	Biscoe, Langley and Ann Biscoe.
		12	Brown, Richard and Ann Darky Long.
		15	Bennett, Richard W. and Mary Biscoe.
		26	Bennett, John and Elizabeth Hardesty.
		28	Brewer, Joseph and Mary Russell.
	May	3	Brown, William and Jane Rock.
		29	Bradburn, James and Eliza. Martin.
	June	25	Brown, Gustavus and Harriot Walker.
	Aug.	5	Bowden, Revd. Jas. J. and Eliza. M. Clagett.
		28	Booth, Thomas and Ann Maryman.
	Nov.	27	Booth, Ignatius and Jane Yates.
	Dec.	19	Biscoe, Richard and Sarah Clarke.
1821	Jan.	1	Brewer, Thomas and Sarah McGee.
	Feb.	3	Bean, John of Robt. and Mary Milburn.
		27	Beavin, John W. and Susan E. Drury.
	May	22	Biscoe, William L. and Britania Langley.
		24	Brewer, Edward and Teresia Greenwell.
	July	7	Buckler, George and Eleanor Gatton.
	Dec.	14	Barber, Walter and Maria Thomas.
1822	Jan.	9	Burroughs, William and Susan Greenfield.
	June	10	Blakistone, Nathl. and Hopey Morgan.
	Dec.	5	Bowles, Gustavis and Susanna Tippett.
		10	Baldwin, George and Mary Wise.
		23	Branikin, Henry and Eliza. Ferroll.
1823	Jan.	9	Booth, William and Jane Aud.
		13	Brown, William and Cath. Branson.
		14	Booth, George and Lydia Maraman.
		21	Bradbond, John L. and Eleanor Rock.
	May	26	Briscoe, John H. and Mary H. Key.
	July	21	Beall, Zadock W. and Margaret Ashton.
		29	Butler, Josiah and Cecelia Carter.
	Sept.	27	Bond, Thomas A. and Eliza. Long.
	Dec.	27	Biscoe, George and Margaret Beale.
1824	Jan.	5	Burroughs, Hezekiah and Mary Ann Weaklin.
		13	Booth, Samuel and Ann Thompson.
		30	Brown, Thomas and Julian Herbert.
	Feb.	21	Bennett, William and Mary Maria Joy.
		23	Butler, Lewis and Polly Mason.
	Apr.	19	Buckler, Alexander and Eliza. Scott.
	June	7	Batty, George and Ann Lynch.
		30	Blakistone, William J. and Mary B. Knott.

1824	July	20	Bowling, William W. and Juliet Blakistone.
	Oct.	16	Barnes, John and Elizabeth E. Murphey.
1825	Apr.	9	Baker, Jesse and Mary Cissill.
		12	Bradburn, Edwd. R. and Mary Thompson.
	June	20	Bean, James and Catherine Boult.
	July	26	Booth, Ign. of Geo. and Susanna Thompson.
	Dec.	20	Bean, Bennett I. and Mary P. Worthington.
1826	Mch.	13	Bennett, Thomas J. and Eliza K. Jones.
	Apr.	8	Brantzell, John and Ann Stone.
	June	3	Brewer, Joseph and Matilda Hutchins.
	Aug.	30	Briscoe, Walter H. S. and Emeline W. Dallam.
	Dec.	21	Blakistone, Henry H. and Ann E. Shanks.
1827	Jan.	8	Brewer, William and Cecelia Russell.
	Feb.	27	Blakistone, Dent and Mary T. Watson.
	Apr.	14	Burroughs, Thomas and Mary Ann Reeves.
	June	1	Bean, Thomas and Mary Lodge.
1828	Jan.	7	Bean, William and Maria Thompson.
		26	Burroughs, Leonard and Eliza. Ann Burroughs.
	Feb.	5	Brookbanks, Elias and Eliza. Mattingly.
		12	Bradburn, Edward R. and Sally Monarch.
	Mch.	8	Beckwith, Nelson and Teresia Ford.
	July	28	Brown, William and Ann P. Greenwell.
	Nov.	6	Bate, John Sr. and Catherine M. Eden.
	Dec.	12	Billingsley, Chapman and Lydia C. Barber.
		17	Buckler, Thomas and Matha Allbrittain.
1829	Jan.	12	Barber, John and Maria Owings.
		13	Beall, Nathl. and Maria Biscoe.
	Feb.	17	Baden, Jeremiah M. and Eliza. A. Greenwell.
	May	12	Bennett, John W. and Eliza. Loker.
	Sept.	7	Boothe, Stanislous and Frances Nelson.
	Nov.	5	Bryan, William and Delila Tippett.
	Dec.	28	Bolds, William and Mary Ann Guy.
1830	Feb.	4	Bond, Henry and Ann Farguson.
		16	Blair, Samuel and Mary Thompson.
		16	Briscoe, Charles and Catherine Leigh.
		22	Brown, John and Ann Maria Aud.
	Apr.	20	Beal, Alex. L. and Eleanor E. Milburn.
	June	1	Biscoe, Thos. H. and Ann Hutchins.
	July	27	Boothe, Lewis and Susanna Boothe.
	Aug.	19	Burroughs, Thos. T. and Casy Tippett.
	Oct.	27	Bean, George and Julian Price.
1831	Jan.	3	Brown, Henry (F. Blk.) and Susan Butler (of Blk.).

1831	Jan.	8	Burroughs, Jesse C. and Susanna C. Burroughs.
	Feb.	2	Buckler, Benjamin and Ann M. Dean.
		3	Beal, George and Mary B. Hall.
		12	Bean, Bennett and Catherine A. Herbert.
		19	Brantzell, William and Eliza. Colton.
	May	31	Bennett, Richard and Matilda Aud.
	Nov.	10	Blakstone, Bernard and Rebecca J. Allstone.
	Dec.	21	Burroughs, Aquila and Susan Eliza. Lyon.
1832	Jan.	9	Brookbank, Elias and Jane Lyon.
	Feb.	28	Biscoe, William D. and Sarah Lilburn.
	Nov.	13	Burroughs, Jno. A. and Eliza. T. Dent.
1833	Jan.	7	Bowes, John and Sarah Wallace.
	Feb.	5	Bowling, Richard and Mary McWilliams.
		12	Bond, William and Ann Cusick.
	June	21	Boothe, Joseph and Mary J. Fenwick.
	Dec.	2	Bradley, John and Cecelia Herbert.
		25	Brian, Richd.—free Blk. and Eliza Reed—free Blk.
		28	Burroughs, John and Cath. Ann Sothorn.
1834	Jan.	24	Bean, William and Ann C. Taylor.
		29	Bowling, Charles and Ann Locke.
	May	24	Burke, Garret and Catherine Brewer Ford.
	Oct.	12	Brewer, Thomas and Ann Hariet Greenwell.
	Nov.	4	Beal, George and Jane Flower.
	Dec.	10	Branekin, John and Eliza. Lacey.
1835	Jan.	3	Baxter, John A. and Ann Adams.
		9	Bohanan, Jonathan and Permelia A. Milburn.
	May	21	Barber, Luke E. and Jane P. R. Causin.
		26	Briscoe, Saml. W. and Ann. L. Barber.
1836	Jan.	7	Beal, Matthias and Maria A. Forrest.
	Feb.	13	Bowes, John and Eleanor Ann Higgs.
	Apr.	16	Buckler, Jas. H. and Jane A. Evans.
	Aug.	5	Brown, Gustavus and Eliza. Greenwell.
		30	Bean, James and Susan M. Price.
1837	May	15	Briscoe, Langley and Juliet Briscoe.
	Oct.	27	Bond, Samuel and Henrietta A. Garner.
	Dec.	2	Bond, Thomas and Eliza. Gatton.
		22	Burch, Albert and Amanda Turner.
1838	Jan.	2	Burch, James and Ann Alvey.
		3	Boothe, Elias and Jane Boothe.
		22	Brantzell, Jno. H. and Mary A. Cullison.
	Feb.	20	Burroughs, Saml. G. M. and Rosetta E. Milburn.
	Apr.	16	Benson, William F. and Susan Wallace.

1838 June 7 Boothe, Joseph and Matilda Nuthall.
Aug. 21 Bennett, Uriah and Mary E. Bean.
Dec. 27 Boothe, Saml. and Clara Fenwick.
1839 Jan. 5 Baxter, Wm. P. and Mary Tarlton.
8 Blakistone, Jno. and Eliza. B. Allston.
Feb. 5 Beavan, Jno. W. and Margaret S. Combs.
Apr. 9 Bowles, Wm. and Susan Ford.
Aug. 26 Bond, Benedict and Lucinda Bedman.
Sept. 17 Briscoe, Robt. M. and Mary A. Brome.
Dec. 30 Bailey, John L. and Eliza. A. Shurcliff.
30 Baggett, George and Mary Ann Garner.
1840 Mch. 16 Brewer, Lloyd and Emeline Thompson.
Apr. 21 Branson, Thos. and Ann Eliza. Gatton.
Nov. 11 Blakistone, Jas. T. and Ann Thomas.
1841 Jan. 11 Blair, William and Mary Eliza Ellis.
May 25 Brome, Jno. M. and Susan M. Bennett.
1842 Feb. 1 Baxter, Jno. A. and Ann Tarlton.
May 28 Beard, Thomas and Barbary Ann E. Bean.
31 Bennett, Joseph P. and Emily Thomas.
Aug. 22 Branson, Jas. A. and Jane E. Cole.
Dec. 31 Barnes, Jno. A. and Susan Buckler.
1843 Jan. 2 Biscoe, Wm. and Jane Y. Barber.
Feb. 1 Burch, James W. and Susan Rebecca Carpenter.
23 Burroughs, Hezekiah and Eliza. A. Sotharon.
June 13 Bean, Stephen L. and Ann S. Cox.
Dec. 28 Burch, Henry Dade and Mary C. Hayden.
1845 Jan. 10 Brewer, Lloyd A. and Mary Ellen Greenwell.
Jan. 25 Blades, Wm. R. and Ellen Price.
Apr. 14 Burnett, John and Mary Wise.
May 20 Blackistone, Geo. W. and Joanna Cheseldine.
1846 Jan. 6 Burroughs, John and Ann Maria Jarboe.
Feb. 6 Berry, George and Mary Jane Scott.
June 22 Burroughs, Aquilla and Marion Knight.
1847 Jan. 20 Buckler, John H. and Martha E. Davis.
Apr. 5 Barber, Robert T. and Mary Ellen Mattingly.
July 30 Buckler, Thomas and Sarah Taylor.
1848 Jan. 25 Brown, Thomas and Mary E. Thompson.
Feb. 8 Bailey, H. and Mary A. Ellis.
Apr. 20 Boothe, Samuel and Larinda Long.
1849 Jan. 15 Bateman, Wm. C. and Sarah A. F. Wainright.
29 Brown, John F. and Mary Susan Harden.
Feb. 12 Bailey, Charles C. and Julia A. Mattingly.

1849	Feb.	12	Blades, William R. and Mary Hopkins.
	Apr.	22	Bean, John H. and Rebecca Loker.
	Feb.	13	Boothe, John T. L. and Eliza. Thompson.
	June	5	Brown, Wellington and Mary E. Hayden.
	July	13	Burroughs, Philip H. and Mary E. Russell.
	Aug.	27	Bean, James C. and Maria L. Bean.
	Oct.	29	Bean, Hezekiah H. and Mary A. Miltimore.
1850	Jan.	15	Bean, John L. and Amanda Stone.
		17	Burroughs, A. M. and Eliza. Knight.
	Feb.	7	Bean, Jeremiah and Mary Mattingly.
	July	23	Brookbank, Samuel and Attaway Norris.
	Nov.	25	Brewer, Edward D. and Mary E. Martin.
	Dec.	10	Brown, Zach. and Susanna E. Carpenter.
1851	Jan.	21	Brewer, James T. and Ann M. Thompson.
		29	Brown, D. and Jane E. Thompson.
	Feb.	3	Bean, John H. and Ann C. Martin.
	Mch.	3	Buckler, James and Lucretia Long.
	Apr.	7	Bunting, James and Jane Ellen Shemwell.
	July	26	Burch, Remigius and Ann B. Blakistone.
		30	Batty, John E. L. and Catherine D. Redman.
	Oct.	7	Biscoe, James and E. S. Anderson.
		16	Burroughs, John A. and Celey M. Spalding.
1852	Jan.	12	Biscoe, James L. and Sarah A. Hammett.
	Apr.	13	Branson, James A. and Rose A. Knott.
	Sept.	21	Baxter, William P. and Mary E. Lee.
1853	Jan.	11	Buckler, Ben and Sallie Wathen.
	Feb.	8	Bell, Thomas and Charlotte Boothe.
	Mch.	28	Bowles, Wm. S. and Celestia Hardesty.
	May	23	Bowles, Gustavus and Zorah Thompson.
	Aug.	26	Beane, Alexander H. and Jane L. Bennett.
	Sept.	13	Brewer, John M. and Ann Castelia Martin.
		18	Boothe, Elias and Sally A. Hardesty.
	Nov.	14	Bradburn, James H. and Mary L. Joy.
		15	Bond, Lorenza D. and Rebecca A. Payne.
		24	Blair, Wm. and Susan Gibson.
1854	Jan.	3	Bradburn, Jno. S. and Ann A. Joy.
	Feb.	6	Brookbank, Elias and Martha Ann Higgs.
	Apr.	15	Bohanan, James H. and Ann Brown.
1855	May	4	Byrd, Thomas J. and Martha Ann Edwards.
		10	Buckler, Solomon and Bettie Ann Bond.
		28	Bradburn, Wm. F. and Mary E. Brewer.
	Dec.	26	Brown, Wm. H. and Mary J. Peacock.

1856	Jan.	26	Blakstone, Henry H. and Harriet L. Hayden.
	Feb.	8	Burroughs, Jno. A. and Eliza. Garner.
	Apr.	1	Barber, Robert T. and Dorsey Ann Penn.
	May	6	Bond, Benedict and Mary B. Chunn.
		17	Bowles, Wm. S. and Mary C. Tippett.
	Aug.	6	Bruce, J. Furgusson and Ellen Forbes Key.
		11	Boothe, Stanis L. and Catherine A. Perry.
	Nov.	25	Bohanan, Ignatius and Martha Ann Peacock.
	Dec.	16	Bean, Robert and Sarah E. Wilson.
1857	Feb.	6	Bailey, James H. and Eliza Ann Hayden.
		10	Bowles, Hillery B. and Elizabeth Bowles.
	May	4	Burroughs, Thomas H. and Eliza. Sothoron.
	Aug.	18	Bean, R. J. and Frannie B. Trowbridge.
		25	Boswell, John H. and Mary C. Ryce.
	Nov.	3	Burgess, Allen and Ann E. Leigh.
	Dec.	8	Biscoe, W. S. and Eliza A. Booth.
1858	July	24	Beal, Thos. W. and Josephine McKay.
	Nov.	10	Biscoe, Thomas R. and Julia King.
	Dec.	22	Bowles, Hillery B. and Margaret S. Tippett.
1859	Jan.	22	Bell, Nathaniell W. and R. Maria Norris.
		24	Bowles, John J. and Mary Matilda Graves.
	Feb.	21	Bond, Wm. Henry and Eliza. Hall.
	Mch.	1	Bowles, Stephen H. and Martha J. Mattingly.
	May	3	Bowles, Wm. J. and Eliza. Herberk.
	Aug.	30	Beacham, Thos. L. and Belinda E. Gardiner.
	Dec.	20	Bohanan, Geo. M. and Maria J. A. Yates.
		27	Bond, Ferdinand H. and Mary Curry.
1860	Jan.	10	Blakistone, Z. D. and Harriet Ann Shanks.
	Apr.	16	Bean, R. J. and Addy M. Taylor.
		17	Bayley, Shirkeiffet and Charlotte A. Graves.
	Aug.	9	Brown, Thomas and Margaret A. Greenwell.
	Nov.	5	Burch, John T. and Mary Margaret Hill.
		20	Biscoe, Robt. B. and Ann Cullison
1862	Jan.	6	Bond, Thos. and Susan A. Dean.
		6	Burch, Wm. E. and Jane E. Guy.
		20	Bell, Thos. E. and Margaret A. Godard.
		27	Bell, Wm. P. and E. R. Paul.
	Nov.	18	Blair, Samuel and Mary C. Maryman.
1863	Apr.	8	Bagley, William A. and Virginia J. Gibson.
	July	9	Buchanan, E. Key and Ann Smith.
	Nov.	3	Bennett, Thos. W. and Mary E. Wheeler.
	Dec.	21	Burroughs, Wm. T. and Mary M. Born.

1794	Sept.	29	Cheseldine, Wm. and Teresia Mason.
	Dec.	23	Cullison, George and Mary Thompson.
1795	Feb.	14	Coard, John and Mary Neale.
		17	Coade, John and Drayden Hebb.
	Mch.	3	Coale, Bennett and Jeane Hendly.
		17	Clarke, George and Mary Doney.
	Apr.	14	Cissell, Zachariah and Catherine Yates.
1796	Feb.	5	Cissell, Thomas and Mary A. McLanan.
	Apr.	26	Campbell, George and Nancy Biscoe.
	May	2	Craig, Peter and Ann Tippett.
	July	15	Clarke, Richard and Eliza. Clarke.
		25	Combs, James and Ann Hendley.
	Sept.	10	Christie, Will F. and Zerbinah Boarne.
	Nov.	22	Campbell, George W. and Ann Biscoe.
		29	Cusic, George and Ann Walton.
	Dec.	5	Cox, James and Sarah Kane.
1797	Mch.	10	Clarke, Charles and Ann Evans.
	May	2	Cheseldine, William and Henny Gibson.
	July	20	Cullins, John and Eliza Thompson.
	Aug.	27	Cecil, James and Eleanor Wathen.
	Sept.	9	Corum, James and Margaret Watts.
	Nov.	28	Clarke, James and Frances Hammett.
	Dec.	9	Chappelear, Benja. and Mary Wood.
1798	Jan.	10	Clarke, James and Eliz. Gibson.
	Feb.	5	Chappelear, Jno. and Dorothy Legal.
	May	1	Cole, Williby and Jane Bean.
		23	Clarke, Thomas and Frances Loker.
	Sept.	2	Cheseldine, Senaca and Eliza. Turner.
		10	Cox, James and Eliza. Aderton.
	Nov.	13	Courtanay, Theodosius and Nancy Clarke.
	Dec.	4	Combes, Nathaniel and Hellen Jones.
		12	Cawood, Stephen Sr. and Jean Hayden.
		15	Carun, Isaac and Decandia Corun.
		28	Cullison, Bennett and Eliza. King.
1799	May	7	Cahay, Nathl. and Lydia Gardiner.
	Sept.	23	Cole, Joseph and Eliza. Morgan.
	Dec.	20	Clarke, Ignatius and Jane Tibboles.
		30	Cole, Robert and Ann Fenwick.
		31	Clarke, William and Mary Sanner.
1800	July	10	Clarke, Walter and Mary Thompson.
	Oct.	28	Clarke, George and Jane Abell.
1801	Jan.	8	Copsey, Enoch and Mary Thompson.

1801	Jan.	13	Combs, William and Rebecca Price.
		31	Cole, Francis and Mary Ann Kelsor.
	June	10	Cooke, Donalson and Anna Wherrett. -
	July	24	Crooke, James and Jane Hazle.
	Aug.	14	Cox, James and Mary Ridgell.
	Nov.	16	Cissell, James and Eleanor McGee.
	Dec.	20	Cidall, Wm. and Catherine Harper.
		21	Cissle, Thomas and Mary Greenwell.
1802	Jan.	22	Cusick, James and Mary Thompson.
	Mch.	19	Cissell, Zachariah and Anna Clarke.
	Nov.	18	Cullison, John and Juliet Greenwell.
1803	Feb.	1	Cissell, Thomas and Sarah Hammett.
		1	Coad, Joseph and Ann Dillaha.
	Apr.	22	Clarke, Joseph and Sarah Langley.
	June	15	Cusick, Philip and Jane Martin.
		13	Carter, George and Ailie Tapler.
	Nov.	1	Chinerel, James and Barthanmie Bean.
	Dec.	31	Cator, John and Eliza. Carpenter.
1804	Jan.	14	Cheseldine, Kenelm and Fanny Tarlton.
		28	Copsey, John and Eleanor Dowell.
	Feb.	13	Clarke, Ignatius and Sarah Davis.
	Mch.	19	Clarke, Cuthbert and Mary Loker.
	Apr.	10	Clarke, John and Mary Evans.
	May	23	Crawler, William and Mary Brent.
1805	Feb.	6	Combs, Lewis and Margaret D. Ford.
	June	11	Cox, Edmund and Eleanor Bond.
	Sept.	17	Clagett, William and Cecelia B. Briscoe.
	Nov.	14	Carpenter, George and Phebe Harris.
		26	Calahan, William and Ann Cowing.
1806	Feb.	18	Carpenter, Allen and Sarah Cissell.
	Apr.	21	Chesley, John and Eliza Biscoe.
	Sept.	9	Cox, William and Eliza. Hopewell.
	Nov.	6	Cinkler, Caleb and Mary Herbert.
1807	Jan.	1	Cawood, James R. and Eleanor Carpenter.
		10	Clarke, Richd. and Mary L. Cissell.
		5	Cheseldine, Richd. and Mary Blakistone.
		5	Carnes, Peter and Margaret Briscoe.
		20	Cusick, John and Eleanor Tippett.
	Feb.	4	Cusick, Charles and Mary Gibson.
	May	20	Cullins, James and Rebecca Brown.
	July	22	Cole, Francis and Eleanor Hopewell.
1808	Jan.	28	Clarke, Joseph and Eliza. Loker.

1808	May	2	Combs, Joseph and Monica Norris.
	Dec.	31	Crismond, Henry and Ann Drayden Dyxon.
1809	Apr.	3	Cusick, Ignatius and Sarah Haskins.
	Oct.	3	Cole, John and Eliza. Guyther.
	Dec.	21	Cole, Thomas and Ann Taylor.
1810	Jan.	5	Cole, John and Ann Tarlton.
	Feb.	19	Cusick, Francis and Ann Hayden.
	May	5	Carum, James and Margaret Mackall.
	Sept.	8	Cawood, Alexander and Mary Clarke.
1811	Mch.	5	Cecil, George and Jane Langley.
		9	Copsey, John and Eliza. Hill.
	Aug.	13	Craig, Reubin and Jane Jarboe.
	Oct.	16	Clarke, William and Eliza. Abell.
	Nov.	30	Carter, Jesse and Clare Hayden.
1812	Jan.	11	Cox, James and Catherine Brown.
	Oct.	12	Combs, Raphael and Margaret Goldsberry.
	Dec.	12	Clarke, John and Jane Joy.
1813	Jan.	12	Clarke, George and Barbara Flower.
	May	27	Cullison, John and Milly Newton.
	July	5	Chapman, William and Mary Ann Bayden.
	Aug.	12	Cox, Peter P. and Eliza. Thompson.
	Oct.	4	Combs, Nathaniel and Susanna Sanner.
		16	Clarke, John and Dorothy Cissell.
1814	Jan.	7	Clarke, Edward and Mary Norriss.
	Feb.	15	Corum, James and Cecelia Semmonds.
	July	28	Clocker, William and Ann Davis.
	Nov.	17	Chrisman, Henry and Catherine Johnson.
1814	Dec.	30	Cusick, William and Ann Gatton.
1815	Jan.	21	Chandler, John and Eliza. Ford.
	Nov.	24	Carroll, Ignatius and Juliet Brigett.
		27	Cecil, William and Mary Williams.
1816	Jan.	8	Clarke, Cornelius and Maria Mathney.
1817	May	14	Cullumber, Joshua and Mary Sanner.
	Nov.	10	Cullison, Cornelius and Eliza. Bohanan.
		20	Cole, Walter and Elizabeth Scott.
	Dec.	31	Carpenter, Saml. and Eleanor M. Wilson.
1818	Jan.	2	Cullison, John and Hellen Cecil.
	Feb.	21	Carpenter, John and Ann Ramer.
	Apr.	25	Clarke, Joshua and Ann Price.
	May	15	Cufonan (Cufman?), Christian and Ann Shermantine.
	Dec.	1	Clarke, William and Ann Norriss.
1819	Jan.	15	Campbell, John and Eliza. Greenwell.

1819 Feb. 2 Cooper, Lewis and Ann Butler.
16 Copsey, Joseph and Juliet Dent Dick.
June 1 Cissell, George and Mary Greenwell.
July 27 Cole, Joseph and Mary Long.
Sept. 23 Cheseldine, Kenelm and Sophia Gardiner.
Dec. 6 Crane, George and Susan Bennett.
1820 Jan. 31 Cheseldine, Richard and Ann Weakly.
1821 June 19 Clarke, Philip and Mary Wilkinson.
Aug. 17 Combs, Raphael and Susanna Redman.
Oct. 8 Cheseldine, Kenelm G. and Maria Thomas.
Dec. 6 Craig, Jesse and Lucy Norriss.
1822 Mch. 26 Crasswell, Thomas and Jane Redman.
Apr. 23 Clements, William and Mary T. Cheseldine.
Dec. 16 Carpenter, George and Eleanor Hayden.
1823 Jan. 13 Clements, Henry H. and Eliza. Thompson.
Feb. 3 Carter, Ignatius and Eleanor Spuck.
Mch. 3 Carsley, Littleton and Polly Hayden.
May 16 Cissell, Peregrine and Ann Bean.
1824 Feb. 9 Carpenter, William and Attoway Hayden.
23 Collison, Samuel and Mary Cullison.
27 Cullison, Joseph and Priscilla Clarke.
Mch. 27 Clark, James and Ann Kirby.
May 25 Carroll, Charles J. and Ann Eliza Holton.
Sept. 4 Campbell, John and Ann Greenwell.
4 Campbell, Danl. W. and Caroline Smith.
Dec. 1 Coad, William and Eliza. R. Smith.
1825 Jan. 17 Chappelear, Henry and Catherine Sothoron.
Mch. 29 Copsey, Joseph and Ann Fenwick.
July 26 Clarke, George and Hannah Clarke.
Nov. 15 Chiseldine, Kenelm and Maria McDaniel.
15 Combs, Henry R. and Maria Hayden.
Dec. 28 Curley, David and Mary Ann Branekin.
1826 Feb. 8 Cheseldine, Kenelm and Teresia Leigh.
Nov. 4 Cissell, John and Mary Ann C. Magill.
1827 Jan. 16 Cullison, Ignatius and Mary A. Greenwell.
Feb. 27 Cullison, Samuel and Charlotte Cullison.
June 19 Cramsey, John and Fanny Massey.
Dec. 19 Cullison, Cornelius and Catherine Wise.
24 Clarke, John and Jane Whealey.
1828 Jan. 10 Carron, Thomas and Mary Gill.
June 24 Clarke, John A. and Eliza Underwood.
Oct. 11 Courtney, Theodius and Julian Milburn.

1828 Nov. 25 Clarke, Robert and Ann Maria Smith.
1829 Jan. 20 Combs, William A. and Ann Woodward.
27 Combs, George and Mary Cath. Coad.
June 15 Cheseldine, John and Ellen Watson.
Dec. 21 Cheseldine, Cyrenus and Margaret Tippett.
1830 Jan. 23 Cusick, Benedict and Ann Lemon.
Apr. 13 Cheseldine, Charles and Ann Gibson.
Aug. 28 Carpenter, Richd. and Ann Maria Howard.
Dec. 20 Clarke, John and Darcus J. L. Clarke.
24 Cahill, William and Delilah Tippett.
1831 Jan. 8 Cissell, James and Maria Milton.
25 Chunn, Henry and Juliet Johnson.
Mch. 31 Cartwright, Alex. W. and Eliza. Chappelear.
June 14 Clarke, Richard and Eliza. Hall.
Oct. 13 Cheseldine, Kenelm and Lucinda Fergusson.
Nov. 28 Cooke, Dr. James and Rebecca W. B. Briscoe.
1832 Jan. 3 Cullins, George and Matilda Gooden.
May 1 Cryer, John and Prudence Spicer.
June 22 Combs, George C. and Mary Davis.
Nov. 20 Catton, John and Darcas Spencer.
1833 Feb. 13 Combs, Henry R. and Eleanor Heard.
May 16 Crane, James E. and Margaret Jones.
June 3 Combs, Peregrine and Ann Tarlton.
July 30 Combs, Edward P. and Henrietta Adams.
Oct. 21 Clarke, Ignatius and Mary P. Bean.
Dec. 23 Clocker, John and Emeline Henning.
1834 Jan. 2 Chappelear, Geo. and Eliza. Tyser.
6 Cissell, John B. and Ann Wheeler.
May 11 Clarke, Nelson and Jane Taylor.
Dec. 9 Catton, Wm. and Mary W. Lodge.
15 Cox, Geo. H. and Sarah G. Bean.
30 Clocker, William and Janet E. Cullison.
1835 July 22 Chin, John and Sarah Herbert.
Aug. 18 Catton, Richard and Sarah Lucellia Hurry.
Sept. 8 Coode, John and Mary D. T. Neale.
22 Combs, William and Matilda Norriss.
Oct. 26 Clarke, Thomas and Eleanor S. Wildman.
1836 Feb. 23 Crane, James E. and Sarah A. Spencer.
Mch. 1 Crane, Robert and Sarah B. Watts.
19 Cullison, Wilfred and Harriet A. Norriss.
1837 Jan. 17 Compton, Wilson and Charlotte W. Hebb.
26 Clements, Benja. D. and Susanna Farr.

1837	Aug.	19	Childs, James and Susan M. Neale.
	Nov.	14	Combs, James G. and Lydia E. McWilliams.
	Dec.	19	Castigin, Sylvester J. and Susan R. Dorsey.
1838	Jan.	22	Carns, Thomas and Ann E. Hopkins.
	Mch.	15	Cheseldine, Kenelm G. and Rachel L. Shaw.
	Apr.	24	Cusick, Aloysius and Susan Thompson.
	Nov.	22	Cuffman, Henry and Martha Beckwith.
1839	Jan.	15	Cheseldine, James and Jane Milburn.
	Mch.	26	Cheseldine, John and Julian Cullison.
	June	18	Combs, George and Charlotte Norriss.
	Nov.	29	Crismond, Elzear and Caroline Hunt.
1840	Apr.	27	Carroll, Henry I. and Lucretia L. Briscoe.
	Oct.	20	Crane, George and Susan Artis.
1841	July	26	Collison, Wilfred and Elizabeth King.
	Nov.	20	Copsey, Enoch and Margaret E. Wood.
1842	Jan.	25	Combs, John C. and Eliza. A. Drury.
	July	12	Chiseldine, Wm. C. and Eleanor Thompson.
	Dec.	20	Combs, John W. and Isabella Hewett.
1843	Dec.	19	Cox, James T. and Eliza. C. Mattingly.
1844	Jan.	24	Clocker, John W. and Ann J. King.
	Dec.	24	Collison, Wilfred and Maria Clopper.
1845	Jan.	2	Clocker, Daniel and Sarah Leigh.
	Dec.	2	Carroll, Henry I. and Mary Eliza. Pile.
1846	Jan.	15	Clopper, Douglas and Mary S. Key.
		27	Collison, H. and Salina C. Wheeler.
	Feb.	23	Cryer, Wm. A. and Eliza. Ann Thompson.
	Aug.	19	Clarke, Edwin and Sarah Peacock.
	Sept.	1	Crane, Geo. and Mary Gough.
1847	Jan.	4	Crismond, Walter and Matilda Saxton.
		5	Cheseldine, Girard and Rebecca Ellis.
		5	Carroll, John and Ann Hooper.
	May	19	Cullisson, George H. and Susan M. Thompson.
	Aug.	16	Coad, J. Edwin and Ellen Ann Manning.
1848	Feb.	9	Catton, John T. and Mary C. Hayden.
	May	10	Clocker, John and Olivia Shermantine.
		23	Campbell, James E. and Emmaranda Brewer.
	June	6	Clocker, H. and Ann M. Haywood.
	July	11	Combs, Lewis C. and Mary E. Coad.
	Oct.	30	Canter, Francis S. and Jane Sotheron.
1849	Jan.	9	Combs, Lewis F. and Eliza. M. Abell.
		22	Combs, P. F. and Virginia Coad.
		30	Carberry, Jas. A. and Julia F. Alvey.

1849	Jan. 30	Cawood, Alex. and Mary Ann Higgs.
	Apr. 28	Cheseldine, Chas. and Henrietta Morgan.
	May 8	Cawood, Hez. B. and Joanna Howard.
	Dec. 29	Combs, Peregrine and Eleanor A. Greenwell.
1850	Jan. 2	Cooke, James C. and Mary B. Briscoe.
	8	Cox, John F. and Susan R. Bond.
	14	Cox, James F. and Eliza. E. Barber.
	Feb. 7	Cheseldine, Wm. E. and Ann M. Cheseldine.
	9	Curry, John and Jane Anderson.
	Mch. 12	Clements, Jno. W. and Susan R. Biscoe.
	May 23	Crane, John A. and Sarah A. Biscoe.
	June 18	Campbell, Jno. G. and Jane E. Yates.
	Sept. 26	Campbell, Geo. E. and Cora A. Smith.
	Dec. 30	Canter, Geo. M. and Clarinda Knott.
1851	Apr. 19	Copsey, Chas. C. and Tresia Scott.
	May 24	Cheseldine, Wm. H. and Susan E. Payne.
	Nov. 18	Craven, Philip and Roba. C. Freeman.
	Dec. 22	Courtney, Theodotius and Harriet P. Thompson.
	30	Clarke, Ignatius and Sarah Ann Greenwell.
1852	June 1	Clarke, John T. and Cecelia A. Hayden.
	Dec. 29	Cullison, John W. T. and Mary E. Cissell.
1853	Mch. 29	Cullings, Wm. T. and Louisa Raley.
	Apr. 13	Copsey, Henry and Susanna Williams.
	May 3	Combs, Wm. F. and Sallie A. Simms.
	June 27	Clarke, Thos. P. and Emily A. Burroughs.
	Nov. 7	Carpenter, Jno. E. and S. C. S. Posey.
	Sept. 19	Canter, Horatio and Eliza A. C. Hayden.
1854	Jan. 9	Cheseldine, A. J. and Mary J. Thompson.
	23	Cole, Wm. E. and E. A. W. Holton.
	Feb. 13	Cox, William and Priscilla McKay.
	24	Campbell, Jno. F. and Susanna Jarboe.
	Aug. 11	Clarke, Henry C. and Julia F. Young.
	31	Combs, Alex. and Mary J. Thompson.
1855	Jan. 25	Copsey, John and Ann Buckler.
	Nov. 5	Chesser, Ephraim and Mary A. Moore.
	5	Collins, Jas. W. and Jane H. G. Merriam.
1856	Jan. 28	Cissell, Jno. L. and Susan E. Brookes.
	June 14	Clements, Jno. W. and Mary E. Greenwell.
	Oct. 21	Cheseldine, Cyreneous and Caroline Herbert.
	22	Crane, John A. and Mary P. Smith.
	Nov. 25	Cheseldine, Biscoe and Ann Rebecca Blakistone.
	Dec. 2	Cheseldine, G. R. and M. S. Hammett.

1857	Jan.	27	Canter, Isaiah and Ellen Jane Hayden.
		29	Cullison, Geo. W. and Ann L. Bell.
	May	13	Clements, Lemuel and Jane A. Abell.
1858	Feb.	4	Combs, Edward P. and Ann. N. Ridgell.
	July	5	Clements, Joseph H. and Josephine Paul.
		21	Combs, Perry and Harriet P. Courtney.
	Oct.	26	Compton, Barnes and Margaret H. Sothoron.
	Nov.	27	Canter, H. A. and Alice Sothoron.
1859	Jan.	10	Curry, Joseph W. and Martha C. Hill.
		15	Cullison, Geo. W. and Catherine R. Clocker.
		25	Cusick, Geo. T. and Jane Ann Howard.
	Mch.	7	Copsey, Henry and Ann Burroughs.
	May	26	Clarke, Geo. L. and Sophia Yates.
	Nov.	7	Clocker, John B. and Margaret A. Greenwell.
		22	Clarke, R. King and E. Rebecca Greenwell.
	Dec.	19	Ching, John F. and Isabell Alvey.
1860	Jan.	30	Cheseldine, Andrew J. and Ann Maria Morgan.
	Feb.	16	Combs, Joseph and Ann E. Wheeler.
1861	Jan.	7	Cecil, James C. and Eliza Ann Hammett.
		22	Corser, James H. and Ellen M. Moore.
	June	20	Clarke, Richard A. and Mary A. Wilkinson.
	Sept.	17	Cheverell, Wm. H. and Ann E. Tarlton.
	Dec.	30	Copsey, C. L. and Elizabeth Wood.
1862	Jan.	27	Cissell, Wm. H. and Marian E. Armsworthy.
	May	10	Combs, John M. and Mary Simmons.
		10	Copsey, Joseph and Mary Knott.
	Nov.	10	Christian, Rev. W. and Sophia Thomas.
	Dec.	30	Cooper, Jas. and Henrietta Joy.
1863	Apr.	3	Courtney, Richard and Mrs. Hennison.
	June	16	Combs, Charles and Rosa H. Stone.
	Oct.	9	Combs, Wm. A. and Ersula E. Taylor.
1794	Oct.	17	Dunbar, Joseph and Draydon Mills.
	Dec.	16	Daffin, Joseph and Mary Heard.
1795	Apr.	5	Drury, Wm. and Ann West.
		21	Drury, John and Ann Jarbo.
	July	8	Dorsey, Walter and Hopewell Hebb.
1796	Oct.	1	Davis, James and Mary Clarke.
	Nov.	7	Drury, Bernard and Catherine Wimsatt.
		18	Dant, John and Elizabeth Hopewell.
	Dec.	12	Dennis, Thomas and Mary Dorant.
		20	Drury, Baptist and Mary Norris.
1797	Jan.	16	Davis, George and Catherine Good.

1797	June	18	Devault, John and Eliz. Gardiner.
1798	Feb.	13	Dorsey, Joseph and Hannah King.
	Mch.	27	Derdain, Lewis and Catherine Clarke.
	May	1	Diggs, Wm. and Dorothy Taney.
	Sept.	6	Downs, Barnaby and Frances Greenwell.
1799	Jan.	23	Dennis, Absolon and Eleanor Morgan.
	Mch.	20	Downs, Igs. and Jane Carter.
		23	Doxey, Jeremiah and Mary Nichorson.
	May	9	Drury, Wilfred and Nelly Bailey.
	June	12	Dyer, Barton and Jane Newton.
	Nov.	13	Davis, Elkanah and Mary Johnson.
	Dec.	11	Dorsey, Clement, and Priscilla Hebb.
	Oct.	14	Dent, Thomas and Rebecca Chappelear.
		15	Drury, Francis S. and Ann Thompson.
		21	Drury, Samuel and Eleanor Jarboe.
	Dec.	22	Davis, Elijah and Susanna Davis.
1801	Jan.	2	Dyer, Barton and Jane Newton.
		19	Dorsey, Charles and Anna Stone.
		28	Dean, John and Henry Stone.
	Apr.	18	Downs, Joseph and Eleanor Adams.
		30	Dent, William and Julia Davis.
	May	25	Dorsey, Thomas and Eliz. Worddiwood.
	Dec.	1	Dorsey, Thomas and Ann Bennett.
		29	Dunbar, John and Ann Richardson.
		31	Dunbar, Wm. and Ann Greenwell.
1802	Jan.	13	Deane, Jno. Baptist and Mary Bridget.
1803	Jan.	14	Deane, George and Eliza Brown.
		16	Dent. Hezekiah and Lavinia Milburn.
	July	12	Dorsey, William and Mary Newton.
	Dec.	29	Drury, Clement and Ann Cissell.
		31	Downes, Jeremiah and Eleanor Norris.
1804	Dec.	10	Dunbar, Wm. and Margaret Smith.
1805	Jan.	19	Daniel, Geo. S. and Sarah Earle.
	Feb.	16	Dorsey, John and Susanna Newton.
		19	Dire, Stephen and Adra Paner.
	Apr.	27	Dudley, John and Sarah Gwinn Garland.
	Aug.	25	Davis, Thos. and Jemima Taylor.
	Sept.	6	Dudley, Landan and Mary Reeves.
	Oct.	28	Dillehay, Thomas G. and Ann Raley.
1806	Jan.	9	Drury, Richd. and Jane Blair.
	Nov.	21	Deane, Joshua and Ann Joy.
	Dec.	6	Davis, Ahaseurus and Sophia Hayden.

1807 Nov. 11 Drury, Francis M. D. and Winifred Greenwell.
23 Diamond, James and Alley Bright.
25 Drury, Enoch and Mary Brewer.
1808 Jan. 21 Dart, Thomas and Eliza Hall.
Feb. 13 Davis, Edzah and Matha Tail.
Nov. 22 Davis, John and Margaret Heard.
Dec. 5 Dixon, Wm. and Mary McClain.
1810 Mch. 5 Drury, Benidick and Mary Simms.
Oct. 12 Davis, Wm. and Margaret M. Hely.
1811 Jan. 16 Duggins, Henry and Nancy Long.
June 6 Drury, Clement, and Dorothy Boyd.
1812 July 10 Drury, Enoch and Lucy Greenwell.
1813 Jan. 18 Davis, Cornelius and Elizabeth Thompson.
June 22 Dawson, John and Elizabeth Humphres.
Aug. 30 Drury, Michael and Catherine Johnson.
Sept. 23 Dameron, John C. and Susanna Winstead.
27 Dillehay, Thos. G. and Margaret Abell.
1814 Jan. 5 Drury, Robert and Mary Cole.
Apr. 10 Dorsey, Ignatius and Barbara Spalding.
Oct. 26 Dorsey, Josiah and Mary Richardson.
1815 Jan. 4 Drury, Enoch and Eleanor Joy.
Feb. 3 Dent, William and Sarah Johnson.
May 31 Downs, Bernard and Poly Allen.
1816 Jan. 23 Drury, Peter and Ann Hayden.
Oct. 8 Dunbar, Jno. A. and Mary Richardson.
1817 Jan. 1 Davis, Edward and Judith Tippett.
Apr. 3 Dunbar, Edward and Mary Pembroke.
Nov. 9 Drury, John and Ann Forrest.
1818 Jan. 9 Deane, Joshua and Eleanor Hardesty.
Dec. 17 Dean, Lewis and Eliza. Long.
1819 Jan. 6 Dart, Joseph and Polly Haskins.
9 Drury, Wm. and Elizabeth T. Edwards.
Apr. 19 Dennis, Edmund and Ann Shercliffe.
June 23 Devy, William and Eleanor Branson.
1820 Jan. 1 Davis, Austin and Jane Lowry.
11 Drury, Henry and Eliza Mattingly.
Dec. 27 Dean, John and Polly Norriss.
1821 Jan. 4 Duel, William and Polly Tippett.
Oct. 16 Dent, Hezekiah and Martha Matilda Hammett.
Dec. 25 Davis, Edward and Ann Milburn.
1822 May 21 Dawson, John M. and Ann Dye.
Dec. 31 Davis, Joseph and Ann Greenwell.

1823	Jan.	23	Dixon, Thomas and Susanna Brown.
	Apr.	23	Donnell, Daniel O. and Mary Tippett.
	July	22	Drury, Joseph and Mary Ann Dixon.
	Aug.	6	Dyer, John and Britainia Downes.
		26	Dick, Alex. and Dicanda Spalding.
	Nov.	24	Drury, Benedick and Susan Fowler.
1824	Jan.	19	Drury, Thomas and Susanna Greenwell.
	Feb.	10	Dukes, John and Mary Ann Dent.
		28	Daley, Timothy and Fidela Adams.
1826	Aug.	8	Dunkinson, Robert and Mary P. Holton.
	Dec.	31	Davis, Amos and Ann Yates.
1827	Jan.	6	Dunbar, George and Sarah Dean.
	Sept.	17	Dement, Thomas and Caroline Shermantine.
		25	Davy, Joseph and Isabella Thornton.
	Dec.	14	Dent, Thomas E. and Susanna Hammett.
		28	Dyson, Thomas and Ann Maria Henning.
1828	Oct.	25	Drury, Cornelius and Mary Dunbar.
	Dec.	29	Drury, Peter and Mary Cox.
1829	July	14	Dyer, Wm. S. and Mary E. Combs.
1830	May	31	Dorsey, Wm. H. and Eleanor Drury.
	June	26	Dorsey, John T. and Matilda Peacock.
	Aug.	3	Dean, John and Susan Thompson.
		16	Drury, Wm. and Julian Thompson.
	Nov.	29	Downs, Noah and Mary A. L. Combs.
	Dec.	1	Dement, Edward and Elizabeth Quade.
		7	Dent, William and Darcus Smith.
		21	Davis, George and Mary Alvey.
1831	Sept.	7	Downs, Henry and Mary B. Goldsberry.
		12	Dyer, George and Ann Redman.
1832	Jan.	22	Davis, Henry I. and Mary Hayden.
	Oct.	27	Dorsey, Wm. H. and Rose Ann Greenwell.
	Dec.	26	Dean, Levy and Susan Barnes.
1833	Dec.	11	Davis, Robert and Elizabeth Caywood.
1834	Feb.	18	Davis, Peregrine and Ann Elizabeth Spencer.
	Oct.	24	Deatley, Washington and Jane Lewis.
1836	Feb.	1	Davis, Jeremiah and Ann Eliza Huntington.
	May	21	Dean, James and Cecelia Ann Dean.
	July	26	Davis, Thomas S. and Charlotte W. Moore.
	Dec.	29	Dimond, Elisha and Susanna Combs.
1838	Jan.	15	Drury, John L. and Frances Greenwell.
	July	23	Drury, Cornelius and Elizabeth Smith.
	Dec.	26	Drury, Ignatius and Ann M. Burroughs.

1839	Jan.	14	Dent, John F. and Lillia D. Blakistone.
	June	27	Dick, Richard D. and Eliza Graves.
1840	June	5	Dean, John and Matilda Thompson.
	Aug.	3	Dunaway, William and Maria Boothe.
	Dec.	22	Dean, Wm. and Sarah Ann Wheeler.
		28	Davis, Kenelm and Violetta Turner.
1841	Jan.	9	Davis, Llewellen and Eleanor Hunt.
	June	29	Dunn, Lewis and Letty J. Mahon.
1842	Aug.	2	Dailey, Daniel and Caroline Martin.
1843	June	14	Dulaney, John and Eliza Coad.
	July	10	Davis, Cornelius C. and Ann Maria Payne.
	Sept.	4	Dean, Thomas and Susan Hazell.
1844	Jan.	2	Dillihay, Wm. and Jane Tarlton.
		6	Dean, Benja. T. and Susanna Bowles.
	June	10	Downs, Joseph and Priscilla Aud.
1845	May	19	Dean, William H. and Susan Eliza Nevitt.
	Sept.	20	Dick, Richard and Eliza Dean.
1846	Oct.	5	Daily, Daniel and Eliza Ann Field.
	Dec.	26	Drury, W. A. and Elizabeth Good.
		28	Dean, John H. and Susan Cox.
1847	Jan.	7	Dillow, Thomas and Margaret Norris.
	Feb.	9	Drury, Cornelius and Sarah Greenwell.
1848	Jan.	3	Downs, Edward and Priscilla Lathrum.
		4	Dixin, Wm. and Mary E. Thompson.
		25	Dyer, James H. and Ann Bradburn.
	Mch.	1	Drury, Robert B. and Mary A. Long.
	June	8	Dunbar, Jos. Jr. and Rebecca Spalding.
	July	6	Diment, Elija. and Mary M. Lee.
	Dec.	19	Dunbar, John A. and Mary M. McKay.
1849	Jan.	8	Dean, Wm. H. and Anna M. Yates.
	May	26	Downs, Noah and Rebecca Norriss.
1850	Jan.	3	Drury, James H. and Cath. A. Mattingly.
		16	Davis, Joseph B. and Julia A. O. Leach.
		19	Dean, Wm. H. and Sarah L. Wood.
	Apr.	15	Dent, Walter L. and Eliza A. Posey.
	July	22	Dean, Thomas B. and Ann C. Hill.
	Oct.	28	Dorsey, Ignatius and Eliza Campbell.
1851	Mch.	4	Davis, Robert and Louisa Bivin.
	Apr.	12	Drury, William H. and Martha E. Dyer.
	May	3	Davis, Jeremiah and Caroline Cahay.
		15	Durant, Clarke J. and Mary E. Dent.
	July	13	Dawson, Benja. and Mary E. Baley.

1851	Nov. 25	Drury, Wm. H. and Eliza Ann Simms.
1852	Feb. 10	Dunn, Wm. and Georgeanna Milburn.
	Apr. 12	Dean, Francis and Julia Suit.
	May 18	Dent, Charles and Sarah M. Hammett.
	July 15	Davis, John A. and Ann S. Howard.
1853	Feb. 10	Dyer, Wm. H. and Henrietta Dyer.
	May 16	Dean, Wm. H. and Ann Maria Dean.
1854	Apr. 17	Dyer, Joseph A. and Mary Norriss.
	Dec. 21	Davis, Thomas L. and Eliza. Catherine Hayden.
1855	Jan. 12	Dean, John F. and Jane R. Howard.
	30	Dement, Merit A. and Sarah A. Evans.
	Dec. 27	Davis, Charles F. and Eliza Cooper.
1856	Jan. 4	Davis, James H. and Mary D. Thompson.
	17	Dean, Levi J. and Eliza C. Buckler.
	Apr. 19	Dingy, Edward and Eliza V. Orm.
	Dec. 1	Drury, John W. and Mary Burch.
	31	Dierling, John and Mary Gatton.
1858	Feb. 4	Dyer, John M. and Mary E. Langmore.
	15	Davis, John and Catherine Johnson.
	July 5	Davis, Jno. F. and Rosetta Williams.
	20	Dyer, Wm. I. and Mary E. Norris.
1859	Apr. 26	Downs, Thomas W. and Dorcas Redmon.
	May 7	Delano, Wm. P. and Susanna Dulany.
	Sept. 26	Dent, Joseph C. and Emeline R. Hammett.
	Oct. 25	Davis, Neale W. and Ann P. Howard.
	Nov. 15	Duke, Geo. D. and Mary A. E. Hebb.
	22	Duckett, Silious and Mary E. Bowes.
1860	Jan. 5	Dean, Jos. R. and Caroline E. Tracy.
	17	Drury, Edward and Attaway Joy.
	May 22	Duke, James T. and Martha A. Dent.
	June 5	Davis, John A. and Josephine Morgan.
	9	Davis, James A. and Martha Ann Cullens.
	Sept. 24	Dameron, Bathomew and Virginia A. Hudson.
	Oct. 29	Davis, W. S. and Elizabeth C. Davis.
	Dec. 26	Davis, John K. and Ann Lovenia Mattingly.
1861	Nov. 5	Davis, John and Regina Peacock.
	Dec. 17	Dare, Richard S. and Carrie H. Shemwell.
	18	Deacons, J. E. and Lydia C. Jones.
1862	Feb. 24	Drury, Robert and Mary Jane Stone.
	July 26	Duvall, Lewis and Henrietta Bullock.
1863	Feb. 9	Dixon, Joseph and Anne Snowden Williams.
	Mch. 28	Davis, Griffin and Charlotte S. McKay.

1796 Feb. 3 Evans, William and Mary Smith.
July 13 Edwards, Stourton and Ann Johnston.
1797 Sept. 26 Edwards, Joseph of Igs. and Mary Parsons.
1798 Dec. 10 Edwards, Benja. and Mary Hambilton.
1800 June 2 Edwards, Jonathan and Esther Barber.
Oct. 1 Ellis, Philip and Eleanor Cawood.
1801 Dec. 2 Edwards, Jesse and Mary Neale.
18 Evans, Ignatius and Susanna Taylor.
19 Edwards, Elkanah and Eliza. Chaplear.
1802 Mch. 4 Estep, Wm. and Mary Greenfield.
Aug. 17 Evans, Wm. and Ann Clarke.
1803 Aug. 30 Edelen, Richd. and Ann Gough.
1804 June 26 Edly, Henry and Eliza. A. Thompson.
Oct. 1 Evans, John and Patty Silence.
Dec. 10 Egerton, James and Eliza. Chesley.
1805 Jan. 3 Ellis, William and Nancy Cox.
Feb. 8 Edwards, Ignatius and Margaret Payn.
May 29 Elliston, Jno. S. and Margaret Blackwell.
1806 Dec. 27 Edwards, Joseph and Deborah Litchwork.
1807 June 16 Ewing, Nathl. and Eliza. Cartwright.
1808 Feb. 27 Elexon, Chas. and Eliza. Winsatt.
1809 Mch. 21 Edwards, William and Sabra Spalding.
1810 Feb. 7 Edwards, Richard and Lydia Dyson.
1811 Feb. 2 Ellis, Hezekiah and Eliza. Brown.
Oct. 28 Egerton, Richard B. and Mary Chesley.
1813 June 5 Edwards, Joseph of Igs. and Eliza. Tippett.
1814 Jan. 28 Evans, Richard and Eliza. Thomas.
Mch. 4 Estep, William and Rebecca Burroughs.
1817 Feb. 1 Evans, Edward and Eliza. Brown.
Aug. 28 Egerton, Charles C. and Susanna Killis.
1818 June 4 Ellis, Alexander and Maria Tippett.
1819 Dec. 28 Ellis, Henry and Susanna Mattingly.
1820 Apr. 5 Eversfield, John and Ann Wailes.
1821 Jan. 6 Ellis, Henry and Sarah Rock.
1823 Feb. 5 Ellis, Samuel and Catherine Payne.
May 21 Egerton, Charles C. Jr. and Rebecca Calliss.
1824 Jan. 20 Ellis, John and Eleanor Turner.
1825 June 21 Edwards, Elkanah and Mary Chappelear.
1827 Jan. 23 Edelen, Wm. E. and Ellen Leigh.
Dec. 15 Ellis, William and Ann Herbert.
1828 Dec. 29 Evans, Daniel and Eliza. Fenwick.
1829 Jan. 26 Evans, Jeremiah and Sarah Price.

1829	Feb.	17	Edwards, William and Mary Drury.
	Apr.	27	Evans, Richard and Eliza Richardson.
1830	Jan.	19	Evans, Sidney and Mary O. Underwood.
	Aug.	5	Evans, William and Delila Armsworthy.
	Dec.	14	Eocret, Joseph M. and Joanna Trotter.
1833	May	7	Ellis, Sylvester A. and Eliza Cheseldine.
	Dec.	23	Edwards, George and Dicanda Dick.
1835	Feb.	9	Evans, John R. and Eliza Martin.
1836	July	28	Evans, Nelson and Maria Underwood.
	Dec.	13	Ellis, Randolph and Emily Long.
1839	Jan.	7	Ellis, Randolph and Nancy Lawrence.
	Feb.	5	Edwards, Harrison and Clarissa A. Harrison.
1842	Jan.	26	Evans, Enoch and Priscilla Johnson.
1843	Oct.	23	Edwards, John and Eliza. Swann.
1849	May	2	Ellis, John and Cath. Tippett.
1850	Jan.	7	Evans, John R. and Mary J. L. Abell.
1851	Jan.	6	Ellis, John W. and Mary Ellen Cheseldine.
	Apr.	22	Ellis, Edward H. and Susanna Harding.
1852	Jan.	6	Ellis, Richard and Melvina Tippett.
		26	Ellis, John N. and Mary M. Cheseldine.
1855	Feb.	15	Evans, Thomas and Rosa Abell.
1856	Apr.	3	Edwards, Richd. M. and Barbary A. Cissill.
	May	13	Ellis, James and Sarah Ann Morgan.
		26	Evans, James N. and Priscilla Armsworthy.
1858	Nov.	15	Edwards, Geo. and Rebecca Armstrong.
	Dec.	6	Ellis, James and Mrs. Caroline Cheseldine.
1861	Apr.	9	Ellis, John W. and Ann M. Cheseldine.
1862	Feb.	3	Edwards, Alex. and Mary E. Suit.
	Dec.	30	Edwards, Benja. and Maria E. Kirby.
1863	July	21	Evans, John B. and Eliza E. Armsworthy.
1796	Apr.	4	Flower, Moses and Ann Richardson.
		12	Fairbrother, John and Mary Kindrick.
	Dec.	12	Ford, Henry and Honny Thompson.
1797	Jan.	23	Flower, Moses and Jean Flower.
	Sept.	20	French, Philip and Eliz. Norris.
1799	Jan.	30	Fenwick, Richard and Susanna Newton.
	Apr.	2	Ford, Edward and Eliz. Greenwell.
1800	Jan.	1	Ford, Benjamin and Margaret Hopkins.
		5	Frier, Thomas and Mary McGill.
	Mch.	23	Forrest, Zachariah and Nancy Ford.
	June	4	Fowler, Edward Teresa Wathen.
	Sept.	6	Ford, Joseph and Mary Greenwell.

1800	Nov. 22	Fenwick, Enoch and Jane Greenwell.
1801	Aug. 7	Farr, John B. and Jane Cawood.
1802	Feb. 8	Ford, Ignatius and Eliz. Thompson.
	June 26	Fowler, Edward and Eliza. Howard.
	Dec. 7	Furgusson, Henry and Mary Tennison.
1803	Dec. 22	Flower, Joseph and Mary Wise.
1804	Feb. 28	Fields, James A. and Susy Evans.
	Mch. 6	Flower, Joseph and Mary A. Norriss.
	May 24	Floyd, Jesse Jr. and Jemima Abell.
	Dec. 6	Ford, Charles A. and Henrietta Lowe.
1805	Apr. 27	Fenwick, James of P. and Eliza. Hcrkins.
1806	Apr. 14	Fenwick, Cuthbert and Eliza. Moore.
1807	Jan. 17	Ford, Athanasius and Mary Heard.
	Sept. 11	Ford, Lewis and Eliza. Plowden.
1809	Nov. 3	Fish, Thomas and Sarah Thompson.
	Dec. 5	Forrest, James (Pilot) and Susanna Fenwick.
	29	Ferroll, Wm. and Mary Thompson.
1810	May 1	Ford, Lewis and Sympho. Rosa Hill.
	8	Ford, Philip and Catherine Hilton.
1811	Jan. 21	Ford, Ignatius and Teresia Peak.
1812	Mch. 31	Fenwick, Ignatius and Mary Fenwick.
	Dec. 29	Ford, John and Rebecca Cloaker.
1813	May 10	Farr, John and Ann Hayden.
1814	Jan. 29	Flower, Sylvester and Mary Peake.
	Feb. 14	Fenwick, Lewis and Teresia Fenwick.
	June 6	Floyd, William and Eleanor Heard.
1815	Feb. 4	Fowler, William and Eliza. Goddard.
	Apr. 20	Floyd, Joseph and Ann Herbert.
	Aug. 14	Freeman, Thomas and Rebecca C. Lynch.
	Sept. 26	Ford, Ignatius and Susanna Herbert.
	Dec. 26	Forrest, Humphry and Mary Leach.
1816	Apr. 19	Feilows, Edward and Janett Martin.
	23	Foster, James and Susanna Tippett.
1818	Sept. 19	Furguson, Jno. and Eliza. Murphy.
	Nov. 14	Ford, John T. and Priscilla Medley.
1819	Feb. 2	Forrest, James and Emily Jackson.
	July 22	Fearson, Samuel and Maria Allston.
1821	July 8	Ford, Joseph and Rebecca Howard.
	26	Ford, Ignatius and Mary Herbert.
1822	Apr. 2	Fowler, Henry and Margaret Melton
	15	Fowler, John and Ann Hayden.
	Nov. 7	Forbes, George and Mary L. Plater.

1822	Dec. 31	Fenwick, Wm. and Eliza. Norriss.
1824	May 22	Fowler, Wm. H. and Katurah Fowler.
	Aug. 30	Flower, Gustavus and Jane Bean.
	Sept. 12	Flower, John B. and Elizabeth Combs.
1829	Jan. 26	Fowler, Charles and Ann Munroe.
	Dec. 26	Farr, John B. and Martha Chinn.
1830	Apr. 10	Fenwick, Joseph and Eliza Greenwell.
1831	Aug. 2	Furguson, William and Jane Jones.
	5	Ford, Edward and Mary Higginson.
	Sept. 20	Fenwick, Bennett and Harriet Simms.
	Dec. 22	Foxwell, George and Eliz. A. Bayne.
1832	Aug. 8	Foxwell, Stephen and Lovy Paul.
	Sept. 10	Foxwell, Shadrick and Mary Ann Paul.
1833	May 28	Floyd, Joseph and Mary Cissell.
	Oct. 24	Forbes, George and Mary E. Harris.
1835	Feb. 17	Ford, Joseph S. and Teresia Wathen.
	Aug. 4	Ford, Henry W. and Priscilla Greenwell.
	Oct. 24	Ford, Joseph and Juliet Dean.
	Dec. 30	Ferroll, Thomas and Catherine Hall.
1836	Sept. 10	Farrand, Thomas A. and Jane Lyon.
	Dec. 24	Flowers, George and Mary McNamara.
1837	Dec. 27	Ferroll, James and Mary Lacy.
1840	Feb. 26	Fowler, Joseph H. and Mary J. Morgan.
	May 11	Fowler, Thomas H. and Ann P. Mattingly.
	June 22	Forbes, James J. and Eliza C. Thomas.
	Nov. 26	Fenwick, Aloysius F. and Charlotte Spalding.
1841	May 3	Ford, Walter and Rebecca Jackson.
	July 6	Ford, Joseph S. and Mary A. Graves.
	Dec. 31	Furgeson, Washington and Ann L. Cheseldine.
1842	Feb. 5	Floyd, Robert and Ann Dyer.
1842	Apr. 19	Furck, Nicholas V. and Eliza. A. Dunbar.
	June 9	Ford, William and Lucretia Greenwell.
	Oct. 17	Farr, Benedick and Catherine Curtis.
	Nov. 25	Forrest, John W. and Ann White Price.
	26	Fenwick, Bened. I. and Ann Maria Long.
1843	Feb. 14	Freeman, Thomas L. and Maria A. Beall.
	May 23	Fenhagen, Edward and Jane E. Norriss.
1845	Jan. 28	Fenwick, John F. and Mary M. Simms.
	May 27	Ford, Henry A. and Jane A. Thomas.
	July 7	Franks, W. D. and Margaret Tarlton.
	Nov. 6	Franklin, Dr. Thos. J. and Josephine Harris.
1846	Dec. 2	Ford, Robert and Ann Taylor.

1847	Feb.	8	French, John R. and Mary L. Jones.
	Oct.	11	Ford, Joseph and Eleanor C. Yates.
	Nov.	15	Flower, John B. and Mary Ellen Bean.
	Dec.	14	Foster, John and Elizabeth Welch.
1848	June	1	Fraser, John and Virginia Armstrong.
	July	25	Forrest, Jos. and H. C. Plowden.
1849	May	26	Fenwick, Wm. H. and Susanna M. Ridgell.
1850	Apr.	8	Fracer, John H. and Sophia Higgs.
1852	Jan.	13	Floyd, F. F. and Mary W. Davis.
1852	Apr.	17	Ferrall, Noble E. and Maria Joy.
1853	Jan.	31	Flanigan, Samuel and Lydia Ann Lemmon.
	Nov.	5	Floyd, Jonathan and Elizabeth Dyer.
1854	Jan.	19	Furck, N. and Mary E. Fowler.
	Mch.	7	Floyd, Jos. and Mary Wootten.
	Nov.	28	Fowler, John W. and Rebecca Saxton.
1855	Feb.	15	Ford, Edward N. and Maria L. Boothe.
1856	Jan.	1	Fenwick, Jas. N. and Susan Wilkins.
	Mch.	24	Floyd, Wm. G. and Mary F. Mills.
	Aug.	26	Frass, John M. and Jane M. Cheseldine.
	Oct.	10	Foxwell, Benja. G. and Mary Jane Bennett.
	Dec.	1	Fareman, Francis R. and Virginia E. Milburn.
1857	Jan.	1	Foxwell, Solomon and L. Kirbey.
		9	Farr, John E. and Mary A. L. Edwards.
	Dec.	4	Fagan, Matthew and Lucindy Wathen.
1860	Jan.	30	Foxwell, J. Van Buren and Sarah J. Cox.
1861	Aug.	12	Farran, John and Jane Burroughs.
1862	Jan.	18	Fowler, John W. and Bettie Taylor.
	Oct.	16	Fenwick, John F. and Ellen Rebecca Dunbar.
	Dec.	17	Ford, Walter and Cassandra Gough.
1863	Sept.	8	Ford, Wm. F. and Alice Pembroke.
1794	Dec.	30	Greenwell, Benedict and Brittania Jones.
1795	Feb.	16	Goldsmith, Thos. and Elizabeth Grant.
	Apr.	12	Gough, Joseph and Eleanor Williams.
	June	1	Gough, John and Mary Jones.
	Aug.	8	Goodwin, Richard and Nancy Woodward.
	Nov.	1	Green, Bennett and Margaret Smith.
1796	July	5	Gibson, Joshua and Mary Cox.
	Oct.	16	Gibson, Jeremiah and Margaret Bond.
	Nov.	22	Greenwell, Edward and Mary Spink.
	Dec.	8	Gray, Randolph and Eleanor Philips.
1797	Jan.	2	Gardiner, Thomas and Mary Llewellen.
		14	Gough, James and Ann Price.

1797 Jan. 19 Greenwell, Peter and Ann Howard.
June 14 Greenwell, Robert and Mary Redman.
July 21 Gibson, John and Sarah Goodwin.
Nov. 23 Gardiner, Samuel and Sarah Gardiner.
Dec. 1 Greenwell, Thomas and Mary Abell.
20 Greenwell, Edward and Hannah Clarke.
1798 Jan. 9 Guyther, Wm. and Ann Cole.
27 Gardiner, John and Nancy Norris.
Feb. 3 Graves, John T. and Ann Edley.
17 Gardiner, John of Jno. and Eliza. Barber.
Dec. 7 Garner, Henry and Nancy Hall.
1799 Jan. 23 Good, Wm. and Sarah Love.
25 Greenwell, Edward B. and Jane Jarboe.
Mch. 23 Greenwell, Jas. of Geo. and Eliza Rhodes.
May 21 Goldsberry, James and Susanna Pierce.
July 6 Graves, Perry and Ann Davis.
31 Goddard, Jeremiah and Susanna Tippett.
Sept. 21 Gardiner, Jno. Chun and Esther Cawood.
1800 Feb. 6 Greenwell, Edmund and Susanna Mureman.
14 Gibson, Jeremiah and Mary Tennison.
19 Greenwell, James and Eliza. Scissell.
Apr. 15 Gough, Wm. and Dorothy Heard.
July 14 Griffin, Philip and Ann Jones.
Aug. 5 Gibson, William and Charlotte Combass.
Sept. 16 Gardiner, Henry and Eleanor Sothoron.
1801 Feb. 14 Goldsmith, John and Susanna Goodwin.
Apr. 13 Goodwin, James and Elizabeth Newton.
May 10 Greenwell, James and Eliza. Wheatley.
July 3 Greenfield, Thomas and Sarah Wayles.
Sept. 26 Greenwell, Jestinian and Susanna Norris.
Oct. 19 Graves, Thomas and Sarah Goldsberry.
Dec. 30 Greenwell, Benedict and Charlotte Thorpe.
1802 Jan. 2 Goldsberry, Ign. and Mary Lusby.
17 Gough, Peter and Nancy Shanks.
Mch. 22 Gough, Charles and Ann Langley.
June 6 Garland, Peter R. and Winefred B. Belfield.
7 Gibson, John and Ann Reeves.
Dec. 23 Gatton, Wilfred and Milly Dixon.
1803 Aug. 18 Green, Frederick and Ann Jones.
Sept. 5 Goldsberry, Cornelius and Margaret Green.
1804 Mch. 24 Grant, Daniel and Ann Cheseldine.
May 19 Gibson, Jeremiah and Ann Yates.

1804	Aug.	28	Gibson, William and Eliza. Booth.
1805	Jan.	6	Greenwell, Ignatius and Monica Roach.
	May	16	Gough, John and Ann Gough.
	June	25	Gough, Thomas and Eliza. Combs.
	July	9	Griffin, Benjamin and Eliza. Fitzjeffery.
	Dec.	11	Gardiner, Hezekiah and Henrietta Hayden.
1806	Jan.	6	Greenwell, Philip and Mary Ford.
		25	Greenwell, Wilfred and Mary Bennett.
	Feb.	10	Gibson, Charles and Nancy Hayden.
	Apr.	24	Goddard, John B. and Mary Lyon.
	July	10	Greenwell, Bennet and Mary Wheatley.
	Sept.	11	Gill, George and Frances Mitchell.
	Nov.	29	Grey, John and Eliza Hayden.
1807	Feb.	5	Goddard, James and Emmy Bond.
	Apr.	1	Gray, Kenelm and Ann Barnes.
	June	25	Grenstead, John and Fanny K. Cloughton.
	Aug.	21	Graves, Zepheniah and Eliza. Newton.
	Sept.	22	Goodridge, Wm. and Winefred Flint.
1808	Sept.	20	Gunn, James and Ann Ford.
	Nov.	2	Greenwell, Jno. L. and Elizabeth Joy.
	Dec.	26	Greenwell, Robert and Ann Wooten.
1809	Jan.	16	Greenwell, Lewis and Mary Heard.
	Sept.	22	Goldsbury, Charles and Ann Goldsbury.
	Oct.	4	Greenfield, Truman and Jane Herbert.
		24	George, William H. and Judith Carter.
		26	Good, William and Ann Forrest.
1810	May	22	Griffin, William and Clarissa Bond.
1811	Jan.	30	Greenwell, Jeremiah and Eliza. Sanner.
	Apr.	20	Greenfield, Thomas and Margaret Briscoe.
1812	Feb.	7	Garner, Hezekiah and Sophia Tippett.
	Mch.	30	Gatton, Joseph and Ann Cusick.
	May	11	Greenwell, Chas. G. and Monica Williams.
	June	26	Graves, Peregrine and Ann Graves.
	Aug.	18	Gardiner, James and Sarah V. Massey.
	Dec.	29	Gibbons, Robt. and Eleanor Manley.
		30	Gibson, Saml. and Ann Gough.
1813	Apr.	29	Gill, Matthias and Mary Fitzjeffery.
	Dec.	19	Gatton, Jno. Lewis and Eliza. Cracroft.
		27	Gray, Richard and Mary Spalding.
1814	Feb.	12	Grumble, James and Margaret Norriss.
		19	Grindall, William and Mary Ann Lathrom.
1815	Jan.	9	Gardiner, Zachariah and Catherine Wathen.

1815	Jan.	10	Gough, Benet and Ann L. Mills.
	Mch.	31	Goodman, Henry and Nancy King.
	May	8	Goldsberry, Cornelius and Eleanor Thomas.
		25	Gatton, Benedict and Susanna Knott.
	Nov.	18	Gray, Walter and Ann Gray.
	Dec.	19	Gough, Peter and Ann Dixon.
		20	Guy, George Thos. and Ann Wathan.
1816	Jan.	18	Greenwell, Wm. F. and Eliza. Heard.
	Apr.	20	Greenfield, George and Teresia Spalding.
	Oct.	8	Greenwell, Ch. G. and Eliza. Combs.
	Dec.	11	Goldsberry, Saml. and Dianna McCowley.
1817	Mch.	18	Gardiner, Henry G. and Juliet R. Bond.
	May	21	Greenwell, Lewis and Mary Mills.
	Sept.	25	Greenwell, Saml. and Monica Jones.
	Dec.	29	Greenwell, Enoch and Ann Green.
1818	Jan.	21	Guy, James and Ann Alvey.
	Apr.	22	Griffin, Benja. and Mary Jefferies.
	May	5	Gough, Stephen and Eliza. Plater.
1819	Jan.	19	Gibbons, George and Mary Manley.
		25	Greenwell, Wm. and Alby Smith.
	Feb.	1	Greenwell, Augustus and Jane Evans.
	June	28	Gray, John and Fanny Clayborn.
	Aug.	12	Goldsmith, James and Mary Tarlton.
1820	Jan.	1	Gibbons, Thomas and Margaret Medley.
		5	Gatton, Bennet and Eliza. Bothick.
		5	Greenwell, Thos. J. and Eliza. T. Floyd.
	June	12	Goldsborough, Ezekiel and Eliza. McKenny.
1821	Jan.	30	Graves, Th. Joshua and Sarah Eliza. Woodward.
	Feb.	27	Greenwell, Philip O. and Mary Eleanor Combs.
	May	11	Gray, Thomas and Charlotte Howard.
	June	26	Greenwell, Philip and Susan Cadees.
	July	28	Goldsborough, James and Nancy Bailey.
	Oct.	19	Goldsborough, Ignatius and Ann Greenwell.
1822	Feb.	11	Gaugh, Thomas W. and Caroline Dunkinson.
	Apr.	15	Goddard, Edward B. Jr. and Eliza. Fowler.
1823	Feb.	3	Gough, Peter and Mary Dixon.
	Apr.	7	Griggs, George and Ann Smoot.
	Dec.	2	Goldsmith, Jno. M. and Ann W. Allston.
		21	Gooding, Charles and Catherine Clements.
1824	Jan.	30	Gibson, Rodolph W. and Susan Herbert.
	June	8	Greenwell, Philip B. and Jane M. Blakistone.
	Aug.	14	Goddard, Lewis and Harriet Norriss.

1825 Jan. 24 Greenwell, Barton and Polly Rennolds.
Feb. 1 Graves, Jeremiah and Mary Betts.
1 Gardiner, Charles L. and Charlotte L. Leigh.
Apr. 2 Goddard, George and Mary B. Knowles.
7 Greenwell, Abell S. and Marthy Hillen.
Dec. 20 Gatton, James and Eliza. Martin.
1826 Jan. 2 Graves, John W. and Barbary Joy.
29 Greenwell, Henry and Ann S. H. Greenwell.
Mch. 27 Gatton, Thomas and Ann Greenwell.
Apr. 5 Greenwell, Sylvester and Maria Goddard.
Nov. 30 Greenwell, Chas. G. and Priscilla Ford.
Dec. 5 Gough, Thomas W. and Margat. McWilliams.
1827 Jan. 6 Greenwell, John and Panny Thompson.
Feb. 10 Greenwell, Jno. Allen and Harriet Stone.
13 Griggs, George and Ann Russell.
May 8 Greenwell, W. F. and Juliana Floyd.
Dec. 31 Graves, Joseph and Eleanor Peacock.
1828 Jan. 21 Greenwell, James and Eleanor Greenwell.
Sept. 22 Gatton, Thomas and Ann Hailes.
Dec. 9 Gardiner, James and Ellen B. Shanks.
27 Goldsberry, Alex. and Christiana Hath.
1829 Jan. 12 Goodrick, John and Mary Mattingly.
Feb. 1 Graves, John P. and Eleanor Thompson.
7 Greenwell, Robert and Ann Joy.
Dec. 10 Grumble, Alex. and Deborah Mattingly.
1830 Aug. 31 Gardiner, Charles Ll. and Eliza. C. Leigh.
Dec. 15 Garner, Edward and Mary Ann Goodrick.
1831 Feb. 14 Graves, John A. and Teresia Wheatley.
Apr. 26 Greenwell, Philip and Mary C. Greenwell.
May 17 Goldsborough, Nicholas and Jane M. Edelen.
Oct. 25 Gough, Stephen H. and Jane Dunkinson.
1832 Feb. 28 Gough, Benedict and Ann E. Edelen.
May 22 Gough, Edward and Ann Eliza Neale.
June 15 Gill, William and Eliza Leigh.
July 23 Greenwell, Samuel (of Wilfred) and Sarah Dorsey.
31 Gough, James J. and Sarah C. Edelen.
Dec. 18 Gooden, Charles and Ann Guy.
31 Gray, Charles and Eleanor Murfy.
1833 Jan. 8 Graves, John T. and Mary Ann Wathen.
May 25 Goldsberry, Elija and Louisa Winsett.
Nov. 1 Goldsberry, Francis and Ann Norriss.
Dec. 28 Guy, Joseph and Christian Langley.

1833	Dec.	31	Greenwell, Aloysius and Ann Brewer.
1834	Jan.	1	Graves, William and Mary Edwards.
		6	Gatton, Elias and Nancy Thomson.
	Feb.	1	Gibson, George W. and Sarah Larance.
		4	Greenwell, John of Philip and Cath. G. Ashcom.
	Aug.	12	Guyther, Henry and Sarah Jane Shadrick.
	Dec.	24	Gatton, William and Maria Graves.
		28	Graves, Samuel and Rachael Graves.
1835	Jan.	9	Guy, John and Emeline Lemon.
		29	Graves, James and Sarah Maria Edwards.
	Feb.	2	Gill, William and Eliza. Tee.
	June	23	Greenwell, Joseph K. and Catherine F. Hebb.
	July	25	Goodrick, —— and Maria Russell.
1836	Jan.	25	Guy, Benedict Joseph and Mary E. Edley.
	Feb.	12	Gibbons, George and Ann Tear.
	Apr.	2	Gatton, James and Ann Joy.
		26	Garner, Samuel and Rebecca Dement.
	May	11	Greenwell, Pius and Mary Ann Winsatt.
	Dec.	3	Greenfield, John and Teresa Gatton.
1837	Jan.	6	Greenwell, Bennet and Jane Greenwell.
		25	Good, Perry and Ellen Cartwright.
	Apr.	4	Gough, Charles E. and Martha E. Rice.
	Sept.	6	Graves, Lewis and Ann Ford.
		11	Greenwell, George W. W. and Eliza H. Dorsey.
	Dec.	20	Guy, Richard and Mary A. M. Peake.
		21	Guyther, William W. and Eliza A. Holton.
		28	Gibbons, Thomas and Catherine Pier.
1838	Jan.	10	Greenwell, Henry and Mary Winsatt.
	Feb.	27	Goodwin, Wm. H. and Ann E. Raley.
	Apr.	21	Greenwell, Bennet and Julian Drury.
	July	11	Goldsberry, John and Eliza L. Stone.
1839	Jan.	1	Greenwell, John A. and Jane M. Fenwick.
	Apr.	30	Goldsberry, Milfred and Susanna Evans.
	Nov.	18	Greenwell, John A. and Celestia Jarboe.
1840	Jan.	20	Gibson, James T. and Ann Joseph.
	Mch.	16	Gatton, James and Susanna Spalding.
	May	2	Goldsberry, John and Eliza Barnes.
	Aug.	3	Goodwin, William and Harriot Thompson.
		3	Grey, James and Sophia Lemon.
	Oct.	5	Goldsberry, James and Catherine Downes.
	Dec.	7	Gatton, Thomas and Mary Ann Carroll.
		21	Graves, James R. and Catherine T. Graves.

1841	Jan.	4	Goddard, James and Sarah A. Thompson.
		11	Griffin, Jas. Harvey and Eliza. Julian Shemwell.
		16	Guy, William, Matilda Gipson.
	Apr.	8	Graves, James R. and Lucinda Long.
	June	8	Greenwell, John F. and Mary Drury.
	Sept.	8	Gray, William D. and Sarah Langley.
		14	Graves, Henry C. and Sarah M. Edwards.
	Nov.	15	Gatton, Henry and Eliza Hill.
1842	Jan.	17	Greenwell, Wm. F. and Ann P. Joy.
	Mch.	1	Greenwell, Jno. A. of K. and Rebecca S. Philips.
	Apr.	1	Greenwell, Alex. and Sarah Ann Tyler.
	July	18	Gatton, Benedict and Catherine Williams.
	Nov.	15	Gilliams, Lewis S. and Charlotte L. Gough.
	Dec.	19	Garner, Henry G. and Cath. Ann Reeder.
1843	Jan.	17	Graves, Jas. T. and Mary S. Barnes.
	May	19	Gough, Stephen H. and Ann Maria Williams.
1844	Jan.	8	Graves, John W. and Lucinda Jones.
	June	10	Greenwell, Joseph K. and Mary E. Wise.
	Oct.	14	Goodwin, Wm. H. and Celestia Joy.
		30	Gough, Wm. H. and Lucinda Bean.
	Dec.	17	Garner, Wm. H. and Josephine Miles.
1845	Jan.	15	Graves, Enoch G. and Mary A. Buckler.
	Mch.	27	Goodrich, John and Susan M. Bean.
1847	Apr.	28	Gatton, Sandy A. and Eliza. Long.
	Nov.	1	Goddard, Geo. W. and Eliza. A. Ware.
1848	May	16	Guy, Thomas and Louisa Winsatt.
		17	Graves, Samuel and Mary A. Graves.
	June	1	Garner, John E. and Mary E. Mills.
	July	11	Greenwell, Thos. C. and Sarah B. Greenwell.
	Nov.	6	Goldsmith, Zach. H. and Anna M. Blakistone.
		20	Grey, George and Matilda Emery.
	Dec.	26	Gray, Robert and Sarah A. Hayden.
1849	Feb.	19	Grandin, Rev. J. M. and Ann D. Shemwell.
	June	25	Greenwell, W. T. and Harriot A. Goddard.
	Sept.	4	Gasley, Louday and Maria E. L. Clarke.
1850	Jan.	29	Greenwell, Jno. L. and Mary J. Bradburn.
	Feb.	26	Greenfield, Geo. T. and Mary Guy.
	Nov.	16	Goldsborough, Washington and Clara Abell.
	Dec.	26	Goldsborough, William W. and Catherine M. Johnson.
1851	Jan.	6	Graves, Wm. Z. and Teresia C. Graves.
	Dec.	29	Goddard, James and Ann Hardesty.
1852	Jan.	13	Greenwell, Frederick J. and Mary C. Yates.

1853 Nov. 19 Gray, Uriah and Elizabeth Gray.
1854 Feb. 27 Goodwin, John and Louisa Cissell.
28 Greenwell, Gustavius and Cornelia A. Davis.
Oct. 31 Greenwell, French V. and Mary Jane Johnson.
Nov. 29 Graves, Lemuel G. R. and Susan C. Greenwell.
Dec. 26 Graves, Jackson and Maria L. Godden.
1855 May 8 Gatton, John H. and Jemima Paul.
19 Goldsberry, Marcellus and Ann S. Long.
Dec. 27 Graves, John A. and Eliza Cheseldine.
1856 Feb. 5 Gray, Uriah and Maria Gatton.
13 Gatton, Jno. W. and Mary J. Newton.
Mch. 3 Goldsberry, Alex. and Ann M. R. Clarke.
19 Graves, Wm. P. and Elizabeth E. Guy.
Apr. 25 Guy, Peter H. and Jane A. Perry.
Sept. 27 Greenfield, Wm. H. and Ann A. Curry.
Dec. 29 Gray, John J. and Ellen Amanda Lathum.
29 Gatton, Robert W. and Mary Jane Knott.
Feb. 16 Greenwell, Wm. W. and Mary T. Ford.
1858 Jan. 1 Goddard, Benedict and Mary E. Stone.
5 Goddard, Lewis and Margaret Wise.
1859 Jan. 4 Goddard, Francis M. and Emma C. Joy.
Mch. 4 Greenfield, Wm. H. and Emeline Gatton.
June 20 Garner, Andrew M. and Sarah C. T. Abell.
Nov. 8 Greenwell, Wm. T. and Mary E. Moreland.
Dec. 26 Goodrich, Wm. W. and Martha Jane Sharpes.
1860 Oct. 23 Guy, Joseph and Mary E. Jarboe.
Dec. 3 Goldsborough, Chas. A. and Sarah A. Dunbar.
22 Greenfield, Geo. T. and Mary Wood.
26 Graves, Lewis and Ellen E. Boothe.
1861 Jan. 23 Graves, Wm. T. and Dorcilla L. Buckler.
31 Graves, Stephen A. and Martha E. Hayden.
Apr. 2 Gatton, James H. and Mrs. Amanda Davis.
29 Garner, Jno. A. and Martha R. Wilkinson.
June 1 Graves Amos M. and Mary R. Heard.
July 8 Graves, James J. and Martha E. Buckler.
Oct. 15 Gough, Jos. T. and E. A. Manning.
1862 Jan. 2 Graves, B. F. and Jane Woodburn.
Apr. 21 Gragan, Patrick and Jane D. Latham.
Aug. 11 Goldsborough, Francis and Ann S. Russell.
1863 Apr. 6 Graves, James T. and Mrs. Ann Maria Thompson.
June 29 Gibson, William G. and Martha Lawrence.
Dec. 21 Good, Thomas W. and Eliza Jane Sinclare.

1794 Dec. 31 Herbert, Philip and Catherine Hazle.
1795 Feb. 9 Herbert, Joseph and Monica Drury.
10 Howard, Bennett and Jane Alvey.
Apr. 26 Hardy, Isadore and Julian Price.
June 2 Hawkins, Doct. and Dorothy B. Tubman.
2 Hammett, William and Mary C. Kennell.
1796 Aug. 26 Hopewell, James and Elizabeth Wise.
Oct. 11 Hall, Philip and Eliz. Armsworthy.
18 Hammett, Robert and Catherine Hammett.
28 Hammett, John C. and Sarah Hammett.
Nov. 22 Hammett, Zachariah and Ann Hackell.
Dec. 31 Harden, Joseph and Susanna Ellis.
1797 Jan. 31 Hammett, John and Eliz. Burroughs.
Feb. 13 Herbert, William and Charlotte Milburn.
Aug. 26 Hammon, John and Ann Campbell.
Sept. 29 Henning, Thomas and Sarah Allison.
Dec. 14 Hardy, Rhd. and Nancy Cook.
1798 Jan. 10 Hammett, Bennett and Dorcas King.
Feb. 28 Harden, Wm. and Eleanor French.
Mch. 13 Hopewell, James and Ann Chesley.
Aug. 30 Hayden, George and Ann P. Maryman.
Sept. 25 Hebb, William and Nancy Thompson.
Oct. 8 Hardesty, George and Elizabeth King.
Dec. 10 Howard, Charles and Rebecca Craig.
1799 Apr. 30 Higgenson, Jno. H. and Brittania Bennett.
Oct. 9 Howe, John and Mary Latimer.
1800 Jan. 29 Hebb, Caleb and Dorothy Brome.
May 22 Hicks, John and Ann Ford.
July 26 Hopkins, John and Elizabeth Hendley.
Nov. 11 Harden, Charles and Henny Cheseldine.
1801 Jan. 13 Headley, James and Ann Beale.
28 Hutchins, Thomas and Ann Clarke.
Mch. 27 Heard, William and Ann Breedon.
30 Howard, Ignatius and Susanna Smoot.
June 13 Hayden, William and Monica Aud.
July 20 Harris, Joseph and Susanna Reeder.
Sept. 11 Hardesty, George and Mary Brown.
Oct. 19 Howard, Francis and Eliz. Riswick.
Nov. 30 Hazle, John and Sarah Hardesty.
Dec. 22 Hardesty, Wm. and Nancy Budges.
1802 Feb. 24 Hammett, Robt. and Catherine Hebb.
Mch. 8 Howard, Benja. L. and Eliza. Barber.

1802	Mch.	31	Heard, William and Eleanor Norris.
	Apr.	25	Hone, Albean and Mary King.
	June	3	Herbert, James and Ann Suit.
		8	Homes, John and Levinah Richson.
	July	6	Hebb, William and Ann Taylor.
	Oct.	26	Herbert, Jesse and Ann Payn.
	Dec.	24	Henning, John and Sarah Henning.
1803	Jan.	1	Hopewell, James and Eliza Cissell.
	Dec.	28	Hayden, Joseph and Ann Hayden.
1804	Jan.	14	Hilton, Henry and Rebecca Tyson.
		24	Heard, Edward and Mary G. Neale.
	May	21	Hayden, James and Betty Hayden.
	Aug.	2	Horn, Henry M. and Eliza Peake.
	Dec.	28	Hardesty, John and Susa Long.
1805	Jan.	16	Henning, Bennet and Ann Kendrick.
		21	Heard, John and Mary Bowling.
	Apr.	13	Hebb, Caleb and Dorcas Broome.
	July	13	Howard, Leonard and Ann Steel.
	Sept.	17	Heard, Joseph and Sophia Abell.
	Dec.	29	Henning, Thomas and Priscilla Sword.
1806	Jan.	7	Hill, James and Eliza. Dixon.
	Feb.	17	Howard, William and Susanna Joy.
	Mch.	18	Hayden, Peregrine and Eliza C. Grindall.
	May	17	Hesledine, Chas. and Mary Barber.
		29	Herbert, Robert and Lydia Cahill.
	July	25	Hill, Wm. and Eliza. Smith.
	Nov.	29	Heard, Mathew and Mary Jordan.
	Dec.	8	Henning, George and Helen Armsworthy.
1807	Feb.	2	Haydon, John and Alla Russell.
	May	14	Haywood, Joseph and Ann Watts.
	Nov.	30	Hamersley, Wm. and Margaret Neale.
	Dec.	16	Hutchins, Bennet and Sarah Breeding.
		18	Heard, Matthew and Ann Jones.
		23	Hall, John and Eleanor Long.
1808	Jan.	20	Hammett, John and Eleanor Johnson.
		20	Haywood, John and Bibianna Goldsberry.
		20	Hatti, William and Laurynia Wherrett.
	Feb.	13	Hayden, James and Mary Smith.
		18	Howard, James and Susanna Ford.
		24	Hebb, James and Sarah Waughop.
		28	Hayden, Joseph and Rebecca Gol sbury.
	June	28	Higgison, John H. and Mary Clarke.

1808 Oct. 13 Henning, Frederick and Sarah McClelland.
Dec. 19 Heard, Walter and Jane Spalding.
29 Hagos, John H. and Mary Spalding.
1809 Jan. 13 Hardesty, Joseph and Susanna Mattingly.
Mch. 8 Hayden, Azariah and Blanchie Pewatt.
10 Hews, Aaron and Elizabeth Boullt.
21 Hebb, William and Sarah Bagley.
Apr. 27 Harris, Walter and Mary Carpenter.
Oct. 24 Haden, John and Elizabeth Corry.
Nov. 19 Hurst, James and Susan Hurst.
1810 Dec. 24 Hall, John A. and Eliza. Aud.
28 Hammett, McKelvie and Lydia Hammett.
1811 Jan. 3 Hayden, Charles and Sarah Grindall.
5 Hammett, Jeremiah and Margaret A. Burroughs.
19 Hewett, John and Clarissa Booth.
29 Howard, Francis and Susanna Manly.
31 Hayden, Richard and Jane Sothoron.
Feb. 4 Hall, Thomas L. and Elizabeth Biscoe.
Mch. 5 Hooe, Bernard and Eleanor Briscoe.
Apr. 13 Hill, Richard and Catherine Dewell.
May 7 Hath, William and Hannah Lynch.
11 Hath, Thomas and Catheline Tarlton.
Sept. 21 Hayden, Azariah and Sarah Murphy.
1812 Jan. 9 Hammett, Enoch, and Jane Johnson.
30 Howard, John and Elizabeth Edwards.
Feb. 17 Hunt, William D. and Martha Davis.
Apr. 25 Hardesty, Richard and Ann B. Lyon.
1813 Jan. 11 Hill, Henry and Margaret Davis.
25 Herbert, Vitus G. and Mary Davis.
May 17 Hayden, Joseph and Maria Mattingly.
Dec. 3 Hebb, Bennet and Eliza Barnhouse.
1814 Feb. 28 Hutchins, Bennet and Ann Hutchins.
1815 June 26 Howard, Leonard and Eleanor Carberry.
July 15 Hays, John H. and Teresia Gatton.
31 Hall, John and Ann Gatton.
1816 Feb. 5 Hayden, Peregrine and Cecelia Alvey.
24 Harden, Jno. Ellis and Mary Ann Barnes.
Mch. 15 Holly, Thomas and Ann Bean.
July 20 Holly, Joseph and Priscilla Mason.
Aug. 6 Howe, Bernard and Clarissa Owens.
Nov. 6 Howard, Cornelius and Sarah Wherrett.
12 Hammett, John and Mary Lock.

1816	Dec.	18	Hunt, Elijah and Mary Ann Dixon.
1817	May	17	Holland, William and Catherine Bohanan.
1818	Jan.	10	Hall, Lewis and Jane Fellows.
		13	Herbert, Thomas and Ann Teresia Milburn.
		13	Hazle, Wm. and Elizabeth Weakling.
		31	Heard, William and Charlotte Davis.
	Sept.	28	Hebb, William and Jane Martin.
	Oct.	7	Hutchins, Bennet and Elizabeth Wood,
1819	Feb.	2	Heard, Ignatius and Eleanor Herbert.
		16	Hayden, George and Jane Charlotte Bradburn.
	June	8	Heard, Benja. I. and Eleanor McWilliams.
		15	Hutchins, John and Clarissa Hebb.
1820	Jan.	22	Howard, Thomas and Charlotte Edwards.
	Feb.	26	Hammett, Saml. and Rebecca Sanner.
	May	23	Hurry, John and Emily Thompson.
1821	Jan.	9	Hooper, Thomas and Mary Drury.
		13	Hammett, Igs. and Elizabeth Sanner.
		27	Hopkins, David and Ann Manns.
	Feb.	5	Hammett, Bennet and Elizabeth Dent.
	Dec.	24	Herbert, Philip and Nancy Gibson.
1822	Feb.	14	Holton, John and Catherine Armstrong.
		26	Harding, Thomas E. and Mary A. Harding.
	May	6	Hazle, Jeremiah and Margaret Hill.
		26	Howard, James and Susanna Edwards.
	July	3	Henry, Vincent and Ruth Ann Laurence.
		10	Hagner, Jacob P. and Sarah Spicer.
	Sept.	22	Huntt, Henry and Mary C. B. Barnes.
		28	Hammett, Williams, and Catherine Tippett.
1823	Apr.	9	Hardy, George and Elizabeth McKay.
	July	21	Hayden, Jonathan and Susan Alvey.
	Oct.	4	Higgs, Samuel and Lucinda Herbert.
1824	Jan.	9	Hardesty, Joseph and Elizabeth Mattingly.
	Feb.	16	Howard, Gabrill and Ann Perry.
	Apr.	27	Hammett, Jas. McKelry and Rebecca Watts.
	May	24	Hutchins, Joshua and Cardine R. Barber.
	June	14	Herbert, John and Ann Catherine Mattingly.
		26	Howard, Thomas and Jane Rodgers.
	Aug.	18	Howard, John and Kitty Wilson.
	Oct.	26	Hammett, Samuel and Mary Ann Corum.
1825	Jan.	17	Heard, Joseph and Ann Bottick.
		18	Herbert, William J. and Ann E. Combs.
		29	Herbert, Phillip Sr. and Mary Davis.

1825 Apr. 8 Hassack, Daniel and Permelia Reanes.
14 Hayden, Thompson D. and Monica Fowler.
May 21 Hamelton, Samuel S. and Mechtildes Brooke.
Dec. 24 Hazell, Alexander and Mary Ann Gurten.
1826 Apr. 3 Hebb, Wm. H. and Priscilla Loker.
Aug. 28 Herbert, Philip and Susan Morgan.
31 Hunt, Wm. D. and Ann Mareman.
Sept. 29 Hammett, Henry and Catherine Wise.
Nov. 13 Hickey, William and Cecelia A. Plowden.
1827 Jan. 2 Harden, John W. and Juliana Gibson.
Feb. 20 Howard, Joseph A. and Elizabeth Fenwick.
May 2 Hardy, Benjamin and Mary Shadrick.
9 Hammett, Biscoe and Ann Eliza Davis.
Dec. 22 Hales, Beverly N. and Elizabeth Joy.
1828 Jan. 8 Hayden, William and Ann M. Hayden.
16 Harden, Wilson Lee and Susanna Gibson.
Dec. 18 Howard, Cornelius and Ann Smith.
1829 Jan. 12 Hayden, Charles and Mary Brown.
26 Herbert, George and Mary R. Fish.
Feb. 1 Harrison, Robert and Maria Hammett.
June 30 Hebb, Thomas and Ann Caroline Wise.
1829 Dec. 19 Hall, Philip and Jane Arnsworthy.
26 Hilton, Henry and Elizabeth Farr.
1830 Apr. 13 Hayden, Bartholomew and Eliza Ellis.
Dec. 18 Hutchinson, Wm. W. and Ann Harbin.
27 Hopewell, James and Elizabeth Hall.
1831 Jan. 10 Hammett, Robert McK. and Jane M. Blakistone.
25 Hayden, Ignatius and Angeline Dillahay.
Feb. 1 Hayden, William and Mary Jane Hayden.
7 Herbert, Joseph and Cecelia A. Payne.
10 Howard, Joseph A. and Jane Maryman.
12 Hayden, James and Sarah Ann Higgs.
Dec. 27 Hilton, William L. and Mary Brome.
1832 Jan. 16 Hardesty, Joseph and Mary Dean.
Feb. 11 Hill, George D. and Caroline Waters.
May 1 Hall, William M. and Ann L. Smith.
31 Harris, William and Ann Wood.
June 18 Hawkins, Jno. T. and Zeorah Hodges.
Nov. 20 Hardy, William G. and Mary P. Dunkinson.
1833 Jan. 8 Hebb, Thomas and Fanny Courtney.
July 10 Holladay, William and Eliza Hudson.
1834 July 7 Hayden, Andrew and Elizabeth Hayden.

1834	Dec. 28	Hayden, Stephen and Maria Mills.
1835	Jan. 24	Howe, Alex. T. and Susan R. Johnson.
	Mch. 30	Hayden, Leonard and Mary Eleanor Ford.
	Apr. 20	Henning, Lewis and Emeline Bean.
	May 5	Howard, Benedict and Martha Rebecca Spalding.
	July 28	Hayden, Charles and Eliza Ann Hayden.
	Oct. 6	Hammett, George and Harriet Loche.
	13	Harper, George G. and Elizabeth Tally.
1836	Jan. 14	Heard, Henry and Elizabeth M. Norriss.
	Aug. 29	Hayden, John and Mary Alvey.
	Dec. 27	Hunton, Benjamin and Jane Davis.
1837	Feb. 4	Hill, William D. and Mary Ann Bleathen.
1838	July 3	Harbough, John K. and Ann Cole.
	Nov. 5	Hill, Thomas and Mary Williams.
	19	Heard, Matthew and Henrietta McKay.
	Dec. 17	Hall, Cornelius and Jane Rock.
	26	Hilton, Henry and Ann Joy.
1839	Jan. 28	Hall, James and Jane Lawrence.
	Mch. 27	Haywood, John A. and Elizabeth Wheatley.
	Aug. 8	Hammond, James and Eliza Ann Bennett.
1840	Jan. 27	Hammett, Joseph A. and Sarah A. Lyon.
	Mch. 23	Hall, Wm. M. and Violetta G. Cole.
	Aug. 4	Higgs, John C. and Susan Hardesty.
	Sept. 28	Hayden, Wm. and Mary E. Guy.
1841	Jan. 12	Hardesty, Richard T. and Ann C. Lathrum.
	Aug. 7	Hilton, Henry and Elizabeth Joy.
	Sept. 8	Heard, James W. and Ann Eliza Johnson.
	30	Hayden, John A. and Elizabeth Wheeler.
	Nov. 17	Hill, James H. and Elizabeth E. Deane.
1842	Jan. 27	Henning, Robert M. and Mary E. Biscoe.
	Oct. 4	Hammett, Henry and Ann E. Thompson.
	Dec. 5	Hardesty, Geo. W. and Caroline Thompson.
1843	Jan. 6	Harrison, John and Sarah Ann Edwards.
	Feb. 3	Harris, John and Sally Wood.
	May 26	Harrison, Gideon D. and Emily Dent.
	Sept. 29	Hutchins, Benjamin and Ann Norris.
1844	Jan. 22	Hazell, Henry and Eliza Elliss.
	Feb. 8	Harding, Francis and Ann Swann.
	Apr. 16	Howard, Bened. I. and Jane E. Davis.
	May 28	Harding, John E. and Mary A. Graves.
	July 9	Heard, Janes M. and Sally Ann Spading.
	Nov. 26	Higgs, Alex. Jr. and Ann E. Boothe.

1845 Jan. 21 Herbert, J. C. and Jane E. Alney.
Feb. 3 Herbert, Augustus C. and Mary E. Alvey.
Aug. 3 Heard, James E. and Jane Maria Dent.
Nov. 24 Harvey, Arcenus J. and Margaret F. Bean.
1846 Jan. 13 Harding, John H. and Jane Rebecca Graves.
Feb. 2 Holmes, John H. and Maria Dunbar.
Apr. 20 Hewett, Benja. and Lucy D. Lumpkins.
June 15 Hebb, Thomas and Eliza. T. Clarke.
Dec. 19 Hazle, William and Ann Long.
29 Hammett, Jas. S. and Ann L. Wise.
1847 Jan. 12 Hayden, John B. and Mary C. Saxton.
26 Higgs, Alex. and Mary Hardesty.
Apr. 12 Hazle, Henry and Jane R. Tippett.
17 Hill, James and Ann C. Wood.
June 1 Harris, John F. and Rosaliee S. H. Brady.
July 13 Hardy, William F. and Eliza M. Millard.
Nov. 1 Harrison, Joseph N. and Ann M. Hayden.
9 Hammett, Geo. E. and Susan S. Dent.
1848 Jan. 4 Hammett, Wm. T. and Margaret Nuthall.
10 Herbert, Philip and Margaret Thompson.
31 Hayden, Jas. Ignatius and Mary E. Abell.
Mch. 6 Hayden, Leonard and Jane E. Monarch.
July 6 Herbert, William and Elizabeth Wheeler.
Nov. 1 Hammett, Abell and Susanna E. Wilkinson.
Dec. 26 Herbert, John and Elvia Thompson.
27 Hayden, George and Martha M. Maddox.
1849 Jan. 26 Huntington, Ignatius and Eliza Jarboe.
Feb. 5 Harden, John W. and Jane R. Brown.
6 Hayden, James W. and Mary A. Mattingly.
12 Howe, John and Chloe Swann.
17 Hill, Zach. and Sarah Harris.
June 7 Hooper, Wm. E. and Jane Wilkinson.
Aug. 1 Hill, George M. and Ann Wheeler.
13 Herbert, John E. and Elizabeth A. Graves.
Nov. 13 Hutchins, Luke W. B. and Lydia A. Slye.
1850 Jan. 4 Hooper, James T. and Ann L. Briscoe.
15 Harding, John H. and Jane M. Buckler.
Feb. 4 Hazell, Judson and Indiana Tippett.
Mch. 18 Harper, John and Sally Ann Thompson.
May 1 Harbin, Saml. and Mary J. Dunbar.
July 1 Hall, William M. and Mary A. Clarke.
6 Hill, Ignatius T. and Ann L. Alvey.

1850 Nov. 26 Herbert, Washington P. and Eliza. S. Higgs.
1851 Feb. 11 Hudgins, William H. and Mary A. V. Braxton.
May 6 Holmes, A. B. and Maria Maddox.
26 Hammett, James McK. and Emeline Watts.
June 9 Harding, John E. and Frances M. E. Dick.
1852 Feb. 17 Hayden, Bernard L. and Maria L. Thompson.
May 3 Herbert, Jno. S. and Rebecca A. Herbert.
27 Hewett, Joshua and Elizabeth Chiveral.
Dec. 27 Herbert, Ignatius J. and Sally Mattingly.
1853 Apr. 5 Hayden, William H. and Harriet H. Heard.
June 4 Henderson, Edward and Adeline Chesser.
July 4 Herbert, Thomas P. and Mary V. Hayden.
Dec. 6 Hooper, Samuel M. and Sarah McCafferty.
1854 Feb. 6 Howe, Philip P. and Mary E. Long.
May 29 Hayden, John B. and Maria Emily Dunbar.
July 12 Hodges, Thomas Ramsey and J. Imogene Coade.
Sept. 8 Hebb, George W. and Mary Eliza Russell.
12 Hayden, Wm. H. and Sarah A. Wilkinson.
25 Harden, Joseph D. and Jane R. Hazell.
Oct. 9 Higgs, Robert H. and Margaret R. Hayden.
18 Hopkins, Stephen and Martha E. Langley.
19 Harrison, Joseph N. and Sarah M. Dent.
1855 Feb. 19 Hayden, Bernard L. and Mary E. Yates.
Apr. 23 Hayden, Leonard and Ann Attaway Bond.
23 Hayden, Ignatius and Rasan A. Greenwell.
May 30 Hadden, Elonza and Cornelia Tippett.
Sept. 24 Harrison, Thomas L. and Eliza A. Bradburn.
Dec. 27 Higgs, Henry E. and Mary J. Hayden.
1856 Jan. 12 Hains, James L. and Martha A. Newton.
Apr. 21 Harden, William S. and Jane Maria Ellis.
June 5 Hayden, Jonathan and Mary E. Bond.
July 9 Herbert, John H. and Mary C. Bradley.
Sept. 2 Huntington, Edward and Mrs. Eliza Foster.
15 Hill, George and Elizabeth Thompson.
Oct. 21 Hayden, James T. and Catherine Burroughs.
Dec. 15 Herbert, George H. and Margaret E. Tarlton.
15 Herbert, Robert H. and Sarah C. Chinn.
27 Hayden, Charles and Leticia Middleton.
1857 Jan. 5 Harden, Robert H. and Margaret S. Elliss.
13 Harrison, Charles and Susan R. Harrison.
July 11 Herbert, John H. and Jane R. Harden.
1858 Jan. 16 Hazell, Patrick and M. Lovinia Guy.

1858	Feb.	7	Hayden, Jerome and Mary L. Mattingly.
		13	Hayden, Thomas F. and Eliza C. Wheeler.
	Oct.	25	Hayden, Jas. S. and Lucinda Russell.
	Dec.	27	Hayden, Henry A. and Sarah Mattingly.
1859	Jan.	10	Hayden, Geo. W. and Rachel S. Cusick.
		15	Hammett, Samuel B. and Ann R. Hammett.
	Feb.	21	Herbert, Joseph S. and Mary Jane Mattingly.
	May	16	Harrison, Thomas and Martha Adaline Harrison.
	Aug.	29	Howard, Leonard and Susan M. Milburn.
1860	Feb.	20	Harding, Benja. L. and Mary Ann D. Graves.
	Mch.	6	Hill, James T. and Mary Thompson.
	Apr.	7	Hill, John H. and Julian Dean.
	May	15	Hammett, Wm. S. and S. E. Tea.
	June	5	Hammett, Chas. M. and Julia A. Maddox.
1861	Jan.	2	Howard, Geo. W. and Dorothy Morgan.
	Oct.	1	Hammett, Jas. H. B. and Eliza. E. Tubman.
		15	Hammett, McKelva and Jane L. Clocker.
1862	Feb.	6	Hubbard, William and Elizabeth Ball.
		25	Harding, Charles W. and Sarah M. Huntington.
	Mch.	1	Hutchington, J. C. and Annie C. Johnson.
	Dec.	29	Hayden, Richard T. and Rosetta Mattingly.
1863	Sept.	14	Hammett, W. A. and Lizie McCarthy.
	Oct.	5	Hammett, Wm. Sidney B. and Rebecca Wood.
1806	Nov.	29	Ireland, Thomas and Sarah Mackall.
1795	Mch.	7	Johnson, John and Eleanor Smith.
	June	2	Jarboe, Ignatius and Susanna Raley.
	Nov.	10	Jarboe, Joshua and Eleanor Elliott.
1797	Jan.	—	Jackson, Doct. Elijah and Mary McWilliams.
	June	14	Johnson, John and Lydia Forrest.
1798	Feb.	17	Jones, John and Elizabeth Monroe.
	Nov.	23	Joy, Barton and Nancy Buckler.
1799	Jan.	15	Jones, Thomas and Mary Bennett.
		15	Jarboe, Joseph and Mary Nelson.
		21	Jones, James and Ann Bennett.
	Nov.	7	Jones, John and Jane Suit.
1802	Aug.	16	Joy, Edward and Barbara Knott.
1803	July	28	Joy, Edward and Elizabeth Wheeler.
1804	Oct.	23	Jones, John and Ann Clarke.
1805	Feb.	8	Johnson, John and Clarissa Shercliff.
	June	13	Jones, Solomon and Monica Reswick.
1806	Jan.	6	Jones, Caleb and Elizabeth Bennett.
1807	Jan.	9	Joy, Ignatius Jr. and Dorothy Drury.

1808	Feb. 20	Jenkins, John J. and Mary Ann Plowden.
	Dec. 6	Jarboe, Matthew Jr. and Elizabeth Nelson.
1809	Mch. 7	Johns, David and Mary Wootten.
	Nov. 23	Johnson, Bennet and Catherine Long.
1811	Jan. 7	Johnson, Philip and Mary Thomas.
	7	Jackson, John K. and Mary Jarboe.
	8	Joseph, Benedict and Alice Guy.
	Aug. 27	Joy, Benedict and Sarah Booth.
1812	Jan. 17	Jackson, Clement and Ann Olivia Winsatt.
	Sept. 22	Johnson, Joseph and Mary Ann Drury.
	26	Johnson, Benedict and Elizabeth Howard.
1813	Oct. 21	Jones, Samuel and Harriet Mac.
1814	Apr. 19	Jarboe, James and Catherine Kerwin.
1815	Mch. 27	Jones, Caleb M. and Rebecca Davis.
	Sept. 30	Jones, Mordicai C. and Eliza. Armstrong.
1816	Feb. 26	Joy, John B. and Mary Ann Spalding.
	Apr. 12	Jones, James and Mary A. Bennett.
	Oct. 30	Joy, James and Julian Alvey.
1818	Feb. 4	Joy, Barton and Ann Saxton.
	Apr. 1	Jones, Walter Moore and Anna Maria Holton.
	Sept. 8	Johnson, Thos. Rinaldo and Sarah Ann Mason.
1819	Jan. 5	Johnson, James and Jane Bothick.
	9	Johnson, John and Martha Drury.
	14	Jones, John B. and Dorothy Alexander.
	Feb. 8	Jordan, Jeremiah and Ann Clarke.
	Dec. 28	Jones, Thomas and Elizabeth Clarke.
1820	Jan. 24	Jones, Basil and Margaret Smith.
	Mch. 16	Jackson, John and Eleanor Butler.
1821	Dec. 24	Jones, Henry and Nancy Worthington.
1822	Jan. 3	Jordan, George R. and Susanna Graves.
	Feb. 7	Jarboe, John and Henrietta Peake.
	Dec. 24	Jarboe, John and Elizabeth Goodwin.
1823	May 14	Jones, Clement and Margaret Ann Goodden.
1824	Feb. 28	Jarboe, Joseph and Darcus Stone.
	July 26	Jones, John B. and Sarah Ann Joy.
	Aug. 2	Jones, William and Sarah Theobold.
1825	Feb. 5	Jarboe, John and Cecelia Hayden.
	10	Johnson, Joseph and Mary M. Yates.
	Mch. 19	Jones, James and Mary Adams.
	Apr. 19	Joy, Joseph and Ann Bullock.
1826	Feb. 2	Joy, John B. and Ann Sanders.
	Mch. 14	Johnson, James and Eleanor Tippett.

1827	Jan.	1	Johnson, Bennet and Mary Ann Power.
	Dec.	18	Jarboe, Basil and Elizabeth Knott.
1829	Jan.	1	Jones, Richard and Mary Catherine Edelen.
	Dec.	26	Jarboe, Charles and Elizabeth Russell.
1830	Feb.	1	Jones, Stephen and Clara Barnes.
	Dec.	24	Johnson, Hewett and Margaret J. Davis.
1831	Jan.	11	Joy, Samuel and Rebecca Leach.
	Apr.	18	Jones, William and Sarah Ann Gill.
	Sept.	25	Jones, Rev. Norris M. and Eliza A. Sothoron.
1833	Jan.	5	Joy, James and Ann Wise.
		7	Joy, Edward and Elizabeth Cissell.
	Apr.	23	Jones, Stephen and Susanna Watson.
1834	July	22	Joy, John and Elizabeth Yates.
	Dec.	22	Jones, Samuel and Mary Johnson.
1835	Oct.	6	Joy, Edward and Mary Goddard.
	Dec.	28	Johnson, Henry and Catherine Herbert.
1836	Apr.	18	Jarboe, John and Catherine Thompson.
	July	25	Jarboe, John B. and Ann M. Hayden.
1837	Jan.	28	Jarboe, John and Ann McClelland.
	July	25	Joy, John B. and Mary E. Evins.
1838	May	22	Johnson, Joseph and Rose Anna Knott.
1839	May	28	Johnson, Thomas and Elizabeth Carroll.
	Nov.	22	Jarboe, Joseph and Mary Johnson.
1841	Aug.	21	Joy, George and Dorothy Melton.
	Oct.	15	Johnson, Jno. of David and Elizabeth Drury.
1842	Jan.	15	Joy, Edward B. and Issabella Bailey.
	Oct.	11	Jarboe, Ignatius A. and Sophia S. Heard.
	Dec.	31	Jones, Thomas S. and Mary S. Harding.
1845	Jan.	6	Johnson, Joseph and Eleanor Lawrence.
1846	Jan.	13	Johnson, Edward H. and Mary Ann Welch.
	Feb.	17	Jarboe, Thomas H. and Ann Mary Clarke.
	Dec.	23	Jarboe, W. J. and Ann C. Drury.
1847	Jan.	13	Johnson, Uriah and Clarissa Sharkley.
	June	1	Jones, Barzillia and Mary L. Sumwalt.
1848	Feb.	8	Jarboe, Matthew and Mary Jane Russell.
	Aug.	7	Joy, James and Mary McCready.
1849	Apr.	16	Jobinson, James and Martha Taylor.
	Oct.	20	Jones, Clement and Eliza E. Lamb.
1850	Jan.	8	Jarbo, James F. and Mary E. Aud.
	Mch.	30	Jones, John J. and Mary J. Cissell.
	Dec.	2	Jones, Joseph H. and Eliza M. Dent.
		30	Joy, Thomas F. and Catherine Peak.

1851	Feb. 20	Jarboe, Robert and Attaway Raley.
1852	Apr. 22	Jones, William H. and Mary C. Stone.
	Aug. 2	Jones, Stephen and Mary F. Posey.
	Dec. 13	Jones, Thomas and Martha A. Stone.
1853	Jan. 18	Joy, John M. and Eleanor Johnson.
	Feb. 1	Joy, Ignatius and Mary E. Morgan.
	3	Johnson, Frederick and Mary E. Mattingly.
	7	Jarboe, John T. and Emeline Stone.
	Sept. 26	Joseph, Aloysius and Tereresa Perry.
	Dec. 1	Jones, Edward S. and Catherine E. Joy.
	20	Johnson, Allen T. and Mary C. Moorland.
1854	Sept. 5	Johnson, Stephen Josiah and Cath. Eliza Mattingly
	11	Johnson, Joseph and Lutha Ann Alvey.
	Nov. 24	Jones, Joshua and Martha Ann Graves.
	Dec. 2	Jones, Jos. H. and Matilda Thorne.
1855	Apr. 9	Joy, Thomas F. and Ann Permelia Jones.
1856	Apr. 9	Johnson, John and Charlotte A. W. Nuthall.
	Nov. 18	Jones, James and Mary E. Foxwell.
	Dec. 30	Jones, John W. and Eliza. Ann Wheeler.
1857	Feb. 17	Jones, W. H. and Mary Lathum.
	Dec. 23	Jones, Hilary and Mary A. Joy.
1859	Sept. 6	Joy, James and Elizabeth Hayden.
1860	Feb. 20	Johnson, Richard and Betty Ann Howard.
	Dec. 17	Joy, James S. and Mary E. Hayden.
1861	Nov. 13	Jarboe, John J. and Anne V. Wathen.
1862	Sept. 23	Jackson, P. J. and Martha E. Evans.
	Dec. 17	Johnson, John E. and Jane M. Good.
1863	Mch. 26	Johnson, James and Susan Moran.
	Apr. 7	Jones, John A. and Susan A. Graves.
	July 7	Jamison, Baker A. and Sallie M. Gough.
1795	June 8	Knott, James and Elizabeth Compton.
	Dec. 25	Knott, Ignatius and Dorothy Hammett.
1797	June 13	Kenny, John and Nancy Barber.
	Oct. 22	Knott, Kenelm and Eleanor Power.
	Dec. 9	King, Stephen and Cloe Nelson.
1798	Nov. 26	Kilgour, William and Sarah Egorton.
	Dec. 11	Kirk, James Jr. and Ann Biscoe
1801	Aug. 28	Keech, John and Clary Hill.
1802	Oct. 12	King, Joshua and Ann Bohanan.
1803	Jan. 23	Keech, Stephen and Mary Warters.
	Dec. 3	Knott, Clement and Mary Blakistone.
	20	Kirby, James M. and Mary Milburn.

1803	Dec.	22	Kirkham, Thomas and Charlotte Betts.
1804	Apr.	19	King, Edmund and Mary Vilender.
	Dec.	4	Kirby, Francis and Ann Greenwell.
		22	Keech, James and Clarissa Sothoron.
1805	July	6	Key, Robert M. and Eleanor B. Beans.
1807	Apr.	11	Knott, Henry and Catherine Fenwick.
1811	Jan.	14	Kilgour, John and Margaret Reeder.
1812	Sept.	25	Knott, John and Susanna Hardesty.
1813	Jan.	13	Knott, William and Elizabeth Johnson.
1818	Dec.	31	Knott, Thomas and Polly Mattingly.
1819	May	25	King, Gerard and Louisa Carpenter.
	Nov.	22	Knott, Nathaniel and Juliet Johnson.
	Dec.	14	Knott, Francis and Mary Knott.
1820	Apr.	1	Keech, John E. and Susanna Burroughs.
1821	Dec.	24	Kirby, Meritt and Jane Price.
		29	Knott, Baptist and Polly Booth.
1824	Feb.	28	Knott, James and Eliza. Thompson.
1825	Apr.	12	Knowles, Wm. B. and Ann C. Goddard.
1826	Nov.	21	King, Rufus and Mary H. Curry.
1828	Dec.	24	Kisch, Stephen C. and Susan Cawood.
1829	Jan.	5	Knight, Henry B. and Henrietta Tennison.
	Oct.	26	Kirk, Henry N. and Charlotte Tabb.
1832	June	23	King, Gerrard and Jane Greenwell.
1833	Apr.	25	Key, Philip B. and Maria L. Sewell.
	Dec.	10	Keech, Samuel and Eleanor Maddox.
1834	Feb.	18	Key, Henry G. S. and Maria L. Harris.
1839	Apr.	9	Knott, Henry and Julia Ann Thompson.
1841	Mch.	20	Knott, John Baptist and Susan Wilson.
1841	Oct.	4	Knott, Thomas R. and Jane M. Greenfield.
		19	King, James and Jane Mattingly.
1842	Apr.	12	Kirby, Cornelius F. and Mary Ann Combs.
	Dec.	17	Knott, William and Mary Ann Bond.
		20	Kirby, James E. and Sarah C. Briscoe.
1843	Feb.	13	Knott, Richard and Susan Dean.
1844	Jan.	1	Key, John Taylor and Mary E. Robinson.
	June	20	King, James and Amanda S. Norriss.
1845	July	8	Knott, James H. and Mary A. M. Cooke.
1846	Apr.	14	Knott, James H. and Susanna Thompson.
1847	Feb.	1	Knott, Richard and Mary S. Jarboe
	Oct.	30	King, George S. and Maria D. Abell.
1848	Nov.	16	Knott, John and Susanna Cusick.
1849	Feb.	20	Keibird, W. S. B. and Ellen S. Turner.

1849 Sept. 11 Keechum, James and Ann E. Blair.
1850 Jan. 7 Knott, Wm. H. and Julia A. Long.
1854 July 11 Krukle, John C. and Martha A. Wheatley.
1858 Jan. 7 King, John F. and A. M. Hayden.
Dec. 21 Keech, Thomas M. and Eva Martin.
1860 May 29 Knott, Richard and Ann Eliza Gray.
29 Kirby, Cornelius and Catherine Taylor.
1861 Jan. 14 King, George W. and Mary G. Russell.
Feb. 12 Knott, Edward and Bettie Wood.
1862 Apr. 28 Knott, Jos. F. and Martha C. Swann.
Dec. 30 Kirby, Charles C. and Mary E. Pegg.
1795 Apr. 3 Lucas, Richard and Ann Smith.
Dec. 22 Loker, Arnold and Jemima Langley.
20 Lyon, William and Rebecca Merphey.
1797 Jan. 16 Laster, William and Sarah Coram.
Feb. 7 Lastre, Samuel and Eleanor Jenkins.
Mch. 28 Lawrence, John and Nancy Mason.
Sept. 25 Lansdale, Will. and Polly Reeder.
Dec. 30 Long, Charles and Eleanor Wathen.
1798 Jan. 10 Long, Joseph and Milicent Panbra.
15 Leach, John and Eleanor Price.
Feb. 28 Leach, Wm. and Mary Tarlton.
Oct. 17 Lawde, James and Ann Lawrence.
1799 Feb. 22 Lee, Henry and Rebecca Knott.
June 1 Langley, Ignatius and Maria Fenwick.
Sept. 23 Lee, James and Elizabeth Manley.
1800 Feb. 4 Loker, William and Elizabeth Thomas.
10 Lyon, Walter and Ann Good.
Dec. 22 Luke, David and Belinder Greenwell.
1801 Mch. 2 Long, John and Barbara McKaney.
Dec. 8 Lindenbayer, Fredk. and Rebecca Hebb.
1802 July 2 Lynch, Stephen and Priscilla Joy.
July 25 Leigh, Philemon and Milly Good.
Sept. 27 Leigh, Arnold L. and Eliza F. Fenwick.
Oct. 14 Lewis, William F. and Rebecca Abell.
Dec. 15 Lancaster, Joshua and Sarah Parsons.
1804 Jan. 12 Lone, Saml. P. and Mary Combs.
Mch. 19 Long, John and Mary Ferrell.
1805 May 13 Leigh, Joseph and Sarah Bean.
June 22 Liderman, Andrew and Eliza Cooper.
May 19 Langley, William G. and Ann P. Cloughton.
Aug. 11 Lynch, Thomas and Elizabeth Hebb.

1805	Dec.	31	Lynch, William and Nancy Bean.
		31	Loker, William and Jannett Thompson.
1806	Jan.	20	Long, Richard and Mary Johnson.
	Oct.	20	Lurty, Thomas and Margaret Shadrick.
1807	Oct.	20	Lyles, William F. and Sophia Bond.
1808	Jan.	11	Leach, James and Mary Stone.
		12	Lee, Wm. T. and Elizabeth Carpenter.
	Apr.	16	Leigh, John and Lucretia Leeds Thomas.
	Dec.	13	Long, Josiah and Eleanor Mattingly.
		13	Lyons, Clement and Sarah Tippett.
1809	Jan.	13	Long, William and Sarah Cusick.
	July	23	Long, John and Mary Brown.
1811	Jan.	4	Lee, Charles and Ann Hutchins.
	Mch.	2	Leach, William and Ann Greenwell.
	May	17	Lynch, Thomas and Elizabeth Coade.
	Dec.	30	Lyon, Richard and Mary Mattingly.
1812	Jan.	28	Loyd, Reubin and Leticia Smoot.
	Feb.	26	Lyon, Gustavius D. and Sarah Mattingly.
	July	21	Leach, William and Mary Drury.
1813	Jan.	11	Lathan, Thomas and Winefred Spalding.
	Feb.	21	Leigh, Lewis and Catherine Johnson.
	Mch.	3	Long, Charles and Elizabeth Dart.
		3	Lodge, Nathan and Mary Hewett.
	Apr.	21	Lyon, John B. and Elizabeth Monroe.
1814	Jan.	10	Lawrence, John and Rebecca Mason.
	Aug.	31	Long, Charles and Sarah Thompson.
1815	May	14	Long, Charles and Ann Long.
		14	Long, John and Mary Bright.
	Sept.	17	Lyon, Alex. and Ann Burroughs.
	Dec.	12	Loker, George and Janet Lilburn.
1816	May	30	Langly, Walter and Rebecca Richardson.
	June	1	Long, Joseph and Margaret Dean.
	Sept.	2	Leach, Wm. and Ann Norriss.
	Nov.	5	Lowe, Saml. P. and Mary A. Brown.
	Dec.	14	Long, Josia and Elizabeth Goldsmith.
		24	Lilburn, Robert and Sarah Martin.
1817	Jan.	1	Lister, David and Ann Craig.
	Feb.	8	Long, John and Ann Herbert.
	Apr.	9	Leach, Samuel and Juliet Fields.
1818	Jan.	14	Loker, Michl. I. and Elizabeth Theabold.
	Oct.	5	Langley, Philip and Mary Thomas.
1819	Jan.	5	Long, Jeremiah and Eppy Buckler.

1819 Jan. 12 Lathum, Thomas and Barberry Knott.
Apr. 13 Love, Samuel and Ann Shammell.
May 4 Locke, William and Susanna Jordan.
28 Long, Thomas and Susanna Spalding.
Aug. 12 Lathram, Matthew and Dorothy Wildman.
Oct. 8 Loker, Thomas and Permelia Biscoe.
Dec. 6 Lyles, William H. and Cecelia B. Claggett.
28 Lathrum, George and Elizabeth Hill.
1820 Jan. 9 Long, Morriss and Eleanor Mattingly.
1821 Jan. 4 Lurty, Cornelius and Elizabeth Flower.
Feb. 14 Langley, James L. and Ann L. Biscoe.
Apr. 27 Long, Joseph and Cath. Knott.
Dec. 29 Lynch, Joshua and Ann Tee.
1822 Nov. 26 Love, Samuel C. and Henrietta Dunbar.
Dec. 2 Legree, John M. and Ruth Hawkins Allder Howe.
14 Long, Charles and Elizabeth Melton.
1823 Apr. 5 Lydeman, Andrew and William Thomas.
Sept. 13 Long, Thomas and Margaret Williams.
Dec. 15 Loker, Wm. and Eliza Aditon.
1825 Jan. 4 Llewellen, John and Mary Booth.
Dec. 14 Leach, James and Catherine Leigh.
1826 Jan. 26 Loker, Meverel L. and Eliza Clarke.
Sept. 2 Loker, Thomas and Lucinda E. Dent.
Dec. 27 Lacy, Joseph and Cecelia Rock.
29 Leach, George P. and Eleanor King.
1827 Feb. 18 Lydaman, Andrew and Diana Thomas.
Dec. 19 Lee, Joseph and Mary M. Gill.
1828 Jan. 2 Leach, John and Mary Johnson.
7 Lathram, James and Ann A. Martin.
22 Leigh, John and —— Thomson.
Mch. 10 Langley, James and Eliza Leach.
Apr. 12 Long, Benedict and Elizabeth Howard.
1829 Apr. 27 Langley, Joseph H. and Emily C. Herbert.
1830 Feb. 10 Langley, Walter and Frances Dunbar.
July 26 Long, Charles and Nancy Newton.
Nov. 20 Lathrum, George and Caroline Raley.
1831 Feb. 24 Langley, William and Eleanor Goldsberry.
1832 May 26 Langley, Ignatius and Charlotte Herbert.
June 14 Leigh, John and Mary Maria Lydaman.
Dec. 18 Lurty, Thomas and Elizabeth Lurty.
1833 May 1 Langley, Robert E. and Ann E. Leach.
Dec. 26 Langley, William and Elizabeth Tea.

1835 Feb. 20 Long, James and Juliann Owings.
June 6 Loker, Thomas and Mary E. Jones.
1836 Jan. 28 Lomax, Walter E. and Ann M. Greenwell.
Feb. 1 Lacey, James and Eleanor Ferrall.
May 23 Lathram, Henry and Miranda Mothersead.
June 15 Lee, Joseph and Mary Goldsberry.
1837 Jan. 7 Lacey, William and Dorcas Ferrell.
10 Langley, William I. and Catherine Bean.
1838 June 21 Lamb, Joshua and Elizabeth E. Dunbar.
1839 Apr. 1 Lomax, Thomas and Ann T. Guy.
June 25 Lawrence, William F. Blk. and Susan Somerville F. Blk.
Sept. 10 Lurty, John R. and Rebecca Baker.
1840 Jan. 20 Long, Peregrine and Mary E. Thompson.
Feb. 26 Lynch, John and Elizabeth Wherrett.
May 18 Lee, James A. and Elizabeth Price.
July 9 Lomax, William and Elizabeth Anderson.
Dec. 28 Langley, Joseph J. and Susan Ford.
1841 Feb. 6 Long, Henry and Jane Newton.
May 11 Lawrence, Henry and Elizabeth Hall.
Dec. 11 Luckett, James H. and Mary Thomas.
1842 Jan. 25 Long, William A. and Jane L. Smith.
1843 Sept. 11 Long, John B. and Sarah Ann Ellis.
1844 Jan. 2 Langmore, Uriah and Mary M. Downs.
Oct. 21 Long, Ignatius H. and Sally St. Clair.
1845 Jan. 4 Long, Joseph and Jane E. Newton.
4 Lang, Richard and Jane Buckler.
Feb. 3 Lathrum, Thomas and Margaret Ann Jones.
June 16 Long, Joseph M. and Elizabeth Alvey.
Aug. 16 Lucas, John and Jane N. Downs.
Oct. 4 Lumpkin, James S. and Mary A. Fenwick.
1846 Jan. 17 Lathrum, Zachariah and Priscilla Lomax.
20 Leigh, Lewis H. and Sympronia Davis.
1847 Jan. 4 Lawrence, John and Elizabeth Johnson.
1848 July 17 Loker, Wm. N. and Anna A. Loker.
Sept. 9 Long, James E. and Susan Mattingly.
Oct. 16 Long, Charles and Catherine Harding.
1849 June 16 Lilburn, John G. and Mary J. Biscoe.
1850 Feb. 11 Lathrum, Elias H. and Ann M. E. Bowles.
Dec. 30 Long, John E. and Mary Herbert.
1851 Jan. 14 Long, Charles and Susan Gatten.
21 Langley, Richd. and Tresia Hayden.
Feb. 22 Lathrum, George W. and Margaret N. Wileman.

1851	Dec. 16	Long, Ignatius H. and Julia Ann Hill.
1852	Feb. 10	Lyon, Wm. S. and Lucinda A. Canter.
	Apr. 6	Locke, William H. and Rebecca Perrie.
	Dec. 22	Lucas, John T. and Clarisa Higgs.
1853	Feb. 28	Lambeth, Job W. and Jane Shemwell.
	Dec. 26	Long, John H. and Mary C. Dixon.
1854	Feb. 22	Leach, Geo. W. and E. E. C. Milburn.
	Apr. 17	Langley, Thomas B. and Rebecca Norriss.
	July 22	Lee, James A. and Ann E. Lee.
	Nov. 18	Long, Charles and Mary Maria Bennett.
1855	Feb. 16	Langley, John H. and Maria E. Hayden.
	Mch. 10	Love, Henry C. and Eliza. H. Woodburn.
1856	Jan. 28	Long, Joseph B. and Mary E. Goodrick.
	28	Laurence, John F. and Martha Ellis.
	Feb. 14	Long, Wm. H. and Mary Bennett.
	Sept. 24	Lathrum, John B. and Mary C. Lathrum.
	Dec. 8	Lennox, Anthony and Maria Guy.
1857	Mch. 13	Love, Wm. H. and Miss Cassa Davis.
	Aug. 5	Love, Walter and Cordelia Frank.
1859	Jan. 12	Lathum, John E. and Rosa C. Martin.
	Apr. 13	Leigh, Lewis H. and Susan C. Howard.
	Dec. 23	Leigh, Wm. G. and Martha J. W. Abell.
1859	May 2	Lathrum, Francis J. and Rachel Ann Thompson.
	Dec. 13	Lathrum, Joseph and Mary Guy.
	26	Long, George S. and Terese. E. Gatton.
1860	Jan. 10	Langley, Ignatius and Susan Langley.
	Feb. 14	Langley, John H. and Marion J. Combs.
	20	Long, John H. and Lydia Ann Long.
	Oct. 29	Long, Alex. and Sarah A. Greenfield.
1861	Feb. 8	Lacy, George W. and Salby Maria Ferroll.
	Sept. 24	Loker, George and Aggie Roach.
1862	June 17	Loker, William A. and Susie E. Combs.
1863	Apr. 7	Long, Harrison and Mary E. Wood
	Nov. 27	Leach, John Holland and Lucy E. Punn.
1794	Sept. 14	McKay, John and Susanna Loe.
	Nov. 15	Morgan, James and Mary Wildman.
	Dec. 23	Moore, James and Amnoy Biscoe.
	30	Mattingly, Gabriel and Eleanor Leigh.
1795	Jan. 20	Mattingly, George and Elizabeth Winsatt.
	Apr. 4	Moran, William and Mary Barber.
	June 9	Medley, John and Eliz. Nottingham.
	Mch. 9	Mattingly, James B. and Jemima Watts.

1795	Sept.	9	Mills, John and Jane Beane.
1796	Nov.	18	McCanvell, Barnabas and Eleanor Spalding.
		17	Minor, John and Jane Oldham.
	Dec.	2	Monarch, Francis and Eliz. Power.
1797	Jan.	7	McClelland, George and Sarah Wherrell.
		7	Morton, George and Dicandia Billingsley.
		16	Morgan, William and Eleanor Far.
	Feb.	3	Mattingley, Jas. B. and Eliz. Watson.
		4	Milton, John and Eliz. Mills.
	May	22	Morgan, Ignatius and "Henry" Far.
	Aug.	1	Milburn, James and Eliz. Redman.
		10	Maryman, Rd. and Lydia Mills.
	Nov.	8	Milburn, Joseph and Eliz. Hopewell.
	Dec.	14	Matheises, Rd. and Eliz. Hardy.
		18	Mattingly, Thos. and Eliz. Greenwell.
1798	Jan.	20	Mattingly, Zachariah and Ann Panny Millard.
	Feb.	3	Medley, Charles and Elizabeth Wheatley.
	Oct.	13	Maryman, John and Jennet Muir.
	Dec.	3	Manning, Wilfred and Nancy Fenwick.
		31	Mareman, Thomas and Eliz. Dapt.
1799	May	15	Mathaney, Daniel and Frances Bean.
	Oct.	11	Murphey, Hezekiah and Eliz. Burroughs.
	Nov.	22	Mattingley, Charles and Ann Hazle.
	Dec.	27	Mattingly, William and Mary Turner.
1800	Sept.	22	Manning, Cornelius and Elizabeth Jenkins.
	Dec.	6	Mattingly, Ignatius and Eleanor Ford.
		27	Mayes, John H. and Mary Greenfield.
1801	Oct.	13	McWilliams, John and Ann Wheeler.
	Nov.	9	Mattingly, Bennet and Ally Spalding.
		23	Melton, Rd. and Sarah Aprice.
	Dec.	26	Mattingly, Igns. and Mary Daft.
1802	Jan.	31	Millard, Joseph and Elizabeth Greenwell.
	Feb.	28	Millard, Joshua and Ann Manning.
	May	24	Merry, John and Mary Long.
	Oct.	28	Mason, Joseph and Sarah Holly.
	Nov.	6	Maryman, Joseph and Jane Maryman.
	Dec.	30	McWilliams, James and Eleanor Neale.
1803	Jan.	1	McHay, Stephen and Sarah Bean.
		1	Mattingly, Alexander and Elizabeth Mills.
	Mch.	12	Mills, Francis and Mary Mattingly.
	Nov.	9	Mattingly, John and Ann Carbury.
1804	Jan.	19	Medley, Philip and Eleanor Neale.

1804 Feb. 25 Milburn, Stephen of Step. and Mary Fenwick.
1805 Jan. 7 Mills, Nicholas Jr. and Mary Greenwell.
12 Mugg, Peter and Sarah Mattingly.
Feb. 14 Mattingly, Joseph and Monica Daft.
Aug. 6 Mitchel, Benja. and Mary E. Downs.
1806 Aug. 26 McWilliams, Alex. and Ann Tabbs.
Nov. 26 Muller, Owen and Mary Smith.
1807 Jan. 6 Magill, Matthew and Dorothy Jarboe.
26 Moore, George and Abigale McCallister.
26 McKey, Benja. and Susanna Anderson.
Feb. 3 McWilliams, Edwd. and Elizabeth Knott.
May 16 Martin, Thomas N. and Sarah Joy.
20 Moss, Chilton and Lucy Templeman.
June 13 McGill, Charles and Rebecca Stone.
25 Maddox, Edward and Maria Porter.
Sept. 1 Morgan, William and Hopewell Goldsmith.
Nov. 28 Millard, Francis and Mary Smith.
1808 Jan. 5 Mattingly, John and Mary Ann Thompson.
5 Morgan, John and Judy Morgan.
16 Moore, Stephen and Ann D. Taylor.
Oct. 4 Mareman, Joseph and Susanna Morgan.
Nov. 26 Morgan, James and Ann Gardiner.
Dec. 12 Milburn, Jeremiah and Drayden McLelland.
1809 Jan. 7 Mattingly, John and Eddy Ellis.
23 Murry, John and Nancy Cole.
1810 Jan. 31 Magill, Benedict and Teresia Howard.
Feb. 5 Martin, Benjamin and Hopewell Hebb.
Sept. 27 Moore, Warren Francis and Mary Maria Greenwell.
Dec. 11 Moran, Richard and Ann Hayden.
21 Martin, John and Margaret Lilburn.
1811 Jan. 16 Mattingly, Luke and Mary Hayden.
July 1 Martin, John B. and Margaret Thompson.
6 Mattingly, Sylvester and Mary Ann Edwards.
Aug. 10 Mackmillion, James and Eliza. Cullins.
1812 Jan. 2 Mills, Lewis and Mary S. Abell.
6 Mattingly, Zachariah and Ann Knott.
28 Monroe, Thomas J. C. and Eliza. Turner.
1813 Feb. 23 Mason, Richd. B. and Mary Armstrong.
Apr. 29 Mudd, Leonard and Clarrissa Reeder.
May 11 Marshall, Philip T. and Jane S. Barber.
Nov. 16 Mattingly, Zach. and Teresia Gatton.
1814 Jan. 19 Martin, Stephen and Elizabeth McKay.

1814	Feb. 4	Maddox, Edward and Polly Kellis.
	Mch. 14	McCormick, John and Eliza. Hazle.
	May 28	Maryman, James and Ann Hayden.
1815	Jan. 2	Moran, Edward and Ann Good.
	6	Mattingly, William and Mary Mattingly.
	Feb. 4	Mattingly, Francis and Eleanor Haskins.
	Mch. 23	Mason, John and Charity Butler.
	June 7	Mattingly, Joseph and Eliza. Monarch.
	Aug. 18	Mattingly, Zachs. and Linder Thompson.
	29	Martin, George and Sarah Milburn.
1816	Jan. 30	Milburn, James and Permilia Taylor.
	Nov. 5	Mason, Benja. and Harret Holly.
	12	Medley, Lewis and Clara Williams.
1817	Jan. 7	Mattingly, Clement and Priscilla Goldsmith.
	Nov. 15	Mapey, Charles and Eleanor Blakistone.
1818	Jan. 19	Miles, Henry and Juliet Mattingly.
	Mch. 20	Mattingly, George and Darky Wheeler.
	June 16	Morgan, Charles and Mary Ann Hayden.
	July 1	Moore, Thomas and Ann Baxter.
	Sept. 15	Morgan, George and Maria Cecil.
	Oct. 27	Martin, George and Anna Norriss.
	Dec. 22	Martin, Thomas and Elizabeth Biscoe.
1819	Jan. 11	Maddox, John and Harriot Turner.
	17	Milburn, John and Ann Theobald.
	Feb. 16	Mason, Peregrine and Sarah Lawrence.
	Dec. 6	Moore, Daniel D. and Mary Langley.
1820	Feb. 9	McGill, Benedict and Eleanor Goddard.
	June 20	Miles, Richard H. and Ann Tarlton.
	Aug. 19	Mattingly, Joseph (of Peter) and Deborah Dick.
	Nov. 28	Manning, Robert and Ann Priscilla Gough.
	Dec. 30	Monarch, Clement and Susan Scott.
1821	Jan. 1	Mick, William and Elizabeth Wise.
	Aug. 20	Mattingly, Richd. and Sophia Johnson.
1822	Jan. 12	Mattingly, Sylvester and Ann Graves.
	May 18	Milburn, Stephen and Clarissa Thomas.
	Sept. 3	Morgan, Ignatius and Eleanor Mills.
	Oct. 29	Morgan, Thomas and W. and Cecelia Ann Lee.
1823	Jan. 4	McKenny, Ruben and Elizabeth Arnold.
	Mch. 11	Moore, James and Ann Thompson.
	Apr. 3	Miles, Dent H. and Mary E. Blakestone.
	June 5	Magee, Charles and Mary Walker.
	23	Mattingly, William and Sabria Bennett.

1823	Aug.	15	Mattingly, Zachariah and Susanna Wathen.
1824	Jan.	7	McClelland, John and Susan Nuthall.
	May	12	Morgan, James and Mary Ann Gibson.
	Aug.	2	Miltimore, James and Nancy Kilgour.
1825	Jan.	24	Milburn, John H. and Caroline Briscoe.
	Feb.	10	Mason, John and Matildai Shanks.
	Apr.	2	Mattingly, Wm. and Henrietta Joy.
	Aug.	24	Maddox, John and Eleanor Burroughs.
1826	Apr.	11	Martin, John B. and Elizabeth Clements.
	June	22	McGeorge, John F. and Evelin B. Powers.
	Nov.	28	Millard, John L. and Sympho Rosa Ford.
1827	Jan.	3	Moore, James and Elizabeth Tear.
	Feb.	7	Mattingly, Alexander and Sophia Herbert.
	July	23	Mareman, Joseph and Mary Fenwick.
	Aug.	20	McKay, Thomas and Ann McClelland.
	Nov.	14	McKay, Benjamin and Ann Worthington.
	Dec.	28	Moore, John T. and Monica Tare.
1828	July	5	Martin, Charles and Maria Thompson.
	Aug.	19	Mason, Nehemiah H. and Jane E. Morgan.
1829	Jan.	6	Mattingly, Henry M. and Peggy Henry.
		12	Milburn, Thomas and Cath. Briscoe.
	Feb.	9	Morgan, Joseph and Catherine Lee.
	June	30	Martin, Marrell and Cornelia Ann Smith.
1830	Jan.	4	Martin, William D. and Sally Maria Dorsey.
		5	Morgan, John Ll. and Elizabeth Morgan.
		7	Maddox, George F. and Julian Burroughs.
		7	Maddox, James and Elizabeth E. Payne.
		23	Monarch, Clement and Nancy Heard.
	Apr.	19	McKay, Benjamin and Susan McKay.
		27	Martin, Henry B. and Elizabeth C. Ashcom.
	May	2	Milburn, John L. and Ann S. Thomas.
		4	Mugg, Thomas N. and Mary Davis.
	Dec.	3	Mudd, Leopold and Mary Ann Millard.
1831	Jan.	1	Mattingly, Clement and Elizabeth Wheeler.
	Mch.	15	Mereman, Benoni and Ann Boothe.
	Dec.	26	Mattingly, Edward and Susan Glassgow.
		30	Moore, James and Mary Tarlton.
1832	Feb.	6	Milburn, William P. and Jane Robertson.
		21	Medley, Robert B. and Jane E. Yates.
	June	7	McLord, Matthew and Eliz. H. Manning.
		11	Maddox, Edmund and Eliza. Neale.
		12	Milburn, John and Susanna A. Crane.

1832 July 2 Milburn, Thomas and Susan Maria Hammett.
Sept. 1 Maddox, John and Mary Hall.
4 Maddox, George F. and Lydia Ann Maddox.
Nov. 10 Milburn, Robert H. and Susanna Richardson.
Dec. 27 Mattingly, William and Jane Johnson.
29 Milburn, Pollard and Susanna G. Wildman.
1833 Feb. 12 Morgan, Joseph and Priscilla Mattingly.
14 Moreland, George W. and Mary E. Burroughs.
Apr. 30 McWilliams, Joseph L. and Eliza Alvey.
June 13 Maderia, Samuel C. and Mary A. Cullison.
July 8 Milburn, John and Mary A. Melton.
Oct. 22 Morgan, Raphael and Elizabeth Edley.
Dec. 10 Maddox, Adolphus and Ann A. Kirk.
31 Mattingly, Richard and Ann Elliss.
31 Morgan, Thomas W. and Eliza M. Spalding.
1834 Jan. 14 Morgan, James A. and Ann P. Howard.
16 Mareman, Joseph and Caroline Morgan.
Feb. 4 Morgan, William and Elizabeth Mattingly.
Sept. 10 Mankin, Edward and Mary Ann Perry.
Nov. 4 Manning, Robert and Henrietta S. Ford.
Dec. 6 Medley, Charles and Eliz. G. Miles.
1835 Jan. 5 McWilliams, James and Emeline Williams.
20 Mareman, James A. and Ann H. Abell.
Apr. 7 Milburn, James C. and Eliza Bennett.
28 Mills, John J. and Cath. Clarke.
Aug. 12 McKay, Gilbert and Jane Louisa Lynch.
Dec. 22 Murry, John and Ann Crowley.
1836 Jan. 2 Mattingly, John and Susan Lathrum.
20 Milburn, John and Eleanor Aderton.
Feb. 22 Moore, Ignatius and Ann Moore.
Mch. 31 McKay, Robert and Maria Taylor.
Apr. 14 McNeal, Andrew L. and Monica M. Medley.
June 11 Milburn, Elias and Roseanna Sabel.
21 Miles, Thomas H. and Caroline E. Campbell.
Sept. 6 Milburn, Nathan and Ellen Peake.
Dec. 27 Marks, James and Elizabeth C. Jackson.
1837 Dec. 12 Mattingly, William and Jane B. Dougherty.
16 McKay, Thomas and Mary E. Clarke.
1838 Jan. 23 Morgan, Joseph and Catherine Abell.
May 1 Morgan, Thomas W. and Wieehell M. Dunbar.
5 McKay, Robert and Rebecca Bohanan.
23 Mitchell, R. H. B. and Susan Benney.

1838	Aug.	21	Marks, Gustavus A. and Jane L. Aud.
	Sept.	17	Magill, Benedict and Mary D. Raley.
	Oct.	16	Magill, James A. and Eliza. Pilkinton.
1839	Feb.	5	McKay, Benjamin and Jane Bean.
	Aug.	20	Mattingly, Henry and Rebecca Burroughs.
	Sept.	9	Miles, Dent H. and Eleanor Medley.
	Dec.	25	Mason, William T. and Mary Ann Amanda Guy.
1840	Sept.	1	Milburn, Alex. and Adeline Wilhelm.
	Dec.	17	Mathaney, James and Charlotte Hewett.
1841	Apr.	27	Morgan, James A. and Mary Ann Dillahay.
	Sept.	6	Martin, Thomas and Harriet S. Wheatley.
1843	Jan.	21	Moore, John and Mary Wheatley.
		26	Magill, Matthew and Mary Jane Jones.
	Feb.	7	Morris, James and Eleanor Haney.
	June	28	Milburn, Joseph and Ann Henning.
	Aug.	16	Mattingly, James H. and Sarah Ann Mattingly.
	Dec.	20	Mills, William and Elizabeth C. King.
		20	Moore, James W. J. and Mary Jane Herbert.
	Feb.	17	Moore, George A. and Sarah Tarlton.
	June	27	Morgan, James H. and May E. Howe.
	Nov.	27	Moore, John and Ann F. Clarke.
	Dec.	26	Mattingly, Fras. L. and Eleanor Drury.
1844	Jan.	16	McCrady, Charles and Ann M. Magill.
	Sept.	9	Morriam, Nathanl. W. and Jane H. G. Kilgour.
	Nov.	21	Mattingly, Richard and Amedia Ching.
	Dec.	4	Monett, John and Elizabeth Ball.
1845	Mch.	25	Moore, Geo. F. and Martha S. Aud.
	June	10	Magill, Joseph A. and Susanna Abell.
	Dec.	30	Mattingly, Edwd. and Cath. Ann Fowler.
1846	July	26	Mattingly, Clement and Emily Hurry.
	Aug.	17	Morgan, Danl. T. and Mary C. Goddard.
	Nov.	3	Matthew, Dr. Tho. and Jane Harriet Stone.
	Dec.	29	Moore, James and Mary Clocker.
1847	Feb.	1	McKey, Benja. (of Jno.) and Sus. J. Taylor.
	Apr.	13	Mattingly, Geo. and Anne R. Bayley.
	May	21	McKay, Wm. and Caroline Bean.
	June	15	McDermott, Michl. and Susan Elliss.
	Sept.	14	Morsell, James S. and Sarah E. Brome.
	Nov.	27	Melton, Philip and Violetta T. Oakley.
	Dec.	13	Morgan, Henry and Martha Ann Howard.
1848	Jan.	4	Mattingly, Wm. and Maria Long.
	Feb.	23	Maddox, Geo. F. and Mary E. Keech.

1848 Dec. 4 McKay, Robt. and Preneal Cole.
21 Melne, William and Ann Armstrong.
1850 Mch. 5 McWilliams, Alex. and Char. T. Kirk.
May 20 Martin, Alex. T. and Margaret E. Ashcome.
Oct. 21 Mattingly, Joseph and Mary E. Dyer.
Nov. 25 Mattingly, James and Ann P. Long.
1851 Jan. 28 Mattingly, Geo. H. and Martha Brown.
Feb. 24 Moore, William W. and Matilda Tarlton.
Aug. 5 Morgan, William and Sarah Ann Bailey.
Oct. 7 Maddox, Chas. John and Mary Lemmon King.
1852 Apr. 20 Maddox, Geo. F. and Lydia Ann Simms.
May 16 Manning, James H. and E. Roach.
30 Martin, Charles and Elizabeth Thompson.
1854 May 31 Mankin, J. R. W. and Lucinda Blakistone.
Aug. 7 Morgan, Thomas and Jane M. Cheseldine.
1855 Jan. 16 Morgan, John D. T. and Lydia Ann Quade.
May 21 Murphy, Owen and Catharon McMahon.
July 24 Mettam, William and Sophia Hammett.
1856 Jan. 30 Morgan, Joseph (of Igns.) and Mary Eleanor Sipes.
Mch. 24 Maryman, John H. and Mary L. Booth.
Sept. 11 Matthews, Edward A. and Mary E. Goldsborough.
Oct. 7 Mitchell, Walter A. and Susan Thomas.
Nov. 11 Martin, Alex. T. and M. Lavinia Hellen.
17 Milburn, John H. and Mary S. Boothe.
Dec. 2 Medley, Wm. B. and Sarah Jane Gatton.
1857 Apr. 21 Mattingly, Wm. of Zach. and Mary J. Hayden.
June 3 Milburn, James C. and Mrs. C. A. H. Abell.
July 23 Medley, Lewis C. and Eliza. Ann Abell.
Dec. 7 Morris, John W. and Bettie A. Mattingly.
21 Moran, Wm. A. and E. Lumpkins.
1858 Feb. 1 McKay, John B. and Ann E. Bean.
16 Mattingly, James H. and Ann S. Abell.
Apr. 9 Miller, Geo. W. and Ann P. Taylor.
June 1 Maddox, G. Fred and Susan R. Harris.
Aug. 24 McWilliams, Alex. and A. C. Gough.
Sept. 13 Mack, John F. B. and Eliza. Hawkins, F. B.
Dec. 28 Maryman, John V. and Ellen J. Russell.
1859 Jan. 4 Mattingly, Peter Hauerman and Clare Emily Johnson.
Mch. 2 McWilliams, Francis and Eliza C. Bennett.
May 17 Martin, Chas H. and Martha E. Thompson.
Nov. 8 Murray, Edward and Margaret Unkle.
16 Milburn, Clement B. and Sarah J. Hammett.

1859	Dec.	5	Murphy, Rev. R. Richardson and Maggie A. Smith.
		12	Medley, James and Sarah Jane Wathen.
		29	Milburn, James L. and Eliza. A. Johnson.
1860	Jan.	5	Mattingly, Jos. and Julia Ann Herbert.
		10	Moore, Wm. W. and Eliza C. Haywood.
	Feb.	14	Maryman, James A. and Mary L. Cusick.
	May	15	McCully, Clinton and Anna E. Spalding.
		22	McGee, Charles H. and Emeline Guy.
		28	Magill, James F. and Sallie A. Russell.
1861	Aug.	19	Mattingly, Jos. H. and Sophia Norris.
	Nov.	18	Medley, Charles and Louisa A. Allston.
	Dec.	9	Mattingly, Thomas D. and Martha Medley.
1862	Jan.	1	Martin, W. H. and Rosa L. Stone.
	Feb.	24	Mattingly, J. W. and Lettie A. S. Jarboe.
1863	Aug.	8	Mathany, John B. and Eliza. Ridgell.
		25	McWilliams, Jerome and Fanny Neale.
1795	Feb.	17	Neale, James and Eleanor M. Coard.
		3	Norris, Joseph and Elizabeth Norris.
		20	Norris, Benjamin and Mary Heard.
		27	Norris, William and Elizabeth Drury.
	Apr.	1	Neale, Lexius and Nancy Epsay.
	Dec.	22	Neale, Jeremiah and Mary E. Fenwick.
1796	Oct.	2	Norris, Stephen and Mary Greenwell.
	Nov.	2	Nuttle, Charles and Ann McClelland.
	Dec.	17	Norris, Philip and Margaret Holton.
1797	Jan.	14	Newgent, Bennett and Aleathia Armsworthy.
	Feb.	6	Neale, Jeremiah and Catherine Rapier.
1798	Dec.	29	Neale, Benoni and Eleanor Neale.
1799	Jan.	2	Nevitt, Francis and Ann Williams.
	Dec.	7	Neale, George and Mary Lee.
		31	Nevitt, John and Susanna Milton.
1801	Apr.	8	Norris, Jno. B. and Henrietta Norris.
	Oct.	20	Norris, James and Sarah Clarke.
1803	Mch.	22	Norris, Wm. of Phil. and Rebecca Norris.
	Aug.	15	Norris, Edmd. and Mary Clarke.
		23	Norriss, James and Henrietta Norriss.
1804	Jan.	4	Norris, Cornelius and Ann Russell.
	Feb.	13	Norris, Thomas and Ann Hopewell.
	Dec.	24	Norris, William and Bebranna Cissell.
1806	Feb.	25	Neale, Thomas G. and Eliza. B. Jordan.
1807	Mch.	21	Norris, Raphl. and Henrietta Greenwell.
1808	Jan.	5	Neale, Henry A. and Jane Neale.

1808	Feb.	27	Nelson, Obadiah and Margaret Alvey.
	Nov.	26	Newton, James and Chloe Graves.
1809	Jan.	9	Neale, Charles Hoskin and Eleanor Brooke.
1810	Nov.	26	Neale, William G. and Mary Williams.
1811	Jan.	7	Norris, Allen and Teaklin Drury.
	Sept.	11	Neale, Thos. G. and Susanna Greenfield.
1812	Feb.	3	Norriss, Cornelius and Eliza. Cusick.
		10	Neale, Charles and Sarah Clarke.
	Dec.	24	Nevitt, George L. and Susanna G. Wailes.
1815	Mch.	28	Neale, Joshua and Mary Clarke.
1817	Feb.	11	Norriss, Thomas and Eliza. Craig.
	May	28	Norris, John L. and Mary Booth.
	Aug.	30	Nuthall, Charles and Mary Gibbons.
	Nov.	25	Newton, James and Rebecca Wathen.
1818	Feb.	2	Nelson, Zephaniah and Frances Winsatt.
	July	6	Norris, Ch. G. and Eliza. Abell.
1819	July	19	Neale, Joshua and Ann Morgan.
1822	Jan.	5	Noxley, Jefferson and Eliza. Tenney)
	Nov.	27	Norriss, Joseph and Eleanor Craig.
1825	Feb.	9	Norris, John B. and Eleanor Norriss.
1826	Jan.	2	Norriss, Henry W. and Rebecca Norriss.
		31	Nuthall, John W. and Maria Norriss.
1827	Feb.	6	Neale, Raphael and Mary J. Smith.
	Sept.	27	Nagh, James and Martha Mathaney.
1828	Dec.	1	Neale, Charles of Jas. and Catherine Gardiner.
1829	Jan.	10	Norris, Samuel and Ann Wheatley.
1830	May	31	Norriss, Benedict and Ann Caroline Norriss.
1831	Feb.	1	Neale, John E. and Mary E. Llewellen.
	Dec.	26	Nelson, Obediah and Caroline Graves.
1833	Apr.	8	Norriss, Henry and Delia Norriss.
	May	7	Nuthall, Levi and Ann E. Edwards.
	Aug.	28	Neale, Presley and Laura I. Martin.
1835	Feb.	9	Norriss, James and Sarah Mattingly.
	Dec.	3	Nowell, William and Margaret Langley.
1836	Jan.	18	Norman, Benedict and Mary L. Cheseldine.
	Mch.	14	Norriss, James and Ann L. Adams.
	Apr.	5	Newton, William and Cecelia Hardesty.
	Dec.	22	Norriss, Judson and Monica C. Hayden.
1837	May	17	Nevett, Charles and Eliza. Weaklin.
1838	Jan.	16	Neale, Thomas and Maria Jarboe.
	Feb.	7	Norriss, Clement (of Jno.) and Eliza. Abell (of Thos.).
1839	Nov.	25	Newton, William and Eliza Watson.

1839	Dec.	12	Nuthall, Charles and Sally Ann Johnson.
		15	Norris, William and Lucretia Davis.
1840	June	8	Neale, Henry C. and Susan E. Maddox.
1841	June	7	Norriss, Joseph A. and Mary A. Ellis.
	Aug.	24	Neale, Leonard and Mary E. Medley.
	Sept.	16	Norris, Edward L. M. and Henrietta Newton.
1842	Jan.	4	Naylor, Geo. Joshua and Margaret A. Woodward.
		8	Norriss, James and Elizabeth Peake.
1843	Jan.	3	Nuthall, William and Mary M. Abell.
		3	Nuthall, John W. and Martha McClelland.
1844	Jan.	8	Norwood, Thomas and Pheba Ann Cissell.
1845	Jan.	6	Norriss, Edmund and Celestia Hammett.
	May	28	Nelson, James and Jane C. Kirk.
1847	Jan.	1	Newton, George C. and Susanna Dixon.
1848	Jan.	17	Nelson, Zepheniah and Mary L. Aud.
	May	16	Norriss, John T. and Mary A. Graves.
	Nov.	29	Nevitt, Charles and Ann M. Cullison.
1850	Jan.	9	Norris, James and Mary Ann Higgs.
		30	Norriss, W. J. and Eliza Ann Shermantine.
	Feb.	1	Neale, Joshua and Julian Payne.
	Mch.	18	Newton, James F. and Sally M. Thompson.
	July	27	Newton, James T. and Martha A. Watson.
1851	Mch.	3	Norris, James W. and Mary J. Dyer.
	July	22	Newton, John F. and Elizabeth Long.
	Dec.	15	Norris, William H. and Mildred C. Weaklin.
1852	Feb.	19	Norris, Ignatius W. and Hannah R. Foxwell.
	Oct.	5	Neale, Francis C. and Rosa H. Millard.
1853	Jan.	20	Norris, Charles J. and Rose Ann Foxwell.
	Feb.	8	Newton, John F. and Ann J. Gatton.
1854	Jan.	30	Norriss, William and Margaret Ellen Downs.
	Apr.	18	Norris, Jetson and Mary E. Brown.
1855	Feb.	19	Norris, William A. and Martha A. Dimond.
	Sept.	1	Norris, Thomas and Jane Ann Wise.
1857	June	16	Norris, Robert and Mary V. Russell.
	Nov.	19	Newman, Thomas A. and Mary E. Van Rywick.
1858	Sept.	28	Norris, John L. and Sarah Goldsborough.
	Dec.	27	Norris, Isadore C. and Rachel A. B. Ridgell.
1859	Feb.	15	Norris, James G. and Mary Elivia Norris.
1863	Feb.	2	Norris, William S. and Margaret E. Redmond.
1797	June	29	Owings, Joseph and Elizabeth Goodon.
1804	Feb.	29	Owens, John and Dicandia Nowelly.
1806	Apr.	2	Owings, George and Susanna Greenwell.

1808	Jan. 4	Owings, Raphael and Elizabeth Long.
	July 27	Owins, Edward and Elizabeth Woodward.
1810	Jan. 12	Owings, John and Sarah Owings.
1812	Nov. 2	Ochler, Andrew and Eleanor Yates.
1813	Dec. 13	Owings, Robert and Teresia Wootten.
1816	June 25	Ochler, Andrew and Rose Ann Carberry.
	July 1	Owings, Alexander and Jane Weaklin.
1830	Apr. 12	Oliver, John and Maria Woodward.
	Dec. 28	Owings, Edward and Ann Rock.
1832	Dec. 31	Owens, Thomas and Eppy Owens.
1833	Oct. 7	Owens, John A. and Sarah Ann Ford.
	Dec. 25	Owens, James and Margaret Lurty.
1834	Feb. 11	Owings, Hanson and Eliza Adams.
1835	Jan. 6	Owens, Alexander and Maria Wheatley.
1837	June 24	Owens, Hilery and Mary M. Owens.
1840	Jan. 8	Owings, Calvert and Priscilla Pilkinton.
1844	July 10	Owens, Robert and Susan Owens.
1846	July 26	Owens, Josiah and Catherine Redman.
1852	Mch. 6	Owens, Raphael M. and Elizabeth Long.
1855	Feb. 14	Owins, James and Sarah Ann Barber.
	17	Owins, Charles and Maria Long.
1858	Feb. 3	Owens, Wm. Edwd. and Henrietta Dyer.
1860	Mch. 12	Owins, Raphael M. and Jane Rebecca Owins.
1861	Feb. 9	Owens, Samuel and Sarah Burroughs.
1794	Oct. 20	Pain, John and Dorothy Drury.
1795	Mch. 9	Plater, George and Cecelia B. Bond.
	Dec. 27	Pilkinton, Uriah and Lydia Stone.
1796	Nov. 21	Peake, Raphael and Ann S. Norris.
1797	Nov. 6	Peacock, Zach. and Elizabeth Joy.
1798	Mch. 22	Plater, George and Elizabeth Somervill.
	Oct. 20	Payn, John and Mary Smith.
1799	Feb. 11	Price, John and Jane Sanner.
1800	July 4	Payne, Joseph and Sarah Beard.
1801	Jan. 6	Ponole, Henry and Milly Greenwell.
1802	Jan. 3	Peack, Joseph and Elizabeth McGee.
	Mch. 24	Perry, William and Appelonia Brown.
	May 22	Payne, Richd. and Catherine Spalding.
	July 26	Price, Jeremiah and Ann Watherton.
1803	Feb. 1	Paul, Sharman and Lydia Carpenter.
1804	Feb. 11	Peacock, Zazhariah and Jane Drury.
	Dec. 31	Price, Archld. and Sarah Hebb.
1805	Jan. 7	Pilkinton, Lewis and Nancy Thompson.

1805	Mch. 2	Price, John and Susanna Maryman.
1806	Apr. 26	Powell, Philip and Judy Norris.
	Aug. 28	Peake, Stephen and Teresia Hayden.
	Oct. 10	Pembroke, Thomas C. and Winefred Dunbar.
	Dec. 20	Peacock, Paul and Dorothy Magill.
	25	Pilkinton, Joseph and Mary Ann Thompson.
1807	Apr. 7	Price, Archibald and Ann Hammett.
	May 20	Pollard, Robert and Agnes Butter.
	Dec. 25	Price, Abraham and Frances Barnhouse.
1808	Jan. 9	Payne, Thomas and Catherine Wildman.
1809	Mch. 7	Penn, William and Clara Tarlton.
	May 20	Potter, Nathaniel and Henrietta M. Ford.
	Sept. 30	Parsons, John and Sarah Gardiner.
	Nov. 6	Pembroke, Thomas and Mary McKay.
1811	Oct. 19	Peake, Ignatius and Elizabeth Millard.
1812	Mch. 25	Patridge, Aaron and Maria Jenkins.
1813	Feb. 6	Pearson, William and Margaret Garner.
	Oct. 25	Peacock, Zachariah and Elizabeth Norriss.
1814	May 17	Powell, James and Susanna Curry.
	Dec. 30	Petherton, Joseph and Winefred Brown.
1815	Nov. 25	Peak, Gustavus and Catherine Cecil.
1816	Apr. 26	Payne, Ignatius and Susanna Thompson.
1817	Jan. 21	Peake, Peter and Mary Wootton.
	July 11	Price, Wm. P. and Ann White.
1818	Jan. 6	Peake, Wilfred and Alley Hayden.
	Nov. 3	Plater, Jno. R. Jr. and Ann E. Plater.
1819	Jan. 17	Pilkinton, Ignatius.
	17	Pilkinton, John and Elizabeth Peacock.
	May 28	Posey, Charles and Henrietta M. Shaw.
1820	Nov. 21	Peake, John and Eleanor Bean.
1821	May 29	Pilkinton, William and Eleanor Mattingly.
1823	Mch. 1	Power, Isaac Newton and Louise Bennett.
	Dec. 23	Power, John and Eliza Lynch.
1824	Mch. 20	Posey, John and Elizabeth Shemwell.
	May 17	Parker, Joseph and Elizabeth R. Sothoron.
1826	Jan. 21	Posey, Thomas and Sarah C. Swann.
1827	Jan. 6	Peake, William and Eleanor Drury.
	8	Peacock, Sylvester and Ann E. Mills.
1828	Mch. 8	Peake, William and Dorothy Heard.
1829	Jan. 19	Pilkinton, Lewis and Elizabeth Thompson.
	20	Pain, Joseph and Elizabeth Saxton.
	Apr. 25	Penn, James and Chloe Wainright.

1829 Aug. 24 Powers, Thomas and Ann Redman.
1831 Jan. 22 Payne, Richard and Eleanor Carpenter.
Dec. 28 Pilkinton, John Lewis and Eleanor Thompson.
1832 Apr. 28 Pilkinton, John and Sidney Leigh.
Dec. 24 Peacock, Philip and Sarah M. Greenwell.
1833 Jan. 17 Paul, Charles and Margaret Bowes.
19 Price, John W. and Susan M. Milburn.
May 21 Posey, Harrison and Ellen Jane Turner.
June 4 Peake, Ignatius and Ann Fenwick.
1834 Jan. 7 Perry, John B. and Teresia Graves.
Feb. 6 Price, Benedict and Ann Morgan.
Apr. 3 Partridge, John and Juletta Edelen.
1835 Jan. 5 Pembroke, Benja. and Charlotte McKay.
Dec. 16 Price, William P. and Ann Maria Biscoe.
30 Pilkinton, Richard and Jane Ferroll.
1836 Jan. 4 Price, John and Elizabeth Haywood.
1837 Dec. 29 Price, William P. and Mary Richardson.
1838 Feb. 13 Payne, Richard and Jane Lee.
Aug. 17 Parsons, John and Elizabeth Leigh.
Oct. 16 Paul, Charles Jackson and Ann M. Bennett.
1839 Jan. 1 Payne, Thomas and Mary Howe.
22 Posey, Zachariah V. and Jane C. Hayden.
May 21 Pembroke, George W. and Ann R. Bean.
Nov. 11 Plowden, Edmd. I. and Charlotte Coad.
1840 Feb. 25 Paul, Charles J. and Savilla Adams.
July 10 Pembroke, Benjamin and Avaline Henning.
Sept. 22 Pegg, James and Fanny Davis.
1841 May 19 Powell, John and Rosa Owen.
24 Pilkinton, Joseph and Dolly Drury.
1844 Jan. 18 Posey, Thomas and Maria Scott.
Aug. 31 Powers, John M. and Joanna S. Crow.
1845 Oct. 16 Prout, Elias and Emeline Bennet.
1846 July 9 Peacock, Henry and Priscilla Jarboe.
22 Price, Archibald and Maria A. Armsworthy.
1847 Aug. 16 Payne, Cornelius and Ann M. Floyd.
Nov. 9 Paul, George E. and Matilda E. Watts.
Dec. 27 Penn, Manuel R. and Mary Wainright.
1849 Mch. 1 Pigman, Bene S. and Ann E. Gardiner.
13 Price, Nehemiah and Sarah J. White.
Dec. 17 Penn, Charles P. and Sophia Mattingly.
1850 July 22 Peake, Lewis R. and Mary S. Raley.
1851 Jan. 27 Price, Thomas B. and Julia A. Goldsborough.

1851 Apr. 21 Palmer, Samuel and Sarah E. Bell.
Nov. 25 Peake, John A. and Mary E. Hilton.
1852 Oct. 3 Peacock, James and Mary E. Clarke.
Dec. 13 Pilkerton, John H. and Eleanor Lacy.
1853 Mch. 28 Pilkinton, Edwd. L. and Jane Sharps.
1854 May 15 Pilkinton, James H. and Serena A. Bohanan.
1855 Jan. 22 Partridge, James A. and Mary F. Jackson.
July 29 Predham, Fleet W. and Miss Isabella B. Pierce.
Dec. 19 Posey, John W. and Judith M. Dyson.
1856 May 12 Payne, John L. and Jane C. Morgan.
13 Posey, James S. and Alice C. Moran.
Sept. 8 Pipseco, Luceon L. B. and Mary T. Rustin.
1857 Nov. 23 Peake, Richard S. and Mary Ann Hayden.
1858 Jan. 19 Peacock, Wm. H. and Mary C. Peacock.
Nov. 24 Pearson, Wm. H. and Mary Ellis.
1859 Mch. 1 Pilkinton, Frederick and Sally Ann Peacock.
Sept. 12 Pilkinton, Joseph and Bettie Ann Lacy.
1860 June 18 Peacock, Wm. Z. and Cecelia Ann Raley.
July 3 Paul, George E. and Priscilla Kirby.
1861 June 4 Potter, Samuel F. and Elizabeth A. Thomas.
1862 Aug. 26 Payne, John H. T. and Martha J. Brown.
1822 Jan. 8 Queen, John and Elizabeth Wootten.
1831 June 3 Quade, James and Cecelia Copsey.
1853 Mch. 21 Quade, Wm. T. and Margaret A. Pilkerton.
1854 May 20 Quade, James H. and Sarah A. Dean.
1856 Dec. 19 Quade, Charles Ll. and Mary Pilkinton.
1859 Aug. 1 Quade, Andrew J. and Dorothy Jarboe.
1860 Sept. 22 Quade, John and Julia Dean.
1795 Apr. 29 Rhynide, Jeremiah and Ann Bullock.
Oct. 17 Redman, John and Mary Greenwell.
Nov. 24 Raley, John and Eleanor Nelson.
1796 Oct. 17 Riley, Michael and Susanna French.
1797 Mch. 9 Rogers, George and Ann King.
May 1 Rhodes, Cornelius and Ann S. Mattingly.
June 3 Redman, John and Henry Greenwell.
Oct. 5 Reeder, George and Margaret Goldie.
1798 May 7 Russell, John B. and Nancy Milburn.
Nov. 28 Rhymn, Jeremiah and Nancy Holly.
1799 Feb. 25 Reintzel, Valentine and Mary Waughop.
June 21 Respess, John and Elizabeth Glasco.
Aug. 6 Richardson, Joseph and Delila Stanpast.
1800 Jan. 21 Rhodes, Igs. and Alina Greenwell.

1800 Dec. 17 Redman, Zachariah and Catherine Gibbons.
30 Rily, Bennet and Ann Brown.
1801 Jan. 19 Ridgell, Jonathan and Polly Davis.
19 Ratliff, James and Linde Goddard.
28 Rice, George and Elizabeth Doney.
Apr. 15 Rock, William and Margaret Dunahoo.
May 18 Richardson, Joseph and Dicandia Mackall.
Sept. 12 Rochester, Thomas and Ann Alice Taney.
28 Reeder, John and Ann Jones.
Dec. 15 Reeder, Henry and Clarissa McWilliams.
19 Rogers, Williams and Ann Johnson.
1802 Mch. 24 Reynolds, David and Luvesia Fowler.
1803 Jan. 10 Russell, Philip and Eleanor Woodward.
May 28 Raley, Zachariah and Ann Wilkinson.
Aug. 19 Redman, Benjamin and Hellen Bean.
Oct. 19 Rawlings, John and Susanna Howard.
Nov. 7 Roland, William and Elizabeth Masse.
1804 Jan. 13 Robertson, John and Sarah B. Sothoron.
16 Redman, George and Winefred Night.
Sept. 25 Reinzell, John and Elizabeth Waughop.
Dec. 30 Russell, William and Jane Russell.
1805 Jan. 7 Roch, John and Sarah Law.
June 15 Reeder, Robb D. and Helen Hebb.
1806 Feb. 6 Roch, James and Susa. Howard.
6 Reswick, Wm. and Nancy Thompson.
Dec. 9 Robertson, Wm. and Ann Thomas.
1807 June 13 Raley, Jno. (of John) and Elefred Drury.
Oct. 31 Rhodes, Cornelius and Margaret Clarke.
1808 Jan. 2 Rockhill, Joseph and Susa. Spalding.
20 Reeves, William and Susa. Wheeler.
Dec. 31 Richardson, Charles and Ann Heikmon.
1809 Dec. 18 Reeder, James and Susanna Loche.
1810 Jan. 27 Russell, Jeremiah and Susann Hayden.
Nov. 13 Reeder, Thomas and Maria Mills.
Dec. 29 Russell, Ignatius and Jane Mattingly.
1812 Jan. 18 Robertson, Henry B. and Levina Loker.
Dec. 4 Roberts, Charles and Ann Loker.
5 Reeder, William and Maria Hebb.
1813 Feb. 24 Ridgely, Wm. G. and Sophia Plater.
Aug. 10 Russell, Charles and Monica French.
1815 Mch. 7 Redman, Zachariah and Panny Mattingly.
1816 Jan. 15 Railey, Benedict and Ann Combs.

1816	Feb. 24	Russell, William and Sarah Cahay.
	Mch. 11	Redmond, Thomas and Ann Bean.
	July 27	Richardson, Wm. and Elizabeth Cole.
1817	Apr. 9	Reevis, Thomas and Elizabeth Watson.
1818	May 6	Ryon, Nicholas and Susanna Boulton.
	July 25	Riggs, Daniel and Elizabeth Minor.
	Dec. 13	Rice, Edmund and Martha Simms.
1819	Feb. 2	Russell, Lewis and Mary Graves.
	June 12	Reeder, Richard and Maria Biscoe.
	Nov. 22	Radford, John and Monica Russell.
1822	Feb. 10	Railey, Ignatius and Dorothy Jay.
	Oct. 5	Railey, Thomas B. and Rebecca G. S. Key.
	Dec. 24	Richardson, Wm. and Darcus Bean.
1823	May 3	Rigell, Thomas R. and Elizabeth R. Adams.
1824	Jan. 13	Railey, Wm. and Mary Morgan.
	26	Reeves, Thomas W. and Ann Wood.
	Oct. 4	Raley, Charles and Mary D. Taylor.
	Dec. 11	Roach, James W. and Caroline Combs.
1826	Dec. 26	Russell, Benedict and Elizabeth Gibson.
1827	Dec. 28	Raley, John and Eleanor Thompson.
1828	Feb. 12	Raley, John B. and Maria Thompson.
	Nov. 4	Roach, Edward N. and Celestia Combs.
	Dec. 27	Redman, William and Ann Floyd.
1829	Jan. 12	Russell, Jeremiah and Eliza Graves.
	Apr. 17	Rencher, Richard M. and Eleanor Smoot.
	July 6	Reeves, Thomas C. and Mary E. Edwards.
	Nov. 16	Ridgell, Uriah and Priscilla Norriss.
	Dec. 21	Russell, Ignatius and Elizabeth Watson.
1830	Jan. 6	Rock, John and Ann Wheeler.
1831	Feb. 1	Raley, John L. and Sarah Weaklin.
	Oct. 3	Raley, Zachariah and Elizabeth Dick.
1832	Apr. 23	Russell, John B. and Mary Tarlton.
	Dec. 29	Russell, Joseph and Elizabeth Eliza Roch.
1833	Jan. 2	Russell, Thomas and Elizabeth Combs.
	14	Raley, William and Maria Shirkley.
	21	Rock, John and Margaret Kitchens.
	28	Russell, Charles A. and Jane L. Hayden.
	July 20	Ridgell, Wm. H. and Elizabeth Cole.
1834	Jan. 13	Russell, Jerome and Susan Rock.
	27	Rock, Charles and Susan Brantzell.
	Feb. 4	Russell, James A. and Mary Eliza. Jarboe.
	Apr. 23	Raley, John and Ann Thompson.

1834 Sept. 15 Rogers, William and Juliet Carroll.
1835 Jan. 20 Raley, William A. and Mary Goodwin.
Dec. 31 Ridgell, Thomas R. and Ann Maria Greenwell.
1836 Jan. 19 Russell, Ignatius and Ruth Ann Haney.
19 Russell, Zachariah and Ann M. Hayden.
1837 Aug. 26 Reeder, Richd. H. and Elizabeth Barber.
1838 Jan. 8 Ridgell, James and Mary Norriss.
9 Raley, Henry S. and Attaway Furgison.
Mch. 8 Redman, Constantius B. and Catherine Lynch.
Dec. 17 Rock, George and Ann Hall.
1839 Jan. 12 Raley, Francis and Elizabeth Spalding.
Apr. 9 Rocke, James and Jane Anderson.
July 23 Raley, Thomas and Lucinda Burroughs.
1840 Jan. 7 Richards, Wm. H. and Eliza. H. Gilmore.
15 Russell, John B. and Ruth Ann Lawrence.
Mch. 5 Russell, George L. and Sarah J. Spalding.
May 28 Russell, Jeremiah and Mary Copsey.
1843 June 19 Redman, James B. and Elizabeth E. Wise.
1844 Jan. 2 Russell, Joseph H. and Cath. Yates.
9 Railey, James W. and Sophia Cissell.
1845 Mch. 3 Rowe, Henry and Jane Saunders.
Dec. 16 Russell, William T. and Rosetta Guy.
1846 Jan. 13 Russell, James M. and Mary Ann Thompson.
1847 Nov. 17 Ridgell, Thomas R. and Ann M. Lomax.
1848 Feb. 28 Russell, Ramond E. and Mary C. Yates.
Apr. 20 Ross, Aaron and Ann R. Drury.
1849 Feb. 10 Russell, Joseph and Cath. Owens.
Oct. 9 Redman, John and Jane Gatton.
Dec. 22 Redman, John F. and Mary J. Norris.
1850 July 26 Radford, John F. and Jane M. Drury.
Sept. 10 Russell, Joseph and Sarah Jane Hall.
1851 Jan. 16 Redmond, Thomas H. and Matilda Dyer.
1852 Oct. 26 Richardson, Geo. W. and Mary E. Yates.
Dec. 9 Robertson, Walter H. and Sarah Anna E. Key.
1853 Sept. 24 Russell, Redmond and Ann E. Bowles.
Nov. 8 Redman, Jefferson J. and Mary S. Lumpkins.
Dec. 12 Russell, John B. and Jane H. Martin.
26 Russell, Jas. H. and Mary J. Stone.
1854 Jan. 30 Reeder, Wm. T. A. and Elizabeth S. Fowler.
Oct. 2 Russell, Wm. H. and Ann Maria Nevitt.
Dec. 23 Redman, James B. and Angeline Hammett.
1856 Jan. 15 Russell, Wm. L. and Mary Jane Graves.

1856	Jan.	26	Raley, Richard T. and Ann Maria Gibson.
		28	Raley, Wm. H. and Mary C. Burroughs.
	Feb.	5	Redman, Jno. F. and Mary Downs.
	May	5	Russell, Jno. A. and Margaret E. Graves.
	Sept.	18	Raley, John B. and Mrs. Jane Radford.
	Nov.	8	Russell, John B. and Jane Ann Lathrum.
1857	June	9	Railey, Charles J. and Jane H. Bean.
	Dec.	28	Rigell, Ignatius and Martha Long.
1858	Jan.	21	Redman, Alex. and Maria A. Norris.
1859	Jan.	10	Raley, Ignatius R. and Margaret L. Bond.
	Apr.	4	Roberson, Hoskins H. and Eliza. A. Mitchell.
	Aug.	20	Russell, John B. and Eleanor Ellis.
1860	Feb.	11	Russell, Joseph E. and Lucilla Cheseldine.
	June	8	Robinson, J. J. and Victoria Morgan.
		20	Ryce, Thomas S. and Elizabeth Ching.
		28	Ruark, George T. and Zora B. Ryce.
	Oct.	15	Reeves, J. R. T. and Elizabeth E. Hayden.
	Dec.	26	Raley, John S. and Jane E. Davis.
1861	Jan.	22	Reintzell, John D. and Viletta G. Armstrong.
	Feb.	4	Russell, John F. and Susan A. Ellis.
	July	23	Russell, Edward and Laurel Ann Gatton.
	Oct.	21	Roach, James and Celestia Smith.
1862	Feb.	24	Raley, J. W. and Mary J. Mattingly.
1863	Feb.	4	Rowe, Charles H. and Chloe E. Wainright.
	Mch.	3	Rozell, Ennels and Maggie L. Thomas.
	July	20	Reed, Wm. R. Washington and Mrs. Ann F. Moore.
		29	Read, Stacy B. and Annie E. Cox.
	Aug.	19	Radford, Robert and Mary A. Hazell.
	Oct.	27	Ridgell, Francis and Mary F. Wise.
1794	Dec.	30	Smith, James and Eliza Lake.
1795	Jan.	16	Simms, Anthony and Eliza Fenwick.
	Feb.	3	Smith, Henry, A. and Dicandia S. Ireland.
	Mch.	9	Smith, John (of Jno.) and Mary Langley.
	June	2	Snow, Charles C. and Eliz. H. Sabery.
	July	11	Shermantine, James and Ann Sword.
		27	Spalding, John and Nancy Bright.
	Dec.	14	Smoot, Revil Charles and Ann Everton.
1796	Jan.	—	Smith, William and Margaret Williams.
	Nov.	11	Sothoron, Henry and Elizabeth Marburg.
	Dec.	28	Stone, John and Mary Goddard.
1797	Feb.	15	Spalding, Bennett and Mary French.
	June	7	Smith, Edward and Elizabeth Combs.

1797	Aug.	12	Spalding, Michael and Susanna Cullins.
	Sept.	16	Spalding, Henry A. and Barbara Abell.
	Nov.	30	Smith, Elwily and Nancy Millard.
1798	Apr.	19	Smith, Bartholomew and Ann Biscoe.
	June	4	Smith, Francis and Jane Heard.
	Sept.	12	Suttle, Francis and Eleanor Drury.
	Oct.	17	Smith, Jno. (of Tho.) and Ann Roach.
	Dec.	29	Stone, Charles and Rebecca Jarboe.
1799	Mch.	28	Sothoron, Zachariah and Margaret Burroughs.
	June	11	Smoot, Charles and Hariet Sothoron.
	Dec.	16	Sweney, Wm. and Jane Turner.
		28	Spalding, Zachariah and Eleanor Abell.
1800	Jan.	4	Smith, Elias and Ann Stone.
	Feb.	11	Sanner, Mathias and Anna Scissell.
	Mch.	31	Smith, John and Mary Walker.
	Apr.	14	Sacton, Bennet and Henry Baily.
	June	22	Shircliff, Francis E. and Clara Walker.
	Aug.	9	Suttle, Ignatius and Ann Winsatt.
	Dec.	29	Smith, James and Ann Price.
1801	June	1	Sothoron, Henry, and Dorothy B. Hawkins.
1803	July	17	Simms, John and Elizabeth Brooks)
	Aug.	2	Spricer, Aaron and Elizabeth Watts.
	Sept.	2	Soot, Jno. H. and Elizabeth Cawood.
	Dec.	19	Smith, Thomas and Ann Doxey.
1804	Feb.	10	Stone, Francis and Myma Lake.
	Nov.	25	Simms, Anthony Jr. and Sarah Brooke.
	Dec.	30	Sacton, Bennet and Mary Morgan.
1805	Jan.	16	Scott, William and Elizabeth Suit.
		19	Stone, John B. and Elizabeth Thompson.
	Dec.	5	Sylance, Thomas and Rebecca Taylor.
1806	Jan.	21	Sword, Urich and Ann Welch.
	Feb.	3	Sacton, Joseph and Eleanor Hayden.
	June	10	Simms, Francis and Teresa Brooke,
	Aug.	22	Smith, Stephen M. and Ann Atwood.
1807	Jan.	27	Smith, Barton and Eleanor Beane.
	Feb.	7	Spalding, Edwd. and Mary C. Radford.
	Mch.	28	Stone, John B. and Jane Stone.
	Apr.	14	Smith, Job and Ann King.
	Dec.	28	Sanderson, Robt. and Brittania Price.
1808	Jan.	4	Stone, Joseph and Harriet Tabbs.
	Feb.	11	Smoot, William and Elizabeth Loker.
	Apr.	15	Scott, Samuel and Mary Biscoe.

1808	Sept.	8	Smith, James and Cecelia Clarke.
	Dec.	13	Sword, John and Sarah Boult.
1809	Apr.	5	Smith, William and Ann Reswick.
		8	Sanner, Joseph and Elizabeth Smith.
	July	7	Starr, Westley, and Philippe Corum.
	Oct.	31	Sothoron, John and Elizabeth A. Briscoe.
1810	Feb.	9	Spalding, Zachar. and Cecelia Reswick.
	July	23	Smith, Lewis and Sarah Clarke.
	Nov.	4	Scott, William B. and Ann Holton.
1811	Jan.	29	Spalding, Clement and Eleanor Alvey.
	Oct.	27	Smith, Robert and Letticea Smith.
1812	June	13	Swann, James and Mary Greenwell.
1813	Jan.	5	Shanks, Thos. and Matilda Blakistone.
		9	St. Clair, George and Sarah Barber.
		12	Slarvin, William and Ann Bean.
		28	Smith, John and Ann Thomas.)
	June	15	Scott, Henry and Dorothy Thompson.
		24	Smith, Basil and Mary Eleanor Mitchell.
1814	Jan.	29	Stone, Joshua and Catherine Stone.
	Apr.	9	Smith, Richard and Mary Fowler.
		29	Spalding, Miel and Elizabeth Stone.
	July	26	Spalding, Clement and Maria Ford.
	Oct.	10	Smith, Charles and Mary Drury.
1815	Feb.	19	Saxton, Joseph (black) and Mary Wheally (black.)
	Sept.	2	Spalding, Edwd. and Catherine B. Smith.
	Oct.	27	Smith, Thomas and Margaret Biscoe.
	Dec.	20	Smith, Charles and Sarah Jefferies.
1816	Jan.	15	Sanner, William and Elizabeth Nowell.
	Apr.	13	Scott, James and Elizabeth Edwards.
		22	Shadrick, John and Rebecca Nottingham.
	Oct.	1	Sanner, Wm. and Ann Hutchin.
		28	Scott, Edward and Henrietta Anderson.
1817	Feb.	10	Slye, George and Mary Barber.
	Sept.	23	Suit, Samuel and Lydia Clarke.
1818	Jan.	27	Stone, Joseph and Maria Shanks.
	Apr.	27	Suit, Nathaniel and Ann Gatton.
	Dec.	29	Sanner, Joseph and Mary Dunbar.
1819	Apr.	24	Spalding, Edward and Mary Floyd.
	July	31	Sanner, Thomas and Ann Newton.
	Sept.	10	Sanner, Jeremiah and Mary Bohnan.
		18	Smith, Thomas and Mary Briscoe.
		29	Spalding, Benedict and Alatha Greenwell.

1819 Dec. 28 Spalding, Edward and Ann Baley.
1820 Feb. 12 Swann, James and Ann Edwards.
14 Stone, James and Juda Wootton.
Aug. 8 Sanner, John Jr. and Margaret Bohanan.
1821 Jan. 14 Stone, John and Ann Stone.
27 Shermantine, John and Susanna Wootten.
Mch. 12 Spalding, Francis and Ann Leach.
Apr. 2 Spalding, Michael and Eliza. Pilkinton.
July 2 Simson, Marcellus and Mary Drury.
Nov. 13 Sanner, Joseph and Mary Taylor.
Dec. 17 Shemwell, Joseph Jr. and Henrietta Biscoe.
1823 Apr. 5 Scott, Samuel and Sarah Tippett.
May 5 Smith, Thomas and Ann Zachary.
Oct. 28 Stonestreet, Nicholas and Ann C. Harris.
Dec. 23 Sothoron, Richard C. and Eliza. Woodburn.
1824 Jan. 27 Spalding, Thomas and Ann Johnston.
Apr. 19 Sutton, Vincent and Mary Bean.
June 15 Shadrick, Thomas and Atteway Guyther.
29 Suit, Samuel and Elspit Jones.
Oct. 12 Smith, William L. and Ann Leigh.
1825 Jan. 11 Simms, Joseph and Sarah Mattingly.
Jan. 24 Simms, John and Teresia Fenwick.
24 Sanner, John and Caroline Drury.
25 Sanner, John D. and Caroline Drury.
June 9 Stone, Joseph and Jane E. Smith.
1826 Jan. 3 Shaw, Charles T. and Rachell Raymond.
6 Stone, Richd. of D. and Mary Bailey.
Aug. 24 Saxton, James and Hannah Kerrens.
Dec. 26 Suit, Kellity and Jane Reeves.
1827 Jan. 18 Smith, Aaron and Ann Langley.
Mch. 17 Stephen, Thomas and Mary Kilgour.
1828 Jan. 3 Stone, William H. and Mary Wise.
11 Smith, Job and Beatrix Redman.
14 Silence, Abell and Teresia Combs.
29 Suit, Thomas A. R. and Emeline Buckler.
Feb. 5 Shanks, Morris and Elizabeth E. Thompson.
July 22 Simms, Joseph and Ann Craig.
1829 May 5 Sutton, James D. and Elizabeth Biscoe.
June 15 Shenwell, James and Caroline Briscoe.
Oct. 20 Swann, Horace D. and Elizabeth Egerton.
1830 Jan. 21 Smith, Richard and Anna H. Key.
Apr. 13 Staniste, Henry and Nancy Silence.

1830	Apr.	19	Sewell, George, free Blk. and Jane Stone.
	Oct.	5	Sothoron, William H. and Susanna Barber.
	Nov.	3	Shelton, Geo. W. and Frances A. Boughton.
	Dec.	20	Swann, Gerard C. and Eleanor Harrison.
1831	Feb.	5	Scott, William and Sarah Ann Thompson.
		8	Spalding, Samuel and Eliza Abell.
	June	13	Smith, William and Mary Moore.
	June	14	Stone, Bennet and Mary Maryman.
1832	Jan.	12	Smith, Rev. John and Susan Hewitt.
	Feb.	14	Simms, John F. and Mary Ann Greenwell.
	June	4	Suit, Calvert and Eliza Scott.
		23	Sword, Henry and Margaret Thomas.
	Sept.	17	Sutton, Samuel and Eleanor Ann Taylor.
	Dec.	31	Smith, Francis and Ann Martin.
1833	Mch.	11	Smith, Joseph and Eliza Owings.
	May	30	St. Clair, William and Maria Barber.
1834	Oct.	31	Saunders, James H. and Rachael Ann Combs.
1835	Jan.	26	Stone, Joseph and Mary Jane Leigh.
	Feb.	17	Spalding, Sylvester and Mary Ann Tennison.
	May	19	Shanks, Peregrine and Rebecca J. Blakistone.
	June	9	Stone, John and Ann Eliza Ford.
	July	4	Stone, John and Susanna Goddard.
	Nov.	16	Smith, Peter P. and Jane Smith.
		23	Stone, Samuel and Eliza Ann Cryer.
1836	Jan.	21	Scott, James T. and Maria J. Ellis.
	June	21	Smith, William and Elizabeth A. Gatton.
1837	Feb.	25	Swann, Llewellen and Catherine Herbert.
	Sept.	12	Sherburn, Wm. L. and Jane Ann Miles.
1838	Feb.	26	Stone, Peter H. and Jane E. Greenwell.
	Apr.	16	Sanner, Samuel A. and Sarah Ann Tea.
	May	15	Stone, Thomas I. and Louisa F. Ford.
	Aug.	31	Scott, Archibald and Sarah Ann Pollard.
1839	Feb.	12	Shermantine, Bened. and Eliza Ann Cullumber.
	Nov.	5	Stone, Matthew A. and Eliza. L. Davis.
1840	Nov.	25	Sothoron, Jno. T. H. or Margaret Hodges.
1841	Jan.	30	Stone, Wm. H. and Sarah Thompson.
	Apr.	20	Spencer, Thomas O. and Catherine M. Hammett.
	June	28	Shermantine, Wm. and Harriott Wootten.
	July	17	Sinclair, John and Susan Cartwright.
	Dec.	7	Shaw, Charles A. F. and Mary L. Swann.
		10	Sanner, James H. and Susan N. Dunbar.
1842	Apr.	4	Spalding, Francis and Caroline Alvey.

1842	Apr. 12	Sanders, James H. and Pamelia Conklin.
	Dec. 15	Spalding, Clement and Eliza. Harding.
1843	May 26	Slye, Thomas B. and Amelia Gwinn.
1844	June 11	Shurkley, John I. and Alice O. Jarboe.
	July 22	Sutton, James D. and Eleanor Hebb.
1845	Jan. 14	Spalding, Sylvester and Hellen Davis.
	Aug. —	Shaw, Charles F. and Margaret P. Estep.
	Sept. 15	St. Clair, Joseph and Eliza. C. Herbert.
1846	June 25	Sanner, Thomas and Mary Buckler.
1847	Jan. 26	Stone, John H. and Ellen C. Abell.
	Feb. 15	Saxton, Robert and Eliza Cawood.
	Apr. 26	Shemwell, Joseph and Mary Barber.
	June 29	Saxton, George and Sarah A. Fowler.
	Sept. 3	Sanner, Abel, and Serena A. Sanner.
	Oct. 21	Spalding, Geo. I. and Margaret Willis.
	Dec. 16	Sothoron, Jno. T. H. and Virginia Sutton.
1848	Jan. 10	Sinclair, John and Ann E. Downs.
	Feb. 19	Sothoron, Zach. H. and Martha Lawrence.
	Apr. 24	Swann, Benja. H. and Lucinda J. Mattingly.
1849	Feb. 12	Stewart, William and Susan Hayden.
	Apr. 16	Scott, William and Mary J. Suit.
	Dec. 29	Sinclair, John and Ann Bowling.
1850	Sept. 6	Sanner, Thomas and Ann Taylor.
	Dec. 31	Stone, Edward F. and Joanah L. Peacock.
	31	Scott, James and Catherine Harding.
1851	Feb. 24	Stone, Marcellus J. and Eliza. L. Jarboe.
	Sept. 12	Suit, Thomas R. and Sarah Ann Anderson.
	Nov. 25	Sutton, Andrew J. and Mary A. Crane.
	Dec. 2	Steadman, Jas. and Mary A. Long.
1852	Feb. 10	Stone, Joseph E. and Mary E. Mattingly.
	June 19	Stone, Francis and Mary Abell.
1853	Apr. 26	Smith, John C. and Semour E. Elliott.
	Dec. 6	Sutton, Robert B. and Julia A. M. Crane.
	17	Swann, Jonathan W. and Mary E. Long.
1854	Apr. 15	Stone, John F. and Martha E. Pilkinton.
	July 5	Smith, George H. and Mary E. Abell.
1855	Jan. 8	Stone, George and Rosa Lathum.
	16	Stone, Hilery J. and Maria L. Peacock.
	Feb. 13	Spalding, James B. and Jane A. Mattingly.
	Aug. 20	Smith, Clement B. and Olivia Kerby.
1856	Jan. 21	Scott, William and Eliza Greenfield.
	Mch. 10	Sanders, John F. and Mary S. Howard.

1856 May 22 Smith, Wm. H. and Georganna Downs.
24 Stone, John F. and Louiza Brown.
1857 July 7 Smith, James and Nannie O. Key.
Nov. 10 Sothoron, Wm. H. and Eliza. Ann Burroughs.
24 Soper, Andrew J. and Mary E. Brown.
1858 Jan. 4 Sinclair, Francis M. and Mary E. Wingate.
4 Smith, Lewis and Mary J. Bailey.
Feb. 6 Soper, Alfred S. and Eliza. A. Cusick.
June 1 Spalding, Zachariah T. and Mary A. Floyd.
July 20 Shanks, Robt. M. and Mary A. Blakistone.
Dec. 7 Slattery, J. T. and Mary E. Bond.
1859 Jan. 15 Scott, Thomas and Mary Howard.
25 Spalding, F. F. and Regena H. Simms.
1860 Jan. 17 Swann, Philip M. and Georgeanna T. Mattingly.
27 Shadrick, John and Mary R. Holton.
Apr. 10 Stone, Cornelius J. and Emily Jarboe.
1861 Apr. 1 Stout, Lansing and Susan C. Plowden.
22 Saunders, Wm. W. and Mary E. Sanner.
Sept. 11 Smith, Peter B. and Mary Heard.
Nov. 26 Slye, G. Robb and Georgeanna Maddox.
Dec. 11 Springer, Thomas H. and Mary Virginia McKay.
1862 May 19 Stone, Wm. M. V. and Mary Wilkinson.
Aug. 11 Sinclair, Geo. W. and E. A. Smith.
1863 Dec. 7 Sothoron, Levin J. and Lydia R. Canter.
1794 Nov. 4 Thomas, Roger and Susanna Hazle.
Dec. 2 Thompson, Ignatius and Mary Steale.
31 Turner, Hezekiah and Eleanor Turner.
1795 Jan. 8 Tippett, Henry and Ann Bennett.
13 Taylor, John and Mary Price.
July 30 Travers, William and Sally Harding.
Nov. 20 Thompson, Arthur and Ann Carberry.
1796 Aug. 30 Tarlton, Stephen and Catherine Hammett.
Dec. 23 Thompson, Ignatius and Lynda Stone.
31 Thompson, John B. and Susanna Norris.
1797 Apr. 17 Tippett, Benja. and Eleanor Hayden.
July 10 Theobald, Samuel and Sarah Doxey.
Sept. 28 Templeman, Augustine and Susanna Higgason.
Dec. 5 Turner, Henry and Eleanor Maddox.
1798 Jan. 3 Tear, Barton and Rebecca Bennett.
Feb. 1 Thompson, Robert and Eliza. Hayden.
Apr. 20 Thompson, Wm. and Lydia Hazle.
July 3 Thackery, Robert and Margaret Gill.

1798	Aug.	16	Taylor, Ignatius and Ann Wise.
		16	Taylor, Elkanah and Eleanor Wise.
	Nov.	24	Taylor, Caleb and Eleanor Headley.
1799	Feb.	13	Thompson, George and Elizabeth Monarch.
		15	Tabbs, George and Lucretia Hopewell.
	Mch.	19	Taylor, Jenifer and Elizabeth Milburn.
	Aug.	18	Tarlton, Elijah and Ann Greenwell.
	Sept.	24	Travers, Thos. A. and Alcey R. Neale.
	Dec.	20	Tippet, Jonah and Susanna Davis.
1800	Mch.	23	Thompson, Wm. and Eleanor Long.
	July	24	Thompson, Richard and Eliza. Kirk.
	Nov.	17	Tippett, John D. and Susannah Hayden.
		18	Turner, Thomas and Mary Coad.
1801	Dec.	17	Tippett, Walter and Margaret Lee.
1802	Jan.	7	Thompson, Saml. and Dorothy Brewer.
	Mch.	10	Tippett, Zachariah and Sophia Tippett.
	Apr.	10	Thomas, Edward and Barbara Corum.
	June	21	Tanner, Jonathan and Frances Dunbar.
	Nov.	27	Thompson, John and Ann Walker.
1803	May	18	Thompson, Geo. and Mary Hackett.
	July	5	Tee, Lomack and Ann Dunbar.
	Aug.	22	Thompson, Joseph and Eliza. Norriss.
	Oct.	11	Thompson, John W. and Eliza. Thompson.
	Dec.	28	Tyler, Thomas and Dorothy Bright.
1804	Feb.	28	Taylor, George and Ann Fenwick.
	Mch.	19	Thompson, James and Jennet Wherrett.
	May	19	Thomas, Zacha. and Mary Eden.
	Dec.	22	Tarlton, Robert and Jane Mills.
		26	Thompson, Joshua and Catherine Edley.
1805	Feb.	15	Tarlton, James and Sarah Chiverel.
	June	1	Tildray, Samuel and Alsie Cottrel.
	Aug.	28	Thomas, Wm. Dr. and Rachael King.
	Oct.	25	Tarlton, Moses and Ann Fish.
	Dec.	21	Thompson, James and Winefred Drury.
		27	Thompson, John B. and Ann Staha Wathen.
		27	Thompson, Charles and Susa. Wheeler.
1806	Feb.	15	Tubbs, Benjamin and Eleanor Aisquith.
	July	21	Thompson, John and Louisa Bath.
	Nov.	20	Thomas, John and Mary Dorson.
1807	Jan.	21	Thompson, Joseph and Rachel Waughop.
	Apr.	27	True, Joseph E. and Sarah Suit.
	Aug.	20	Thomas, Edward and Clariey Thompson.

1807	Sept.	2	Tarlton, Robert and Elizabeth Cox.
1808	Jan.	7	Thompson, James and Eleanor Joy.
		16	Tarlton, Moses and Margaret Norris.
		25	Thomas, Doc. James and Eliza Courts.
		30	Tarlton, Elijah and Ann Milburn.
	June	22	Thomas, Elisha and Eliza Smoot.
	July	23	Thompson, Jesse and Mary How.
1809	Dec.	19	Tippett, John and Mary Fergurson.
1810	Jan.	1	Thompson, John and Mary Thompson.
	Mch.	24	Thompson, Wm. and Monica Walker.
	June	12	Thompson, Barzillai and Catherine Greenwell.
	Nov.	14	Turner, Edward and Margaret A. Cooke.
1811	Jan.	19	Turner, Charles and Teresia Alvey.
	Feb.	11	Thompson, Henry and Susanna Tippett.
	Feb.	23	True, James and Ann Thompson.
1812	Mch.	4	Travus, Nicholas and Mary Shamell.
		14	Turner, Jesse and Margaret Jordan.
		31	Thompson, Lewis and Eleanor Johnson.
	Dec.	16	Tippett, Thomas and Ann Stone.
		30	Tippett, Thos. and Mary Newton.
1813	Jan.	14	Tarlton, John and Margaret Blakistone.
	Apr.	27	Tarlton, Edmund and Teresia Bean.
	Aug.	28	Tarlton, George and Elizabeth Daffin.
1814	Jan.	10	True, John and Jane Thompson.
	Jan.	28	Tarlton, George and Mary Yates.
	Sept.	2	Thomas, Joseph and Darca White.
1815	Jan.	24	Thompson, Peter U. and Larience Dent.
	Apr.	17	Thompson, James and Charlotte Bennett.
	Aug.	31	Turner, Philip and Eliza. A. Bond.
	Oct.	23	Tippett, Thomas and Cath. Mattingly.
1816	May	1	Thompson, Thomas and Maria Peacock.
	Aug.	5	Thomas, William and Eliza. Tubman.
1817	Dec.	29	Tarlton, Dololph and Sarah Combs.
1818	Jan.	23	Thompson, Charles and Rebecca Green.
	Feb.	17	Turner, James and Priscilla Thornton.
	Mch.	10	Teal, George and Laurence Thornton.
		26	Tarlton, Basil and Mary A. A. Norriss.
		27	Tyer, John and Susanna Ferroll.
		31	Taylor, George and Jane Fenwick.
	Nov.	17	Thompson, Barza. and Mary Williams.
	Dec.	10	Thompson, Henry and Elizabeth Clarke.
1819	Feb.	9	Thompson, Joshua and Dorothy Wathen.

1819 July 24 Tippett, Thomas and Ann True.
Aug. 10 Thompson, John and Sarah Wimsatt.
Dec. 26 Teal, George and Eliza Corum.
1820 Jan. 10 Thompson, Ignatius and Kitty Thompson.
Feb. 8 Thompson, Rapl. and Mary McGee.
Apr. 11 Thompson, James and Ann Coad.
Aug. 28 Thompson, John and Eleanor McKay.
Nov. 7 Tennison, John and Matilda Greenwell.
1821 Feb. 12 Thomas, Henry and Cath. Butler.
June 14 Turner, Hatch and Eliza Hammett.
Dec. 10 Turner, Edward and Sarah Ann Raymond.
1822 Feb. 8 Tippett, Robert and Mary Allston.
1823 Mch. 5 Thompson, Ralphl. F. and Ann Blair.
1824 July 19 Thompson, James and Eliza J. Long.
Nov. 19 Tarlton, George and Julia Ann Edwards.
1825 Jan. 1 Tippett, Samuel and Margaret Smith.
May 30 Tippett, John and Susan Tippett.
Oct. 17 Thompson, Chas. and Mary Cheseldine.
1826 Jan. 19 Thompson, Aloysius and Eleanor Mareman.
Apr. 12 Thompson, James and Hannah Lacey.
Nov. 27 Thompson, Clement and Eliza Powers.
Dec. 20 Tippett, George and Mary E. Burrage.
1827 Jan. 6 Tippett, Peregrine and Susan Leigh.
Feb. 20 Thompson, Charles and Lucretia Spalding.
Nov. 27 Thompson, Uriah and Clara Thompson.
Dec. 26 Thompson, George and Sybill B. Garner.
1828 Jan. 14 Taylor, Henry and Eliza L. Bohanan.
Feb. 12 Thompson, George and Susan Knott.
Apr. 8 Thomas, Dr. Wm. and Eliza. Lansdale.
Nov. 29 Tysix, William and Rebecca Farr.
Dec. 29 Taylor, Jeremiah and Susanna Bennett.
1829 Feb. 28 Thompson, Ignatius and Eleanor Dean.
May 2 Thomas, George and Ann Smith.
14 Tippett, Walter and Maria Hardesty.
June 9 Thompson, Thomas and Eliza Saxton.
Nov. 26 Thompson, Benedict and Mary Brown.
1830 Jan. 12 Thomas, Richard and Celia Butler.
May 4 Taylor, Wm. M. and Sarah E. Talton.
Aug. 3 Tennison, Robert and Frances Dunbar.
Nov. 23 Thomas, Moses and Ann Eliza Cullison,
Dec. 24 Tippett, Uriah and Mary Welch.
1831 Feb. 9 Thompson, George and Eliza. Cusick.

1831	Dec.	22	Taylor, James and Nancy Wallas.
		30	Tarlton, Barzillai and Eliza Price.
1832	Feb.	7	Tippett, Philip D. and Ann Neale.
		14	Taylor, Wm. B. and Eleanor Guyther.
		20	Tippett, Jonathan and Fanny Thomas.
	July	18	Thomas, Thomas C. and Mary Thomas.
	Aug.	6	Thompson, John B. and Matilda Higgs.
	Oct.	8	Tippett, Zach. H. and Jane Heard.
1834	Apr.	18	Thomas, Jonathan and Ann E. White.
	June	10	Thompson, Charles and Eliza Yates.
	Dec.	23	Thompson, Jas. R. and Mary E. Abell.
1835	Jan.	3	Tarlton, John A. and Ann Eliza. Baxter.
	May	19	Thompson, Geo. H and Gracey E. Cheseldine.
	Sept.	14	Thompson, Robert and Mary B. Bean.
	Oct.	20	Thompson, Wm. H. and Sarah Ann Jones.
	Nov.	16	Turner, Lewis E. and Anna M. Neale.
1836	Apr.	19	Thomas, Roger and Lydia Hammett.
	June	1	Thompson, John and Mary Drury.
	July	25	Ticer, Julius C. and Milita Ann Harrison.
1837	Oct.	30	Tippett, Zacheus and Emma A. Tippett.
1838	Jan.	2	Tarlton, Basil and Sarah Haywood.
		9	Thomas, William and Matilda Edwards.
		16	Tarlton, John H. T. and Susan Hammett.
	Sept.	3	Townsand, Samuel and Amelia C. Washington.
		17	Thompson, John B. and Aleck B. Gatton.
1839	Jan.	1	Taylor, Wm. J. and Maria J. Jones.
		8	Thompson, James and Charlotte Cusick.
	Apr.	30	Thompson, George and Teresia Graves.
	Nov.	11	Thompson, John B. and Mary L. Tarlton.
		25	Tarlton, Jerome and Mary Haywood.
1840	June	6	Tea, James Thomas and Ann E. Lydaman.
		15	Tucker, John H. and Priscilla Underwood.
1841	Feb.	1	Thompson, James and Jane M. Tippett.
	May	3	Turner, John H. and Margaret Ellen Green.
		4	Tennison, Edward F. and Ann Hellen Thompson.
	June	9	Thompson, Benedict and Mary Thompson.
	July	31	Tarlton, Alfred and Susan Haywood.
	Nov.	2	Thompson, Joseph and Elizabeth Drury.
1842	Jan.	14	Tarlton, Jerome and Margaretta Wootton.
	Feb.	1	Turner, John H. and Monica C. Gough.
	Apr.	19	Tennison, John E. and Catherine Thompson.
	Nov.	15	Thompson, John H. and Harriet Priscilla Moore.

1843 June 19 Turner, Wm. F. and Eliza Redman.
1844 Apr. 18 Thomas, Joseph I. S. and Hester A. R. Bennett.
June 10 Thompson, Uriah and Mary G. Boothe.
29 Tippett, William and Cecelia Thompson.
Nov. 12 Tennison, Wm. H. and Dorothy Peake.
Dec. 17 Turner, John H. and Eleanor S. Smith.
1845 Jan. 4 Thompson, Geo. F. and Ann M. Fenwick.
Feb. 3 Thompson, John B. and Ann Maria Bean.
Dec. 2 Tippett, Jonathan and Sarah Watts.
1846 Jan. 13 Turner, Wilson and Eliza Hayden.
Feb. 2 Thomas, John W. and Cath. J. F. Jackson.
June 2 Taylor, Daniel J. and Caroline Davis.
Dec. 14 Thompson, Wm. F. and Susan Ann Knott.
1848 Feb. 28 Tarlton, Geo. and Ellen A. Brewer.
Apr. 5 Tear, Henry and Mary J. Bennett.
Dec. 2 Tarlton, John H. T. and Mary E. Hammett.
1850 Jan. 15 Thompson, Sebastian and Mary R. Hayden.
Feb. 5 Thompson, Alex. J. and Mary Bailey.
May 2 Tucker, Wm. B. and Mary F. Wilkinson.
22 Tarlton, Albert and Ann Norris.
1851 Feb. 6 Tippett, Thomas and Mary Lacey.
Sept. 24 Tarlton, W. T. and A. P. Hammett.
Nov. 4 Tennison, Wm. H. and Jane J. Watts.
27 Thompson, Aloysius and Ann M. Gough.
Dec. 29 Tippett, Daniel and Mary E. Gooden.
1852 July 13 Thompson, George and Mary L. Cheseldine.
1853 Apr. 5 Tarlton, Basil and Ann E. Wheatly.
1854 June 5 Thomas, James R. and Jennett E. Briscoe.
Nov. 4 Thompson, Thomas M. and Emily Hancock.
Dec. 23 Tippett, Robert B. and Susan E. Cheseldine.
1855 Jan. 18 Turner, John F. and Rebecca Ward.
Nov. 17 Turpen, Joseph B. and Mary E. Stone.
1856 Mch. 31 Tennison, Geo. W. and Julia A. Herbert.
Apr. 14 Tippett, M. A. K. and Catherine L. Higgs.
Dec. 15 Tippett, George and Elizabeth Ryce.
15 Thompson, Crawford and Emely Ryce.
1857 Feb. 9 Tippett, John P. and Mary Raley.
24 Tippett, J. W. and Joseph Ann Bean.
Oct. 5 Thompson, Clement S. and Cecelia A. Simpson.
Dec. 31 Thompson, Moses and Monica Radford.
1858 Jan. 4 Thomas, Wm. H. and Mary E. Quade.
Mch. 9 Thompson, Thomas and Eliza Herbert.

1858	Apr.	28	Tarlton, Wm. P. and Sarah Jane Moore.
	Sept.	6	Thompson, Benedict and Ann E. Goodwin.
		28	Thompson, Geo. R. and Ellen A. Diment.
1859	Jan.	3	Thompson, James A. and Martha E. Jones.
	May	2	Turner, Wm. B. and Rebecca Adams.
1860	Jan.	3	Tucker, Ausa (?) A. and Scotia Ann Stone.
	Apr.	23	Tarlton, Jas. Pinkney and Mary Ellen Moore.
1861	Jan.	3	Turner, Joseph H. and Susan R. Sinclair.
		5	Tippett, Uriah and Susan O. Donnell.
	May	4	Thompson, Jas. R. and Amanda McKay.
1862	Nov.	10	Tucker, Michael and Sarah Ann Beverly.
1863	Feb.	4	Tennison, Jas. A. and A. M. Baily.
1798	Oct.	3	Unddiwood, Jeremiah and Eliza Pembroke.
1859	Mch.	24	Unnigh, Chas. and Eliza. J. English.
1820	Oct.	10	Van Reswick, Tho. and Juliet Abell.
1849	Apr.	16	Van Reswick, Joseph and Mary E. Simms.
1851	Apr.	1	Venson, William F. and Ann Abell.
1857	Sept.	9	Vanwart, Wm. and Jane Morgan.
1795	July	28	Winsatt, Joseph and Mary Howard.
1796	Jan.	12	Wherrett, William and Dorothy King.
	Jan.	—	Wise, Richard and Ann Wiseman.
	Feb.	3	Watts, William and Louisa Harwood.
	Apr.	1	West, James and Eleanor Gardiner.
	July	21	Wood, Leonard and Eleanor Bath.
	Aug.	7	White, Peter and Ann Barnhouse.
	Nov.	28	Wailes, George and Dorothy Greenfield.
	Dec.	10	Winsatt, Robert and Margaret Mattingly.
	Dec.	11	Wise, Richard and Eliza. Goddard.
		30	Wiseman, John and Sarah Fenwick.
		31	Worthington, The. and Nancy Greenwell.
1797	Jan.	16	Wise, James and Catherine Hutchins.
	Nov.	24	Watts, George and Susanna Smith.
	Dec.	24	Wise, Mile and Monicai Jarboe.
1798	Mch.	22	Williams, James and Ann Jones.
	Apr.	10	Wherrell, James and Mary Taylor.
	July	24	Watts, Barton and Eliza Goodwin.
	Sept.	6	Wise, John Y. and Mary Knott.
		15	Winsatt, Bennett and Belender Smith.
1799	Jan.	8	Woodward, Joseph and Margaret Jordan.
		22	Watts, Henry and Sarah Guyther.
	Sept.	3	Willner, Thomas and Eleanor Hennen.
	Oct.	10	Walten, James and Dorothy Hayden.

1800	Jan.	2	Weakley, Peregrine and Ann Fowler.
		3	Winsatt, Joseph and Sally Stone.
		22	Winsatt, John B. and Margaret Boothe.
	Apr.	11	Wilkinson, John and Nancy Thompson.
	Nov.	11	Wise, Richard and Mary Long.
	Dec.	17	Wheeler, William and Terecy Hamilton.
1801	Jan.	13	Watts, Williar and Eleanor C. Barber.
		17	Walker, Daniel and Ann Joy.
		19	White, Peter and Mary Bransel.
		26	Wooton, Richard and Mury Sanner.
	Aug.	6	Ward, Benjamin and Jane Burroughs.
		19	Wherrett, Wm. H. and Mary Clarke.
	Nov.	26	Walker, John and Eleanor Davis.
1802	Feb.	20	Wheatley, Enoch and Mary Wheeler.
	Apr.	27	Walker, Bennet and Milly Reeder.
	June	14	Wills, John B. and Ann C. Floyd.
		18	Walker, John and Mary Davis.
	July	26	Watherton, Thomas and Ann Coalton.
	Sept.	29	Waughop, Harry and Sarah S. Watts.
	Nov.	20	Walker, William and Eliza. Bridget.
1803	Jan.	4	Wherrett, John and Sarah Armstrong.
		16	Watts, Thomas and Polly Tarlton.
		16	Wartes, Sandy and Eliza Buckler.
	Apr.	20	Wise, Miel and Jane Cullison.
	Oct.	11	White, James and Maria Chesley.
	Nov.	7	Wood, Henry and Ann Brawner.
	Dec.	31	Walker, Joseph and Rebecca Davis.
1804	Feb.	4	Walker, Daniel and Ann Clarke.
		6	Williams, Benja. and Mary Combs.
	Mch.	26	Winsatt, Benedict and Eleanor Cole.
	June	8	Watson, William and Eliza. Coade.
	Mch.	30	Williams, George and Mary Wherrett.
1805	Jan.	4	Williams, Thomas and Eliza. Hardesty.
	Feb.	28	Watts, Daniel and Ann Hammett.
	Mch.	15	White, Joseph C. and Mary Jones.
	Apr.	4	Williams, John and Mary Beetley.
	June	17	Wise, James and Monica Williams.
	Aug.	21	Wise, John and Mary Wise.
1806	Mch.	15	Williams, James and Eliza. Neale.
	Apr.	16	Winsatt, James and Eleanor Lurty.
	May	14	Welch, John and Ann Artis.
1807	Apr.	14	Winsatt, John G. and Eliza. Williams.

1807	Apr. 20	Woodward, William and Susanna Medley.
	Sept. 30	Wheat, Benoni and Mary Jordan.
	Nov. 30	Wildman, James and Dorothy Greenfield.
1808	Jan. 11	Wheatley, Joseph and Mary Wootten.
	May 17	Wootten, Benedict and Judy Abell.
	Aug. 13	Wootten, John B. and Mary Fenwick.
1809	Mch. 21	Woodland, Primas and Ann Wood.
	Sept. 13	Wise, Adam and Polly Thomas.
1810	Nov. 31	Walker, John B. and Henrietta Lowry.
1811	Feb. 14	Wilder, Edward and Susanna K. Egerton.
	20	Watson, Henry and Elizabeth Harrison.
	Mch. 28	Watts, Joshua and Eleanor Nelson.
	Apr. 12	Winsatt, William and Eliza. Moore.
	June 18	Winsatt, John and Winefred Hutchins.
	Sept. 1	Weeden, William and Ann Fras. Scott Harrable.
	21	Wheatley, Joseph and Ann Norriss.
	4	Wilkinson, John and Sarah Brewer.
	Nov. 20	Wathen, Faban and Ann Suttle.
1812	Jan. 3	Williams, John G. and Eliza. Saxton.
	June 15	William, Lewis and Eleanor Medley.
	Aug. 24	Wills, John B. and Ann Jarboe.
1813	Jan. 1	Walker, William and Milly Suttle.
	11	Watts, George H. and Ann Armstrong.
	Jan. 18	Watson, George and Sarah Coard.
	Aug. 17	Williams, Jos. C. and Priscilla A. Thomas.
	Oct. 23	Wise, James and Ann Booth.
	Nov. 23	Wise, George and Sophia Hammett.
	Dec. 27	Williams, Joseph and Clara Greenwell.
1814	Dec. 20	Wheeler, Bennet and Ann Avis.
1815	July 31	Williams, Benja. and Monica Combs.
	Sept. 4	Winsatt, Wm. and Ann Radford.
1816	June 11	Worthington, Thos. and Mary Leach.
	July 8	Welst, John and Mary Bennett.
	Sept. 3	Wheatley, Matthew and Eliza Wootten.
	7	Wheatley, John and Jane Norriss.
	Dec. 30	Walker, James and Penelope Reeder.
1817	Apr. 23	Williams, James and Eliza. Spalding.
	July 25	Woodburn, Hezekiah and Attaway Barnes.
1818	Jan. 1	Watts, Richd. H. and Catherine Crane.
	26	Woodland, Ignatius and Lucinda Butler.
1819	Jan. 16	Whitman, Benja., Jr. and Eliza. Lilburn.
	Feb. 8	Wherett, James H. and Henry Doxey.

1819	June	21	Winters, John and Ann Maria Smith.
1820	Jan.	1	Woodburn, William and Ann Edwards.
		10	Wootten, Ignatius and Ann McKay.
		10	Wootton, Joseph and Harriot Clarke.
		22	White, Nelson B. C. and Sarah C. Kirk.
	Feb.	3	Wathen, James and Susanna Graves.
	Apr.	29	Wise, John and Rancha Wise.
	Nov.	9	Wheeler, Ignatius and Elizabeth Morgan.
1821	Jan.	13	Wood, Charles and Fanny Thompson.
	Aug.	9	Wood, William and Rebecca Power.
	Dec.	24	Wherrett, Benja. and Sally McKay.
1822	Feb.	2	Wilkinson, James and Caroline Clarke.
	June	17	Walton, John and Mary Dukes.
	Sept.	17	Wood, Henry S. and Lydia Ann Maraman.
	Dec.	10	Williams, Joseph C. and Harriot Clarke.
1823	Jan.	4	Wise, Thomas and Sophia Wise.
		27	Wathen, Hanson and Mariel Bowes.
	Feb.	3	Wootten, James and Ann Shearmontine.
		6	Wathen, Benedict and Catherine Graves.
	Apr.	9	Wainright, Richard and Eleanor A. Scott.
	Dec.	30	Wheeler, Raphl. and Ann Pilkinton.
1824	Sept.	11	Williams, Charles and Mary Hill.
	Dec.	14	Woodburn, Wm. and Margaret Edwards.
1825	Jan.	27	Wooten, James and Sally Selence.
	Feb.	7	Woodward, Bennet and Eliza. Bowling.
	June	14	Wright, Henry R. and Eliza Davis.
	Oct.	10	Woodland, James and Eliza. Butler.
1826	Jan.	18	Washington, John and Mary Moore.
		20	Wise, John A. and Catherine Thompson.
	Mch.	27	Woodland, Thomas and Elizabeth Butler.
	Apr.	17	Wathen, Clement and Ann Spalding.
	Nov.	27	Walker, Richard and Elizabeth Spalding.
1827	Jan.	8	Wilkinson, Thomas and Caroline Cissell.
		9	Wherrett, John and Maria Bealle.
		13	Winsatt, George and Ann Spalding.
	Feb.	10	Woodburn, Michael and Catherine Burroughs.
		13	Wheeler, George and Ann Fenwick.
	Apr.	16	Woodland, Henry and Mary Ann Butler.
	Oct.	16	Williams, James and Mary Ann Hayden.
	Nov.	8	Wise, George H. and Ann Bohanan.
1828	Apr.	15	Ward, Saml. B. and Eliza. Cartwright.
	Nov.	19	Willhellam, Abraham and Mary Milburn.

1828	Dec.	30	Williams, and Emeline Alvey.
1829	Jan.	5	Woodburn, Daniel and Eliza. Davis.
1830	Feb.	23	Wood, Jeremiah R. and Susanna Wood.
	Aug.	14	Wood, Isaac and Ann Stone.
	Dec.	14	Wood, Alexander and Jane Alvey.
1831	Jan.	31	Wathen, Hanson and Emily McDaniel.
	Apr.	21	Wilson, John and Louisa Suter.
	May	24	Wilson, Joshua and Priscilla Hebb.
	June	10	Webster, Samuel and Mary Eliza. Sothoron.
1832	Jan.	7	Wise, Samuel and Rebecca Drury.
	Feb.	7	Williams, Charles and Mary Hill.
		7	Wherrett, William and Ann Sanner.
	Apr.	19	Wootton, Turner and Olivia C. Hopewell.
		30	Welch, John B. and Harriet E. Ford.
	May	1	Woodward, William and Mary E. Gough.
	June	8	Ward, Thomas F. and Sarah Wherrett.
	July	5	Watts, Joshua and Levinia Martin.
1833	Jan.	2	Wheatley, John Lewis and Eliza Tarlton.
	Feb.	12	Wood, Richard and Jane Parker.
	June	11	Woodward, William and Eliza Jane Neale.
	July	9	Weiss, Joseph E. and Ann Adelade Bailey.
1834	May	18	Wilkinson, Geo. W. and Mary Dillihay.
	Oct.	31	Wathen, Bennet and Eliza A. Howard.
	Nov.	26	Wilhelm, Abraham and Ann E. Milburn.
	Dec.	30	Wood, William and Susanna Heard.
1835	Jan.	19	Wootton, James and Elizabeth Cole.
	Feb.	2	Wathen, Martin and Jane Boothe.
	May	9	Wheatley, Joseph and Lora Ann Cramsley.
		27	Wood, Henry and Susan Hill.
1836	Feb.	2	Winsatt, Ignatius R. C. and Ann Eliza Johnson.
1837	Feb.	20	Wise, Elkanah and Mary H. Cissell.
	Nov.	7	Williams, Robert M. and Eliza Ann Anderson.
		14	Weisel, Samuel and Susan M. Turner.
1838	Mch.	3	Wise, Francis and Catherine Price.
	June	26	Warring, James and Ann Maria Thomas.
	July	31	Woodward, and Ann Maria Tarlton.
1839	Jan.	1	Wood, Richard and Jane Sothoron.
		17	Williams, John H. and Susan Ann Burroughs.
	Feb.	1	Wooten, James and Mary Goldsberry.
	Apr.	8	Wilkinson, Geo. W. and Rebecca Greenwell.
	Dec.	15	Wheatley, Wm. C. and Ann M. Armsworthy.
1840	Aug.	25	Wathen, John F. and Priscilla Ford.

1840	Nov. 12	Wood, Clement and Susan Ann Bennett.
	Sept. 26	Wheeler, John M. and Leaher Ann Paul.
	Dec. 15	Woodward, Geo. and Philipi Sanner.
1841	Jan. 18	Wheatley, John H. and Mary E. Evans.
1842	Mch. 29	Winsatt, Benedict and Frances E. Rust.
1843	May 16	Wise, James H. and Johanna Combs.
	Oct. 31	Welsh, William W. and Susan Bean.
1844	Jan. 8	Woodburn, Hezekiah A. and Adeline Lyon.
	Feb. 3	Wood, Charles C. and Mary E. Scott.
	15	Wise, James C. and Mary S. Beavan.
	29	Watts, Richard and Eliza. E. Powers.
	Aug. 19	Wheatley, Matthew and Jane Clarke.
	Nov. 21	Washington, Daniel H. and Martha M. Keech.
1846	Jan. 3	Watson, John J. and Jane Dean.
	10	Wheatley, John F. and Mary E. Haywood.
	12	Wathen, James F. and Susanna Radford.
	Apr. 28	Woodward, Robert W. and Charlotte Bennett.
1847	Feb. 6	Wise, Elkanah and Mary A. Jackson.
	Nov. 17	Weaklin, Thomas and Ann Mason.
1848	June 28	Wise, John N. and Jane Thompson.
	Oct. 20	Woodburn, Michael and Clarissa Hill.
	Dec. 6	Wise, John H. and Lucretia J. Watts.
	27	Wathen, Martin and Sarah J. Russell.
1850	Apr. 23	Wathen, Clement and M. S. Missouri Morgan.
	May 14	Woodburn, Richd. and Sarah Burroughs.
	July 6	Wood, W. W. and Cath. Hill.
	20	Wilkinson, Geo. N. and Jane C. Hayden.
	Nov. 4	Wilson, James and Mary Ann Suter.
1851	Oct. 23	Weems, Francis W. and Eliza V. Harris.
1852	Jan. 20	Wieners, Charles and Antoinette Forster.
	21	Wood, William H. and Mary Burroughs.
	Apr. 10	Wheeler, James and Lydia Ann Goddard.
	Dec. 22	Williams, William H. and Mary Wood.
1853	May 19	Watts, Joshua and Margaret Abell.
	Sept. 18	Wilkinson, McKeldry and ——— Greenwell.
	21	Whitney, James O. and Sallie M. Moore.
	26	Ward, Jos. T. and Lucretia C. Johnson.
	Nov. 28	Wooten, Joseph S. and Sophia A. Burroughs.
1854	Mch. 17	Wheatley, John F. and Sarah A. Clarke.
	July 11	Wheatley, John and Jane L. Booth.
	Dec. 18	Welch, William C. and Mary A. Bond.
1855	Jan. 1	Wathen, Robert H. and Mary P. Dukes.

1855	Jan.	2	Wise, John H. and Ellen Watts.
		22	Woodburn, Jno. W. and Ann C. Graves.
	May	30	Warren, Leonard and Laura Tippett.
1857	Jan.	7	Wood, Julius and Catherine A. Langley.
	Apr.	13	Wood, Albert A. and Mary Ellen Alvey.
		21	Wheeler, Wm. and Ann Armsworthy.
	June	2	Wells, Edwd. A. and Mary L. Hammett.
1858	Jan.	4	Wilkinson, James M. and Martha Heard.
	Apr.	3	Wood, Joseph T. andMary E. Graves.
	Aug.	24	Wise, Benedict and Jane Eliza Russell.
		9	Wheatley, Mathew and Eliza Smith.
1859	Jan.	25	Wilkinson, Thomas and Mary Rebecca Gray.
	Mch.	7	Wood, John and Charlotte A. Bean.
	Dec.	13	Williams, Wm. Benja. and Eliza Etta Ann Taylor.
1860	Jan.	11	Wood, Charles J. and Mary J. Dean.
	Feb.	16	Wilson, Edwin A. and Ann C. Bean.
	May	26	Woodburn, C. and Josephine Bond.
	Aug.	9	Wherrit, John C. and Emily Conly.
	Oct.	30	Walton, Dr. J. Randolph and Margaret R. Ihrie.
	Dec.	5	Wheeler, Francis and Susan Owings.
		15	Wathen, Joseph and Ann R. Hayden.
1861	Jan.	5	Wood, Thomas J. and Snowden Dean.
	Apr.	9	Wise, James A. and S. R. Unkle.
	June	3	Wise, Robert H. and Margaret Ann Briscoe.
	Nov.	4	Wise, George and Mary Brewer.
1862	Jan.	14	Wheeler, John T. and Mary J. Fenhagan.
		28	Wise, Wm. S. and Mary E. Joy.
	Feb.	12	Woodburn, Jno. W. and Ann R. Mattingly.
	Apr.	22	Wise, Alex. and Celestia Cullison.
1863	June	25	White, Hanson and Zilah A. Langley.
1798	Oct.	19	Yates, James and Mary Scott.
1799	Jan.	13	Yates, William and Mary Raley.
1802	Dec.	31	Yates, Ignatius and Rebecca Greenwell.
1803	Aug.	8	Yates, John and Jane Stone.
1804	Nov.	2	Yates, Noch and Cecelia Hendley.
1806	June	10	Young, Thomas and Margaret Loker.
1808	Feb.	3	Yates, Edward and Margaret Peacock.
1826	Nov.	27	Yates, Martin and Mary E. Hayden.
1827	Jan.	5	Yates, James and Clarisa Johnson.
1829	July	14	Yates, William I. and Julian Norriss.
1830	Oct.	26	Yates, William and Caroline Hayden.
1832	June	19	Yates, James T. and Eliza Moore.

1834	Jan. 20	Yates, James T. and Mary Ann Yates.
1836	Dec. 27	Young, Thomas and Mary Crane.
1837	Jan. 4	Yates, John G. and Matilda Tennison.
1839	Feb. 11	Yates, John T. and Ann M. Watts.
	Dec. 6	Young, Notley and Mary E. Smith.
1840	Jan. 21	Yates, Benedict and Sarah J. Thompson.
1845	May 28	Young, Albert and Rachael Ann Briscoe.
1847	July 19	Yates John F. and Mary E. Watts.
1853	Apr. 25	Yates, George A. and Catherine Burroughs.
1857	Feb. 4	Yohe, Joseph and Mary J. Clements.
1858	Jan. 18	Yates, John D. and Annie E. Greenwell.
1859	Jan. 13	Yates, John H. and Ann Louisa Russell.
	Nov. 22	Yates, Matthew A. S. and Mary F. Drury.
1862	May 12	Yeatman, Wm. and Annie Maria Lamb.

HUNDREDS OF ST. MARY'S COUNTY

It is the oldest county in the State, being established in 1637; and is divided into the following hundreds, viz., Upper Resurrection, Chaptico, Upper St. Clements, Lower St. Clements, Upper Newtown, Lower Resurrection, Lower Newtown, Poplar Hill, Harvey, St. George's, Upper St. Mary's, Lower St. Mary's, St. Inegoes, and St. Michael's.*

* *A Geographical Description of the State of Maryland and Delaware,* Joseph Scott, Philadelphia. 1807, p. 64.

ANNE ARUNDEL COUNTY

A LIST OF THE NUMBER OF INHABITANTS IN ALL HALLOWS PARISH

Number of Inhabitants in All Hallows Parish

A List of the Number of Inhabitants in All Hallows Parish taken by John Jeams Junr Anno Dom 1776.

Name	White Men	White Women	White Children	Black Men	Black Women	Black Children	Taxables
William Rees	1	3	8				1
John Ilman	1	1	1				1
Francis Guynn	1	1	5				1
Richard Rawlings	1	2	4			1	1
Ralph Bazill	2	2	1	1	1	1	3
Joseph Williams	2	4	4				2
Richard Jacobs	1	/	1				1
John Jacobs	1	2					1
William Jacobs	1						1
John Nicholson Junr	1	1	2				1
Henry Jones	2			1	2	3	5
John Onion	1	1	3				1
Capt James Sanders	2	2			2	2	4
Thomas Elliott	2	2	3	1			3
Sarah Collings	–	2	1				
Leonard Romalls	1	1	8				1
James Sanders	2	1	3		1	2	3
Robert Welsh Elliott	1	2	1				1
John Lee	1						1
Matthew Elliott	3						3
Marmaduke Morgan	1	1	2				1
Thomas King	1	1	1	1	2	4	4
John Stell	1	2	4				
John Jacobs	1	1					1
Mary Jacobs	–	4	1				
Rachel Stell	–	2	1				
George Newsom	1	1	2				1
William Jeams Son John	2	2			1	3	3
William Lockwood	1	1	1			4	1
John Cowman	2	2	6	2	3	6	6
Gerard Hopkins Junr	3	3	1	3	3	7	7
Thomas Philps	1	1	5				1

[2]

	White Men	White Women	White Children	Black Men	Black Women	Black Children	[illegible]
Amount Brought over							
James Disney Son of Wm	1.	1.	2.	1.			2
William Davis Junr	2.	2.	4.	2.	2.	6.	6.
Isaiah Phelps	1.	3.	3.				1.
Joseph Howard Junr	1.	1.	2.	5.	1.	7.	6
Joseph Williams Son of Benn	1.			1.	1.	4.	3
Thomas Rutland	2.	1.	2.	6.	2.	6.	10.
Elizabeth Williams		1.					
Denune Howard	1.						1.
John Givans	1.	1.	2.				1.
Benjamin Selby	1.	1.	4	1.	1.	4.	3.
Jonathan Selby	1.	3.	1.	2.	1.	1.	2.
Stockett Williams	1.						1
Richard Elliott	3.	1.	5.				2
Robert Ross	1.	1.	4				1
Abraham Short	1.	1.	3				1.
Ruth Elliott		3.	1.				
John Basil	1.	1.	4				1.
William Turner	1.	1.	4				1.
Elizabeth Letton		1.	3.				
William Ryan	1.	2.	4				1.
John Elliott	1.						1
Hester Beard		3.	6				
George Hurst	1.	1.	2				1
	1.	1.	9				1
Richard Tydings	3.	3.	2.	2.	1.	8.	1
John Nelson Gray	1.	1.	6.				1
Joseph Pearce	1.	3.	3.		2		3
Jane Knighton	1.	1.	1.	3.	3.	7.	1
William Harwood	2.	1.					1
Otho French	1.						1
William French	1.	1.	3.				1
William Pearce	2.	2.	5	1.	1.	1.	3
Daniel Davis	1.	1.	1.				1
Benjamin Welsh	1.	1.		3	2.	4.	6.
Edward Lee	1.	4.	1.	2	1.	3.	1
Robert Welsh							

[3]

Name	White Men	White Women	White Children	Black Men	Black Women	Black Children	Taxables
Amount Brought Forward							
Philip Richardson	4	3	1	1			5
Samuel Poole	2	3	4				2
Richard Phelps	1	1					1
Catharine Stewart	1	2	2				1
Robert Stewart	1						1
John Burgess Son of Wm	2	2	6			1	2
William Anderson Junr	1						1
James Anderson Senr	3	1		1	1	4	5
Aaron Rawlings	1	1	9		1	7	2
Matthew Beard	1						1
Deborah Phelps	1	3	2				1
Mordecai Barry	2	2	5				2
John Basford	1	1	3			1	1
Thomas Bassford	2	1	4				2
Henry Hall	1	1		4	3	8	8
John Chaplain	2	1	6				2
David Evans	1	1	3	4	3	7	7
Ann Gaither	[illegible]	1			1		1
Ann Stewart	1	3	1			1	1
Hugh Jones	1	1	1				1
Samuel Taylor	1	1	7				1
Nachel Howard	1	1	7				1
Ann Taylor		1	2				
Benjamin Williams	1	1	2	1			2
Matthew Robinson	[illegible]			1			2
John Phelps	1	2		1	1		2
Thomas Fowler	1	1				1	1
Mr Francis Linthicum	1	1	1				1
Jacob Iiams	1	2	3				1
Eleanor Drue		2					
Sarah Jones	1	3	3	1			2
George Hayden	1	1	4				1
John Myers	1	3					1
Auther Thompson	2	2	1				2

[4]

	White Men	White Women	White Children	Black Men	Black Women	Black Children	Wag[illegible]
Amount Brought over							
Burton Linthicum	1.	1.				1.	1
William St. Laurence	1.			1			2
Elianor St. Lawrence		1.	1.		1.	2.	1.
Philip Brown	1.	1.	3.				1.
Zachariah Cheney	1.	1.	3.				1
Edmund Wayman	1.	2.	1.	1.			3
Caleb Taylor	1.	1.	5.				1.
Joseph Jones	1.	1.	2.				1.
Susannah Phelps	5.	3.	3.				3
Joseph Owens	1.	1.	3.				1.
David Stuart	1.	1.	4.	1.	2.	1.	4
Samuel Fowler	1.	1.	2.				1
Henry Onion	1.	1.	3.				1
Abraham Woodwards (Quarter)				2.	2		4
Stephen Basford	1.	2.			2	10.	3
John Connoway	1.	2.	6		1.	1.	2
Thomas Orrick	1.	1.					1
Thomas Pawley	1.	1.					1
Edward Edwards	3	3.	5	2.	4.	7.	9
Philip Thomas's (Quarter)				2.	3	6.	2
John Linthicum	1.	2.	4.	1.	3.		5
Elizabeth Linthicum	1.	2.	2.				1
Benjamin Talbott	1.	2.	3.	5.	2.	6.	8
William Andrews	1.	1.	2.				1
Nicholas Saint Laurence	3.	1.					3
Joshua Adams	1.	1.	5.				1
Thomas Tucker	1.	1	1.				1
Sarah McCauley	1.	6.					1
Daniel Atwell	1.	1.					
Susannah Johns's (Quarter)				5.	2.	5.	
Francis McCauley	3.	2.	1.	2.	1.	1.	
Mary Tucker	2.	2.					
William Hood	2	6.		7.	7.	8.	
John Hammonds (Quarter)	1.			3.	1.	2.	
Sarah Elliott	1.	2.	1.		1.	4.	

[5]

	White Men	White Women	White Children	Black Men	Black Women	Black Children	Taxables
Amount brought forward							
Alexander McClain	1	1	2				1
Amos Gaither	1	2			3	6	4
Benjamin Cadle	1	2	1				1
James Cadle	1	2	6				1
Samuel Cadle	1	1	6				1
Elizabeth Ridgely	3	1	1				3
Cornelius Barry	2	1	2			1	2
Edward Gaither	3	3		3	3	6	6
Cassandra Ducker	—	2	2	1	2	4	3
Gideon Gary	1	3	5	3	2	6	6
Elijah Golden	1	3	3	2	1	3	4
Thomas Fowler Basford	1	1	1				1
Leonard Wayman's (Quaker)				5	3	7	8
Zachariah McCauley	1	1					1
Edward Halls (Quaker)				4	2	2	6
Thomas Henry Hall	1	1	1	5	5	11	11
William Hall	1	1	1	3	1	5	5
Jeremiah Crabb	2	2	1	6	5	7	13
Samuel Brogden	1			3	4	5	8
Joseph Mayo Junr.	1	1	5	1			2
Thomas Philnett	2	1	3				2
Benjamin Gravel	1	2					1
Isaac Jones	1	1	6	0	1	5	2
Elizabeth Jones		1		2	3	3	5
Robert Whittaker	1	1	7				1
John Beard	2	1	3	1	1	2	4
Joseph Watkins	1	1	6	3	2	1	6
John Iiams Son of John	3			1			4
Capt. John Iiams	1	2	2	1	3	7	4
Richard Beard Junr.	2	1	7	2	1	4	5
Robert John Smith	3	1	6		1		4
Richard Beard Senr.	3	5		1	2	4	6
Richard Watters	1	2	2	1		1	2
Ann Battee	1	2	1	3	4	4	6

[6]

	White Men	White Women	White Children	Black Men	Black Women	Black Children	[illegible]
Amount Brought over							
Gassaway Watkins	2.	1.	4.	1.	1.	2.	4
James Elliott	1.	1.	4.	.	.	—	1.
John Thomas's (Quarter)		—	—	3.	1.	8.	4.
Mary Strachan	—	—	—	3	1.	—	6
John Bishop	1.	1.	.	.	.	.	1.
William Brown	4.	1.	5.	2.	1.	—	7.
Sarah Carter	—	3.	2.	—	1.	—	[illegible]
William Thrift	2.	2.	3.	.	—	—	2
George Stolker	2.	1.	1.	.	—	—	2.
Stephen Beard	2.	1.	2	1	1.	1.	4
John Selman Senr	3.	3.	4.	1.	1.	5.	6.
Thomas Fowler Son of Wm	1.	6.	5	.	—	—	1.
John Tidings	2.	1.	8.	2.	1.	—	5.
John Glover	1.	1.	3.	.			
Lewis Lee	1.	2.	2.	2.	1	4.	4
Ann Rawls	—	2.	1.	.	—	—	
Thomas Harwood's (Quarter)	3.	.	.	4.	3.	11.	10.
Richard Burgess	2.	1.	10.	2.	1.	4.	5.
John Carvill	1.	1.	2.	1.	—	—	4
Alexander Carvill	1.		—	—	—	1.	[illegible]
Stephen Rawlings	2.	2.	3.	.	—	1.	2
William Carvill	1.	1.	1.	—	1.		2
Thomas Chips	2.	1.	1.	.	—	—	2
Samuel Watkins	2.	1.	6.	2.	2.	4	6.
Ann Chambers	.	1.	—	—	1.	—	[illegible]
James Disney	2.	3.	3.	2.	2.	1.	5
William Disney	1.	1.	2	.	—	—	[illegible]
James Davidson	1.	.	.	.	—	—	[illegible]
Mary Walsh	.	3.	1.	.	—	—	
Margaret Williams	.	3.	3.	.	—	.	
John Harwood	1.	2	—	9.	7.	11.	[illegible]
Colo Richard Harwood	1.	1.	5.	4.	6.	5.	[illegible]
Henry Oneal Walsh	1.	.	—	8.	7.	13.	[illegible]
Samuel White	1.	1.	2.	.	—	—	[illegible]
William Ryan	1.	1.	.				
Hugh Champain	1.						
William Powell	4.						

[7]

	White Men	White Women	White Children	Black Men	Black Women	Black Children	Taxables
Amount brought fforward							
Eleanor Butler	1.	1.	3.			-	2.
John Orely	1.	1.					1.
Samuel Jacobs	2.	2.	6.	1.	1.	1.	3.
Daniel Pearce	1.	2.	2				
Nicholas Macubbin (Quarter at Beards Creek)	1.			4.	6.	9.	21.
Plummer Iiams	2.	2.	1.	3.	3.	9.	8.
Jeremiah Watkins	1.	1.	6.		1.	2.	2.
Samuel Galloways (Quarter)	-	-	-	6	5.	12.	11.
William Iiams Son of George	1.	1.	1.	4.	4.	11.	9
William Davis Senr	2.	2.	2.	1.	1.	2.	4.
John Powell	1.	1.	4.				-
Philip Chambers	1.	2.	5.			-	1.
Lewis Stockett	1.	1.	7.	4.	3.	2.	8.
Thomas Noble Stockett	1.	2.	2	7.	5.	12.	10.
Rachel Stockett	1.	1.	3.	-	1.	3.	2.
Gassaway Rawlings	2.	3.	3.	8.	7.	21.	17.
Joseph Cowman	3.	2.	2.	5.	6.	10.	13.
James Owens Junr	1.	1.	3.			1.	1.
John Watkins son of Gassy	1.	1.	4.		-	1.	1.
William George McCain	1.	1.	1.				1
Joseph Howard Junr	2.	2.	1.	6.	3.	10.	11.
Rachel Sullivan		1.	2	-			+
Thomas Sprigg	1.	3.	-	23.	16.	29.	40.
Capt Thomas Watkins	1.	2	4.	4.	2	10.	7.
Richard Welsh	1.	2.	2		-		1.
Dinah Sparrow		2.	1.			-	
Edmund Purdy	1.	1.	2			-	1.
Richard Watkins	1.	2.	4	1.	1.	1.	3.
Elizabeth Brookes	1.	1.	-	3.	2.	1.	6
Ephraim Duvall	1.	1.					1.
Thomas Gibbs	1.	2.	3	1.	1.	12.	3.
William Rawlings	1.	1.	1.			-	1.
Charles Stewart	2.	2.	-	3	5.	13.	10
Benjamin Burgess	1.	2.	1.	1.	:	2	2
Isaiah Burgess	-	3.	-	-	1.	1.	1.
Thomas Mancear	1.	1.	5.			-	1.
Jane Inch	-	2.		-	1.	1.	1.
Capt Thomas Walker	1.		-	-	1.	1.	2
Eleanor Hall		1.		-	-		

[8]

	White Men	White Women	White Children	Black Men	Black Women	Black Children	[illegible]
Amount brought over	–	1.			1	–	1
Elizabeth Buchanan	2.	1.	3		–	–	[illegible]
Joseph Gibson		2.		1.	2.	3.	3.
Elizabeth Scougall	–	3.	1.	1.	1.	4.	2.
Elizabeth Ferguson	2.	1.	4.	1.	1.	5.	4.
John Sifton		1.	1.		–	–	
Sarah Mitchell	2.	1.	2.	–	2.	4.	4.
William Thornton	1.	–	–	1.	1.	–	2.
The Revd David Love	1.	1.	–	3.	3.	3.	3.
Capt Thomas Pearson	–	4.	2	–	1.	1.	[illegible]
Dinah Gassaway	1.	1.	1.	6.	4.	7.	[illegible]
Nicholas Gassaway	1.	2.	6.	3.	2.	7.	6.
Nathan Waters	1.	2.	7.	1.	1.	1.	3.
Francis Linthicum	1.	1.	4		–	–	[illegible]
William Purdy	1.	1.	4.		–	–	1.
Henry Purdy	2.	1.	3.	1.		–	3.
John Holton	1.	1.	2.	5.	4.	8.	8.
William Sanders	1.	1.	–	4.	5.	13.	10.
Elizabeth Sanders	1.	3.	2.		–	–	1.
Francis Wayman	1.	1.	3.	–	–	–	1.
William Roberts	3.	3.	5.	8.	5.	7.	10.
Joseph Mayo	1.	7.	3.	3.	4.	6.	8.
Robert Crain Davis	1.	1.	5.	–	2.	6.	3.
William Brewer	1.	2.	4.	2.	6.	9.	9.
Eleanor Brewer	1.	1.	5.	1.	2.	3.	4.
Joseph Brewer Senr	1.	1.	4.	[illegible]	1.	3.	2.
Samuel Guest	2.	–	1.		–	–	2.
Henry Brewer	1.	1.	1.		–	–	[illegible]
William Jennings	–	2	–	2.	4.	7.	6.
Alice Nicholson		–	–	11.	11.	25.	22.
Nicholas Maccubbin's (Quarter Squirrel Neck)	2.	1.	–	1.	2.	3.	5.
Joshua Yeates	2.	3.	–	7.	3.	7.	10.
Jonathan Selman	–	1.	1.	–	–	–	[illegible]
Sarah Pearce	1.	2.	4	–	–	–	[illegible]
William Ward	1.	2.	2.	–	–	–	[illegible]
John Litton	1.	1.	4.	–	–	1.	[illegible]
Kelly Lewis							

[9]

	White Men	White Women	White Children	Black Men	Black Women	Black Children	Taxables
Amount brought forward						1.	1.
John Smith	1.	1.	3	-	-		
Margaret Hunter	-	2.	1.	-	-	-	1.
Eleanor Reed	-	1.	-	2.	-	-	3.
William Bennett	3.	3.	5	5	3.	8.	9.
Benjamin Gaither	1.	-	-				1.
Capt. Nachel Gaither	1.	-	-	-	-		
Catharine Lusby	-	1.	2.	-	-		
Ann Rankin	1.	3.	3.	-	1.	2.	2.
Edward Stewart	1.	1.	2.	2.	1.	4.	4.
Francis Belmear	2.	2.	5.	1.	1.	4.	4.
William Anderson	1.	1.	4.	1.	2.	1.	4.
Moses Donaldson	2.	1.	4		-	-	2.
Thomas Benson	3.	3.	3.	.	.	-	3.
Samuel Cheney	3	1.	4	-	-	-	3.
Thomas Mulliken	1.	2.	6.	3.	4.	13.	8.
Jeremiah Mulliken	1.	1.	-	4.	1.	6.	6.
Belt Mulliken	1.	1.	4.	3.	2.	5.	6.
Absalom Anderson	1.	3.	6.	1.	2.	2.	4.
Johns Hopkins	3.	1.	8.	6.	12	25.	23.
Girrard Hopkins	3.	2.	-	9.	7.	16.	19.
Joseph Hopkins	1.	1.	2.	2.	1.	5.	4.
Revd. John Ashton's (Quarter)				2.	2.	6	4.
Samuel Cheney Junr.	3.	3.	2	-	-	-	3.
Joseph Cheney	1.	1.	3.	-		-	1.
Hugh Jean Harris	1.	-	-	-	-	-	1.
Mary Holliday	-	3.	4.	4.	2	6.	6
Rebecca Wilson		1.	1.		1.	2.	1
Benjamin Holliday	1.	.	.	.	.	1.	1
Thomas Jarmes	1.	2.	4.	1.	1.	2.	2.
John Jones	2.						1.
Daniel of St. Thomas Jenifer	2.	1.		5.	2	3.	10.
James Dick	3.	3.	7.	8.	6.	11.	18.
Charles Stewart	4.	4.	-	35.	22.	26.	61.
John Nicholson	2.	2.	5.	1.	2.	-	5.

[10]

	White Men	White Women	White Children	Black Men	Black Women	Black Children	[illegible]
Amount Brought over							
Zachariah Duvall	1.	1.	3.	.	- -	-	1.
Samuel Galloway's (Quarter)	.	.	-	5.	4.	5.	9.
Capt. William Brogden	4.	2.	3.	6.	7	27.	17.
John Brogden	3.	2.	5.	3.	5.	13.	11.
Thomas Watkins	2.	1.	- -	8.	8.	18.	18.
Elizabeth Hall	1.	3.	4.	4.	7.	16.	12.
John Magg	1.		. .	-	-		1.
James Hunter	1.	1	4.			-	1.
Anthony Stuarts (Quarter)	-	.	.	3.	3	6.	6.

[Page 1]

A list of the Number of Inhabitants in St. James Parish by Order of Ann Arundel County Committee

Saml. [illegible]

White Men	Wt Women	Wt Boys	Wt Girls	men	Wom	[illegible]	[illegible]
Saml Chew	3		12	36	26	20	20
Richard Pollage	—	—		—	—	—	—
William Crutchs	—	—	—	—	—	—	—
Lewis Scrivener		—	—		—	—	—
Francis Scrivener	1		4	5	4	3	4
Morgan Jones	2	3	2	2	1	2	4
Joseph Fraiser	1	5	1	2	2	—	—
William Fraiser	—	—	—	—	—	—	—
Jos. Fraiser	—	—	—	—	—	—	—
William Parker	2	—	1	—	—	—	—
Saml Burkhead	4	—	5	3	6	6	5
Samuel Burkhead Junr	—	—	—	—	—	—	—
Lebon Burkhead	—	—	—	—	—	—	—
Nehemiah Burkhead	1	—	—	—	—	—	—
Thos H Burkhead	—	—	—	—	—	—	—
John Reed	—	—	—	—	—	—	—
John Burkhead	2	8	—	2	1	—	2
Nehemiah Burkhead	—	—	—	—	—	—	—
John Burkhead Junr	—	—	—	—	—	—	—
Francis Burkhead	—	—	—	—	—	—	—
Hopefull Wood	3	3	—	—	—	—	—
William Harris	—	—	—	—	—	—	—
Robt Boughton	1	1	—	—	—	—	—
[illegible]emiah Burkhead	1	—	—	5	3	1	3
[illegible]n Burkhead	—	—	—	—	—	—	—
[illegible]thew Burkhead	—	—	—	—	—	—	—
[illegible] Wood	1	1	1	—	—	—	—
27	22	16	16	45	43	32	

[2]

White Men	Wt. Women	Wt. Boys	Wt. Girls	N. men	N. Wom	N. Boys	N. Girls
Richard Wood	1		1				
Robt. Ward	3	1	—	6	3	—	4
	Sarah Woods 1	4	1				
John Skinner	1		5	1	5		4
Richard Randel	2	1	4	—	—	—	—
Thos. Cheyney	1	1	—	—	—	—	—
John Ballson	3	3	2	2			1
John Welch	2	5	2	—		—	—
John Ward	1	—	1	—	—	—	—
Robt. Ward Junr.	1	—	—	—	—	—	—
James Tasker	2	—	—	—	—	—	—
James Tasker Junr.		—	—	—	—	—	—
David Sells	1	1	2	—	—	—	—
Isaac Stevens	1	1	—	—	—	—	—
Morgan Wood	1	2	4	—	2	—	1
Gedean Shoemaker	1	—	—	—	—	—	—
William Whitington	2	—	—	—	—	—	—
Stephen Lambath	1	—	—	—	—	—	—
Joseph Warner	1	1	1	—	—	—	—
William Simmons	2	2	3	1	3	—	—
Saml. Harrison	1	—	—	3	4	5	3
Doctr. Andrew Pisser	1	—	—	—	1	—	—
William Earnott	3	3	3	—	—	—	—
Thos. Earnott	1	2	1	—	—	—	—
William Davenport	1	—	2	—	—	—	—
Richard Brown	1	2	2	2	—	—	2
Captn. Thos. Smith	1	—	—	2	1	2	3
Richard Dowell	1	2	2	—	—	—	—
	Elizb. Lewin	1	2	4	3	5	11
Samuel Lewin	1	—	—	—	—	—	—
[illegible] H. Smith	1	—	1	2	4	3	1
[illegible] Chew	1	3	—	2	3	6	3
[illegible] Lane	1	—	—	6	4	3	—
27	22	16	16	43	43	32	41
	66	51	55	76	80	59	76

[3]

White Men	Wt Women	Wt Boys	Wt Girls	N men	N Women	N Boys	N Girls
Thomas Shields	1	4	1				
Richard Hopkins	1	3	2	1	1	1	
Henry Plummer	1	3	3	1		1	
Richard Richardson	1	3	4	4	7	3	3
Joseph Richardson	3			5	9	7	10
John Hall	4	1		2	0	11	5
John Coal	1	4	2	4	4	8	1
Joseph Galloway	2	1	1	7	5	6	7
Jona Dawlings	1					3	2
Richard Dawlings						1	
Saml Dawlings							
Richard Harwood				7	4	6	5
Stephen Watkins	1	3	3	5	4	6	9
Elizb Smith					3	2	2
Richard Wells	1	1	2	3	3	3	1
John Sullivan							
Thos Mean							
Thomas Medcalf	1	2	1	1	1		1
John Watkins Junr	1		1	4	3	6	6
Frances Tophouse	1	2	3				
Benjamin Lane	4			3	7	0	7
Thomas Lane							
Gabriel Lane							
Jonas Galtivith	3		2		1	1	1
John Deal				4	4		6
John Plummer	2	2					
William Marnsbury	1	1					
Elizb Taylor				3	4	3	2
Thomas Tillard	1						
William Dove	3	3	1				
Saml Shuttles	2	2	3	1	1	4	1
Jonn Brushearie	1			1			
Wt Men 59	66	51	55	76	00	50	76
(09)	105	03	03	132	143	137	115

Carried over

[143]

White Men	Wt Women	W. Boys	Wt Girls	N men	N women	N Boys	N Girls
Charles Cheyney	3			1	2	3	4
John Cuny	1		2				
Richard Wells	1	2	5				
Richard Simmons	2			2	1		1
William Simmons	1	2		3	4	2	
Benjamin Cheyney	4	2	2	1			
Benjamin Cheyney							
James Sutton	1	1	1				
	Abigl Simmons		4	3	4	6	5
Saml Galloway	1			7	0	7	3
Phillip Thomas	2			10	13	12	0
Phillip Thomas Junr							
Robt Welch							
Joseph Pemberton	3	3	2	0	1	2	1
George Neal	2	1		4	1	1	1
John Pindell	1		1	1	1	1	1
Thomas Warner	1	3	4				
					F Harry	3	
John Eddings	1						
Benjamin Gaiter	3	3	2	3	5	5	6
Joseph Ward	1	2	2	3	3	3	4
John Welch	3	2			1		
Thomas Owens	1						
Joseph Owens	1		1				
Richard Shekells	1	1	1		1	1	
Saml Ward	2	4		3	3	4	4
				F Polly			2
Saml Ward Junr							
John Welch Junr							
	W. J. Henwood	2	3				
Charles Henwood							
Solloman Story	1	1	1				
Richard Deale	1	1	1				
Bt Over 09	105	03	03	132	143	137	143
110	145	113	110	101	194	100	106

Carried Over

Men	W. Women	W. Boys	W. Girls	N. Men	N. Women	N. Boys	N. Girls
Willm Hutton							
Jos Hutton Jun							
Henry Hutton							
Daniel Armiger	1	1	3				
	Ann Smith	4	2	5	7	9	10
	Ruth Hall	3		6	3	4	4
Addaim Allin	1					1	1
Ezekiel Gott	1	1	1	2	3	4	4
	Ann Gott		1	3	2	1	2
Jno Shekells	1	3	3				
Henry Darnell	2			23	21	36	30
Richd Darnell							
Phillip Darnell				21	17	42	31
	E. Hammon			2	3	2	2
Phillip Hammon							
Lewis Jones	5			3		5	1
Jond Jones							
Absolom White	1		1				
Willm Wivell							
Benj Mungiff	1			4	2	2	3
Thos Whittington	1	3	4	1	2	1	2
Thos Westmecoat							
Willm Armiger	1	7	6	1			1
Jno Warden	1	1	2				
Capt Jno Kelly	1	1		1	2		1
Marshall Stone	1						
George Ross	1	1	1				
Jno Lambath	1	3	2	1	1	1	1
Richd Scrivener	1	1	3				
Jno Trott	1		1				
Jno Trott Jun	1	4	2				
Hugh Griffith	3	4					
Allen Ball	1						
Brot 110	148	113	110	101	194	100	185
147	170	130	152	334	337	376	206 Carried Over

White Men (struck through)	W. Women	W. Boys	W. Girls	N. Men	N. Women	N. Boys	N. Girls
	Sarah Wood	1	1	—	—	—	—
Willm. Turner	4	1	2	—	1	1	—
Thos. Tucker	—	—	—	—	—	—	—
Seborn Tucker	1	2	1	—	—	—	—
Isaac Tucker	1	—	1	—	—	—	—
Jno. Griffith	1	3	2	—	—	—	—
Jno. Griffith Junr.	1	—	—	—	—	—	—
Marshall Griffin	1	2	1	—	—	—	—
David Price	1	1	—	—	—	—	—
	Mrs Farman	2	—	—	—	—	—
Benj. French	1	6	1	1	1	—	—
Mazel. French	—	—	—	—	—	—	—
	Mrs Hughes	2	3	—	—	—	—
William Ollion	1	3	1	—	—	—	—
	Mrs Brown	5	—	—	—	—	—
William Childs	3 / 1	1	2	2	2	3	1
Henry Childs	2	2	6	1	1	3	3
Harrison Lane	1	4	1	—	—	—	—
Thos. Lane	—	2	1	—	—	—	—
Henry Griffith	1	—	2	—	—	—	—
Thomson Trott	1	1	4	—	—	—	—
Sebert Trott	1	1	—	—	—	—	—
Richd. Trott	1	—	1	—	—	—	—
Saml. Childs	1	1	2	1	1	3	2
Richd. Joys	1	4	2	—	—	—	—
Nathan Hammond	—	—	—	—	—	—	—
Saml. Maynard	1	1	3	3	0	5	5
James Whitington	1	1	—	—	—	—	—
Evan Roberts	1	3	—	3	7	4	6
David Weems	6[?]	1	—	14	15	17	0
David Weems Jr.	1 Sen.	1 Sen.	—	2	—	1	1
Willm. Weems	—	—	—	—	—	—	—
	Mrs Gover	—	2	3	2	4	1
Thos. Morton	—	1 Jun.	—	—	—	—	—
Mr. Com[?] 187[?] / 576	170 / 213	150 / 202	132 / 191	134 / 161	137 / 175	176 / 217	206 / 313 Carried Over

White men	Wt. Women	Wt. Boys	Wt. Girls	N. men	N. Women	N. Boys	N. Girls
Thomas Miles	—	0	0	—	—	0	0
Jno. Dove	1	2	4	—	—	—	—
Augustes Randel	—	1	5	—	—	—	—
Jno. Galloway	—	—	—	2	—	—	—
Jno. Williams	1	—	3	—	—	—	—
Edward Blunt	1	1	2	—	—	—	—
Nathan Forster	1	1	2	—	—	—	—
Jno. Phips	1	—	4	—	—	—	—
Phillip Smith	1	1	2	—	—	—	—
Jos. Crutchley	1	1	2	—	—	—	—
Thomas Crutchley	—	—	—	—	—	—	—
Saml. Osburn	1	—	—	—	1	—	—
Benj. Atwell	1	—	2	—	—	—	—
Jno. Franklin	1	3	2	—	2	3	—
Jno. Dowel	—	—	—	—	—	—	—
Robt. Jackson	—	—	2	—	—	—	—
D. Allengim	—	—	—	—	—	—	—
William Pellman	—	—	—	—	—	—	—
Jno. Huonig	—	—	—	—	—	—	—
Jos. Cornfz	—	—	—	—	—	—	—
Quinton Cemp	—	—	—	—	—	—	—
William Franklan	—	—	—	—	—	—	—
Jos. Allen	1	2	3	4	5	10	3
Thomas Nash	1	2	1	—	—	—	—
Thomas Dodson	—	—	—	—	—	—	—
Jno. Burkhad	—	—	—	—	—	—	—
Nathaniel Phips	1	—	1	—	—	—	—
Edward Colloson	1	—	1	2	—	2	1
Nathaniel Clew	1	—	1	2	—	2	3
William Scott	—	—	—	—	—	—	—
Jno. Parsons	—	2	1	—	—	—	—
Thos. White	1	2	1	—	—	—	—
Thos. Laughlin	1	1	3	—	—	—	—
Bt. Over 176	215	202	191	164	175	217	313
209	232	221	233	174	183	234	320 Carried over

White men	Wt. Women	Wt. Boys	Wt. Girls	N. men	N. Women	N. Boys	N. Girls
	M. J. Wood	—	—	—	—	—	—
William Tucker	1	3	1	—	—	—	—
[illegible] Parrish	1	4	3	—	—	—	—
Thomas Phelps	—	—	—	—	—	—	—
					M. N. Parker 5 6	—	—
Jno. Tims	1	3	1	—	—	—	—
George Gardiner	—	1	—	—	—	—	—
Thos. Shaubert	—	2	1	—	—	—	—
Richd. Shaubert	—	—	—	—	—	—	—
Jno. Ferguson	—	—	—	—	—	—	—
Jno. Winterson	1	1	2	—	—	—	—
Jno. Chew	1	—	1	1	1	4	1
William Easton	1	1	1	—	—	—	—
Willm. Griffin	—	—	—	—	—	—	—
Benj. Norman	1	6	2	2	1	2	2
Thos. Norman	2	4	—	1	—	2	2
Griffith Collins	1	—	1	—	—	—	—
George Gardell	1	2	—	—	—	—	—
Jos. Tucker	1	—	—	—	—	—	—
Thomas Ditty	1	2	1	—	—	—	—
Selah Tucker	1	6	4	—	—	—	—
James Tucker	—	—	—	—	—	—	—
William Atwell	1	3	—	—	—	—	—
Benj. Atwell	1	1	1	1	1	—	—
Benj. Atwell Junr.	1	—	—	—	—	—	—
Jno. Atwell	1	2	2	—	—	—	—
Jos. Atwell	1	1	1	—	—	—	—
Jno. Hunt	1	—	—	—	1	1	—
Robt. Atwell	1	1	—	—	—	—	—
Jos. Tims	—	—	—	—	—	—	—
Peter Tims	—	—	—	—	—	—	—
Jno. Barker	1	3	2	—	1	—	—
Jno. Barker Junr.	—	—	—	—	—	—	—
Brt. Over 209	232	221	233	174	103	234	320
240	255	276	257	179	109	243	325

[9]

White men	Wt. Women	Wt. Boys	Wt. Girls	N men	N Women	N Boys	N Girls
William Barker	—	—	—	—	—	—	—
Benja. Brashears	3	—	—	3	5	2	5
William Hillard	1						
Saml. Wells	—	—	—	—	—	—	—
James Butler	—	—	—	—	—	—	—
Jno. Sheckells	2	..	—	4	2	2	2
Francis Sheckells	—	—	—	—	—	—	—
David Stewart Over Sear for David Stewart				2	4	2	6
Capt. Thos. Harwood	2	1	2	5	4	3	2
Isaac Simmons	1	3	3	—	1	2	1
Jos Owens	1	—	4	—	—	—	—
James Cowley	—	—	—	—	—	—	—
William Childs	—	—	—	1	2	2	1
Jno. Brown	1	2	4	—	—	—	—
Dowel Brashears	—	3	3	1	—		1
Zadock Brashears	1	—	1	—	1	—	—
Jemima Childs		4	2	1	1	1	—
William Jenney	1	2	5	—	—	—	—
Rachel Harrison 3		2	—	10	10	12	14
Saml. Harrison	—	—	—	4	0	3	3
Jno. Weems	1	—	—	10	13	16	22
Richd. Harrison	—	—	—	—	—	—	—
Walter Harrison	—	—	—	—	—	—	—
Benja. Ward	2	3	1	—	—	—	—
Abram Tanquary	1	1	3	—	—	—	—
Jno. Marshall Junr. 3	2	4	1	1	3	9	3
Jno. Turner	—		—	—	—	—	—
Richd. Chew	3	1	1	20	14	10	16
James Boys	1	1	1		—	—	—
Willm. Scrivner	—	—	—	—	—	—	—
Jos: Hutton Over Sear for Wm. Fitzhugh Esqr.				4	4	3	—
Charles Drury	1	—	1	1	—	1	1
Mrs. Drury		2	2	4	3	2	6
Bt. over 240	255	276	257	179	109	243	325 Carried over
270	204	329	291	252	264	313	400

White Men	W. Women	W. Boys	W. Girls	N. men	N. Women	N. Boys	N. Girls	
Benj. Darnell	—	—	—	4	6	2	4	
William Cowel	1	1	—	—	—	—	—	
William Drury	1	1	—	1	1	3	1	
Jno Brown	—	—	—	3	2	6	6	
Jno Holladay	1	1	1	—	—	—	—	
Jno Gatterwood	1	2	1	—	—	—	—	
Joseph Parker	2	2	—	—	—	—	—	
Henry Roberts	1	5	3	—	—	—	—	
[illegible] Hill	1	1	1	—	2	1	1	
	Ann Parker	1	2	—	—	—	—	
Jno Lambath	1	1	1	—	—	—	—	
Saml Mead	1	6	5	1	1	—	1	
	Rachel Ratliff 3	—	—	—	—	—	—	
	Sarah Holliday	—	—	—	2	1	—	
Waymack Brushears	1	8	1	1	1	4	1	
William Crandel	—	—	—	2	1	—	—	
Saml Varnel	1	—	4	—	—	—	—	
	M. J. Miles	2	4	3	4	—	1	
Thos Miles	—	—	—	—	—	—	—	
William Miles	—	—	—	—	—	—	—	
Jno Door	1	2	4	—	1	—	1	
Jno Carr	3	—	1	—	1	—	1	
John Carr Junr	—	—	—	—	—	—	—	
Jno Lane Junr	1	—	—	—	—	—	—	
Saml Lane	1	4	2	0	4	4	4	
John Richmond	—	—	—	—	—	—	—	
John Scrivenor	1	2	4	—	1	—	1	
Walter Carr	2	2	2	—	1	—	2	
Nathan Brushears	1	4	1	2	1	1	2	
Gassaway Watkins	1	1	1	5	3	6	1	
Rubidee Wood	3	—	—	—	—	—	—	
Peter Leith	—	—	—	—	—	—	—	
Saml Wells	—	—	—	—	—	—	—	
Bro. over 270	204	329	291	252	264	313	400	Carried
299	313	370	339	204	297	341	434	Carr.

[17]

White men	Wt. Women	Wt. Boys	W. Girls	N men	N Women	N Boys	N Girls	
Thos. Cowley	1	3	1			4	1	
	Ellinor Marriott	1	1		1		2	
	My Phillips	1	1					
Jos. Gott	1	2	3		1	4	1	
Adam Crandel								
Jno. Attadell	1	2	1					
Thos. Crandel	1	1						
Frederick Griffin								
Jos. Crandel	1	2	1	1				
Hezekiah Orm								
Benj. Crawford	2	3						
Isaac Simmons / Jno. Arnold Sr.				1	1		2	
Richd. Noarl	2	1						
	Rachel Allin		2					
Charles Mushy	1	2						
Willm. Hayes / Jno. Doaty Sr.	1		1	6	4	4	8	
Willm. Fisher	1	1						
Jeremiah Simmons	1	4	2	1	2			
Jno. Medcalf	3	6						
Luke Wirth	1	3	3	2	3	4	6	
Capt. Abram Simmons	1	2		1	3	4	5	
Walter Magowan				2	2	1	3	
Thos. Teal / James Haymes	1	4	4	6	6	3	9	
Moses Williams	1							
	Ann Dace			2	3	0	2	
Thos. Tongue	1	3		2	2	1	3	
Jno. Gibbs	1							
	Susn. Fisher	2	3	2	7	7	2	
	Sarah Hill 2			3	2	4	1	
Jos Hill / Thos. Mackey	1			1			1	
Jacob Welch	1	6	1					
Brt. Over 299	313	370	339	204	297	341	434	Carried
320	345	420	367	314	338	307	474	Over

Wt. men	Wt. Women	Wt. Boys	Wt. Girls	N men	N Women	N Boys	N Girls
Jno. Stone	2	4	1				
Agnes Tatter		2	1	3	5	7	1
William Arnold	1	1					
James Rendel	1				1	1	3
Capt. Richd. Weems	1	5	1	5	2	2	4
Capt. Benj. Harrison	1			3	2	1	5
Mrs. Franklin				4	2	6	2
Jacob Franklin	1			3	2	4	6
Saml. Harris		3	1				
Robt. Daniel							
David Griffiths	1	1	1				
Wm. Franklin	2			2			1
Charles Spencer		2		2	3	0	3
Robt. Atwell	1	1					
Jno. Gardener	1	2	2				
Thos. Crandel	1	1	3		1		
Willm. Deal				1	1	1	2
Capt. Jno. Deal	1	2	1	2			3
Ralph Flowers	1	3					
Jno. Davie	2	3					
Richd. Gott	1	2	4				
Anthony Gott			1	2	4	0	4
Anthony Gott Junr.	1		1				
Anthony Woods do	1	1	1				
William Crandel	1		1				
Jos. Ford	1	3					
Hanr. Howard		1					
Jno. Lane	3		1		1		1
Jno. Lane Junr.							1
Jno. Lane Junr.	1						
Saml. Lane	1	4	2	0	4	4	4
Jno. Richmond							
Jno. Scrivner	1	2	4		1		1
Walter Lane	2	2	2		1		
Wt. men [2]30	345	420	367	314	330	307	474 came
359	370	464	395	349	360	429	515 carr.

[8]

White Men	W^t Women	W^t Boys	W^t Girls	N. men	N. W^ms	N. Boys	N. Girls
John Marr	2	2	—	—	—	1	1
John Marr Junr	—	—	—	—	—	—	—
	Sus^n Williams	—	—	—	—	—	—
	Sarah Maccen 1	·	1	3	2	6	6
Abram Sollars	1	1	2	—	—	—	—
Richard Green	—	—	—	10	4	11	10
Charles Mushears	1	2	—	—	2	—	—
Richard Sawyer	—	—	—	—	—	—	—
Wilkinson Mushears	1	3	—	1	1	—	—
George Gardner	—	—	—	2	2	—	—
George Gardner Junr	—	—	—	—	—	—	—
James Owens	3	2	—	4	3	6	3
	Eliz^h Hopkins 1	1	3	1	1	2	4
William Hopkins	—	—	—	—	—	—	—
Jarrard Hopkins	1	2	2	—	1	—	—
Thomas Marriott	1	3	2	—	—	—	—
	Sus^n Wells	2	2	—	—	—	—
John Clarke	1	1	5	2	1	—	—
Saml Atwell	2	1	1	—	—	—	—
Frederick Mills	1	5	1	—	3	2	6
Joseph Hill	1	1	1	4	3	1	2
	(M^y Johns 3	2	—	9	7	0	11
	Eliz^t Shearbut	1	4	—	—	—	—
Thomas Shearbert	—	—	—	—	—	—	—
Richard Shearbert	—	—	—	—	—	—	—
	Eliz^t Joys	2	—	—	—	—	—
	Sarah Pavey	2	—	—	—	—	—
William Kingston	10	1	3	—	—	—	—
William Shearbert	1	2	4	—	—	—	—
John Thomas	3	—	1	10	12	25	11
William Evens	1	—	—	2	1	1	2
Daniel Olliver	1	—	4	—	—	—	—
William Olliver	1	5	—	—	—	—	—
Br^t Over'd 359	370	464	395	349	360	429	515 Carr[illegible]
304	414	503	435	403	411	491	570 Over[illegible]

148

White Men	Wt Women	Wt Boys	Wt Girls	N Men	N Wmn	N Boys	N Girls
Basil Gest	—	—	—	—	—	—	—
	Sarah Clark 2	—	1	—	—	—	—
Allen Ball	2	2	1	—	—	—	—
John Bowie	1	2	1	—	—	—	—
John Simmons		—	—	1	1	2	3
Richard Crutchley	1	2	3	—	—	—	—
	Eliz. Mount	—	—	—	—	—	—
Benj. Galloway	1	—	—	—	—	—	—
James Weems	—	—	—	5	6	5	6
Joseph Richardson	Eastern Shore			1	2	3	6
Stephen Steward	3	—	—	16	0	0	11
John Parsons	0	—	—	—	—	—	—
Joseph Gilbert	0	—	—	—	—	—	—
William Westly	0	—	—	—	—	—	—
Thomas Neal	0	—	—	—	—	—	—
Amos Harrison	0	—	—	—	—	—	—
James Medcalf	0	—	—	—	—	—	—
William Medcalf	0	—	—	—	—	—	—
William Willson	0	—	—	—	—	—	—
Benjamin Ward	0	—	—	—	—	—	—
William Spencer	0	—	—	—	—	—	—
Richard Wason	—	—	—	—	—	—	—
Jn Norris	3	5	2	3	1	—	1
John Barker	1	5	2	—	—	—	—
Thomas Norris	1	2	1	11	7	5	6
	Susa Tucker	1	—	—	—	—	—
John Tucker	—	—	—	—	—	—	—
	Eliz. Shearbert	1	3	—	—	—	—
Nicholas Norman	—	—	—	1	1	3	2
Thomas Roberts	1	2	2	—	1	—	1
Benjamin Lane Junr	1	1	1	—	1	2	—
Stephen Steward Junr	—	—	—	—	—	—	—
				R. Mash / Pistolle	—	—	—
William Fisher	1	1	—	—	3	0	4
Wm Boen 304	414	503	435	405	411	491	570
333	439	530	449	443	442	526	610

	W. Women	W. Boys	W. Girls	N Men	N Woms.	N Boys	N Girls	
…le Allen								
…on Welch	—	0	0	—	—	0	0	
	Sarah Fowler	1	—	1	1		1	
…er Tipps	1	1	—	—	—	—	2	
…m Harrison	—	—	—	7	4	2	6	
…n Norman	—	—	—	3	—	—	2	
…liam Kirby	1	2	—	—	—	—	—	
…cob Fuller	1	3	—	—	—	—	—	
…n Tipps	—	—	—	—	—	—	—	
333	439	530	449	443	442	526	610	
…d Doc. 340	443	537	449	454	447	520	621	37…

INDEX*

* Name of slaves are omitted, where only "given names" occur in the records. Figures in parentheses (2), mean that the name occurs that number of times on the page indicated.

*Duckett added when father died in 1797.

C

D

G

* Erroneously appears as "John and Mary" on p. 259.

* Separate names of hundreds not indexed.

I

J

K

L

MC.

M

N

O

P

Q

S

U

V

W

Y